Contents

■ ■ ■ ■ ■ ■ ■ ■ ■ ■ ■ ■ ■

Chapter 5

MARKETS AND MARKET SEGMENTATION 123

Chapter 6

CONSUMER PRODUCTS AND BUYING BEHAVIOR 151

Chapter 7

BUSINESS PRODUCTS AND BUYING BEHAVIOR 181

Chapter 8

PRODUCT BRANDING, PACKAGING AND WARRANTIES 211

Preface

■ ■ ■ ■ ■ ■ ■ ■ ■ ■ ■ ■ ■

I keep six honest serving men,
(they taught me all I knew);
their names are What and Why and When
and How and Where and Who

Rudyard Kipling

Applied Marketing is student friendly. This textbook was created to present the basic concepts and terminology of the marketing field in a readable, understandable format. Students generally want to learn, and the mission of education is to provide the tools, methods and motivation so that learning happens. Extensive classroom testing has shown that students enjoy reading *Applied Marketing*.

The concepts and principles in this textbook are stated simply and clearly, with examples of "real-world" products, companies and situations that help in the learning process. These examples are both current and appropriate, creating the freshest text on this subject on the market. The pedagogical materials are purposely designed to be attractive and interesting, and the **Marketers At Work** boxes have been especially well received. These inserts feature former students who are now working in the field of marketing and provide the career orientation that is setting new paradigms.

Applied Marketing recognizes the importance of services, ethics and global marketing. These special topics are woven throughout the text. Descriptions and examples of intangibles are included frequently. Discussions of marketing ethics can be found in each chapter under the boxed headings **Marketing and Society.** Ethics issues are also handled in the management areas of each chapter where appropriate. **Global Marketing** vignettes also appear in each chapter. This pertinent subject is further covered in great detail in chapter 18.

The table of contents in *Applied Marketing* reflects the book's student friendly approach. Marketing management is explained early in this textbook, and most chapters contain management components relating specifically to that material. The planning function is dealt with in chapter 3, and appropriately, **Marketing in Practice: Components of the marketing plan** immediately follows. The chapters on the elements of the marketing mix (product, price, distribution and promotion) are laid out in logical order. Products are developed and priced before being distributed and promoted. Marketers do not operate in a vacuum, but work closely with other parts of the business venture. Accounting functions are of particular interest because they provide the information required to measure the results of the marketing effort. **Marketing in Practice: Accounting for marketing decisions,** is located within the text after the chapters on pricing (10 and 11). This discussion helps students better to understand pricing and its relationship to financial statements. *Applied Marketing* devotes a portion of the final chapter to look at what the future holds for marketers and students. This section focuses on areas of potential growth in the field of marketing. Immediately following is **Marketing in Practice: Careers in Marketing and Job Search Tips.**

The chapters in *Applied Marketing* are presented in a question/answer format. Chapter subheadings are in the form of questions; the following text supplies the answers. Material in the text that relates to the specific question is highlighted to supply the reader with the immediate reference to concepts and terms. In addition, these important definitions appear in the margins for quick referral. Explanation of the terminology and concepts is clear, and relevant examples, chosen from the world of business, clarify the terms and ideas.

Each chapter begins with **The Job to be Done,** which asks the major questions raised in the text that follows. Students are urged to look for the answers that form the backbone of the material found in that chapter. A complete, end of the chapter summary, labeled **Summing it Up** reviews the answers to the opening questions. **Key Concepts and Terms** are presented at the end of each chapter, along with discussion questions under the heading **Building Skills.** Practical application of text material is supplied through the inclusion of case studies. These cases, created from recent events in the business community, include questions to help stimulate further discussion.

Applied Marketing provides the potential to explore and expand. The currentness of the chapter material and cases provides an atmosphere that stimulates student thought and classroom discussion. By giving the student room to search and examine, this text becomes the helpmate of professors without binding them to rigid models. Students are the ultimate consumers of textbooks. *Applied Marketing* provides this audience with a comprehensive yet comfortable presentation of the basics of marketing. This text strives to make the task of learning easier for the student and the job of teaching more pleasant for the professor.

Acknowledgments

Many people contributed to the "final product" that has become *Applied Marketing*. The helpful and cooperative reviewers, whose schools are listed below, cannot be overlooked. In the textbook industry one also gives deserved credit to the experienced, knowledgeable, and professional editors that lend so much to the development of such a project. Without this expertise, no college text would get off the ground.

This work is a little different from most because it is student friendly. Students not only modeled its creation, but played a major role in its development. The current edition was classroom tested by literally thousands of students across the country. These were the ultimate reviewers, and the finished goods that you are now holding in your hands is largely the result of their input and critiques. While these students may be nameless in this acknowledgment, they will always be recognized and appreciated.

Thank you from the author and the editor to the instructors at these institutions for their insight and commentary: Essex County College; Appalachian State University; Arizona State University; Midland Lutheran College; Tulsa Junior College; Mohawk Valley Community College; Southwest Texas State University; Mountain View College; Clark State Community College; and Shasta College.

Suppplemental Material

The entire program for this course includes elements for enhancing lectures and encouraging self-assessment. Options include an Instructor's Manual complete with test questions options, transparency masters, guided exercises, lecture notes, and a guide for collaborative projects where students assess their own work. ABC News Video clips from the Wall Street Journal Report present current ethical and social marketing issues in the real world. Prentice Hall Custom Test provides an electronic testing service.

Other options for classroom enhancements can be accessed through On-line College through America-on-Line or from the JWA video catalog. America-on-Line and Prentice Hall offer instructor training and student chat sessions on a variety of topics. JWA offers corporate training videos across diverse skills areas. JWA videos are adaptable to any classroom environment.

Marketing, The Marketing Concept, and The Marketing Mix

The Job to be Done

There is no mystery to marketing. One does not need a great deal of education to be a successful marketer. A creative mind and a good dose of common sense helps. The willingness to help people and firms satisfy their needs is what marketing is all about. This opening chapter gives you the tools to:

- understand what marketing is, how the exchange process operates, and the ways that marketing affects our lives,

- explain how form, time, place and possession utility help satisfy needs and wants,

- describe the ways that marketing has evolved,

- define the marketing concept and the elements of the marketing mix, and

- identify the functions of marketers and the people and firms that carry them out.

Marketers at Work

Mark Highfill

Many students have a desire to work for Fortune 500 companies after completing their studies. As glamorous as the "big names" of the business world might sound, most graduates find their initial opportunities greater with smaller, less well-known firms. Although some may aspire to entrepreneurship, most realize that such dreams usually are realized after gaining experience in the employ of others. Few have the drive, ability, or good fortune to jump directly from college into business ownership. Mark Highfill is just such a person.

Throughout his college career, Mark strove to gain the experience and knowledge needed to compete in the world of private enterprise. While attending Old Dominion University and Virginia Commonwealth University, this go-getter developed an appreciation for marketing and its role in the business arena. He credits the internships that he served with giving him the hands-on experience necessary to put his coursework to good use.

On graduation, Mark founded Austin's of America, a marketer of promotional items primar-ily for the retail trade. This Richmond, Virginia firm specializes in inflatable, point-of-sale pieces such as balloons, moonwalks, human fly traps and air tents. Austins is not limited to air-filled promotions, and can provide its customers with banners, searchlights, printed materials and a variety of other promotional items. The firm prides itself on being "Your *Total* Promotional Source."

Hard work and tough decisions are all part of running an enterprise. Although the admits that his is no standard nine-to-five career, Mark enjoys the freedom and financial rewards of being in business for himself. the success of Austin's of America led him to be selected as Young Entrepreneur of the Year by the Virginia Small Business Administration. Mark Highfill truly exemplifies applied marketing at its best.

What Is Marketing?

Ask a group of students to define marketing and most will describe selling or advertising—its most visible and glamorous elements. Marketing includes much more.

MARKETING DEFINED

Through time, marketing has been described as the pipeline for our standard of living or as business activities that direct the flow of goods from producer to user. While de-emphasizing the physical transport of goods as an outdated synonym for marketing, the American Marketing Association adopted this definition:

> Marketing is the process of planning and executing the conception, pricing, promotion and distribution of ideas, goods, and services to create exchanges that satisfy individual and organization objectives.[1]

---

[1]Editors, "AMA board approves new marketing definition," *Marketing News,* March 1, 1985, p. 1.

In other words, **marketing** provides the goods and services when and where they are required to **satisfy customer** needs or wants. Consider a **need** as a void that requires filling. Needs include more than just the necessities of life, such as the lack of anything that might provide gratification. A **want** is a desire for a particular something that would produce the most satisfaction. Each of us has different levels of comfort or pleasure that will quench any particular need. What pleases one person may do nothing to please another. Similarly, businesses and organizations have different needs and wants than individuals. While supplying satisfaction to others, companies and individuals must also fulfill their organizational objectives.

Needs may vary depending upon the culture where the buyer lives. A citizen of Japan may receive more satisfaction from a lunch of sushi and rice than from one of a hamburger with fries. For a woman in India or Iraq, jeans of any brand might not provide a stitch of satisfaction. A city dweller in Houston prefers a high rise condominium, while a family living outside Orlando opts for a three bedroom, two bath house on the edge of a lake or golf course. Any of these choices would fill a need for food, clothes or housing. Only one choice would be satisfying to each of these different consumers.

Marketing—Providing the goods and services when and where they are required to satisfy customer needs or wants.

THE EXCHANGE PROCESS

The **exchange process** is the hub of marketing. Marketers exchange their products for money or other things of value. The products can be either goods or services. In most of the world's economies, goods and services are traded for money. Buyers receive the satisfaction that the products bring and are willing to give up money for that reward. Sellers gain income and profits from such dealings.

Transactions occur when people or businesses exchange assets with others. In business transactions, goods or services are typically exchanged for money. If the transaction does not involve finances, it is called barter. Bartering, once a common type of transaction in our society, continues today on a lesser scale. An example would be the exchange of the labor used in wood cutting for some of the firewood produced.

Before a grocery shopper can purchase a can of Campbell's chicken noodle soup, a chain of exchanges must precede that transaction. First, the poultry farmer sells chickens to the Campbell Soup Company. This marketer buys equipment, cans, labels, and shipping containers to present the product in a form that the consumer needs. Trucking companies deliver the soup to wholesalers, who in turn resell the product to supermarkets. Each of these exchanges is a buying/selling transaction that places the products in locations where they ultimately produce satisfaction for the user.

Customers in market economies decide which products will be produced by choosing one good or service over another. Goods will not be manufactured or services provided if there is no market demand for them. This control over the exchange process is called **consumer sovereignty.** Consumer sovereignty means that buyers dictate which products will or will not be produced and distributed. If more people demand Campbell's chicken noodle soup, more chickens will have to be processed and more noodles cooked. Additional cans and labels will be needed, and supermarkets may require more shelf space.

Exchange process—exchanging something of value (usually money) for goods or services.
Transaction—the exchange of valuable assets, (usually money) by the buyer for goods or services from the seller.

Consumer sovereignty—in market economies, the consumer is "king" by choosing the products that will be made.

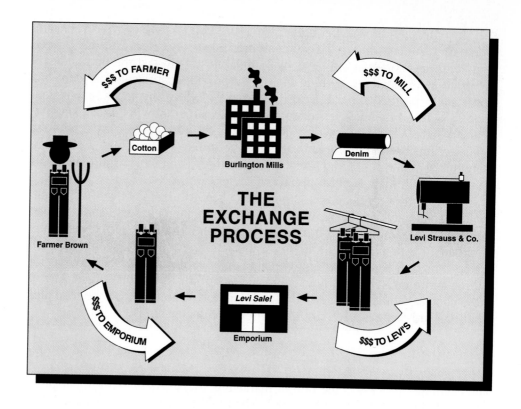

THE EXCHANGE PROCESS

$$$ TO FARMER

$$$ TO MILL

Cotton

Burlington Mills

Denim

Levi Strauss & Co.

Farmer Brown

$$$ TO EMPORIUM

Levi Sale!

Emporium

$$$ TO LEVI'S

The level of the consumer's role in determining which goods and services are available in the marketplace varies greatly from country to country. This principle of consumer sovereignty dictates economic conditions in most Western industrialized nations. When products are not purchased, manufacturers stop making them. On the other hand, needed or wanted goods and services will usually be marketed.

In command economies, such as those in the countries of the former Soviet Union, government decides what will be manufactured and by whom. In many socialist nations of Europe and Asia, consumer needs receive little attention. The breakup of the Soviet Union and the independence gained in Eastern European countries alter such centralized control. These economies are struggling to adapt to a business climate where the needs and wants of consumers and organizations are not dictated by a central authority, such as government.

How Does Marketing Affect Our Lives?

Marketing affects everyone. Every member of our society becomes part of the marketing scenario. As buyers of groceries, appliances, cosmetics, garden supplies and gasoline, consumers form a powerful group. They control what products are made and how they are distributed. By choosing one product over another, buyers actually determine the courses of action taken by major marketing businesses. When consumers choose jeans over flannel

Many manufacturers, such as the Pozzi Window Company, are finding new markets for their products overseas.

slacks, manufacturers must scramble to find denim. If people demand more fiber in their diets, marketers of breads and cereals find new ingredients and modify production processes.

Local businesses market their establishments as well as the products they offer for sale. The development of an appealing and enduring image is a necessary function of any business. The retail establishment, the dentist, the auto repair shop and the real estate broker search out and respond to customer needs. Without this marketing effort, it may be difficult to develop a positive and lasting image.

Elements of marketing are everywhere. Stores and shops line the streets, and trucks crowd the freeways. All around us we see someone or some business directly involved in marketing. Billboards line our roads and highways. Television is loaded with commercial messages. Newspapers and magazines display an array of goods for sale.

Our society's standard of living depends in part upon marketing. The variety of goods and services available to consumers is a direct result of the marketing effort. Without stores and warehouses, how will consumers have the products necessary to fill their needs? Without advertising, how will consumers know what products are available and where? Marketing is a significant contributor to the lifestyles found in the United States.

Similarly, world markets clamor for the standard of living enjoyed by people in developed nations. As new economies lurch toward free market determination for individual satisfaction, marketing takes on new dimensions. How can the distribution of goods function in areas where refrigeration and highway networks are inadequate or nonexistent? Is it possible to advertise when centralized authorities control the media? In many areas of the global community, marketing principles are just beginning to be understood.

Both individuals and organizations use the principles of marketing. For example, people must market themselves when applying for employment. Applicants must learn the needs of prospective employers and package their talents to satisfy those needs if they hope to be hired. The candidate who best markets herself or himself is more apt to be selected for employment.

School districts use marketing when asking taxpayers to support operating levies. If the product is not what the public desires or if the price is too steep, the tax-paying consumer may not "buy." Effective marketing enables communities to understand and value the role of education. The price of the product and the cost of the marketing effort play heavily on such decisions.

Politicians, too, market themselves. They are careful to promote an image of competence and integrity. Consistency and appropriateness are important to political candidates. Those in the running may wear tuxedos and ball gowns to fund-raising banquets, but they roll up their sleeves when visiting the factory or put on jeans when stumping the rural areas. The universal appeal of a candidate is often a product of marketing efforts.

Marketing is an important part of our lives. An understanding of how and why it works is basic to our education.

ow Are Needs Satisfied?

Determining the needs of people and businesses is the goal of marketing and marketers. Only when these needs or wants are known can the means of satisfying them be created. More than just the product itself may be required. The time and place that the need arises are also important considerations. The ability of a good or service to satisfy will depend upon meeting all of these requirements.

UTILITY

Utility—the ability of a good or service to provide satisfaction.

The habits and tastes of buyers span a range as wide and varied as the products designed to satisfy them. **Utility** is the ability of a product to satisfy a need or want. This term defines the value of a specific product for the individual user. The vast number of types, sizes and brands of goods and services attest to the variety of tastes and needs of consumers. Cosmetics, airlines, household goods, automobiles and clothing come in different forms for different people. Business firms purchase raw materials, parts, equipment and services from a host of suppliers depending upon their organizational needs. Consumers and business buyers, not marketing companies, decide the satisfaction that products provide.

Form Utility

Form utility—the type, quality, size, shape, taste or other physical characteristics of a product that provide satisfaction.

The need for a product often demands a particular type or quality of good or service. **Form utility** supplies that satisfaction, based upon the physical characteristics of the product. For instance, a person shopping for summer clothing will look for specific sizes, fabrics and styles to fit her or his needs. Although the form that a product takes may be created through manufacturing, marketers dictate the requirements for customer satisfaction.

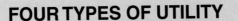

FOUR TYPES OF UTILITY

FORM

Form utility provides satisfaction by shaping raw materials into different products.

TIME

Time utility provides satisfaction by making products available when needed.

PLACE

Place utility provides satisfaction by making products available where they are needed.

POSSESSION

Possession utility provides satisfaction by allowing the exchange of ownership or service.

In many cases the marketer alters the form of a product to provide for a specific need. For example, Thor-Lo Inc. manufactures athletic socks for a variety of activities. Taking a page from shoe marketers such as Nike and Reebok, this innovative company produces sport-specific socks for aerobics, walking, cycling, hiking and just about any other type of human physical performance. Although they are more expensive than the average sports socks, Thor-Lo's are widely acclaimed by people who wear them for work or play.[2]

Time Utility

The form a product takes provides satisfaction for one set of needs. Goods and services also must be available when needed. **Time utility** provides this benefit. Products that are available when needs arise bring satisfaction. However, as valuable as the form of a product might be, its quality, shape, size or taste may be worthless if not received on time.

    Because certain products are more in demand at certain times or for specific occasions, prices for these goods or services may reflect this increased need. The demand for flowers is high around Easter and Mother's Day, and prices typically increase at these holiday times. Plumbers doing emergency service at night or on weekends charge more than they do during regular working hours.

Time utility—the ability of a good or service to be available when needed.

Place Utility

Similarly, **place utility** assures that what is needed can be obtained where it is needed. The texts still on the shelves at the bookstore cannot provide satisfaction for the student studying for the exam. Nails at the building supply center

Place utility—the ability of a good or service to be available where needed.

---

[2]Gretchen Morgenson, "The foot's friend," *Forbes*, April 13, 1992, pp. 60-62.

are of no help to the carpenter on the job site. The sweatshirts provide little warmth to the football team if the wrong college receives them. All goods and services must be available where required if they are to satisfy needs.

Similar to time utility, place utility also has an effect upon price. Service stations that locate at off-ramps along interstate highways or main thoroughfares often price their gasoline higher because of the additional place utility offered. Camera film at vacation or resort areas typically costs more. Medical supplies delivered to the home are more expensive than those purchased at the pharmacy.

Possession Utility

Possession utility— the ability of a good or service to be owned or acquired.

Possession utility relates to having use of the good or application of the service and is important for satisfaction. The right products, available when and where needed, must be possessed to be fulfilling. The rock concert held at a convenient time nearby provides little satisfaction to the fan if no tickets are available. The birthday gift held in the store on layaway will not be satisfying unless presented. Whether a person owns or rents, the product in hand is what provides ultimate satisfaction.

Form, time, place and possession utilities are interrelated. To guarantee full satisfaction, each must be present. Time utility will not substitute for form utility, and vice versa. Suppose a prospective buyer has the money to buy a pair of needed slacks. If the only pair available is three sizes too small, how can satisfaction occur? The aim of marketing is to maximize the utility of the goods and services. When marketing does a thorough job, the result is satisfaction.

Quality and Variety

The quality and variety of goods and services provided must meet a broad range of human and organizational needs. For instance, Dole Food Company can no longer be concerned with just providing fresh and canned vegetables and fruit to a needy public. The increasing interest in healthier foods has caused this huge produce supplier to switch from using pesticides to using ladybugs to rid its products of unwanted, harmless bugs. By growing toxin-free fruits and vegetables, Dole hopes to differentiate its brand from standard supermarket produce.[3]

Modern science has made great strides in bioengineered agricultural products. Such futuristic items as Posilac, a growth hormone for cattle, and Flavr Savr genetically altered tomatoes have left many growers and consumers wary. In fact, the hype over many bioproducts caused somewhat of a backlash, with some farmers and marketers promoting "unaltered" beef, milk and produce. Fresh Fields and Whole Foods Markets are two grocery retailers that are experiencing remarkable growth by offering shoppers a product mix that is primarily free from additives and preservatives.[4]

---

[3]Craig Torres, "Finding brand name loyalty may sway investors," *The Wall Street Journal,* April 6, 1993, pp. C1 and 2; Dan Koeppel, "Dole wants the whole produce aisle," *Adweek's Marketing Week,* October 22, 1990, pp. 20-26.

[4]Cyndee Miller, "Food fight rages over bioproducts," *Marketing News,* March 14, pp. 1 and 19; Betsy Spethmann, "Nature's bounty," *BRANDWEEK,* September 6, 1993, pp. 19-25.

Dole, a leader in differentiating its products from others, stresses its use of lady bugs instead of pesticides

The business community is placing greater emphasis on determining market needs before producing goods and services. These products become the means for satisfying needs and wants. The emphasis on satisfying customer needs has become the focal point of business today, but such was not always the case.

ow Has Marketing Evolved?

Business activity has gone through three distinct phases since the Industrial Revolution: the production, selling and marketing ages. Early in this evolution, most businesses concentrated on production as the key to profitability. The next stage emphasized selling, distribution and promotion. Today, the age of marketing stresses determining and satisfying the needs of customers.

THE PRODUCTION AGE

Business ventures from the Industrial Revolution through the early 1920s were typically production oriented. Business people generally believed that mass-produced goods would sell themselves. Often this was the case. With consumer demand growing at a rapid rate, it was difficult to argue with this philosophy. The economy was driven to produce more and more goods to feed this soaring demand. Many businesses of today were started during this **production age.**

Although technological advances continued to feed a market with countless products, consumer demand was so great that shortages were common. The company that could come up with faster or more efficient methods of production was often the most profitable. Management planning was directed

Production age—the period noted for heavy demand yet short supply for goods and services; management efforts directed toward improved production.

internally toward increasing production output and lowering costs. Little effort was aimed outward toward buyers or markets. Production capability dominated the world of business.

THE SELLING AGE

As manufacturing increased prior to World War I, competition continued to produce "better mousetraps." Selling the output of production became the primary task of the business community. The company with the most outlets and the best fleet of salespeople was often the most profitable. The **selling age** had arrived.

The goods that resulted from the production age filled the warehouses of manufacturers. The need to get rid of excess inventory became a major drive of the selling age. Businesses directed their emphasis toward the distribution system. Increasing the number of outlets was the typical plan of attack. Advertising grew rapidly. Inventories that once burdened manufacturers were transferred to the showrooms and shelves of shops and stores, distributors and dealers.

> **Selling age**—the period characterized by over production and excess inventories; management stressed increased distribution.

THE MARKETING AGE

The stock market crash of 1929 signaled the start of the Great Depression and rocked the world. Consumers and users had little money to buy the wonderful products that were available as the result of the selling age. Outstanding distribution efforts were not enough to clear the shelves. Business people began to determine that to work their way out of these difficult times, they must first learn what customers need. Before a company could be successful making or selling products, there had to be a demand for them. This was the advent of the **marketing age.**

> **Marketing age**—the period featuring increased competition and selective demand; management activities focused on determining and satisfying customer needs.

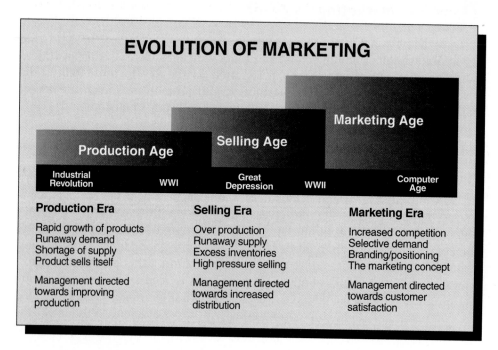

EVOLUTION OF MARKETING

Marketing Age

Selling Age

Production Age

| Industrial Revolution | WWI | Great Depression | WWII | Computer Age |

Production Era

Rapid growth of products
Runaway demand
Shortage of supply
Product sells itself

Management directed towards improving production

Selling Era

Over production
Runaway supply
Excess inventories
High pressure selling

Management directed towards increased distribution

Marketing Era

Increased competition
Selective demand
Branding/positioning
The marketing concept

Management directed towards customer satisfaction

Since the late 1930s, with time out for the shortages caused by World War II, most businesses have begun to realize the importance of marketing. The marketing evolution is real, yet the time periods and lines between the different stages are not distinct. Some marketing oriented firms were doing business in the production and sales eras. Today, a few firms still have a production bent, but many changes in philosophy have occurred since the early days of business development. There is presently a national trend toward quality and customer service, which leads to further development of the marketing concept.

What Is The Marketing Concept?

Today's most successful businesses are usually those that have created a company-wide marketing orientation. Wal-Mart and Victoria's Secret, with their satisfaction guaranteed policies, are companies that fit this image. Even giant Procter & Gamble tailors its massive product line to satisfy consumer needs. The development of a quality image by Japanese automobile marketers is another prime example of a marketing effort directed toward customer satisfaction. These types of endeavors illustrate the advancement of the marketing concept.

MARKETING CONCEPT DEFINED

Businesses that totally direct their efforts toward the satisfaction of customer needs have the **marketing concept.** Companies that show such concern try to gain complete understanding of customers and their needs prior to introducing a product. The basic principle of marketing oriented companies is understanding buyer requirements.

Marketing concept— directing business effort toward satisfaction of customer needs.

The Whirlpool Corporation, Xerox and Carnation are three examples of marketing minded firms. These businesses show their customer orientation by using toll-free telephone numbers in their advertising or on product packaging. This encouragement of comments and complaints demonstrates a commitment to the marketing concept. The marketing oriented company exhibits this sense of caring for customers who buy their goods or services.

Anne Klein II takes the marketing concept one step further with its "At Your Service" program. By supplying a toll-free telephone number, this upscale women's wear marketer provides fashion tips and shopping information for today's female executive. This innovation generates names for the company's marketing database and mailing list while solidifying its customer loyalty. Where else can a harried professional find the inside scoop on what to wear for the "big meeting" at the last minute? Anne Klein II, owned by Takehiyo Inc., offers a plus to customers at its new retail shops as well as department stores by providing this simple service.[5]

---

[5]Pat Sloan, "Anne Klein II campaign," *Advertising Age,* July 13, 1992, p. 3; Cara Appelbaum, "Anne Klein blitzes direct marketing," *Adweek's Marketing Week,* October 8, 1990, pp. 20-21.

Product Quality and Customer Service

Product quality and customer service are the most important characteristics of marketing oriented companies. Satisfaction fades quickly without quality and service. Customers must be made aware of these product and company attributes. The marketing oriented firm assures that its employees believe in the goods and services being marketed. Everyone within the organization needs to buy into this philosophy if it is to succeed. Such businesses concentrate their efforts on customer satisfaction rather than on winning competitive battles.

Product quality has reached new heights of importance. Markets worldwide are crowded with overproduction, and price competition will likely get even tougher. One company that learned the quality lesson early was Plumley Cos., a supplier of hoses to the automobile industry. The firm was dropped by Buick in 1983 because of poor quality. Instead of giving up, the company fought back through training and a stronger management emphasis. Today, Plumley's sales are over $80 million and it can proudly point to quality awards from car manufacturers worldwide. The successful marketers of the future are those that give customers all of what they want and nothing that they are unwilling to pay for.[6]

One would be hard pressed to argue against the marketing concept as used by Procter & Gamble. Often accused of a no-frills marketing policy, P&G can point to its more recent ventures into the world of cosmetics for increasing its awareness of the consumer. Largely created through acquisition, this branch of the world's largest consumer goods marketer is growing rapidly. Having shed its staid image, Procter & Gamble is marketing Oil of Olay, Pantene, Cover Girl and other new lines with an eye aimed directly at the female consumer's needs and wants. Providing what is needed is the essence of the marketing concept.[7]

There are many examples of firms that did not understand or adhere to the marketing concept. *The National Observer,* a newspaper/magazine produced primarily to put to use idle Dow-Jones presses between runs of *The Wall Street Journal,* was published for production reasons. The Edsel, an automobile that only filled the manufacturing needs at Ford Motor Company, is another example of a nonmarketing reason for product development. Both were failures.

Team Effort

Achievement of the marketing concept requires a total effort by everyone within the business. Each department and each individual must think in terms of providing customer satisfaction. Knowledge of market needs must permeate

---

[6]Polly LaBarre, "Management tools must be managed," *Industry Week,* September 5, 1994, p. 78; Randy Kirk, "It's about control," *Inc.,* August 1994, pp. 25-26; James B. Treece, "A little bit of smarts, a lot of hard work," *Business Week,* November 30, 1992, pp. 70-71; Otis Port, John Carey, Kevin Kelly, and Stephanie Anderson Forest, "Quality," *Business Week,* November 30, 1992, pp. 66-72; Otis Port and Geoffrey Smith, "Beg, borrow—and benchmark," *Business Week,* November 30, 1992, pp. 74-75; Stratford Sherman, "How to prosper in the value decade," *Fortune,* November 30, 1992, pp. 90-103.

[7]Gabriella Stern, Suein Hwang, "Procter & Gamble agrees to buy Avon Product's Giorgio fragrance line," *The Wall Street Journal,* July 27, 1994, p. B4; Seema Nayyar, "Procter & Gamble's prescription for the future," *BRANDWEEK,* July 20, 1992, pp. 14-19; Zachary Schiller, "P&G is turning into quite a makeup artist," *Business Week,* April 8, 1991, pp. 66-69.

Global Marketing: A Close Shave!

There can be little doubt that worldwide markets hold a tremendous potential for American marketers. Trade agreements such as NAFTA, APEC and GATT, the acronyms that have flooded the news media recently, continue to open new doors for trading overseas. Many companies have taken advantage of ready and waiting foreign markets by adapting their products to new and different cultures. Others have jumped in with both feet without first determining customer needs. Globalization dictates the wise use of the marketing concept.

Not content to sit on its domestic laurels, Gillette was one of America's first multinationals. However, this well-known marketer of men's shaving needs and toiletries did not just jump into the global arena without a plan. The company realized that consumers were not the same worldwide, nor were promotional opportunities and messages. Gillette spent considerable time analyzing markets and media before entering the fray.

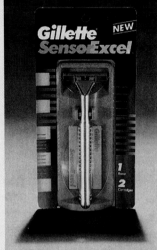

Once deciding to go global, Gillette developed a single communications strategy. Having learned that the value sought in shaving products was generally the same throughout the world, the firm decided to lead with its premiere brand, the Sensor. Although many brands are squeezed into foreign cultures where there is little chance of acceptance, Gillette was confident that both the product and the brand would be universally accepted.

SOURCE: Gavin Chalcraft, "Beware the perils of wanton globalization," BRANDWEEK, December 5, 1994, p. 17.

the entire business. Management must constantly work toward a goal of team effort in providing the utility needed by customers. Many companies are breaking down the typical management hierarchy to produce more horizontal organizations featuring the creation of teams. Firms such as Motorola, Xerox and AT&T swear by this move toward emphasizing the process rather than the task. Without this cooperation among everyone on the team, no effort by the marketing staff will produce customer satisfaction.[8]

Achieving the team effort offers many challenges. Many of today's businesses and business people are products of the production age. The idea of coordinating the firm's total effort toward customer satisfaction is a fairly new concept. Many companies still slip into the old "production comes first" rut. Continuing to offer the same products without developing a concern for the needs of the marketplace leads to failure.

Some firms understand the needs of the customer, yet may find that production modifications that allow them to respond to these needs are too costly. Some marketers opt to supply one type of product to everyone, instead of targeting smaller groups. Such firms can minimize costs and maximize profits by catering to mass rather than specific needs. But customers alter their

---

[8]John A. Byrne, "The horizontal corporation," *Business Week,* December 20, 1993, pp. 76-81.

preferences over time, and the environments within which the marketing company operates may change.

Many companies apply the marketing concept. For instance, mail order retailer L. L. Bean's telemarketing personnel provide outstanding service. In addition, this firm offers to resole its famous Maine hunting boots, if the tops are still in good condition, for only $24. This policy shows genuine concern for customer satisfaction. Embassy Suites offers free breakfasts and cocktails to its guests. This hostelry also promotes customer orientation by giving monthly bonuses to its employees. This marketing attitude flows down from the top. When management displays the marketing concept, employees follow.

The needs of the market must govern production decisions. Knowledgeable salespeople cannot overcome poor product planning. Expensive, slick advertising will not replace inadequate distribution systems. The companies exhibiting the marketing concept control the ability to provide utility and value to the customer. The tools such firms use make up the marketing mix.

hat Is The Marketing Mix?

Marketing does not just happen. Those companies that choose to be marketing oriented must adapt their firms to provide the utility needed by people and businesses. Businesses with the marketing concept manage and control the marketing mix in their pursuit of customer satisfaction.

MARKETING MIX DEFINED

In striving for customer satisfaction, businesses use what is known as the **marketing mix.** The marketing mix includes the product itself, its price, distribution systems and promotion. Most companies attempt to control these factors to provide the most satisfaction. Marketing oriented companies create the goods and services and adjust prices to fit demand and competition. Marketers also plan their distribution systems to provide time and place utility. Promotional efforts are geared toward creating product awareness and desire.

Marketing mix—the elements of product, price, distribution and promotion that create utility.

Product

The **product** is the first element of the marketing mix. Physical goods or intangible services are basic to customer satisfaction. Marketing oriented firms are able to modify their products to bring about the greatest benefit. Not all goods and services are viewed in the same way by all consumers or organizations. Features that bring satisfaction to one buyer may not be desired or accepted by another.

Each of these product traits has an impact upon the individual buyer. For instance, one consumer looking for an automobile may be interested in styling, room, economy of operation and warranty. To another buyer, only a Porsche or a Lexus will bring satisfaction. One baseball lover may be satisfied with watching any ball game, but to many avid Chicagoan's, it's the Cubs or nothing. Such loyalty may be crucial in making a satisfying purchase.

Packaging may be a deciding factor in satisfying the buyer. Food available in individual serving sizes may be the major characteristic that appeals the most to single people, while bulk packs at lower prices are a boon for shoppers

Product—a good or service used to provide satisfaction.

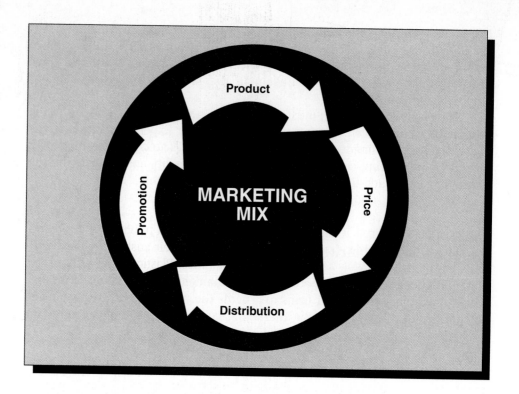

with larger families. Jars of pickles, plastic vials of medicine, boxes of picture puzzles, cartons of milk and sacks of flour come in different sizes to appeal to different markets.

Many products, such as appliances, computers and automobiles, require technical assistance or repair. An important factor in the purchase of such products could be a conveniently located, local facility to handle repairs or adjustments. Products from a manufacturer that offers servicing might be preferred by some buyers.

How well the manufacturer provides for replacement, repair or refund can have a decided effect on consumer satisfaction. Some products carry warranties from the manufacturer and/or the retailer. Others do not. Customers often prefer products that offer a better warranty. This is often true with the current consumer emphasis on quality.

Design, packaging, convenience and warranty are all components of the complete product. The marketer may create or modify each of these product characteristics to assure the greatest degree of satisfaction. The characteristics of goods and services and their effect on buying behavior will be covered in detail. Product is just one of the controllable elements of the marketing mix.

Price

Price—the perceived value of a product.

Another element of the marketing mix is **price,** or the perceived value of the product. Product price must be affordable for the targeted customer, yet affordability varies from buyer to buyer. For example, hardly a household can be found that does not have at least one pair of sneakers in a closet. Originally worn for sports, this footwear has become part of the native costume of teenagers and young adults. Prices depend not only on the quality of construction but on the image as well. Discount merchandisers sell some no-name sneakers for as little as $10, while Reebok, Nike and New Balance, many with built-in air pumps, may retail for more than ten times that amount.

An important component of a complete pricing program is the company's policies regarding payments or offering credit. Many of this country's largest retailers offer terms that include a liberal return policy. When the customer is not completely satisfied with the goods or services purchased, the product may be returned for replacement or refund. Because of these policies, buyers have learned to trust marketers such as Wal-Mart and Land's End.

Companies that allow customers to pay for products over time often have a competitive advantage. Visa, MasterCard, American Express and the Discovery Card exist because firms realized this need to supply credit to buyers. By convincing retailers that accepting credit cards is a bonus to their customers, these suppliers have created buying habits unique to our times. Plastic money and instant credit have become permanent fixtures in consumer goods and services markets.

Distribution

The **distribution** process gives the "when-and-where" satisfaction that consumers and users require. It makes little difference how attractive or functional the product might be if it is not available when needed. To many, the purchase of a good or service may be postponed for awhile if the desired item is not readily at hand. To others, if the product is not available now, there is no satisfaction.

Distribution—the process of supplying goods and services to consumers or firms with need.

If the particular style and color of a pair of shoes cannot be found in the right size, some buyers will place a special order. Other shoe purchasers may opt for a different model. For one, having the footwear now is more important than waiting for a specific brand or style. A person might be willing to delay a haircut for a week until his or her favorite stylist returns from vacation. On the other hand, waiting may not be an option if the Whitney Houston concert is tonight.

Promotion

Promotion, also known as marketing communication, is perhaps the most familiar element of the marketing mix. The glamour and sheer volume of advertising make promotion more evident than the other elements. Promotion is the vehicle marketers use to inform, remind or persuade potential buyers. This element of the marketing mix can be a powerful and influential force in determining consumer preferences.

Promotion—marketing communication that informs, reminds or persuades potential buyers.

The best products may never find their way to needy buyers without proper promotion. Advising consumers about the quality of goods and services and where they can be purchased is important to the marketing effort. Promotion has the added effect of boosting competition. By informing prospective buyers about the attributes of one product over another, advertisers are supplying the data needed for critical choices. As a result, product quality often improves. When rival brands gain favor with buyers, companies often realize the need to increase the quality of their own products. Improvement or redesign is often the only course of action for a marketer whose goods or services have been labeled as inadequate by customers.

Marketing and Society: The Great Condom Debate

Few maladies have had the impact on society as has the AIDS epidemic. The dramatic change in course from the free-sex era of the seventies and eighties to the safe-sex message of the nineties has captured the public's attention. Certainly, Earvin "Magic" Johnson's painful revelation gripped the world. The early stigma of AIDS as a disease transmitted only by homosexuals and drug addicts is changing.

During the 1980s, condom sales climbed mercurially. Once relegated to drawers behind the counter at pharmacies, many brands are now openly displayed on point-of-purchase merchandisers. Some condoms are now found for sales at upscale boutiques and stores. To coin a phrase often heard in government circles, using condoms has become "politically correct." Even

with this widespread acceptance, condom sales have tapered off lately, and poor marketing is being blamed.

Many people in our society show concern over the spread of AIDS. Celebrities and business people have joined forces in raising funds to aid in research and increase public awareness. Meanwhile, the media have been caught in the dilemma of wanting to satisfy the need for intelligent education while at the same time trying not to offend.

Although television has been cleared by government agencies to advertise condoms, many networks and stations have chosen not to air these commercials. Many magazines have rejected ads by Benetton, the international clothing marketer, extending its "United Colors of Benetton" slogan to disease control sheaths. On the other hand, such promotional messages in Europe face little of the resistance found in this country. The debate over the importance of having an informed public versus the desire to keep from offending any segment of society is likely to continue.

SOURCE: Cyndee Miller, "Condom sales cool off; carefree attitudes of youth, poor marketing are blamed," *Marketing News*, February 28, 1994, pp. 1 and 9; Barbara Lippert, "Benetton's condoms raise a hue and cry," *Adweek's Marketing Week*, February 18, 1991, p. 37. (Photo courtesy of Benetton)

The marketing mix contains those tools that can be largely controlled by management. A marketing oriented company has the ability to modify the products it offers, adjust prices, select distribution and develop a wide range of promotional activities. Managed use of the marketing mix is exactly what occurs as businesses seek to satisfy the needs of customers.

What Are the Functions of Marketing?

In managing the marketing mix to provide customer satisfaction, businesses carry out a number of related functions. In large firms, each of these activities may be controlled by different individuals or departments. Managers of small companies often do multiple tasks.

BUYING AND SELLING

Buying and selling are two of the primary tasks facing today's marketers. Whether the company is in manufacturing or in distribution, things must be bought and sold to accomplish the goals of the business. Industrial firms purchase raw materials or component parts to manufacture other products. Intermediaries buy goods to be resold. Each of these acquisitions depends upon the ultimate needs of the consumer.

Marketers of services also carry out the buying function. The beautician must create the latest styles to please customers. The tax preparer will not produce satisfaction by using last year's forms to file this year's taxes. The hairstylist and the accountant must be equipped with the latest information and supplies. Good purchasing helps service marketers prepare to satisfy customer needs.

TRANSPORTATION AND STORAGE

Transportation and storage are also functions of marketing people. A necessary goal of distribution systems is to have products available when needed. Retailers must keep goods on hand in sufficient quantities to provide a consistent supply to the markets served. Toys 'R Us, Wal-Mart and Home Depot are important cogs in the marketing wheel that supplies needed goods and services.

Consumer goods marketers need to have influence over members of the distribution channel. Such control is necessary to assure that transportation and storage tasks are carried out properly. If Gillette runs a nationwide promotional campaign on its Right Guard deodorant, the retailers' shelves must have adequate stock. Computer software giant Microsoft must assure a supply of programs for its service centers and industry users.

STANDARDIZING AND GRADING

Standardizing and grading are necessary because of the staggering number of products available to the consumer or user. Placing goods or services into specific categories assists buyers in understanding what products are available. Clothing comes in a variety of sizes which are fairly uniform from brand to brand. Laundry detergent from different manufacturers appears on the supermarket shelves in cartons with the same capacity. Marketers provide this standardization.

Government agencies set some standards and grades. Trade associations or industries establish others. The U.S. Department of Agriculture classifies meat and dairy products according to established standards. The Society of Automotive Engineers creates rigid specifications for many automobile parts. The Coca Cola Company regulates the ingredients in its soft drinks. Manufacturers and service providers determine the level of quality they will offer consistent with the need to satisfy their customers.

sparkle...sparkle...sparkle...sparkle...sparkle

feel the difference ...
Coke puts you at your sparkling best!

Anyone for fun? The fountain's the place to find it!
And part of the fun, for millions, is the real great taste
and sparkling refreshment of ice-cold Coca-Cola. Why
not let Coke give your next lunch a nice happy sparkle?

The Coca-Cola company takes great pains to keep the specifications and formulas for its products secret.

CREDIT

Credit functions are often under the control of the financial department, yet marketers cannot afford to overlook this important facet of most transactions. Setting sensible prices for products is necessary. The need to establish terms of sale is equally important. Buyers often compare these selling terms against other product attributes. Setting prices and selling terms are tasks for marketers, not accountants. If financing from General Motors Acceptance Corporation were not available to GM's dealers, fewer cars would be sold. Credit policies affect marketing.

In establishing competitive terms, marketers strive to assist businesses generate a profit. Applying the marketing concept does not mean that satisfaction of customer needs voids the need for sound business judgment. Two of the factors that led to the demise of the selling age were the unwarranted granting of credit and the offering of expanded buying terms. Free and easy credit creates more problems for companies than it solves.

COMMUNICATION

The communication function involves the transmission of ideas and strategies both internally and externally. Passing of information to current and future customers is part of this function. Further, in a typical marketing oriented company, since employees work together in teams, everyone should be familiar with the goals and tactics of the marketing policy. When the production department grasps the market needs for certain standards of quality, its workers are more apt to minimize rejects. Shipping departments must understand customer requirements for delivery. Credit people have to keep apprised of competitive selling terms.

Marketers, through their promotional efforts, communicate product quality, price and availability to prospective customers. The best products will do little to satisfy needs if potential buyers are not aware of their existence. Accurate and effective promotion of the business's goods and services is one of the major roles played by marketing people.

MARKETING RESEARCH AND MANAGEMENT

Promotion often depends upon input from research efforts. Learning about the effectiveness of advertising and publicity is important for all firms engaged in providing products to needy customers. Marketing businesses rely upon research to manage the job of meeting the marketing concept criteria.

No discussion of the functions marketing people perform would be complete without the mention of management. Marketers by nature must be managers. Controlling the functions marketing oriented companies perform is a standard management task. In addition, supervision of product planning, including design and packaging, is necessary to assure that marketing functions run smoothly.

Buying and selling, transporting and storing, standardizing and grading are a few of the tasks confronting marketers. Financing, communication and managing complete the marketing effort. These typical functions are a part of almost all marketing operations.

ho Carries Out These Marketing Functions?

Individuals or departments within the marketing company carry out many of these functions. Most larger businesses employ staffs to accomplish these tasks. Smaller operations may have only a few people to handle the marketing duties. Other firms may opt to use independent specialists.

■ ■ ■ ■ ■

Marketing functions and who performs them

FUNCTION	WITHIN FIRM	OUTSIDE AGENCY
Buying	Purchasing Department	Independent buyers group
Selling	Sales Department	Manufacturers' agents
Transportation	Traffic Department	Shipping specialists
Storage	Traffic Department	Public warehouse
Standardizing/Grading	Marketing Department	Trade association/ government
Credit authorization		
Marketing research	Finance Department	Banks, credit bureaus
Advertising	Marketing Department	Marketing research firm
Public relations	Advertising Department	Advertising agency
	Advertising or PR Department	PR agency

■ ■ ■ ■ ■

MARKETING DEPARTMENTS

Most large consumer and business product manufacturers have internal marketing departments. The men and women working in this group have training and expertise in these functions. These sections direct and control the marketing mix within or outside their companies.

Marketing departments of major corporations include specialists who handle personal selling and advertising. Other groups include marketing research, new product development or product design. Some consumer product manufacturers follow the lead established by giant consumer goods houses such as General Mills, Kraft General Foods or RJR Nabisco to include product specialists within the marketing organization.

OUTSIDE FIRMS

Some manufacturers lack either funds or know-how to employ their own staff in marketing areas. Such companies seek the services of independent, outside firms that specialize is specific marketing functions. The same types of personnel found in marketing departments staff these agencies and firms. Expert marketing help is the key to success whether provided from within the company or from outside.

Advertising and Public Relations Agencies

Advertising agencies are organizations that create, plan and schedule promotional materials and campaigns. While many large consumer products manufacturers have in-house advertising departments, others elect to use the services of professional agencies. Creative people, media specialists and customer liaison personnel staff these organizations. Some advertising agencies do prod-

uct design, branding, package creation and marketing research. These full service agencies sometimes act as independent marketing firms.

Advertising agencies promote their clients' products. Public relations
agencies are more concerned with the image of the company itself. How the
public views the marketer is just as important as the look, taste, function or
feel of the product. Shaping the image of a business may require the special
talents of public relations experts. These firms have particular expertise in
developing and promoting the corporation. Their staffs have contacts and good
rapport established with the editorial members of the media. Public relations
experts are in great demand by firms under public scrutiny, such as in the
petroleum and defense industries.

Marketing Research Firms

Some departments in companies, outside marketing firms or advertising agencies conduct market research. Other organizations work exclusively in this field.
These marketing research firms usually locate in major metropolitan areas.
They conduct surveys, evaluate markets and test the effectiveness of promotional efforts for clients.

Many staff members in marketing research firms have scientific or academic backgrounds. Economists, mathematicians and even anthropologists are
found on the staffs of these support businesses. The ability of these professionals to analyze and develop theories about research questions greatly
assists the research effort. While the internal organization within a company
may perform many marketing functions, scientific research is often left to outside firms.

Marketing Intermediaries

Marketing intermediaries include wholesalers, distributors, dealers, jobbers
and retailers. These individuals and firms provide a vital link in the marketing
process by assuring the delivery of products between producers and customers.
Grand Union supermarkets, Kinney shoe stores, Burger King fast food outlets
and the college bookstore all fit this description of marketing intermediaries.
They are often the parties responsible for seeing that satisfaction is reached.
Some intermediaries carry out more functions than others, but all serve as an
important part of marketing distribution systems.[9]

While some marketing oriented companies choose to control their own
distribution systems through company owned intermediaries, most consumer
goods marketers use independent businesses in their distribution systems.
Whether performing as company subsidiaries or as independent operators,
marketing intermediaries carry out those tasks that assure that the when-and-
where requirements of customers are met.

**Marketing
intermediaries**—those
individuals and firms
that assure delivery of
products from produc-
ers to customers.

---

[9]The term *marketing intermediaries* was first suggested by Boone & Kurtz in *Contemporary
Marketing* (New York: CBS Publishing, 1986), Preface, p. xiv.

SUMMING IT UP

Marketing involves company or individual efforts to satisfy the needs and wants of customers. The exchange process describes where marketing transactions occur. Customers receive satisfaction when they exchange money or other assets for goods and services that provide benefit. Through market demand, consumer sovereignty prevails in market economies. Government usually determines what goods and services will be offered in command economies.

Marketing affects everyone. Each individual and business is impacted daily by some aspect of marketing. It is important to understand how marketing works. Satisfaction of needs or wants is supplied by form, time, place and possession utility. Products must be in the form needed to provide benefit. Goods and services must also be available when and where they are needed. Buyers must also be able to possess the attributes of these products.

Early businesses strived to provide as many products as possible. The mass production of goods describes the production age. In the selling age, focus turned toward distribution. Companies aimed to increase the number of outlets where their products could be bought. The marketing age brings an emphasis on determining and satisfying customer needs.

Companies that focus their attention on satisfaction of customer needs have the marketing concept. This orientation must be a team effort involving all members of the operation.

The marketing mix includes the product, price, distribution and promotion. Products include either goods or services. Prices vary depending upon internal and external influences. Distribution provides the when and where benefit needed. Promotion informs buyers of product availability. The firm's ability to satisfy customers is determined by its marketing mix.

Buying and selling, transportation and storage, standardization and grading are all functions of marketers. The offering of credit, marketing communication and research are also part of the role played by marketers and managers. Many of these tasks are carried out by individuals within marketing firms. Sometimes independent organizations provide these services.

KEY CONCEPTS AND TERMS
FROM CHAPTER ONE

Consumer sovereignty	Possession utility
Distribution	Price
Exchange process	Product
Form utility	Production age
Marketing	Promotion
Marketing age	Selling age
Marketing concept	Time utility
Marketing intermediaries	Transaction
Marketing mix	Utility
Place utility	

BUILDING SKILLS

1. Describe how marketing might be conducted in other countries and economic settings. Explain the kinds of problems one might expect in the countries of the former Soviet Union to face in developing free market economies.

2. Contrast the different types of utility, citing examples to support your case.

3. Describe the phases in the evolution of marketing, including the management emphasis in each.

4. Define the marketing concept, citing examples to support your case.

5. Describe the marketing mix, citing examples of how it varies between different products and companies.

6. Describe and discuss some of the typical marketing functions that are conducted by companies such as Apple Computer, Gillette, Dole, Marriott.

7. Explain why one firm might decide to use outside sources rather than do the marketing with their own personnel.

Making Decisions 1-1: "It Takes a Licking and Keeps on Ticking...er, Glowing."

The growth in the number of brands of wrist watches has exploded in the past decade. Many of the new entries have gained popularity due to lower prices. Others have tapped special markets, such as Swatch's move toward the teenage sector. As one of the veterans in this industry, Timex has always had a loyal following from those who appreciated the durability of the product. The firm's classic slogan, "It takes a licking but keeps on ticking" has stood the test of time among consumers.

In the early 1990s, Timex appeared to be somewhat stagnant. Competition in the "less than $100" category was fierce as Swatch, Seiko, Lorus and Casio vied with Timex for a somewhat limited market. The time was ripe for something new to shake up this humdrum market, and Timex did just that. Enter Indiglo, the watch with the blue, glow-in-the-dark face. Developed in cooperation with Motorola Inc., Indiglo is an electroluminscent light powered by the watch's battery.

The novelty of Indiglo caught on immediately. Timex credited its 30% increase in sales during 1993 largely to this new product, and similar jumps continue. Letters from customers with unique stories have inundated the firm's marketing department. Los Angeles earthquake victims wrote about how their Indiglos helped them tiptoe through broken glass strewn halls. Some capsized fishermen from Florida talked about the comfort of the blue dials helping them through the night. Such publicity has helped move this somewhat mundane timepiece from the drugstore counter to trendier displays at department stores. Although no one knows for sure how long the market will last, Indiglo from Timex is quite a hit...for the time being.[10]

Describe the types of utility that Indiglo from Timex offers its buyers, along with the ways that Timex has demonstrated the marketing concept.

Making Decisions 1-1: 1-2: Where the Boys Are.

One would be hard pressed to find a more successful, long-standing product than Barbie, from toy giant Mattel Incorporated. The year was 1959 when this star was born, and the old girl is still going strong. Roughly half of this California company's revenue has come from sales of this venerable cutie and her friends. A Valley Girl talking model, reintroduced in 1992, could lead to revenues of over $1 billion by the mid 1990s. In recognition of her thirty-fifth birthday, Mattel came out with a special reproduction of Barbie in 1994, complete with the original zebra striped bathing suit she first introduced. The giant toy marketer also expanded the accessory line to include a cruise ship with detachable swimming pool and a motor home that converts into an outdoor camping scene, complete with twinkling stars.

[10]Editors, "Indiglo watch lights up better times for Timex," *BRANDWEEK,* April 25, 1994, pp. 30-32.

As successful as Barbie has been, Mattel still feels that there is room for growth. Recent strategies call for additional distribution in Europe and Latin America. The company is also broadening the appeal for this world-famous doll by creating new wardrobes. Barbie can now be seen wearing everything from standard business attire to leather miniskirts. The sales of clothing and accessories form a major portion of the continued growth in sales of this superstar. This venerable cutie even has her own store, Barbie on Madison, located in the Manhattan outlet of FAO Schwarz.

While Mattel management is thrilled with the success saga of Barbie, they want the world to realize that the company also makes toys for boys. One of the company's recent triumphs in this field is Bruno the Bad Dog, a toy truck that transforms into a ferocious barking dog. Other additions to the male side of its line of toys include figures from the film Hook and from television's popular show American Gladiators. Mattel is also heavily promoting colorful baseball gear for kids and the latest rival to Silly Putty, Gak, an oozy, gooey stuff.[11]

Explain, in marketing terms, the tremendous success of Mattel's Barbie, along with the ways that the company used its marketing mix.

Making Decisions 1-3: B&D courts the DIY.

Face it, some people are handier than others. There are those who can build decks, landscape the backyard, repair their own cars and even add a room or remodel the kitchen. These folks who are "good with their hands" have formed an entire market niche called Do-It-Yourself, or DIY. Although the market for DIYers has been around for sometime, it has taken a big jump in the past decade with the advent of giant home improvement retailers, such as Home Depot, Hechinger and Lowe's. For some companies that manufactured tools and supplies for this field, an opportunity presented itself.

In the early 1990s, Black & Decker, a well-known product name in America, reintroduced its DeWalt brand as a pricey line of tools targeting professional builders. While the average consumer has a high regard for this giant appliance and power tool manufacturer, the industrial user had a lesser image. In order to recapture the building professional, B&D brought back the old brand name that had once held a quality position. By ignoring any mention of the parent company, Black & Decker rejuvenated sales in this profitable sector.

Black & Decker quickly learned that the DeWalt professional tools were too expensive for the typical DIYer. To learn what this market really needed, B&D elected to study a small group of male consumers who owned and used power tools regularly. Coupled with other research, the results obtained from this consumer group showed what this market needed and how the company could reach them. The company then established project teams to design a new line of tools from the ground up, quickly. In August 1993, Black & Decker launched its Quantum line—the brand name and colors were the direct result of consumer input. Post-purchase interviews with buyers confirmed that B&D had indeed met the needs of this fast growing market.[12]

Describe Black & Decker's use of the marketing mix and the ways this company epitomizes the marketing concept.

---

[11]Cyndee Miller, "Finding next big toy is not child's play," *Marketing News*, May 23, 1994, pp. 2 and 14; Editors, "Mattel's Barbie's got a new billion-dollar figure," *BRANDWEEK*, February 8, 1993, pp. 32-33.

[12]Susan Caminiti, "A star is born," *Fortune*," November 29, 1993, pp. 44-47.

2

Managing the Marketing Environments and Society

The Job to be Done

Marketing doesn't just happen. Marketers may have control over the marketing mix, but there are other variables that affect all plans.

Chapter 2 covers the outside influences that impact marketing and the affect of societal demands on marketing strategies, allowing you to:

- identify the environments in which marketing operates,
- analyze the economic, demographic, cultural, governmental, technological and competitive changes that influence marketing decisions,
- explain how professionals manage marketing in face of these constant fluctuating environments, and
- comprehend the impact that the demands of society have upon marketing management.

Marketers at Work

Working as an assistant to the Special Events Coordinator for the Southern California Division of PepsiCo sounds like a fascinating and glamorous job. According to Maryann Sugawara, "it was anything but." Oh sure, the events were exciting and she was fortunate to meet lots of marketing people, but the demand for split-second timing and execution were stressful, to say the least. Still it was this experience that pointed her toward a career in advertising.

Maryann received her first taste of marketing while employed as a "gofer" with a small advertising agency in Orange County, California. She began working for PepsiCo while attending Orange Coast College, and continued in this capacity after transferring to California State University Solidus/Fullerton. Although admitting that her college courses in marketing and advertising were helpful, it was practical experience that really hooked her this career path.

After graduation, Maryann landed a job with Muse Cordero Chen, Inc., an award-winning minor-

Maryann Sugawara

ity advertising agency in Los Angeles. This fast-growing firm won acclaim for creating powerful ads for Nike, Snapple and Supercuts that targeted specific ethnic audiences. The firm's work on the anti-smoking campaign for the California Department of Health Services was especially noteworthy.

Maryann began work for Muse Cordero Chen as an Assistant Account Coordinator. She has worked with most of the firm's major clients in developing complete marketing campaigns. Although she finds the human contact exciting and rewarding, Maryann's real interest lies in art. To this end, she has enrolled in the Los Angeles Art Center's College of Design, turning toward the creative end of the business. Whatever direction she selects, Maryann Sugawara has the talent and ambition to succeed.

What Are the Marketing Environments?

Marketers do not work in a vacuum. Business ventures are constantly facing upheaval due to environmental changes. Fluctuations in the economy, demographics, cultural areas, government laws and policies, technology and changes among competitors are common. Marketing management often has very little control over these external factors.

The changing **environments** in which marketers operate include the economic, demographic, cultural, political, technological and competitive arenas. As their surroundings shift and fluctuate, companies must alter their marketing mix to deal with new situations. Each environment has its own dimensions, yet they are often interrelated. Economic change regularly creates political action. The cultural environment often experiences changes in customs and traditions, as well as demographic movement. New technology stimulates competitive activity. Marketers must adjust strategies to handle each event.

Large movement in any of these environmental areas may be gradual, but sudden changes of a smaller nature have a dramatic impact on marketing strategy. Fluctuation in the business cycle or the influx of immigrants may take place over time. Trade quotas imposed by governments or price cuts by competitors can occur at a moment's notice. Shifts in these external climates

Marketing environments—the economic, demographic, cultural, political, technological and competitive arenas in which marketing operates.

impact each element of the marketing mix. Changes in product design caused by technological developments impact prices. Distribution moves in response to demographic shifts modify promotional campaigns. Modifications of these marketing environments create opportunities as well as problems.

ECONOMIC ENVIRONMENT

The business climate is not static. Cyclical or seasonal changes in the **economic environment** influence buying power. This in turn places pressure on prices and on product development. Historically, business has tended to progress through a series of up turns and down falls. These fluctuations in the business cycle affect all aspects of marketing. While some of these seasonal moves are predictable, others are not.

> **Economic environment**—the fiscal and financial factors influencing buying power.

The business cycle typically passes through stages known as prosperity, recession and recovery. Severe recession is usually called depression. During the upward spiral of prosperity, unemployment remains low and consumer spending is high. Although economic conditions are good, real individual income may decrease due to inflation. These environmental changes seriously impact disposable and discretionary income.

Disposable/Discretionary Income

Disposable personal income is the money that a person or household can save or spend after deductions for taxes. **Discretionary income** is what is left from disposable income after covering the necessities of life. Following the subtraction of money to pay taxes, housing costs, food, clothing and medical care, what is left can be used to purchase other goods and services. Discretionary income is a measure of consumer buying power.

Fluctuations in the business cycle influence an individual's buying power. Discretionary income is generally high in prosperous times. People tend to spend more until the upward spiral of inflation takes over, and they begin to receive less value for their dollars. As the economy slips into a recession, spending drops and unemployment rises. This downward trend impacts discretionary income and buying power.

> **Disposable personal income**—The amount of money available to spend or save after deductions for taxes.
> **Discretionary income**—disposable income minus necessities, such as housing, food and clothing.

In a severe recession, business conditions have deteriorated drastically. Businesses lay off workers due to lack of demand for the firm's products. The unemployed lack the money to buy goods and services, causing additional people to lose their jobs. Although wise marketers forecast such economic trends, they can do little to prevent them.

DEMOGRAPHICS

America has often been described as a nation that cannot sit still. The country certainly has seen its share of change since its birth over two hundred years ago. The population has grown and has aged. An increasing number of immigrants entering our society come from countries such as Nicaragua, Haiti, Hong Kong and the former Soviet Union. Americans are filling new jobs and moving to new locations. The demographics of the United States are in a constant state of change.

ENVIRONMENT	CHARACTERISTICS
Economic	Changes in the business cycle; inflation and recession; the effect on disposable and discretionary income
Demographic	Changes in the make-up of our society based upon age, gender, ethnic background etc.; the "graying of America" and the traits of the "X" generation; population shifts to Sun Belt states and away from urban centers
Cultural	Changes in our perception of the role of men and women, along with changes in the family life style; increased multicultural influence; the "wellness" movement and "green" marketing
Political	Changes in government laws and regulations; deregulation; consumer and environmental protection; actions of government agencies
Technological	Changes involving the creation of new products and systems; superconductivity, cold fusion and the information highway
Competitive	Changes in competition; new products and new packaging; pricing pressure; nontraditional channels of distribution; effective advertising and increased selling pressure

■   ■   ■   ■   ■

Demographics—the study of populations by size, location, age, gender, ethnic background and other factors of its people.

Demographics is defined as the study of populations by size, location, age, gender and ethnic backgrounds. Occupations, incomes, wealth and other characteristics are also part of this statistical description. People move from area to area, new jobs arise as old ones fade; whole sections of a country or state may have a change in makeup. Political upheavals and economic revolts in other countries have changed the faces of Americans. The ebb and flow of birth rates, population shifts and immigration impact many marketing decisions.

Demographic studies are statistical in nature and provide marketers with vital information. The age and ethnic makeup of given locales raise the demand for different products. Income levels and occupational data affect the pricing strategy. The channels for distribution may need to be created or abandoned as populations shift. Promotion often takes on different flavors as the ethnic quality of a region changes.

Consumer Groups

One good example of changing demographics is the population shifts experienced in the United States since World War II. The increase in the number of babies born in the late 1940s and early 1950s impacts entire industries. Children born during this period were called "baby boomers." Their numbers triggered a rush of products targeted toward infants.

BABY BOOMERS Many baby boomers became the young, upwardly mobile professionals, or **yuppies,** of the 1980s. As a group, these consumers displayed purchasing patterns different from those of previous generations.

Yuppies generally spent more and saved less. Their retirement plans are less stable and more indefinite than those for their parents. Collectively, these people had a tremendous impact upon the types and numbers of goods and services that were provided. Mature baby boomers are just hitting their stride, reaching their earnings peak during the 1990s. The year 1990 brought a mini-baby-boom, as women who had waited to start families began giving birth. Although the blizzards of the winter of 1993-1994 extended this period a bit, the baby boomlet definitely appears to be ending.[1]

Although much has been written about the baby-boomer era, most experts agree today that the group does not act as one giant market. Although some 77 million Americans count themselves as boomers, they do respond differently to products and promotion. As a group, they generally place a greater emphasis on personal needs, yet many boomers are now fighting the aging process, becoming major purchasers of anti-aging products. As this group of consumers, born between the mid-1940s to the mid-1960s matures, their buying habits will continue to impact savvy marketers.[2]

THE "X" GENERATION, OR BABY BUSTERS Following the baby boom years, the number of children born to the average U.S. family declined, even reaching ZPG (zero population growth) around 1980. The generation of children born to boomers are now reaching maturity and, though a sizable market, their numbers are declining. Sometimes called "baby busters," this group of eighteen to thirty-four year olds is facing the world differently than their boomer parents.

Sometimes referred to as "Generation X," these consumers are a bit more jaded than their predecessors. The freedom spawned in the boomer years carries over to this new generation in the form of intense individualism. Busters typically are not as trusting of business and business people, and are likely to look upon marketing as little more than hype.

The tension between these two generations is especially evident in office environments, where busters are apt to look upon boomers as slow moving and inefficient. The blossoming of the information age has created opportunities for X generation members that their predecessors did not have. Taco Bell demonstrated the importance of this market with a promotional campaign begun in 1994. Featuring alternative music, television commercials and print ads promoted the in-store sale of tapes and CDs, as well as contests for "South of the Border" trips.[3]

---

[1]Diana Crispell, "The baby boomlet may end with a blizzard," *American Demographics,* March 1994, pp. 16-17; Editors, "The rich autumn of a consumer's life," *The Economist,"* September 9, 1992, p. 67; Gene Horetz, "Baby boomers are just hitting their earnings stride," *Business Week,* April 6, 1992, p. 14; Joseph Spiers, "The baby boomlet is for real," *Fortune,* February 10, 1992, pp. 100-104.

[2]Campbell Gibson, "The four baby booms," *American Demographics,* November 1993, pp. 36-40; Cheryl Russell, "The master trend," *American Demographics,* October 1993, pp. 28-37; Howard Schlossberg, "Survey sheds light on 'typical' boomer," *Marketing News,* January 31, 1994; Robert A. Rosenblatt, "Boomers: Keeping up with the folks," *The Oregonian,* September 19, 1993, pp. A1-29; Judith Springer Riddle, "Fountain of growth," *BRANDWEEK,* August 16, 1993, pp. 19-22.

[3]Laura Keaton, "New magazines aim to reach (and rechristen) Generation X," *The Wall Street Journal,* October 17, 1994, pp. B1 and B8; Suneel Ratan, "Why busters hate boomers," *Fortune,* October 4, 1993, pp, 56-70; Cheryl Russell, "The power of one," *BRANDWEEK,* October 4, 1993, pp. 27-32; Mark Landler, "Move over, boomers," *Business Week,* December 14, 1992, pp. 74-82; Jon Berry, "Consensus on the new census—a key demo plummets in numbers," *BRANDWEEK,* December 7, 1992, p. 8.

ALTERNATIVE DINNER MUSIC.

CD $4⁹⁹   TAPE $3⁹⁹

Stop by Taco Bell today and pick up a Do Something CD or tape featuring 10 of today's hottest alternative bands, including Sarah McGlachlan...General Public...Cracker... and Spin Doctors...CDs are only $4.99 and tapes $3.99. A portion of the net proceeds goes to Do Something, helping young people help their communities. So crank up the tunes. Cross the Border.™ And Do Something.

Purchase required. Offer valid at participating Taco Bell® locations while supplies last. Price does not include tax. Guaranteed minimum donation $200,000. For information about Do Something, Inc. call (212) 978-7777. Void where prohibited.

Taco bell targets the X generation with its new advertising campaign

The Graying of America

As birth rates decline and life expectancy increases, the composition of our population changes. People over the age of fifty make up a larger group of our residents today than ever before. This **graying of America** will likely become the most significant external change to impact marketing in the next century. The impact of the baby boom will continue to be felt as this portion of our population enters middle age and then becomes senior citizens. By the year 2025, a far greater percentage of the U.S. population will fall into the over-60-years-old category than during any time in our society's history.

Graying of America— the increasing market for goods and services among people over 50.

As the mature market materializes, marketers are responding quickly to determine the needs and wants of this sizable group. Just as all segments of the population differ, so do those in the over 50 category. Certain characteristics, such as declining materialistic values and increased flexibility, appear common, but marketers have learned to avoid stereotyping the mature adult. While as a whole the group purchases more sunscreen and painkillers than younger markets, where and how they shop covers a broad spectrum. Analysts expect to see greater emphasis on spending versus saving as baby boomers begin to infiltrate the gray market.[4]

Several titles for these aging, former baby boomers have appeared. One gerontologist refers to the group as YEEPIES, standing for "Youthful, Energetic Elderly People Involved in Everything." Another writer calls this demographic category GRAMPIES, or "Growing Retired Active Moneyed People In an Excellent State." Whatever buzzwords are used to describe these consumers, a few facts are evident to marketers. On the whole, this older population is living longer and retiring earlier. Middle-aged Americans have the energy, time and money to make a sizable market.[5]

One thing that mature adults and marketers have learned alike is that the body does not last forever. This is certainly true with oral hygiene. Where at one time the typical oral care section of a drugstore or supermarket held a few brands and sizes, today's shopper often faces up to seven dozen different types of toothbrushes and over 150 toothpastes. No longer does dental hygiene attack just cavities. Many of the newer products fight effects of aging such as tartar buildup and yellowing.[6]

Population Shifts

The size and makeup of the population are among the demographic factors affecting marketing. The shifts of population centers are other elements of concern to marketers. Increased numbers of people living in the Sun Belt, or those areas with warmer and sunnier climates, have had significant influence

---

[4]David B. Wolfe, "Targeting the mature mind," *American demographics,* March 1994, pp. 32-36; Carol M. Morgan, "The psychographic landscape of 50-plus," *BRANDWEEK,* July 19, 1993, pp. 28-32.

[5]Frank L. Conaway, "The mature consumer," *Discount Merchandiser,* May 1994, pp. 150-151; J. Waldrop, "Old money," *American Demographics,* April 1992, pp. 24-26; V. Goodhead, "Marketing to mature adults requires a state of being," *Marketing News,* December 9, 1991, p. 10.

[6]Editors, "The American oral orgy is just beginning," *BRANDWEEK,* February 7, 1994, pp. 28-

on distribution systems. Florida, Texas, Arizona and California have been major gainers in this population trend. Researchers estimate that by the year 2000 one out of every eight Americans will live in California, which will have a GDP greater than all but six nations of the world. Southern and Western areas will need an increase in the number of intermediaries and transportation systems to ease distribution to an increasing population.[7]

A number of smaller cities are experiencing population explosions. The quest for clean air, recreational opportunities and affordable living caused a flood of employees to seek out places such as Chattanooga, Tennessee; Boise, Idaho; and Madison, Wisconsin. Amarillo, a smallish city in the Texas panhandle, sent checks worth millions of dollars to businesses, but the businesses could only redeem the checks if the firms set up shops in the town.

Quality living has replaced income opportunity as the choice of many. Technological advances trigger many of these population shifts. The information era sparked by the computer makes the location of business less reliant upon suppliers or customers. San Diego, Salt Lake City, Minneapolis-St. Paul, Orlando and Austin have become hot spots for growth due to this technological explosion.[8]

Another phenomenon is the increased importance of "edge cities." These population centers, located around major metropolitan areas, gain increasing importance as downtown areas become less desirable. Once again, technology

GEOGRAPHIC POPULATION MOVEMENTS THROUGH THE YEAR 2000

■ Winners   ■ Losers

SOURCE: Anne Murphy, "Hot Spots," *Inc. 500*, 1994, pp. 37-40; Joseph Spiers, "Areas where prospects are best," *Fortune*, January 27, 1992, pp. 21-22

---

[7] Jon Berry, "Where the growth is," *BRANDWEEK*, March 22, 1993, p. 32.

[8] Louise Lee, "Move your company to Amarillo; it's a nice place, and they'll pay," *The Wall Street Journal*, September 14, 1994, p. B1; Kevin Kelly, Joseph Weber, Janin Friend, Sandra Atchison, Gail DeGeorge and William J. Holstein, "Hot spots," *Business Week*, October 19, 1992, pp. 80-88.

plays a role on where people locate. In spite of this trend of entrepreneurs locating away from major cities, many of the older northern cities such as Boston, Chicago and Minneapolis are still rich in the talent and brainpower that some employers seek. However, today's marvelous communication systems allow women and men to exchange information from all parts of the country or the world.[9]

CULTURAL ENVIRONMENT

The **cultural environment** includes all of the customs and traditions of a society that influence marketing decisions. Changes in family structures impact the needs of people and the ways that marketers operate. The health and well-being of a population influences new product development, distribution and promotion. Influxes of peoples from foreign lands have a striking effect on both populations and their businesses. Sometimes these changes create new opportunities. Other times they appear to be disruptive. Regardless, the culture of our or any society has a decided effect upon marketing and marketers.

Cultural environment—the customs and traditions of a society that influence marketing.

Women in Business

The increasing number of women entering the workforce is a significant cultural change that affects marketing. As more females take full-time positions in business, changes in living patterns and habits develop. In 1980 fewer than 20 percent of American kitchens had microwave ovens. Today most of these family centers are equipped with these radar ranges. Such a change in lifestyle has created a staggering number of new products aimed at microwave cooking. Many of the foods found on supermarket shelves today were not available just a few years ago. Marketers have reformulated products and redesigned packaging to meet the demand of microwave owners.

With more women working, the number of two paycheck families is increasing. In 1990, over one-third of U.S. households lived off double incomes. This number will climb to over 50 percent before the turn of the century. Two income families account for more than two-thirds of the personal wealth of the country. In addition, single, head-of-household families continue to increase. Such cultural changes result in an increase in the demand for more convenience items and easier maintenance of households.[10]

An increased number of women launching business and professional careers has sparked dramatic changes in product lines from clothing and leather goods marketers. The over 57 million working women in America is a formidable market. Executive garb for women is a prominent addition for many garment manufacturers. Jockey International doubled its sales with the creation of a line of underwear for women. Automobile makers, credit card

---

[9]Joel Garreau, "Edge cities in profile," *American Demographics,* February 1994, pp. 24-33; Kenneth Labich, "The best cities for knowledge workers," *Fortune,* November 15, 1993, pp 50-56.
[10]U.S. Bureau of the Census, Current Population report.

Coach Style Nº 6750

To order the bag shown, or for your free copy of the Coach Leatherware catalogue, call 800-262-2411.
Nº 6750 Riding Bag Spectator, five colors, $154.
Nº 4715 Organizer, $170.
Nº 2050 Silk-lined gloves, $64.
Also available at The Coach Store nearest you.

New York • London • Tokyo

The increasing number of women holding executive positions in business opens new markets for many established products (Courtesy of Coach Leatherware)

companies and computer marketers realize the potential of this market and adapt their products and promotion to appeal to this growing segment. Advertising is also reflecting the changing role of women, increasingly portraying women in non-stereotyped roles. Maidenform dropped its former "I dreamed...in a Maidenform bra" ads in 1992 in favor of a campaign that stressed self-esteem and empowerment of women.[11]

---

[11]Gerry Meyers, "Targeting the new professional woman," *BRANDWEEK*, January 31, 1994, pp. 18-24; Cyndee Miller, "Liberation for women in ads," *Marketing News*, August 17, 1992, pp. 1 and 2.

Singles as Buyers

Another phenomenon of our changing society is the increase in the number of singles, or one person consumer units. While stereotyping is popular with this buying group, many of the clichés referring to young bachelors and old widows are changing. Although the percentage of single women over the age of 55 is greater than that of men, the gap is narrowing.

Buying patterns are changing as well. Single men do spend more than women, but once again the difference is slowly evaporating. More and more females are delaying marriage and developing careers, which in turn leads toward greater discretionary income. This same cultural change has led to an increase in spending by women on items associated with dating. Entertainment and vacation expenditures, previously the purview of men, are becoming more equally divided among the genders.[12]

The Wellness Movement

Awareness of good health and nutrition created a surprising cultural change. People in the United States are taking better care of their bodies. Exercise has taken on new importance, spawning such companies as Soloflex and Diversified Products. More and more homes are becoming gyms, with consumers opting to exercise in their garage or bedroom rather than at a health club. Home fitness products such as Stairmaster and Nordic Trak are gaining in popularity. One of the latest and fastest growing entries in this arena is SportRope from Spalding. This innovative exerciser combines aerobics and weight conditioning.[13]

Although fitness participation has dwindled lately, the aging population is not to blame. Many feel that the initial spurt in the field of fitness was overkill, and more and more exercisers are practicing sensibility versus exhaustion. The wellness movement reaches kids as well. Targeting the latchkey set, Al Fong, a gymnastics coach, and Ron Matsch, a fitness center owner from Kansas City (MO), created an indoor playground called Discovery Zone. These 8,000 to 9,000 square foot units offer an alternative to afternoon television addiction and are now franchised nationwide.[14]

Diets have changed. As a nation we are consuming more fish and fowl and less red meat, causing a drastic decrease in the demand for beef. Because of its lower fat content, even buffalo meat is promoted as a beef replacement. One Denver area purveyor of bison meat estimates its sales will increase tenfold by the middle of this decade. In the face of this trend away from consumption of beef, the Beef Industry Council continues to advertise. A two year, $42 million campaign started in the summer of 1992 stresses flavor and different ways to cook beef.[15]

---

[12]Patricia Braus, "Sex and the single spender," *American Demographics,* November 1993, pp. 28-34.

[13]John P. Robinson and Geoffrey Godbey, "Has fitness peaked?" *American Demographics,* September 1993, pp. 36-42; Cyndee Miller, "Convenience, variety spark huge demand for home fitness equipment," *Marketing News,* March 16, 1992, p. 2.

[14]Jeanne Whalen and Jeffrey D. Zbar, "Why big Mac leaped from kids' play," *Advertising Age,* August 15, 1994, p. 12; Monica Roman, "Discovery Zone, fitness for the latchkey set," *Business Week,* July 27, 1992, p. 76.

[15]Fara Warner, "Call of the wild," *Adweek's Marketing Week,* February 3, 1992, p. 14; Carrie Goerne, "Don't blame the cows," *Marketing News,* June 22, 1992, pp. 1 and 2.

Consumers are flocking to natural products. These goods, containing no unnecessary chemicals, have become standards among a growing sector of buyers. Dental care products, shampoos and deodorants have joined an expanded list of foods as being free from additives. Mouthwashes without alcohol, pure cotton fabrics and swabs, chemical free sunblockers and undyed/uncolored bathroom tissue fill the ever expanding shelves of retailers everywhere.[16]

Smoking continues to lose favor, spawning the introduction of nicotine patches. More healthy alternatives are finding their ways onto supermarket shelves and restaurant menus. The battle against foods high in cholesterol has become the major effort of many marketers. Packages in grocery stores proudly sport labels reading "cholesterol free," and even Dunkin' Donuts has modified its recipe to contain no animal fat products. Kentucky Fried Chicken changed its name to KFC to avoid any stigma attached to fried foods. KFC also offers unfried items on its menus. Nabisco's Mr. Phipps Tater Crisps are baked rather than fried in oil.[17]

Most of the push toward a healthier life seems to have centered on the food industry. Vegetarian meals are showing up in supermarket cases rather than wallowing in nature stores. Meat free meals on buns, Gardenburgers, are popping up in such "in" spots as the Hard Rock Cafe and Mickey's Kitchen, the new restaurant chain from Disney. The alleged health benefits of garlic and ginseng are also making marketing headlines. One company, Ginseng Up Corporation is even offering a soda flavored with the oriental herb.[18]

Multicultural Influence

Changes in the cultural environment occur with the influx of people from other countries. The immigration of other cultures into this society enriches the food and restaurant industries more than others. Not only have Mexican eateries flourished in the past decade or two, but Hispanic foods are becoming readily available through supermarkets. Grocery shelves and cafe menus reflect the increasing interest in this flavorful foreign cuisine. Fast food outlets are serving breakfast burritos. Burger King offers tortillas filled with combinations of eggs, meats and potatoes for the breakfast lover. Border Breakfasts is a microwaveable Tex-Mex breakfast sandwich from Owens Country Sausage sold through supermarkets.[19]

---

[16]Editors, "Putting it mildly, more consumers prefer only products that are 'pure,' 'natural'," *The Wall Street Journal,* May 11, 1993, pp. B1 and B8.

[17]Emily DeNito, "Oreo, Ritz join Nabisco's low-fat feast," *Advertising Age,* April 4, 1994, p. 3; Joan Warner, "Confessions of a nicotine-patch wearer," *Business Week,* November 9, 1992, p. 134; Alison Sprout, "Healthier chips," *Fortune,* August 24, 1992, p. 99; Matthew Grimm, "KFC test its first non-fried chicken," *Adweek's Marketing Week,* May 11, 1992, p. 7.

[18]"Profiting from a global mindset," *Nations Business,* June 1994, p. 6; Yumiko Ono, "Shoppers look for healthier items," *The Wall Street Journal,* May 10, 1994, p. B1; Cyndee Miller, "Marketers tout health benefits of garlic and ginseng," *Marketing News,* June 24, 1991, pp. 1 and 28.

[19]Bob Ortega, "Restaurants see 'health-Mex' as hot cuisine," *The Wall Street Journal,* August 9, 1994, p. B1; Richard S. Teitelbaum, "Taco cabana," *Fortune,* February 2, 1993, p. 91; Pat Baldwin, "Tex-Mex for breakfast," *Adweek's Marketing Week,* April 2, 1990, p. 24.

LadySmith

THE DIFFERENCE IS OBVIOUS

And we couldn't think of any reason why a woman should have to adapt to a handgun designed for a man. That's why Smith & Wesson developed the LadySmith series, based on two years of research and suggestions from more than 6,000 women.

Lightweight, forged for strength, these compact .38 Special revolvers are powerful--but not overpowering. And, from slim rosewood or Goncalo Alves stocks to reduced reach for easier straight-through double action trigger pull, they've been redefined to fit a completely different "average" hand.

Add the choice of two- or three-inch barrel, frosted stainless or blue finish, and a handsome morocco-grained carrying/storage case, and the result is four revolvers that manage to be elegant without losing any of their practicality.

The LadySmiths from Smith & Wesson. Because a handgun should fit the hand that's actually going to hold it.

Smith & Wesson
SPRINGFIELD, MASSACHUSETTS 01102

1·800·331·0852

For additional information about safety, the LadySmiths, or a dealer in your area, please call between 8:00 am and 5:00 pm E.S.T.

Due to significant changes in the cultural environment, Smith & Wesson finds it important to target the female market with its Lady Smith model. (Courtesy of Smith & Wesson)

As the cultures of our society change, so must marketing strategies. Many companies, such as Kmart, Coors, Campbell Soup and Kodak, are responding to these changes with better training of personnel and new products targeting these markets. Advertisers show recognition of this changing culture by showing more ethnic groups in the ads and commercials. The growth of the Asian-American community triggered new products and new

WINNING THE DEREGULATION BATTLE, STATE BY STATE

AMERITECH

Profit caps have been replaced with rate regulation in three of its states, giving Bells more flexibility. Ameritech is asking for entry into long distance in exchange for competition in local service.

BELL ATLANTIC

First of the Bells to win federal court approval to provide cable TV in its own markets. Flexible pricing has replaced profit caps in all of its states. MFS Communications was granted a license in Maryland to compete on an equal basis in local service.

BELLSOUTH

Flexible pricing plans exist in seven states; North and South Carolina continue to use profit caps. An Alabama federal court has approved BellSouth's entry into cable TV.

NYNEX

New York proposed a plan to allow Nynex freedom in setting rates, in return for open competition in intrastate long distance. New York's plan is the first that allows competitors to offer direct dialing.

PACIFIC TELESIS

California looking to open up competition in the long-distance market, giving Pactel rate relief.

SOUTHWESTERN BELL

Three states have pricing regulations, while the others use profit caps. Texas is considering legislation to open its telecom market to outside competition.

U S WEST

Six states have profit caps. A Seattle federal court gave US West the right to offer cable TV in Washington.

---

media, as have increases in Hispanic and European populations. No consumer goods marketer can ignore these explosive markets.[20]

POLITICAL/LEGAL ENVIRONMENT

Political environment—the actions of government bodies and agencies that influence marketers.

The **political environment** affects marketing in many ways. The actions of government bodies and agencies often initiate economic change. Cultural shifts may cause bureaucratic or legislative action. City, county, state and federal agencies act and react to numerous business and economic forces. Whatever the trigger, there is little doubt that actions of government bodies can have a significant effect upon marketing.

---

[20]Yumiko Ono, "Food firms cook up more oriental fare," *The Wall Street Journal*, February 22, 1994, p. B1 and B6; Cyndee Miller, "Hispanic media expand; TV has strongest appeal," *Marketing News*, January 21, 1991, pp. 1 and 10; Editors, "Breaking out the Hispanic market," *Adweek's Marketing Week*, October 1, 1990, p. 33; Pamela Sherrod, "Advertisers learn how to reach Hispanics," *The Oregonian*, October 21, 1990, p. B4.

Legislation

Perhaps the most obvious political impact is the enactment of laws or the creation of regulations by legislatures and government agencies. For example, in 1994 the Senate Finance Committee of Congress debated implementation of the GATT (General Agreement on Tariffs and Trade) treaty. Lobbyists for the textile industry attempted to persuade legislators to add an amendment that would have limited the export of imported clothing. Such a move would have been a major blow to retailers such as The Gap, J.C. Penney and Wal-Mart, driving up prices and severely hampering supply. The measure was defeated at that time, but serves to illustrate how legislative action can impact marketing.[21]

When the Justice Department spearheaded the move to break up the telecommunications giant AT&T, new marketing opportunities emerged. MCI and Sprint now actively compete with "Big Blue" for dominance of the long distance service. The "Baby Bells" that were the offshoots of AT&T now compete worldwide and are increasing their presence in related fields such as cellular phones and cable television. The field of telephone equipment manufacturing, once the sole realm of Western Electric, a "Ma Bell" subsidiary, now finds itself with a number of competitors selling designer phones and high-tech answering machines. Again, government action resulted in marketing changes.[22]

Taxes

As mentioned earlier in this chapter, taxes have a direct impact on buying power, the amount of money that individuals have to spend on goods and services. As government levies increase, spendable income goes down for consumers and for businesses. Political action at the federal, state and county levels can increase or decrease the cost of doing business.

Taxes that governments impose can have a positive as well as a negative effect on some industries or areas. As the federal government spends tax dollars through the Department of Defense, the Seattle area benefits when Boeing receives a contract. New Haven suffers when no more orders are issued for submarines from General Dynamics. Many state governments are learning that the ability to attract new businesses to their areas can be tied directly to existing tax structures. Marketing positions are now commonplace in many government organizations.

Foreign Trade

Global marketing occurs between companies located in different countries, and political action often impacts this trade. Government bodies often regulate foreign trade by imposing barriers. Used as a protection for domestic industries, tariffs or quotas placed on imports have the effect of making imported goods more expensive. Government action can also have a direct effect on the exchange rate, which is the price of foreign currencies.

---

[21] Alicia Mundy, "Fruitless," *BRANDWEEK,* August 8, 1994, pp. 1 and 6.

[22] Mark Lewyn, "Grab your partners for the wireless ball," *Business Week,* August 15, 1994, p. 95; Andrew Kupfer, "The baby bells butt heads," *Fortune,* March 21, 1994. pp. 76-90; Peter Coy, "The bells' sibling rivalry turns into sibling warfare," *Business Week,* October 25, 1993, p. 38

American businesses may benefit or suffer from such political activity. Tariffs, or import duties, on imported items have the effect of increasing their prices. Domestic producers may find their goods more competitively priced due to the taxes on foreign products. Limiting the number of imports through quotas imparted by government has the similar effect of making domestically produced goods more attractive. Action by foreign governments on American exports has the same impact.

As with economic and cultural fluctuations, marketers have little control over the political environment. While businesses are able to lobby with congress and legislatures for passage of favorable laws, legislation and regulation are not directly in the control of marketers. As big business exerts more power in political arenas, more of these lobbying practices have fallen under public scrutiny.

TECHNOLOGICAL ENVIRONMENT

Technological environment— changes in science, engineering and manufacturing that influence marketing.

The **technological environment** of marketing includes the fields of science, engineering and manufacturing. Scientific developments impact how and how long we live. Breakthroughs in engineering areas help to create new methods and processes. Manufacturing builds on these technological changes to bring new products to needy markets. Changes in any of these technical areas affect the marketing effort.

Marketing oriented companies adjust to these technological changes, with an eye toward satisfying consumers and businesses. Research and development departments are constantly seeking new methods to make existing products and new products for existing processes. Small businesses often find themselves in the position of leading industry because of their entrepreneurial spirit. Many larger companies copy this effort through intrapreneurial emphasis. No firm can afford to let technological advances catch it unaware.

Computerization

One of the most significant technological changes in the latter part of the twentieth century is the emergence of the computer. Rare is the business or individual not touched by this electronic marvel. Color graphics and laser printers have created a new industry, desktop publishing. Laptops and modems give users mobility and diversity. New products and opportunities are constantly being created because of the computer. Kitchen and laundry appliances, watches, office equipment, automobiles and many other products are predominantly computer controlled. Computer controlled robots have progressed from assembly lines to hospital operating rooms where their pinpoint precision is often superior to that of the human hand.[23]

The use of microprocessors affects many industries. The auto-focus and automatic features of the new 35mm cameras, for instance, have proven to be highly successful. Even the photo industry giant Eastman Kodak altered its marketing plans for a disc camera due largely to the popularity of the computer

---

[23]Stephen Baker, "A surgeon whose hand never shakes," *Business Week*, October 4, 1993, pp. 111-114.

Computer chips control many of the goods that we use on a daily basis, including the alarms clocks that start our day.

operated picture takers. One of the latest photographic innovations is Nikon's underwater SLR. The Nikonos eliminates the need for bulky housings, using a liquid tight aluminum body to achieve its integrity. At $4,000 each they are still a bit expensive for the average vacationer.[24]

The dash toward multi-media has created some unusual and amazing partnerships in the world of electronics. Apple and IBM formed a joint venture, Kaleida, to develop multi-media software. Toshiba is collaborating with Apple on a multi-media player, and Kodak is working with Macintosh's creator on digital photography. Paul Allen, co-founder of Microsoft with Bill Gates, is spending hundreds of millions of dollars on multi-media development. Many industry leaders feel that this latest electronic passion will ultimately have an impact on the publishing industry as more people "read" using laptop computers.[25]

---

[24]Alison L. Sprout, "Seaworthy camera," *Fortune,* February 24, 1992, p. 103.

[25]Edward C. Baig, "Love at first byte," *Business Week,* May 18, 1994, p. 128; Stephen H. Wildstrom, "You name it, they got it," *Business Week,* May 18, 1994, pp. 180-182; Mark Lewyn, "Going places," *Business Week,* May 18, 1994, pp. 176-178; Myron Magnet, "Who's winning the information revolution," *Fortune,* November 30, 1992, pp. 110-117; Dori Jones Yang and Kathy Rebello, "Microsoft's other pioneer jumps into multimedia," *Business Week,* November 30, 1992, pp. 106-107.

Information Highway and Virtual Reality

The use of computers is no longer restricted to the boundaries of any one country or region. Internet allows users to communicate worldwide as easily as punching a few keys or moving the mouse. This international network is perhaps the first milestone on the information highway. Also known as the electronic superhighway, national information infrastructure or more informally as infobahn, this system of networked equipment may revolutionize the way that we do business and live.

Much of the infrastructure for the information highway already exists. The fiber optic systems installed by telephone companies form the basis for a delivery mechanism. Coupled with satellites and cables, visual and audio messages can be transmitted almost anywhere. Computer firms, such as Hewlett-Packard and Digital Equipment, work on perfecting set-top boxes that will serve as the off-ramps from the highway into television sets or computers.[26]

Although often linked with games, virtual reality is a virtual cinch to become a standard product received via the information highway. This development gives viewers the opportunity to create simulated events. Knowledge Adventure Worlds markets an Internet-based service that allows one to look at a billboard advertising an automobile and be transported, via electronics, into a test-driving experience. The viewed personas, called digital actors, interact in a variety of simulations. Customers must own CD/ROM equipment and connect to Internet, but the company forecasts 500,000 subscribers by 1996.[27]

Other Developments

VCRs, CDs and FAX machines are gadgets of the 1990s. The increase in purchases of VCR equipment has led to changes in the motion picture industry. Although movies are still being produced in large number, more studios are turning to the home viewing market as their leading income producer. Compact discs are having similar effects on the record industry. Almost impossible to damage and boasting superlative reproduction quality, CDs threaten to make the long-play record obsolete. Automobile manufacturers now modify the dashboard design of their cars to allow CDs as optional equipment. Individual and portable CD players are almost as popular as Sony's Walkman.

Natural Environment Influence

The natural environment often influences changes in technology. Scarcity of raw materials creates the need for new developments. The general concern by global societies over the depletion of renewable resources and the fears over pollution have prompted many businesses to look for new sources of energy. Products that do not destroy scarce resources are finding their way to the market.

---

[26]Andrew Kupfer, "Set-top box wars," *Fortune,* August 22, 1994, pp. 110-118; Andy Reinhardt, "Building the data highway," *Byte,* March 1994, pp. 46-74.

[27]Debra Aho Willamson, "Virtual reality via the Internet," *Advertising Age,* October 31, 1994, p. 17.

THE ENVIRONMENT & THE MARKETING MIX

Technological Environment

Economic Environment

Demographics

Cultural Environment

Product

Promotion | MARKETING MIX | Price

Distribution

Competitive Environment

Legal/Political Environment

Society's desire for more durable and less wasteful products stimulates development. Many marketing oriented companies meet this need through the use of recycled materials. Weyerhaeuser, the lumber and paper company recognized as a leader in reforestation, is among those socially conscious firms involved in recycling. Many paper goods, plastics and metals can be used over and over, reducing the amount of energy needed for raw material refinement. The search for innovative solutions to the problems of society often leads to the creation of new products and processes.

COMPETITIVE ENVIRONMENT

The impact of the **competitive environment** is similar in many respects to that of new technology. Product improvement or development can render another good or service obsolete. Also, the actions of competition may outdate a firm's marketing plan. Sometimes competition comes from the introduction of better products. Competition also results from improved marketing.

Competition often leads to the process of acquisition, merger and joint venture. Firms sometimes find that it is better to join with rivals in some manner rather than to try to duke it out in the arenas of the marketplace. Fair competition also stimulates new product development, as marketers constantly strive to be one step ahead of their friendly or unfriendly associates.

A marketing oriented company cannot afford to keep its efforts focused on only domestic rivals. Much of the new product innovation and price competition of today comes from overseas firms. The consolidation of Europe, increased free market capacity in the Eastern Bloc and the continued

Competitive environment—the actions and policies of rival firms influencing marketers.

industrial growth of Asia will impact U.S. firms in a far greater degree during the next few decades. Much of this competitive thrust will come in the high-tech industries.

Apple's strong marketing program for its Macintosh line has seriously eaten into the MS/DOS domain of business computing. Once ruled by IBM and the clone makers, these fields are increasingly being penetrated by mouse driven systems. The development of Microsoft's Windows for MS/DOS operations and the marvelous graphics available today on computers is the direct consequence of this competitive battle.

Even while operating within these rather uncontrollable environments, marketers retain significant control over the marketing mix. Changes in the environments of economics, demographics, culture, politics, technology and competition affect the success of all of these programs. Companies must carefully manage their products, price, distribution and promotion to meet these challenges.

How Is Marketing Managed?

Marketers need to exercise sound management practices that involve the functions of planning, organizing, directing and controlling. Marketing mistakes are as prevalent as marketing successes. Wise marketers strive to overcome these errors. The fickleness of customer preference, the problems associated with distribution channels, and the unpredictability of competitors influence the ability to produce a profit. Also, marketing must be compatible with company objectives while satisfying customers.

In the management process, marketers are constantly weighing costs against benefits. Costs include dollars spent and the effects on corporate image or on society. Marketers must decide whether production and distribution costs are too great to provide a reasonable profit even when demand is high. When Bausch & Lomb decided to enter the mouthwash market, many decisions had to be made. The company had to weigh the added costs of developing a product foreign to their usual eye care business versus potential income. The success of the product overcame initial drain on reserves.

POSITIONING

Positioning—creating an image of the product or the marketing company in the minds of the buyers.

Positioning means creating an image of the product in the minds of the buyers. The marketing company develops this position for consumer goods and services. With industrial type goods, positioning usually refers to the image of the company. Marketing management must be constantly aware of product images to balance price, distribution and promotion efforts. All facets of the marketing mix must be in harmony. Positioning is basic to marketing success.[28]

---

[28]Jack Trout and Al Reis, *Positioning: The battle for your mind* (New York: McGraw-Hill, 1981).

The war is not a recent one. It has been going on for years. The influx of foreign cars has kept executives from the American automobile industry busy crying for stiffer tariffs and quotas. On the other hand, consumers have long blamed Detroit for poor quality, poor gasoline economy and poor response to their needs. Industry executives fought hard to convince both consumers and government officials that their problems are real. "Buy American" themes permeate advertising for U.S.-made cars.

Today, most Japanese automobile companies have production facilities stateside pumping out the same high quality products to which buyers have become accustomed. In fact, the Toyotas, Nissans and Hondas assembled here are actually more American than many of Detroit's models. Chrysler makes cars in Mexico, Canada and Japan. The Dodge Stealth and Summit wagon are imported from Mitsubishi. The Crown Victoria, marketed by Ford, contains over 26 percent foreign-made parts, which enables the manufacturer to evade fuel-economy standards. The Pontiac LeMans is built in Korea from a German design.

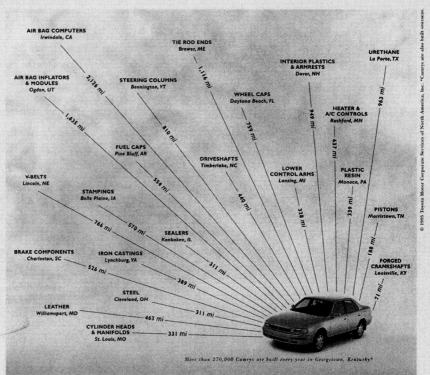

Before you buy a Camry CHECK THE MILEAGE.

More than 270,000 Camrys are built every year in Georgetown, Kentucky*

EVERY YEAR, Toyota buys thousands of parts from communities right across the country. In fact, we buy more than $4.6 billion per year in parts for both domestic and overseas production, from more than 440 U.S. suppliers. Whether it's engine blocks from Ohio, batteries from Tennessee or wiper systems from New York, our investment in local industries is paying off in the form of thousands of jobs across the United States.

INVESTING IN THE THINGS WE ALL CARE ABOUT. **TOYOTA**

For more information about Toyota in America write Toyota Motor Corporate Services, 9 West 57th Street, Suite 4900-J14, New York, NY 10019

© 1995 Toyota Motor Corporate Services of North America, Inc. *Camrys are also built overseas.

Most Toyota Camrys sold in America are assembled in the firm's Georgetown, Kentucky plant from parts manufactured throughout the United States. Toyota's investment in these local communities

continued to page 50

continued from page 49

results in thousands of jobs across the country. Although some of the American suppliers are firms in which Toyota has an ownership interest, many are independently owned. Many of the parts purchased in the U.S. are shipped to Japan for further production or assembly.

sources: Terry Lefton, "What's an American Car," Adweek's Marketing Week, July 27, 1992; David Versical, "Hey Aunt Millie: Did Honda make your U.S. car?" Automotive News, February 17, 1992, pp. 4 and 66; Eric Hollreiser, "Brand America takes a beating in Japan," Adweek's Marketing Week, January 13, 1992, p. 5; Paul Magnusson, James B. Treece, and William C. Symonds, "Honda. Is it an American car?" Business Week, November 16, 1991, pp. 105-112. (Photo used with permission of Toyota Motor Sales, USA)

Many consider positioning as the foundation of marketing strategy. Marketers position their products as unique among the available alternatives. Product attributes, price, distribution systems and promotion all must remain consistent with the image viewed by consumers. Positioning must remain accurate and appropriate if it is to achieve buyer acceptance.

Positioning can be subtle or bold. Marketers create images for individual products or lines and for the entire firm. Mazda, for example, has repositioned the company along with the company's cars. Perhaps realizing that it could not win a head to head battle with Honda, Toyota and Nissan, the "other Japanese" car maker counts heavily on the success of niche models. Building on Miata's success, Mazda continued its image building with a redesigned RX-7. The firm bills itself as the automobile marketer that has brought the pure sports car back for the American driver.[29]

What Social and Ethical Demands Face Marketers?

Within the constantly changing environments of the business world, marketers strive to balance the marketing mix. Businesses and business leaders must also practice social responsibility while striving to provide satisfaction. Success in the marketing effort will be measured against its costs to society.

CONSUMERISM

Consumerism—a movement to protect the rights of consumers.

As our economy exploded after World War II, product quality generally decreased and consumer complaints went up. **Consumerism,** born in the 1960s, was sparked in part by John F. Kennedy's pronouncement of the Consumers' Bill of Rights. President Kennedy stated that consumers had the

---

[29]Jack Keebler, "Subtle exchange: You have to look hard to see the transfer of technology from racing to street cars," *Automotive News,* May 16, 1994, pp. 6i-7i; "Rx-7 makes 10 best," *Japan 21st,* March 1994, p. 85; Eric Hollreiser, "Mazda hitches its image to the RX-7," *Adweek's Marketing Week,* March 16, 1992, p. 5; Patricia Sellers, "New selling tool: The Acura concept," *Fortune,* February 24, 1992, pp. 88-89.

Wheeler-Lea Act (1938)

Prohibits unfair and deceptive acts and practices regardless of whether competition is injured; places advertising of foods and drugs under FTC jurisdiction.

Automobile Information Disclosure Act (1958)

Prohibits car dealers from inflating the factory price of new cars.

National Traffic and Safety Act (1958)

Provides for the creation of compulsory safety standards for automobiles and tires.

Fair Packaging and Labelling Act (1966)

Provides for the regulation of the packaging and labeling of consumer goods. Requires manufacturers to state what the package contains, who made it, and how much it contains. Permit industries' voluntary adoption of uniform packaging standards.

Child Protection Act (1966)

Bans sale of hazardous toys and articles. Amended in 1969 to include articles that pose electrical mechanical, or thermal hazards.

Federal Cigarette Labelling and Advertising Act (1967)

Requires that cigarette packages contain the following statement: "Warning: The Surgeon General Has Determined That Cigarette Smoking Is Dangerous to Your Health."

Truth-in-Lending Act (1968)

Requires lenders to state the true costs of a credit transaction, outlaws the use of actual or threatened violence in collecting loans, and restricts the amount of garnishments. Established a National Commission on Consumer Finance.

National Environmental Policy Act (1969)

Establishes a national policy on the environment and provides for the establishment of the Court on Environmental Quality. The Environmental Protection Agency was established by Reorganization Plan No. 3 of 1970.

Fair Credit Reporting Act (1970)

Ensures that a consumer's credit report will contain only accurate, relevant, and recent information and will be confidential unless requested for an appropriate reason by a proper party.

Consumer Product Safety Act (1972)

Establishes the Consumer Product Safety Commission and authorizes it to set safety standards for consumer products as well as exact penalties for failure to uphold the standards.

Consumer Goods Pricing Act (1975)

Prohibits the use of price maintenance agreements among manufacturers and resellers in interstate commerce.

Magnuson-Moss Warranty/FTC Improvement Act (1975)

Authorizes the FTC to determine rules concerning consumer warranties and provides for consumer access to means of redress, such as the "class action" suit. Also expands FTC regulatory powers over unfair or deceptive acts or practices.

Equal Credit Opportunity Act (1975)

Prohibits discrimination in a credit transaction because of sex, marital status, race, national origin, religion, age, or receipt of public assistance.

Fair Debt Collection Practice Act (1978)

Makes it illegal to harass or abuse any person and make false statements or use unfair methods when collecting a debt.

FTC Improvement Act (1980)
Provides the House of Representatives and Senate jointly with veto power over FTC Trade Regulation Rules. Enacted to limit FTC's powers to regulate "unfairness" issues.

Toy Safety Act (1984)
Gives the government the power to recall toys quickly when they are found to be unsafe.

Trademark Law Revision Act (1989)
Updates the Lanham Act to reflect changes in business practices relating to trademark usage and protection. Among other actions, it reduces trademark registration and renewal periods, requires the removal of unused trademarks, permits registration of a trademark before its use in commerce, and provides new remedies for trademark infringement.

■　　■　　■　　■　　■

right to safety, the right to choose, the right to be informed and the right to be heard. Later, President Gerald Ford added a fifth commandment for the right to consumer education. This movement toward responsible marketing includes interested citizens, government agencies and civic minded businesses. The purpose is to strengthen the buyer's position in relation to sellers.

The consumer movement caused many marketing oriented companies to correct procedures and alter the products they offer. A general awareness of consumers' rights has led to improvement initiated by industry instead of by government. Responsible marketers recognize that correcting marketing wrongs protects the product, the company image and the consumer.

ENVIRONMENTALISM

Environmentalism—
a movement to protect the environment.

Concern for the protection of the **environment** impacts marketers. Water and air pollution problems do not disappear without concentrated effort. The earth's natural resources are being depleted. Smoke and smog, litter and garbage, strip mining and destruction of rain forests are all issues that marketers must face. Providing the right product to those in need can no longer be the only goal of marketing. Proper care of the environment must be addressed along with prices and advertising campaigns.

The buying public's concern about depletion of the ozone layer has deeply impacted the aerosol industry. The chlorofluorocarbons, or CFCs, which are a major culprit, have largely been replaced with hydrocarbons. These propellants are also under attack because they contribute to smog and are flammable. Most consumer goods houses are following the lead of industry giants such as DowBrands, which now packages its cleaners and hairsprays in both aerosol and trigger spray bottles. Aerosols have acquired a negative image that may never be overcome.[30]

---

[30]Terry Lefton, "Still battling the ozone stigma," *Adweek's Marketing Week,* March 16, 1992, pp. 18-19.

The standard methods for the manufacture of styrofoam, such as that used in packages and packing materials, also used CFCs. Heeding the warnings about environmental damage, Dunkin' Donuts converted to using paper cups, the city of Portland, Oregon, banned the use of styrofoam packaging. McDonald's, long a user of polystyrene "clamshell" containers, bowed to public pressure and switched to paper in 1990. Lever Bros., Procter & Gamble and Colgate-Palmolive conduct ongoing research for environmentally sound packaging materials.[31]

GREEN MARKETING

The term **green marketing** relates to the promotion of products or manufacturing processes that are beneficial or safe to our environment. In a poll conducted by Roper Starch Worldwide in 1993, a number of respondents said they would refuse to buy products that might harm the environment. Many marketers call this "green movement" a revolution, and consumers are leading the charge. Companies and brands that are wasteful or that harm the environment may face buyer boycotts.[32]

Green marketing— the promotion of products or manufacturing processes that are environmentally sound.

Many firms are joining the green parade. Bonjour International, an apparel marketer, places messages on its hangtags urging consumers to join environmental groups. Converse has introduced its Windstar hiking and walking boots with the brand name taken from the Windstar Foundation, a Colorado educational agency. London based Body Shop markets "cruelty-free" cosmetics, which have had wide acceptance in Europe. Earth Mercantile in Salem, Oregon, and Table of Contents in Ardmore, Pennsylvania, specialty stores that stock environmentally safe products, find business booming. Books, like *Shopping For A Better World* and *The Seventh Generation,* help to locate environmentally sensitive products and socially responsible companies. The 1990s will bear "the green decade" label when consumer reaction to social and environmental responsibility impacts marketers where it counts...in the wallet.[33]

Green marketing has fostered the birth of dozens of new products, many from small, niche marketers. One of the market areas receiving the greatest attention is household cleansers. Often made from harsh chemicals and solvents, this group of consumer goods was a natural for the promotion of "natural" products.

Life Tree, a Northern California company, markets an herbal cleanser named Fresh & Natural Bathroom Cleaner. From Boulder, Colorado, Earth Wise Inc. has introduced Earth Wise Superior Cleaning Products made from 100 percent biodegradable ingredients packaged in recycled plastic containers. A

---

[31]Fara Warner, "What happened to the truth?" *Adweek's Marketing Week,* October 28, 1991, pp. 4 and 5; P. Berman, "McDonald's caves in," *Forbes,* February 4, 1991, pp. 73-74; D. Kiley, "McDonald's repaints the arches green," *Adweek's Marketing Week,* August 27, 1990, p. 6.

[32]Peter Stisser, "A deeper shade of green," *American Demographics,* March 1994, pp. 24-29.

[33]Kathy Dimond, "A value at any price," *Oregon Business,* March 1994, pp. 62-63; Marilyn Marter, "Green products go mainstream," *The Oregonian,* July 27, 1993, p. D3; Robert McMath, "Keeping precious rainforest, and themed products, green," *BRANDWEEK,* October 11, 1993, pp. 34-35; Philip Elmer-Dewitt, "Anita the agitator," *Time,* January 25, 1993, pp. 52-54.

Marketing and Society: Soda Pop Jeans!

Green marketing is not new. Many firms have been promoting their products and their company as being environmentally friendly for years. Biodegradable and ozone-safe products are common, and many cosmetics are promoted as never having been tested on animals. Packages proudly proclaim "made from recycled paper," and trigger sprays are replacing aerosols in many cases. Companies who clean up their processes to reduce pollution tell the world about their efforts. Others boast of their contributions to worthy, "green" causes.

One of the more startling uses of recycled materials is called Soda Pop denim. Manufactured by Swift Textiles from a weave of 80 percent pure denim and 20 percent a spun plastic fiber created from used softdrink bottles, this material looks, and almost feels, like the "real" thing. Jeans marketers were a bit stunned to find that pants made from organically grown, dye-free cottons did not catch on with envi-

ronmentally conscious consumers. These same marketers are hoping that the appearance of regular denim will be a big plus for soda pop jeans.

THE ORIGINAL ARIZONA JEAN COMPANY™

Lee and Code Bleu began test marketing in the fall of 1994. VF, the parent company for Lees, placed the new item under its Ecolojeans label, and is targeting the younger set. Code Bleu, sold mostly through department stores, is going after a similar age group. J. C. Penney, on the other hand, is bringing out Soda Pop jeans under its red hot Arizona label, directed toward a slightly older market. Although it is still a little early to tell, these marketers are expecting big things from this new, recycled fabric.

SOURCE: Elaine Underwood, "While manufacturers open stores, retailer J. C. Penney builds a $500 million private-label powerhouse," *BRANDWEEK,* January 9, 1995, p. 26; Elaine Underwood, "Green jeans and pop bottles," *BRANDWEEK,* October 10, 1994, p. 8.

Cleveland, Ohio, firm called Sunshine Industries has been very successful selling Pik Up Stik, a lint remover with a sticky surface that can be cleaned and reused. Then there is the Green Paint Co., from Manchuag, Massachusetts, that sells recycled paint.[34]

Green Marketing—The Down Side

Some marketers have gone too far in wooing environmentally conscious customers. Green marketing can cause some firms to stretch the credibility of their claims. Roper Starch Worldwide concluded a two-year survey in 1994 indicating that many consumers do not believe exaggerated claims found in advertising. The publishing arena, which once flourished with "green" books and newsletters, has seen a definite downturn. The Federal Trade Commission has shown new muscle in going after marketers who exaggerate.

At the same time, many businesses are quietly producing items that do provide some environmental benefit. Garden Botanika is a cosmetics retailer

---

[34]Editors, "Green Paint Co.," *Marketing News,* April 25, 1994, p. E8; Robert McMath, "The greening of cleaning," *Adweek's Marketing Week,* March 16, 1992, p. 33.

that blends its products from natural ingredients. Tree of Life, Inc., a Florida health food firm, distributes Small World animal crackers, cookies in the shape of endangered species.[35]

RECYCLING

Society demanded cleaner air and water, and the safe disposal of waste materials. New business ventures arose to address that need. Biodegradable packaging is a direct result of concern over trash disposal. Ridding the country of its excess trash is a major task as traditional landfills become saturated and new ones are placed farther from urban areas. Many ocean side metropolitan areas investigated the feasibility of using giant ships with super-heated furnaces for trash disposal at sea.

Disposable diapers came under fire because of the unbelievable volume of the non-biodegradable trash that they created. Many young parents resorted to using cloth diapers as a statement against this waste. Apparently the major producers of disposables have convinced many that they should not feel guilty, because the nation's leading producer of cloth baby diapers, Gerber Products Co. announced in 1992 that they would stop making this variety. Debate over disposable diapers took another step toward marketing creativity when Safe-Fence, an Idaho firm, announced that it was recycling throwaway diapers into fence posts. Supposedly, they last for a long time.[36]

Diapers are not the only product being recycled. Enviro Lumber, an Oregon company, makes lumber from used plastic milk containers. Although the product is not suitable for structural uses, it can be adapted as decking, siding, sign posts and park benches. Overseas markets are also opening up for recycled products. Members of the National Office Products Association are actively involved with refurbishing used office furniture for global markets. Used tires are being used as fuel to generate electricity in England and other European countries.[37]

CAUSE MARKETING

American business is also digging into its pocketbook to support worthy causes, such as wildlife protection. Firms such as Waste Management and Times-Mirror have earmarked substantial sums for the preservation of the California condor and the checkerspot butterfly. Such activity has created the new buzzword, cause marketing.

---

[35]Kevin Goldman, "Survey asks which 'green' ads are read," *The Wall Street Journal*, April 11, 1994, p. B5; Howard Schlossberg, "Two environmental advocates say green has lost its luster," *Marketing News*, January 17, 1994, pp. 13 and 15.

[36]Dave Kansas, "Maine repeals U.S.'s only ban on drink boxes," *The Wall Street Journal*, April 7, 1994, pp. B1-B6; Terry Lefton, "The end of the great diaper debate," *Adweek's Marketing Week*, January 20, 1992, p. 6; Kevin Kerr, "Disposable versus cloth diapers," *Adweek's Marketing Week*, February 18, 1991, p. 24.

[37]Jim Kadera, "Company changes milk jugs into logs," *The Oregonian*, April 7, 1993, pp. D10-11; Tim Triplett, "Old furniture finds home in secondary market," *Marketing News*, April 25, 1994, p. 2; Carla Rapoport, "Fuel from old tires," *Fortune*, November 15, 1993, p. 14.

WE CAN SAVE THE WORLD.

No matter who you are and where you're from, there's one thing we all have in common: the earth is our home. A home is something to take care of and protect, not abuse and destroy. We know this and yet we continue to contribute toward the destruction of our planet. Why? Perhaps we say, "I can't make a difference." Well we can. But only if every one of us decides to take action. That's why at the beginning of the summer, we are issuing millions of hangtags containing simple instructions on how we can save our world. Different tags will be found on each BONJOUR fashion item for every woman, man and child in stores all over the world. Get hold of them, read them, have your family, friends and neighbors read them, and do your share.

Let's save our world.
We have nowhere else to go.

Charles Dayan
President,
BONJOUR INTERNATIONAL

ENDORSED BY THE UNITED NATIONS
WORLD GLOBE PHOTO DONATED BY NASA

Bonjour International, through its "Save the world" campaign, is among a host of companies which promote social responsibility. (Courtesy of Bonjour International, Ltd.)

Good turns by marketers do much for enhancement of the corporate image and positive public opinion. The donation of money, time or promotion to worthy causes is known as **cause marketing.** Johnson & Johnson donates over $1 million annually in hotlines and shelters for battery victims. Campbell Soup Company sponsors a Walkathon for The March of Dimes, with a guarantee of $150,000. Plasticard donates to Alzheimer's, Helping Hand to leukemia, and Bird's Eye to the food bank, to name just a few worthy ventures helped by marketers. Waldenbooks actively participates in the Team Read program of the Reading Is Fundamental foundation, aimed at reducing illiteracy.[38]

> **Cause marketing—** gaining positive public opinion through the use of donations of money, time or promotion to worthwhile causes.

Clairol, the cosmetics marketer, takes a special interest in its customer, today's woman. Originally devised as a public relations campaign, the company's "Clairol partnership with women" has become a prime example of cause marketing. This program spearheads scholarships for deserving women, and offers "take charge" awards for females over the age of thirty who have overcome adversity. Clairol also sponsors a mentor program, where successful women "adopt" newcomers to the world of business. Clairol's work on these programs has led to a strong following of women loyal to the company and its products.

SUMMING IT UP

Marketing operates within constantly changing economic, demographic, cultural, political, technological and competitive environments. Management must adapt the marketing mix to meet these changing conditions.

Economic change relates to the business cycle. Disposable and discretionary incomes fluctuate through the stages of prosperity, recession and recovery. The demographics of our economy are in a constant state of flux. The baby boom of the 1950s has progressed to the mature audience of today. Population shifts, brought about by economic change and the aging of the market, impact all aspects of marketing.

The increasing and diverse roles of women in business have sparked new products and new needs awareness. The wellness movement and multicultural influence affect product development and distribution patterns. Legislation and regulation are the major components of the political environment. Deregulation and foreign trade policies impact the ability to carry out marketing mix plans.

Ever changing technology creates new products and makes others obsolete. Computerization has fostered technological development through the latter part of this century. Superconductivity and cold fusion may well lead the way into the year 2000. Competition influences all of the decisions created by changes in these marketing environments.

Marketers manage product, price, distribution and promotion to adapt to these changing conditions. Positioning products to create images in the minds of buyers is one of the key marketing strategies. Management activity is tempered by consumerism and environmentalism.

---

[38]Yumiko Ono, "Advertisers try 'doing good' to help sales do better," *The Wall Street Journal,* September 2, 1994, p. B8; Nancy Arnott, "Marketing with a passion," *Sales & Marketing Management,* January 1994, pp. 64-65; David D'Alessandro, "Event marketing winners: Olympics, local, causes," *BRANDWEEK,* July 12, 1993, p. 16.

KEY CONCEPTS AND TERMS FROM CHAPTER TWO

Cause marketing
Competitive environment
Consumerism
Cultural environment
Demographics
Discretionary income
Disposable income
Economic environment

Environmentalism
Graying of America
Green marketing
Marketing environments
Political environment
Positioning
Technological environment

BUILDING SKILLS

1. Explain, citing some examples, how upward and downward moves in the economy would affect product, price, distribution and promotion.

2. List some products that are specifically designed to capture the "gray market" of older consumers. Describe some of the reasons for population shifts.

3. The actions of the government have caused environmental changes. Describe the effect of these changes on marketing.

4. List some of the products that have appeared as the direct or indirect result of the increased number of working women and of a multicultural influence.

5. Identify as many products as possible that have been made obsolete by technological change.

6. Describe how the marketing mix has changed for the competitors in the "cola wars."

7. List some examples of product positioning.

Making Decisions 2-1: Belly Up To the Bar.

Some products seem to defy any of the glittery, marketing promotions that impact TV viewers and everyday consumers. For example, what can a company do with a bar of soap? Granted, Procter & Gamble, Colgate-Palmolive and a host of other industry giants have concocted quite an array of personal hygiene products. We have soaps that deodorize, moisturize and beauticize, and sometimes perform their magical mix of all things for all bodies.

For Unilever, the omnipresent multinational corporation headquartered in Europe, bodies are what its all about. Many a year has passed since a bar of soap made a real impact on this highly competitive market. Lots of formulas have been sampled, many promotional schemes have been exposed. But for Lever's 2000, bodies have become the focal point.

When Lever Brothers Company, the U.S. subsidiary of the Anglo-Dutch giant, first introduced its new, all encompassing soap branded "2000," management was not sure which marketing tack to take. Granted, the new 2000 bar was all things to all users. It deodorized, it moisturized, and, one would like to think, it also made a person feel cleaner, if not better. Rather than positioning this soap as a "me too," Lever created an entirely new niche. No other bath soap did what Lever 2000 could do.

With a futuristic name like 2000, promotional geniuses immediately began to look at a space age concept for advertising. Instead, Lever's advertising agency, J. Walter Thompson, decided to feature the 2,000 body parts that the soap cleaned, softened and made odor free. The provocative, yet tastefully done television commercials helped this new product make a big splash in an already sodden market.[39]

Describe Unilever's use of the marketing mix, including environmental factors, that might have affected the consumer's decisions.

Making Decisions 2-2: Pretty Women.

Few will question the increased importance of women buyers in a variety of markets. With the rise of the double income family since the 1960s, the number of working women skyrocketed. As the earning power of females climbed, so did the influence that they wielded over household purchasing decisions. Perhaps no buying decision, formerly relegated to men, was impacted more than that of the automobile. Once the domain of males, car purchases are now split about 50/50 between the genders and some suggest that women influence up to 80 percent of these decisions.

Although it took a while, car makers are realizing the importance of this market. More females work as automobile designers, and many manufacturers have established in-house groups to specifically work on marketing to women. This awakening has even spawned a magazine, *American Woman Motorscene,* designed to educate and enlighten women regarding this major buying decision. On the down side, this cooperative move to appeal to a sizable, previously untargeted market has not trickled down to many dealers. Female buyers still complain about the condescending,

---

[39]Christopher Power, "Everyone is bellying up to this bar," *Business Week,* January 27, 1992, p. 84.

patronizing way they are treated in many automobile showrooms.

The car market is not alone in recognizing the purchasing power of women. Led by Tandy, computer marketers are also wooing female consumers. Once considered "too technical" for the average female to comprehend, high-tech products are now being designed, packaged and promoted to appeal to female audiences. Even Midas, the muffler people, have joined the parade of companies specifically targeting this demographic group. Wise marketers are finding women a pretty market indeed![40]

Discuss the changes in marketing environments that prompted the move to target women and the ways that marketers modify the marketing mix to be more appealing to the female market.

Making Decisions 2-3: An Ecological Lunch?

Much has been said and done lately regarding the need to protect the environment. Conservationists and government agencies have kept the public aware of the dangers of everything from automobile exhaust to styrofoam packaging. Many companies have joined the movement by eliminating waste, cleaning up production operations and refusing to use dangerous products. Others have not.

One firm that has taken an innovative route toward environmental concerns is Rubbermaid ncorporated, the Wooster, Ohio, marketer of household items. The smart management at this company not only realized the impact of the green movement on its production, but also saw an opportunity to turn consumer concerns into product acceptance. In the fall of 1991, just in time for the back-to-school buying crunch, Rubbermaid introduced its Litterless Lunch Box.

By downsizing one of its popular insulated beverage chests, the company had the perfect shape and configuration for a lunch box. In addition, the product features Rubbermaid's Servin' Saver reusable sandwich holders and drink containers. This marketing oriented firm promotes the

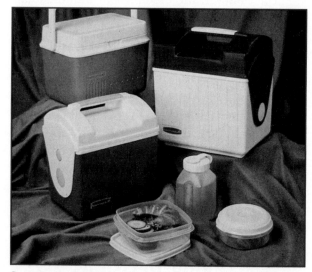

© 1993 Rubbermaid Incorporated, Wooster, Olt. (used with permission).

fact that the Litterless Lunch Box not only eliminates "brown bags" but also plastic wrap, paper cups and aluminum foil as well.[41]

Discuss the benefits and pitfalls of the green movement and the ways that Rubbermaid positioned its products and itself.

---

[40]Tim Triplett, "Automakers recognizing value of women's market," *Marketing News,* April 11, 1994, pp. 1 and 2; Kyle Pope, "High-tech marketers try to attract women without causing offense," *The Wall Street Journal,* March 17, 1994, pp. B1 and B8; Fara Warner, "Midas increases bid to attract women," *BRANDWEEK,* March 14, 1994, p. 5.

[41]Rahul Jacob, "America's best," *Fortune,* February 7, 1994, p. 54; Jon Berry, "The art of Rubbermaid," *Adweek's Marketing Week,* March 16, 1992, pp. 22-25; Jon Berry, "Rubbermaid packs an ecological lunch," *Adweek's Marketing Week,* September 9, 1991, p. 10.

3

Marketing Planning

*T*he Job to be Done

Proper planning is the key to marketing success. Whether done by the company, department, or product, the planning process is imperative for success. The planning process hinges upon the proper development of the marketing mix. In this chapter you learn how to:

- identify the process and the characteristics of marketing planning,
- describe the steps of a marketing plan and recognize the factors that affect the performance of marketing plans,
- explain the methods marketers use to organize and plan for growth,
- analyze the ways image and positioning impact marketing plans, and
- explain the forecasting methods marketers use.

Pam and Jeff Martin

This dynamic duo took a rather circuitous route to their current marketing success. Pam first entered El Camino College with the goal of earning a degree in early childhood education. She always had a bent for dealing with and for children, and this seemed like a natural career choice. Unfortunately her scholastic endeavors were cut short, primarily by a need to eat, and she found herself in the workforce. It was at her job with the Hawthorne Community Medical Group that she got her first taste of marketing...and she fell in love with it. A later position with Economics Research, where she was in charge of marketing educational software, solidified her interest in providing customer satisfaction.

Jeff, on the other hand, first wanted to follow in his father's footsteps and enrolled in the fire science program at Cypress Community College. However, he soon found himself bitten by the show biz bug and changed his major to theater arts. An elective course in marketing also heightened his interest in business. An early childhood love of magic was unshakable, and Jeff soon found himself struggling in the entertainment field. Supplementing his income by hanging wallpaper, he gradually built a reputation as an outstanding young magician, performing in clubs, for children's parties and at county fairs.

As capable as Jeff is, he experienced trouble marketing his talents. The Southern California entertainment industry was crowded in the early 1990s, and the gigs were few and far between. Then Jeff met Pam, and the magic began. Her organization strengths and marketing savvy quickly turned things around, and Jeff Martin, "The Blond-Curly-Haired Magician" was in demand throughout the West. From the Spokane County Fair to a convention in Yuma, Arizona, Jeff's schedule quickly filled with lucrative and exciting performances. Today, as wife and husband, the magic continues.

What Is Marketing Planning?

The first, and primary, function of marketing is planning. Marketing is no different than any other business discipline in that it needs guidance and direction to succeed. Any marketing mix that is thrown together without planning is doomed. Whether created for the whole company, for a department or for individual goods or services, a marketing plan is a must.

Few marketing efforts succeed without an analysis of what needs to be done and how. A **marketing plan** can be compared to a road map; the plan is a set of guidelines for establishing and controlling marketing activities. This tool that marketing management uses may be extensive and detailed or brief and to the point, but should cover all of the necessary mileage. Planning should be both long-range and immediate.

STRATEGIC PLANNING

Strategic planning— long-range planning.

Strategic planning is long-range in nature. Top level management must decide the "what" and the "why" of marketing decisions. These decisions fall into the realm of far-reaching, strategic planning. Strategic planning always takes into consideration the marketing company's goals and objectives. The image of the company and its capabilities play key roles in this process.

Suppose the board of directors of Sara Lee decides their strategic plan calls for an increase in its share of the market and sales for its Hanes Hosiery division over the next two fiscal years. Each part of that business unit, such as the L'eggs and Bali lingerie groups, could be charged to produce its own tactical plan describing in detail how to reach this goal. In this case, both the pantyhose and undergarment areas have become strategic business units.

Strategic Business Units

Strategic business units, or **SBU**s, are independent profit centers that may operate as separate entities. Any group within the company, a collection of products or individual good or service that requires a separate marketing plan classifies as a strategic business unit. Large multinational corporations often designate individual products or product lines as SBUs. In smaller firms, the entire company may act as a single profit center.

Strategic Business Unit (SBU)—an independent profit center.

TACTICAL PLANNING

Tactical planning is short-term in nature, spelling out the how, where, when and who of the marketing effort. Once upper management decides on the strategic objectives of the unit, middle level managers must wrestle with the problems of reaching those goals. How will the products be made, and where will they be distributed? When will production be started, and who will do the marketing tasks? These are the details that are spelled out in tactical planning.

Tactical planning— immediate, or short-term, planning.

PLANNING RESPONSIBILITY LEVELS

Management Level	Planning Responsibility	Results In
Functional Areas	Pricing and product development	Objectives & strategies
	Distribution Marketing communications	Tactical plans
Strategic Business Units	Product line management	Marketing plans
	Brand management	Sales and market share objectives
Corporate	Corporate vision, mission, and strategic plans	Long-range plan Corporate objectives and strategies
	SBU organization	Yearly business plans Financial objectives

The tactical plan for the L'eggs group would address specifics in each part of the marketing plan. Product and packaging changes could create an increase in market demand, as would pricing policies. More extensive distribution could also be a tool to gain added share of the market. Finally, promotional campaigns could be undertaken to boost sales of this one product. Together, the increased sales of the combined products of Hanes, each with their separate tactical plans, would provide the means toward achieving the corporate end.

What Are Some Characteristics of Marketing Planning?

Since planning is an important function of marketing management, such forward thinking should not be constrained. Goal setting is a serious effort, and no potentials should be avoided or overlooked. Planners often use brainstorming to arrive at their ultimate goals. The process of planning is in itself a useful procedure that strengthens any organization.

RESEARCH

Since planning relates in both the long and short term to customers and product acceptance, research becomes an important prerequisite. In order to satisfy needs, marketers must first know what the needs are. One of the reasons why the planning function is ongoing is that customer needs and product preferences change on a regular basis. Similarly, images and product positioning face continuous tests by customers and competitors.

Because of the scientific nature of marketing research, which is discussed in the following chapter, planning often becomes somewhat technical in nature. A thorough job of looking into the future takes into account many variables. Company changes, customer moods and competitive actions all impact the planning process. Some of the information influencing planning may be statistical in nature, such as economic trends or demographic changes gathered through marketing research. Other data might involve taste test panels or customer surveys.

FLEXIBILITY

Above all, planning should be **flexible.** Rigid, academic exercises that leave no room for change are doomed from the onset. The business of doing business is dynamic, especially in the marketing field. Rigid plans are usually not adaptable to the sudden changes that regularly occur in the environments in which marketing operates.

The marketing venture often mushrooms at rates the planners could not foresee, making both the plan and its authors woefully out of sync. Sometimes an original marketing plan becomes lost in the chaos that often occurs with rapid growth. Many consumer electronic firms find themselves unable to keep up with the rapid product changes and customer demands of today's markets.

REACTION TO MARKET CHANGES

Businesses that have not spent time planning are often the ones that have difficulty reacting quickly to market changes. Market demand increases or decreases may be the result of environmental changes that are beyond the marketer's control. Just as automatic withdrawals from paychecks force employees to save, planning requires marketers to look at their complete operating arenas. Competition can change rapidly and drastically. Once marketers learn through the planning process to watch for such movements, their ability to respond and to act is enhanced.

One of the most dramatic changes on the American buying scene in the past few decades is the emergence of the male consumer. The cultural and economic revolutions that created the need for two family incomes also brought about an increase in the number of males doing the household shopping. Men are now purchasing many consumer products, breaking the traditional mold of both genders. Marketers reacted to this environmental change by targeting more product and promotion toward this newer buying segment. Advertising for Kmart shows men shopping for baby shampoo, and Johnson & Johnson displays a hairy arm hoisting an infant in its ads for Baby Diaper Rash Relief. A clever TV commercial for Procter & Gamble's Jif peanut butter shows two fathers, and only one female parent, at a children's playground. Reaction to changes in markets is important to every aspect of marketing planning.[1]

Market Share/Market Growth Analysis

One of the more important planning decisions involves the share of the market a product currently holds compared to the status of the market in terms of growth. Analyzing the position of each good or service in relation to how the market is behaving gives the strategic planner some indication as to where emphasis should be placed. For example, if a good or service falls within a market that is showing little sign of growth, no amount of product revision or promotional activity can create a tremendous return. On the other hand, when the marketer finds that its entry into a high growth market is stalled, the marketing plan should address that problem.

A commonly used matrix, developed by the Boston Consulting Group, labels the products in these categories. A cash cow has a high share of a low growth market. An item with low market share in the same low growth market would be called a dog. Those products that take a sizable chunk out of a fast growing market are stars, where a product that has not taken advantage of such an arena is a question mark, or problem child.

IN-HOUSE COOPERATION

Marketing planning promotes **in-house cooperation.** When other areas within a business know what marketing is doing and understand why, teamwork

---

[1]Laura Zinn, "Real men buy paper towels, too, *Business Week,* November 9, 1992, pp. 75-76.

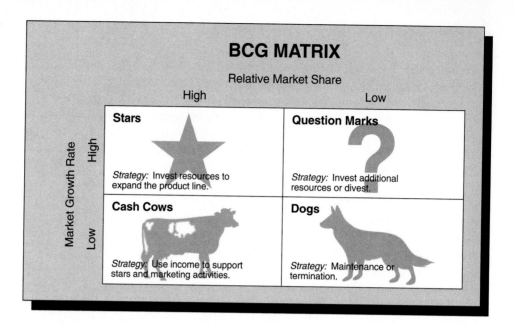

BCG MATRIX

Relative Market Share

High — Low

Market Growth Rate — High / Low

Stars

Strategy: Invest resources to expand the product line.

Question Marks

Strategy: Invest additional resources or divest.

Cash Cows

Strategy: Use income to support stars and marketing activities.

Dogs

Strategy: Maintenance or termination.

results. Products are not made in a vacuum. Marketing research verifies market needs, finance assists in establishing prices, and the traffic department ships the goods. Marketing needs the cooperative effort of all facets of the business to move toward customer satisfaction.

Even in the marketing oriented companies where all groups work toward the goal of customer satisfaction, proper planning is a big help in developing cooperation and teamwork. Production departments need to plan in advance for tooling and equipment. Financial groups must prepare the firm for cash flow and accounts payable. The transportation area requires advance notice to line up storage and shipping. The marketing plan alerts all departments so that internal glitches can be minimized.

What Are the Steps of a Marketing Plan?

Companies both large and small should develop marketing plans for their businesses. This formal report should contain provisions for its continual update. Most marketing oriented companies swear by the planning process and the plans that are the fruit of those exercises. In order to plan for the future, one must first look at the present.

SITUATION ANALYSIS

Situation analysis— the first step in a marketing plan that spells out present conditions and company capabilities.

The first step in any planning process is a **situation analysis,** which spells out the present market conditions and company capabilities. Setting goals and strategies is meaningless without such an examination. These factors are analyzed based upon competitive postures, future trends, present production and marketing capabilities and corporate motives. Since planning addresses individual products or groups, many plans may be necessary. The planning posture for Gillette's Good News disposable razors may be considerably different from that company's position with its Paper Mate pen division.

This opening section of the marketing plan examines all aspects of the present conditions. Product mix and distribution systems are scrutinized. The plan also looks at the organization of the firm and department and describes the strengths and weaknesses of the strategic business unit. Market conditions, economic trends and competitive analysis are important parts of this initial stage of the marketing plan.

MISSION STATEMENT

Completion of the situation analysis leads to a **mission statement.** This portion of the plan describes the broad purposes or roles of the strategic business unit. Knowing the present conditions and future prospects, the marketing plan addresses what needs to be done. Planning for planning's sake is a waste of time. Planning with direction is meaningful. Mission statements should be realistic and specific. Many companies, such as Marriott, Johnson & Johnson and Avis post their mission statements in conspicuous places so that all employees know what the firm stands for.[2]

In assessing the company resources to be used in grasping opportunities, marketers should first **define their business.** This definition should include the markets served, the products offered and the technology available for expansion. If the firm is a manufacturer, the production capabilities and distribution systems presently available may dictate which road the company takes. In service sectors, changes in direction or expansion more often depends upon financial resources.

For corporate planning, the mission statement includes the business in which the company sees itself operating and how it wants to be recognized in that field. This portion of the planning process addresses the role and vision of the strategic business unit as seen by its managers. The direction of each individual operating center may be different, yet should be in tune with the overall company prospectus. Bread Loaf Construction Co., a Middlebury, Vermont, building construction firm, encourages all employees to participate in developing mission statements.[3]

Missions change just as strategies change. At VF Corporation, the company that markets Wrangler and Lee jeans, Vanity Fair lingerie and Jantzen swimsuits and sportswear, the situation was tough in the latter 1980s. Heavy competition from Levi Strauss, especially with its Dockers line, and from Sara Lee, with the Hanes and Bali divisions, called for action. Management rewrote the marketing plan and changed the mission statement, stressing a consumer driven emphasis. Focus groups and customer interviews provided the needed information.[4]

Mission statement— describes the purposes or roles of the strategic business unit.

---

[2]Gilert Fuchsberg, "'Visioning' missions becomes its own mission," *The Wall Street Journal,* January 7, 1994, pp. B1-B5.

[3]Teri Lammers, "The effective and indispensable mission statement," *Inc.,* August 1992, pp 75-77.

[4]Elaine Underwood, " A high-tech marketer in disquise," *BRANDWEEK,* February 8, 1993, pp. 14-17; Janet Bamford, "After careful retailoring, VF is looking smart," *Business Week,* June 22, 1992, pp. 66-68.

Encouraging participation from its employees, Bread Loaf Construction Co. completely rewrote its mission statement to accent customer service. (Courtesy of Bread Loaf Construction Co.)

GOALS AND OBJECTIVES

Each strategic business unit needs direction. A planning document should state specifically what the organization expects to accomplish and when. If the SBU controls several different products or product lines, the targets for each may vary. Similarly, future plans may be long or short range in nature. Regardless of the situation, the statement of **goals and objectives** should be complete, conclusive and comprehensive.

Goals should not be established lightly or without thought. These objectives ought to be reachable, yet challenging enough to stretch the company or division to reach its potential. Setting easy-to-reach or undemanding targets does little to strengthen the organization or its people. Since these planning documents are flexible, goals and objectives are subject to continual modification.

Long-Range Strategies

While determining objectives and goals, marketers often devise and create **long-range strategies.** These strategic processes for reaching the objectives or purposes are usually stated rather simply at this stage. How the company or unit wants to be perceived within its industry or niche is an important basis for the further development of the details or tactics. Broad areas of responsibility need to be established and methods of measurement or control spelled out.

During this stage in the planning process, marketers assess their resources in relation to market opportunities. What advantages the company or strategic business unit possesses need to be spelled out. The potentials and pitfalls of its operations should be examined. Once the goals are determined and the direction decided upon, the details of how to get to that end can be created.

TACTICAL PLAN

The **tactical plan** lists the specific procedures, people, equipment and finances needed to reach the stated goals. Areas of responsibility and timetables are a part of this implementation area. When Apple Computer first introduced the Macintosh, specific share of market or sales figures were objectives. The tactics needed to reach those ends appeared in detail in the marketing plan. The tactical plan included how rapidly and where the product would be introduced and how it would be promoted, complete with budgets and distribution timetables.

Objectives are not met simply because they are stated. The tactical plan addresses these issues. What are the product features and benefits, including branding and packaging? How might pricing changes or discounts affect previously set goals? Does distribution need modifying or expansion? What new promotional schemes will make the objectives real? This section of the marketing plan tackles all of these questions in detail.

Tactical plan—lists the specific procedures, people, equipment and finances needed to reach goals.

Evaluation

The tactical portion of the marketing plan also includes a section regarding the **evaluation** of the marketing operations. A continuing process that gauges how well objectives are met and how effective individual strategies or tactics perform is necessary during the operation, not afterward. When Gallo introduced the folksy boys for their Bartles & Jaymes ads, the objectives of brand recognition and increased sales were part of the plan. Close monitoring of these award-winning commercials was necessary to assure that the goals were reached, or in this case, exceeded. In 1992, Gallo dropped the long-running, clever ads, but the characters live on in other advertising efforts.

The final phase of the marketing plan involves the measurement of the results and evaluation of the entire marketing process. A continual process of checking the progress must be put into motion. Marketing plans and tactical procedures are useless without constantly evaluating them against the standards set by the company.

Product acceptance and promotion evaluation must be continual in order to be effective. Are the mission statements and objectives current and accurate? Is the market clearly defined? How well is the tactical plan meeting strategic goals? What is the status of sales and profits? How does the product or strategic business unit stack up to the competition in share of market? The best way to obtain necessary control information is by conducting regular marketing audits.

Marketing Audit

The **marketing audit** is a systematic process of evaluating results. This measure of control looks at the original objectives and measures the results in reaching those goals. By auditing the status of the marketing plan, companies can keep better control over strategic opportunities and marketing resources. No changing of the marketing mix should occur without the evaluation factor of an audit.

Marketing audit—a continual or periodic process used in evaluating the marketing effort.

If the Carnation Company decided to market split pea puree under its Contadina label, close monitoring of product acceptance would be necessary even after favorable pre-testing. What effect would a 10 percent cut in price

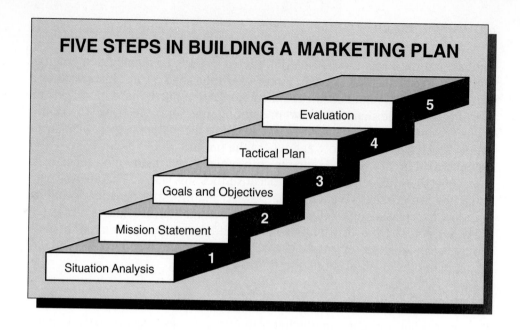

FIVE STEPS IN BUILDING A MARKETING PLAN

5 Evaluation
4 Tactical Plan
3 Goals and Objectives
2 Mission Statement
1 Situation Analysis

have on the sale of a bar of Dial's Tone soap? Can Tandy gain market share by selling computers through Safeway, and if Sophia Loren were to endorse L'eggs, what impact would it have upon product awareness? If the marketers of these major consumer products were to make such significant changes in their marketing mix, early determination of the results would be necessary. Since information is needed continuously, annual marketing audits would be useless.

Audits must cover all of the factors that affect the marketing mix. Changes that may occur in outside areas, such as the economy, culture or government, are particularly important. Subtle changes in competitive strategy or technology can have significant effect on results. Each element of the marketing mix must be audited to ensure that the marketing plan is performing as desired.

hat Affects the Performance of Marketing Plans?

The tactical section of the marketing plan includes the procedures necessary for reaching the objectives. How these tactical plans are carried out will determine the direction that the marketer takes. Tactics depend upon strategies. The long-range plan dictates what is to be done in the shorter time span.

Even with well-conceived blueprints, marketers are aware of factors that might detour their plans. Good turns of events are just as important as the potholes. Strategic business units should be prepared to jump at any valid opportunity that comes along. They should also be ready to abandon ship quickly if the need arises. Marketing plans are not rigid, unbending documents that commit a company or its people to only one avenue of attack.

STRATEGIC WINDOWS

During the situation analysis portion of the planning process, marketers explore both market opportunities and available resources. In searching for opportunities, companies try to locate the **strategic window.** This opening blends the best abilities of the marketer with market opportunities. The objective is to find those market needs that can be satisfied using the available assets of the marketing company.

Not all possible roads lead to success. Just because a new potential comes along does not mean that all firms or all units should jump at that opening. Some strategic business units may be better equipped to win than others. The chance for increased sales, share of market or profit will depend upon a variety of factors. The internal readiness of the marketer must be up to the challenge presented by the external opportunity.

Strategic window—
the opening that combines the best abilities of the marketer with market opportunities.

SWOT ANALYSIS

In determining the course of marketing direction, businesses look to their **strengths** and **weaknesses** in light of the **opportunities** and **threats** they face. Using the acronym **SWOT,** marketing management assesses the readiness of its planning. The marketing plan may be designed to save or protect present products instead of developing new ones to meet opportunities. In this regard, marketers need also be wary of the closing of the strategic window. Many a marketing oriented company has jumped toward the window only to find it closed.

SWOT—acronym meaning strengths, weaknesses, opportunities and threats.

Strengths

The strengths of a company or a marketing group are many. Some may be apparent, others hidden. Companies that hold patents or control raw material supplies have obvious advantages. Rich capital resources and sound production capabilities are other obvious strengths. Not all of the pluses need be present for a strategic business unit to take advantage of potential opportunities.

An assessment of the resources of a business should include more than the physical assets of the company. The talents of the employees and the image of the company are also assets. Firms possessed with innovative management have an outstanding resource that can open windows not available to those businesses less endowed. Marketers with a "can do" aura gained from past successes often win competitive battles simply because it is expected of them.

Weaknesses

Many firms, realizing their own shortcomings, simply acquire other companies to gain the resources needed. Certainly, Colgate-Palmolive Company has the capability of developing almost any cosmetic or health care product needed. The manufacturing and research and development departments of this giant trade goods house are among the largest and most respected in the industry. However, seeing a market niche that blended with their product mix, Colgate

■ ■ ■ ■ ■
Swot analysis

STRENGTHS	WEAKNESSES	OPPORTUNITIES	THREATS
Unique product, brand awareness, package design, outstanding positioning	"Me too" image, obsolete or outdated product, lack of significant image	Discovery of niche market, change in demographics, lack of competitive awareness	Market size limited, change in demographics, easy market entry
Low-cost position, prowess in manufacturing/ processes, raw material advantage	Outdated manufacturing processes, lack of capital for expansion	Technological breakthrough, markets not yet stagnant, global opportunity	Superior capability of competition, inability to spread overseas
Current distribution system, integrated distribution systems in place	Lack of distribution system, perishable or fragile product, no in-house delivery capable	Competition stymied with outmoded channels, direct marketing potential	Easily adapted channels by competitors, small and flexible competition
Superior product/firm image, promotional capabilities already established	Poor product/firm image, no promotional plan in place	Poor competitive image, inadequate competitive promotional activity	Image or positioning unimportant in market, good promoters in market

■ ■ ■ ■ ■

purchased Mennen Company in early 1992. This move was a bit of a departure for a firm that is noted for developing new products from within.[5]

Archrival Procter & Gamble, on the other hand, has been gobbling up other companies as fast as it can open its pocketbook. Outright purchases of Richardson-Vicks and Noxell pushed P&G quickly into the over-the-counter medicine field and into the lower end cosmetics game. During the 1980s, the company also picked off several key lines from Norwich-Eaton Pharmaceuticals, Revlon and G. D. Searle, strengthening its position in these markets.[6]

Weaknesses in personnel are less apparent. Managers who might be capable in one type of strategic move, may falter in another. A shallowness in management depth can also be taken as a people weakness. Many times company image and positioning are not strong enough to tackle new tasks or markets. The narrowness of the product mix may act as a lack of strength. The Clorox Company found this out when it attempted to expand into the detergent field, an unsuccessful venture.[7]

---

[5]Seema Nayyar, "Colgate mulls a new course for Mennen," *Adweek's Marketing Week,* June 8, 1992, cover and p. 5; Seema Nayyar, "Building on its strengths," *Adweek's Marketing Week,* June 15, 1992, pp. 18-20.

[6]Gabriella Stern and Suein L. Hwang, "Procter & Gamble agrees to buy Avon Product's Giorgio fragrance line," *The Wall Street Journal,* July 27, 1994, p. B4; P. Sloan, "Courting Revlon," *Advertising Age,* March 11, 1991, p. 37; Cara Appelbaum, "A new world of beauty for P&G," *Adweek's Marketing Week,* April 15, 1991, pp. 4-5; Zachary Schiller, "Procter & Gamble is following its nose," *Business Week,* April 22, 1991, p. 28.

[7]Michael Jankofsky, "Clorox in bid to streamline sells frozen foods to Heinz," *New York Times,* July 1, 1993, p. D5; Fara Warner, "Clorox dumps its detergents and sticks to core brands," *Adweek's Marketing Week,"* May 27, 1991, p.6.

Opportunities

Some opportunities knock like Charles Barkley played basketball, boldly. When chances for expansion, redeployment or new products come along, prepared companies are ready to move quickly. One does not need to be a genius to realize that the wellness movement is here to stay. Those firms taking advantage in the shift in eating habits, such as Campbell's Soup, ConAgra and Tyson Foods have profited.

The green movement has been building over a longer period of time, but has also attracted a major following. Too many firms seemed to jump in this direction without much thought. Others decided being green looked nice, but were unable to back up their claims of being good for the environment. Deja Inc. is a company from Portland, Oregon, that manufactures footwear entirely from recycled materials. The firm takes maximum advantage of the public's growing concern about waste and environmental decay. The marketers that make the best of this opportunity blend good ethics with sound business.

Many of the opportunities lie in the area of expansion. New products, new lines or new markets all hold a degree of awe or intrigue to marketers. Creating goods or services from scratch is exciting. To take advantage of opportunities, marketers have to have the plans in place, ready to move when the time is ripe. Since potential windfalls are not always evident in advance, planning for such events is difficult. However, the planning process itself acquaints everyone and every group within the firm or unit with the capabilities, or lack of them, that are present. Knowing the strengths and weaknesses of the SBU in advance allows managers to jump at the right opportunities when they arrive.

Threats

No firm has a monopoly on intelligence or street smarts. One of the downfalls of some marketers is the belief that they, and they alone, are the only ones who really know what is happening. Recalling the environments in which marketing operates is valid when dealing with opportunities and threats. When nationally acclaimed economists cannot agree on the future ups and downs of business cycles, only a Pollyanna would think that its crystal ball is the one tuned to the right channel. Business conditions change, and even the best forecasts can go astray.

Government action that impedes opportunity becomes a threat. Local, state and federal bureaucracies have a knack for upsetting the best of plans. Wise marketers also keep their eyes and ears open to cultural movement. Technology and competition go hand in hand at undermining opportunities. Just as a venture begins to cough up a return on the original investment, along comes a "better mousetrap" or a shrewder competitor. Perhaps the most critical threats facing marketers relate to new developments and competitive actions. As a good example, when Colgate announced its decision to enter the men's cosmetic field with the purchase of Mennen, Procter & Gamble cut its prices on competing brands.

CRISIS AS OPPORTUNITY

(wéi jī)

The Chinese word for "crisis" is made up of two parts: "danger" and "opportunity".

危 "Danger", originally pictured as a man on the edge of a precipice 产.

机 "Opportunity"—a reminder of the seemingly small but important opportunity that can come out of danger.

A **CARAVAN**® Storycard

The *Calligraphy Presentations*® Collection brings together the ancient oriental art form of brush calligraphy with the rich, multi-layered meanings of Chinese characters. One of a series of multicultural "Storycards" by Caravan (catalog avail.). This card created by artist Yunn Pann, Shanghai-born calligrapher and designer, and writer Linda Jade Stearns.
CARAVAN INTERNATIONAL, INC., P.O. BOX 17936, BOULDER, COLORADO 80308   PH. (303) 449-0305
Copyright 1988 Caravan International, Inc. All rights reserved. Printed in U.S.A.   GA20-200

Many of the applications of SWOT analysis relate to growth strategies. Most marketers adhere to the philosophy that standing still can be fatal. Rarely does one find business ventures that do not at least dream of expanding. For major firms, such development can take a variety of courses. The opportunity may lie with the creation of new products, or perhaps just strengthening the present market position. Whatever the goals, growth is a prime motivator of plans.

How Do Marketers Plan for Growth?

There are a number of possible tacks that a marketing firm might take in relationship to growth. Remembering that strengths and weaknesses affect the ability to take advantage of opportunities and overcome threats, marketers look

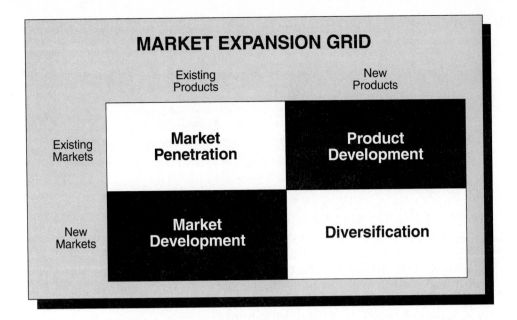

MARKET EXPANSION GRID

	Existing Products	New Products
Existing Markets	Market Penetration	Product Development
New Markets	Market Development	Diversification

to growth individually. For some strategic business units, expansion means new. New products, new markets, or new partnerships. To other companies, growth is the steady progress of existing business.

MARKET PENETRATION STRATEGY

Market penetration strategies attempt to increase sales of existing products in their primary markets. To increase share of market for given products, marketers use a variety of product improvements or promotional schemes. Packaging changes are common among mature products. When Kraft General Foods created the single service pouch for Maxwell House coffee, the company hoped to increase its share of a rather stagnant market. Delta Air Lines unleashed a massive promotional campaign to crack the Dallas–Ft. Worth market dominated by American Airlines. This effort included television commercials and newspaper advertising, along with personal selling to corporate accounts.[8]

This type of growth strategy is sometimes necessary to just maintain market position. In large, mature segments with lots of competition, keeping the present percentage of the sales is often more important than expansion. Product or package redesign and increased promotion are the two primary tools for maintaining market share.

NEW MARKET STRATEGY

Some strategies involve presently established products that are looking for **new markets.** By creating a new or extended market for a product entrenched in

New market development— creating new markets for existing products.

New product development— creating new products for existing markets.

---

[8]Elaine Underwood, "Delta does Dallas vs American," *BRANDWEEK,* September 28, 1992, p. 4.

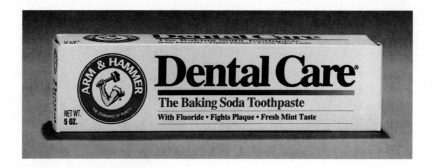

The first toothpaste incorporating baking soda, often recommended by the dental community, carries the Arm & Hammer name.

one market area, the marketer expands the potential while enhancing the original position. This strategy is especially helpful for mature products and is one method for extending product life.

Medical reports have unleashed some new markets for two old standards, aspirin and oat cereals. Doctors recommend aspirin for people who have suffered from a heart attack, and oatmeal is touted as helpful in reducing cholesterol. Before the medical industry backed these existing products, this particular market did not exist. Marketers of waxed paper promote its use as a food covering in microwave ovens, a new market for an old product. Club soda manufacturers promote this established item as a stain remover. All of these examples show new market development for old products.

NEW PRODUCT STRATEGY

Using a different strategy, older, more established markets are targeted by **new products.** The fact that a particular market segment may already have sizable product representation does not exclude the introduction of newer items. This strategy, the introduction of a new product to an existing arena, works well if the previous market can be broken into smaller pieces.

Arm & Hammer, the same firm that adapted new markets for baking soda, was the first to incorporate this natural abrasive into toothpaste. Although the dental community had suggested brushing with baking soda for some time, the taste left a bit to be desired. The blend of paste and soda made for an acceptable product. Not to be upstaged, Procter & Gamble introduced a similar toothpaste in 1992. Mentadent, Chesebrough-Pond's entry into this market, takes the product one step further using a refillable pump, a green marketing ploy.[9]

Several firms are in the hunt for the lucrative market for fat substitutes. NutraSweet was the first to gain FDA approval for its Simplesse, a milk and egg white based material for use in cold products such as dressings and frozen desserts. This company also markets Simple Pleasures, a fat free ice cream product. Procter & Gamble's Olestra is a synthetic that retains its fat-like qualities when heated, but P&G has struggled to gain approval for this product.

---

[9]Pay Sloan, "Peroxide push in toothpaste," *Advertising Age,* May 16, 1994, p. 46; Pam Weisz, "Mentadent gets buyer-, eco-friendly," *BRANDWEEK,* February 21, 1994, p. 10.

Global Marketing: Here Come the Chinese!

Most people equate global marketing with the "big boys." Giant multinationals like Boeing, Coca Cola and Caterpillar get most of the export news. The major trade goods houses all have a presence in overseas arenas. Procter & Gamble, Unilever, Nestlé and other giants of the industry sell their products worldwide. Many smaller multinationals are finding opportunities in global marketing as well, but the volume of their sales is hard to track. The price tag on a giant earth mover or a jet liner cannot be easily hidden.

Although global markets exist almost everywhere, much attention has been placed on the biggest of them all—China. American firms have joined other multinationals in drooling over the potential in the world's most populous country. As its economy struggles between free market desires and controlled leadership, China continues to open up its trading policies to allow foreign goods to flow in. One point overlooked by many global managers, however, is that the bridge moves traffic both ways and exports from the "big dragon" are burgeoning.

One of the major areas where Chinese products are making inroads is the toy industry. Walk into any Toys 'R' Us store and you will find shelves jammed with goods from the Far East, but most notably originating in China. From moderately priced games such as Turbo Blaster Raceway to small items such as Matchbox vehicles, the presence of this Oriental giant is being felt worldwide. One will shortly be seeing even more sophisticated goods arriving across the Pacific, as China changes its emphasis away from labor intensive manufacturing.

SOURCE: Joyce Barnathan, Douglas Harbrecht, Ann Therese Palmer and William J. Holstein, "A tidal wave of Chinese goods," *Business Week,* December 12, 1994, pp. 56–57.

Unilever, Kraft General Foods and Frito-Lay are other players developing new products for basically old markets.[10]

DIVERSIFICATION STRATEGY

Many factors influence growth strategy. Some long-range plans call for **diversification,** the branching into new and different ventures. This strategy may be necessary because of the deterioration of present markets or may come about because of opportunities spotted in new arenas. At times, this philosophy relates solely to the personality or style of the management.

For example, Coppertone is a brand name familiar to most sun lovers throughout the world. Shering-Plough, a multi-faceted pharmaceutical giant, has profited handsomely from just this one product. Now, this company lends

Diversification—
branching into new areas or products not currently being covered.

---

[10]Jennifer Lawrence, "Whatever happened to Olestra?" *Advertising Age,* May 2, 1994, p. 16-18; Camela Zarcone, "PandG's Olestra makes headway," *Chemical Marketing Reporter,* November 22, 1993, p. 7; Ann M. Thayer," Food additives," *Chemical & Engineeting News,* June 15, 1992, pp. 26-44.

the Coppertone name to a variety of sun goods. Jacques Moret of New York markets swimwear carrying the famous Coppertone brand. Beach footwear, waterproof watches, towels and tote bags help diversify the Coppertone line.[11]

Many innovative products crop up in the electronic industry. Some relate to functional applications. Others are a bit more fanciful. Recoton, an electronics accessories house from Long Island City, New York, markets a whole range of clever items for the gadget freak. An adapter that allows for listening to CDs over a car's tape deck and wireless headphones are just two of this company's products. The company's diversification strategy is more evident through its acquisition of other firms with complimentary lines, such as antennas, headphones, and CD cleaners. In a less serious vein, TeleFire is a screen that fits the front of a television set. The cells in the translucent plastic act much like a kaleidoscope, changing the picture into what the inventors labeled "kinetic mosaic." Created by Western Light Lab of Mill Valley, California, TeleFire is a fresh break from the humdrum of the tube.[12]

How Do Image and Positioning Impact Plans?

Marketing plans that fail to consider the position of a product are often a source of trouble. The product design, pricing methods, distribution set up and promotional efforts all relate to the product's position. How the market views a product has tremendous bearing upon the performance of the marketing plan. Performance often depends upon the **image** of the company as well as its goods or services.

As was discussed in chapter 2, **positioning** describes the image of the product or company in the minds of buyers or the public. These images form the basis for marketing planning. Positioning impacts every aspect of the marketing mix and must be coordinated between each element. If the marketer creates an upscale image for the product, the pricing of that product must remain constant with that image. Products targeting a more affluent group of consumers need to be priced to reflect the value expected. Similarly, distribution and promotion must remain in character with the position established for the product.

For instance, Volkswagen is usually viewed as being economical and unsophisticated, while Cadillac carries a plush and costly image. Consumers would have just as much trouble picturing a VW as posh, expensive or luxurious as they would have believing that Cadillac produces an economy car. To illustrate, Volkswagen's Quantum has yet to make the quantum leap, and the Cadillac Cimmaron did not live up to original projections. The public perception of these products clashed with the position conceived by the marketers.

---

[11]Cara Appelbaum, "Coppertone says good-bye to summer," *Adweek's Marketing Week,* September 16, 1991, p. 6; Cyndee Miller, "Coppertone plans swimsuit line and additional licensing ventures," *Marketing News,* February 5, 1990, pp. 2 and 5.

[12]Richard S. Teitelbaum, "Recoton," Companies to Watch column in *Fortune,* July 27, 1992, p. 97; Alison Sprout, "Psychedelic screen," Products to Watch column in *Fortune,* July 27, 1992, p. 107.

CORPORATE POSITIONING

The strategy section of the marketing plan will define the overall position of the company, department or other strategic business unit. This area establishes the image that the unit wants customers or the public to accept for itself. If the marketing plan is created for a specific product, the positioning of that product might be stated here prior to moving into the tactical plan where more detail is found.

For example, Polaroid has a corporate strategy of positioning itself as the only producer of instant cameras, leaving the lucrative 35mm market to a host of other camera marketers. The company has identified a marketing opportunity that meshes well with its resources. The success of the Spectra has confirmed the segmentation strategy of this old line company.[13]

The dairy industry has positioned butter as the higher priced, richer tasting spread. Margarine producers, on the other hand, taking advantage of increased health consciousness, position their products as low in cholesterol and saturated fats. Carnation ice cream is positioned as the low price, quality favorite, whereas Breyer's promotes the naturalness of its brand. Ben & Jerry's positions its products as upscale, almost sinful, gourmet treats.

UPSCALE VS UTILITARIAN IMAGES

The market position and image of the A. T. Cross Co.'s pens is one of quality, prestige writing implements. This old-line company began to market thin, 0.5 mm, graphite pencils in the spring of 1989, a move viewed by industry analysts as a long-awaited strategic change. Cross still promotes in such prestige media as *Smithsonian, The New Yorker,* and *The Wall Street Journal* to maintain its prestige image.[14]

The retail trade reflects basic positioning principles. Both Sears and J. C. Penney have undertaken drastic image changes in the recent past. The change in policy at Sears to "go discount" is well documented. Penney's move was a bit more subtle. Gradually, this old line mass merchandiser has changed its product lines and its image to become more "upscale." Although repositioning on this scale takes years to assess, early reports indicate that Penney's move is paying off.[15]

As a further illustration of positioning and its influence on tactical plans, check out Applebee's. This Kansas City, Missouri, chain of family

---

[13]Iris Rosendahl, "Polaroid unveils Captiva camera and new high speed films," *Drug Topics,* July 5, 1993, p. 54; David Kiley, "Polaroid's Spectra targets the practical-minded with a new pitch," *Adweek's Marketing Week,* February 26, 1990, p. 5.

[14]Michael Schuman, "Thin is out, fat is in," *Forbes,* May 9, 1994, p. 92; Debora Toth, "A. T. Cross gets the lead out and expands into finer-point mechanical pencils," *Adweek's Marketing Week,* May 29, 1989, pp. 32-33.

[15]Jay Palmer, "Penney for your thoughts: concentration on affordable fashion, J. C. Penney mounts a comeback," *Barron's,* April 11, 1994, pp. 12-13; Marianne Wilson, "J. C. Penney's new look," *Chain Store Age Executive,* June 1993, pp. 70-71.

Marketing and Society: It's Deja Vu!

Target marketing is often a scary proposal. One has to be sure that the selected group will behave in the right manner. In addition, distribution channels and promotional venues must be available to support the effort. Many firms have joined the "green" bandwagon with products or promotion that claim to make the world a better place. One company that has taken this strategy to the utmost is Deja Inc.

Julie Lewis, a noted recycling advocate, founded Deja. Several of the original officers of the company

came from another Northwest shoe marketer, Avia. Most of the initial funding came from grants and venture capitalists. Borrowing from the French phrase *deja vu*, meaning already seen, the firm marketed its first 5,000 pairs of DejaShoes in 1992. The unique aspect of this line of casual footwear is that it is manufactured almost entirely from recycled products. Sawdust, tire treads, trim from disposable diapers, coffee filters and almost any other discarded object goes into the manufacture of these attractive and comfortable shoes.

WHAT'S INSIDE A DEJA SHOE?

milk jug

soda bottles

recycled cotton canvas or recycled polypropylene

wetsuit trim waste

coffee filters and file folders

seat cushion trim waste

polystyrene cups

trim waste from diaper manufacturing

recycled EVA foam

tire rubber and recycled rubber

magazines and cardboard

World's first shoe made from recycled materials

continued to page 81

continued from page 80

From the beginning, the company felt there was a market of individuals who would be attracted to the recycling philosophy. Although the company does little advertising, point-of-sale displays and brochures carry the complete story of the DejaShoe. In addition, the firm trains retailer salespeople to be conversant about recycling and environmental protection. Deja Inc. hopes one day to branch into clothing and other items aimed at this same target market.

SOURCE: Jim Hill, "Earth friendly shoes," The Oregonian, October 30, 1993, pp. E1–E5; Richard Colby, "Deja gets a kick out of shoes," The Oregonian, June 17, 1992, pp. D1–D2.

restaurants carved an unusual niche in the fast food market. Offering a casual dining atmosphere and frequent menu changes, this fast growing franchise operation continues to post record earnings compared to lower priced outlets. Even competitors such as TGI Friday's and Chili's have not been able to overcome the positioning offered by Applebee's of upscale surroundings at a modest price.[16]

MASCULINE VS FEMININE IMAGES

As marketers target specific groups of buyers, they often position their products with a specific image. Chunky and Man-Handler soups appeal to a masculine audience, yet carry that aura of Campbell's position as the number one soupmaker. L'Orient frozen dinners and Fresh Express packaged snacks, both from Campbell, have a lighter, definitely more feminine feel. Promotion for these different convenience goods from the same house is affected by the image that they carry.

Gender positioning does not only relate to the target markets. Certain goods just seem to take on an aura that is masculine or feminine. Once such an image is established, marketers generally avoid changing it. Safeguard, the deodorant soap from Procter & Gamble, is one of those products that, on its own, assumed a more masculine image among consumers. The success of Unilever's Lever 2000 has P&G scrambling to reposition its leading brand to be a little less manly. New packaging and advertising are used to soften the male image.[17]

Beer carries a masculine image, with most brewers traditionally targeting male consumers. Michelob, the upscale brew from Anheuser-Busch, departed from the norm in a campaign that featured women, dressed in suits and jeans, drinking beer. One print ad that broke in 1992 showed four women in a restaurant enjoying themselves and, of course, a Michelob. This repositioning of a beer suitable for both sexes featured ads in *Vogue* and *Cosmopolitan*.[18]

---

[16]Shelley Neumeier, "Applebee's International," Companies to Watch column in *Fortune*, February 24, 1992, p. 93.

[17]Fara Warner, "Safeguard's risky mission," *Adweek's Marketing Week*, March 16, 1992, pp. 36-37; P. Sloan and B. Johnson, "P&G slips on soap," *Advertising Age*, September 30, 1991, p. 3.

[18]Cyndee Miller, "Michelob ads feature women—and they're not wearing bikinis," *Marketing News*, March 2, 1992, pp. 1-2.

TARGET MARKETS

Target markets should be specified for each item in the product mix or line. Team members within and outside the marketing department need to know the characteristics of each target. Buyer profiles are often provided through research. Targeting specific markets will define many of the needed tasks to be undertaken in the more detailed tactical plan.

Sometimes the target market dictates product design. For example, green marketing has been hot for a number of years, yet the clothing industry had trouble coming up with products to appeal to those who prefer natural products. At Christmas 1991, both Levi Strauss and Esprit introduced lines made from a cotton that contains its own natural coloring. By eliminating potentially harmful dyes and chemicals, these apparel leaders offer goods that appeal to the environmentally conscious shopper, a specific target.[19]

How Does Management Style Impact Performance?

Management and leadership styles vary. What works in one business may not be effective in another. One trend is the evidence of a less rigid, more casual management style. Young managers, often found in the highly technical industries spawned by the computer boom, are less rigid and more informal than their predecessors. Dictated by corporate strategy and organization, leaders and their styles guide the tactical plan, but can be significantly different.

INTRAPRENEURSHIP

Intrapreneurship— the entrepreneurial quality of restraint-free thinking used in an organizational setting.

New management styles encourage innovation and **intrapreneurship.** By permitting and encouraging employees to develop restraint-free thinking, not tied to rigid doctrine, management benefits from increased flow of ideas and information. For example, management by walking around, known also by the initials MBWA, is a system that has worked well for United Airlines. Instead of confining themselves to offices, United's managers roam freely throughout their facilities, getting to know their workers and the tasks that they carry out. A spirit of teamwork results.

To foster intrapreneurship, some companies place the responsibility for the development process in a separate company or division. Colgate Venture Co. operates separately from Colgate-Palmolive. This subsidiary firm, staffed with entrepreneurial types, is constantly eyeing specialized products and looking for niche markets that have growth potential. Similarly, Kraft General Foods uses a subsidiary called the Culinova group to look at new product and new market opportunities. Management style is more intrapreneurial in these arms, operating separately from potentially stifling corporate structures.

---

[19]Susan L. Oliver, "Seeds of success," *Forbes,* July 15, 1994, p. 98; Cyndee Miller, "Levi's, Esprit spin new cotton into eco-friendly clothes," *Marketing News,* April 27, 1992, pp. 11-12; Elaine Underwood, "Jeans take on greener hue," *Adweek's Marketing Week,* June 8, 1992, p. 4.

THE FABRIC OF OUR LIVES™
®Registered Service Mark/Trademark of Cotton Incorporated.

COTTON INCORPORATED FOR AMERICA'S COTTON GROWERS, 1370 AVENUE OF THE AMERICAS, NY, NY 10019
Dockers® and the Dockers® logo design are registered trademarks of Levi Strauss & Co. ©1990 Levi Strauss & Co.

Although 501 jeans remain an important part of business, Levi Strauss has seen its Dockers product line soar. (Courtesy of Levi Strauss & Company)

Some studies have also shown that intraprenuerial managers are less susceptible to stress and burnout that often accompany business decision making. Some firms, such as AT&T and PepsiCo, and many graduate business schools are even offering training or courses in introspection. Many feel that this sort of exercise helps develop the intuitiveness that is so important to management. As hectic and competitive as today's business environment is, a cool head is a major advantage to the individual and the company.[20]

ow Do Marketers Forecast?

Marketing management "looks into the future" to modify today's plans and strategies. Production, distribution systems and promotional campaigns take time to complete. To prepare for the future, marketers need methods for predicting buyer demand. Such predictions cannot be made with a flip of the coin or a peek at a tarot card.

Sales of new products are particularly difficult to forecast. Without past data on performance, testing the product among potential buyers becomes the best tool for estimating market demand and product acceptance. Forecasting for established products is made easier by checking ongoing performance.

TREND ANALYSIS

Trend analysis— looking into the past to predict the future.

Looking into the past to predict the future is a common approach to forecasting. Such **trend analysis** looks into the past to predict the future. Studies of previous success of products in different economic and competitive settings may give clues on future performance. This glimpse at what has happened previously helps in developing an estimate for what is likely to happen later. Simply observing the previous year or two may not produce an accurate estimate of what will happen in the next twelve months. These backward looks can be tempered by weighted factors to provide more accurate data.

By weighting the data to account for unusual economic conditions such as these, forecasters gain a clearer picture of what is ahead. Weighted or not, trend analysis has a weak point. Too often forecasters and marketers become lulled into assuming that past performance will continue unaltered. Estimates of the future should use past information that is tempered by other factors, including good judgment.

---

[20]Stratford Sherman, "Leaders learn to heed the voice within," *Fortune*, August 22, 1994, pp. 92-100.

SALES FORCE COMPOSITE

Other methods of gathering information for planning the future involve using input from the selling team or from company management. The judgment offered by these marketing sectors is often more realistic than the data supplied by past performance. The **sales force composite** method of forecasting assumes that the foot soldiers of the selling staff are closer to the pulse of customers and markets. By asking for customer input from the sales force, marketing management can forecast future expectations based upon customer needs.

Sales force composite—the forecasting method that collects information from the field sales force to predict the future.

Surveys of Buying Intention

In cases where input from the sales staff is insufficient, marketers may need to poll customers and prospects directly. **Surveys of buying intentions** may supply a more accurate picture than that generated solely by company salespeople. Knowledge about the plans of buyers can be invaluable in setting marketing goals. Such information usually depends upon the willingness of the customers to reveal their future plans.

JURY OF EXECUTIVE OPINION

Jury of executive opinion is a forecasting method that surveys various managers in different functional areas. This cross section of information provides a broader base for forecasting if it is not limited to the marketing staff alone. It is not difficult to find an audience of "experts." Although these leaders often provide unusual insight, management should be careful to ferret out wild, unfounded or impertinent opinions.

Jury of executive opinion—the forecasting method that polls managers with differing expertise to predict the future.

    Forecasting should not overlook management expertise. Top managers often achieve their success because of their innate ability to use good judgment and reflection. Marketing executives often develop such intuition through knowledge and experience, which cannot be ignored in sales forecasting. The hunches and feelings of these executives are valuable additions to quantitative information.

THE DELPHI TECHNIQUE

Similar to the jury of executive opinion method, the **Delphi technique** asks questions of business executives. In this case, however, these experts are usually from outside the company. A researcher, after collecting and tabulating input from the sample, sends the individual predictions back to the group. Members are then asked to refine their choices. Ultimately, the Delphi technique will narrow the choices down to a single pattern. The quality of the panel has considerable effect on the outcome of both the jury of executive opinion and the Delphi technique.

    The purpose of forecasting attempts is to arm marketers with the necessary data regarding changes and trends in the environments. This allows for successful management planning and decision making. Managing the marketing mix can be a difficult job. So many variables can change in so many ways. While the process may be strenuous, the results are sweet.

How Do Marketing Departments Organize?

To use the tools of the marketing mix efficiently, marketers must develop organizational structures. Rarely do any two marketing oriented firms staff or group themselves in the same manner. There is no one preferred method of organizing. Some structures work better for certain industries or companies than do others. Companies or departments have latitude in selecting the format that best suits the objectives and personnel available. Whatever organization is picked, the functions and tasks of marketing remain the same.

BY FUNCTION

Functional organization—one designed according to the role or purpose of the individuals or groups.

One common way that marketers organize their staff is by **function.** Dividing the company or SBU according to role or purpose makes a lot of sense for marketers. In marketing departments, typical functions include product design, advertising, sales, research and customer service. With smaller organizations, a few people may be responsible for one or more categories. In larger companies, additional functions, such as marketing administration or communications, are included as need arises.

Functional organizations are by far the most common and most practical. Marketing functions must be carried out regardless of the personnel available or type of market served. Although the exact arrangement of the functions in relation to staff or line positions may vary, the tasks remain.

BY GEOGRAPHY

Geographic organization—one designed according to region or location.

A **geographical** organization, designed according to region or location, is the best choice for some firms. For sales oriented companies conducting business nationwide, the organization might assign areas of responsibility according to areas. The Eastern seaboard, upper and lower Midwest, and the Pacific coast would be typical. In firms with global marketing activities, geographic organization might include an international department, further divided into specific areas of responsibility.

This type of arrangement requires a larger organization. Small firms or groups might not have a sufficient number of personnel to fill the slots in such a widespread department. Some functional areas of control might be found under each section within a geographic organization. Others would locate in a central or headquarters slot.

BY CUSTOMERS OR MARKETS

Market organization—one designed according to customers or markets served.

Instead of breaking into geographical segments, many marketing firms organize based upon **customers** or **markets** served. Since many customer groups or market areas have distinct characteristics, different management styles or marketing needs may exist that are more easily addressed separately. The Boeing Aircraft Company realizes that there are decidedly different needs to be met in the Government Services or in the Aerospace divisions that are not present with the Commercial Aircraft group. An organization based upon markets is more manageable for this firm.

This type of organization fits best when the types of goods or markets are very dissimilar. Many companies take this arrangement one step further with the description of divisions or subsidiaries. The market or customer organization is also found frequently when firms acquire other businesses.

BY PRODUCT

A common method of organizing used by consumer goods marketers is by **product.** This type of organization places individual products or product lines under separate managerial control. Product or brand managers are especially prevalent in the food industry. Procter & Gamble was one of the first consumer products companies to adopt this form of organization. RJR Nabisco, Carnation, Kraft General Foods, Ralston Purina and others organize their marketing groups according to product.

Product organization—one designed according to products or groups of products offered.

In organizations that employ product or brand managers, many of the marketing tasks are carried out by these people. Even so, a few common functions, such as sales or research, might be handled by corporate staff. The exact duties of product management personnel will vary from firm to firm.

SUMMING IT UP

Marketing planning is essential for success. Strategic or long-range planning is typically carried out by top management. Tactical, or day-to-day, planning is the charge of mid-management. Successful marketing planning is usually characterized by its flexibility and by in-house cooperation by all employees.

The marketing plan begins with the situation analysis, laying out the present market conditions, product characteristics, competitive posture and economic trends. The mission statement describes the broad role of the organization, which is followed by a more specific account of the goals and objectives of the individual SBU. Broad strategies, particularly regarding positioning and target marketing, are determined before the tactical plan is developed. The tactical plan spells out the details of how the profit center plans to accomplish its goals. This portion of the marketing plan should contain a continuing process for evaluation of the whole plan.

The marketing plan is affected by strategic windows of opportunity. The strengths and weaknesses of the organization should be weighed against market opportunities and threats (SWOT analysis). In planning for growth, marketers often attempt to increase the share of market for existing firms. This market penetration strategy may be augmented with a new market emphasis. New product strategies aim at creating brand new items for existing items. Diversification strategies look for new markets for totally new products. Image and positioning play key roles in all growth strategies.

Management style often impacts the implementation of the marketing plan. Forecasting market demand often uses trend analysis to look at past performance in predicting the future. Sales force composite, jury of executive opinion and the Delphi technique are also major forecasting tools. Marketers typically organize by function, geography, customers or markets, or product.

KEY CONCEPTS AND TERMS FROM CHAPTER THREE

Diversification
Evaluation plan
Functional organization
Geographic organization
Intrapreneurship
Jury of executive opinion
Market organization
Marketing audit
Mission statement
New market development

New product development
Product organization
Sales force composite
Situation analysis
Strategic business unit (SBU)
Strategic planning
Strategic window
Tactical planning
Trend analysis

BUILDING SKILLS

1. Describe the steps in a marketing plan and any ideas of different methods for organizing the marketing planning process.

2. Discuss the application of SWOT analysis, citing some examples of firms that have either successfully taken advantage of the window of opportunity or missed that fleeting moment.

3. Discuss the specifics needed to establish a system of control for a marketing program.

4. Describe the types of strategies available to marketers, and how marketers can implement them in different situations.

5. Discuss the various forecasting techniques, focusing on both their contrasts and their uses.

6. Compare the relative advantages and disadvantages of the different types of marketing organizations.

Making Decisions 3-1: You Have No Option.

In many European companies, notably France and Italy, men spend more on cosmetics than women. That trend is just catching on in the United States. The American male is a bit picky when it comes to trying new products. Men are also less likely to forgive a product that does not perform.

An area of great potential for cosmetics houses is hair coloring for men, and Clairol has risen to the challenge. Introduced in 1989, this company's Option brand is battling Combe's Grecian Formula for the number 1 spot in men's hair coloring.

Clairol's management felt that the male market held some real challenges that could not be overcome simply with name familiarity. Although the company has 60 percent of the female market, men could not be won over easily. Option has the three main qualities that marketing research uncovered as important. The product gives barely detectable results, is easy to use and is trustworthy. After ten years in development, Clairol's Option looks like the right choice.[21]

Describe any differences in the marketing mix and marketing plans between hair coloring for men versus women.

Making Decisions 3-2: The Perfect Atmosphere.

People have eternally tinkered with their atmosphere. Cave dwellers wore animal pelts and built fires when cold. Some evidence exists that crude air conditioners were in use when the heat turned up. In more modern times, the heating and cooling of the air around us is common. In addition, we play with lighting, aromas and noise to create our own, individual envelope. Now along comes the Atmosphere Manager to do it all for us.

Created by Norm Automation, a Sunnyvale, California, firm, this air conditioner-like machine purports to create the perfect climate for romance or a variety of other settings. The window unit not only controls the temperature and humidity, but also manages the flow and amount of air. In addition, Atmosphere Manager is capable of raising or lowering the lights and supplying the area with a variety of scents. If the room is fairly tightly sealed, this mood maker can even adjust the air pressure.

When work needs to be done, this marvelous machine controls its five settings to provide the best of conditions to keep you alert. Different settings are available for solo work versus conferences. Feeling romantic? Just say the word, and Atmosphere Manager reduces the fresh air input, dims the lights by remote control, and releases a soft fragrance of roses and rum into the air. The rest is up to the individual.[22]

Identify the growth strategy that Norm Automation employed for Atmosphere Manager, and describe how you might position this new product.

---

[21]Johanna Omelia, "Men's hair color grows by leaps and bounds," *Drug and Cosmetic Industry,* April 1994, pp. 40-41; Bill Susetka, as told to Judith D. Schwartz, "What Clairol learned while developing 'Option' for men," *Adweek's Marketing Week,* October 9, 1989, pp. 52-53.

[22]Alison Sprout, "Atmosphere Manager," Products to Watch column in *Fortune,* July 27, 1992, p. 107.

Making Decisions 3-3: Put on a Happy Face.

Some marketers thrive on competitive battles. Others avoid them. But, whatever the industry, one can always find friendly or not so friendly rivals. Personal care products offers an arena in which only the bravest and best equipped usually play. At the top of the heap are such well-known names as Unilever and Procter & Gamble. These are major players.

Then there is the new kid on the block, Scott's Liquid Gold Inc. You heard me right. The maker of Liquid Gold wood polish and Touch of Scent air fresheners bellied up to the bar with the big boys. A subsidiary of this Denver based firm, Neoteric-Cosmetics Inc., is marketing a line of skin care products branded Alpha Hydrox. The line of face creams and lotions will snuggle up on the shelves next to P&G's Oil of Olay and Unilever's Pond's.

Tiny compared to its competition, Scott's Liquid Gold feels that it has an advantage. Its products contain extractions from sugar cane and citrus known as alpha hydroxyl acids. Called glycolic acid in its skin cream formulas, this substance is alleged

to reduce the effects of aging. The company fully expects to succeed in the big leagues, and line extension of toners and gels will follow.[23]

Identify the growth strategy Scott's Liquid Gold Inc. used, and describe the probable components of the company's marketing plan.

---

[23]Seema Nayyar, "Scott's polishes its skin-care pitch," *BRANDWEEK,* February 1, 1993, p. 2; Seema Nayyar, "Scott's extends from furniture to skin care," *Adweek's Marketing Week,* June 8, 1992, p. 5.

Marketing in Practice: Development of the Marketing Plan

SITUATION ANALYSIS *(what are the present conditions?)*

- Overview of organization, its product(s) and general condition
- Market conditions, including economic forecast
- Competitive analysis
- SWOT analysis
  organization's strengths and weaknesses
  market opportunities and threats

MISSION STATEMENT *(what is the organization's philosophy?)*

- Social responsibility analysis

OBJECTIVES AND BASIC STRATEGIES
(what does the organization want to do?)

- Strategic window analysis

TACTICAL PLAN *(how, who, when and where can the objectives be met?)*

- Products
  new product development
  positioning
  target markets
  branding strategy
  packaging strategy

- Pricing
  market level
  discounts/concessions
  freight considerations

- Distribution
  channel strategy
  inventory management
  physical needs

- Promotion
  media plan
  creative strategy
  *   sales promotion activities*
  public relations needs
  personal selling plan

EVALUATION PROCESS *(what are the procedures for regular, periodic review?)*

- Marketing audit

MISSION STATEMENT

DEJA, Inc. will create and market comfortable and attractive lifestyle products such as footwear, apparel and accessories manufactured predominantly from recycled materials as well as plant materials obtained in an ecologically sensitive and sustainable manner. In so doing, the company will promote new uses and markets for these materials in accordance with our commitment to the principles of sustainable development and our passionate dedication to environmental stewardship.

STRATEGIC OBJECTIVES

BASIC STRATEGY: To give the "green" concept a mainstream appeal.

FINANCIAL GOALS: To go from zero to $50 million in sales revenue in roughly six years, to be profitable in the third year, and allow for an exit strategy by the venture capital backers after roughly seven years. DEJA strives to keep as much as possible of its total costs in the variable category, including the selling and distribution contributions, and handle design, public relations, and marketing through consultants. All management decisions will be made with the goals of keeping fixed costs to a minimum and stretching the initial cash investment to the maximum.

SITUATION ANALYSIS

STRENGTHS: Uniqueness of the concept; catching the front end of "green" wave; the management combination of "green" experience (environmental science and knowledge of environmental issues) with "mainstream" footwear experience; solid financial backing.

WEAKNESSES: Lack of brand identity; deficiency of funds for marketing, when compared to the major footwear competitors; lack of history of consumer demand for the primary product classification.

OPPORTUNITIES: The redefinition of "green" consumer products and companies; for DEJA to assume a leadership role in the most significant and sweeping market trend to emerge in decades.

THREATS: Large competitors, with substantial resources, entering this arena; inconsistency of recycled materials, in terms of both quality and quantity.

Target Audience

Most new product development processes include the creation of a customer profile, with demographics playing a key role. DEJA found that psychographic considerations are more important than sex, race or income in determining the target market. A strong concern for environmental protection exceeds most demographic categories, although younger generations do exhibit more knowledge and interest in saving our precious environment. This sense of the needs of our target audience pervades both the product design and our promotional efforts.

Product

While environmental concerns are basic to the design of DEJA products, the company recognizes the need for equal or superior quality coupled with attractive cosmetics. While the products must be designed to be appealing to all markets regardless of customer knowledge of DEJA's "green" philosophy, it is expected that consumers will be "won over" by the accompanying benefit to society. The company accepts the challenge to produce quality products, recognizing a consistent attitude toward environmental protection yet acknowledging the fashion realities of a diversified target market.

PROMOTIONAL PLAN

Positioning:

DEJA, Inc. positions itself as an environmentally active and socially responsible firm, not as a marketer of footwear. The company must "walk it's talk," stressing its mission statement rather than marketing hype. This approach has proven to be an incredibly cost effective method of reaching the target market. The founder of DEJA, Julie Lewis, is the perfect messenger. This very credible, non-corporate type spokesperson is her own story within the DEJA story, and publicity regarding her background and the company's roots in green marketing provides great leverage with retail customers. DEJA includes retailers in this company publicity at the local level, which in turn creates a "green" image in the community's eyes for those outlets carrying the DEJA line. National publicity generates local interest, and local publicity adds to the global campaign, a major promotional emphasis.

Personal Selling:

Personal selling at DEJA becomes a marketing communications tool, spreading the word about the company mission. Education is as important in selling the DEJA concept as is closing the sale. Retail customers must be made aware of both what DEJA is doing and why DEJA is doing it. Such a promotional effort requires an integrated communications link from management through the sales force to retailers and their salespeople to the ultimate consumer. Such an integrated communications network is necessary to provide and deliver the common message that is such an integral part of success.

Point-of-Purchase:

The final link in the education process includes point-of-purchase materials. Many consumers may have received the publicity messages and understand what DEJA is doing. Point-of-purchase materials will solidly link that publicity with the actual product, supporting the DEJA mission by once again emphasizing what the company is doing and why. The ability to couple the DEJA message with product at the point of sale is crucial.

PRICING AND DISTRIBUTION

Pricing is used by DEJA as an effective marketing tool to assure retailer customers that all are treated equally and that profits can be maximized. The basic elements of the pricing policy include:

- selective distribution, no discounters;
- one price to all customers regardless of order or account size;
- minimum 100 percent mark-ups are encouraged; and
- for mark-down sales, maximum 35 percent discounts, two times a year, for no longer than three weeks per sale are suggested.

4

Information Systems and Marketing Research

The Job to be Done

Information is important to marketers. Controlling the marketing mix is difficult without knowledge. Chapter 4 provides answers that help to:

- explain why marketers need information and the makeup of marketing information systems,
- recognize the types of information marketing research produces, including the available types of data,
- describe the marketing research process and the methods of identifying sources of information,
- define the methods of collecting data and surveys,
- compare the types of error occuring in marketing research, and
- analyze the management of marketing information.

Patty Shea

How Do Marketers Use Information?

If the function of marketing is the satisfaction of customer needs, then the logical first step is to determine what prospects desire. The requirements of the market include all aspects of the marketing mix, not just products. To successfully serve customers, marketers need information to identify markets, to develop or modify products and to make other marketing mix decisions. Without marketing information, the marketing management process becomes a coin toss. Information is the keystone for marketing planning.

IDENTIFY MARKETS

Information helps the marketer to **identify potential markets.** The size of the market potential must be resolved before the product is introduced, not afterward. To select specific targets, marketers require knowledge about who is buying what and for which reasons. Understanding the profile of potential buyers helps marketers decide how their goods and services should be designed, packaged, priced and promoted.

Illustrating this point, disposable camera marketers might never have identified all of the potential uses for these throwaways without first gathering

Identify markets	Determine total number of potential buyers, develop buyer profiles, describe location of buyers, calculate purchasing power of buyers.
Product development or modification	Analyze product features, determine packaging and branding requirements, develop product positioning, assess service requirements.
Distribution needs	Analyze present system in light of buyer needs, determine additional requirements, contrast competitive delivery systems, examine economies of scale.
Pricing concerns	Determine manufacturing and marketing costs, compare industry standards, examine competition.
Promotional evaluation	Determine present costs and potential savings, analyze effectiveness of promotional effort, contrast competitive effort, develop new promotional tactics.

■ ■ ■ ■ ■

information. This fast growing segment of the film market was pioneered by Fuji Photo Film back in 1986, followed quickly by giant film house Eastman Kodak, whose product was promoted during the 1993 Super Bowl. Agfa Photo Imaging Systems launched its Le Box in Europe in 1992. While disposables have become the favorites of many amateur photographers, especially teens and seniors, they are also used by insurance claims adjusters and law enforcement officers. Some hosts supply their guests a throwaway at weddings or parties to record spontaneous moments.[1]

PRODUCT DEVELOPMENT AND MODIFICATION

Targeted markets often give clues as to how the goods or services should be designed to bring about satisfaction. **Product development and modification** should be the result of information from present and potential markets. Knowing what is needed and how it should be packaged are part of the marketing decision process. Good marketers rarely put products into a marketplace without first checking to see what is needed.

Marketing information regarding needs and product design help a firm position its goods or services early. If the marketer does not establish an image at the beginning of its efforts, customers will likely do it themselves. It is important for the selling company to control product positioning to assure success. Similarly, it is important to maintain an appropriate company image.

---

[1]Terry Lefton, "Kodak teaming with NFL on single-use cameras," *BRANDWEEK*, December 14, 1992, p. 3; Alison Fahey, "The single-use picture brightens,"*BRANDWEEK*, November 9, 1992, p. 2; Mark Maremont and Robert Neff, "The hottest things since the flashbulb," *Business Week*, September 7, 1992, p. 72.

Product preferences impact other areas of the marketing mix. Input regarding customers helps the marketing company establish pricing policy, set up distribution channels and create promotional campaigns. Information regarding competition is another factor in the decision making process. Knowing what rival firms charge for their products impacts pricing decisions. Distribution systems must be in tune with market locations and customer needs for servicing products. Promotional efforts then can be tailored to match segmentation and positioning strategies.

To aid in the decision making process, marketers convert raw data into useful information. The fact that sales are at a certain level in one area is important. However, the statistics take on added value when compared to sales from a different period, or another territory, or in relationship to those of a competitor. The more information available to marketers, the better job they can do.

For example, since the mid 1980s jeans marketers have spent more effort targeting the older market. The idea being that the thirty-to-fifty-year-old segment was the group that began the big jeans movement of the fifties and sixties. As this group aged, Levi's, Wranglers and Lees have strived to maintain the brand loyalty developed when these jeans wearers were young. Now, these same major jeans houses are rediscovering the teenage offspring of this group, finding that a message of down-to-earth basics works best on this market.[2]

Marketers obtain data from a variety of sources. For example, Frito-Lay, a division of PepsiCo, outfits its field sales force with hand-held laser scanners to check stock levels at customers' stores. After transmitting the data collected back to the company, management converts it to information helpful in making decisions on a daily basis, when it previously took weeks or months. Advanced computer software has greatly enhanced inventory control systems.[3]

hat is a Marketing Information System?

Some information is readily available, while other valuable facts may be difficult to gather. A single piece may mean little, but when assembled with other data it becomes meaningful. The collection and analyzation of odd bits and pieces creates a marketing information system. This bank of data is needed for planning and strategy development.

---

[2]Elaine Underwood, "Jean-etics 101,"*BRANDWEEK*, August 17, 1992, pp. 14-15.

[3]Susan Reda, "Floor-ready merchandise," *Stores,* April 1994, pp. 41-42; "Levi Strauss marks ten years of pioneering Levilink," *Chain Store Age Executive,* October 1993, p. 42; G. M. Fodor, "Software helps you keep stocks level," *Industrial Distribution,* February 1992, pp. 28-29.

MARKETING INFORMATION SYSTEMS
DEFINED

A **marketing information system** includes all of the procedures and sources needed to collect and analyze pertinent data. Sound marketing decisions are based upon the availability of this information. To be effective, the system used to accomplish marketing goals must operate smoothly. Marketing information systems receive their direction from and deliver their output to marketing management.

To gather the input necessary for making marketing decisions, a firm's marketing information system looks to both internal records and external data sources. Individually and collectively, these areas provide management with the fuel necessary to aid in effective decision making. A marketing information system is fundamental to any marketing oriented organization.

Marketing information system— the procedures needed to collect and analyze marketing data.

In-house Data

Much information regarding market performance can be gathered **in-house.** Too often businesses overlook those sources that are underfoot, but the company itself has a variety of useful records. All departments within a business firm have potentially helpful data. The marketing department itself has records of customer activities. Which customers are buying what products and in what quantities can tell much about purchasing trends.

SOURCES FOR THE MARKETING INFORMATION SYSTEM

OUTSIDE SOURCES
• Independent Agencies
• Shopping Services
• Media Reports
• Trade Journals
• Suppliers
• Experts: Economists, Lawyers, etc.

MARKETING INFORMATION SYSTEM

IN-HOUSE
• Marketing Dept.
• Field Sales Force
• Accounting Dept.
• Shipping/Receiving
• Managers
• Data Processing

MARKETING RESEARCH
• Secondary Data
• Primary Data

Whether using company salespeople or independent representatives, this field sales force is an excellent source for gathering information regarding market trends and customer preferences. Accounting departments can supply data regarding marketing costs and profits. Back orders from customers might give a feel for market demand. The shipping/receiving department can provide records showing frequency of shipments to a variety of locations. An often neglected in-house source is the talent and intuition of the company's marketing people. This knowledge, gained from experience, is important for planning marketing programs. These internal sources offer an unlimited source of pertinent marketing information.

Outside Data

The second part of the marketing information system is the collection of data from sources **outside the company.** Marketers must be constantly aware of competitive moves. At times, one can simply ask, and one's competitors will provide a wealth of information. On other occasions, deeper research is necessary. Employers, government agencies and directories are other good sources of data. Retailers often use "mystery shoppers" to check on the service provided by clerks and salespeople.

Experts, such as lawyers, economists and consultants can supply specific information that might not be available from internal departments. Although consultants in many areas of expertise are available, many companies have similar specialists on their staffs. Other firms gather data from private agencies or government bureaus. These outside sources make up an important part of the marketing information system.

Marketing Research

Marketing research— the systematic gathering, recording and analyzing of pertinent marketing information.

Marketing research, defined as the systematic gathering, recording and analyzing of pertinent information, is another component of information systems. As important as the other sources of data are, more detailed and specific knowledge will be gained through a professionally operated marketing research program. Marketing research supplies the bulk of the ammunition needed by management for effective decision making.

In defining marketing research, the emphasis should be placed on the word *systematic.* This process is anything but casual or happenstance. Detailed demographic and lifestyle information about potential buyers usually requires marketing research. Evaluation of these facts, figures, activities and opinions received from all sources is part of the marketing research function. Without such analysis, much of the data might be useless.

What Types of Information Does Marketing Research Provide?

Marketing research is capable of supplying a wealth of information to management. Management must determine the type of data it needs to carry out

Global Marketing: Viva la Mexico!

There was a time when our neighbors to the south were not considered a market for anything more than tourist dollars. Mexicans were generally poor, and American goods were expensive. Outside of vacationing in the United States, the wealthy of Mexico spent few pesos outside their country. Today, the rejuvenated Mexican economy is producing more spendable income, hence more demand for imported merchandise.

Fueled largely by the manufacturing boom, and the potential offered by the North American Free Trade Agreement, Hispanic workers are beginning to climb out of poverty. With American as well as Japanese firms moving more and more of their industrial capacity to their country, Mexican workers are finding more money in their pockets than ever before. This new found buying power has created an overwhelming demand for imported goods, especially those from America.

From Haggar slacks to Gatorade, from Domino's pizza to Pampers disposable diapers, few U.S. products are not in demand. Ironically, even salsa and picante sauces made and marketed by American firms are selling in the country that virtually invented them. Because the increases in income levels are recent and the buying power growing, few American firms have any significant research on this market. As is the case with any new market, the more information available, the better the marketing effort. Exporters will have a difficult road ahead of them without sound marketing information.

Source: Dan Koeppel, "Mexico, USA," *Adweek's Marketing Week,* February 17, 1992, pp. 20–23; Stephen Baker, David Woodruff, and Elizabeth Weiner, "Detroit South," *Business Week,* March 16, 1992, pp. 98–103; Stephen Baker and S. Lynne Walker, "The American dream is alive and well—in Mexico," *Business Week,* September 30, 1991, pp. 102–105.

---

marketing mix decisions. Details regarding economic change are important, as is information about product acceptance and market demand. Marketing research also gathers opinions and feedback concerning the value of promotional efforts and the image of the business or corporation.

ECONOMIC DATA

Some marketing research effort gathers **economic data.** Environmental changes occurring throughout the world impact marketers. These trends in business activities are important in making forecasts. Marketing companies must keep current on these changing global conditions. Firms dealing overseas use such research to isolate problems in material sources or opportunities for international expansion.

In some industries, such as utilities and banking, firms have economists on staff. In most cases, outside sources supply most of this research information. The gathering process can be costly. Large, multinational businesses have greater opportunity for collecting economic data firsthand because of the availability of funds. Smaller firms often need to refer to published reports, such as those found in federal government reports. *The Wall Street Journal,* and other trade, economic or business periodicals also supply economic data.

PRODUCT DATA

Some marketing research is **product** oriented. Early confirmation of market acceptance of new products, including packaging, is important. For instance, consumer reaction to the design of a good or service may be caused by factors other than the product itself. Input from prospective buyers helps in design considerations during new product development. Much of the design in Ford's highly successful Probe is the result of design data gathered through marketing research.[4]

Marketing research may also produce package design recommendations. Packages must be functional and must have promotional qualities. Listening to consumers is the most practical avenue for gaining this information. As an illustration, a major cookie marketer was considering the introduction of a new package. The company wanted to find out whether an easy opening packet would be more favorable than an easy closing one. Researchers found that children were the ones who typically opened this brand's package by physically ripping it apart, destroying the means for either opening or closing. This information eliminated costly package redesigns for the cookie maker.

MARKET DATA

In addition to product information, marketers need details about the **target markets.** Research in this area should include current characteristics and potential targets. The percentage share of the market captured by a company and by its competition may be the basis for setting prices or planning promotional campaigns. Data on sales quotas or territory modifications help marketers anticipate and prevent problems with the sales staff. Store audits, including surveys of customers and employees, are helpful in determining acceptance and satisfaction.

Computer databases make it easier for companies to keep track of market needs. For example, Pioneer Hybrid International Inc., a major agricultural product supplier out of Des Moines, Iowa, charts over 700,000 farm operators. The database includes customers, and more importantly, prospective customers. Much of the information is gathered by Pioneer's field sales staff who are connected with the firm's mainframe through individual microcomputers. Marketing management uses the database to segment markets and analyze needs.[5]

EVALUATION OF PROMOTION

Businesses also conduct research regarding the effectiveness of their **promotional efforts.** Marketing communications must be received, understood and

---

[4]Raymond Serafin, "Ford 1-2 punch leads Detroit sportscar resurgence," *Advertising Age,* February 2, 1994, p. S4; C. Sawyers, "Ford targets California, younger buyers for Probe," *Automotive News,* June 29, 1992, p. 30; C. A. Sawyers, "The more things stay the same: After $650 million redesign, Taurus and Sable are greatly improved. But who can tell?" *Automotive Industry,* October 1991, p. 53.

[5]Tom Eisenhart, "Dell, Polaroid use databases to target customers, link internal units," *Business Marketing,* March 1991, pp. 41-43.

Types of information gathered through marketing research

Economic	Status of present economic activity, retail purchases, forecasts, foreign trade figures.
Product	Packaging, color, taste, service and warranties, physical traits.
Market	Size of market, determination of needs, demographic makeup, geographical location, competitive presence.
Promotion	Market acceptance and preference, media selection, effectiveness.
Corporate Image	Company policies, reputation with employees or union, general public or community acceptance, relationship with customers and competition.

believed by the targeted market if the product is to be successful. An important function of marketing research is the comparison of the impact of different ads or commercials.

Research to resolve the relative merit of the media used by the marketer should be gathered regularly. Management needs to know which media are the most effective and which messages are being absorbed. Market researchers continually test other promotional activities, such as the use of store displays and coupons, for effectiveness.

CORPORATE IMAGE DATA

It is also important for marketers to keep tabs on their **corporate images.** The reputation of the company influences acceptance of its products. This fact is especially true for firms that market products to other businesses. Regardless of a company's size or reputation, the way customers and the public view it changes from time to time. How marketers react to environmental or consumer safety issues is important in maintaining widespread approval.

Today's emphasis on product quality and customer service demands that the firm's information be updated regularly. One easy way to find out how customers feel about the quality and service they are receiving is to ask. Granite Rock Company, Watsonville, California, sells its rock, concrete, asphalt and other building materials for a premium price. The company claims that it can command more due to the quality and service that it gives customers. To keep on top of its corporate image, Granite surveys its market annually. Company management then posts the results of the image survey for its employees' benefit and to aid in maintaining the high level of customer service.[6]

---

[6]Lior Arussy, "Don't upgrade your image if that's not what you really need," *Marketing News,* February 28, 1994, p. 4; George M. Zinkhan, "Advertising design and corporate identity," *Journal of Advertising,* December 1993, pp. vii-ix; Tricia Welsh, "Best and worst corporate reputations," *Fortune,* February 7, 1994, p. 75; Edward O. Welles, "How're we doing?" *Inc.,* May 1991, pp. 80-83.

Secondary vs. primary data

TYPE OF DATA	ADVANTAGES	DISADVANTAGES
Secondary	Inexpensive	Out of date
	Easy to locate	Limited in scope
	Availability	Mostly demographic
	Easily created	
Primary	Current	Expensive
	Must be collected	Takes time to collect
	Difficult to formulate	Needs expertise
	Custom tailored to fit needs	

What Types of Data Are Available?

Research provides marketers with information needed to make intelligent decisions. Some of the statistics and facts are readily available and easy to find. Other information needs to be physically collected. Both secondary and primary data are valuable in setting marketing strategies.

SECONDARY DATA

Secondary data— previously collected and tabulated marketing information.

Secondary and primary data are the two broad categories for available information. **Secondary data** is information previously collected and tabulated. Typical sources for this information are government agencies (such as the U.S. Census Bureau), trade associations, colleges and universities, libraries and private computerized databases. Secondary data tends to be demographic in nature, although some lifestyle information is available from these previously gathered sources. The advantages of secondary data are easy access and low cost. However, previously collected data is often out of date.

Secondary data is part of most major research projects. If the marketer needs to know the percentage of elderly living in Tucson, Arizona, or the number of black males unemployed in Cleveland, secondary data can supply the answers. Since this information is less expensive to collect, it should always be included early in the marketing research plan.

PRIMARY DATA

Primary data— marketing information that must be collected.

Primary data is information gathered for the first time to satisfy the objectives of a specific research project. If the attitudes and interests of customers or prospects are needed, primary data is the answer. Typically, the way to amass lifestyle information is by collecting primary data, usually by survey. Because facts are gathered as research projects need them, primary data can be both current and accurate. The collection of primary data is usually more expensive than simply referring to secondary data sources.

Specific surveys or observations of organizations or groups of people provide primary data. The process of collecting this information is the mainstay of marketing research. To find out the brand preference for dry cereals or the average income of owners of VCR equipment, primary data must be gathered.

hat Is the Marketing Research Process?

Whether conducted by staff within the firm or by outside specialists, all marketing research projects typically follow the same pattern. The process used for conducting a scientific undertaking can be equated to taking a voyage or trip. Just like steering a ship or driving a car, one first needs to understand where one wants to go. Research projects begin with a goal in mind.

DEFINE THE PROBLEMS AND SET THE OBJECTIVES

The first step in the marketing research process is to **define the problem and set the objectives.** Without problems or questions, there is little need for research. The goals of the project must be weighed against other factors, including budgetary constraints. Because marketing research can be expensive, costs must be weighed against benefits received.

Researchers and management often have some difficulty in identifying marketing problems. In fact, the objectives of a given research project may be simply to isolate and define specific problems. Defining problems is useful when it gives management the information needed to set objectives. Marketers are goal oriented, and research projects typically reflect that orientation.

IDENTIFY THE SOURCES OF INFORMATION

Once the objectives are known, the next step is to **identify the source group or area** from which the information will be gathered. In seeking secondary data, the researcher must decide which institutions or depositories can supply what is needed. For primary data, individuals or firms will be the sources from which information must be collected.

Age or gender distribution of a population might be found in secondary data. If the research goal is to determine the market size for pantyhose in New England, census figures would be a good source for this information. A project to evaluate corporate image will most likely require the collection of primary data. The sources for this type of project would include customers, suppliers, community leaders, and employees. Accurately identifying sources from whom or about which information is needed has a significant bearing on the next steps to be taken.

SELECT THE DATA COLLECTION METHODS

Once the objectives and the sources are known, the next step is to **select the methods** used to gather the data. Depending upon the goals of the project,

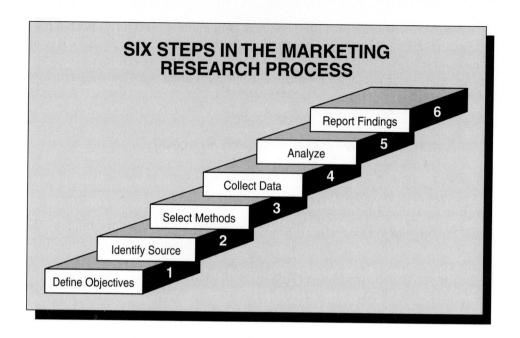

SIX STEPS IN THE MARKETING RESEARCH PROCESS

- 6 Report Findings
- 5 Analyze
- 4 Collect Data
- 3 Select Methods
- 2 Identify Source
- 1 Define Objectives

several ways are open to proceed in the collection process. Secondary data might be found in company records or in outside sources. Primary data would require a survey. Suppose the objective is to determine a consumer profile of buyers of Honda lawnmowers. Some data could be collected by including a survey along with the warranty card. More detailed information might demand personal contact with buyers or prospects.

COLLECT DATA

The next stage of the research process is the **collection of data.** By using the available sources, information gathering can produce a wealth of material. The project might be small, such as observing the number of people entering Sak's Fifth Avenue in New York City on the first day of spring. This data would require little time or effort. On the other hand, a national survey to determine the demographics of the cola drinking market might be time consuming and costly.

The method of data collection varies depending upon the objective and the source. Accuracy is essential to good marketing research. Steps should be taken when collecting data to minimize all possible errors. Some collection methods produce sharper results, but greater accuracy generally means higher cost.

ANALYZE AND REPORT DATA

Once gathered, the **data is analyzed** by the researchers. Even with the clearest methods and the best collection processes, correct interpretation of the facts can be difficult and tedious. To be converted to usable information, data must be assembled in readable form. Using computers reduces human error, thereby increasing accuracy. Many statistical programs are on the market to provide this capability for researchers.

The final step in the marketing research process is to **report the findings.** Management may need a detailed explanation and clarification to fully grasp the meaning of the findings. Reporting usually includes an oral as well as a written presentation.

ow Are Sources Identified?

Once the objective or purpose of the project comes into focus, the sources for information are usually obvious. This group includes those people or firms from whom or about which information is needed. Sources may be large or small, easy to locate or difficult to find.

POPULATION

The entire group of people or firms from whom or about which information is required is labeled the **population.** Sometimes called the **universe,** this body includes every possible source of information. When the objective relates to characteristics of target markets, all potential buyers in that category would be the population. If the goal regards raw material requirements for businesses in a specific field, all firms in that industry would make up the population.

Suppose the researcher is trying to determine the sneaker buying habits of married females under the age of thirty-five in Kansas City, Missouri. In this case, all women fitting that description would be the population. In a study to investigate the image of the Standard Oil Company of California, the population would include all of those people and organizations that have contact with the company. This would include suppliers, customers, employees, and, perhaps, the general public.

Population, or universe—the group of people or firms from whom or about which information is required.

SAMPLE

Marketing researchers know that a relatively small number of contacts within a large population may provide significant and accurate information about the entire group. It would not be physically or economically feasible to contact every married female under the age of thirty-five in Kansas City, or all people who are familiar with the Standard Oil Company of California. To gain enough information about or from a population, researchers select a **sample,** a small segment that represents the entire population. People or firms who contribute information are known as respondents.

In sampling a population, researchers strive for accuracy. Statisticians claim that the larger the sample the more accurate the results, but there is a limit to the amount of additional accuracy one can achieve. Doubling the sample size of the same population may significantly reduce the error. However, further increases

Sample—a small segment of the population that is representative of the whole.

in the sample size might add little additional accuracy. The size of the population affects sample size, as does the detail of the information needed.

Simple Random Sample

Simple random sample—the sampling method where each member of the population has an equal chance of being selected.

Marketing researchers need accuracy. The type of sample chosen is as important as the size of the sample. While there are many methods of selecting a portion of the population, the **simple random samples** produce the most accurate results. In this sampling procedure, every member of the population has an equal chance of being selected. An accurate comparison would be to that of a lottery, where selections are completely unbiased and random.

Take the case of the married women from Kansas City. A simple random sample would occur if all of the names of the entire population were placed into a giant bowl and selected by a blindfold draw. Using this sampling method, every name in the bowl would have an equal opportunity of being chosen. Although this method maximizes accuracy, simple random samples are rarely feasible.

Convenience Sample

Convenience sample—the sampling method that chooses respondents from the handiest locations.

When needing information from large and varied populations, researchers may cut some corners to save time and expense. By selecting a **convenience sample,** the investigator is collecting information in the most economical manner. This usually means that respondents are chosen for the convenience of the interviewer. In using this sampling method, the element of chance selection is lessened, and accuracy diminishes.

Stopping the women of Kansas City at shopping centers or on street corners would be an example of convenience sampling. This would be an easier survey to conduct than randomly selecting places and times for such interviews. Since not everyone may shop at that mall or be on a specific street corner at a given time, some potential respondents will be missed. Consequently, this sampling method would produce less accurate results than the simple random sample.

Cluster Sample

Cluster sample— the sampling method that divides the population into groups, usually geographically.

Cluster samples are preselected geographic groups of the population. This method of determining the source selects people or firms from specific areas, where the data is then collected. The cluster method is cost effective, especially when targeting large populations. Since the opportunity for any individual being chosen in a cluster sample is less than equal, accuracy suffers when using this method.

Quota Sample

Quota sample— the sampling method that selects a limited number of respondents from any group.

The **quota sample** is one that selects a limited number of people or firms from specific categories. Usually, the researcher arbitrarily sets the quotas. Not only does this method reduce the possibility for chance or random selection, but the sample quantity is predetermined. The potential for error in affixing a limit on the number of respondents compounds the reduced accuracy.

An example of a quota sample would be talking to one hundred Kansas City women from groups including students, office workers, business executives and professionals. Once the quota was reached, no more responses could be taken from that classification. Such a sampling method could produce error

RESEARCH OBJECTIVE	POPULATION	SAMPLES
Customer profile for women buyers of sports utility vehicles in California	All potential women of driving age residing in California	**Simple random:** all women in population have equal opportunity to be selected **Convenience:** women interviewed on street corners in cities and towns **Cluster:** women selected from major cities in northern and southern California **Quota:** 100 women are chosen from each of three age groups, income levels and ethnic types
Corporate image for major department store chain	All individuals and firms that have any contact with firm including customers, suppliers, employees, stock holders, competition and local community	**Simple random:** all parties have an equal opportunity to be selected **Convenience:** mail survey sent to representative number from each public **Cluster:** sample chosen from each area where a store is located **Quota:** focus groups limited to ten people are held with each of the specified publics

■ ■ ■ ■ ■

in the group selected and in the number of responses called for in each group. Accuracy is lower when using this sampling method.

How Is Data Collected?

Whatever sampling method is chosen, the next task for researchers is the actual gathering of information. Several data collection methods are available. The mode selected is dependent upon the information needed, the accuracy desired and the marketer's financial resources. The entire research process may be conducted by in-house personnel or by professional agencies.

Mystery shoppers help assure that retail sales-people provide good customer service.

OBSERVATION

Observation—the collection method that gathers data by watching the sample and noting activities.

A simple way of collecting primary data is by **observation.** Determining what people are doing or how they are doing it is the objective of this research method. Information can be amassed by humans or machines. A researcher standing near the entrance of a store in a shopping mall counts the number of entering customers using a hand-held device. Another type of observation is tallying the number of people watching a television show or listening to a radio station. Arbitron and A. C. Nielsen develop ratings for these media by totaling the viewers and listeners for networks, stations and individual programs.

Another use of the observation method involves "mystery shoppers." Checks on customer service performance by employees are made using anonymous "customers" who report on the results of their shopping visits. Many retailers monitor sales and service activities in their own locations as well as at competitors' stores. Some independent firms specialize in this type of research. For example, Atlanta-based Shop 'n Chek employs over 35,000 professional shoppers who report on the customer service skills of employees. Another firm, restaurant chain Au Bon Pain, devised its own questionnaire with employee help, which is used by mystery shoppers.[7]

Remember, marketing research is intended to be scientific by nature. Observation means more than merely counting people. People's actions are as important as the number of bodies involved. In addition to counting the

---

[7]Kevin Helliker, "Smile: that cranky shopper may be a store spy," *The Wall Street Journal,* November 30, 1994, pp. B1 and B8.

number of people entering a given store, researchers want to know where the customers travel within the store and what types of merchandise catch their eye. Shoppers are often watched, sometimes by hidden cameras, to see the aisles they travel and the shelves or displays that capture their interest. The reasons for a person's actions may not be learned through observation, but it is a good tool for exploratory research.

EXPERIMENTATION

Another collection method is **experimentation,** a controlled, scientific procedure. Unlike observation, this gathering mechanism gives the researcher some insight into cause-and-effect relationships. Experiments are often used to test specific product attributes. By altering characteristics one at a time, the research can produce optimum design without going through the expense of trial and error or through test marketing. As in any scientific research, experimentation should be conducted in a laboratory setting. Tight restraints on the control factors are important. This research is often expensive and sometimes difficult to control.

Experimentation—the collection method that gathers data through controlled, scientific test procedures.

Computer simulations are one type of experimentation gaining the favor of marketing researchers. By introducing variables in a software program, the researcher can manipulate a synthetic market, and the computer will produce suggested consequences. Although the results may not be as accurate as those obtained in an experiment using direct responses, the process is faster and much less expensive. The use of computers in marketing research will grow rapidly as additional software becomes available.

SURVEY

Surveys are the most common way of collecting primary data. Consumer surveys help in finding product preference and aid in gathering demographic or lifestyle information. Learning what buyers look for in product attributes gives guidance to the design of products. The development of psychographic profiles through marketing research provides management with an insight into buyers' needs and wants.

Survey—the collection of information by asking people or businesses questions.

By using surveys, researchers can often probe for information that might not be obvious. This research method is especially helpful in unearthing public opinion or image data. For example, Epson America was having a difficult task converting business buyers to using its computers. Marketing research surveys determined that, among corporate buyers, the Epson name was primarily associated with printers. To overcome this positioning problem, the firm embarked on an extensive advertising and promotion campaign to build brand name familiarity and image. Research uncovered information that might otherwise have gone undetected.[8]

---

[8]Terry Lefton, "Brand strategy: Epson shifts to product ads,"*BRANDWEEK,* June 28, 1993, p. 3; Terry Lefton, "Ad hike to fuel first image blitz," *BRANDWEEK,* October 5, 1991, p 2.

■ ■ ■ ■ ■

Effectiveness of survey methods

	TELEPHONE	MAIL	FACE-TO-FACE	FOCUS GROUP
Quality of information	Very good	Good/poor	Excellent	Excellent
Quantity of information	Limited	Limited	Very good	Excellent
Control of sample	Good	Poor	Very good	Excellent
Time required	Fast	Slow	Medium	Slow
Cost	Medium	Medium	High	Very high
Versatility	Fair	Fair	Excellent	Excellent

■ ■ ■ ■ ■

How Are Surveys Conducted?

Among the variety of information gathering procedures at the disposal of marketing researchers, surveys are preferred. Typically, surveys are taken using one of four methods; telephone, mail, person-to-person or focus group. The process selected may vary depending upon the degree of accuracy required and the details of the data needed. Cost factors will also influence survey methods, as some are more expensive to conduct than others.

TELEPHONE

The fastest and least expensive way to conduct surveys is **by telephone.** Although a variety of subjects can be approached using this method, interviewers have only moderate control over the accuracy of the sample. Asking the right question of the wrong respondent produces error. For instance, it is difficult to verify over the telephone whether the person giving the information is actually the head of the household or the baby-sitter.

One major problem in conducting telephone surveys is the limited amount of available time. Generally, the average person will respond to telephone interviews for only two minutes. This time span may not be sufficient for the interviewer to complete the survey. Lengthy interviews necessary to gather large amounts of data need a different survey approach. In addition, many people are leery of telephone surveys, or resent being interrupted at home, and refuse to participate.

MAIL

Another common form of data collection is **by mail.** Some of these surveys are ongoing, such as the warranty cards included with appliances or the "How-are-we-doing?" questionnaires featured by airlines and hotels. A significant advantage of mail surveying is the amount of information that can be gathered at a low cost. The interviewer again has little control over who responds to the survey. Mail questionnaires can be filled out by anyone.

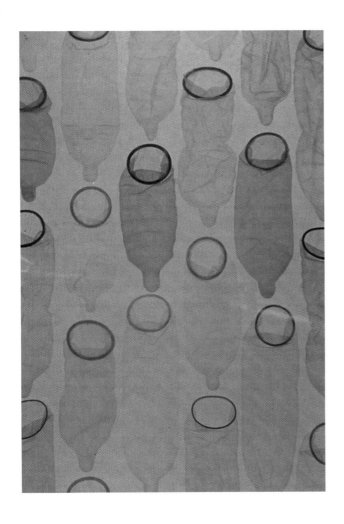

THE 90ᵀᴴ ANNIVERSARY BUICK LeSABRE

Leave the sticker on,
and show everyone how
smart you are.

Or take it off,
and let them think you
paid thousands more.

$18,999

Value. It's spelled out right there in black
and white, at the bottom of the sticker. The
price of the 90th Anniversary Buick LeSabre.*
    If you need more proof of LeSabre's
incredible value, consider that LeSabre has
the highest resale value in its class.** Then

look at the sticker again.
    You'll see that this car comes equipped
with a long list of standard equipment, including:
• 3800 V6 engine • power driver seat and
antenna • air conditioning • driver air bag
• ABS brakes • power windows and door locks

• AM-FM stereo cassette (with seek and scan)
• DynaRide® suspension • PASS-Key®
theft-deterrent system • special 90th
Anniversary badging.
    The 90th Anniversary LeSabre is
our anniversary gift to you. So drive

one home. Oh, about the sticker—go ahead, take
it off. Keep them guessing. For more
information, see your Buick dealer today
or call 1-800-4A-BUICK.

BUICK
90ᵀᴴ ANNIVERSARY

LeSabre is a registered trademark of GM Corp. ©1993 GM Corp.
All rights reserved. Buckle up, America!

*MSRP includes dealer prep and destination charge. Tax and license are additional. **Information from IntelliChoice, Inc.'s 1993 *The Complete Car Cost Guide.*

Come to Bowling Green...

Introducing
Bowling Green
a new men's fragrance
by Geoffrey Beene

Figure #3—ad reprint—Geoffrey Beene
Geoffrey Beene (*above*) and Calvin Klein (*right*) target the same audience for their fragrances, but each adopts a decidedly different positioning strategy. (Courtesy Sanofli Beauty Products)

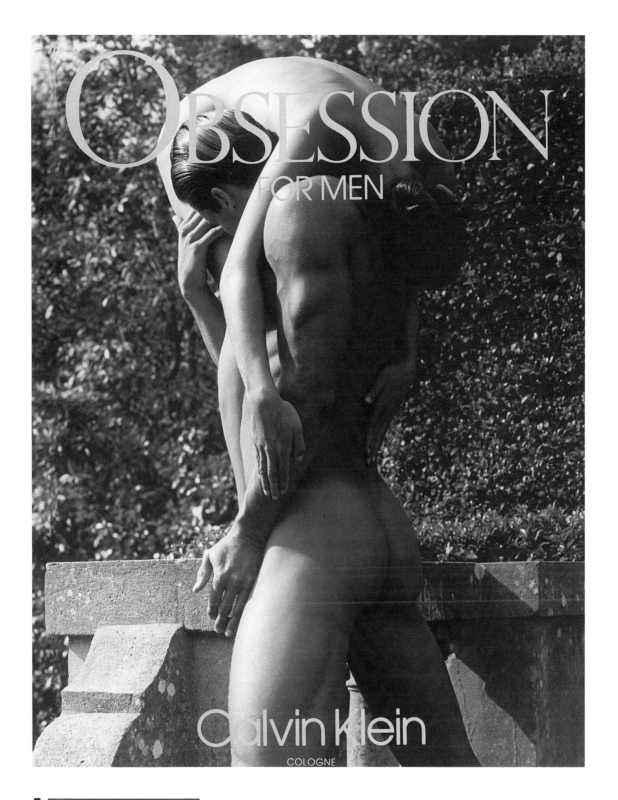

Figure #4—ad reprint—Calvin Klein

(Courtesy Calvin Klein Cosmetics Corporation)

It'll know you care
even when you don't talk to it.

ONEIDA

Shown: Calla Lily pattern in stainless.

Figure #5—ad reprint—Oneida

This classy ad for Oneida typifies the promotional treatment given to upscale products. (Courtesy of Oneida Ltd. All right reserved)

People often take their time in returning mail inquiries, which can slow the tabulation of the results. Although speed is secondary to accuracy, responses that dribble in over a period of months may be of little value. Consequently, most researchers put a time limit on mail surveys and disregard late responses.

PERSON-TO-PERSON

The best way to assure sampling accuracy is by the **person-to-person** survey method. By meeting individually with the respondent, the interviewer has a better chance of being sure that the interviewee represents the type of sample desired. Also, questionnaires to be answered in a face-to-face meeting may be a bit more complicated because the interviewer is present to clarify any misconceptions. Normally conducted by professionals who have been trained in this type of work, person-to-person interviews are expensive.

People responding to in-person interviews may be inclined to answer in the way that they think the interviewer desires rather than how they actually feel. This is particularly true when the person conducting the survey can be identified as having particular biases. If the interviewer wears labels or insignia that relate to a certain company or product, the answers received may reflect this bias. Even with this tendency for the respondents to hide their true feelings, face-to-face surveys are the most accurate.

FOCUS GROUP

Another survey method is the **focus group.** Typically, focus groups should consist of no less than six and no more than twelve respondents. These people meet in a quiet, isolated place with a well-trained moderator who asks a limited number of questions and records the answers. Sometimes hidden cameras photograph the group to watch facial expressions and body language. By maintaining a casual atmosphere, the moderator can gain responses that might not appear in a typical survey.

Focus group—a group of six to twelve people who respond to questions posed by a moderator

Focus groups are used extensively to gain information about consumer product preference. When the marketer needs to know which version of the product tastes better, what package is the easiest to open or why one advertisement is more attention grabbing than another, focus groups are often the answer. This survey method is especially useful in spotting trends. Business marketing products to other businesses are also major users of focus groups. NCR Corporation and Digital Equipment Corporation, to name just two, frequently use this research method to determine business customer needs and to build buyer profiles. Some researchers have questioned an overuse of this technique, pointing out that other, less costly methods might provide an adequate return.[9]

[9]Joe Whalen, "Qualitative research adds the 'why' to measurement," *Marketing News,* May 9, 1994, p. 8; Don E. Schultz, "The customer and the data base are the integrating forces," *Marketing News,* November 22, 1993, p. 14; Cyndee Miller, "Focus groups: A useful crystal ball for helping to spot trends," *Marketing News,* May 27, 1991, p. 21; T. L. Greenbaum, "Focus groups vs one-on-ones," *Marketing News,* September 2, 1991, p. 10.

Focus groups are marketing research collection methods that are especially helpful in determining customer preferences.

ELECTRONIC DEVICES

Gimmicks, such as recording eyeglasses and wristwatches, are among new developments in research techniques. For instance, computers have made it possible to put sensing devices into a pair of plain eyeglasses that record the television shows watched. The same technology produces wristwatches that show radio listening preferences of average commuters.

People Meter

People meter—a television monitoring device that records the programs being watched and makes video note of attentiveness and reaction.

Another research method used to evaluate television advertising is the **people meter.** This device gives more detailed and sophisticated data regarding the viewing habits of television watchers. Linking these electronic tools to a centralized computer, research firms record not only the programs people are watching, but when viewers leave the room or mentally tune-out. People meters have shown that regardless of the popularity of the show, commercials are often ignored. Major changes in television rate schedules may result.

The major television networks are concerned that people meters may not be all that they were meant to be. A. C. Nielsen and Arbitron continue to experiment with a number of devices to streamline and improve their ratings services. Advances in technology should make research involving the evaluation of advertising even more meaningful. One advance in the people meter,

CHAPTER 4 INFORMATION SYSTEMS AND MARKETING RESEARCH

announced in the spring of 1992, was a device that could read facial expressions. One major concern for society and advertisers regards the question of invasion of privacy.[10]

What Types of Errors Occur in the Survey Process?

The intent of marketing research is to supply management with accurate and current data from which decision can be made. To be beneficial, this input must be as accurate as possible. Researchers go to great lengths to assure accuracy, yet some error is inevitable. Three types of errors are typically encountered: nonresponse, sampling and measurement.

NONRESPONSE ERROR

One type of misinformation that researchers encounter is **nonresponse error.** This occurs when people refuse to take part in the process. A number of studies have reported that quite often people who are asked to participate in a survey refuse. Concern over the authenticity of the surveyor and lack of time were the major reasons given.

A major concern shared by researchers regarding nonresponse error is the possibility of biased results. Suppose the objective is to discover the color preference of prospective customers of ski parkas. When those who favor green do not respond, the information received is not completely accurate. Marketing management could be misled by nonresponse error.

Nonresponse error— error due to lack of response from the sample.

SAMPLING ERROR

Another problem faced by researchers is **sampling error.** When the wrong group of people responds or nonselected people give input, the results will show sampling error. Suppose the survey of the married women of Kansas City under the age of thirty-five included responses from men, or women over that age, or from St. Louis females. The results would not be accurate.

Selection of the proper survey method helps to minimize sampling error. Interviewers can be trained in telephoning procedures so that the sampling error is negligible. Questionnaires can be written to reduce the potential of this inaccuracy in mail surveys. If accuracy of the sample is very important, most researchers will still opt for the person-to-person method.

Sampling error— error due to receipt of input from the wrong sample.

---

[10]Joe Mandese, "People meters shake up global TV ratings," *Advertising Age,* July 18, 1994, p. 116; James D. Peacock, "Active meters require active inquiry," *Journal of Advertising Research,* May/June 1993, pp. RC6-RC9; S. McClellan, "New Nielsen system is turning heads," *Broadcasting,* May 18, 1992, p. 8.

MEASUREMENT ERROR

Measurement error—error due to receipt of erroneous information from the correct sample.

Measurement error, such as when respondents give incorrect answers, is the most difficult to police. If interviewees give answers that are false, the accuracy of the survey suffers. If the women of Kansas City say that they prefer Reebok when in reality Nike is their favorite, the results of the survey are skewed.

Researchers have little control over measurement error, and there is no positive method of completely eliminating this problem. Assuring that person-to-person researchers do not convey prejudice or favoritism is helpful. The interviewer who wears a Coors jacket while conducting a survey to determine beer preferences is likely to generate sizable measurement error.

Measurement error also occurs with the introduction of bias into the survey. Questionnaires that guide the respondent toward specific answers produce inaccuracies. Measurement error is often the product of poorly written or untested survey documents. If a respondent must choose between only two brands of tooth paste, a true response is impossible if neither of the products listed is preferred. The women of Kansas City may not like sneakers at all.[11]

How Is Marketing Information Managed?

The results of research surveys are **tabulated, cross-tabulated** and **coded.** In some telephone surveys, the data is fed directly into the computer. Results from mail and person-to-person surveys are either hand tabulated or entered from a terminal where a computer program handles the coding and filing. Many highly sophisticated statistical programs that can manipulate tremendous amounts of data are available.

Marketing oriented firms, such as Gillette, generate many marketing research projects annually. The processing of this information is made easier by the use of innovative computer software. Programs, such as A-CROSS, a tabulating tool produced by Strawberry Software, make the presentation of the statistical results of marketing research meaningful to marketing management. The use of these tools has greatly simplified the researchers job, while reducing error.

Researchers must **analyze** and **interpret** the data that has been collected and assembled. They must be aware of management's reasons for wanting the information. Marketers are interested in the significance of the information to their planning and strategy. Information gained from the interpretation of the data makes it worth the expense of time and money.

ETHICAL CONSIDERATIONS

In their zeal for collecting information, some marketers have overstepped the boundaries of ethical behavior. The computer provides the industry with the

---

[11]S. A. Long, "Pretesting questionnaires minimizes measurement error," *Marketing News,* May 27, 1991, p. 12.

Marketing and Society: The Pursuit of Privacy

Most Americans value their privacy. We become fiercely defensive when someone or some company steps over the boundaries that outline our individual space. A major area of controversy is the invasion of our privacy by computer databases. This form of marketing research is used to build a statistical storeroom of knowledge about individuals and firms. However, people do not always want to have details of their lives and habits available to others.

It seems lately that these electronic probes often know more about us than we know about ourselves. Even supermarket scanners are capable of collecting a variety of information that can be traced to individuals when checks or credit cards are used for payment. Writers for a major trade journal showed how easy it was to get information by exposing a credit report on Dan Rather, the CBS newscaster. Although the gathering of information may be beneficial to marketers, consumers and businesses are screaming loudly about invasion of privacy.

This fact became painfully evident recently to Lotus Development Corporation, the giant software house. Working with its Atlanta based partner, Equifax Incorporated, Lotus created a database of over 120 million consumers to be sold to mail order houses and direct marketers nationwide. Called Marketplace Households, the software had some built-in safeguards to insure a degree of privacy. However, the company was quickly besieged by tens of thousands of irate citizens demanding that their names be removed from the database. Under such overwhelming pressure, Lotus wisely killed the project.

Sources: E. I. Schwartz and M. Galen, "Snooping on behalf of the right to privacy," *Business Week*, June 29, 1992, pp. 39–40; D. Schroeder, "Life, liberty, and the pursuit of privacy," *American Demographics*, June 1992, p. 20; "Who cares, wins," *The Economist*, May 16, 1992, pp. 19–20. D. Seligman, "The devil in direct mail," *Fortune*, March 11, 1991, pp. 123–124; S. Caminiti, "What the scanner knows about you," *Fortune*, December 3, 1990, pp. 51–52; Laura Bird, "Amid privacy furor, Lotus kills a disk," *Adweek's Marketing Week*, January 26, 1991, p. 9.

ability to gather tremendous amounts of data, much of which might be personal. Companies that freely divulge this information are rightfully being charged with invasion of privacy. One area of business that is especially sensitive is credit and collection. While data regarding one's credit ratings and payment records are important, some organizations go too far in delving into personal matters. If this information is then freely given to other groups or individuals, the invasion of privacy escalates.

The manipulation of data and statistics is a constant concern of the public and for marketing researchers. This problem is especially true with the results of experiments. Studies that purposely look for preconceived or biased results produce misleading information. Research concluded by both Procter & Gamble and the American Paper Institute in 1990, for example, contradicted previous research regarding disposable diapers, which was, by the way, conducted by manufacturers of cloth diapers. Similarly, when Wonder Bread sponsors a study on the weight gain effect of eating white bread, and M&M/Mars supports research on chocolate inhibiting cavities, the entire field of marketing research becomes suspect.[12]

Marketing researchers are learning that their work must be free from stereotyping. Often marketers have invented groups just to meet what they felt were the demands for the product. Marketing researchers cannot afford to overlook people who do not fall into preconceived niches. Only when research contains no labeling and biased hypothesis, is it a useful tool of marketers.

GLOBAL RESEARCH

Because of the lack of a marketing framework and suitable talent, conducting research overseas becomes more difficult. Language barriers and customs differences heighten the dilemma. Many U.S. firms operating in foreign markets employ research organizations from the home country to gather data. Most American marketing research agencies have branches in key overseas locations.

Researchers operating in global arenas must be conscious of cultural differences that may impact or color the information gathered. What is considered a typical inquiry in America may be offending in India or Yemen. The lack of infrastructure, such as telephone, mail systems and broadcast media, may make the collection of data a true challenge. Also, many lesser developed countries have little or no secondary data on hand.

SUMMING IT UP

Marketing hungers for information. Markets need to be identified, products developed or modified and marketing mix decisions made. A marketing information system, gathering data from in-house, outside sources and research, feeds this hunger.

Marketing research provides information about the economy, products, markets, promotion and corporate image. Secondary data contains primarily demographic material that has already been gathered, collated and tabulated. For information regarding activities, interests or lifestyles of a group, primary data usually must be collected.

The marketing research process begins with defining the problem and setting objectives. The sources of information must be identified, and the methods of gathering data established. After data is collected it is tabulated and reported to management.

---

[12]Joseph Weber, "Lies, damn lies, and product research," *Business Week*, August 1, 1994, p. 13.

The sources of information lie in the population, the entire group from whom or about which information is needed. Small samples of the population usually provide accurate input. The simple random sample is the most accurate, but the convenience sample is more widely used and is more economical.

Information is collected through observation, experimentation or survey. Surveys are conducted by telephone, mail, person-to-person and focus groups. In-person interviews supply the most accurate information, and focus groups typically are used to determine product preferences.

Accuracy is important to marketing research. Nonresponse error is difficult to predict, but sampling error can be largely overcome through proper selection of the sample. Measurement error, where respondents give incorrect answers, is almost impossible to eliminate.

KEY CONCEPTS AND TERMS FROM CHAPTER FOUR

Cluster sample
Convenience sample
Experimentation
Focus group
Marketing information system
Marketing research
Measurement error
Nonresponse error
Observation

People meter
Population, or universe
Primary data
Quota sample
Sample
Sampling error
Secondary data
Simple random sample
Survey

BUILDING SKILLS

1. Explain how a small firm without large resources can create a viable marketing information system.

2. Describe where one might find meaningful information to market infant teething rings, hair coloring, motorbikes and bridles for horses.

3. Discuss the relative merits of the various sampling methods, noting especially where each might be used to the best advantage.

4. Identify the best methods for gathering data about age, gender, income level or degree of education; the type of person who might purchase a VCR; the brand preference for cereal and coffee; the activities conducted by respondents while wearing sunglasses; packaging suggestions for a new shampoo.

5. Describe the types of information needed by marketing researchers trying to resolve the corporate image of a firm that manufactures automobiles, television sets and plastic baggies.

Making Decisions 4-1: To Market, to Market, to Buy a . . . .

Evidence abounds showing that today's consumers have changed. Gone are the times when marketers could rely heavily on brand loyalty. Perhaps it was the recession of the early 1990s, or maybe heavy competition among products. Whatever the reasons, the average grocery shopper is becoming increasingly concerned with saving money.

Advertising agency Warwick Baker & Fiore conducted a nationwide survey in 1992. The research results showed that most consumers arm themselves to save money when they do war with the supermarket. In this shopper survey, over 90 percent responded that they were bargain hunters in one way or another. Whether it is clipping coupons or reading the sales flyers, an increasing number of grocery shoppers are watching their pennies. Redemption of coupons rose steadily in the early part of this decade as buyers continued to search out the "deals."

The statistics gathered by Warwick Baker & Fiore cut across a wide range of demographics. Men as well as women, young alongside old, and almost all income levels are similar in their cost cutting forays into the world of grocery shopping. The study does not refute brand loyalty . . . it merely states that brand loyalty is taking a back seat to saving money. As more and more consumer goods marketers turn to promotional gimmicks and sales, this trend seems destined to continue, with or without bad economic times.[13]

Identify the types of data you would expect to be collected by such a research project, and the ways that such information might affect the decisions of consumer goods marketers.

Making Decisions 4-2: That's Amore!

Segmentation strategy plays a key role in any marketing effort, and information about how segments act and react is crucial to success. Today, more attention is being paid to psychological drives as important indicators of consumer preference. Having this ammunition in advance, marketers can position their goods and services to satisfy these basic behavioral needs. This information would be particularly helpful in repositioning brands by targeting personal drives not presently covered by competitors.

New York based advertising agency BBDO uses a technique known as Personal Drive Analysis (PDA). Using this in-house developed system, the company can survey individuals within segments to determine psychological drives such as indulgence or ambition. Using PDA, the agency uncovered the psychological rewards that attract people to certain brands.

For example, BBDO applied this technique to the athletic shoe market and found that Nike was viewed as the brand of choice for consumers

---

[13.] Laurie Petersen, "The strategic shopper," *Adweek's Marketing Week,* March 30, 1992, pp. 18-

motivated by drives of winning or ambition. Reebok was favored by people seeking stability, and L. A. Gear was associated with sexiness and indulgence. Interestingly, from a high point in the mid-1980s, sales of L. A. Gear have dropped rapidly in the past few years. In imported beer markets, both Beck's and Heineken share a user profile of upscale, confident males. Within this group, Beck's is associated with individuality, while Heineken has an aura of status. A study of spaghetti sauces showed that brand preference was influenced by one's romantic mood. Ah . . . that's amore![14]

Describe the types of survey you would select to gather psychological information, the types of error you might expect in such a project, and ways to maximize accuracy.

Making Decisions 4-3: One Size Fits All.

Over the past decade, there has been a steady increase in products designed to accommodate people with disabilities. Some of this attention came about as the result of government action, such as the Americans with Disabilities Act, signed in 1992. In other cases, smart and socially responsible marketers saw an opportunity to profit by solving customer needs. Whatever the reasons, many of the goods that are helpful to those with physical problems are being enjoyed by a wide sector of the consumer market.

AT&T designed its Big Buttons telephone for the elderly. The device's oversized numbered push buttons make dialing easy for those with failing eyesight. Much to the communications giant's surprise, the style appeals to a broad range of consumers. Similarly, Procter & Gamble created a new easy open plastic top on its detergent packages for the ease of elderly or arthritic consumers. This design change has

(Courtesy of AT&T)

proven to be a delight for anyone who previously fumbled with these cartons.

Many of the trends to make products easier for the older segment of the market also prove to be a boon for younger users. OXO International tackled the problem of modifying kitchen utensils

[14]Cyndee Miller, "Spaghetti sauce preference based on whether you're in the mood for love," *Marketing News,* August 31, 1992, p. 5.

to be easier to use by consumers whose arthritis impaired their grip and dexterity. These big handled potato peelers, openers, and flatware were so attractive that they became in demand by many gourmet kitchen equipment stores and catalog houses. Kids, too, loved the way these tools felt and worked.[15]

Design a research project to gather information for kitchen utensils, including the sources you would contact and the methods you would use.

---

[15]Bruce Nussbaum, "What works for one works for all," *Business Week,* April 20, 1992, pp. 112-113.

5

Markets and Market Segmentation

The Job to be Done

Not all products are needed by all people or all businesses. In the process of satisfying customer needs, marketers usually create goods and services that benefit only a few people or firms. Chapter 5 provides the data needed to:

- describe the markets for consumer products,
- identify the factors needed for successful market segmentation,
- define the methods for segmenting consumer goods and business goods markets, and
- analyze the ways that segmentation strategy impacts the management of business markets.

Tom Shepansky

Tom Shepansky fell in love with marketing while attending Northern Alberta Institute of Technology in Edmonton. Courses in advertising, salesmanship, marketing research and public relations confirmed his desire to enter the promotional arena. It was not just the coursework that turned him on but the method of instruction. The faculty at NAIT believe strongly in hands-on instruction. Case study analysis in marketing and, especially, applied advertising, that demanded full student participation truly prepared him for what lay ahead.

After graduating with honors, Tom realized his dream of a career in the field of his choice and joined Intergroup Advertising. As Senior Account Supervisor, he has responsibility for a number of national and international clients. Although there have been many positive aspects of moving up the ladder at this firm, Tom looks back at his stint handling the McDonald's account as one of the most fulfilling. Working for this major client allowed him to become involved with all facets of promotion: advertising, marketing research and public relations.

As a student, Tom was active in extracurricular activities. He credits these associations with broadening his horizons and extending his knowledge base. Even before graduation, Tom had a natural feel for the business pulse of his city; his involvement continues today. Along with memberships in many business organizations in his community, he is especially active in the Advertising Club of Edmonton, serving as president and board member.

What Are the Markets for Consumer Products?

There are many consumer products markets, some big and others small. More people buy Chevrolets than Porsches. Although both are jeans, Wranglers appeal to a greater potential audience than do Jordache. Lots of people buy ice cream, but only a small percentage prefer Ben & Jerry's.

CONSUMER PRODUCTS MARKETS DEFINED

Consumer products market—a group of people with purchasing power and demand.

A **consumer products market** is a group of people that have the need and the money with which to buy goods and services to satisfy those needs. Having desires or needs for products is not enough. A market exists when people having need also have the finances to satisfy that need by making a purchase.

Aggregate Markets

Aggregate market—a large, undifferentiated market where individual needs do not alter the marketing mix.

Some marketers design and distribute their goods and services for large, undifferentiated markets. This group of buyers represents a total or **aggregate market.** To serve an aggregate market, companies develop their marketing mix without regard for individual differences among the potential consumers. These products can appeal to anyone, no matter what income level, ethnic background, gender or occupation.

Consumer product marketers selling to the trade rarely target aggregate markets. Fresh produce and some paper products are among the few items that

In marketing its T100 pick-up truck, Toyota is specifically targeting a mostly male audience with a lower household income than that of Camry or Corolla owners. (Used with permission of Toyota Motor Sales, USA)

are available to an unspecified group of buyers. It is far more common, however, for consumer goods sellers to create products, packages and images that appeal to a specific group of buyers. Such a market may be smaller, but the rewards are often greater.

Segmented Markets

Market segmentation is the process of breaking an aggregate market into specific targets for buyers who respond similarly. This strategy takes a large group of potential buyers with different characteristics and separates it into smaller groups which exhibit common buying habits. Most consumer products marketers direct products toward segmented or targeted markets. These pieces of an undifferentiated market contain consumers who respond alike to specific changes in the marketing mix.

Most automobile marketers design individual models of vehicles toward specific segments of the driving market rather than to an aggregate group. Pick-up trucks are rugged or tough, and compacts are economical to buy and own. Station wagons and minivans carry swarms of kids and bags of groceries, and luxury cars appeal to those who have arrived and are anxious to let others know it. The products attract those specific targets, and the promotional efforts position the automobile to appeal to that market segment.

The grocery industry offers many illustrations of segmented markets. Kellogg's, the giant cereal house, makes cereal for children, adults, dieters and the health conscious. Mother's bakes several varieties of cookies to tickle different taste buds. Swanson markets frozen dinners, but introduced the Lean Cuisine meals to appeal to the segment that consciously watches calorie intake. Even bathroom tissue comes in soft or softer, scented or unscented, colored or white, small or family package arrangements. Each type appeals to a totally different group of consumers. These products target portions or segments of the total market instead of trying to appeal to the masses.

Market segmentation—the process of breaking an aggregate market into specific targets of buyers who respond similarly.

The decisions regarding whether to segment and how to segment are the basis for tactical planning. Most marketers of consumer products practice some form of segmentation strategy. Picturing Close-Up as the toothpaste with sex-appeal is a segmentation strategy. Targeting successful executives as the market for Hartmann luggage and aiming Kix cereals at kids also breaks aggregate markets into smaller parts.

Marketers practicing segmentation strategies design a marketing mix that will appeal to that particular portion. Product, price, distribution and promotion must be geared toward satisfying the needs of the targeted section for marketing success. Prices may be more easily altered to meet demand because of the lack of competitive pressure. Similarly, smaller markets do not necessarily mean limited distribution. Promotion must maintain the image that relates to the isolated segment.

Campers are the target market for the Coleman Company's primary line of products. The stoves, canoes, lanterns and tents Coleman makes would look out of place if advertised in the magazine *Computer World*. Similarly, promotion for Moore Business Forms will not appear in *Better Homes & Gardens*. The image created by Vaurnet sunglasses might be tarnished if the company promoted by using a flyer placed on car windshields. Product image, promotion message and market segment must relate.

What Is Needed for Successful Market Segmentation?

Positioning becomes an important aspect of segmentation strategy. The total image of the product includes its price, the distribution outlets where it can be purchased and the promotion methods and messages. This position in the minds of buyers solidifies brand loyalty. To be successful, the entire marketing mix must stay in character with the target segment.

SUCCESS FACTORS

Successful segmentation— markets must be large enough, similarly responsive and reachable.

Realizing that not all buyers are alike, marketers segregate portions of the total market to direct their efforts more efficiently and profitably. Competition is often less active, at least initially, if a firm selects a small segment that does not affect the total market. For instance, many pain relievers are on the market today. Competition in this field is intense. Bayer, the aspirin people, have been successful in the pain remedy market by targeting their products toward small segments. For its aspirin-free Bayer Select, the company pinpoints specific pain sufferers with headache, arthritis, menstrual and other ailments.

Market Size

The market segment must be **large enough** to make the effort profitable. Packaging and promotion for special brands may be costly. If the segment is too small, economies of scale in production may be lost. This could cause a raise in prices to a level that would impair sales, and thus profits.

Segmentation success factors

SUCCESS FACTOR	GOOD EXAMPLE	POOR EXAMPLE
Large enough	Mature "boomers"	63 year olds
	"X"generation	29 year olds with acne
	Texans	Texans weighing 90 pounds
	Golfers	Ambidextrous golfers
Mutually responsive	Heads of households	Single parents with 9 kids
	Incomes over $100,000	Billionaires
	Suburbanites with lawns	Penthouse dwellers
	Golfers	Golfers in Dallas, Texas
Reachable	Working mothers	Blue-eyed blondes
	African-American men	Left-handed males
	California teenagers	Teenagers with long hair
	Tennis players	Tennis elbow sufferers

■　■　■　■　■

For instance, a detergent specifically created to remove raspberry stains targets too narrow a market. The product may be satisfactory, but the number of prospective buyers would not be sufficient to produce adequate profits. Many women make clothes for themselves and others, and this group could be a substantial market segment. Yet, buttons made from mink fur would probably not create much of a stir with these consumers. Although the sewing market is large, not all seamstresses have similar needs.

Similarly Responsive

The market segment should be **similarly responsive.** The potential buyers within the targeted group must have somewhat the same tastes, habits or needs so that they can be distinguished from other potential customers. As a target, the consumers within the segment must react in the same manner to changes in the marketing mix. Individuals need not show identical physical characteristics, but they must be similarly responsive to outside stimuli. Uniformity of response in the target market is mandatory for successful segmentation.

The segment selected by General Mills for its Fiber One cereal includes both males and females, young and old, from a variety of ethnic backgrounds. The product is a high-fiber-content cereal that appeals to a more health conscious target, regardless of gender, age or race. In this case, different demographics of the market will not affect the success of the segmentation. The size of the market segment is important for success, and the target must be similarly responsive.

American males between the ages of 21 and 35 constitute a large enough segment for a successful target market. Yet it is unlikely that such a huge group would respond similarly in the selection of a soft drink or motion picture. The expanding number of women executives might not exhibit the same buying behavior when purchasing a new automobile, but could show similar needs for clothing. There are enough people in California to form a significant target market, but one brand of mouthwash will not appeal to all Californians.

Reachable

If a market segment is large enough and responds similarly, it also must be **reachable.** Distribution channels have to be established so that the target can purchase the goods. Products created to appeal to specific segments are useless if the market is not accessible. Consumers also need to be informed. Otherwise, the product cannot supply economic utility. Segmented markets need to be reachable by promotion as well as distribution.

Marketers may use established intermediaries or create completely new channels. Procter & Gamble introduced its Cover Girl skin-care line late in 1992 targeting teens. Hoping to build early brand loyalty, P&G asked retailers to place this teen product group next to its Cover Girl cosmetics, rather than with similar items from other marketers. Distribution was already in place. On the other hand, Freeman Cosmetics, a family owned niche marketer out of Beverly Hills, expanded its line of cosmetic and skin-care products at about the same time. This small firm distributed mostly through beauty salons, but the company wanted to expand its coverage with the new brands. Attracting competitive shelf space in traditional channels was more difficult.[1]

To be reachable, the marketer must be able to communicate with the target. Advertising and other promotional means need to inform buyers of the product's benefits and qualities. To illustrate, Embassy Suites Hotels has targeted the traveling business person as its prime market. This innovative hostelry chain places its clever advertisements featuring Garfield the cat in trade journals such as *Business Week, Fortune* and *Inc.* These media reach the desired audience.

ow Are Consumer Markets Segmented?

Consumer markets can be segmented in several ways. Geographic, demographic and psychographic segmentation are the three most common methods of breaking up a total market. Segmentation strategy does not dictate that only one method of targeting a market can be used. Many consumer product marketers use combinations of these segmentation methods to define the targeted audience.

GEOGRAPHIC SEGMENTATION

Geographic segmentation— breaking a market into target segments according to location.

Breaking a market into segments according to location is **geographic segmentation.** Products may be designed and promoted for specific regions of the country because of the characteristics of buyers in that area. Marketers sell more dune buggies in the desert regions of the Southwest than in other parts of the country, although Oregon and Michigan also have sandy areas. Snowmobiles, on the other hand, are not big sellers in Florida or Louisiana.

---

[1]Seema Nayyar, "Cover Girl aims to capture teen set," *BRANDWEEK,* September 28, 1992, p. 2; Seema Nayyar, "Family-owned Freeman runs at beauty kings," *BRANDWEEK,* September 14, 1992, p. 2.

Geographic segmentation can also mean differentiating between urban and rural markets. Marketers of air conditioners find a larger potential in metropolitan areas and will plan their distribution and promotion toward satisfying that segment. Although sold by some dealers in large cities, four-wheel drive vehicles appeal to a more rural group of buyers. Suburban dwellers are the target market for such things as lawn and garden supplies.

DEMOGRAPHIC SEGMENTATION

Demographic segmentation targets markets according to age, gender, national origin, income or religious preference. Demographic data provides the basis for targeting numerous consumer goods. Products are marketed specifically for women, teenagers, African Americans, blue collar workers or the affluent. Additional segmenting can easily occur within any demographic sector. Each of these specific target markets must still meet the criteria for successful segmentation.

Demographic segmentation— breaking a market into target segments according to age, gender, national origin, income or religious preference.

Age

One common method of using demographic segmentation is to target according to **age.** Products designed for children or senior citizens target demographically segmented markets. Pampers disposable diapers are not for everyone, nor is Geritol or Dentu-Cream. These products appeal to users in a particular age group. Our population is living longer. As discussed previously, the "graying of America" is an important demographic change facing today's marketers. The marketing of products specifically designed for an older generation is growing increasingly popular. As the percentage of people over the age of fifty-five increases during the next decade, more marketers will be targeting this affluent and receptive segment.

Age also impacts the clothing industry. As the older markets grow, so does its waistline. Many of the top names in the fashion industry are marketing larger sizes. Liz Claiborne led the way with Elisabeth, a line designed especially for larger women. Givenchy followed with En Plus, and a host of designers joined the parade, including Gianni Versace, Tamotsu, Criscione and Albert Nipon. Saks opened a boutique, named Salon Z, that caters to the larger sizes. High fashion is not the only industry niche that recognized that an older market needs more room. Jeans marketers, notably Levi Strauss & Company, Wrangler and Gitano, all let out the seams a bit for the fall 1992 season. Even Wrigley's, the chewing gum people, targets the older market with increased promotion of its Extra Sugar Free brand.[2]

Children form another major age oriented segment. Although the practice of targeting youngsters is not without critics, some of the marketing effort in this arena is well done. Nike is one company that has gained some success, realizing that the way to reach kids is through their parents. The children's

[2]Fara Warner, "Wrigley aims gum at gums," *BRANDWEEK,* December 6, 1993, p. 9; Amy Feldman, "Hello Oprah, good-bye, Iman," *Forbes,* March 16, 1992, pp. 116–117; Cyndee Miller, "Jeans marketers loosen up, adjust to expanding market," *Marketing Week,* August 31, 1992, pp. 6 and 7.

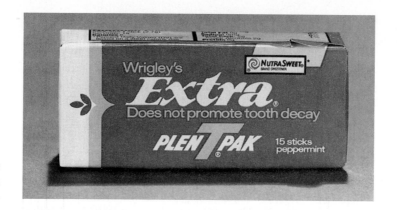

Wrigley targets the "mature market" with its sugar free gum.

market may "know Bo," but it is mom and dad who must be convinced that one sneaker is better than another. Nike's advertising has received plaudits from both kids and parents.

The teenage market is gaining new respect from marketers. Realizing that this segment has plenty of discretionary income, firms such as Bausch & Lomb, MasterCard and Procter & Gamble have all target this 25 million strong segment. Using media such as MTV and *Rolling Stone,* marketers take advantage of the increased moxie and knowledge of this younger group of buyers. The teen market is not confined to America either. Europe, Asia and Latin America are all experiencing a boom in teenage spending.[3]

Demographic segmentation by age is not limited to the old or the young. Some marketers specifically target a range of ages. An example would be L'Oreal's V by Vanderbilt line of cosmetics targeting women in the 18–34 age group. The company specifically differentiates this brand from its Chaps and Vanderbilt brand, which sells to an older target.[4]

Marketers that overdo promotional efforts in children's markets usually find opposition among parents and society. Promotion aimed at the younger set has sometimes bordered on being deceptive. The Quaker Oats Company found its claims for Gatorade roundly questioned when the firm began to promote to the younger market. Initial ads that were in poor taste were withdrawn or modified.[5]

Family Life Cycles

People progress through various stages of life and **family life cycles.** We move from single status, through stages of marriage and divorce, with or without children, and often back to single status again in later years. Parents with babies,

---

[3]Laura Zinn, Jonathan Berry, Kate Murphy, Sandra Jones, Marti Benedetti and Alice Z. Cuneo, "Teens," *Business Week,* April 11, 1994, pp. 76–86; Laura Zinn, "Never trust anyone over 30?" *Business Week,* April 11, 1994, p. 86; Paula Dwyer and Russ Mitchell, "The Euroteens (and how to sell to them)," *Business Week,* April 11, 1994, p. 84; Shawn Tully, Teens—the most global market of all," *Fortune,* May 16, 1994, pp. 90–97.

[4]Judith Springer Riddle, "L'Oreal readies new V line," *BRANDWEEK,* September 27, 1993, p. 13.

[5]Laura Bird, "Gatorade for kids," *Adweek's Marketing Week,* July 15, 1991, pp. 4–5; Jon Berry, "Did marketers overhype the kids' market?" *Adweek's Marketing Week,* December 10, 1990, pp. 18–19.

TRADITIONAL AND CONTEMPORARY FAMILY LIFE CYCLES

1. **Young single or divorced without children**
   Few financial burdens. Fashion opinion leaders. Recreation-oriented. Buy: basic kitchen equipment, basic furniture, cars, equipment for the mating game, vacations.

2. **Young married without children**
   Better off financially than they will be in near future. Highest purchase rate and highest average purchase of durables. Buy: cars, refrigerators, stoves, sensible and durable furniture, vacations.

3. **Young married with children**
   Home purchasing at peak. Liquid assets low. Dissatisfied with financial position and amount of money saved. Interested in new products. Like advertised products. Buy: washers, dryers, TV, baby food, chest rubs and cough medicines, vitamins, dolls, wagons, sleds, skates.

4. **Young single or divorced with children**
   Less buying power, one income, but otherwise same as number 3.

MIDDLE-AGED FAMILIES

5. **Middle-aged single or divorced without children**
   Few financial burdens. Opinion leaders. No costs of raising children. Buy: foods, luxuries, clothes, cars, sports and hobby equipment, new furniture, travel.

6. **Middle-aged married without children**
   Financial position better. No costs of raising children. Buy: food, clothes, cars, sports and hobby equipments, new furniture, vacations.

7. **Middle-aged married with young children**
   Financial position better. Some wives work. Less influenced by advertising. Like larger-sized packages, multiple-unit deals. Buy: many foods, cleaning materials, bicycles, music lessons, pianos.

8. **Middle-aged married with older children**
   Financial position still better. More wives work. Some children get jobs. Hard to influence with advertising. High average purchase of durables. Buy: new, more tasteful furniture, auto travel, nonnecessary appliances, boats, dental services, magazines.

9. **Middle-aged single or divorced with children**
   Less buying power, one income. Otherwise same interests as number 7 and 8.

OLDER FAMILIES

10. **Older married, no children at home, at least one working**
    Home ownership at peak. Most satisfied with financial position and money saved. Interested in travel, recreation, self-education. Make gifts and contributions. Not interested in new products. Buy: vacations, luxuries, home improvements.

11. **Older married, retired**
    Drastic cut income. Keep home. Buy: medical appliances, medical care products that aid health, sleep, and digestion.

12. **Older, one partner or divorced or unmarried, working**
    Income still good but likely to sell home.

13. **Older, one partner or divorced or unmarried, retired**
    Drastic cut in income. Buy: medical appliances, medical care products that aid health, sleep, and digestion.

whether mom and dad are in their 20s or 40s, will need diapers and baby food. Yet other requirements of different families may vary. Specific groups within the family life cycle are targeted by many products. Crest toothpaste appeals to families with young children who need the cavity fighting protection of fluoride. Procter & Gamble also created a special children's version of Crest to appeal to this younger market. Tarter Control Crest, on the other hand, will more likely attract an older audience that experiences greater-than-normal build up of calcium deposits.

Gender

Consumer goods specifically designed for women or for men abound. Deodorants, bicycles, athletic shoes and vitamins may be marketed to a broad ranged, mass market, or may be specifically aimed at one **gender** or the other. Shulton, another division of Procter & Gamble, markets both Lady's Choice and Old Spice deodorants. Schwinn makes bikes for both genders. Advertising vitamin supplements with extra iron targets females.

Gun manufacturers have taken aim at women. Led by Smith & Wesson, which introduced a specially designed handgun for women in 1988, advertising for these products appears in traditionally female magazines. The Lady-Smith, as S&W branded its product, has become popular among women concerned about their safety. *Ladies' Home Journal* carried ads from Colt, The Arms Manufacturer, stressing self-protection and responsibility toward family. Although targeting women for firearms has not met with universal support, this segmentation strategy has been successful.[6]

Among the more recent moves by Nike, the footwear giant, is an athletic shoe branded Air Huarache. This ultra-lightweight footwear features modern materials such as neoprene and lycra in its design. Nike received complaints from rock music aficionados for the use of John Lennon's song "Instant Karma" in advertising these new shoes. The firm's agency, Wieden & Kennedy, confirmed that Nike had licensed the rights to the classic hit, but some still felt its use in a commercial was wrong.[7]

Long noted for targeting males, the beer industry has begun to creatively go after women. For example, Coors Brewing Co. of Golden, Colorado, introduced a beer cooler in 1992. This combination beer-wine refresher is clear and fruity tasting. Coors created this product specifically to target women. Currently ranked number three in the giant beer market, the company hopes that beer coolers will bring relief from the often bloody competitive battles in this market.[8]

---

[6]John Maines, "Can females be friends with firearms?" *American Demographics,* June 1992, p. 22; Carrie Goerne, "Gun companies target women; foes call it 'marketing to fear', " *Marketing News,* August 31, 1992, pp. 1 and 2.

[7]Cyndee Miller, "Pitch for sneakers is also campaign to end violence," *Marketing News,* December 6, 1993, p. 13; Matthew Grimm, "The sneaker warriors gun for women," *Adweek's Marketing Week,* March 23, 1992, p.12; Nena Baker, "Nike's ready to go all out to promote latest sneaker," *The Oregonian,* March 14, 1992, p. B1.

[8]Kathy Brown, "Coors brews a 'beer cooler' for women," *Adweek's Marketing Week,* April 6, 1992, p. 4.

Marketing and Society: Roots in Nature!

No one would deny that the cosmetics industry is very competitive. Upscale products sold through department stores are among the more active markets, where rival brands try to outdo one another with glitzy packaging and trained beauty consultants. It would take a special kind of company with a particularly different product to want to enter this battleground. But just such a marketer, Origins Natural Resources Incorporated and its Origins line of natural cosmetics, entered the fray with an innovative philosophy and a different line of products.

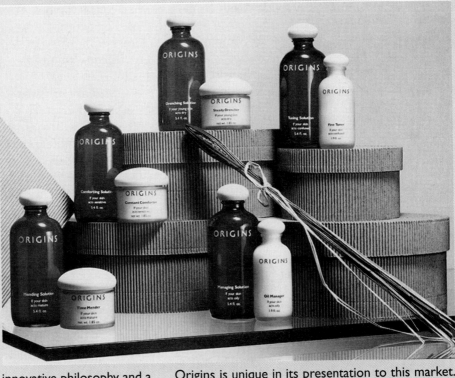

To begin with, Origins was determined to express its environmental concerns. The company did away with flashy metal trim on packages that make them difficult to recycle. The firm's glass bottles are wrapped simply in brown paper. Another step taken by the company is the Origins Empties program, which encourages customers to return empty containers for recycling. The sizable reduction in packaging costs is passed on to the customer via lower prices. Origins uses natural ingredients, including essential oils extracted from plants.

Origins is unique in its presentation to this market. Calling its salespeople "guides," the company trains its department store personnel in the art of soft-sell. Origins shows a genuine respect for its customers and does not want them to feel that they have been pushed into making a purchase. The firm's advertising is low key, featuring the product rather than beautiful faces. Although its market niche is small, Origins is making quite a splash in this industry known for its flash.

SOURCE: Judith D. Schwartz, "Natural cosmetics line seeks distinction as 'mind-set' brand," *BRANDWEEK*, March 15, 1993, pp. 29–31.

National Origin

Cultural heritage has an impact on the types of foods preferred by individuals. Marketers segment specific ethnic or national origin groups of consumers that display common tastes in food. People with Mediterranean or Latin American heritage often prefer spicier dishes than do people with a Scandinavian background. Realizing this preference, the Campbell Soup Company targets specific regions of the country that contain heavier concentrations of ethnic groups creating seasoned products to appeal to those segments.

Many companies have targeted the African American market. For example, Revlon realized the different needs among this group when it introduced its Darker Tones line through Almay in 1991. Another cosmetics house to follow suit is Prescriptives Inc., a subsidiary of Estee Lauder. This company's All Skins line produces cosmetics especially formulated for black women. In segmenting this market, Prescriptives needed to establish the right distribution channels and create the promotion to complete the strategy.[9]

The cosmetic industry is not the only section of American business to target the African American market. Cadillac began a promotional campaign to woo black customers early in 1994, and Nike has long maintained advertising targeting this market segment. Major retailers, such as J.C. Penney and Sears, set up special departments in those geographic areas where ethnic populations are large. Despite the efforts of some marketers to reach ethnically segmented markets, minorities often feel that promotion does not reflect the true needs or feeling of their culture.[10]

Religion

Markets are also demographically segmented by **religious preference.** Some sects favor certain foods, and some religions restrict certain activities, on specific days of the week. These factors may influence distribution patterns. Some firms cater to the habits dictated by specific religions, such as Mogen David wines and kosher products marketed to the Jewish community. Marketers of products designed to appeal to religious groups distribute to those areas where concentrations are located. More kosher goods appear on supermarket shelves in the New York City area and in southern Florida.

Many churches and some denominations are becoming more marketing oriented. A good example is the Willow Creek Community Church outside Chicago. Before commencing operations, the founder made extensive marketing research, determining what turned people on or off with organized religion. The church was then established to satisfy the needs of its audience. Today, the Willow Creek Community Church draws about 15,000 people to its weekend services.[11]

---

[9]"Penney's models Iman's cosmetics," *Advertising Age,* March 7, 1994, p. 17; Judith Springer Riddle, "Cosmetics niche markets go mass market," *BRANDWEEK,* November 18, 1993, Superbrands edition, p. 76–79; Maria Mallory and Stephanie Anderson Forest, "Waking up to a major market," *Business Week,* March 23, 1992, pp. 70–73; Cara Appelbaum, "Ethnic makeup goes mainstream," *Adweek's Marketing Week,* August 19, 1991, p. 11.

[10]Cyndee Miller, "Cadillac promo targets African-Americans," *Marketing News,* May 23, 1994, p. 12; Michael J. McDermott, "Marketers pay attention! Ethnics comprise 25% of the U.S.," *BRANDWEEK,* July 18, 1994, pp. 26–27; Karen Benezra, "Tactics may not translate but strategies often do," *BRANDWEEK,* July 18, 1994, pp. 28–30; Editors, "Where blacks, whites diverge," *BRANDWEEK,* May 3 1994, p. 22.

[11]Cyndee Miller, "Church keeps message but changes medium," *Marketing News,* April 11, 1994, pp. 5 and 7.

Keeping the message but modifying the medium, the Willow Creek Community Church markets its programs toward the ". . . unchurched Harry and Mary" using multimedia packaging. Courtesy William Fasata.

Income Level

Markets may be demographically segmented by **income level.** By price alone, Calphalon cookware aims at the more affluent market. Although there are many men's aftershave lotions and colognes on the market, Caswell-Massey prices its products to target a wealthier segment. Bally markets its leather goods for people with expensive tastes and sufficient income to support them. Even the rich do not act, respond or buy in the same manner.

On the other end of the scale lies lower income consumers. Often called the have-nots, this segment is sometimes overlooked as marketers assume there is little discretionary income available. Many discount retailers, such as Wal-Mart and Dollar General realize that this downscale market still has buying power. When over 40 percent of U.S. households have incomes of $25,000 or less, the numbers alone speak of a sizable segment. Although most firms that target this group are ethical, some companies have been known to exploit poor consumers who may be less educated as well.[12]

Geodemographic

A recent development in the field of market segmentation is the creation of a geodemographic study. This process links consumer traits with specific regions and is especially helpful for retailers.

---

[12]Tim Triplett, "The rich are even different from the rich," *Marketing News,* August 1, 1994, pp. 2 and 3; Aaron Bernstein, "Inequality," *Business Week,* August 15, 1994, pp. 78–83; Cyndee Miller, "The have-nots: Firms with the right products and services succeed among low-income consumers," *Marketing News,* August 1, 1994, pp. 1 and 2.

Sears, public utilities, health care facilities and financial institutions benefit from this segmentation method. For example, the marketing information system at Kraft General Foods pointed out that one particular supermarket was selling more cans of ground coffee than another. Researchers determined that customers at the second store preferred to grind whole beans. This geodemographic data enables KGF to convince the store manager to stock its Private Collections Brand to capture this market segment.[13]

PSYCHOGRAPHIC SEGMENTATION

The ways in which people act and react also form the basis for breaking up aggregate consumer markets. **Psychographic segmentation** is the method of targeting smaller markets according to the lifestyle, or interests, opinions and activities. People who enjoy cooking, who are into photography or who actively participate in athletics fit this description. Further segmentation occurs even within these broad categories. For example, some consumers specialize in certain types of cuisine, such as Thai or French, or are involved in home brewing. There are specific products designed to appeal to each type of psychographic segment.

For example, in promoting Bowling Green, Geoffrey Beene's fragrance for men, the scene is woodsy and idyllic with a casually dressed male lounging in the background. Obsession, a men's cologne from Calvin Klein, advertises in a sensual, often risqué, atmosphere. Both products are directed toward men, but each to a different segment. The marketers of these similar products segment according to lifestyle as well as gender.

Using psychographic segmentation can lead to rather small niche markets. To illustrate, look at a firm in Escondido, California, called All-In-One-Faith Inc., led by a self-proclaimed Ph.D. Mr. Emanuel Bronner. After immigrating from a long line of soap makers from Europe, Bronner hit on the idea of creating a natural soap and using the bottle as an easel on which to scribe his "Moral ABCs." His peace and love philosophy caught on during the hippie counterculture movement of the 1960s and today attracts fans and customers from all walks of life. Bronner's Peppermint Pure-Castille Soap, the mainstay of his line, is sold primarily through natural food and health stores and rings up over four million dollars in sales annually.[14]

Many consumers refuse to worry about things such as cholesterol or sodium intake. Directly opposite is a large group of people who avoid anything that even hints of being artificial or unhealthy. Quaker markets cereals containing sugar, salt, and artificial flavorings through supermarkets. Barbara's breakfast foods, from Barbara's Bakery in Novato, California, contain no additives or preservatives and are typically found at health or natural food stores. Bowing to consumer pressure, some advertisers are replacing unrealistically thin models with everyday types or drawings to avoid creating an "unnatural" image.[15]

[13]Lynn G. Coleman, "Marketers advised to 'Go regional'," *Marketing News,* May 8, 1989, pp. 1, 8.

[14]Wendy Bounds, "Suds and philosophy lather up business for odd Dr. Bronner," *The Wall Street Journal,* November 26, 1993, pp. A1 and A4.

[15]Kevin Goldman, "Pretty models are supplemented by drawings of a hummingbird," *The Wall Street Journal,* February 10, 1994, pp. B1 and B8.

**Examples of products that target segmented
consumer markets**

PRODUCT	PRIMARY TARGETED SEGMENT
Hominy grits	Southerners (geographic)
Rainbird sprinklers	Rural/suburban areas (geographic)
Tomato seedlings	Rural/suburban gardeners (geographic/psychographic)
Acne medicine	Teenagers (demographic)
Sports bras	Women athletes (demographic/psychographic)
Hair straightener	Blacks (demographic)
Imported crystal	Affluent entertainers (demographic/psychographic)
Fly rod	Anglers (psychographic)
Snowmobile	Winter outdoors enthusiasts (geographic/psychographic)
Microwave ovens	Households/businesses (aggregate)
Frozen peas	Consumers everywhere (aggregate)

■ ■ ■ ■ ■

Concern about health and wellness even impacts the pet food industry. The multi-billion dollar pet food industry is coping with the new wave in pet foods, thanks to Iams Company, from Dayton, Ohio, and Hill's Pet Products, now owned by Colgate-Palmolive. These two firms created the health food craze in pet foods. Iams and Hill's began by offering special diets that eliminated some of the irritating fillers often found in other varieties. Part of the marketing strategy for these healthier pet foods involved distribution, as marketers turned veterinarian offices into retail stores.[16]

In a daring move, some marketers, including MCI, American Express and Apple Computer, have singled out the gay market for promotion. Using media such as *Out, Advocate* and *Victory,* firms attempt to reach an audience that by some estimates may exceed 25 million people in the United States alone. Ross Products, a division of Abbott Laboratories, markets Advera, a flavored drink fortified with vitamins and minerals, that targets the over one million Americans infected with HIV.[17]

MULTIPLE SEGMENTATION

Geographic, demographic and psychographic segmentation often do not stand alone. Many marketers target products toward combinations of these segments. To illustrate, Reebok, Nike, Converse, L.A. Gear and Adidas sell many styles of their footwear for sports use. This is psychographic segmentation. These marketers have lines of shoes for tennis, running, walking, aerobics, basketball and

---

[16]Julie Liesse, "Purina bites back into pet food," *Advertising Age,* April 20, 1992, p. 45; Laura Bird, "Iams and Hill's wage a high-fiber, low-cal war against Ralston Purina and Carnation," *Adweek's Marketing Week,* October 1, 1990, pp. 20-22.

[17]Meg Cox, "New magazines cater to people with HIV," *The Wall Street Journal,* March 1, 1994, pp. B1 and B8; Cyndee Miller, "Top marketers take a bold approach in targeting gays," *Marketing News,* July 4, 1994, pp. 1 and 2; Judith Springer Riddle, "Advera drink launch eyes HIV consumers," *BRANDWEEK,* October 18, 1993, p. 2.

a variety of other athletic activities. These companies also produce shoes for men, women and children, all of which are definitely demographic segments. Such market segmentation is both psychographic and demographic.

USAGE PATTERN

Because smaller segments may account for heavy sales, many marketers attempt to segment based upon this **usage pattern.** The marketing effort can be targeted either toward keeping the heavy users or toward bringing in non-users. For example, an overwhelming percentage of beer consumers are male, and promotion for top brands reflects this usage pattern. Brewers, however, realize that women are often the purchasers of the brew that their male partners consume, hence there has been a tempering trend in some advertising.

The marketing company often modifies the marketing mix depending upon the usage rate in different segments. To illustrate, Rockwell makes a complete line of circular saws. The product, promotion and pricing for worm-drive models, the type generally used by building contractors, are distinct from those employed by Rockwell for the do-it-yourself market. The buying habits of professionals varies greatly from that of amateurs.

What Are Business Products Markets?

Most manufactured goods are sold by one business to another, a business-to-business transaction. Even those items ultimately purchased by consumers may pass through at least one other business before reaching consumers' shelves, closets or garages. Wholesalers and retailers are business organizations that first handle these items. In addition, most enterprises require a variety of equipment, supplies and accessories that again are purchased from commercial entities . . . businesses.

BUSINESS MARKETS DEFINED

Business products markets— Manufacturers, marketing intermediaries, institutions and government.

Individuals buy consumer products for themselves or for their families. Businesses and other organizations make up **business products markets,** which include manufacturers, marketing intermediaries, institutions and government agencies. Just as with items purchased by consumers, the products found in business markets include both goods and services. These organizations purchase items manufactured by business for business. Some of these products are used directly or indirectly in the making of other finished items. Others are manufactured for resale.

MANUFACTURERS AND SERVICE INDUSTRIES

Manufacturers comprise a major market for business goods and services. This category defines all of those businesses that are either manufacturing other goods or that are creating a service. Maytag buys steel, paint, electric motors

Global Marketing: Shh!

The "quiet shoe" is making loud noises. Once known as the preferred footwear for youngsters, sneakers are finding their way into the closets of every age group and gender. Although they got their start in athletic arenas, rubber-soled shoes are now an integral part of everyone's wardrobe. One can probably even go to the opera in sneaks, if the shoes sport the right brand name.

The sales of sneakers go up and up and up. Sales have increased 150 percent since 1983, and there appears to be no end in sight. Although dominated by big names such as Reebok, Nike and Adidas, the market has plenty of room for smaller manufacturers. Fila Footwear USA, a unit of Fila Sport S.p.A. of Italy, ran ads during the 1992 NCAA basketball telecasts in competition to Nike and Reebok. Keds and P.F. Flyers are making a comeback, and L.A. Gear is climbing again after a brief plateau.

The market for sneakers exceeded 400 million pairs in 1990, and is expected to double that figure, worldwide, by 1996. Of this total, nearly 97 percent will be manufactured overseas, principally in the Asian countries of South Korea, Taiwan and Hong Kong. Domestic production has not been able to compete with lower cost imports. Expected growth

in the 7 percent to 10 percent per year range will continue to benefit foreign manufacturers.

SOURCES: Matthew Grimm, "Gearing up—for the long run," *Adweek's Marketing Week*, February 2, 1992, pp. 12–13; Editors, "The latest contender," *Adweek's Marketing Week*, April 6, 1992, p. 29.

and electronic controls that become part of finished washers and dryers. This major appliance manufacturer also purchases welding equipment, robots, lubricants, solvents, desks and computers. These items are purchased from other business entities.

Service providers, such as Four Seasons hotels, American Airlines and One-Hour Martinizing dry cleaners, do not manufacture goods, but do create activities that require business products. These companies purchase beds and furnishings, aircraft and fuel, cleaning solvent and clothes pressers. These items are used directly or indirectly to produce the service. In this way, providers of services function as manufacturers.

MARKETING INTERMEDIARIES

Those markets where products are sold by manufacturers to **marketing intermediaries** for resale are typically called **"the trade."** This group of buyers, made up of wholesalers, distributors, dealers and retailers, is a major segment of the organizational market. Intermediaries purchase goods from businesses for resale to manufacturers, to other resellers or to consumers. These members of the distribution system form that vital link between manufacturers and the ultimate consumers.

SuperValu is a grocery wholesaler, purchasing products from leading food and sundry goods manufacturers. This company resells the merchandise it buys from manufacturers to retail supermarkets. Some retailers buy goods directly from manufacturers. Music instruments, such as pianos, normally bypass wholesalers to proceed directly to the retailer's showroom. Each of these intermediaries services the trade. Many of these business customers develop their own specifications for the goods that they purchase from manufacturers.

The consumer goods sold by giant mass merchandisers, such as Kmart, J.C. Penney and Wal-Mart, are often standard, off-the-shelf type items. The corner grocery, the jewelry outlet in the mall and the local shoe store are also retailers that purchase goods for resale to consumers. Whether reselling groceries or apparel, sporting goods or appliances, fertilizer or typewriters, these smaller outlets provide significant market for manufacturers.

INSTITUTIONS AND GOVERNMENT

Institutions and governments form the third market of business or organizational buyers. Public and private schools, hospitals, federal, state and local government agencies, and non-profit associations are all prime targets for these marketers. The X-ray equipment for the hospital and the football pads and jerseys ordered by the prep school are products purchased by organizations. The desks for the county office building and the trucks for the city road department are part of this market.

Similar to some marketing intermediaries, many of these organizations create the specifications for the manufacture of the goods. This is especially true with government agencies. An elaborate system and exhaustive number of "Milspecs" appear on almost every article purchased by the Pentagon. Agencies and bureaus in fields other than defense also create their own requirements for the products they buy. For instance, schools select athletic jerseys in the colors and sizes needed for a particular organization.

Many legal and budgetary restrictions are found in this market. For example, many government agencies purchase only on a competitive bid basis. These buying groups often require sealed bids as well. Thorough inspection of ordered goods usually occurs before the government agency accepts delivery for the entire shipment. Because of the unique quality of this market, many suppliers specialize in dealing strictly with institutions or with government organizations.

 ## ow Are Business Markets Segmented?

Some business markets are aggregate, and others are segmented. Lotus, for example, markets general business software for a variety of users, but McDonnell Douglas, the aircraft manufacturer, creates computer programs strictly for the healthcare industry. Cessna markets a broad line of business airplanes suitable for the needs of almost any company. Gulfstream Aerospace, a Chrysler company, caters only to those businesses needing large, corporate aircraft. These examples describe the segmentation of organizational markets, which is somewhat different than targeting in consumer goods arenas.

GEOGRAPHICALLY

Geographic segmentation is as common in business markets as it is with consumers. To illustrate, in the United States, there is a definite concentration of manufacturers in certain areas. Many sellers locate in the heavily populated areas in the East and Midwest to be near industrial facilities. The automobile industry in and around Detroit and the manufacture of tires in the Akron, Ohio, area show this geographic concentration. The Silicon Valley of California, the research triangle in North Carolina and the Boston beltline demonstrate geographic segmentation in the high-tech industry that has arisen in the past two decades.

Businesses tend to group in certain locales for many reasons. Initially, industrial concentration had much to do with the availability of energy or labor or shipping access. This was the case with the woven goods industry in New England and the aluminum business in the Northwest. Closeness to markets and proximity to raw material sources have also played a part in area selection. Concentration of steel manufacturing around the Great Lakes region placed the industry close to sources of iron ore and to major users.

Manufacturers of auxiliary or secondary equipment often settle in the same area where the major industry headquarters are located. Support services are more readily available in these locations. Also, there are often informal networks of people in comparable lines of work that allow for the exchange of ideas and interests. Former employees of the major companies often start up these support or service firms. Most of these entrepreneurs naturally locate in the same region. This growth of related, new businesses is common in Silicon Valley.

Survey of Industrial and Commercial Buying Power

A major effort in classifying businesses is undertaken by *Sales & Marketing Management,* a marketing trade journal. *S&MM* annually creates the **Survey of Industrial and Commercial Buying Power.** This report lists the number of firms by state and county. The survey includes exact location, size, dollars of shipments/receipts and other pertinent information. This journal is an excellent guide for use by organizational marketers.

BY TYPE OF BUSINESS

Some industrial markets are segmented according to the buyers' **type of business.** We have learned that a marketer of consumer apparel might select, for example, young female athletes as the target segment. Similarly, a manufacturer of products for organizational markets may choose to concentrate on customers from one type of business or industry. To illustrate, there are many manufacturers of fasteners, such as nuts and bolts and rivets. Among these

Media market profiles
S & MM ESTIMATES: 01/01/94

STATE S&MM/NIELSEN MEDIA RESEARCH MEDIA MARKET (DMA)	TOTAL POP. (THOUS.)	HOUSE-HOLDS (THOUS.)	BLACK POP. (THOUS.)	HISPANIC POP. (THOUS.)	POPULATION BY AGE GROUP (THOUS.)						EFFECTIVE BUYING INCOME TOTAL EBI ($000)	RETAIL SALES ($000)	BUYING POWER INDEX
					2-11 YEARS	12-17 YEARS	18-24 YEARS	25-34 YEARS	35-49 YEARS	50 & OVER			
WISCONSIN													
GREEN BAY-APPLETON	**981.2**	**367.0**	**3.0**	**8.1**	**153.9**	**84.6**	**88.5**	**151.6**	**211.5**	**263.1**	**14,629,315**	**7,987,989**	**.3662**
metropolitan	534.0	198.4	2.3	4.4	84.2	44.8	54.7	89.3	117.8	127.0	8,515,659	5,148,491	.2174
nonmetropolitan	447.2	168.6	.7	3.7	39.7	39.8	33.8	62.3	93.7	136.1	6,113,656	2,839,498	.1488
LA CROSSE-EAU CLAIRE	**445.8**	**165.9**	**1.4**	**2.6**	**68.5**	**37.1**	**51.9**	**62.8**	**92.6**	**120.4**	**5,968,294**	**3,481,003**	**.1560**
metropolitan	261.9	97.8	.9	1.5	39.8	21.1	34.1	38.1	55.1	66.2	3,628,312	2,439,615	.0990
nonmetropolitan	183.9	68.1	.5	1.1	28.7	16.0	17.8	24.7	37.5	54.2	2,339,982	1,041,388	.0570
MADISON	**795.6**	**303.9**	**20.2**	**10.2**	**116.8**	**62.2**	**91.4**	**129.9**	**178.0**	**194.8**	**13,003,452**	**7,694,094**	**.3282**
metropolitan	527.7	203.8	19.6	8.8	74.5	38.4	69.2	92.4	122.7	115.2	9,280,093	5,110,588	.2258
nonmetropolitan	267.9	100.1	.6	1.4	42.3	23.8	22.2	37.5	55.3	79.6	3,723,359	2,583,506	.1024
MILWAUKEE	**2,116.6**	**789.4**	**241.2**	**80.6**	**324.2**	**175.8**	**199.2**	**338.9**	**465.2**	**548.6**	**35,557,872**	**17,345,176**	**.8400**
metropolitan	1,890.3	708.6	239.3	76.0	290.9	157.1	174.2	305.5	416.9	487.1	32,153,517	15,875,199	.7604
nonmetropolitan	226.3	80.8	1.9	4.6	33.3	18.7	25.0	33.4	48.3	61.5	3,404,355	1,469,977	.0796
WAUSAU-RHINELANDER	**453.0**	**168.7**	**1.2**	**2.7**	**70.7**	**40.2**	**39.1**	**65.0**	**94.7**	**130.9**	**6,273,133**	**3,547,345**	**.1613**
metropolitan	119.6	43.2	.1	.5	19.5	11.0	10.2	18.2	26.8	30.4	1,749,146	960,775	.0441
nonmetropolitan	333.4	125.5	1.1	2.2	51.2	29.2	28.9	46.8	67.9	100.5	4,523,987	2,586,570	.1172
WYOMING													
CASPER-RIVERTON	**126.1**	**48.4**	**.6**	**5.5**	**22.0**	**12.3**	**8.8**	**18.1**	**29.3**	**31.9**	**1,876,821**	**956,002**	**.0464**
metropolitan	62.0	24.6	.5	2.4	10.7	5.6	4.8	9.6	14.5	14.9	1,016,774	577,740	.0253
nonmetropolitan	64.1	23.8	.1	3.1	11.3	6.7	4.0	8.5	14.8	17.0	860,047	378,262	.0211
CHEYENNE-SCOTTSBLUFF-STERLING	**126.2**	**49.1**	**2.6**	**15.0**	**20.3**	**11.4**	**10.7**	**19.0**	**28.2**	**32.8**	**1,907,133**	**1,145,371**	**.0488**
metropolitan	76.8	29.6	2.5	8.1	12.4	6.7	7.1	12.6	17.7	17.8	1,236,792	722,934	.0311
nonmetropolitan	49.4	19.5	.1	6.9	7.9	4.7	3.6	6.4	10.5	15.0	670,341	422,437	.0177
TOTAL UNITED STATES DMA'S	**259,414.8**	**95,842.1**	**32,452.1**	**25,596.9**	**38,175.2**	**21,245.9**	**25,940.8**	**41,684.6**	**57,877.7**	**66,546.7**	**4,166,928,868**	**2,078,093,757**	**99.9381**

SOURCE: *Sales & Marketing Management*, October 28, 1994, p. 48

firms, several companies market strictly to the aircraft and aerospace industry. In the furniture business, some firms rely on the institutional or school markets whereas others concentrate on office or business customers.

With some manufacturers dealing in organizational markets, the same product may be targeted toward a variety of different markets. Marvin Windows sells much of its product line of wooden windows for new construction. Building supply houses are Marvin's customers for this product. Building owners and remodelers are also users of windows. The do-it-yourself buyer usually frequents lumber yards and builders emporiums for windows. Each of these targets has different needs. Design and function are the concerns of architects and builders of new homes, while building renovators worry more about cost. Each type of segment deserves different treatment from the marketer.[18]

Standard Industrial Classification (SIC)

The **Standard Industrial Classification** is a system the U.S. government designed to segment markets by industry types. This network divides the total organizational market into specific industry categories, such as agriculture, construction, manufacturing, the resale trades and finance. Each of these segments is further broken down in more detail using well-defined codes. Within the SIC code, each business fits into an industry that carries a four digit number. This code signifies a group of firms that are involved with the same primary activities.

Standard Industrial Classification (SIC)— a system the U.S. government designed to segment markets by industry types.

Standard Industrial Classifications have some drawbacks. Categorizing all businesses according to the products that they produce can be difficult. Many companies shine in several product areas that are dissimilar. For example, Procter & Gamble markets detergents, pharmaceuticals, food products and much more. This consumer goods giant falls under several different codes. Litton Industries is listed in the SIC under both microwave ovens and shipbuilding. Additionally, lists are not updated on a regular basis. Many new companies, or entire industries, such as superconducting filament manufacturers, might not appear for years.

BY MARKET SIZE

Some suppliers in the organizational field break their markets into segments according to **size.** The total number of business buyers may look small when compared to millions of consumers, but the volume of goods changing hands in the industrial sector is gigantic. Picture the amount of terry cloth purchased by the average consumer compared to the orders placed by Fieldcrest. The gallons of paint needed by the typical do-it-yourselfer is minute compared to what is used by the Pontiac Division of General Motors.

Many firms find that it is uneconomical to manufacture goods in small quantities, concentrating their efforts on major users. Other companies, seeing an untapped segment free from competition, will go after the leftover, smaller markets. At times, these niche markets can produce sizable volume and profits for specialty marketers.

---

[18]Kate Bertrand, "Divide and conquer," *Business Marketing*, November 1989, pp. 48–54.

SIC EXPLAINED

This system, that the federal government developed, is a means of collecting information regarding all of the industries in the economy. The first two digits of an SIC number represent an area of major activity, such as agriculture, mining or manufacturing. This portion of the code is the division. For example, all manufacturing businesses receive a division code between 20 and 39. Each of these numbers denotes a major group. Companies with the major group code of 20 are manufacturing in the food industry.

The latter two numbers of the four-digit code represent specific industries. The SIC system has the potential for 99 specific industries under each major group or each division. A food manufacturer could be further listed in the bottled or canned soft drink industry. This firm then would carry an SIC code of 2086. The SIC designation is helpful to other businesses searching for specific firms in specific industries. For example, an inventor with a new type of soft drink looking for an established manufacturer under private label could use this SIC code. Carton suppliers interested in locating cola marketers could also use the SIC system to locate all of those firms in that same line of business.

Niche market—a very small, selective group of prospects or buyers.

A **niche market** is a very small, select group of prospects or buyers. These smaller markets exist in a variety of industries and can produce outstanding profits for suppliers. Data on these smaller segments, with buying power ranging from $10 to $200 million, is often hard to come by. Many private research firms have developed databases that are helpful to marketers of products such as protective legwraps for racehorses, hot melt adhesives and residential door knobs.

Consumers goods marketers may also target small, niche markets. A suede shoe cleaner from Kiwi and Casabar's costume jewelry cleaner illustrate this point. Another example in the consumer arena would be Republic of Tea, founded by the former owners of Banana Republic, which created a market for very exotic, super expensive teas, referring to this niche as the "elite of the elite."[19]

[19]Robert McMath, "Niche marketing is the buzzword as manufacturers polish their pitch," *BRANDWEEK*, January 17, 1994, pp. 36–37; Russell Mitchell and Sandra D. Atchison, "You are relaxed. You are content. You are approaching 'tea mind'," *Business Week*, November 30, 1992, p. 44.

Largest manufacturing industries

RANK	SIC	INDUSTRY	TOTAL SALES ($ MIL)	EMPLOYEES
1	3714	Motor vehicles and car bodies	$38,978	420,132
2	2911	Petroleum refining	36,695	78,222
3	3089	Plastic products	32,162	424,755
4	3714	Motor vehicle parts and accessories	29,694	274,036
5	3721	Aircraft	28,808	305,082
6	3571	Computers and peripheral equip	28,726	162,562
7	2752	Commercial printing	28,296	437,871
8	3674	Semiconductors and related devices	24,167	209,851
9	2869	Organic chemicals	22,559	122,623
10	3312	Blast furnaces and steel mills	22,473	216,685

SOURCE: "Largest manufacturing industries," *Sales & Marketing Management,* July 1991, p. 58.

How Does Segmentation Strategy Impact Management of Business Markets?

Most business product marketers tailor their goods and services to satisfy specific needs. These needs may be found in aggregate markets, or segmented ones. Some manufacturers find that offering their products to broad, undifferentiated markets generates greater sales. Others opt to bypass the competition, service a smaller sector and earn greater profits on fewer sales.

For instance, IBM, Apple, Compaq, DEC and a host of other companies tangle over the gigantic personal computer market. Meanwhile, Cray Research Inc. targets the much smaller world of supercomputers. Only about 250 of these superfast, supercomplex machines exist, but at prices of up to $20 million each. The company does well in this highly segmented market. Seymour Cray, founder of the Minneapolis based company, left in 1989 to form Cray Computer Corp., located in Colorado Springs. The going has been tough since the end of the cold war cooled the demand for supercomputers, but Cray Computer recently received a government contract to assist in building a high-tech spying machine.[20]

The criteria for successful segmentation are just as valid for items used in manufacturing as they are for products sold to the trade. The target segment must be large enough. The prospects must be similarly responsive, and they must be reachable. In organizational markets, a few customers can generate sizable volume. Typically, businesses in given industries will react in a similar fashion to products. Most business customers are reached through direct

[20]John Markof, "Cray snares $4.2 million deal for high-tech spying machine," *The Oregonian,* August 18, 1994, p. E2; Lawrence M. Fisher, "Cray can't sell new supercomputer," *The Oregonian,* February 22, 1992, p. D2.

channels of communications and personal selling. Market segmentation rarely succeeds if these criteria are not met.

As a rule, in organizational markets, positioning regards the image for the firm more than its products. Buyers of these products depend heavily upon the reliability and dependability of suppliers. Therefore, a company's reputation and performance are often more important than the goods or services it provides. Organizational sellers develop images as quality leaders, low priced specialists or premier service providers. A firm's products may have independent images, but the positioning of the company usually takes precedent.

Market segments are the result of more than just a research exercise. Marketers should not attempt to pigeon-hole groups of buyers who really do not show similar needs or behavior. If the products offered perform well and need is generally evident, pursuing the aggregate market might be the best strategy. Trying to target a segment that does not exist will lead to failure.

GLOBAL CONSIDERATIONS

Global marketers have more of a challenge when it comes to segmenting markets. Demographic strata may be blurry, especially in lesser developed nations. The poor may comprise the entire population, and in some societies there is no market for females. Even in more advanced economies, the needs or opinions of women are often ignored or debased. In most cases, consumer goods markets must be reduced to the simplest of targets.

Similarly, psychographic segmentation is more difficult to define in global markets. The recreational facilities found in abundance in the U.S. are lacking in much of the rest of the world. Even in more advanced countries, people often spend more of their time working and commuting than engaged in leisure activities. Waiting for a tee at a Los Angeles golf course does not compare to the long lines found in Japan.

Segmenting business markets can be equally trying. Few countries in the world can match the industrial might of North America, Europe and countries from the Pacific Rim. Many production goods, especially manufacturing equipment, must be brought in from outside the economy. Many third world countries lack sophisticated distribution systems needed for highly segmented markets. Then, too, advertising media might not be available to reach such targets.

SUMMING IT UP

Consumer goods markets consist of individuals purchasing for their own use or for that of their households. This group of buyers may operate as a mass or aggregate market or show specific buying patterns that differentiate them from other purchasers. Marketers that target only certain consumers who show similar buying patterns are practicing market segmentation.

To be successful, target marketing selects segments that are large enough, show similar responsiveness and are reachable. Consumer goods markets are typically segmented according to geographics, demographics or psychographics. Some of these groups are targeted by a combination of these methods.

Manufacturers, intermediaries, institutions and government make up the organizational markets. These aggregate markets are typically segmented according to their location, size and type of product. The criteria for successful segmentation is the same in organizational markets as in consumer goods arenas.

KEY CONCEPTS AND TERMS FROM CHAPTER FIVE

Aggregate market
Business products markets
Consumer products markets
Demographic segmentation
Geographic segmentation
Market segmentation

Niche market
Psychographic segmentation
Standard Industrial Classification (SIC)
Successful segmentation

BUILDING SKILLS

1. Compare the characteristics of aggregate markets with target segments, explaining how segmentation affects the marketing mix.

2. Describe the target markets for Healthy Choice frozen dinners, Obsession scents from Calvin Klein, Apple laptop computers, the Ford Bronco II and Starbucks coffee.

3. Explain how the criteria for successful segmentation apply to Dove beauty bar soap, Converse tennis shoes, Haggar sports clothes, Weber barbecue kettles and Pentax automatic cameras.

4. Compare the differences between geographic, demographic or psychographic segmentation strategies, classifying the segmentation of Yamaha snowmobiles, Head 'n Shoulders dandruff removing shampoo, Swatch wristwatches, Soft Soap liquid hand soap and Isotoner slippers.

5. Describe the methods for segmenting business markets, explaining how they differ from those used to target consumer goods.

6. Analyze the positioning of a business marketer, explaining how marketing management controls these factors.

Making Decisions 5-1: You Old Softie, You!

Samsonite Corp. of Denver, the world's largest manufacturer of suitcases, grew dramatically during the past decade, while many competitors stumbled. Headquartered in Denver, the company initially built its reputation and sales by marketing functional, hard-sided luggage, briefcases and carrying cases, targeting the adult market of business travelers. Many business firms ordered custom built carriers for handling instruments and machines from Samsonite.

Today, soft luggage has become a significant portion of the industry. Business and recreational travelers find that "softies" are easy to handle, resist damage and remain attractive. In addition, to avoid subjecting their possessions to potential loss or damage, more people are carrying their baggage onto airplanes. Soft items are more resilient and easier to squeeze into tight overhead racks. Samsonite has led the way in developing innovative soft luggage, with about half of the "luggage leaders" sales generated from soft-sided items.

Several years ago, Samsonite introduced Sammies, a nylon product of nine different styles. Back packs lead the line that included duffels and other casual items. The marketer aimed this line at the segment of 16 to 24 year-olds, hoping to capture and keep this younger market. By establishing brand loyalty early, Samsonite expects to maintain its grip on these buyers when they become older and more affluent. To reach this segment, the company advertised on MTV and in magazines such as *Rolling Stone*, *Glamour*, and *Cosmopolitan*. Although no longer labeling these items "Sammies," the company has been very successful with this segmentation strategy.[21]

Explore the reasons why Samsonite chose to segment its market for Sammies, explaining the advantages or disadvantages of segmentation strategy.

(Courtesy of Samsonite)

---

[21]Mark Hudis, "Leo Burnett for Samsonite luggage: It's in the bag," *Mediaweek*,. June 27, 1994, pp. s10–s11; Cara Appelbaum, "Samsonite's sporty set," *Adweek's Marketing Week*, September 9, 1991, p. 10.

Making Decisions 5-2: Not Just for Kids.

There was a day when blue jeans were worn by men for work. The granddaddy of blue denim marketers, Levi Strauss & Company, got its beginning by supplying miners, cowboys, and millers with hard wearing canvas pants. Most of the sales for these utilitarian trousers remained in the arena of working males until teenagers made them a cult emblem in the 1960s. Jeans became the symbol of rebellion in those days. By banning the wearing of dungarees to class, school officials promptly labeled jeans as the ultimate twist in turning against authority.

During the 1970s and 1980s, jeans became a fashion statement. Designer labels began to fill the racks and shelves of boutiques and department stores. Men wore them with jackets and ties, and women dressed them up by wearing high heels, silk blouses and floral scarves. Hardly a yuppie's closet was bare of at least one pair of "dress up" jeans.

But the yuppies of yesterday are today's "grays," and to capture this aging market, jeans makers have resorted to new strategies. Fewer ads feature teenagers. New promotions depict people in their 40s and 50s, predominantly women. Television stars Betty White and Dixie Carter are replacing the likes of Brooke Shields. Designs, too, are changing to accommodate this more mature market, with more room and softer styles.[22]

Describe the methods the jeans industry used to segment its market, using the criteria for successful segmentation to comment on the possibility for success.

Making Decisions 5-3: Playing It Safe!

It is often difficult to understand how products take on a particular image. Sometimes even the marketing company has trouble grasping the position that consumers select for certain brands. Take Safeguard, for example, one of the best selling bar soaps from Procter & Gamble. When the company first introduced this deodorant bar in the 1960s, it was not expected that the product would acquire a male image . . . but it did.

The marketer was satisfied with this positioning until recently, when arch-rival Lever Bros. had such success with its Lever 2000 brand. When Lever gained the number one position in this convenience good category, P&G got busy. The giant packaged goods house from Cincinnati began a face lift for Safeguard, hiring the New York design firm of Gerstman + Meyers. By changing the type style to a less masculine look and using contemporary colors on a white metallic wrap, G + M hoped to create a softer image that would appeal to both men and women.

Procter & Gamble took one additional step to reposition this brand. Creating a liquid antibacterial soap carrying the Safeguard name, P&G plunged

---

[22]Cara Appelbaum, "Not-for-teens blue jeans," *Adweek's Marketing Week,* August 5, 1991, pp. 20–21; Barbara Lippert, "From Spike Lee to Matisse," *Adweek's Marketing Week,* August 5, 1991, p. 29.

into a definitely feminine arena. The company banked on the original imaging to hold the male market while the new positioning would draw in the other gender. Although it is not easy to change the image of established products, Procter & Gamble is gambling on its marketing clout.[23]

Describe the methods used by Procter & Gamble to segment the market for Safeguard. Using the criteria for successful segmentation, analyze the potential for success for this strategy.

---

[23]Fara Warner, "Safeguard's risky mission," *Adweek's Marketing Week,* March 16, 1992, pp. 36–37.

6

Consumer Products and Buying Behavior

■ ■ ■ ■ ■ ■ ■ ■ ■ ■

The Job to be Done

As consumers we buy many different products. Some are goods or services that we use ourselves; others are bought for our households. Chapter 6 explores consumer buying, providing students the ability to:

- describe consumer products and the characteristics of convenience, shopping, and specialty goods,
- identify the classifications of consumer services,
- analyze the consumer buying process and the factors affecting consumer buying decisions,
- compare the personal and social factors influencing the consumer buying process, and
- recognize the ways that consumer behavior influences marketing management.

What Are Consumer Products?

Consumer products— goods or services purchased to satisfy individual or household needs or wants.

Consumer products are goods or services that are purchased to satisfy individual or household needs or wants. These goods and services can be found in supermarkets and Saturday markets, road-side stands and multi-stored shopping malls. Few goods are delivered, but services are often provided where people live, work or play.

CONSUMER GOODS DEFINED

A **consumer good** is a physical product, something that has form, shape and size. Individuals buy these items to satisfy their hunger or thirst, clothe their bodies, or carry them around town. Some are purchased because of a loyalty for a given brand. Other items are bought based upon price. Still others are purchased after exhaustive research.

Cereal and cat food, shirts and sneakers, perfumes and powders are all consumer goods. So are fertilizers and lawn mowers, convertibles and pickup trucks, toasters and washing machines. These goods are available in an endless number of styles, sizes and prices. Although having such a selection can make the choice difficult, consumers are usually grateful for this wide variety.

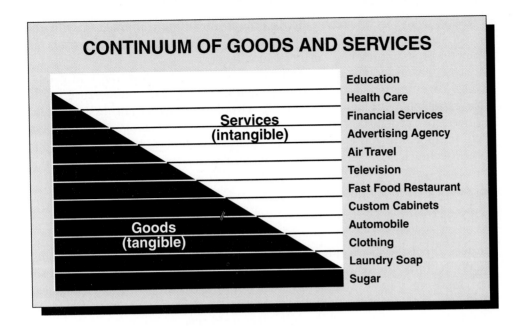

CONSUMER SERVICES DEFINED

Services are intangible activities or tasks that cannot be stored, resold or transported. These products include the use of a facility that is owned by another or the act of work performed by someone else for the benefit of the purchaser. The traveler on a Greyhound bus going from one city to another does not own the transportation, but uses it. The golfer plays the golf course, and people with hampers full of dirty clothes avail themselves of the services of coin-operated laundries. The dentist performs a service, as does the gardener and the engineer. In these cases, the receiver of the service pays for its use. While the buyer does not purchase anything physical, satisfaction still results.

> **Services**—intangible activities or tasks that cannot be stored, resold or transported.

Services have become the dominant part of our American society. Three out of every four Americans work in the service sector, which accounts for about two-thirds of the U.S. Gross Domestic Product. Although economists differ on the methods for measuring the value or impact of services, the average consumer easily agrees that a major portion of one's income goes to pay for intangibles. Our economy has become service oriented. Banking, medical care, travel and lodging, advertising, utilities and automobile repair all fall into the service category.

The Growth of the Service Sector

The rate of growth of services has been phenomenal. More than 35 million jobs have been added to the U.S. economy since 1966, yet manufacturing employs fewer people now than it did twenty years ago. Experts estimate that 90 percent of the growth in the American economy between now and the year 2000 will be in the service sector. Much of this growth will occur in the health and education fields. Technology remains a big factor in the continued upswing of the service boom. Technological advances include such high-tech areas as computer programming and artificial intelligence.[1]

One reason for this increase in services is the growth in physical goods. As new consumer goods appear on the market, repair and maintenance needs arise, especially with high-tech items. Electronic ignition systems in cars create the need for specialists trained to repair these parts. As compact disc players begin to appear in more automobiles, homes and offices, the need arises for trained technicians to service entertainment centers.

DIFFERENCES BETWEEN GOODS AND SERVICES

Services themselves are intangible, yet the performance of these products usually requires the assistance of physical things. Banks keep their depositors' funds in vaults. Mechanics need tools to repair cars or appliances. Gardeners cut the grass with lawn mowers and feed it with inorganic or organic fertilizers. Television broadcasters need towers and transmitters, and pet groomers need shears and shampoos. Few services are completely divorced from goods.

Production and Consumption are Inseparable

Neither customers nor providers can separate the production of services from their use. Services are consumed at the time they are produced. When consumers put their money into video games, or business people sit down with consultants, the services are provided and used simultaneously. When the skier buys a ticket on the chairlift, the value received from that purchase is immediate. While the benefits from using the service may live on, the performance of the service is complete when it occurs.

The person performing the service or persons allowing the use of their equipment become extremely important for customer satisfaction. People provide services. Performer and performance are inseparable. If the tune-up on the car is not satisfactory, it is the mechanic's fault. When the plane arrives late, travelers blame the airline, not the weather or the crowded skies. The people providing the services are responsible for satisfactory results.

Services are Perishable

Services are **perishable.** They cannot be stored. Once a service goes unused, such as a seat at the baseball park or an appointment with a physician, it cannot be regained. Airlines offer reduced fares for advance purchase of tickets. If the traveler cannot make the trip when scheduled, refunds may not be available. The airline company selling the use of its equipment in advance is trying to cut down on the number of empty seats. Although the passenger may rebook for another flight, these missed opportunities are gone forever.

---

[1]Ronald Henkoff, "Service is everybody's business," *Fortune,* June 27, 1994, pp. 48–50.

Because services cannot be stored, providers must meet market demand with sufficient supply. Since these activities often involve physical goods, such as meals and trucks, the coordination of the resources needed to provide the service becomes critical. When the local Sizzler franchise runs out of baked potatoes, consumers blame the restaurant not the farmer or the restaurant supply house. If trucks fail to show up at the loading dock because of equipment breakdowns, traffic managers go after the freight company, not the manufacturer of the vehicles.

Services are Less Standardized, Involve More Buyer Participation

Less standardization exists in the services arena. The quality of any service activity varies from provider to provider and from day to day. A can of Bumble Bee brand tuna fish is the same no matter when or where it is purchased, but haircuts by two different barbers may vary greatly. Although the flight from Atlanta, Georgia, to Columbus, Ohio, follows the same course, traveling with Delta may differ from the same trip on American. Since people are involved with the performance of services, providers must monitor the quality of their activities on a continuing basis. Most airlines point out the card ". . . in the seat pocket in front of you" for comments on in-flight service. Car rental companies and hotels ask for customers to report on the personnel, the equipment, or the accommodations.

The purchaser also has the opportunity to **participate** in the production of a service. The doctor and the accountant need information from the patient or client. If the car owner does not explain what needs attention, the mechanic has no starting point. Sometimes buyers assist in specifying how the service will be conducted. When contracting for lawn care, the homeowner often describes what needs to be done and how. The bride and groom select the wedding music to suit their own tastes.

The Ownership of Services Does Not Transfer

The **ownership of services cannot be transferred.** When a customer has a pair of scissors sharpened, the sharpening equipment used does not become the property of the buyer. The air traveler does not own the seat on the airplane. Tourists who use beds in Ramada Inns cannot claim rights to the mattress and bedding. The benefit of getting the lawn mower sharpened may last for a while. The buyer may receive lasting value, but the service itself does not go on. Ownership of the tools for providing the service remains with the seller.

■ ■ ■ ■ ■
Characteristics of goods vs. services

TRAIT	GOOD	SERVICE
Physical attributes	Tangible	Intangible
Production	Prior to use	During consumption
Storage	Exhibits varying shelf life	Perishable
Standardization	Usually the same	Rarely the same
Buyer participation	Seldom	Regularly
Ownership	Transfers to buyer	No transfer

■ ■ ■ ■ ■

How are Consumer Goods Categorized?

Generally, consumer goods are categorized by their availability and the reasons why they are purchased. Typically, the physical products consumers purchase are classified as convenience, shopping and specialty goods. Although their characteristics are different, some customers may place a given product in a different category than other buyers. Consumer needs and wants vary greatly, and how one buyer pictures an item might be quite different from another's viewpoint of the same product.

CONVENIENCE GOODS

Convenience good— frequently purchased item that requires little effort by the consumer.

Convenience goods are frequently purchased items that require little effort on the part of the buyer. Typically these goods are widely distributed staples bought through retail stores that offer self-service. These outlets carry a large variety of competing brands of convenience goods. Snack foods and soft drinks, pantyhose and popcorn, paper towels and paperback books are found in many stores and shops. Even the silent retailers, vending machines, handle many of these goods.

Convenience goods are most often nondurable and low priced. Brand name is important to the consumers of these products. In spite of similarities, most buyers assume different brands have different qualities. Promotion of convenience goods is primarily the responsibility of the manufacturer. While brand loyalty is important to buyers of these items, it may not be very deep. Marketers are counting on purchasers to be swayed by the advertising messages and try something different. RJR Nabisco, for example, has done an exceptional job in promoting Oreo cookies. Today, one out of every ten cookies sold in the United States is an Oreo.

One out of every ten cookies purchased in the United States is an Oreo from Nabisco.

SHOPPING GOODS

Consumers compare both competing products and stores when purchasing **shopping goods.** Contrasted with convenience goods, distribution for shopping goods is more selective. Buyers take more time in making their decisions, and the service offered by retailers is usually important when selecting these products. Shopping goods are usually more expensive than convenience goods. Price is a key factor in the buying decision, and a greater range of prices may be available for similar items. Stores may offer Sunbeam, Black & Decker, Proctor Silex and West Bend steam irons, but the prices for each may vary.

In addition to price, physical characteristics of the product, including style and quality, influence the consumer's buying decision. More risk is attached to the purchase, adding greater anxiety to the buying decision. Many shopping goods last longer, falling into the durable goods category. Manufacturers advertise these consumer products, but retailers provide much of the promotional effort. Clothing, small and large appliances, furniture and automobiles are examples of shopping goods.

The electronics explosion illustrates the purchasing patterns common to shopping goods. Personal computers are now available through department stores, warehouse clubs, specialty office equipment outlets and mail-order houses. Whereas one used to shop for television sets at appliance dealers, a wide variety of retailers now vie for the consumer's business. Although one may receive a greater degree of in-store assistance when buying from specialty retailers such as Radio Shack and Circuit City, CostCo and Wal-Mart often have much lower prices. Buyers of shopping goods are interested in both good service and low prices.[2]

Shopping good— a good that requires the comparison of competing products and stores.

SPECIALTY GOODS

Specialty goods include items that are less widely distributed than either convenience or shopping goods. Many grocery stores carry fresh produce. Few handle organically grown fruits and vegetables. Various retailers sell glassware, but only a handful carry Orrefors or Baccarat crystal. As the name implies, specialty goods are special in the buyer's eyes. Buyers may be unwilling to accept substitutes and travel a considerable distance to find the selected retailer.

Although specialty goods are usually more expensive than convenience or shopping items, price is seldom a factor. Similar to convenience goods, branding is important for these items. However, unlike the fickle convenience goods buyers, those who seek specialty goods frequently exhibit strong brand loyalty. Since the market itself is smaller, widespread promotion of specialty goods would not be efficient. Advertising is usually directed toward preferred audiences, using select media, such as direct mail or magazines. Cartier watches, Wedgwood china, Ferrari automobiles, Clos Du Vol wine, and Godiva chocolates are a few examples of specialty goods.

Specialty good— a unique, and narrowly distributed, item that takes special effort to locate.

---

[2]Doug Stewart, "Comparison shoppers," *Inc./Technology Guide*, Winter 1994, pp. 22–28.

Characteristics of consumer goods

		TYPE OF GOODS	
CHARACTERISTIC	CONVENIENCE	SHOPPING	SPECIALTY
Distribution	Wide	Less Wide	Narrow
In-store service	Self-serve	Heavy assistance	Light to heavy assistance
Durability	Non-durable	Durable	Durable
Branding	Important	Not important	Important
Brand loyalty	High	Low	High
Promotion	Mostly by manufacturer	By both manufacturer and retailer	Mostly by manufacturer
Price	Not important	Important	Not so important

■ ■ ■ ■ ■

CONSUMERS DETERMINE
ULTIMATE CATEGORY

Although it is easy to categorize merchandise according to the above descriptions, the consumer is the one who makes the ultimate classification. Fierce brand loyalty may turn what would ordinarily be a convenience or shopping good into a specialty item. If the buyer prefers Haagen-Dazs ice cream or Jojoba shampoo, these normal convenience items become specialty goods.

Loyal buyers will not consider substitutes if one store is out of the preferred brand. To the beginning angler, the purchase of a fly rod may mean going from shop to shop talking to salespeople. When enough information is available, he or she makes a satisfying decision. A dedicated flyfisher may buy only a Fenwick rod. This shopping good becomes a specialty good.

ow Are Consumer Services Classified?

Services are categorized differently than goods. Some services require tools or equipment to provide satisfaction. Others are more people oriented. In most cases, the buyer travels to the seller's place of business, although there are some services which go "on the road."

EQUIPMENT BASED

Equipment based services—those services provided primarily through the use of equipment.

Many consumer services are **equipment based.** Machinery or mechanical apparatus is necessary to provide satisfaction. People cannot take train rides without a train. A consumer cannot have a suit pressed or a car washed if the service provider does not have the proper equipment. Even accountants and the medical profession require tools to practice their trade.

A service that uses physical apparatus does not escape the need for people. The equipment used is worthless without people to run it. Buyers may participate. The customer at a self-service car wash provides a portion of the work. Some service operators may be semi-skilled, such as those who clean carpeting in the home. Others are highly trained or educated, such as airline pilots, accountants or nurses.

PEOPLE BASED

Some services are **people based.** Professionals, although they might use various types of equipment, fall into this category. Dentists use drills, attorneys rely upon law libraries and accountants need pencils, forms and computers. With these services, the work is carried out by the person, not by the tool. The janitorial service uses a variety of equipment, but people do the greater portion of the work.

People based services—those services provided primarily through the talents of people.

Whether the service is performed primarily by equipment or by people, different levels of skill are apparent. Airlines and automatic car washes are equipment oriented services. Few would argue that it takes more skill to fly an airplane than it does to operate a car wash. Similarly, guard duty and plumbing are activities performed primarily by people. Although the security patrol needs a certain degree of training and expertise, the plumber is usually seen as being more skilled.

Professional services are delivered by trained and educated people. Doctors and lawyers, economists and consultants are highly skilled in their work. Similarly, photographers, air traffic controllers and X-ray technicians need to have a high level of experience and knowledge to perform their tasks well. The level of skill involved in the performance of the service usually dictates the price that the buyer will pay.

AT THE SELLER'S OR BUYER'S PLACE

Services are also categorized by where they are used. Many are provided at the **seller's place.** Doctors rarely make house calls anymore. United Airlines does not pick up passengers at their homes, nor does the body shop bring its equipment to the location of the mangled car. These services typically occur at locations chosen by the seller. Services carried out at the seller's place of business are usually equipment dominated. Often, the facilities needed to provide the benefit are immovable, such as hotels, hospitals or health clubs. Also, the equipment itself may be too expensive or fragile to risk movement.

Some service providers work at the **buyer's place.** The U.S. Postal Service delivers mail to the home or place of business. The plumber and the gardener will travel to the location where needed. Towing companies pick up stalled vehicles wherever they are. Most of the service suppliers that travel to the buyer's location are people oriented rather than equipment dominated. Although businesses such as landscapers, electricians and carpet cleaners do use equipment, they are classified as people dominated.

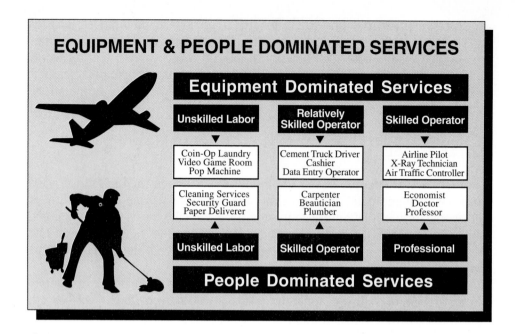

EQUIPMENT & PEOPLE DOMINATED SERVICES

Equipment Dominated Services

Unskilled Labor	Relatively Skilled Operator	Skilled Operator
Coin-Op Laundry Video Game Room Pop Machine	Cement Truck Driver Cashier Data Entry Operator	Airline Pilot X-Ray Technician Air Traffic Controller
Cleaning Services Security Guard Paper Deliverer	Carpenter Beautician Plumber	Economist Doctor Professor
Unskilled Labor	Skilled Operator	Professional

People Dominated Services

On Neutral Ground

Some services are available in places where neither the seller nor buyer locate. One of the more visual of these intangibles offered today is consumer credit. Visa, MasterCard and Discover offer the use of their buying services in thousands of outlets all over the world. The actual activity is carried out at locations away from where the transaction occurs. Many credit cards are now offered by firms other than banks, such as AT&T and General Motors. Both buyer and seller benefit from this service. A number of service providers operate in all three arenas. Insurance agents may sell protection policies by calling at the home or business of the insured. Much of the processing of the forms and transmission of paperwork is done at the office of the seller. On the other hand, in the case of a claim, the insurance person is often found at the scene of the accident.[3]

How Do Consumers Decide What to Buy?

A variety of factors trigger each individual buying decision. Sometimes the judgment is based upon a critical need. At other times it is simply a preference for a particular brand that causes the purchase. On still other occasions the consumer buys purely on impulse. Whatever affects the final determination, buyers follow a standard process for selecting the goods or services that satisfy needs.

---

[3]Terry Lefton, "Real universal card on line, topping tele-giants," *BRANDWEEK*, November 9, 1992, pp. 1 and 6; Terry Lefton, "New plastic alliances will follow court decision," *BRANDWEEK*, November 9, 1992, p. 3.

THE CONSUMER BUYING
DECISION PROCESS

The usual purpose behind any purchase decision is the satisfaction of need or want. Sometimes these needs are evident, other times they are not. That initial step toward a satisfactory purchase begins with the understanding that something is needed.

Need Realization

This realization of needs or wants is the first step in this buying process. Need occurs when the consumer lacks something that has usefulness or value. When the shoelace breaks or the floppy disk is full, it is easy to understand that something must be purchased. Otherwise, the shoe or the computer might not be usable. Needs are not always this evident.

The routine stocking of the refrigerator or the replacement of worn out clothes can satisfy a need. Perhaps there is neither milk for the morning bowl of cereal nor a top that goes with the skirt or shorts. The smell of pizza might trigger a need to satisfy hunger, and a stalled engine may signify time to get a tune-up. In either of these cases, the person becomes aware that something must be purchased to do away with the anxiety of not having. As these needs arise, consumers take steps to purchase those products necessary for satisfaction.

Search for and Evaluation of Alternatives

Once a need is realized, consumers typically go through a pattern of search and evaluation. When there is no immediate rush, a list or mental note may be made for the next trip to the store. If timing is crucial, a special trip might be in order. Shopping goods may call for a different buying pattern than convenience goods. Before deciding to buy a television set, one usually makes at least a brief search to check out special sales or gather information. When the TV picture tube blows out on the day before the Olympics, the decision to buy becomes more urgent.

Any trauma associated with making a decision is usually the result of perceived risk. If there is risk involved with the buying decision, perhaps because of the high price of the purchase or a lack of knowledge about the product, the finality of the decision may become intense. Usually, higher priced items create more concern. So do those buying decisions where the consumer must carry out a detailed search for the right good or service.

Looking for alternatives may be entirely a mental exercise. A given brand that was successful in the past and is known to satisfy the need can be an easy choice. On the other hand, present information may override past experience. Recent media advertising can influence a buyer. Sometimes the cold soft drink just advertised seems sure to be the perfect thirst quencher even if it is not the usual choice.

At other times, finding suitable solutions for satisfying the need may take more effort. Reading manuals or reports, talking to salespeople, or consulting with friends or relatives can become part of the evaluation process. Alternative solutions may be ignored or overlooked for many reasons. Buyers may be busy, or impatient, or maybe prejudiced against certain products. An unwillingness to frequent a certain part of town or to drive on the freeways may reduce the number of choices available. In addition, consumers may not consider products that they have not tried before.

Make Purchase

Once the search is over and an evaluation made, consumers then **decide to buy.** The decision regarding what product to buy often includes the place to buy it, especially with shopping goods. Whether the actual purchase involves satisfying a spontaneous whim or the filling of a longtime desire, the purchase may bring a feeling akin to euphoria. On the other hand, if funds are scarce, the occasion is unpleasant; or if the purchase is too expensive, the feeling could be very different. Depression, guilt or unhappiness sometimes follow purchase decisions.

In selecting the product and retailer, consumers may keep second or third choices handy in case the favored selection is not available. A grocery shopper may prefer Sanka brand instant coffee, but may take a substitute if the supermarket is having a sale on Taster's Choice. A motorist who usually frequents one parking lot may have to drive to another if the original choice is full.

With shopping goods, the decision may be based upon the type of retailer where the item may be purchased or by other outside factors. For instance, many women traditionally bought upper-end cosmetics at department stores. Today, similar quality merchandise is available at considerable savings from Rite-Aid, Long's Drugs or even Wal-Mart. In fact, distribution for the entire cosmetics industry is changing, for both women and men, with the addition of such exotics as essential oils and scents. Aromatherapy reportedly makes one feel good inside while smelling good on the outside.[4]

Postpurchase Evaluation

The final step in the consumer decision-making process is the evaluation that takes place after the product is purchased. Postpurchase evaluation is the conscious or subconscious process of determining the satisfaction gained from the buying pattern. Whether aware or not, all consumers will evaluate the worth of the buying decision, and this information then becomes the basis for making future decisions. Additional input regarding the goods or services bought may come up after the purchase has been made. Outside influences that were not available earlier may now color the buyer's thinking. A comment from family or friends about the florist or pizza parlor can alter the purchase evaluation.

Cognitive dissonance—the sometimes subliminal feeling, akin to "buyers remorse," felt by consumers after making a significant purchase.

Buyers often wonder if they have made the right choice. This syndrome is called **cognitive dissonance.** This phenomenon is not limited to bad purchases. The feeling of concern may simply be the aftermath of making a "risky" choice of products. Is the color or fit just right, or will it really last? Perhaps another item or a different store might have produced better results. Consumers may harbor doubts about the purchase made. Cognitive dissonance breeds **buyer's remorse.**

---

[4]Pam Weisz, "More than a cosmetic makeover," February 21, 1994, pp. 18–24; Pam Weisz, "New adventures in the skin trade," *BRANDWEEK*, April 4, 1994, p. 9.

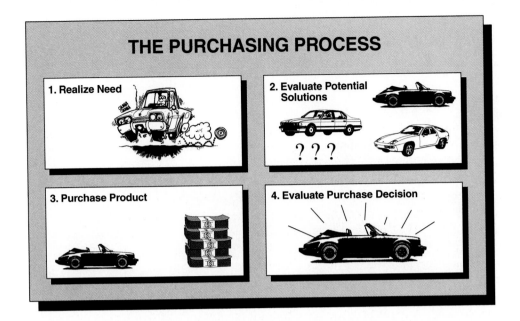

THE PURCHASING PROCESS

1. Realize Need

2. Evaluate Potential Solutions

? ? ?

3. Purchase Product

4. Evaluate Purchase Decision

When strong enough, this feeling that the purchase was a mistake can lead to hesitancy in making future buys. Consumers may feel that the risk of making a wrong decision is very great if they have been "stung" in past buying situations. The unwillingness to make another purchase mistake may lead to a more thorough search in the future. Cognitive dissonance becomes more acute as the price of the product increases.

What Influences the Consumer Buying Decision?

Although the actual process of making a decision to buy something may appear to be simple, several factors affect the purchase. Internal traits of an individual and external influences impact the decision to select one product over another. All consumer buying decisions respond to these personal and social factors.

Buyers react to both **internal and external stimuli** in making decisions. The stimulus might be physical, such as a growling of the stomach signaling the need for food. It could also be emotional, such as a desire to feel appreciated. External forces, such as a picture of a mouth-watering morsel or the aroma wafting from a bakery, can trigger hunger.

MASLOW'S HIERARCHY OF NEEDS

Psychologist A. H. Maslow developed a theory that human needs could be described in a hierarchical manner. Maslow's five-tiered description of needs starts with the basic physiological requirements of food and drink. His description of needs progresses through the stages of safety, belonging and esteem, to

Global Marketing: Innkeeper to the World.

Perhaps no name is more familiar to American travelers than Holiday Inn. The green and white signs of the roadside motels spelled relief for tired and hungry tourists or business people. The chain has expanded over the years to include upscale Crowne Plaza hotels and the Holiday Inn Garden Court. Many of the country's favorite vacationlands are now dotted with Holiday Inn resorts under the SunSpree banner, many of which include golf courses and tennis facilities.

(Courtesy of Holiday Inns Worldwide)

One of the characteristics about Holiday Inns that many Americans are not familiar with is the fact that the Inns are no longer American. The company, originally named after a Bing Crosby movie title, was purchased in 1990 by Bass PLC, a British conglomerate known mainly for its ale. The firm is now named Holiday Inn Worldwide and is headquartered in Atlanta. Even the familiar green sign is undergoing change, as the new ownership works on a different marketing emphasis.

One of the first things that Bass set out to accomplish was a greater global presence. Although Holiday Inn had always been a worldwide chain, most of the marketing effort was directed toward the domestic market. Now, under the leadership of Bass, the theme line "Stay with someone you know" is translated into dozens of languages throughout the world. Europe is a key target market, where the company hopes to change travelers' resting habits from city center to highway locations.

SOURCE: Greg Foster, "Innkeeper to the world," *BRANDWEEK*, November 9, 1992, pp. 15–19.

reach the final stage of self-actualization. Many marketers relate Maslow's theory with consumer drives.

Why each person responds to a stimulus is unknown. Physical needs create drives that require somewhat urgent decisions. One cannot comfortably exist without food or shelter. A very hungry person cares little about the particular form that food takes. To a homeless person, an abandoned shed, or even a large cardboard carton, is better than a park bench or alley. The lower level of Maslow's hierarchy provides markets for many convenience goods, but the social needs of consumers also create marketing opportunities.

PERCEPTION

The consumer's **perception** of the product influences the ultimate decision of what to buy. The manner in which an individual interprets stimuli affects the image of the product. This impression or mental image of a good or service may govern a person's buying habits. Different consumers react to projected images differently. Waterford, the classy Irish crystal house, had to wrestle with a difficult decision because economic hard times dictated the need for machine-made products from Germany. This conflicted with the handcrafted image that the company once enjoyed. The big question is whether consumers will accept this new image.[5]

Similarly, the image of Breck shampoo has been made over by Dial Corporation., its new parent company. Gone are the likes of Kim Bassinger, Brooke Shields and Cybill Shepherd. The Breck girl is a thing of the past. The latest Breck bottles and ads offer a classier, more upscale image. Dial has also reformulated this old standard to compete head on with Procter & Gamble and Helene Curtis for the premium shampoo market. The company is banking on this repositioning of Breck to change consumer perceptions.[6]

Perception— an individual's manner of interpreting stimuli.

PERSONAL INFLUENCES

The **personal factors** which influence consumer buying behavior revolve around a person's attitudes and determines why one individual may favor one specific brand while another person makes an entirely different choice. Attitudes are often based upon beliefs, but may be modified through learning experiences. Although these personal influences play a major role in what and how people buy, the final decision may be based upon a combination of internal and external stimuli.

Personal factors affecting consumer behavior—attitudes, governed by one's beliefs and learning.

Attitudes

Attitudes are personal factors that often cause shifts in consumer behavior. Described as the way one feels about things, a consumer attitude translates into a like or dislike for certain products. One's positive or negative feelings about goods or services may be the result of a deep seated belief. Attitudes are also subject to change based upon learning experiences. Consumer attitudes can be shaped by several forces, reflecting favorable or unfavorable reactions to products or retailers. Consumer attitudes can be changed, but the task is not an easy one.

Attitude—the like or dislike of a product.

---

[5]Frederick Studemann, "Mixed fortunes at Waterford," *International Management,* May 1993, p. 34; Mark Maremont, Mark Landler, and Stewart Toy, "Has Waterford set loose a bull in its shop?" *Business Week,* November 5, 1990, p. 58.

[6]Pauline Yoshihashi, "Reviving Breck: New bottles no girls," *The Wall Street Journal,"* April 6, 1992, p. 4; Pat Sloan, Bradley Johnson, "Dial's personal-care push opens with?" *Advertising Age,* April 6, 1992, pp. 3 and 41; Carrie Goerne, "Dial repositions Breck as a premium brand," *Marketing News,* May 11, 1992, p. 6.

Beliefs

Belief—an opinion, impression or concept that an individual accepts as being true.

Beliefs have a major effect on attitudes. A belief is an opinion, impression or concept that an individual accepts as true. Beliefs may be developed during the growing years or later in life. Parental influence plays a major role in how one feels about goods or services. With the receipt of new input, beliefs may change. Added knowledge gained from information or exposure to different viewpoints may affect an original belief.

Individuals raised in households where Ford automobiles were considered inferior might develop a negative buying attitude toward those cars and their dealers. If *Motor Trend* magazine votes a Ford model as "car of the year" or friends laud the performance of the new Explorer, these attitudes may change. The additional information overcomes an original belief.

Attitudes may change through the **learning** process. The likes or dislikes of consumers can be altered by experience or by outside forces. These factors may cause a change in buying behavior. The anti-Ford person who rides in the Explorer in a car pool may learn to modify his feeling about that brand of car. The purist who refuses to drink instant coffee may develop a taste for that drink after tasting it at a friend's house. Learning occurs by chance or on purpose.

Conditioned Learning

Conditioned learning—repeated experiences that affect one's attitudes either positively or negatively.

Many buying patterns displayed by consumers are the result of learned behavior. Repeated experiences which affect or alter one's attitudes is described as **conditioned learning**. The results often are influenced by a reward or penalty

■   ■   ■   ■   ■

Conditioned vs. cognitive learning

BUYING EVENT	TYPE OF LEARNING
Ran out of cold cereal and remembered having a new sugar free, healthful brand while visiting Aunt Tillie	Conditioned if you tried the cereal and enjoyed it; cognitive if you read the labels on cereal boxes to see which were most nutritious
Winter came early and you realized that your old coat was not going to make it through another season	Probably conditioned, because you tried on numerous models at a variety of stores
Having just been chosen as member of the cross-country ski team, you realize that your equipment needs upgrading	Cognitive as you collected info from a variety of sources, both through team members, manuals and journals, and from in-store personnel
Facing your second year at college, the weight of composing essays and writing term papers causes you to consider the purchase of your own computer	Cognitive because you collected information from professors, classmates, computer lab people and through computer magazines
After a strenuous afternoon of mountain biking, you stop at the convenience store on the way home for something cool and refreshing	Conditioned, because you tried it before and found it the best thirst quencher

■   ■   ■   ■   ■

received from a previous decision. Finding that one product is more tasteful or beneficial than another may alter brand preference. This new buying habit could change again and again. Often an outside influence, such as advertising or referral by family or friends, initiates shifts in buying patterns.

Marketers promote convenience goods heavily to maintain or change these buying patterns. The attitudes developed by consumers may be fickle, especially for convenience goods. Marketers strive to keep their consumers loyal while at the same time trying to convince new prospects to switch brands. Advertising, coupons, free samples and a host of other promotions tempt attitude change. Since convenience goods are generally low in price, the consumer takes little risk in trying a new brand. Once switched, the consumer usually develops different attitudes. Conditioned learning maintains the new buying habit.

A study conducted by the Promotion Marketing Association of America in 1990 found that the success of the promotion depended on many factors. Typically, older, more educated and affluent buyers were most affected by sales enhancers such as coupons, contests and rebates. The least effective merchandising tool appeared to be sweepstakes. Good promotion often overcomes entrenched brand loyalty.[7]

Cognitive Learning

Other learning may be the result of thinking, or the understanding gained through the accumulation of knowledge. **Cognitive learning** is the conscious effort to gain information about products. Buyers give little thought to simple decisions when buying convenience goods. On the other hand, the purchase of shopping or specialty goods often requires the collection of information about the comparative values of competitive products.

Cognitive learning— conscious effort to gain knowledge about products that affects one's attitudes.

Retailers play a major role in the cognitive process of consumers looking for shopping goods. By explaining the relative merits of the brand of VCR, the television and stereo dealer educates buyers. This information may alter the consumers' attitudes. Similarly, advertisements for specialty goods often include detailed, technical copy. Marketers use descriptive literature to inform prospective buyers. Bausch & Lomb, the marketers of the Interplak electric toothbrush, want to educate consumers before they make a purchase. By providing informative literature and through detailed advertising, Bausch & Lomb impacts cognitive learning, thus influencing the prospect's decision.

SOCIAL FACTORS

Social factors also affect consumer buying decisions. Group associations, family, social status and cultural background shape this behavior. Often these external elements have a greater influence on changing attitudes than learning. As an example, psychologists have proven that in group situations, people are apt to compromise their judgment. The urge to follow the crowd overcomes principle. The desire to be accepted as a member of an association is powerful.

Social factors affecting consumer behavior— reference groups, family, social status and culture.

---

[7]Murray Raphel, "What do customers want?" *Direct Marketing*, June 1994, pp. 22–23; Editors, "Study: Some promotions change consumer behavior," *Marketing News*, October 15, 1990, p. 12.

"It doesn't get any better than this."®

For many consumer goods houses, the target market is clear, as illustrated by the ad for Old Milwaukee beer. (Courtesy of The Stroh Brewing Company)

Reference Groups

Influence from **reference groups** is perhaps the most crucial environmental factor influencing consumer behavior. Most people are members of groups, whether in the communities where they live, the companies where they work, or the churches or schools they attend. These groups can be either organized or informal associations. Because of the buyer's membership in a group or association, he or she may make purchases based on what other members are buying. Most peer pressure is by inference.

Not all reference groups are those to which people belong. Buying habits are also influenced by the groups consumers would like to join. This is the essence of positioning. American Express ads typically feature celebrities or other successful people. Poor people have little use for and can ill afford credit cards. If consumers aspire to be members of a particular crowd, they often buy the products used by this group. This association occurs whether the person is an actual member or not. For the young person on the way up the corporate ladder, an important goal could be owning an American Express card.

Reference groups usually develop designated or accepted **opinion leaders.** These people are the ones whose decisions influence other members of the group. As these leaders' choices of goods or services become evident to other members, they often follow suit. These influences may also affect people outside the group.

Reference groups— the formal or informal associations to which consumers belong or wish to belong.

Opinion leaders—the people whose decisions influence other members of the group.

Family

Family, either by birth or by marriage, is another social factor influencing consumer behavior. Buying patterns develop while people grow up with parents or other parental figures. Young adults frequently continue to use the same toothpaste or brand of cereal after leaving the "nest." When people marry, they frequently purchase different brands than they used while single. He used to brush with Crest while she favored Close-Up. Together they choose Aim.

In the United States, the high incidence of divorce increases the possibility for change in buying habits. These splits affect all parts of the family. Hallmark's "To Kids With Love" line of greeting cards tries to boost the morale of children caught in the middle of separation. Because of change in income status that often occurs with divorce, many households select new brands or types of products after a breakup. If the divorced person remarries, a new pattern of buying habits surfaces. As this new family grows, the learned attitudes from each partner affect the buying patterns of the other.

Individual family members make some purchases. Other purchases are made jointly. The changing roles of family members alter buying habits. The increased income producing role of women and greater participation of male members in household management create different purchase patterns. More men are active with cooking and are participating more as food shoppers. Therefore, males are grocery shopping in greater numbers, a role typically reserved for women.

On the other hand, females are more involved in buying decisions that were traditionally male dominated. Buying a car is no longer the sole domain of men. More than 35 percent of all automobiles sold in the United States are purchased by women, and an increasing amount of the grocery shopping is

Family—relations by birth or marriage who influence buying decisions.

done by males. The changing roles of men have fashioned new images of them in advertising. Increasingly, advertisers are dumping the macho look in favor of sensitive, nurturing portrayals. Pictures and scenes of young fathers with babies are especially effective.[8]

Social Status

Social status—groups of people viewed by others as approximately equal in rank, wealth or power.

Social status is another social influence that impacts consumer buying behavior. A social class is a group of people viewed by others as being approximately equal in rank, wealth or power. Many factors affect social status. These include source of income, education, family background, political clout or religious position. Members of a particular level or class often share similar interests, values and activities. Terms such as lower-upper, upper-middle, and lower-lower commonly describe the various socio-economic levels. Claritas Inc., an Alexandria, Virginia, research firm, has identified sixty-two distinct classes, each with its own standards.[9]

The social status of a consumer often affects what and where goods and services are bought. Buying habits for certain products may be traceable to social levels. Other consumer decisions are the direct result of the amount of

SOCIAL STATUS LEVELS

Upper-upper Old line families with inherited wealth; socially active; expensive tastes; usually highly educated (less than 1% of US population)

Lower-upper New rich from successful business or professional experience; conspicuous consumption; moderate education (2% of US population)

Upper-middle Doctors, attorneys, educators, and managers; purchasers of "big ticket" items; highly educated (12% of US population)

Lower-middle "Do-it-yourselfers"; white and gray collar workers and skilled craftspersons; many two-income families; careful buyers (30% of US population)

Upper-lower Blue collar workers with moderate education; high brand loyalty but low priced taste (35% of US population)

Lower-lower Poorly educated, often unemployed, unskilled labor; buying pattern dictated by available funds (20% of US population)

---

[8]Laura Zinn, "Real men buy paper towels, too," *Business Week,* November 9, 1992, pp. 75–76; Zachary Schiller, Mark Landler, and Julia Flynn Siler, "Sex still sells—but so does sensitivity," *Business Week,* March 18, 1991, p. 100.

[9]Kenneth Labich, "Class in America," *Fortune,* February 7, 1994, pp. 114–126.

disposable income available. People from all levels may share common tastes for corn flakes or dill pickles, but discretionary income dictates purchases of designer clothes or Caribbean cruises. Yet social status is losing some of its significance. In today's market driven economy, increasing one's social status is difficult if not impossible without sacrificing time. Numbers of aspiring young people are beginning to forgo the materialistic pleasures associated with status in favor of more time to spend with family and friends.

THE GROWING AFFLUENT MARKET Perhaps fueled by the aging baby boomers, the 1990s have experienced an increase in spending on luxury items. Long held in the doldrums, affluent consumers began opening their wallets and purses in the early part of the decade and have not slowed down yet. Sales of luxury automobiles, luggage, imported champagne, travel and jewelry have climbed steadily as the number of households in the $100,000 class rose by almost 50 percent since 1988.[10]

Culture

The last defined social factor affecting consumer behavior is **culture.** Culture includes the laws, customs, traditions, mores and moral codes of any group of people. Peoples from many countries, ethnic backgrounds and cultures populate the United States. This country is often viewed as having no culture of its own. In reality, true American culture flourishes and is the combination of its varied parts.

> **Culture**—the laws, customs, traditions, mores or moral codes of a group of people, often ethnic in nature.

The mixed cultural background of our society produces a multitude of customs. In addition, some of our traditions are uniquely American. Turkey at Thanksgiving and fireworks on the Fourth of July originated here. Baseball and modern jazz were born in the United States. Mother's Day is predominantly an American custom.

Subcultures

Cultures from many countries have created pockets of common activity within their communities known as **subcultures.** Not all Chinese living in our society speak the same dialect. The black community has numerous groups within the whole that practice distinct customs or follow specific traditions. The dialect and habits of natives of New York City are very different from those found in New Orleans.

> **Subculture**—a group within a culture that displays distinctive buying behavior.

The cultural makeup of America continues to diversify. Many economists and sociologists expect 50 percent of the U.S. population to be of African, Hispanic or Asian background by the middle of the next century. These subcultures typically show different habits and buying behavior, opening new opportunities for marketing and marketers. Many major consumer products companies already promote products specifically tailored to meet ethnic or cultural tastes.[11]

---

[10]Elaine Underwood, "Luxury's tide turns," *BRANDWEEK*, March 7, 1994, pp. 18–22 and 30.

[11]Steve Rabin, "How to sell across cultures," *American Demographics*, March 1994, pp. 56–57.

Marketing and Society: That's the Esprit!

Many businesses and business people shun political connections. The fear of offending even a small segment of their market means that most firms keep their opinions and preferences confined within the corporate walls. Although top management at some companies contribute to certain campaign funds, such activity is usually done without fanfare or publicity. After all, why take a chance of offending a potential customer, right?

"Wrong," says Susie Tompkins. Never a shy one, the founder and present driving force behind Esprit de Corp has often put causes ahead of fashion. During the 1980s, Esprit was one of the brightest lights of the world of women's clothing. Despite some bitter public battles with her former husband, Tompkins is back at the helm leading Esprit on its comeback. She is pinning the company's future on targeting the older, more mature audience.

Perhaps redirecting the company's image to target a more adult market will help it reach the sales performance it once knew. However, will this new segment be as tolerant of Tompkins' social forays on behalf of drug abusers, AIDS victims and battered women? Competition for this consumer group is keen. The Gap, The Limited's Express and DKNY have a head start in capturing this lucrative market. Still, industry analysts are betting that Tompkins and Esprit will win their way back, and an aggressive advertising campaign stressing style rather than issues is sure to help.

SOURCES: Elaine Underwood, "Esprit returns to fashion," *BRANDWEEK*, February 22, 1993, p. 4; Cara Appelbaum, "A tight fit," *Adweek's Marketing Week*, March 16, 1992, p. 28; Laura Zinn and Michael Oneal, "Will politically correct sell sweaters?" *Business Week*, March 16, 1992, pp. 60–61. (Courtesy of Esprit)

How Does Consumer Behavior Influence Marketing Management?

Marketers work toward satisfying the needs of customers. To be successful, they must understand how the purchaser behaves. It is impossible to put together the correct marketing mix without knowing what influences the actual purchase. Development and distribution of needed products rely upon knowledge of consumer behavior.

Buyers see a variety of attributes in goods and services. Not all product attributes are necessary or valuable to all consumers. One consumer purchases Ry Krisp because it contains fewer calories than many other snack foods. Meanwhile, Ralston Purina is busily repositioning these crackers, pitching the natural flavor of the rye enhancing the taste treat of various toppings. Using new ads and a redesigned package, the Checkerboard company hopes to win new fans for this perennial favorite.[12]

---

[12]Jon Berry, "Ry Krisps duck their diet image," *Adweek's Marketing Week*, March 4, 1991, p. 9.

PRODUCT ATTRIBUTES VS BUYER NEEDS

Marketers must match product attributes with buyer needs. The quality or satisfaction derived from a good or service must be adapted to the requirements of specific groups of buyers. Knowing how internal and external forces impact these needs is necessary for product design. The selection of which coffee to buy could be primarily impacted by conditioned learning. On the other hand, buying a car may be more likely influenced by family, reference groups, social status and, perhaps, culture. Marketing management must design programs that will get buyers to listen to their promotion or sample the product.

The American automobile industry has gone through just such introspection. Catering to middle-aged baby boomers, Detroit has redesigned and repromoted its products to be more attractive. Chrysler, for example, designed its three LH model cars for distinct groups within the boomer market. Through improved quality, the American manufacturers grabbed an increased share of market, but the Japanese firms are fighting back. Marketing prowess will likely prove to be the key factor in the battle for the automobile market.[13]

Marketing management must control the entire marketing mix. Product design is only one of the factors to consider. Understanding how buyers might react to changes in price, distribution or promotion is also essential. The image of any good or service is reflected in every element of the marketing mix. Marketing management must be aware of the image projected by its company and products. Promotional efforts or product designs at odds with consumer perception seldom succeed.

REPOSITIONING

It seems to be fashionable today for marketers to change the image of their products. This is especially true with goods that became tainted with the growth of the wellness movement. KFC dropped the word "fried" from its name, and offered up a whole new menu of healthier items. Cereal and cracker manufacturers changed to baking and lowered the amounts of fat in their products. Even the California Milk Processors Board has had to rethink the ways that it promotes what "every body" once thought was good.[14]

Even if profitability looks promising, company and product image affects the marketing effort. Honda first entered the American market with a small, economical car that soon gained popularity for its low maintenance and quality. When the firm entered the luxury car field, the company wisely decided to avoid any relationship with the original line, distributing the Acura through independent dealers. This was a management decision.

---

[13]Krystal Miller, "Catering to middle-aged baby boomers, Detroit creates a new generation of cars," *The Wall Street Journal,* March 11, 1994, pp. B1–B5; Larry Armstrong and Hiromi Uchida, "Detroit, check your rearview mirror," *Business Week,* June 6, 1994, pp. 26–27.

[14]Jon Berry, "Repositioning? Forget it. Sales are all that count," *BRANDWEEK,* August 23, 1993, p. 13.

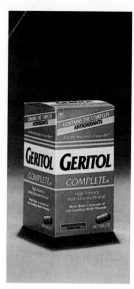

Although it targets the "gray market" with its Geritol products, SmithKline portrays these customers as active and vibrant.

Geritol is one brand that was initially associated with the elderly. During the 1980s, its manufacturer, SmithKline Beecham, reformulated this heavily promoted vitamin supplement, renamed it Geritol Plus, and targeted a younger female audience. This change in positioning was very successful, and the company shed much of its identity with the more mature market. The emergence of this important, older market could not be ignored. Rather than try to reposition an already profitable product, SmithKline created Geritol Extend, positioned to attract an over-fifty clientele. Wisely, the company did not portray this "gray" market as ancient and doddering, but rather as active, animated, and alert. Once again, proper positioning of the product has proven successful.[15]

GLOBAL CONSIDERATIONS

Although the basic buying process for consumers might be similar around the globe, greater emphasis may be placed on need in some societies than others. Many economies do not offer the discretionary income found in most advanced industrialized countries. While some populations may feel the need, they might not have the means to satisfy that need. In many instances, few alternatives are available, making the buying decision rather meager. This is certainly true today in many of the nations that made up the former Soviet Union, where supplies of consumer goods are quite scarce, and often expensive.

In struggling economies, consumer buying decisions are more often based upon social than personal factors. Family and culture weigh heavily, and reference groups as we know them in the U.S. may be nonexistent. Without a broad assortment of merchandise, conditioned and cognitive learning may be less of an influence than what is available for whom.

SUMMING IT UP

Consumer products are physical, tangible goods or intangible services purchased by individuals for their own use or for use in their households. Services now account for a sizable portion of consumer purchases. Services differ from goods in that their production and consumption are inseparable. They are perishable, less standardized than goods and involve more buyer participation. Title to services does not transfer from seller to buyer.

Convenience goods receive wide distribution primarily through self-service outlets. They are generally inexpensive and nondurable, and brand plays an important role. Promotion effort is carried out primarily by the manufacturer of convenience items. Shopping goods are price sensitive, durable items that undergo narrower distribution. With these products, branding is relatively unimportant and the store where the shopping good is purchased is as important as the good itself. The distribution of specialty goods is very narrow, but

---

[15]Cynthia Klaja and Renee Grandchamp Davis as told to Aimee L. Stern, "Geritol Extend goes for the old," *Adweek's Marketing Week*, February 17, 1992, pp. 30–31.

the select stores where they are found often provide a great deal of customer service. Branding is important with specialty goods, and manufacturers are the dominant promoters. Consumer services are categorized as equipment or people based. They can be provided at the seller's or buyer's place, or even on neutral ground.

Consumers go through a routine, systematic purchasing process. After needs are realized, buyers evaluate the alternative solutions that will bring satisfaction. After decisions are made and products bought, consumers conduct a post-purchase evaluation, which may include cognitive dissonance.

The evaluation of products that will satisfy needs is influenced by personal and social factors. The personal influences include beliefs, attitudes and both conditioned and cognitive learning. Reference groups, family, social status and culture are the social factors influencing buying behavior.

Marketing management must adapt to the influences on consumer behavior. The marketing mix is modified according to the personal and social influences on buying habits. Product positioning and ethical considerations impact management decisions.

KEY CONCEPTS AND TERMS FOR CHAPTER SIX

Attitude
Belief
Cognitive dissonance
Cognitive learning
Conditioned learning
Consumer good
Convenience good
Culture
Equipment based services
Family
Opinion leaders

People based services
Perception
Personal factors
Reference groups
Services
Shopping good
Social factors
Social status
Specialty good
Subculture

BUILDING SKILLS

1. Describe how you would categorize the following as either convenience, shopping or specialty goods: jeans, a toaster oven, bulk macaroni, shampoo, mouthwash, Colorado blue spruce seedling, diamond engagement ring, Oriental oyster sauce.

2. Define the factors of shopping goods that would tend to make buyers of these items less brand conscious.

3. Classify the following consumer services: a miniature golf course, a mobile pet grooming service, a horseshoe farrier, an automobile detailing shop, a marketing consultant.

4. Describe the consumer buying process, contrasting it in the purchase of convenience, shopping or specialty goods, or between equipment or people dominated services.

5. Compare the difference between conditioned and cognitive learning, citing examples of products where either might influence a decision to buy.

6. Identify the social factors that might influence the purchase of used automobiles, hamburger from a fast food restaurant, bathing suits, cologne, bathroom tissue, a VCR, camping equipment, ski boots, hair spray.

7. Discuss the repositioning of Oldsmobile, Olive Garden restaurants, Advil, Kellogg cereals.

Making Decisions 6-1: Here Kitty, Kitty.

Cat owners are well aware of the classic, aloof and independent personality most feline creatures display. Roughly 30 percent of American households appreciate these qualities in a pet. Whether purebred or of the alley variety, these pets appear to have a mind of their own that human needs or interests cannot sway. These furry, purry animals are often finicky eaters. Many an owner has discovered this trait while forced to dump a week's worth of food down the drain. Not all cats have the same appetite as Morris.

Keeping cats as indoor pets has spawned the $350 million per year cat litter industry, crowded with seventy-five different brands. No company has taken better advantage of the habits of cats than has Edward Lowe Industries. The company founder is often credited as being the one who created the cat box filler industry. Not all cats have the same tastes, as giant paper marketer Crown Zellerbach learned when the ultimate customer, the feline pet, rejected a waste paper product the company developed for litter boxes. Although it fit the purpose, cats would not use it.

One problem litter marketers faced in trying to please the household cat is the elimination of odor. Since these pets have adapted to city life from an original desert habitat, their urine is especially concentrated and pungent. Lowe found that Fullers earth, a form of crystalline clay, was a great replacement for sand or sawdust. The material has natural deodorant properties coupled with excellent liquid absorption. Many companies add extra ingredients that slow bacterial growth or disinfect.

Clumping products that absorb moisture rapidly, forming readily disposable nuggets, entered the market in 1992. Initial reaction by both cats and owners was favorable. Only time will tell how much of a foothold these items make in a competitive marketplace. Regardless, although the cat does not make the purchase, it certainly affects the decision. Brand loyalty appears to be very important in marketing cat box fillers.[16]

Categorize cat box litter as a consumer good, citing factors of consumer buying behavior that would affect the purchase of this product.

---

[16]J. Kelly, "Cat litter marketers snarl over claim," *Advertising Age,* June 1, 1992, p. 45; Robert McMath, "Cat litter: Myth and reality," *Adweek's Marketing Week,* February 3, 1992, p. 24; Penny Ward Moser, "Filler's the name, odor's the game," *Fortune,* April 25, 1988, pp. 107–118.

Making Decisions 6-2: Answer the Phone!

The breakup of the Bell System in 1984 was at the time the largest move ever made by the Justice Department against American business. The vast holdings of giant AT&T were spun off into seven regional companies, with independent owners and managers. The Baby Bells, as they are called, cover the following areas:

Nynex	New York and New England
Bell Atlantic	Mid-Atlantic states
BellSouth	The Deep South
Ameritech	The Midwest
Southwestern Bell	Texas and surrounding area
USWest	Pacific Northwest and mountain states
Pacific Telesis	California and Nevada

The Baby Bells have struggled since their forced birth. Once out from under the parental umbrella of AT&T, many of these new companies tried to go too many directions too soon. Each of the seven jumped rather quickly into global marketing. Nynex is in Thailand and Bell Atlantic shares New Zealand's telephone system with Ameritech. Southwestern quite naturally does business in Mexico. Pacific Telesis is big in Australia and Britain, while USWest has gone after Eastern Europe and Russia. While these overseas ventures hold promise, most produce a drain on cash.

Mind boggling advances in technology caught many of these adolescent firms unaware. Some of these advances opened the doors to local competition, including subsidiaries of GTE Corporation. Many of Ma Bell's offspring dove into such high-tech fields as computers, cellular phones and cable television. Southwestern Bell even bought an architectural design firm. As these fledgling firms struggle toward adulthood, continued pressure will be brought by the publics served and by stockholders to maintain quality and to produce profits.[17]

Categorize the Baby Bells as services, discussing the expansion of these firms into international arenas, focusing on the potential for success.

Making Decisions 6-3: When Your Ship Comes in . . . Docker.

The products marketed by Levi Strauss & Company are known worldwide. 501s and jeans and Levis for Men are worn by all ages and both sexes. The product lines of this San Francisco based company are constantly expanding. The company, whose founder began stitching together canvas pants for miners and farmers over a century ago, has become the largest apparel manufacturer in the world.

Company size does not always dictate success. As the "baby boomer" generation has matured, fewer are buying jeans. An ill-fated attempt by Levi

---

[17]Katherine Arnst and Gail Edmondson, "The global free-for-all," *Business Week*, September 23, 1994, pp. 118–126; Peter Coy, Robert D. Hof, and James E. Ellis, "The Baby Bells' painful adolescence," *Business Week*, October 5, 1992, pp. 124–134.

to move into suits and sport coats triggered a massive decline in sales and profits in the 1980s. One of the major reasons for the failure of this line was that it did not fit the Levi image. Consumers had positioned Levis as casual, durable clothing. An upscale, traditional product clashed with such positioning.

A solution to this downward trend in sales was necessary. Marketing management found it in a product branded Dockers. This line of pants is a little dressier than jeans, yet maintains that casual Levi image. These cotton trousers offer a looser fit, which suits the more mature buyer just fine. The pants line also offers contemporary styling that pleases younger consumers as well. Dockers are doing so well for Levi Strauss & Co. that if they were marketed by an independent company, the firm would be in the *Fortune 500.*[18]

Describe the factors of consumer buying behavior that might influence the purchase of Dockers, and the ways that Levi Strauss & Co. managed the marketing mix to appeal to these buying behaviors.

---

[18]Elaine Underwood, "Category wars: Levi's unfolds $40 no-iron Dockers push," BRANDWEEK, April 4, 1994, pp. 1 and 6; Bob Garfield, "Levi's for women ads pack powerful punch," *Advertising Age,* August 16, 1993, p. 38; A *New York Times* news release, "Levi takes casual path," *San Jose Mercury News,* June 27, 1989, pp. 4D and 11D.

7

Business Products and Buying Behavior

■ ■ ■ ■ ■ ■ ■ ■ ■ ■ ■ ■ ■ ■

The Job to be Done

Businesses are major buyers of goods and services. These organizations purchase products for different reasons than do consumers. This chapter describes business products and examines the buying behavior of organizations, giving the student access to what is needed to:

- understand the arena of business products, and contrast production goods with trade goods,
- recognize what types of businesses buy accessory equipment and supplies,
- differentiate between business buying from consumer buying,
- describe the characteristics of business buying behavior, and
- analyze the impact of business buying behavior on marketing management.

Jeff Adams

Jeff Adams developed an interest in medicine while serving as a medical corpsman in the military. After serving Uncle Sam, he returned to his Minnesota roots and worked towards an Associate of Applied Science degree in Sales and Marketing. It was at Inver Hills Community College that Jeff first received recognition, earning citations for Outstanding Achievement—Sales and Marketing, a Motivational and Leadership Award and an Outstanding Student Award. There was little doubt in Jeff's mind that he would pursue a career in sales in the medical industry.

He began his career with Zimmer Inc., and soon began to experience the same success that he enjoyed at Inver Hills, being selected as Success Story of 1987 from a field of over 400 salespeople. Jeff was wooed to Biomet, Inc./R. H. Medical, Inc. in 1989, where he remains today as Senior Sales Associate. Biomet is the world's leading manufacturer of reconstructive orthopedic inserts, such as hip, shoulder and knee replacement parts. The firm markets its products through local distributors and sales associates in over 100 countries worldwide.

Orthopedic devices have undergone significant change in the past decade, as has the medical profession. Not only have materials changed, with the inclusion of more exotic metals and plastics, but the industry has undergone mergers and buyouts, becoming highly technical and competitive. Jeff's drive has helped him achieve recognition within his firm and the trade, as well as financial awards. Seeing patients walking or throwing and knowing that his firm's products were involved provides him with all of the personal gratification anyone can need.

What Are Business Products?

Manufacturers, marketing intermediaries, institutions and government agencies are the markets for business products. Each of these types of organizations purchase both goods and services. Although needs may vary, business organizations and nonprofit groups display similar buying patterns and behavior. While the customers are fewer, they typically purchase in very large quantities. Many of the buying firms or organizations are concentrated in specific geographic locations, often in the heavily industrialized states or cities.

BUSINESS GOODS

Business goods— tangible products purchased by businesses from businesses.

Business goods are tangible products purchased by businesses from businesses. These goods differ from consumer goods in that they satisfy the needs of commercial ventures and institutions rather than of households. Manufacturing firms buy the materials and equipment needed for production. Wholesalers and retailers purchase items to be resold to other companies or individuals. Nonbusiness and nonprofit organizations have special needs. All of these organizations also buy products for their own internal use.

Business goods are not sold directly to consumers. The minimum order quantities for these items are usually high. In addition, business buyers require a great degree of training and technical expertise. Marketing intermediaries are

IN THE LOOKALIKE WORLD
OF FINANCIAL SERVICES, ONE STANDS OUT.

Everywhere you look, there's another one.
Another financial network. Another financial service.
Which one's for you?
Look for the one with the long record—at least
120 years of financial success.
The one who has *never* missed a dividend in all
those years.
The one with a solid foundation—over
$40 billion in assets.
The one with the diversity that protects against
adversity.
The one who knows when to fund ventures and
when to buy Treasury notes.
The one who knew how to say "no" when every-
one else was saying "yes." And who knows how to say
"yes" now that some are saying "no."
The one that America's most demanding corpora-
tions count on for pension plans, employee benefits
and risk management.
Look for The Travelers.
One of the most respected financial experts
in the world.
Have you looked under The Travelers
Umbrella lately?

TheTravelersﺝ

The Travelers Companies, Hartford, Connecticut 06183

Travelers offers a variety of insurance packages aimed exclusively at the business market. (Courtesy of The Travelers Corporation)

involved in the distribution of some types of business goods, but others commonly move directly from seller to buyer.

BUSINESS SERVICES

Some services are provided strictly for consumers, some are used exclusively by businesses, and still others are shared. Consumers purchase haircuts, lawn care and dry-cleaning services. Businesses and organizations are heavy users of consultants, engineers, advertising agencies and marketing research firms. Both markets need the services provided by accountants, banks and equipment repair.

Many organizations attempt to perform the necessary services from within the firm or association. Cost savings can take precedence when deciding who is to supply which business services. At times, however, outside agencies can provide the service more economically than internal groups. Sometimes, the expertise of a service provider might exceed the capabilities in-house.

ow Are Business Goods Categorized?

Products required to satisfy business or organization needs are categorized differently than those for consumers. Business goods are typically placed in groupings according to their use. These categories include production goods, trade goods, accessory equipment and operating supplies.

PRODUCTION GOODS

Production goods— business goods used directly or indirectly in the manufacture of other items.

Production goods are those used either directly or indirectly in the manufacture of other items. Some of these products are the ingredients of the finished good being made. Others are the implements or machinery used in the manufacturing process. Materials and supplies used in packing, shipping, maintenance and repair are also production goods, if they are utilized in the manufacturing process.

The potash mixed with silica in the manufacture of glass are ingredients in a finished bottle. The giant bottle blowing machinery used to manufacture these containers are tools, or implements. The storage and mixing bins for the raw materials, the lubricating oils for the machinery and packing cartons for storing and shipping the bottles also qualify as production goods. For clothing, the ingredients might include fabrics, thread and zippers; the sewing machines are production equipment. Each of these products is used directly or indirectly in the manufacture of other goods.

Raw Materials

Raw materials— production goods that are refined or changed in the process of becoming part of a finished good.

Raw materials are production goods that are refined or changed in the process of becoming part of a finished good. Almost all finished goods are made from raw materials that have been processed in some way. A production good that is altered in any way during manufacturing is a raw material. Raw materials form the basis of all manufacturing operations.

For example, the iron ore mined from the earth is a raw material used in the production of steel. Using heat and pressure, the ore becomes a different product. The steel produced from iron ore is also a raw material when it goes through additional manufacturing processes. A stamping process may alter the shape of the original steel to form the seat frame for a bicycle or corrugated roofing.

Component Parts

Some ingredients used in the manufacture of other goods are not raw materials. Premanufactured items that become an integral part of a finished good are

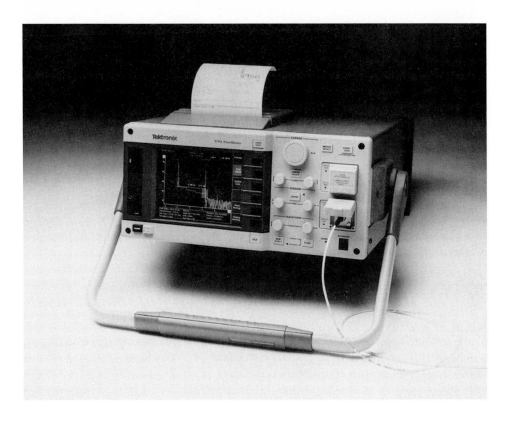

Electronic equipment, such as the FiberMaster from Tektronix, are largely assembled from component parts. (Courtesy of Tektronix)

component parts. These items are not altered, modified or processed during the manufacturing process. Instead they are inserted into and become part of the final product, or finished good.

Component parts— premanufactured items that become part of a finished good.

Automatic transmissions, brake light assemblies and windshields are pre-manufactured component parts that become a part of the finished automobile. The bolts that attach the transmission to the engine, the plastic lens of the brake light and the gasket around the windshield are also component parts. Most of today's machinery, appliances and electronic equipment are assembled from these production goods. Computer hardware, garden equipment and tele-vision sets contain many component parts.

Production Equipment

The machinery and tools used to manufacture products are called **production equipment.** The heavy break presses and gigantic stamping machinery that shape steel into fenders for automobiles or doors for refrigerators fit this description. So do the intricate soldering jigs used in making printed circuit boards for computers. These business goods are used directly in the production process to convert raw materials or component parts into finished goods.

Production equipment— machinery and tools used to manufacture other items.

The sewing machines that make shirts and shorts for Ocean Pacific are production equipment. Ovens for the corner bakery and etching tools used by engravers at Franklin Mint provide the same utility. Lathes that spin table legs for Drexel furniture, and microwelders used in the assembly of hand-held cal-culators for Hewlett-Packard are production equipment.

Production Supplies

Production Supplies

Production supplies— miscellaneous items used indirectly in the production process.

Production supplies are miscellaneous items used indirectly in typical manufacturing processes. This category would include mold releases, lubricating oils and packing materials. Production supplies do not become a part of the finished goods the way raw materials and component parts do, nor are they used as utensils. These products often service or maintain production equipment, and, without them, tools and machinery might not function properly.

The use of production supplies is limited to the manufacturing process. While most organizations expend a number of nondurable products in the course of doing business, only those used in manufacturing are known as production supplies. The silicon mold release used on plastic injection molding machines by Western Electric is a good example. The oil for the sewing machines at Levi Strauss and the shipping crates for Toro lawnmowers are also production supplies.

TRADE GOODS

Trade goods—business goods purchased by marketing intermediaries for resale.

The second major category of goods purchased by business organizations is **trade goods.** These items are sold to the trade, or marketing intermediaries, which in turn resell them to other businesses or individuals. When a manufacturer sells its output to either wholesalers or retailers, the products at the time of transfer fit the definition of business goods. A case of Skippy peanut butter, a truckload of Buick Park Avenues or a gross of Nike sweat socks all qualify as trade goods, sold by one business to another for resale. It is only when individuals purchase these items from the store or dealer that they become consumer goods.

It is not uncommon for trade goods to be altered or modified by the intermediary. Many wholesalers and retailers buy in bulk from manufacturers and repackage the products using their own, individual brand names. Supermarket chains and wholesalers sell goods that are made for those outlets under a private label brand. Some retailers add performance or service warranties to products purchased from manufacturers for resale. This adds a degree of value for the consumer. For example, Computerland customizes hardware systems with software packages to fit the needs of particular customers. Les Schwab offers additional warranties on tires over and above those provided by the manufacturer.

ACCESSORY EQUIPMENT

Accessory equipment—durable goods that are neither used in production nor for resale.

Coffee makers, vehicles, office computers and fork lifts a business or organization purchases are classified as **accessory equipment.** These durable products are not directly or indirectly employed in making other products, nor are they resold to other businesses. Firms buy these items for use in their own facilities. Conveyor belts and forklifts purchased by FedEx are not part of a manufacturing process. The tanks of oxygen and adjustable beds purchased by Cedars-Sinai Hospital do not produce other goods. The U.S. government does not purchase space shuttles for resale.

Client: Steelcase Inc.
Agency: Saatchi & Saatchi DFS/CCG
Product: Context
Comm no: ZSSO0101
Length: 30

Steelcase ®(sm)

The Office Environment Company®

LEAD IN MUSIC.
MALE ANNOUNCER:
Context, by Steelcase.

FLORINDA:
You move the components around like little blocks

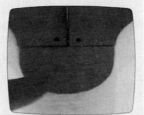

to create an environment.

A traditional panel-based system

is a two dimensional planning concept.

This system invites you to think in the third dimension

and in terms of the functional

requirements of the user.

It's in a world by itself. It's the most complete freestanding furniture system ever. You simply have to see it in the flesh, so to speak.

FADE TO BLACK WITH LOGO AND MUSIC.

Steelcase, one of the world's largest marketers of office furniture, specializes in accessory equipment. (Courtesy of Steelcase, Inc.)

Accessory equipment cannot be confused with production equipment because it is not part of the manufacturing process. Since these types of products are not offered to intermediaries for resale, they also do not qualify as trade goods. The desks in offices at Scovill Manufacturing Company are accessory equipment, as are the corporate aircraft flown by Dow Chemical Co. Chalkboards on the walls at Middlesex Community College are not for resale, nor are the computers and word processors used by the Indiana State Police. These business goods are accessory equipment.

Descriptions of business goods

PRODUCTS	TYPE OF BUSINESS GOOD
ABS Plastic molding powder (production good):	
Acrylonitrile, butadiene, styrene monomers	Raw materials
Catalytic chambers, extruders, exhaust systems	Production equipment
Cartons, gaylords, pallets.	Production supplies
Trash bins, conference tables, employee showers	Accessory equipment
Bathroom supplies, fluorescent tubes, disinfectants	Operating supplies
Computer (accessory equipment):	
Microprocessor chips, plastic for printed circuit board	Raw materials
Cabinet, keyboard, cathode ray tube for monitor	Component parts
Soldering equipment, work station benches	Production equipment
Solder, foam packaging materials	Production supplies
Letterhead, lunchroom supplies, floor wax	Operating supplies
Corn Flakes (trade good):	
Corn flour, wheat flour, sugar, salt	Raw materials
Ovens, conveyor belt, packaging machinery	Production equipment
Lube oil, hot melt adhesives	Production supplies
Office computer, forklift	Accessory equipment
Paper towels, pencils, computer paper	Operating supplies

■   ■   ■   ■   ■

OPERATING SUPPLIES

Operating supplies—
miscellaneous
nondurable supplies
neither used in
production nor offered
for resale.

Operating supplies are the final category of goods sold by one business to another. These nondurable supplies are not used in production nor are they for resale. Commercial ventures and nonprofit organizations alike consume these items in their day-to-day operations. Janitorial and office supplies make up the largest portion of this category.

Operating supplies are nondurable. They do not have an extended shelf life and many are expended during use. Paper towels, coffee cups, paper clips, stationery, bottled water and light bulbs may all be necessary purchases for any organization. Typically, less expensive than other types of business goods, these products are still important in day-to-day operations.

How Does Business Buying Differ from Consumer Buying?

Factors affecting business buying decisions are unlike those that impact individuals. While taste preferences and brand loyalty may influence consumers, other factors affect business buying behavior. Demand for consumer goods varies according to the whims of the buying public. Availability, fashion trends, the time of the year and even weather influence consumer demand. The need for business goods often depends, at least indirectly, on these same factors.

DERIVED DEMAND

Market demand for business goods evolves from market demand for consumer goods, referred to as **derived demand.** This means that the ultimate needs for consumer goods create the demand for products purchased by businesses. To illustrate, the Ford Explorer has become a popular four-wheel-drive vehicle. As individuals demand more of these cars, Ford develops increased need for steel, transmissions, brake assemblies and seats. The seat manufacturer will require more fabric and springs, and the fabric supplier will need additional thread and dyes. All of these transactions grew from the consumer demand for the vehicle.

Derived demand— demand for business goods evolves from and varies directly with demand for consumer goods.

The demand for consumer goods often triggers multiple or joint demand for different business products. As consumers clamor for Dockers, Levi Strauss & Co. requires fabrics, zippers, rivets, packaging materials and a number of other goods purchased from a variety of separate suppliers. As more individuals, schools and businesses buy computers, there is a joint demand created for both hardware and software. Introduction of Intel's Pentium microprocessing chip and commercialization of MicroSoft's operating system Chicago have caused an explosion in the personal computer industry.[1]

Demand in the electronics industry is not limited to the United States. Pacific Rim and European countries clamor for up-to-date hardware and software. Developing nations are also in the hunt for increased internal capability through external supply. As this demand for modernization spreads globally, more and more businesses feel the impact. Needs are not limited by national boundaries.

PROFESSIONAL BUYERS

Business organizations often hire **professional buyers** who have specific education or training in the buying function. Although some consumers claim a degree of skill in buying, the expertise of household shoppers usually cannot match that of business purchasers. The selection of the proper products and suitable suppliers to satisfy business needs requires highly trained personnel.

Professional buyers— purchasing staff having specific education and/or training in buying functions.

The common title for professional buyers is purchasing agent. Small firms may assign buying tasks to an individual who has other duties, such as someone in manufacturing or warehousing. Larger industrial firms usually employ a staff of purchasing experts, with different buyers handling specific items.

MULTIPLE BUYING INFLUENCE

The business buying process often involves more than one person. In many firms, people from other areas within the company decide the products needed and the suppliers to be used. These choices are passed to the purchasing department where the professional buyers complete the actual transaction. This **multiple buying influence** is common in production goods markets.

Multiple buying influence—more than one person making the business goods purchase decision.

---

[1]G. Pasqual Zachary and Jim Carlton, "Software rivals vying to define how PCs work," *The Wall Street Journal,* March 7, 1994, pp. B1 and B8; Jim Carlton and Don Clark, "PC makers to launch machines using new version of Intel's Pentium chip," *The Wall Street Journal,* March 7, 1994, p. B8.

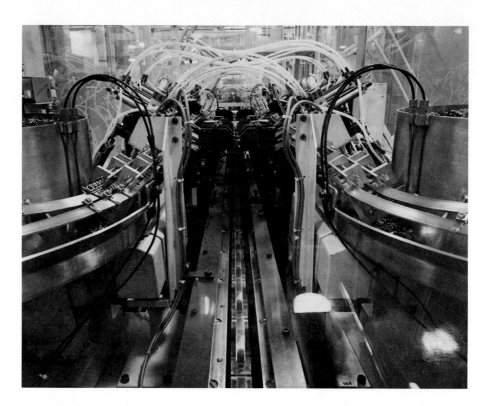

The contact insertion line at Allen-Bradley's World Contactor Automated Assembly Facility is an excellent example of robotics. (Courtesy of Allen-Bradley Co., Inc.)

Many businesses prefer a policy of multiple sourcing, where the purchasing staff buys similar products from a number of different suppliers. Highly technical goods often require more input regarding both needs and product specifications and demand that additional people, outside the buying office, be consulted. Even when a firm relies on a single source, the ultimate decision of what to purchase and from which supplier is often made by committee.

Buying Centers

Buying center— personnel from different functional areas within a company who collectively make purchasing decisions.

Many large business goods users refer to this core of interested parties as the **buying center.** This informal, interdepartmental group feeds information, preferences and specifications to the purchasing department. The professional buyers then place the actual orders with appropriate vendors. These groups are usually small, with four members considered optimal, allowing the needs of each area to be addressed. Buying centers are common in high-tech industries.[2]

Sometimes the initial contact between buyer and seller is through the purchasing department, which then may draw in additional interested parties. On other occasions, the engineering or manufacturing group may be the one to initiate the process. Firms which have successfully integrated buying centers into their operations feel that the better communication between all departments leads to wiser, less costly purchases.

[2]S. Joe Puri, "Industrial vendors' selling center," *Journal of Business and Industrial Marketing,* Summer 1992, pp. 59–69; Robert D. McWilliams, Earl Maumann, and Stan Scott, "Determining buying center size," *Industrial Marketing Management,* February 1992, pp. 43–49.

NEGOTIATED TERMS OF SALE
AND CUSTOMER SPECIFICATIONS

In business buying arenas, **negotiated terms of sale** are common. Buyers often provide input to sellers regarding terms of sale. The nature of business markets dictates customer involvement in the pricing products. Consumers rarely have this opportunity. Depending upon the product, industry and companies involved, buying groups often bargain with sellers to customize the terms of sale. The length of time required for payment, final price and type of warranty provided are typical items included in negotiated terms of sale.

The average consumer cannot walk into a clothing store and tell the proprietor what he or she is willing to pay for the shirt or blouse. Consumers usually buy according to the store's terms of sale. Business buyers, on the other hand, often have the opportunity to bargain with suppliers over payment terms and discounts. Such price negotiation is especially common with non-standard or custom products.

Business buyers often influence the form of the products they buy. **Customer specifications** of product design or tolerances are common in these markets. Consumers usually do not tell the grocer that only the sweetest oranges will be acceptable. Nor can consumers demand only half of the frozen pie or one pat of butter. When purchasing goods for households, shoppers normally accept what is offered for sale.

On the other hand, the buying process used by businesses often dictates special considerations. The corrugated cartons ordered by Apple Computer require specific printing. Western Datacom uses different circuitry in its modems than do its competitors. The cheddar needed by Stouffer's for its frozen cheese soufflé needs additional aging. These requirements may be non-standard, but buyers at such firms can still specify what they need.

SAMPLING

Production goods buyers commonly request **samples** of raw materials or component parts prior to placing a large order. Since businesses usually buy in volume, purchasers are typically cautious before making major commitments. To assure that a new product from an old supplier or an old product from a new vendor works satisfactorily, production goods buyers request samples. Consumers do not have this opportunity when purchasing shampoo, dog food or chain saws.

Arcata Graphics would request samples of a new coated paper before printing books or brochures for its customers. Lea & Perrins will want to be sure that the new non-drip bottle insert from Owens-Illinois Glass Company is compatible with its Worcestershire sauce. Even the purchasing department's simple task of adding a new company to the list of approved suppliers often means sampling.

Sampling—the process of testing small quantities before placing a production order.

LEASING

Leasing occurs much more frequently in business goods markets than it does among consumers. Many firms find this to be a cost effective alternative to buying outright. Production equipment, vehicles, office furniture and

Many businesses prefer to lease equipment, including exterior signs.

computers are examples of products that are suitable for leasing. Raw materials and component parts must be purchased.

Most retail establishments lease their outdoor signs rather than purchase them outright. A company with a large sales force may find leasing company vehicles more economical than purchasing them. The hassle of reselling used cars and adjusting for various rates of depreciation is often less desirable than renting. Many businesses and organizations lease office or production equipment.

INTERPERSONAL RELATIONSHIPS

With business goods, more people may be involved in the buying decision. The products themselves can be complex, hence, buyer and seller must work closely together. The **interpersonal relationships** between user and supplier are usually more significant than those found with consumers. These close ties with vendors give purchasers a feeling of confidence that the materials received will be what was ordered. Significant hardship on the purchaser can result if the correct order does not arrive when needed. When buyers rely heavily upon suppliers, stronger relationships automatically develop.[3]

Purchasing agents at Kraft General Foods realize the need for fresh and contamination-free ingredients. Procter & Gamble would not switch its suppliers of tubes for Crest toothpaste without knowing the shipping and quality control capabilities of the new firms. To keep assembly lines producing the test equipment that its customers require, Siemens must receive the cathode ray tubes, knobs and dial faces it requires on time.

---

[3]Kate Bertrand, "With customers, the closer the better," Business Marketing, July 1989, pp. 68–69.

Global Marketing: Siemens Gears Up for Europe '92.

It seems as though the entire world watched as the clock ticked toward December 31, 1992. That was the date when many of the countries of Europe were to unify into one major economic force. This event was not meant to create a United States of Europe ... at least not yet. What it signified was the merging of product specifications, currencies, and trade policies that would allow Europe to reach star status as a major force in global marketing. Companies the world over were active in investing in Europe over the past decade in anticipation of 1992 and the potential for restrictions on outside opportunities after that target date.

Before unification, the giant German conglomerate, Siemens, was struggling to make its mark outside its own backyard. The rebuilding boom in eastern Europe pumped up the firm's building systems division, but the computer group suffered. With most of the company's profits coming

from sales within the European Community, time was running out for Siemens to make its mark in other global markets. The company had to expand its operations while the window of opportunity was open.

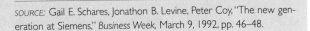

The innovative and aggressive management of this firm pushed ahead. The company captured a bulk of the fuel injector business for the world's automotive industry. State-of-the-art engineering and production control have led Siemens to the top of global enterprises. The company name has become synonymous with quality and productivity. This German giant is a force to be reckoned with in a global economy often thought to be dominated by Japanese multinationals.

SOURCE: Gail E. Schares, Jonathon B. Levine, Peter Coy, "The new generation at Siemens," *Business Week*, March 9, 1992, pp. 46–48.

The need to develop trust in vendors dictates close working relationships. Because of the interrelationships developed between business goods buyers and sellers, it is often difficult for competition to make inroads. Business goods buyers usually do not switch suppliers carelessly or without thorough investigation. Once a buy/sell relationship is entrenched, it often lasts.[4]

RECIPROCITY

The buying and selling of business goods often involves **reciprocity.** This sometimes controversial process occurs when one company purchases needed products from one of its customers or competitors. When a manufacturer has a requirement for a product that is being made by one of its customers, it makes

[4]Robert B. Settle, Pamela L. Alreck, "Risky Business," *Sales & Marketing Management*, January 1989, pp. 48–52.

good sense to purchase from that source. Similarly, purchasing necessary material from competitors leads toward better industry relations and less bickering.

In the chemical and paint industries, for example, this mutual exchange is a common practice. A major market for the output from any one company could be a firm in the same general industry. Shell Chemical buys acetone from Monsanto which in turn purchases ethylene from Shell. Flecto, a leading spray paint marketer, buys its latex bases from a variety of manufacturers who in turn purchase urethane paints from Flecto.

Reciprocity must be carefully controlled by those firms involved to assure that there is no restraint of trade. One firm cannot refuse to sell to another if the buyer meets the credit standards of the seller. Sellers cannot favor one customer over another by offering price concessions or special considerations. Even without any unethical or illegal practices, reciprocity tends to dampen competitive zeal.

hat Characterizes Business Buying Behavior?

Many differences are apparent between consumer and business buying behavior. The quantities are greater and the needs often are more urgent when businesses buy from businesses. The factors influencing organizational buyers differ from those impacting typical consumers.

MORE RATIONAL AND FORMAL

The buying decision is **more rational** and **less emotional** in business markets. Professional buyers do not make decisions based upon personal preference for the product, but rather on what is best for the organization. The purchasing agent for John Deere tractors will not order blue paint if the production department specifies green. Just because the dairy department manager for Safeway Stores dislikes cottage cheese, it does not mean that this taste preference will influence the purchasing decision with a supplier. A buyer for Bloomingdale's orders cosmetics based upon customer demand, not on her or his personal desires.

Although interpersonal relations are more important in business buying, the actual purchasing process is usually more formal. Dress is typically more conventional in the business buy/sell arena, although there is a trend away from three piece suits and wing-tipped shoes. Led by the Dockers line from Levi Strauss and the wrinkle resistant pant from Haggar, corporate America is redefining how it dresses.[5]

Appearance and the decor of the business purchasing arena are more professional than those found in the consumer area. Appointments are more common in this market. This is not to say that the exchange process for business goods is necessarily somber, but the practice is more reserved. Although the philosophy of conducting trade may vary greatly from customer to customer and from seller to seller, businesses still follow more orderly procedures than do consumers.

[5]Teri Agins, "Between suits and jeans: The corporate casual look," *The Wall Street Journal*, January 21, 1994, pp. B1 and B4.

DELAYED DECISION, MAKE OR BUY CHOICE

Negotiations for business purchases usually take time, necessitating **delayed decisions.** While some consumers may make quick choices on which shirt to buy or what meat or fish to have for dinner, these options involve considerably less money and impact fewer people than those made in business buying. Negotiations regarding customer specifications, terms of sale and sampling do not occur over night. The initial visit by a salesperson rarely results in an immediate purchase.

Delayed decision—negotiations for the purchase of business goods take place over time.

Businesses often face the dilemma of whether to manufacture needed items in-house or to purchase them from outside vendors. **Make or buy decisions** are unique to business markets. Some manufacturers have the capacity in-house to produce much of their needed production equipment and component parts. These products are also available from outside sources that specialize in this type of work. For example, Ford Motor Company makes most of its own manufacturing jigs and fixtures. That company has the machinery and know-how to also make merchandisers for dealer showrooms, yet chooses to buy these items from point-of-purchase display businesses.

Make or buy decision—determining whether to manufacture needed items in-house or to purchase from outside vendors.

RELIABILITY

Business buyers are very conscious of the **reliability of the supplier.** The goods purchased and the delivery schedule promised must meet the purchaser's requirements. No business buyer wants to be placed in the position where the firm's production facility would have to shut down due to lack of materials or equipment. To illustrate this point, Caterpillar, the heavy equipment marketer, suffered severely in 1994 because of engine failures and parts shortages. Customers relying on truck engines canceled orders because of these delays. Although Caterpillar is second only to Cummins Engine, many of its truck manufacturing customers were seriously hampered because of delays in shipping.[6]

Reliability is especially important with businesses dealing with production and trade goods. The Gates Rubber Company markets hoses and belts for a variety of industrial uses. This marketer relies heavily on its reputation for dependability. Customers of this Denver based firm cannot afford to shut down their own manufacturing process because of a faulty belt or a late delivery.

Kimberly-Clark Corporation recently reentered the bathroom tissue market with its Kleenex Premium brand using a new process. This technology produces a single ply toilet paper that matches the twin layer competition in softness and strength. The company could not afford to run out of raw material or packaging for this heavily advertised item because of an unreliable supplier.[7]

---

[6]Bill Vogrin, "Poor quality forces Cat customers to cancel," *Marketing News,* May 9, 1994, p. 7.

[7]"Tissue: Producers strive to overcome impact of premium bath tissue decline," *Pulp and Paper,* February 1992, p. 13; Fara Warner, "Kleenex goes national with high-tech bathroom roll," *Adweek's Marketing Week,* November 25, 1991, p. 7.

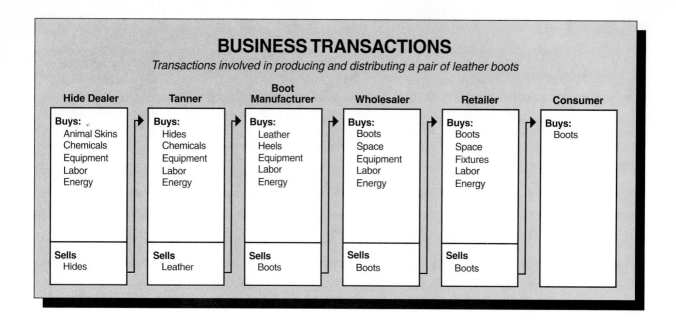

BUSINESS TRANSACTIONS

Transactions involved in producing and distributing a pair of leather boots

Hide Dealer	Tanner	Boot Manufacturer	Wholesaler	Retailer	Consumer
Buys: Animal Skins Chemicals Equipment Labor Energy	**Buys:** Hides Chemicals Equipment Labor Energy	**Buys:** Leather Heels Equipment Labor Energy	**Buys:** Boots Space Equipment Labor Energy	**Buys:** Boots Space Fixtures Labor Energy	**Buys:** Boots
Sells Hides	**Sells** Leather	**Sells** Boots	**Sells** Boots	**Sells** Boots	

TECHNICAL ASSISTANCE

The **technical assistance** available to the buyer has an impact on the purchase decision. Many business goods are complex, scientific or very technical in nature. These factors are especially significant with raw materials or component parts that need further processing. The firm that offers the best technical assistance or current and accurate instructions often has the edge over companies that do not provide such help. Xerox, General Electric and Honeywell are just a few of the many companies who have good reputations for employing highly trained, technical specialists. These people serve in the field to help when something goes wrong with the products those companies sell. To business buyers, technical service is often as important as the product itself.

What Is the Business Purchasing Decision Process?

With the myriad of factors that impact purchasing, business buyers have their hands full. While the process of making the buying decision might be very similar to that of consumers, a different set of factors influences the final business buyer's conclusion. The process includes the recognition of a need, followed by the selection of alternatives to satisfy that need. The purchase decision requires post purchase evaluation.

DETERMINE NEEDS

Raw materials, component parts and production equipment purchases relate to the finished products manufactured using these items. New finished goods require new purchasing decisions. The needs of buyers depend upon whether the purchase is for a new product or an established one. New task buying needs refer to products that have recently been developed. Reorders and modified reorders relate to stable goods.

New Task Buying

A newly developed product or change in a production process often creates a **new task buying** need. In these cases, different production goods may be necessary for the manufacturing process. For example, when Hershey, the candy firm, decided to market Reese's peanut butter, this new product required a variety of raw materials, production equipment and production supplies not previously used by the company. Similarly, when 3M introduced its Privacy Filter, a device that shields computer screens from all but the user, the company needed plastic film, venetian blind type slats and mounting brackets which were not normal purchases for this firm. In both of these examples, demand grew out of the creation of a new task buying need.[8]

Not all new task buying purchases are the result of brand new products. Significant production changes may also create these types of buys. Pepsi is not a new product, but when PepsiCo changed its can design for this popular soft drink, a new task buying need developed. Shipping cartons and the containers themselves were like new products for PepsiCo's purchasing department. These requirements for packaging materials resulted from a new task buying need.

Reorder and Modified Reorder

Orders for business goods that result from the need for previously purchased products are reorders. Most of the purchases are routine. Manufacturers in constant production of a given item develop procedures to assure that materials and equipment are available when needed. Procter & Gamble is in constant need of surfactants and containers to make its dishwashing liquids. Estee Lauder cannot afford to run out of colorants and tubes for its line of lipsticks. Such purchases would be considered standard reorders. For production goods, it is usually the manufacturing group that establishes reorder specifications. Although some reorders are routine, not all are ordinary.

Some reorders require slight changes from previous purchases. The color of the product might not have been right for the customers, or the tolerance could be a bit too loose. Either of these cases would cause a change in the needs and require **modified reorders.** For example, a "25% more FREE" special that International Delight ran on its non-dairy coffee creamer increased the size of the carton. This caused a change in the standard reorder for shipping containers to accommodate the taller packages. A modified reorder was necessary to reflect this special promotion. Although these materials may be purchased from the same original suppliers, the order itself is not routine.

[8]Alison Sprout, "Computer privacy," *Fortune,* March 9, 1992, p. 69.

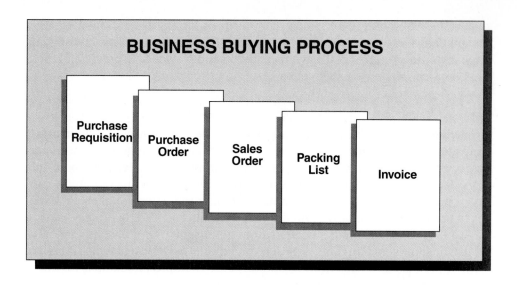

BUSINESS BUYING PROCESS

Purchase Requisition · Purchase Order · Sales Order · Packing List · Invoice

EVALUATE ALTERNATIVES

After establishing needs, business buyers go through a similar search and evaluation process that occurs with consumers. With business goods, this step is more detailed and complex. In the purchase of these items, analyzing the available alternatives requires investigation of both products and suppliers. With more people involved with the purchase of business goods, arriving at a consensus on the right product from the right supplier may be complicated. The individual members of the buying center, although often working as a team, often have different priorities. Multiple requirements make it difficult to chose the best suppliers.

Business goods are often technical, and their purchase may reflect a sizable investment. These products go through a more thorough investigation than would consumer goods. Testing of samples received and the issuance of trial orders occur before making large purchases. If many suppliers are submitting samples and proposals, the purchase decision can take a long time.

SELECT SUPPLIERS

Based upon the previously discussed need to assure reliability and develop solid relationships, business purchasers select their suppliers. In some cases the buying firm may decide upon multiple sources of supply. This is especially true in highly competitive industries. Other firms may opt for a single source for goods or services, reasoning that the buyer may enjoy a closer relationship with the seller if they represent a major source of income.

Once vendors are determined, a regular, formal procedure is carried out by most business goods buyers. The need for accountability dictates a more professional approach to buying than that found with consumers. This process includes the submission of formal paperwork that solidifies the purchase into contractual form.

Purchase Requisition

Purchases by businesses follow a standard procedure. In larger firms or agencies, employees from a department, or a member of the buying center, starts the process with documents called **purchase requisitions.** This form tells the purchasing department what is needed, by when and often from whom. Smaller firms may eliminate this step as the person doing the purchasing is often the one in need of the goods or services.

Purchase requisition—the first step in purchasing paperwork flow, created by the department or person in need.

Purchase Order

The department, or person, who does the actual purchasing creates a **purchase order,** or **PO,** using the information found on the requisition. POs may be transmitted verbally, electronically, or by mail. The purchase order, which is an offer to buy, is the first step in a business contract. The second stage of this contractual process occurs when the seller receives and accepts this offer to buy. These actions complete the offer and acceptance, resulting in an agreement between two or more parties.

Purchase order (PO)—document created by the buyer that transmits order information to the seller.

Sales Order

Upon accepting the purchase order, the seller submits a **sales order,** or **order acknowledgment,** to the buyer. The purchase order offers to buy, and the sales order confirms acceptance of that offer, completing the contract. At this point, both parties are obligated to live up to the terms of the agreement and bring the transaction to a close. The quantity and types of products ordered, price and payment dates, and the delivery schedule are all spelled out in detail. Most firms check and double check these documents to assure their accuracy.

Sales order (order acknowledgment)—document created by seller that confirms receipt and acceptance of the order and specifies selling terms.

Packing List

The next document in the paperwork process is the **packing list.** This item travels with the goods shipped to the customer. This form spells out exactly what is being shipped, which may not include everything that was ordered. Sometimes the complete order is not shipped at one time. The portion that was not shipped is considered back ordered, and the packing list will show this information.

Packing list—document that travels with the shipment that describes the contents.

Invoice

The final step in the purchasing process is submission of the **invoice,** or bill. Since most business goods transactions are on an open account basis, similar to a consumer charge account, payment is not always necessary before the goods are shipped. The terms of sale contained on the sales order spell out when the invoice is to be paid and if certain discounts are allowed. To promote prompt payment, most sellers transmit invoices when the merchandise is shipped. Again, the paperwork may be sent electronically or by mail.

Invoice—the bill

POSTPURCHASE EVALUATION

Business buyers go through the same postpurchase analysis that occurs with consumers. Since the relationship with suppliers may be much closer, this process often includes the sellers and the buyers. With multiple buyers influencing the decision, deciding whether the actual purchase was beneficial and should be continued can be complicated. Some members of the buying group may be satisfied, while others may not.

Most manufacturing companies utilize **quality control** departments or procedures to evaluate incoming materials. This group or individual also has the job of simplifying the postpurchase evaluation function. This inspection occurs in the production facility where incoming shipments arrive.

hat Is Nonbusiness Marketing?

Not all businesses have profit as their motive. Associations which do not operate for profit still carry out marketing tasks. Unique opportunities occur in these arenas. The marketing mix used by nonbusiness organizations may be quite different from that used by profit seeking ventures.

NONBUSINESS MARKETING DEFINED

Nonbusiness marketing relates to all activities that do not attempt to generate profits. These programs may be undertaken by a business venture or by a nonprofit organization. General Motors conducts campaigns to enlighten the public on the use of seat belts, and Anheuser-Busch promotes programs for the responsible use of alcohol. The American Lung Association warns of the dangers of cigarette smoking, and the U.S. Armed Forces conducts extensive recruiting through the media.

Similar to services, nonbusiness marketing is intangible and perishable. Sometimes, physical goods are used to raise funds for the organization, but generally, nonbusiness groups act as service providers. In what has become an American tradition, the Girl Scouts sell cookies to raise funds for local troops. Kiwanis Clubs vend candy to earn money for the operations and community service work. In most cases, however, nonbusiness marketing does not involve physical goods.

IDEAS AND CAUSES

The marketing of **ideas** or **causes** are nonbusiness ventures. Many corporate giants contribute directly or indirectly through foundations to support worthy causes. The Levi Strauss Foundation donates a major portion of company profits to combat social problems. From AIDS to poverty to illiteracy, the world's largest clothing manufacturer gives roughly 2.5 percent of

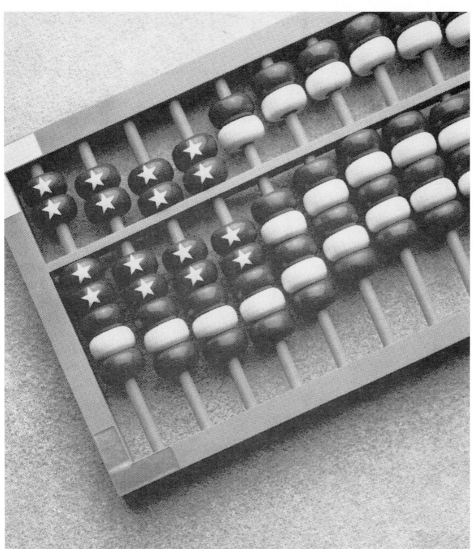

Anyway we add it—
it makes good sense to answer the Census.

We all add up. Each and every one of us make up a part of America. Everybody counts.

Census findings help the government reach important decisions when planning for schools, hospitals, roads and basic needs for our community.

So make a difference. When you receive the Census form, please take a few minutes to fill it out. And mail it in.

Answer the Census.

CENSUS '90

©1990

Many advertising agencies, such as Muse Cordero Chen, donate their services to nonprofit organizations like the U.S. Census Bureau. (Courtesy Muse Cordero Chen, Inc.)

its pretax earnings to charitable projects. Many of America's business-es encourage their employees to become involved with such community benefiting activities.[9]

Like services, ideas and causes are intangible. In addition, since they are not purchased, convincing a market to embrace and endorse these opinions or propositions is a challenge. Marketers strive for understanding and believabil-ity to counteract the negativism that faces these, sometimes, controversial arguments. The abortion issue is one that receives intense participation from both proponent and opponent.

NONPROFIT ORGANIZATIONS

Similar to organizations that promote services, ideas and causes, the market-ing efforts by **nonprofit** organizations differ from those firms marketing goods. These entities gain status by performing selected tasks that benefit society but do not generate net income. Most such groups collect donations and funds which are then dispersed to needy recipients.

Nonprofit organizations generally engage in philanthropical activities. As such, these groups or associations typically receive tax-free status from feder-al and state governments. Churches and other religious bodies are in this cat-egory. Most associations that collect funds for distribution to the needy or for special medical causes are nonprofit organizations. The United Way, American Red Cross and American Cancer Society are typical examples.

TRADE ASSOCIATIONS

Not all nonprofit organizations are philanthropic. Nonprofit industry groups, called **trade associations,** promote the success of a specific field. These groups are very marketing oriented. Trade associations exist for almost every industry or business type imaginable. Marketing executives and educators form the joint membership of the American Marketing Association. Paint and wallpaper dealers, manufacturers and interested parties make up the National Decorators and Paint Association. Dog and horse breeders organized years ago, and llama owners have followed. Similar groups represent point-of-purchase display manufacturers, the dairy industry, aerospace firms and the garment industry.

As with other nonprofit groups, trade associations marketing involves multiple publics. These industry groups count on contributions or dues from members to fiscally survive. On the other hand, those donations are usually spent outside of the organization to provide general benefits for its members. Directors of these groups are constantly weighing requests for lower dues with demands for greater benefits.

---

[9]Jon Berry, "Pro bono marketing," *Adweek's Marketing Week,* March 25, 1991, pp. 18–22.

Marketing and Society: Bad Credit Is Bad Business.

Everyone, it seems, wishes to have a good credit rating. As we strive to climb that slippery ladder to success, we are constantly being badgered to buy more. At some point, we must purchase homes, cars and everyday consumer goods "on time." Parents and teachers make suggestions that we should establish credit early in our lives so that we have it when we need it. Sometimes we overextend.

With millions of people in this country buying things with plastic money or on installment plans, keeping track of credit has become big business. Fortunately, computers have eased the pain of these reporting organizations. Unfortunately, those very same computers do not always process the right data. The Federal Trade Commission receives more consumer complaints about inaccurate credit reporting than about any other subject.

For consumers, most of the aggravation arises from incorrect information being dispersed to creditors or lenders. Many reports say that the wrong data is being recorded for the wrong person. Upon checking up on why credit was denied, people find that the computer has listed information under their names that belongs to someone else. Even the names of spouses and children are found to be wrong, to say nothing of the misinformation about prompt payment and outstanding balances.

Congress has been under the gun for years to clean up this credit reporting mess, but to little avail. Just when it seems as though some muscle will be applied to this industry, lawmakers back down under pressure from lobbyists and business groups. Of course, if one looks at the financial prowess of the members of Congress, it is no wonder that little is accomplished.

SOURCES: Evan I. Schwartz, "It's time to clean up credit reporting," *Business Week*, May 18, 1992, p. 52; Michele Galen, "Getting the kinks out of your credit report," *Business Week*, May 25, 1992, pp. 132–133.

How Does Business Buying Behavior Impact Marketing Management?

Business buyers are demanding and often hard to please. Purchasers scrutinize products and service carefully, and competition is rough. Marketers must be quality conscious, timely and flexible. Because the quantities in purchasing dollars can be substantial, satisfying these purchasers is not an easy task.

QUALITY AND RELIABILITY

In the selling age, producers paid little attention to customer needs. Today's business goods marketers know the importance of staying on top of the market. Product requirements can change rapidly. Firms which do not stress close personal relationships with customers may find their lines outmoded. Sellers must prove the **quality of their products** and the **reliability of their company.** To succeed in this area of business, marketing companies must be constantly aware of customer needs and competitive challenges.

Business goods buyers need quality products and service from suppliers, although the quality needed by one customer may be at a different level than that required by another. To illustrate, the polyurethane film purchased by U.S. Divers for scuba diving vests must be pinhole free to assure safety. Insta-Graphics uses the same basic material for stamping out letters and numerals to be heat sealed onto athletic jerseys, a less quality-conscious application. Although requirements are different for each firm, both need their orders for materials serviced promptly and properly.

Defects in raw materials and component parts may have direct impact upon the quality image of their buyers. When incorporated in the purchaser's products, problems in the goods received lose their original identity. Suppose IBM were to sell a computer with a defective silicon chip. That firm's customers will find fault with the computer, not the chip maker. When the waste water hose on the commercial washing machine springs a leak, angry laundromat operators point the finger at Speed Queen, not the hose maker.

PRICING AND DISTRIBUTION

Setting **prices** is a critical process with businesses. Since the quantities purchased are very large, accurate pricing is crucial to sellers. Underestimating demand or miscalculating costs can have a disastrous effect on profits. Marketing management also may be forced into a much more flexible pricing policy when selling goods to other businesses. Price setting by firms in these arenas can create greater challenges than those found in retailing.

The primary **distribution** challenge for business product marketers is one of timing. Assuring that goods arrive at the buyer's place when requested is mandatory for maintaining good customer relations. Production and trade goods sellers equally share this management responsibility. Industrial customers cannot afford to close down manufacturing for want of raw materials or production equipment. Wholesalers and retailers need their warehouses and shelves stocked in order to resell to hungry customers.

PROMOTION

The **promotion of production goods** is often not as flamboyant as that used for trade goods. Celebrity studded television commercials would not be appropriate for the industrial market. Usually, personal selling plays the starring role in production goods promotion. Interpersonal relationships are built through one-on-one communications rather than through mass advertising. Management must create the proper amount of promotion while exercising good cost control. Keeping a handle on costs is imperative to provide satisfactory profits while maintaining the desired market position.

Positioning

Positioning is just as important in business product marketing as it is with consumer goods. In this market, positioning normally relates to the company, not

With Gates Power Cable™ belts, you can put 'em in the sheaves and forget 'em.

Because of the way Power Cable is built, it turns a lot of severe problem drives into no problem drives.

□ Aramid fiber cords.
□ Extra rugged green cover. Doesn't matter what makes a problem drive a problem,

the green is mean enough to take it in stride.

□ High horsepower
□ Heavy shock loads.
□ Harsh environment.
Power Cable. From Gates.
There's another green belt from Gates for light duty uses up to 17 HP. Gates Powe Rated®.

Both are available through your local Gates distributor.

The Gates Rubber Company, 990 South Broadway, P.O. Box 5887, Denver, CO 80217. 800/678-5283.

Gates
GNDV31F

The world's most trusted name in belts and hose.

Some things you can depend on.
Like the sun coming up.
And Gates Power Cable.

Business goods marketers, such as Gates Rubber Products, usually position the company rather than the company's products. (Courtesy of The Gates Rubber Company)

its specific products. Close relationships develop between buyers and sellers in this arena, and delivery is crucial in business-to-business transactions. Therefore, the selling company often gains a reputation for quality and reliability first and its products second.

Once a business product marketer gains a reputation for delivering quality products and **providing good service,** that company may be positioned in buyers' minds as an industry leader. Competition will have a difficult time unseating an entrenched supplier from the mind of a professional buyer. In addition, once a manufacturer gets a name for having poor quality or unreliable shipping, that stigma is hard to dissolve.

Business product marketing makes up a significant portion of the U.S. economy. Management needs to be flexible, aggressive and alert to know what is best in determining needs and satisfying customers. In the business arena, the quantities are large, the stakes are high and the competition is keen.

SUMMING IT UP

Business products are purchased by businesses from businesses. They can be either goods or services. Business goods are typically categorized as production goods, trade goods, accessory equipment and operating supplies.

Production goods are those items purchased for use directly or indirectly in the manufacturer of other products. Production goods include raw materials, component parts, production equipment and production supplies. Trade goods are purchased by marketing intermediaries for resale to other businesses or to consumers. Wholesalers buy these goods and resell to retailers or to other business entities. Retailers purchase goods from businesses for resale to consumers. All consumer goods have their beginning as trade goods.

Accessory equipment are durable goods not involved in production or for resale. Items such as computers and office machines, vehicles and material handling gear are an important part of the operation of any organization. Operating supplies are those more inexpensive and nondurable purchases that still play an important role in day-to-day business affairs. Janitorial and office supplies form a major portion of this category.

The demand for business goods is derived from the ultimate demand for consumer goods. The process usually involves professional buyers and is influenced by many people within the buying organization. Negotiated terms of sale, sampling and leasing are common in the business buying arena. Customers are more likely to specify product design than consumers, and the purchases take place at the buyer's place of business rather than the seller's.

Business buyers behave in a more rational, less emotional manner. The buying atmosphere is more formal, and the decision takes a longer time to gel. Purchasers place a good deal of importance upon the reliability of the supplier. Technical assistance is important in production goods markets. The decision process for business buying parallels that of consumers. Needs assessment begins with whether the purchase is a new task buy, or merely a reorder. The paperwork flow begins with purchase requisitions and purchase orders by the buyer. The seller returns a sales order, or order acknowledgment. The packing list travels with the shipment, and the invoice serves as the bill.

Business buyers rely primarily on product quality and reliability of the supplier. Price is a secondary consideration. Positioning in these markets tends to be toward the company rather than the company's products.

KEY CONCEPTS AND TERMS FROM CHAPTER SEVEN

Accessory equipment
Business goods
Buying center
Component parts
Delayed decision
Derived demand
Invoice
Multiple buying influence
Operating supplies
Packing list
Production equipment

Production goods
Production supplies
Professional buyers
Purchase order (PO)
Purchase requisition
Raw materials
Reciprocity
Sales order (order acknowledgment)
Sampling
Trade goods

BUILDING SKILLS

1. Describe the differences between raw materials and component parts, indicating the types of businesses that purchase accessory equipment and operating supplies.

2. Give some examples of consumer goods that are **not** sold to the trade, and discuss why.

3. Explain the concept of derived demand as it relates to business buying behavior.

4. Explain the reasons why business buying is more professional and demanding.

5. Explain the terms and concepts relating to business buying behavior, such as multiple buying decision, negotiated terms of sale and sampling.

6. Describe the most important considerations for a buyer at a hospital looking for new beds, the purchasing agent at Hewlett-Packard needing printed circuit boards, the millinery buyer at Saks.

7. Differentiate the factors that influence the purchasers of metal working equipment, food colors for pharmaceuticals, fabric and buttons used in manufacturing clothing, batteries for electric toothbrushes.

8. Contrast the different types of business purchases citing examples to support your statements.

9. Analyze the factors of business buying behavior that influence marketing management.

Making Decisions 7-1: A Paper Tiger.

Paper is one commodity that consumers and businesses cannot do without. From paper bags to bathroom tissue, newspapers to automotive air filters, paper is an important part of every consumer's household. Computer paper and letterhead, credit card receipts and trade journals are of major importance to the business community, and all are paper based.

Many people think of paper as "ground-up trees." For sure, most paper products do originate from timber. Yet many of the finest quality paper products use cotton as the prime ingredient. No one produces better "rag" paper than Crane & Co., Incorporated. Crane supplies 100 percent cotton based papers to the U.S. Mint, which uses the paper in printing our nation's currency. High rag content also appears in fine writing papers produced by Crane. This stationery is said to be among the finest available. This diversified marketer also makes tracing paper for drafting, the material used in passports, the glass fiber base for Formica and other specialty paper items.

Crane purchases most of its cotton from Texas and California, where much of the prized long-fiber varieties are grown. The company also contracts to buy the cutting scraps from companies that make and sell men's underwear. This cotton content produces an extremely durable paper—one that can be manufactured only a few thousandths of an inch thick yet still maintain its beauty and strength. In the paper industry known for massive equipment and a heavy hand, Crane also employs a light touch. This company's fine writing papers are decorated with hand-painted borders and individually tied ribbons before they reach "Milady's desk."[10]

Define the different types of business goods that Crane markets, describing how buying behavior might vary between purchasing agents at the U.S. Mint, a Formica manufacturer, and a writing paper wholesaler.

Making Decisions 7-2: Killer Worms!

Insects are the bane of the agricultural community. Farmers the world over have waged a never-ending war against these crop destroyers. The U.S. chemical industry appeared to have won the battle over the last decade with the invention of dozens of pesticides. However, two major problems have arisen which have intensified the battle. First, many bugs have become immune to many of all but the most recent chemical killers. Secondly, many pesticides have been found to be detrimental to the health of humans as well as to crawly critters. Enter the killer worms.

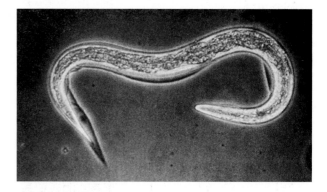

(Courtesy of BioSys)

---

[10]L. Killian, "Crane's progress," *Forbes*, August 19, 1991, p. 44; Christopher Knowlton, "A real paper tiger in the papertrade," *Fortune*, March 28, 1988, p. 52.

Nematodes are a family of miniature worms that just love to eat insects, but not the crops. A Silicon Valley company called BioSys pioneered development of these microscopic worms. The firm puts them in a semi-frozen state, packages them and ships them to farmers and to agricultural products companies such as Ortho. The worms, when sprayed in a solution, burrow underground where they seek out soil-born insects.

After settling in the larvae of pests, the worms emit a bacterium that kills the insect. The nematodes and their offspring feast on the dead bug until the food supply is exhausted. They then move on to yet another pest picnic. The work of firms such as BioSys promises to revolutionize the agricultural business.[11]

Identify the types of business goods marketed by BioSys. Describe the factors that would influence the purchase of nematodes.

Making Decisions 7-3: Down by the ol' Mill . . . .

Many businesses pick up nicknames that stick with them over the years. IBM is Big Blue, Kodak is often called Big Yellow and UPS carries on the large theme with Big Brown. Even after divesting most of its far flung offspring, AT&T is still labeled Ma Bell. In the heavy industrial field, Cincinnati Milacron is a firm noted for its tool making expertise and is affectionately called "the Mill."

Cincinnati Milacron has had its ups and downs during the past decade. With Japanese firms invading the field of machine tools, the Mill found the core of its business fading. Although the company picked up some new technology, enabling it to enter fields such as laser production, increases in business in one area were often greeted with drops elsewhere.

One of Milacron's premier product lines includes plastic injection molding machines. Here,

again, Pacific Rim companies were eating into the Mill's sales and profits. Forming a venture team of individuals from purchasing, manufacturing and marketing, the company created a new piece of equipment for the plastics molding industry.

This group's effort paid off handsomely. The Vista, as the machine is called, is a competitively priced injection molding machine that far surpasses its predecessor in speed and efficiency. Cincinnati Milacron has used this concept of team development on other equipment redesign. As they say in the industry, "the Mill is back."[12]

Describe the types of business goods Milacron markets and the factors of business buying behavior that might affect the purchase of equipment from this firm. Discuss the positioning of production goods marketers.

---

[11]Gene Bylinsky, "Killer worms to the rescue," *Fortune*, April 20, 1992, p. 20.

[12]Edmund O. Lawler, "Reclaiming market share on the trade show floor," *Business Marketing*, March 1993, p. 45; Zachary Schiller, "Milacron: Simpler is better," *Business Week*, May 18, 1992, p. 101; Peter Nulty, "The soul of an old machine," *Fortune*, May 21, 1990, pp. 67–72.

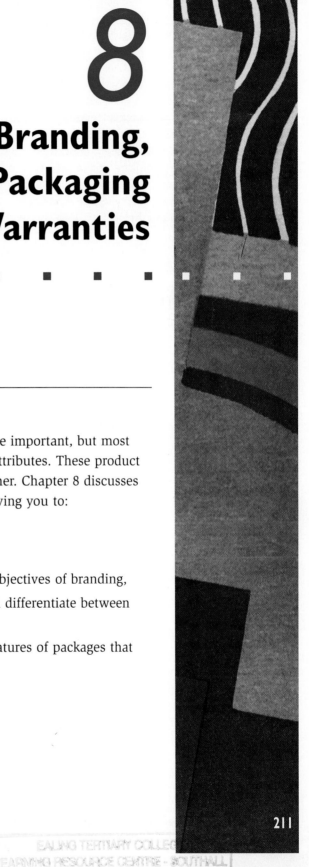

8

Product Branding, Packaging and Warranties

The Job to be Done

The physical characteristics of goods and services are important, but most consumers buy products based upon the associate attributes. These product attributes help buyers to choose one item over another. Chapter 8 discusses these points about products and their attributes, leaving you to:

- describe products and brands,
- understand the process for protecting brands,
- define the ways brands are classified and the objectives of branding,
- identify the characteristics of a good brand and differentiate between branding strategies,
- recognize the functions of packages and the features of packages that benefit consumers, and
- contrast the different types of warranties.

Marketers at Work

Raymond Melendez

The retail tire industry is highly competitive. Once the domain of American giants with names like Firestone, General Tire and Uniroyal, the business has broadened to include imports from around the world. Michelin (France), Hercules (Korea) and Toyo (Japan) are just a few of the many overseas competitors in this crowded arena. Although price and quality are, and always have been, important, customer service has become one of the keys to success for tire marketers. In this area, perhaps no firm does it better than the industry leader, Goodyear.

Raymond Melendez helped to work his way through El Paso Community College by working in a local Goodyear store. Although he also took coursework at the University of Texas at El Paso, he fell short of receiving a degree. Still, he progressed quickly from Credit Manager to Store Manager in the Goodyear organization. As his retail operation grew, so did Ray's reputation for providing outstanding customer service. It was not long before he was promoted to Product Service Manager for the entire region, a position he held until recently.

The whole state of Texas was not big enough to hold Raymond Melendez, and Goodyear decided that he could best serve their needs by transferring to Akron. Although it was difficult to leave his home, Ray accepted the position of Senior Customer Services Representative at Goodyear's Ohio headquarters. Here his knowledge of tire and mechanical warranties, and experience in customer service, have paid off handsomely for both Goodyear and Ray Melendez.

What Is A Product?

A product is not just a physical good or an intangible service. A product is the sum of its characteristics, which, when lumped together, bring benefit or satisfaction to the user. Some of these attributes are within the product itself. Others are less obvious, yet still important to buyers.

A BUNDLE OF VALUES

The features of products could include the texture, taste or color of goods, or the comfort, attractiveness, or pleasure received with the purchase of services. Some of these characteristics are physically part of the product, whereas others are linked by association. Since satisfaction brings value to both people and business buyers, it makes sense to refer to these various facets of products as the **bundle of values.** A product's bundle of values includes both the physical and associate attributes that individually or collectively satisfy needs.

Bundle of values— those physical and associate attributes of a product that individually or collectively satisfy needs.

The chemicals in Almay's hypo-allergenic skin cream are part of its physical attributes. However, product image, brand and package are equally important parts of any cosmetic. The color, fabric and style of a dress or suit is a physical attribute, but the way that it makes you feel is intangible. The taste of Coke is a physical part of that soft drink; its brand name is an associate characteristic.

Once considered taboo, black has become as "chic" in packaging as it is in fashion, as this bag of Smartfood illustrates.

PHYSICAL ATTRIBUTES

The **physical attributes** of products are important. How the item tastes, feels or looks, and whether the service is prompt, handy or complete are parts of the process of satisfying customers. Toasters must make toast and plumbers need to stop the leaks. The electric motor that drives the lathe and the engineering report on the new construction project must do the jobs required. All of these goods and services need to arrive on time to benefit the business buyer. The physical attributes of goods are easy to understand. Being tangible, there is something to feel, or to "get one's teeth into."

Color is important to the way people perceive a product. Many foodstuffs would be uninviting without the addition of dyes. Auto manufacturers often paint pickup trucks a yellowish red, which is more attractive to men, the major market. Bluish reds appeal more to women and are used on cars targeting female audiences. To enhance their products, many marketing companies turn to experts, such as the Color Marketing Group which works years in advance to decide which colors will be in or out of favor. Long avoided by food marketers, some grocery items are now packaged using the "chic" color, black.[1]

Although services are not material goods, the particular style of the service provider becomes a physical attribute. The room offered by the Hilton, the physical examination performed by the doctor and the concert by Whitney Houston are the primary characteristics of these services. However, the availability of reservations, the physicians cold hands and the concert hall restroom facilities are important extras or associate attributes.

Physical attributes— the tangible properties of products, such as taste, color, size and shape.

[1]Randall Lane, "Clash of the color czars," *Adweeks Marketing Week,* April 20, 1992, p. 18; Randall Lane, "Does orange mean cheap?" *Forbes,* December 23, 1991, pp. 144–146; Laura Bird, "Packaging paints it black," *Adweek's Marketing Week,* September 17, 1990, p. 17.

Associate attributes—The nonphysical characteristics of a product, such as brand, package, serviceability and warranty.

It is apparent that products offer more than physical qualities. **Associate attributes** are sometimes the most important aspects of goods and services. All factors other than the product itself are associate attributes. Consumer and business goods marketers alike strive to develop loyalty. Identifiers, such as brand names or symbols, the package and the serviceability of goods, are associate attributes that help create a loyal following.

The companies that market the products also have images or auras. Sometimes, the stature of the marketing company itself is more important to the buyer than the actual good or service. Business goods marketers are especially interested in creating reliable, dependable images. Marketing oriented firms depend upon associate attributes to build brand loyalty and company preference.

Image and Brand

Consumers develop feelings about goods and services. Impressions created by the promotional efforts of the marketer and **images** of the product itself attract some people while turning others away. Chevrolet created a masculine, "outdoorsy" feeling for the Blazer, designed to appeal to a small segment of the driving public. On the other hand, the positioning of Mercedes Benz as the ultimate in engineering has drawn an entirely different audience than the one attracted to the Chevy Blazer. Although this German manufacturer has tried to alter its sometimes aloof image, positioning for the car and the company remains upscale.[2]

To consumers, and at times to business product purchasers, brand names may be the sole reason for buying a good or service. Branding identifies and becomes part of the product. Marketers of groceries, air travel, cosmetics, hardware, appliances, lodging, clothing and a myriad of other goods and services spend billions of dollars annually to develop loyalty for specific brands. The brand names Kleenex, Charmin' and Sunkist are important associate attributes. The nicknames "Ma Bell" for AT&T and "Big Blue" for IBM have become part of the auras of these companies, indicating special feelings of strength and protectiveness.

Package

The **package** containing the goods is also an associate attribute. To many consumers, a particular item may be purchased simply because the package fits buyers' needs. In these cases, the product may take a secondary role to its container. Loyalty for one brand can be cast aside if a competing good offers a better, more useful package. When Prell shampoo first appeared in plastic tubes, advertising emphasized the shatter-proof package. The container became a key attribute of the product itself and helped to launch Prell's success. Today, most hair care products and cosmetics are found in break-resistant tubes or bottles.

---

[2]Jim Henry, "Mercedes S: Slimmer, rounder flagship caters to U.S. tastes," *Automotive News,* June 6, 1994, p. 24; Lindsey Brooke, "Benz in Bama," *Automotive Industries,* June 1994, pp. 63–64; Carrie Goerne, "New Mercedes campaign focuses on 'relationships' ," *Marketing News,* April 27, 1992, p. 2.

Physical vs. associate attributes of selected products

PRODUCT	PHYSICAL ATTRIBUTES	ASSOCIATE ATTRIBUTES
Toyota Camry	Styling	Brand name
	Engine	Warranty
	Economy	Service availability
Safeguard soap	Ability to clean	Brand name
	Deodorant protection	Bar sizes
	Color or aroma	Masculine image
Guess clothing	Styling	Brand name
	Fabric	Durability image
	Color	Fashion image
Apple's laptop computer	Size	Brand name
	Electronic components	Warranty
	Carrying case	Take anywhere image

■   ■   ■   ■   ■

Business buyers may also be influenced by packaging. Giant steel fabricators need tank cars of perchlorethylene, but dry cleaners buy this same cleaning solution by the drum. Both businesses benefit from the size of the container. In the latter case, the chemical may also be shipped in polyethylene drums to produce a significant savings in freight charges due to their lighter weight.

Warranty

The **warranties** offered by consumer and business goods manufacturers offer a clue to a product's marketability. To buyers, knowing that a given product will be repaired or replaced, or that the purchase moneys will be refunded, becomes an important factor influencing the purchase decision. Consumers often show preference for products that are backed by warranties. Sears and Goldwater's are retailers with corporate images that assure customer satisfaction.

Although most warranties are associated with consumer products, sellers to business markets also back their products. Because of the need to maintain a positive image, these marketers are also anxious to assure customer satisfaction. Defective products must be replaced or credited quickly and efficiently if the supplier is to retain the good customer relations so important in the business arena. Those firms that develop negative images because of reluctance to back up their products may find themselves at a competitive disadvantage.

What Is A Brand?

A brand may be a name, a symbol, an emblem, a logo or any other form that positively differentiates one product from all the rest. Even mottoes and slogans are used to distinguish one product from another. The particular identifiers that the marketer selects may include any combination of these items. The brand names Coca-Cola and Coke relate to one specific soft drink, but the can with its distinctive color and stripe and the slogan used by the Coca-Cola Company uniquely identify this product, too.

AN IDENTIFIER

A **brand** is any name, symbol or other device that identifies a good or service. Just as ranchers brand their herds to indicate ownership, so do marketers label their products as being different from the competition. Consumers often purchase by brand and develop loyalties toward certain makes of products or for specific companies. Marketers develop their pricing, distribution and promotion strategies largely based upon such brand loyalty.

There are any number of ways to identify products. Ford Motor Company uses many brand names, such as Mustang, Aerostar and Taurus, to label individual cars in its automobile line. In addition, the vehicles and advertisements from this company carry the distinctive blue oval, which is the symbol of the corporate entity. The slogan "Quality is Job One" also refers to the vehicles from Ford.

BRAND NAMES

A **brand name** is a word or phrase used to identify a product. When General Mills chose Cheerios as the name for one of its cereals, the company declared ownership. Noxell, owned by Procter & Gamble, picked Cover Girl as an identifier for makeup. Sunshine Bakeries coined Cheez-It, while RJR Nabisco chose Better Cheddar for cheese flavored crackers. Sears uses Allstate for its insurance wing, and General Motors created Mr. Goodwrench to identify service capabilities of its dealers.

Sometimes goods or services are named after the company manufacturing or providing the product, such as Estee Lauder cosmetics, Black & Decker tools, B. F. Goodrich tires, Marriott hotels or IBM computers. In some cases, the product carries its own distinctive brand name. Cascade, Kleenex, One-a-Day, Cougar, Whopper, AquaFresh, Macintosh, Allstate, Oshkosh B'Gosh and Weedeater are just a handful of the many brand names created by product marketers.

HOUSEMARK

On many consumer goods, the manufacturer includes an emblem or symbol called a **housemark** that identifies the marketer of the product. 'Nilla Wafers is a brand name, but the housemark of Nabisco appears in the corner of the package. This familiar red triangle identifies the company that made the product. General Mills also incorporates its company symbol, a blue script "G," along with brand names on the individual products that the firm markets.

Housemarks are useful to marketers in expanding product lines because they create continuity between the new and the old brands. Consumers, being aware of the quality or price image of established products, are inclined to accept the new offerings as similar in quality and value. Grocery shoppers

The familiar red triangle on products from Nabisco is a housemark that identifies the marketing company.

familiar with French's red flag accept that company's Dijon brand mustard as equal quality to other items from French. S. C. Johnson & Sons uses the distinctive logo on both its floor care waxes and its household products to kindle brand loyalty for each. The housemark for Delta Airlines appears on its airplanes, employee uniforms and at airport counters.

LOGOS AND SYMBOLS

Logos and symbols play an important role in identifying the product. When these identifiers take human-like or cartoon form, they are referred to as brand characters. Pillsbury's Doughboy, the Keebler Elves and Ronald McDonald do as much to promote the individuality of the producer as do the brand names of the products that these firms offer. The pentastar is about as well known as the name Chrysler, and NBC's peacock broadcasts the network's identification without the announcer saying a word.

Chiquita Banana, the Jolly Green Giant, the Snuggles bear and the Noid who cannot destroy a pizza from Domino's identify their products. These symbols have become an associate attribute of the product without relating to the physical characteristics of the good or service. Charlie Tuna, now over twenty-five years old, identifies Star-Kist, but consumers do not expect to see horn-rimmed glasses on the fish when they open the can.

MOTTOES AND SLOGANS

As identifiers, **mottoes** and **slogans** are also brands,. After all, ". . . the friendly skies" belong only to United Airlines, and the trucks built ". . . Ram tough" must be from Dodge. To "reach out and touch someone," we use AT&T. Sherwin-Williams paints ". . . cover the earth" and Charlie Brown and friends urge us to "Get Met. It pays."

Nonprofit organizations share the same desire for easy recognition. The symbol for the Wool Industry is often visible in ads and on garments. Easter Seals employs a different spokesperson each year; and every four years, five interlocking circles tell the world that it is time for the Olympic Games. United Way employs its own special logo, as do the American Cancer Society and the American Red Cross.

How Are Brands Protected?

By branding a product, the marketer is saying "This is mine, and mine alone!" Such identification is at the heart of product differentiation, giving a firm's marketing management the opportunity to promote the differences and advantages of its goods or services over other suppliers. Brands are an important part of any marketing strategy and warrant being defended and protected.

TRADEMARKS

Trademark—an identifier registered for protection with the Commissioner of Patents and Trademarks.

Consumer product marketers use a number of branding options to create a complete image. The Coca Cola Company, for example, uses the brand names Coke and Coca Cola and also the distinctive stripe or swirl. All of these identifiers are **trademarks,** which means that they have been protected under the terms of the Lanham Act of 1946. To be trademarks, brands must be registered with the Commissioner of Patents and Trademarks, U.S. Department of Commerce. The owner of the brand, not the government, has the responsibility to obtain this protection.

Failure to protect the brand name can lead to the possible loss of the trademark rights. For example, nylon, aspirin, kerosene, linoleum, shredded wheat, zipper and thermos were brand names at one time. Because the marketers of these products were lax in insisting upon proper usage of the trademark or failed to register them, these names are now generic. Tough new trademark laws offer immediate nationwide protection, but punish firms that give only token use to registered identifiers.

To be protected, the brand must be dissimilar from others that are already registered. To be accepted by buyers, the identifiers should also carry a degree of truth. For example, to capitalize on the wellness movement, many brands try to give the impression that they are low in calories by using the word "light." This identifier has been so misused that it has become meaningless. To illustrate, Bertolli Extra Light 100 percent pure olive oil has exactly the same number of calories as its standard version. New federal regulations are designed to eliminate misleading or deceptive types of identification.[3]

How Are Brands Classified?

Identifying products is a major task for marketers. Most consumer goods and services are named by the manufacturer or provider. Other brands are selected by marketing intermediaries. In production goods markets, products often carry letter or number designators rather than names. Most of the time with these items, the marketing company itself is also identified. Rohm and Haas sells VS100 acrylic molding powders and Digital Computer labels its mainframe computer Vax.

---

[3]Dan Koeppel, "After five years, the FDA decides 'light' mayo is not what it seems," *Adweek's Marketing Week,* October 15, 1990, p. 6.

To protect its NutriSweet identifier, Monsanto registered it with the Commissioner of Patents and Trademarks.

MANUFACTURERS' BRAND

Brands created by the maker of a good or the provider of a service are **manufacturers' brands.** These identifiers may be on individual items, such as Tone soap, Windex glass cleaner, Contadina tomato paste or Visa charge card. Manufacturers' brands also appear on a series of products, such as Swanson soups and frozen dinners, Kraft cheeses and dinners or Levi's jeans, shirts and casual clothing.

Manufacturers' brands identify the products made by that company. Even when specific names or symbols are created by outside agencies, these brands become part of the product itself. The marketer retains exclusive rights to the use of these identifiers when they are properly protected. Aqua Net is a manufacturer's brand used by a division of Fabergé for hair spray. Georgia-Pacific produces MD brand bathroom tissue. Spred is the identifier coined by Glidden for its latex based exterior paint.

Manufacturer's brand—an identifier created by the maker of a product.

DEALER BRAND

Marketing intermediaries also create brands. These **dealer brands** are as distinctive as manufacturer brands. Also know as **private label,** these identifiers battle toe-to-toe with other merchandise and often win the war. President's Choice, for example, is a line of upscale food items marketed by Loblaw Cos. Ltd. of Toronto that competes successfully against manufacturers' brands in both Canada and the United States. Many dealer brands also come in packages that are similar to more famous products, which often leads to court battles. So far, manufacturers have their hands full trying to compete, as private labels continue to grow in popularity.[4]

Dealer brand—an identifier created by a marketing intermediary, also called private label.

---

[4]Michael J. Silverstein, "Exposing the five myths of private label brands," *BRANDWEEK*, June 20, 1994, pp. 17–18; Richard Gibson, "Pitch, panache buoy fancy private label," *The Wall Street Journal,* January 27, 1994, pp. B1 and B10; Judith Springer Riddle, "There just ain't no cure for the store brand blues," *BRANDWEEK*, July 19, 1993, pp. 16–17; Jon Berry, "If you have nothing to say, why not be a store brand," *BRANDWEEK*, October 11, 1993, p. 14; Jon Berry, "Now, the new generation of store brand products," *BRANDWEEK*, November 29, 1993, p. 13; Jon Berry, "Even Perry Mason may not have the store-brand solution," *BRANDWEEK*, May 17, 1993, p. 15.

Sears has an ownership interest in some of its suppliers, but this legendary retailer does not actually make the products it sells. Yet Craftsman tools and Kenmore appliances are well known as brands that belong to Sears. In the same fashion, United Grocers, a grocery wholesaler, has penned the name Western Family to identify paper goods, pasta and other grocery items made for them by manufacturers. Weyerhaeuser, the timber products company, makes Ultra Soft disposable diapers for Wegman's, a regional chain store. Actually, Wegman's, with forty-five supermarket outlets located in upstate New York, is involved very heavily with private label brands.[5]

Kmart uses Nature's Classics and Oral Pure as in-store brands. The Bon Marché carries its own menswear under the Carl Michaels and Saville Row names. To upgrade the image, if not the prices, some retailers redesigned the packages for their store brands to include the company name. Dominick's, a supermarket chain out of Chicago, included the company name on its new packaging, and sales and profits increased dramatically. The battle between manufacturers' brands and private labels is bound to continue throughout the 1990s, and beyond.[6]

FAMILY BRANDS

Family brand—an identifier that appears on a group of products.

Manufacturers or intermediaries sometimes create **family brands** which identify an entire group of products as uniquely their own. When consumers relate to a series of items having the same name, they often develop loyalty for the entire family. Preference for Kleenex facial tissue may be transferred to Kleenex dinner napkins. Satisfied users of Minute Maid frozen orange juice are apt to show the same brand loyalty to frozen juice bars with that same family brand.

Kraft General Foods markets a variety of family brands. These include Good Seasons salad dressings, Birds Eye frozen foods and Baker's chocolate and coconut baking products. Each of these families of brands contains a variety of individual names or descriptions given to specific products. Betty Crocker, the well-known family brand for cake mixes and budget meals from General Mills, is now found on a variety of kitchen utensils, such as pizza pans, clocks and knives.[7]

Most of the goods and services described so far are consumer products. While branding is more common with trade goods, some production goods marketers also use brands. For example, Salespacer, Drummer and Huckster are brand names of merchandising displays manufactured and distributed by Stor-Rite Metal Products. Mylar and Lucite are DuPont's brand names for polyester plastic film and acrylics.

---

[5]Gerry Khermouch, "Wegman's builds its local base with private label," *BRANDWEEK*, March 8, 1993, p. 23; James Lileks, "Brand names loom large in consciousness," *The Oregonian*, March 17, 1991, p. L3.

[6]Patricia Sellers, "Brands: It's thrive or die," *Fortune*, August 23, 1993, pp. 52–56; Elaine Underwood, "Kmart private label: Haste makes waste," *BRANDWEEK*, August 17, 1992, p. 4; Elaine Underwood, "Re-store brands," *Adweek's Marketing Week*, June 18, 1992, pp. 28–30.

[7]Elaine Underwood, "Betty Crocker heads for junior high," *BRANDWEEK*, November 11, 1991, p. 10; Cara Appelbaum, "Spreading Betty's name around," *Adweek's Marketing Week*, May 25, 1991, p. 6.

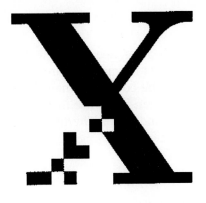

Xerox, The Document Company, changed its corporate identifiers to better describe the company's operations. (Courtesy of Xerox Corporation)

CORPORATE BRANDS

Just as the branding of a product is important, the naming of a business, organization or retail outlet may be a significant marketing tool. The Southland Corporation selected 7/Eleven for its convenience stores because the name identified the hours of operation. It was also catchy and easy to remember. Although many of these franchise operations are now open 24 hours a day, the name remains a classic.

Similar to product brands, business names indicate ownership and attempt to build loyalty. Instead of relating to a product quality or benefit, business names often refer to the type of business the firm conducts. Overhead Door Company, International Paper, United Technologies, and Data General are company names illustrating this point. Federal Express is another corporate brand that describes the business activity. In 1994, the company went through a complete restructuring of its image including a name change to FedEx. Xerox is another major company that has undergone an identity crisis and change.[8]

Many retail firms and business goods marketers take the name of the founders of the company. Robinson's and Goldwater's are department stores labeled for their organizers. Other production goods firms named for their originators include Hewlett Packard, Pitney Bowes, B. F. Goodrich and Boeing Airplane Company. Some businesses select unique and memorable corporate identifiers. Compaq, Tektronix and Nike fit this description.

What Are the Objectives of Branding?

Identifiers are expected to do more than merely separate the marketers of one product from another. While establishing ownership is important, marketers use branding to accomplish a variety of other objectives. The branding strategy used by a marketing company depends upon these aims.

---

[8]Tim Triplett, "Generic fear to Xerox is brand equity to FedEx," *Marketing News*, August 15, 1994, pp. 12–13; Elaine Underwood, "Proper I.D.," *BRANDWEEK*, August 8, 1994, pp. 24–30.

MAINTAIN PRODUCT LOYALTY

Many products compete for the satisfaction of customer needs and wants. **Product loyalty** is one key to increased sales and profits for manufacturers and for intermediaries. If a product creates an image for the consumer that makes the buying decision easier, then the buyer will more than likely use that brand regularly. A study by the Boston Research Group found that many of the top brands of fifty years ago had amazing staying power.[9]

IDENTIFY VALUE AND QUALITY

Marketers also use brands to **identify the level of value and quality** of their products. Marketing management expects that buyers will recognize the value and quality of their products through the brand. For example, consumers attach an image of economical driving to the Geo Metro and luxury to the Cadillac Seville. General Motors strives to maintain these perceived levels of value and quality throughout all elements of the marketing mix.

Conversely, when a marketer introduces a new product at a different level of quality, the company will often change brand names. As an illustration, Holiday Inns generally positions itself as a moderately priced motel chain that caters largely to vacationing families. When the company targeted traveling business people who visit major metropolitan areas, Holiday Inns started a new chain of more expensive and extravagant hotels branded Crowne Plaza. Little or no reference to Holiday Inn ownership is made at these hostelries. Other Holiday Inn properties, such as Homewood Suites and Hampton Inns do not stress the corporate name so as to establish their own brand/quality perception.

An EquiTrend study from Total Research, a Princeton, New Jersey, firm, ranks brands on an annual basis according to their quality appeal. In a survey of 2,000 randomly selected households, consumers were asked to rate brands on a scale of one to ten based upon quality. Although the results are acknowledged to vary according to a wide variety of conditions, including the state of the economy, several brands have dominated the top ten for the past five years. Disney, Kodak, Hallmark, Mercedes, Fisher-Price, AT&T and Levi's have yet to fall out of the select front-runners.[10]

The same company, using a model designed by John Morton, divides consumers into seven primary categories; intellects, conformists, popularity seekers, pragmatists, actives, relief seekers and sentimentals. The demographics of each group can be plotted along with perceptions of brand quality. Taking the process one step further, the magazine *Financial World* calculates a dollar

---

[9]Martin J. Beck, "Building brand equity where it really counts: In the store," *BRANDWEEK,* June 13, 1994, p. 20; George S. Low, Ronald A. Fullerton, "Brands, brand management, and the brand manager system," *Journal of Marketing Research,* May 1994, pp. 173–190; Tracy Carlson, "Brand burnout," *BRANDWEEK,* January 17, 1994, pp. 23–24.

[10]Terry Lefton, "Measuring quality perception of America's top brands," *BRANDWEEK,* April 4, 1994, pp. 24–26.

The equitrend top 20

1994	1993	BRANDNAME	1994 SCORE
1	1	Disney World	84.1
2	1	Disneyland	82.8
3	3	Kodak Photographic Film	82.5
4	4	Hallmark Greeting Cards	81.4
5	8	Mercedes Automobiles	80.3
6	5	Fisher-Price Toys	80.2
7	—	Reynolds Wrap Aluminum Foil	79.9
8	6	AT&T Long Distance Telephone	79.4
9	10	Levi's Jeans	79.1
10	—	Ziploc Bags	78.9
11	—	Sea World	77.8
12	9	Arm & Hammer Baking Soda	77.7
13	—	Duracell Batteries	77.7
14	12	Lego Toys	77.2
15	16	Tylenol Pain Reliever	77.1
16	21	IBM Personal Computers	77.1
17	13	Hershey's Milk Chocolate Bar	77.0
18	22	Campbell's Soup	76.9
19	26	Lexus Automobiles	76.7
20	19	Michelin Automobile Tires	76.4

NOTE: Because Total Research changes the number of brands, as well as the identity of the brands it ranks in each year's EquiTrend study, past rankings are adjusted to reflect ratings in accordance with the brands being ranked in the current survey.

■   ■   ■   ■   ■

value for globally familiar identifiers in a variety of categories including apparel, electronics, food, and personal care products.[11]

Preserving an Upscale Image

Attaching quality and value to an image is especially important with upscale products. These items which cost more than average brands are expected to provide more quality as well. Although many of the products that fall into this category took a beating during the recession of the early 1990s, some are making a comeback. In the same annual EquiTrend survey cited above, researchers note that such brands as American Express, Estée Lauder, Lexus, Marriott and Cadillac are just a few upscale brands that continue to shine.[12]

PRODUCT COMPARISON

For the consumer or user, branding promotes **product comparison.** The consumer describes his or her tastes or feelings by referring to a product by its

---

[11]Alexandra Ourusoff, with Meenakshi Panchapakesan, "Who said brands are dead?" *BRANDWEEK*, August 9, 1993, pp. 20–33; John Morton, "Brand quality segments: Potent way to predict preference," *Marketing News*, September 14, 1992, pp. IR-8 and 14.

[12]Cyndee Miller, "Upscale brands regaining popularity," *Marketing News*, May 23, 1994, p. 3.

identifier. This usually leads to a quality evaluation of the goods or services being described. If the buyer prefers French's mustard, then he or she has established a taste preference. In addition, the consumer has the freedom to choose by brand and can challenge the manufacturer's promises by selecting one brand over another. Those who purchase by brand name are trusting that the product does what the manufacturer claims it does.

While helping buyers to compare product value and quality, branding also promotes convenience. For those consumers who may not read the complete labels on packages nor have time to try a variety of products before each shopping, branding simplifies decision making. These buyers can choose more quickly with more assurance because of images created by product identifiers. Shopping becomes more convenient once brand loyalty is established.

What Makes a Good Brand?

Although there are no hard and fast rules for the selection of brands, most marketers follow some general guidelines. It is important that the brand fits the image of the product and of the marketer. Identifiers should be distinctive, easy to communicate and relate to the use or benefit received.

FITS THE IMAGE

The brand name must **fit the product and/or company image.** Since marketers position their products to create images in the minds of consumers and industrial users, branding of the good or service needs to reinforce and strengthen that representation. Said another way, brands must keep in character with the entire marketing mix. Rugged products need rugged names. Companies marketing toward children usually develop light, fanciful branding. Upscale products avoid trite or mundane brands to avoid conflicts in positioning.

An identifier that fails to suggest stability or conservatism might not fit the image of a financial company. Soft, feminine names would not help sell a line of men's toiletries. Prudential chose the Rock of Gibraltar as their symbol for solid financial strength, and Gillette uses Right Guard for its deodorant. Ortega and Old El Paso are appropriate names for Mexican food products. The name Continental suits a Lincoln better than Mustang or Tempo.

DISTINCTIVE

The brand name should be **distinctive** and should stand out from the competition. Marketers spend considerable effort to develop product differentiation, hence the brands should also stand out from the competition. Dannon created the name Danimals for its line of yogurts for kids, and McDonald's adopted the slang term for the company, Mickey D, for its dinner sized hamburger. One would be hard pressed to create a list of brands more distinctive than Apple computers, Ziploc plastic bags, Duracell batteries, Playskool toys, Tylenol pain relievers and the all-time winner L'eggs hosiery.

Global Marketing: Hugs and Kisses.

What could be more American than a Saturday afternoon at the movie munching on Milk Duds or Good & Plenty candies? Well, while the movie may be a product of the good ol' USA, those two brands of candy are the product of Leaf, a division of the giant Finnish conglomerate Huhtamaki Oy. Other well-known brands from this Scandinavian firm include Heath toffee bars, Whoppers malted milk balls and Pay-day peanut bar. The global candy business is not the private domain of American marketers.

For years, the U.S. candy business has been dominated by Hershey and Mars. Each maintains about one-third of the domestic market, and any move by one company is quickly matched by the competitor. When Hershey increased its share of the market in 1989 with the purchase of Peter Paul/Cadbury, Mars cranked up its new product development process, coming out with twelve new brands. One of these, a premium priced, European style chocolate bar named Sussande bombed, costing the company an estimated $100 million.

With the American market becoming more calorie conscious, both companies have turned their atten-

tion overseas. At the end of World War II, Hershey had unbelievable brand recognition in both Europe and Asia. American GIs handing out candy bars as they occupied former war zones created an awareness for Hershey chocolate bars that rivaled Coke's familiarity. Unfortunately, conservative corporate policies failed to take advantage of this market position.

Hershey is now actively pursuing business overseas. The company gained an immediate presence in Europe by purchasing Gubor, a German chocolate marketer, and has since bought a major candy firm in Scandinavia. Swiss giant Nestle still controls a bulk of the European market, but Hershey is making inroads. New product development is active at this Pennsylvania company. A white chocolate confection branded Hugs is the same shape and size as the famous Hershey's Kisses. The Hershey brand Reese's is also scoring well in the peanut butter market.

SOURCE: Fara Warner, "Turning over a new leaf: Aggressive branding awakes," BRANDWEEK, July 4, 1994, pp. 18–20; Rita Koselka, "Candy wars," Forbes, August 17, 1992, pp. 76–77.

Names that separate one brand from the rest of the pack are often easier to remember. Ralph Lauren's Polo brand of clothing is unique in the garment industry. Many fashion lines use only the designer's name, such as Charlotte Ford, Geoffrey Beene or Amy Vanderbilt. Fling disposable cameras from Kodak and Royal Velvet towels by Fieldcrest stand alone, yet accurately describe the product. Breeze from Airwick, Option hair coloring for men from Clairol and Calphalon pots and pans from Commercial Aluminum Cookware Company are distinctive brands. In one of the most innovative promotional campaigns in decades, the Price Pfister division of Black & Decker used a play on its Pfunny spelled name to create Pfixer-upper awareness of its Pfabulous Pfaucets.[13]

---

[13]Pam Weisz, "Price tools for Pfixer-uppers," BRANDWEEK, April 18, 1994, p. 8.

EASY TO COMMUNICATE

The brand name should be **easy to say, spell, write,** and **remember.** Gatorade, Dentine, Dockers, Lumina and WordPerfect fit this requirement. Other easily communicated brands include Silk Bright, Spudsters, TheraFlu, Silent Sentry and Motorola. The list of good brand names is endless and memorable. Companies look for brands that are easy to communicate globally. Knowing how a brand translates into a foreign tongue avoids embarrassment.[14]

Corporate brands must be easy to communicate. Apple and Compaq are computer firms that follow this practice. Franchise operations such as Burger King, Big 5 Sporting Goods, Mail Boxes Etc. and MinitLube reap the benefit of descriptive, easy-to-remember names.

RELATES TO PRODUCT OR BENEFIT

Many successful brand names **relate to the product or its benefit.** This relationship may refer to the use of the product, to the needs filled, or to the user benefit. Die-Hard batteries, Easy-Off oven cleaner, Beautyrest mattresses are good examples. Cling-Free anti-static fabric softener and Off insect repellent refer to the functions or benefits of these products.

hat Are Branding Strategies?

Branding strategies are the methods used by marketing management to distinguish goods and services from one another. Some marketers select brands that relate to a family of products, while others create distinct names for each good. To identify its products, the marketing company looks to previous successes and present needs. Outside consultants or branding specialists frequently aid in this important decision. The strategy used depends upon the company philosophy, the firm's product mix, and the competitive situation.

BRAND EXTENSION

Brand extension— adopting the name of a successful brand for a new one.

To build brand loyalty, some firms continue exploiting a proven, well-excepted brand name by using it on new or additional products. Such **brand extension,** sometimes referred to as line extension, is quite popular with consumer goods marketers. For example, PepsiCo uses brand extension in creating its family of products that include Pepsi Cola, Diet Pepsi, Pepsi Light, Crystal Pepsi and Pepsi Free. Kraft General Food's success with Jell-O brand gelatin dessert prompted

---

[14]France Leclerc, Bernard H. Smith, Laurette Dube, "Foreign branding and its effect on product perceptions and attitudes," *Journal of Marketing Research*, May 1994, pp. 263–270; Editors, "Firms pick their names to fit new global economy," *Marketing News*, October 1, 1990, p. 2.

■ ■ ■ ■ ■

Some examples of good branding

BRAND	CHARACTERISTICS OF IDENTIFIER
Certified Stainmaster Carpet (DuPont)	Describes product; fits image; distinctive; a bit wordy
Lunch Buckets microwaveable meals (Dial)	Distinctive; relates to product usage; communicable
Fab 1 Shot detergent (Colgate-Palmolive)	Fits image; relates to benefit; catchy
Lean Cuisine frozen dinners (Stouffer)	Distinctive; fits image; rhythmical and almost poetic
Mevacor cholesterol reducer (Merck)	Fits image; sounds mediciny
Fling disposable camera (Kodak)	Relates to use; distinctive; short and snappy
Reatta sports car (Buick)	Relates to design origin (Italy); short; racy sounding
Firespice hickory chips (Weber)	Relates to benefit; relates to use; unique
Bull's-Eye barbecue sauce (Kraft)	Distinctive; sounds strong or masculine; memorable
Lend Lease truck rental (Lend Lease)	Relates to service; sounds business-like
The Guardian Life Insurance Co.	Relates to benefit; gives aura of protection and security
Swatch watches (Swatch)	Pertinent; retainable; winning
Rent-A-Wreck car rentals	Descriptive; unforgettable; easy to say

■ ■ ■ ■ ■

additional products under that familiar trademark. Frozen treats, puddings and packaged cheesecakes all carry the Jell-O brand.[15]

The original Wheat Chex cereal brand from Ralston has been extended to include Rice Chex, Corn Chex and Honey Graham Chex. Dole, a popular brand of fresh fruit, uses brand extension with its line of raisins, dates and nuts. Nabisco uses this tactic when it adds Apple Newtons and Strawberry Newtons to the original Fig Newtons brand. L&F leveraged the Lysol brand into drain openers in 1994, and Chesebrough-Ponds added Mentadent mouthwash to the toothpaste line in 1995. Another niche marketer, Heluva Good Cheese, has salsa and cocktail sauces using the same, catchy brand name.[16]

Brand extension is not limited to convenience goods. The strategy appeals to shopping goods marketers, too. A good example is Conair which acquired bankrupt Cuisinarts in 1989. Conair, noted for marketing hair dryers, kept the Cuisinart name on its upscale product line. The company extended the Cuisinart brand to microwave ovens and espresso coffee machines.[17]

The idea behind brand extension strategy is to capitalize on the popularity of an accepted brand by using that same identifier on other items. Although some argue that this strategy is overused, the policy still remains popular, especially in the highly competitive convenience goods arenas. Several big names in consumer goods marketing are now moving into branded produce. Pillsbury, Kraft General

---

[15] Judith D. Schwartz, "New recipes, repositioning put the jiggle back in Jell-O," *BRANDWEEK*, May 10, 1993, p. 26; David Kiley, "Finally, branded vegetables are on the shelves," *Adweek's Marketing Week*, October 30, 1990, pp. 20–24.

[16] Pam Weisz, "Lysol family grows into drain category," *BRANDWEEK*, June 27, 1994, p. 9; Pam Weisz, "Mentadent mouthwash in '95," *BRANDWEEK*, June 13, 1994, p. 4; Karen Benezra, "Heluva good time to repackage, line extend," *BRANDWEEK*, May 2, 1994, p. 25.

[17] Debra Chanil, "Personal cair appliances," *Discount Merchandiser*, September 1993, p. 74; Ariane Sains, "Conair extends the Cuisinart name to other upscale goods," *Adweek's Marketing Week*, March 19, 1990, pp. 20–21.

**Some examples of brand extension
and flanker branding**

COMPANY	BRANDS
Continental Baking	Hostess cupcakes, pudding cakes and Twinkies (brand extension)
Drackett Products	Windex, Endust (flanker brands)
Procter & Gamble	Ivory soap, liquid and flakes (brand extension) Tide, Cheer, Bold, Oxydol and Dash (flanker brands)
Golden Grain	Rice-a-Roni, Noodle Roni (brand extension)
Unilever	Lipton tea, soup, rice and sauces (brand extension)
Ralston Purina	Lucky Dog, Dog Chow, HiPro, Chuck Wagon (flanker brands) Wheat Chex, Rice Chex, Bran Chex (brand extension)

■ ■ ■ ■ ■

Foods, Green Giant, a division of Metropolitan PLC, and Campbell Soup are seeking consumer acceptance of their well-known names in the fresh fruit and vegetable departments of supermarkets. Niche marketer Frieda's Incorporated specializes in exotic items, including spaghetti squash, Asian pears, arugula and kiwis, for its line of branded produce.[18]

FLANKER BRANDING

Flanker brand—a new product with an individual brand.

Some marketing oriented companies create new branding for each product they produce. Procter & Gamble and General Mills are noted for bringing **flanker brands** to the market. A flanker brand is a new product with an individual brand name. These products often compete with existing items in the same product line as well as with brands from other marketers. Each of the laundry detergents marketed by P&G, such as Tide, Bold, Cheer and Dash, carries its own distinctive identifier.

The automobile industry thrives on flanker branding. Although most carry the housemark name, such as Dodge, Ford or Buick, individual models each have separate identifiers. Caravan, Taurus and Riviera narrow the broad manufacturers' identification to a more specific, distinct flanker brand. In many ways, the use of this branding strategy increases the uniqueness of the product to a greater extent than does brand extension.

COMPUTER ASSISTED BRANDING

DuPont was perhaps the first major corporation to use the computer in selecting brand names for its products. The ingredients and potential uses for the

---

[18]Judith Schwartz, "Searching for the next kiwi: Frieda's branded produce," *BRANDWEEK,* May 2, 1994, pp. 46–48; Robert McMath, "Produce market is ripe for branded fruits, vegetables," *BRANDWEEK,* June 7, 1993, p. 26; Jonathan Prinz, "Extending your brand? Consider what's at stake," *BRANDWEEK,* April 4, 1994, p. 17; Laura Zinn, "Does Pepsi have too many products?" *Business Week,* February 14, 1994, pp. 64–66.

prospective item are fed into dataprocessors which then select the most appropriate identifier. Dacron, Tedlar, Orlon, Kevlar, Tyvek, Teflon and a host of distinctive brands result.

The use of computers has fostered businesses whose sole task is to dream up attractive brand names. Sentra, one of Nissan's models, the Acura Legend, Zapmail and Compaq are the creations of NameLab, a brand creating company. A similar firm, Interbrand, coined Priazzo for Pizza Hut and Affinity for Johnson & Johnson. The SALINON Corporation markets a computer program called Namer to help companies select brand names and another titled Headliner to create slogans and jingles.[19]

hat Are the Functions of a Package?

Branding is not the only facet of a product's attributes that builds loyalty. The way that the product is boxed, canned, bottled or wrapped aids in creating a faithful following. Modern packaging is both functional and attractive. Consumers will remember easy handling or reusable packages. When buyers are attracted to the package, they are likely to develop loyalty toward the contents. Positioning of products includes packaging.

CONTAIN

Packages **contain** the product. This is the primary function of packaging. Boxes, cans, plastic bags or glass bottles in a variety of shapes and sizes hold the goods that consumers purchase. It would be difficult to shop for shampoo or peanut butter without containers to hold these items. Similarly, industrial goods arrive at buyers in gaylords, drum or shrink wrapped. Cost savings occur if large quantities of goods can be accommodated by forklifts and other materials handling equipment. A plastic film-wrapped pallet holding forty-eight cartons of motor oil can be loaded and off-loaded from vehicles more efficiently than by man-handling individual cases.

A nostalgic move to return to the old, general store merchandising method of offering dry goods in bulk has become popular in some areas. Supermarkets offer select products in bins where customers can scoop out nuts, candies, cereals or pasta in just the amounts needed. With this notable exception, the largest percentage of items purchased from consumer retailers are available in some sort of package.

PROTECT

The modern package also **protects** its contents. Delicate, high-technology parts are typically packed in boxes lined with foam to guard against the rigors of shipment. Blister packaging protects smaller items from handling while providing

[19]Casey McCabe, "What's in a name," *Adweek's Marketing Week*, April 16, 1990, p. 22.

the customer with a view of the product. Many foods come sealed in multi-layer plastic packages that keep discoloring gasses out while retaining tasteful moisture. Among the innovative designs used to protect contents include a glass coated plastic by Flex Products Inc. called Transpak.[20]

The package also serves to protect the seller from possible theft, especially of small items. Cassette tapes and compact discs are typically sold in larger packages than the contents, making them more difficult to conceal. The backing card of a blister or shrink wrapped package is likewise harder to hide in a would-be thief's purse or pocket. These containers also offer a degree of protection from damage to the enclosed products. The plastic cover is usually troublesome to break or tear, thus the product and its package remain intact and losses are minimized. Some packages contain sensors that will trigger electronic scanners designed to deter shoplifting.

PROMOTE

A product's package often becomes the key identifier of the product itself. Because so much of the package is involved with **promoting** the product, the package is often included as part of the overall promotional effort. Recipes, directions, helpful tips and many other promotional aids add to the appeal of packages. Package labels inform buyers of the ingredients and any cautions about the contents.

Action by the Food and Drug Administration in 1994 led to major changes in the labeling of food packages. A list of ingredients is no longer enough. All food containers must now clearly tell consumers the fat, cholesterol and caloric content of each serving. The FDA also set stringent standards on what can or cannot be labeled as "low fat" or "healthy." This type of packaging enhances safety for the consumer.[21]

For many consumer goods marketers, distinctive packaging is an equity protector of the brand itself. Coca-Cola spent millions in developing a plastic version of its famous curved bottle. PepsiCo has endeavored to build the same ready awareness for its own line by giving the packages names, such as "Fast Break" and "Big Slam." Mentadent's double pump and the easy-to-open yet childproof cap on Aleve are likely to cement a certain segment of consumers to those brands. Perrier added unusual artwork to its bottle, and a new process by Brandt Technologies Incorporated out of Windsor, New York, promises to make its uniquely painted bottle more common.[22]

---

[20]John Holusha, "New packaging that spares the environment," *The Wall Street Journal,* March 28, 1990.

[21]Cyndee Miller, "Food industry faces sweeping label requirements," *Marketing News,* June 6, 1994, pp. 5 and 12; John Carey, "Food labeling: The FDA has the right ingredients," *Business Week,* November 23, 1992, p. 42; Elaine Underwood, "Labeling rules a boon to package designers," *BRANDWEEK,* December 14, 1992, p. 9.

[22]Cyndee Miller, "The shape of things," *Marketing News,* August 15, 1994, pp. 1 and 2; Betsy Spethmannn, "The mystique of the brand: Jarred, bagged, boxed, canned," *BRANDWEEK,* June 27, 1994, pp. 25–28; Karen Benezra, "Crystal Pepsi gets new look for youth," *BRANDWEEK,* February 28, 1994, p. 5; Betsy Spethmann, "Patented packages become equity guard," *BRANDWEEK,* August 9, 1993, pp. 1 and 6; Gerry Khermouch, "Painted bottles: The next wave in niche packaging," *BRANDWEEK,* March 8, 1993, p. 10.

Marketing and Society: Getting a L'egg up.

It would be difficult to conjure up a better example of expertise than the marketing of L'eggs. Twenty years ago this division of Hanes called on the Howard Marlboro Group to design a complete program for the merchandising of pantyhose. The brand name, novel package and original egg-shaped free standing display unit launched a two-decade career for this product that has seen few equals. So unique was this approach that it not only won numerous marketing awards, but also is exhibited at the Whitney Museum of American Art in New York City.

L'eggs was the first pantyhose to be nationally branded and distributed through grocery, drug and discount stores. This brand literally transformed the industry and led to the 55 percent share of market that it enjoys today. Although the package has endured with little more than color changes for decades, marketing management at this innovative company recognized the problem of keeping an "endangered species" like a styrofoam eggshell before sensitive consumers. In 1991, L'eggs introduced a new, ovoid shaped cardboard package that promises to be more acceptable to an environmentally conscious audience. Once again, the Howard Marlboro Group did the design.

SOURCES: Laurie Petersen, "Shed the egg, spare the image," *Adweek's Marketing Week*, July 15, 1991, p. 9; Associated Press release, "L'eggs to scrap plastic 'egg' package," *Marketing News*, August 19, 1991, p. 20.

The color, shape or texture of the package identifies and enhances the image that the product is trying to promote. The yellow Pennzoil bottle, the green can of Comet cleanser and the white Johnson & Johnson first-aid packages all single out the contents by color. The shape of the Quaker Oats box, the Planters' peanuts jar and Pepperidge Farms bags help promote by their distinctive shape. The L'eggs package is a prime example of the promotional value of creative design.

Creative Environments Incorporated added another promotional twist to packages, smell. Shoppers strolling the supermarket aisles will now get a good whiff of the product if they pass within two feet of its shelf. These scented containers have been created to promote brands using this innovative packaging concept. Shopping goods marketers are experimenting with talking packages that give assembly directions to buyers. Andrew Jergens has even begun to package its famous lotions in refillable pouches, promoting that these packages help to save money and the environment.[23]

---

[23]Seema Nayyar, "Refillable pouch a lotions first," *BRANDWEEK,* October 26, 1992, p. 3; Editors, Packaging Notebook, *Adweek's Marketing Week,* January 20, 1992, p. 44; Cyndee Miller, "Hey, listen to this: a talking package!" *Marketing News,* April 15, 1991, pp. 1 and 25; Laura Bird, "Romancing the package," *Adweek's Marketing Week,* January 21, 1991, pp. 10–14.

Uniform Product Codes appear on packages for everything from Adams peanut butter to Zee paper towels. Laser scanners at the checkout stand read the bar codes on packages. The UPCs give the grocery shopper a speedy check out at supermarkets while recording up-to-the-second inventory control for the merchant. This excellent method for stock management is spreading from the grocery business into a variety of other industries, including clothing and auto parts.

OFFER CONVENIENCE

Packaging multiple units in one container provides **convenience** to the buyer and potential cost savings to the manufacturer. The use of six-packs for soft drinks or giant economy sizes of laundry detergent make it easier for the shopper. The manufacturer benefits from increased sales and lower production costs because of the larger purchases and increased consumption. Marketing hot dog rolls or batteries in multiple unit packages increases the unit sales for the marketer.

Campbell Soup Company targets college students as a prime market for Chunky brand soups. Ring-pull tops make it easy for buyers to pull, pour and zap in the microwave oven. Seneca Foods conveniently packs its applesauce that ends up in lunch buckets with wooden spoons. McCormack markets black pepper in a bottle with a built-in grinder. In these cases, customer convenience produces loyalty.[24]

Package convenience also relates to serving size. Although once shunned by consumers, individual portion packs are reemerging. For example, TheraFlu and Metamusil are over-the-counter remedies available in single servings. The fast-food industry favors premeasured condiments, and test marketing for jams, dressings and coffee creamers in such packages looks promising.[25]

PROVIDE SAFETY

Modern packaging provides **safety.** This package function is particularly evident in over-the-counter medicines and drugs. Since the Tylenol scare in 1982, where cyanide was found in capsules, most pharmaceuticals feature safety devices. Many now include seals which when broken indicate that the package has been violated. Labels ask consumers to check for broken seals. With the number of different types of containers used in the food industry, tamper protection may be complicated. One solution is the inclusion of a chemical within a food pouch, such as the inner package of a boxed product, that when punctured reveals a latent image on the package that says "opened."

Safety of the environment is another consideration. Many packagers have eliminated plastic foams from packages because of the potential harm to the atmosphere. Since the fluorocarbons used in aerosols deplete the ozone layer,

---

[24]Robert McMath, "Eye on: Packaging," *Adweek's Marketing Week,* January 8, 1990, pp. 76–77.

[25]Eben Shapiro, "Mini products have mini sales," *The Wall Street Journal,* October 12, 1993, p. B1; Dan Koeppel, "From salad oils to jams to laxatives, tiny 'packables' are enjoying a mini-boom," *Adweek's Marketing Week,* February 12, 1990, p. 5.

UPC CODE AND SYMBOL

The Universal Product Code symbol is a graphic representation of the UPC code. It is in the form of a series of parallel light and dark bars of different widths. The numbers printed below the machine-readable symbol allow for human reading of the code number. To accommodate the ranges in quality achievable by various printing processes, the symbol size is variable. Nominal size is 1.020 inches in height by 1.469 inches in width. The symbol size can vary from 80% to 200% of nominal. It is readable in an omni-directional manner by fixed-position scanners. This feature increases checkout productivity by allowing the items to be machine read without the need for the checker to orient the symbol in relation to the scanner.

The symbol prevents tampering, and even poor printing should not result in scanning devices reading a wrong number. The symbol is also readable using hand-held devices.

The UPC code number 12345 67890 printed below the symbol is for human use as is the number system character printed to the left of the symbol and the modulo check character printed to the right. The symbol, in addition to containing the UPC code number, number system character, and modulo check character, also includes left and right guard bars, center bars, and left and right light margins. Each character in the symbol is made up of two dark bars and two light spaces.

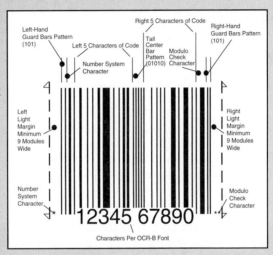

marketers across a broad spectrum of product lines are switching to pumps. Old and new products alike are finding their way into trigger dispensers. Procter & Gamble uses pumps for deodorants and cleansers, and S. C. Johnson has put its Pledge cleanser in a triggered spray bottle.[26]

Which Features of Packages Benefit Consumers?

Proper packaging offers a variety of benefits to both buyers and sellers. Consumers and users receive fresher, safer products, and suppliers gain cost savings and promotional value. Modern packagers are often innovative and creative. New materials and advanced technology produce advantages for both maker and user. The lowly package is not an insignificant part of the product.

---

[26]Robert McMath, "It's all in the trigger," *Adweek's Marketing Week,* January 6, 1992, pp. 25–28.

ECONOMY AND REUSABILITY

Different sized packages may offer **economy** to the consumer when the manufacturer passes its savings on to the buyer. By purchasing the exact amount needed, buyers reduce waste and save money in the process. Single people might need milk by the quart to maintain its freshness. The family with three teenagers may find it hard to keep the refrigerator stocked even when buying milk in gallon containers. As the use of individual serving packages has increased, so has the number of packages designed to serve just two people. The size of the household has become a major factor in determining the size of the package.

Some packages are **reusable,** producing a benefit to consumers. Peanut butter tubs or cookie tins make attractive containers for a variety of items. The consumer gains a useful receptacle, and the marketer benefits from increased demand for its product. Coffee cans and empty jars have long been favorites for use in holding nails or sewing supplies. Some product packages have even more useful reapplications, as consumers collect empty packages because of their unique design. Some distillers of spirits market their products in one-of-a-kind bottles or attractive tins that collectors accumulate and trade.

DISPOSABILITY

Disposability of used packages continues to concern conservationists, consumers and manufacturers alike. Packagers are making headway in the fight to cut the costs associated with disposing of used packages. Easier and safer means of discarding old packages benefits both society and consumers. Containers that are easy to dispose of mean lower costs for the trash industry and governments and less time and effort exerted by users. Biodegradable materials are more common, and new types of packaging are being researched.

Recycling

Recycling—the process of reusing scrap packaging materials.

Many municipalities promote **recycling,** the process of collecting scrap packaging for reuse. Some area trash collectors are required to collect recyclable materials when placed alongside regular waste pickups. The recycling of packages results in lower material costs by reusing raw materials while providing a cleaner environment. Plastics manufacturers are joining the recycle bandwagon. Many communities took action to ban the use of foam cups and serving containers made from this polystyrene. Mobil, Dow, Amoco and four other polystyrene makers have created the National Polystyrene Recycling Co., with plans for five national locations.

 hat Is a Warranty?

Many consumer goods and services carry warranties or guarantees. These associate attributes may be the feature that sways the buying decision from one item to another. With shopping goods, the willingness of the manufacturer to back its products often influences the purchase decision. A solid reputation for quality, reinforced by the integrity of the marketing firm, goes a long way toward providing customer satisfaction.

WARRANTY DEFINED

A **warranty** is a promise to replace or repair defective products, or provide a refund. Warranties can sometimes produce competitive battles between the makers of goods. The automotive industry is noted for using product warranty as a promotional tool. When Chrysler first began the "5 year/50,000 mile" campaign, competitors quickly responded. Other car manufacturers from Detroit have since engaged in a "war of warranties" that has produced 6/60 and 7/70 versions of this warranty protection. In times of massive recalls, such as 1993, warranties become a major concern to both buyer and seller.[27]

Warranty—a promise to replace, repair or refund defective merchandise.

The serviceability of products, and the warranties that manufacturers give with their goods, have considerable promotional effect. One reason that IBM was so successful in selling its personal computers over the years was at least in part due to the availability of service on its electronic equipment. Maytag, too, is renown for its serviceability. Retailers also benefit from policies that provide customers with repair or maintenance. Sears proudly promotes that it services what it sells.

IMPLIED VS EXPRESSED WARRANTY

All products carry an **implied warranty.** Products must perform the tasks they were designed to carry out. Although the degree of control or level of operation may vary from product to product, consumers and users are entitled to goods that work. Scissors are supposed to cut, bicycles should carry a person from one place to another and washable garments must last through the rinse cycle. Although pinking shears cut differently than flower snippers, each should cut as intended. Ten-speed bicycles are used differently than mountain bikes, but both are means of transportation. Cottons need different washing care than do polyesters. These product capabilities are implied warranties.

Implied warranty—assumption that product will perform as intended.

Some products carry an **expressed warranty.** An expressed warranty is a performance or durability statement made about a good or service, either by the manufacturer or by the selling intermediary. Expressed warranties can be either verbal or written. Although legal recourse is more difficult without physical proof, a salesperson's claim made to a prospect about the performance of the product is enforceable. When in writing, these warranties are often called **guarantees.**

Expressed warranty—specific statement regarding performance or durability.

If a paint manufacturer states on the can that its paint can be cleaned off brushes and rollers with soap and water, the company offers an expressed warranty. When the salesperson at the garden shop states that the lawn mower will never need oil, an expressed warranty has been given. Products that do not

---

[27]Douglas Lavin, "In the year of the recall, some companies had to fix more cars than they made," *The Wall Street Journal*, February 24, 1994, p. B1.

perform to the standards made in expressed warranties are subject to return, replacement or refund. The amount of credit may vary.

FULL VS LIMITED WARRANTY

Full warranty—covers all necessary parts and labor to return the product to working order.

A **full warranty** covers the work necessary to bring a product back to complete and workable condition. Such a warranty can include replacement of the entire item with a new one. Full warranties include the repair of a defective good so that it performs as intended. If neither of these options is satisfactory, full warranty can mean refund of the entire purchase price. The famous "satisfaction guaranteed" promise by Sears is a good example of a full warranty. Many mail-order houses, such as L. L. Bean, Eddie Bauer and Land's End, offer full warranties. This policy counteracts potential consumer concern about selecting merchandise from a catalog and receiving it from distant providers.

Limited warranty—only a portion of the repair or replacement cost is covered.

Companies covering only a portion of the repair or replacement cost offer a **limited warranty.** By limiting the warranty to parts only, no labor, the marketer considers that the parts are usually reliable and that labor for replacing them may be costly. Although this type of warranty does not have as great a promotional value in attracting customers, the plan still has merit. This limitation on the liability is very common with appliance manufacturers.

Radio Shack warrants its telephones and computers for a certain length of time. After this period expires, the retailer will replace the parts free, but charges for the labor. This retailer supplies a limited warranty. Many automobile service

The L. L. Bean Guarantee

"Our products are guaranteed to give 100 percent satisfaction in every way. Return anything to us at any time if it proves otherwise. We will replace it, refund your purchase price or credit your credit card, as you wish. We do not want you to have anything from L. L. Bean that is not completely satisfactory."

Mail order retailers, such as L. L. Bean, typically offer liberal warranties to help ease customer concerns over dealing sight unseen over long distances. (Reprinted by courtesy of L. L. Bean)

policies carry the same warning; parts only, no labor. Sometimes the limited warranty restricts the time period for repair or refund, such as ". . . within one year from date of purchase."

PRO-RATA WARRANTY

Many makers of automobile equipment, such as tires, and batteries, offer **pro-rata warranties** on their products. This type of warranty means that a portion of the value will be reduced due to the amount of use or wear. After thorough testing, Uniroyal believes that a certain grade of its tires should last for 40,000 miles. The company could not afford to unconditionally replace all tires that failed short of the full mileage suggested. Since the product diminishes in value through wear, the warranty should be appropriately less as the item ages. This is a pro-rata warranty.

Pro-rata warranty— the value of the repair or replacement is reduced by the amount of wear on the product.

SUMMING IT UP

Products are a collection of physical and associate attributes known as the "bundle of values." The physical aspects of products include those tangible characteristics such as taste, shape, size, feel and color. Associate attributes, those "untouchable" traits, include brand, package and warranty.

A brand is a name, symbol, logo or other means of identifying products. Manufacturers and dealers create brands. Housemarks distinguish the marketing company, whereas brand names, logos and mottoes identify the product. Sometimes whole families of goods adopt the same brand name.

Branding is used to distinguish one product from another. This strategy reinforces loyalty for the good or service, and serves to establish quality and produce comparison. Good brand names are distinctive, fit the image of the product and are easy to communicate. Marketers that choose individual brands for different products are using a flanker branding strategy. Coupling an established brand with a new product is a form of brand extension.

Packages contain, protect, offer convenience, promote and provide safety. Packaging supplies economy, disposability and reusability to consumers. Warranties are a promise by the marketer to replace, repair or pay a refund on defective goods or services. Implied warranties mean the product will perform as intended, whereas expressed warranties state a specific level of performance or durability. Warranties may be full, limited or pro-rata.

KEY CONCEPTS AND TERMS
FROM CHAPTER EIGHT

Associate attribute
Brand
Brand extension
Brand name
Bundle of values

Dealer brand
Expressed warranty
Family brand
Flanker brand
Full warranty

Housemark
Implied warranty
Limited warranty
Manufacturer's brand
Physical attributes

Pro-rata warranty
Product liability
Recycling
Trademark
Warranty

BUILDING SKILLS

1. Describe the parts of the bundle of values that have contributed to the success of the Lexus from Toyota, Swatches, Cheerios, Toro lawn mowers, and Patagonia jackets.

2. Name the different kinds of identifiers, citing examples of each. Discuss the differences between manufacturer's, dealer and family brands.

3. Explain why branding is less common with production goods than with trade goods.

4. Give some examples of brand extension and flanker brands, explaining the advantages and disadvantages of these different strategies.

5. Give some examples of effective and ineffective branding, explaining why you feel they have succeeded or failed.

6. Give some examples of package design that promote the product; that offer convenience; that provide safety.

7. Give some examples of implied warranties, expressed warranties, limited warranties and pro-rata warranties.

Making Decisions 8-1: On a Roll.

What fits on the feet, is used for recreation and fitness conditioning, and is one of the hottest and fastest growing products to hit the streets in a decade? If you answered in-line skates, you got it. If you answered Rollerblades, watch out for legal recourse. The fact is that Rollerblade Incorporated, the Eden Prairie, Minnesota, company that owns the Rollerblade trademark, does not cotton to folks using its registered brand name loosely.

Spiritblade™ ABT™ Skate by Rollerblade, Inc.   Photo Courtesy of Rollerblade, Inc.

(Courtesy of Rollerblade)

In-line skates were developed in 1980 by a couple of minor league hockey players looking for a way to keep in shape during the off-season. The venture was purchased by a Minneapolis advertising entrepreneur who brought in a new management team. By expanding the target market and increasing its promotional budget, Rollerblade finally connected. Sales took off, growing at better than 150 percent during 1990–1991.

Although Rollerblade maintains over half of the market for in-line skates, the company is not without competition. First Team Sports, also from Minnesota, markets a brand called Ultra-Wheels, and several standard roller and ice skate firms have similar products on the market. However, with its jump start on the market, Rollerblade has achieved cult brand status. This innovative company's major concern now is protection of its trademark lest Rollerblade become a generic term.[28]

Explain why Rollerblade is a good brand name. Discuss the purposes and processes of protecting brands.

Making Decisions 8-2: Here Piggy, Piggy!

Cherrios, Hush Puppies, Aerostar, Mr. Coffee and Tabu. Brand names such as these are descriptive, distinctive, communicative and provocative, the stuff consumer marketers thrive on. Give a good product a name that buyers will remember and you have come a long way toward cementing brand loyalty.

The word "pigs," on the other hand, could only describe overweight, mud wallowing sources of bacon . . . or the offensive line of the Washington Redskins. Not so, says Don Beaver Jr., owner of the company and developer of the product that grosses over $5 million annually, with profit margins of close to 15 percent. As a former

---

[28]Pamela Sebastian, "Roller skate innovator tries to protect its lead," *The Wall Street Journal*, January 16, 1992, p. A1; Carrie Goerne, "Rollerblade reminds everyone that its success is not generic," *Marketing News*, March 2, 1992, pp. 1–2.

contractor, Beaver always had problems cleaning up oil and grease spills from factory floors. Rags and sawdust, two often-used methods of getting rid of this goo, were both messy and not thorough enough. Clay pellets, similar to kitty litter, gave off dust that often clogged machinery and was constantly being tracked through the facilities on employees' shoes.

One day Beaver experimented with some of his wife's old stockings stuffed with industrial absorbents. The product worked beautifully. This entrepreneur then tried a variety of stuffing materials, settling upon a corn based absorber, and called the sausage shaped products "pigs." Pigs could be wrapped around machinery bases, were easy to dispose of, and soaked up four times their weight of oil, grease, grime and dirt.

Soon pigs were in such demand, Beaver sold his janitorial business and began to produce these innovative bundles of grease cleaning power on a full-time basis. Although the company has had its rough times, it now appears to be off and running. Oh, and the name of Beaver's company? New Pig Corporation, of course![29]

Explain why the branding of production goods differs from trade goods, pointing out the factors that would make a production good brand effective.

Making Decisions 8-3: The Unjunk.

One would be hard pressed to find a marketer of trade goods who did not believe in the value and importance of establishing brand loyalty. Most things purchased by consumers carry some sort of identifier. Often these items have names, symbols, characters and slogans that are as much a part of the product as the product itself. Similarly, packages often have as much if not more promotional value than the product they contain.

One of the keys to selecting brands is to make these identifiers as unusual and distinctive as possible. Whether a name or a slogan, the means of pinpointing a specific product should relate to that good's or service's features and benefits. Brands should also be catchy, easy to communicate and current. The good ones are memorable; the others are not.

In tune with the concern with the wellness movement, two New York chefs collaborated on the creation of Terra Chips. Dana Sinkler and Alexander Dzieduszycki chose this earthy sounding brand name which seems perfect for a collection of sweet potato, taro, batata and parsnip snacks cooked in pure peanut or canola oil. Enhancing these colorful and healthful finger foods is a distinctive black and silver package. Realizing that the higher price of their product might be a disadvantage if they were shelved next to other snack foods, these niche marketers display Terra Chips in the deli or gourmet sections of supermarkets and specialty foods stores. In-store sampling and appearances in motion pictures, such as Star Trek VII, help to make up for the lack of an extensive promotional budget.[30]

Analyze the brand name and promotional scheme of Terra Chips as relates to their targeted market. Examine the functions of the package for these items in light of enhancing their image. Identify the types of warranty you might expect Terra Chips to carry.

---

[29]"Top draws," *Industrial Distribution,* September 1993, pp. 35–36; C. J. Barchfeld, "Do what works best," *Marketing News,* July 9, 1990, p. 2; B. Posner, "The phantom customer," *Inc.* September 1989, p. 21; Lucien Rhodes, "High on the hog," *Inc.,* March 1987, pp. 77–84.

[30]Karen Benezra, "How to veg out and live life in the chips at the same time," *BRANDWEEK,* June 27, 1994, pp. 30–31.

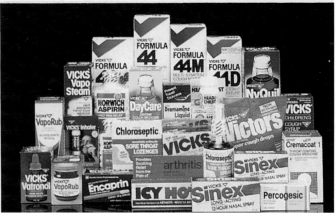

Figure #6–photo–Procter & Gamble product lines

Procter & Gamble (*above*) has an extremely wide and diversified product mix that includes a variety of consumer goods. Carver Tripp, on the other hand markets only paints.

Figure #7–photo– Carver Tripp display (*left*)

(Courtesy of Stor-Rite Metal Products)

F igure #8—ad reprint—Jantzen

Jantzen has expanded its market by selling its line of summer sportswear and swimwear in markets south of the equator. (Courtesy Jantzen)

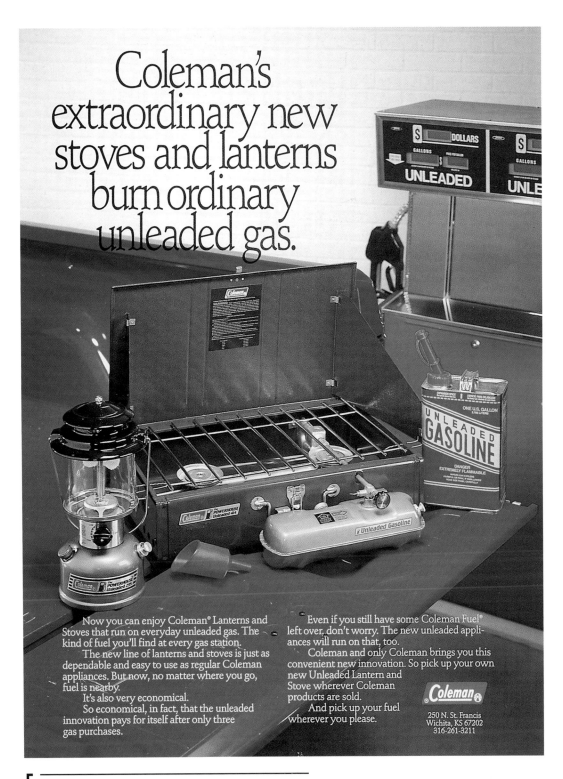

Coleman's extraordinary new stoves and lanterns burn ordinary unleaded gas.

Now you can enjoy Coleman® Lanterns and Stoves that run on everyday unleaded gas. The kind of fuel you'll find at every gas station.

The new line of lanterns and stoves is just as dependable and easy to use as regular Coleman appliances. But now, no matter where you go, fuel is nearby.

It's also very economical.

So economical, in fact, that the unleaded innovation pays for itself after only three gas purchases.

Even if you still have some Coleman Fuel® left over, don't worry. The new unleaded appliances will run on that, too.

Coleman and only Coleman brings you this convenient new innovation. So pick up your own new Unleaded Lantern and Stove wherever Coleman products are sold.

And pick up your fuel wherever you please.

Coleman.®

250 N. St. Francis
Wichita, KS 67202
316-261-3211

F igure #9—ad reprint—Coleman

Coleman promotes its line of high quality camping gear through consumer goods magazines. (Courtesy of Coleman Company)

When your financial future is at stake, there's nothing more important than someone you can trust.

There's only one thing we can be absolutely sure the future will bring. Change.

The ups, downs, twists and turns that stand in the way of achieving your financial goals.

At Merrill Lynch, we know change. We've understood it, managed it and turned it to our clients' advantage for over 70 years. And they've come to trust our ability to deal with it.

You see, we're determined to be a firm in which your trust, as well as your money, is well placed.

 **Merrill Lynch**
A tradition of trust.

©1989 Merrill Lynch & Co., Inc.

F igure #10—ad reprint—Merrill Lynch

Merrill Lynch reaches its market of business people through trade journal advertising. (Courtesy of Merrill Lynch &Co., Inc.)

9

Product Life Cycle, Product Mix and New Product Development

The Job to be Done

Like all living things, products have lives that pass through stages. Marketers typically offer a variety of products with different characteristics. The development of new products feeds this product mix. This chapter answers the questions that allow you to:

- identify the stages of the product life cycle,
- determine the characteristics of the product mix and product line,.
- describe the process for new product development,
- understand what causes some products to fail and others to succeed,
- recognize the reasons for new product success or failure, and
- analyze the problems associated with product management.

Amy George

College students often find that learning how to get a job is just as important as attaining an education. While most colleges offer some employment or placement services, these are often not enough to assure the best start. Many find that searching for the right career niche can be as rewarding as absorbing the knowledge to be used once on the job.

Amy George is a believer. While attending Westmoreland County Community College, she took advantage of all available opportunites to make career decisions. She had many discussions with faculty and advisors and attended job fairs. With a few courses under her belt, such as marketing, finance and management, she began to research the options available for young people with an Associate of Applied Science degree. Assistance

with résumé writing and practice at handling interviews added to her confidence and preparedness.

This groundwork paid off. Amy decided that the financial services industry offered a significant opportunity to use her skills and to grow into management positions. She landed her first job with the Southwestern National Bank of Pennsylvania. Enlightened management appreciated her bent toward public relations and customer service and rewarded her by opening up career opportunities within the organization. By attending evening classes at the University of Pittsburgh, Amy has high expectations of accelerating her career.

What Is The Product Life Cycle?

Products have a life span just as people do. Some products last a short time; others continue on for years. The life of a product is influenced by competition and technology, but is also impacted by the ability of the marketer to determine needs and design the goods or services to satisfy them. Despite the marvelous innovations of the NeXT computer, the company learned that customers just did not want an optical drive. Despite the massive advertising by the big brewers, consumers would not accept dry beers.

PRODUCT LIFE CYCLE DEFINED

Product life cycle— the introductory, growth, maturity and declining stages of a product.

The **product life cycle** includes the stages of introduction, growth, maturity and decline. As products pass through these phases, sales and profits grow and then taper off. Product life cycles relate to entire industries or reflect the activity of a single brand. One can measure how long eight track tapes were on the market, or the total life span of Cheerios. The length of time that a product remains active depends upon many factors.

Life cycles of different goods or services are not the same. The product life cycle often shrinks with technological advances. As new products are born, others suffer premature death. Clorox liquid bleach has been on the market seemingly forever, but Salvo laundry detergent tablets lived only briefly. Color Bright Clorox 2 is at an earlier point in its product life cycle.

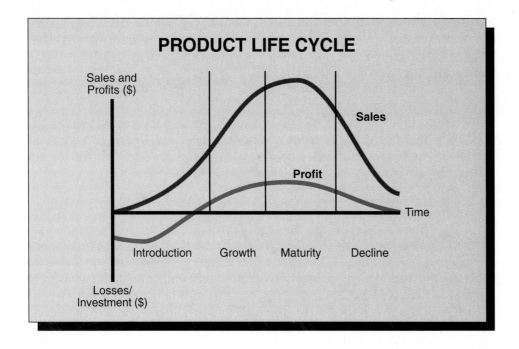

PRODUCT LIFE CYCLE

Scope, the popular mouthwash from Procter & Gamble, has been around for a while, but the company's new addition, with baking soda, is still an infant.[1]

INTRODUCTORY STAGE

The first step in the life of a product is the **introductory stage.** Lots of experimenting with design features usually takes place during this beginning phase. Since immediate profit is not a major corporate goal, the introductory stage is the time in the life cycle to iron out the bugs. Development and production costs are sizable, so profits are minimal or nonexistent. At this point, prices are typically kept high, unless the firm wants rapid market acceptance.

By being selective in their choice of intermediaries, marketers help distribute products to those people or firms who are most likely to try new items. This careful distribution allows marketing management to exercise more control and gain greater feedback regarding market acceptance. Competition may be limited, so advertising tends to stress product features more than brand. Samples, coupons, contests and store displays are common, arousing initial interest.

GROWTH STAGE

The next step of the product life cycle is the growth stage. During this period, the products face stiffer competition. While many companies may take a "wait

---

[1]Pam Weisz, "Procter to scope out more profit in baking soda mine," *BRANDWEEK*, February 7, 1994, pp. 1 and 6; John Sinisi, "Clorox cleaner push may be costly," *BRANDWEEK*, August 10, 1992, p. 5; John Sinisi, "Clorox adds $15 million to '93 budget," *BRANDWEEK*, July 20, 1992, p. 4.

and see" attitude toward new arrivals, once the good or service is established and showing signs of good potential profit competition steps forward. Newer, improved models are likely to appear. In this phase, prices usually feel this competitive pressure and start to decrease.

Distribution typically grows rapidly and may not be as selective as earlier. Advertising and promotional efforts now build upon brand image to build loyalty. Expenses for this increased effort tend to be high during the growth stage, and profits may be slow until the period is well underway. During this growing-up time in the product life cycle, marketing management learns whether or not the good or service will progress to full-fledged maturity.

MATURITY STAGE

In the maturity stage, sales usually tend to flatten out. Prices become more competitive, and profits, while initially high, begin to taper off as the life nears its end. Rivalry is heavy during this adult stage, with numerous marketers striving to keep a share of market and industry position. During this period, marketers often use package redesign and product improvements in the attempt to prolong life. Even with successful, old-line products like Cheerios and Wheaties, General Mills discovered that reformulation was necessary to differentiate even further from competitive, private label cereals.[2]

For consumer goods, pricing competition is common. Heavy promotion creates an additional strain on profits, which typically reach their highest point early in this stage. As the product continues to age, sales and returns ultimately decline. Distribution is somewhat stable, as competition continues to fight for the preferred outlets. Location within stores often becomes as important as the number of retailers handling the item.

Promotional efforts target protection of brand loyalty and undermining the similar efforts by competition. Heavy use of coupons, contests and premiums occurs with consumer goods, and old standards lead the way at association trade shows featuring production goods. Point-of-purchase displays are likewise common during the maturity stage and are used to place one particular product in a better in-store position than the competition.

DECLINING STAGE

The final phase of product life is the **declining stage,** where the product nears the end of its useful life. All but the strongest competition fades, and declining sales typically mean a drop in profit. Once again, distribution becomes selective as less profitable outlets are weeded out. Promotion tails off rapidly as marketers attempt to hold on to the last remnants of profitability.

Sometimes products earn a reprieve as marketers bring them back to usable life simply because buyers will not let them die. Some marketers try to replace a brand with a newer version only to find that consumers remain loyal

---

[2]Richard Gibson, "Classic Cheerios and Wheaties reformulated," *The Wall Street Journal,* August 31, 1994, pp. B1 and B3.

PRODUCT LIFE CYCLE EXAMPLES

STYLE

FASHION

FAD

to the original. Classic Coke is a classic example. Although Coke II was originally marketed to replace regular Coke, a loyal following demanded the original be retained. After exhaustive testing, the new brand has yet to gain significant share of the multi-billion dollar soft drink market.[3]

Not all products exhibit the same life cycles. Brands within certain categories of goods may show markedly different periods of growth or maturity. Neutrogena, the amber colored beauty soap in the clear plastic wrap has been on the market for over three decades and is not showing any signs of weakening its position. Tone, on the other hand, is a brand still struggling to make its way to profitable maturity.

Business products go through life cycle stages, too. This phenomenon is best illustrated in the high-technology field. The robotics systems used in manufacturing are in a rapidly climbing growth stage. The use of computers in organizations is not new, yet the networking of data processing systems has just begun. As the use of computers by businesses grows, new products emerge.

FADS AND FASHIONS

Different product life cycles graphically illustrate the different rates of the growth stage and extensions to the maturity phase. These differences are particularly evident when looking at the life cycle curves for fads. A **fad** is a product with a short life that goes through a mercurial growth stage only to come to an abrupt end. Looking at a graph of its product life, it is difficult to see whether or not the fad ever reached the maturity stage. "Clear" soft drinks, deodorants and dish washing detergents clearly illustrate fads. Pet rocks, hoola-hoops and the wet look in footwear and clothing are other examples.[4]

Fad—a product with a short life which never reaches maturity.

[3]A. Fahey, "Coke II sneaks into colas combat zone," *Advertising Age,* May 11, 1992, p. 1; News Briefs column, "Coke II hits new markets," *Adweek's Marketing Week,* May 4, 1992, p. 8.
[4]Kathleen Deveny, "Anatomy of a fad: How clear products were hot then suddenly were not," *The Wall Street Journal,* March 15, 1994, pp. B1 and B5.

Fashion—a product with a short life cycle which reaches maturity but only for a relatively brief period of time.

A **fashion** does reach the maturity stage, but usually for a shorter period of time than for non-trendy products. The life cycle graph for this type of product shows a more bell shaped curve than one for a fad. A fashionable product is not restricted to the garment industry. Many of the goods associated with the wellness movement, such as All-Bran or Fruit & Fiber cereals and Nordic Trak or Sierra exercise gear, are considered fashions. The forecasts for these items still show substantial life.

hat Is The Product Mix?

The length and shape of life cycle curves will vary from product to product. Different offerings from a specific marketer within the same product line may behave differently through their life cycle stages. Diet Coke was successful from the onset, but Coke II struggled. Cheer and Bold grabbed market share in the competitive laundry detergent field, whereas Salvo did not. Some marketers believe in having many items in their product baskets. Others companies limit their product mix.

PRODUCT MIX DEFINED

Product mix—the number of different products offered by a marketer.

The **product mix** is simply the number of different products that a marketer offers for sale. Some consumer goods manufacturers, such as RJR Nabisco, Kraft General Foods and Standard Brands, have an extensive array of products. Clarins, a skin care products marketer from France, and James River Corporation, the maker of Northern bathroom tissue, have smaller product mixes.

The size of the mix does not necessarily translate into profits. Many large consumer goods marketers have low profit margins. On the other hand, companies with smaller product mixes often find market niches that provide a substantial bottom line. This phenomenon is especially true in the high-tech arena. The laptop DTR-1 from tiny Dauphin Technology of Lombard, Illinois, touted as three computers in one, met with instant success when introduced in 1993. In this crazy, fast-paced industry, one wonders if a product that is four, five or six in one is not just around the corner.[5]

Most consumer goods marketers offer more than a single item. Many entrepreneurial efforts begin with a single good or service and expand into more complete product mixes. Frank Perdue, the chicken king of the Northeast, is now marketing turkey lunchmeats and franks, adding these varieties to its previously all-chicken lines. Giant Procter & Gamble had a humble beginning marketing only candles. Today this massive marketer claims a mix that includes detergents, food items, health-care products and industrial cleaners.

---

[5]Alison L. Sprout, "Pen-ultimate computer," *Fortune*, May 17, 1993, p. 89.

Marketing and Society: The fountain of youth...

Ever since Ponce de Leon searched the new world for the fabled fountain of youth, people have been awed by the prospects of looking younger. Fashion and cosmetics industries thrive on consumers attempting to look like someone who they really are not. Our entertainment media, from television to magazines to the big screen, constantly portray "youth and beauty" as the norm. As a result, any product that boasts the ability to help us retain a younger appearance is often an instant success.

This fascination with turning back age, or at least the look of age, led to the overnight success of skin creams that claim to reverse the aging process. Avon Products Inc. says its Anew line sold more than $175 million in 1993, and Chesebrough-Ponds, a division of global giant Unilever, claimed similar success for its Age-Defying Complex. These potions contain alpha-hydroxy acids, the primary ingredient found in leather tanners and tile cleaners. The cosmetic industry claims that these products work by sloughing off layers of skin cells, thereby exposing a younger appearing layer underneath. Consumers hope that creams and lotions containing alpha-hydroxy acids remove wrinkles.

All is not rosy in the cosmetics industry, however, as consumer complaints continue to mount. One Canadian import brought enough protest over skin irritations that the Food and Drug Administration was able to pull that product off the U.S. market. In general, the FDA has been somewhat stumped in its efforts due to lack of consumer uprising. So long as manufacturers do not make unsubstantiated medical claims, this agency's policing power is stymied without evidence of harm from users. Many industry watchdogs still feel that insufficient research is reason enough to move slowly on alpha-hydroxy based cosmetics, but try telling that to the buying public.

SOURCE: Suen L. Hwang, "Acid-based wrinkle creams: Fountain of youth or snake oil?" *The Wall Street Journal*, April 13, 1994, p. B1; Seema Nayyar, "Scott's extends from furniture to facial care," *Adweek's Marketing Week*, June 8, 1992, p. 5.

PRODUCT LINE

A group of products with similar characteristics or usage form a **product line.** Some marketers offer several product lines, while others concentrate on a few related products within a single line. The line of soft drinks marketed by PepsiCo includes Pepsi Cola, Pepsi Lite, Diet Pepsi, Pepsi Free and Crystal Pepsi. Each member of this product line is distributed by PepsiCo through the same types of wholesalers and retailers; one sales staff handles the entire group.

Product line—a group of products that have similar characteristics or usage.

Products within a line are often priced about the same. However, it is possible to find items within a product line that vary from upscale to economy. The line of beers offered by Anheuser-Busch range from Michelob to Busch Bavarian. How the goods are used is more important in defining lines than the prices of those articles. Fashion socks from Hanes and support hosiery from Easy Spirit are extensions of in-place lines from those marketers. Even though Fingos are positioned by General Mills as a snack food, the product is really another cereal product.[6]

WIDTH OF THE MIX

Width of the product mix—the number of different product lines within the product mix.

The number of product lines offered by a marketing firm is known as the **width of the product mix.** The more lines that a company offers, the wider its mix. A company that offers only one or two product lines is said to have a narrow product mix. The Carnation Company has product lines that include dairy products, flour, canned foods, farm supplies and a host of other items. Toshiba makes copiers, televisions, telephone systems, appliances and computer equipment. In contrast, Lindsay International markets only olives, and Mita advertises that copiers are its only business.

Philip Morris has a wide product mix. That firm sells everything from cigarettes and beer to cold cuts and pickles. On the other hand, Bel-Tronics Limited manufactures only radar detectors, a narrow product offering. McDonnell Douglas markets military and commercial aircraft, space and missiles, information systems, helicopters, financing and health care. Cessna is in general aviation aircraft, period.

DEPTH OF THE LINE

Depth of the product line—the number of individual brands within any one product line.

The **depth of the product line** refers to the number of individual brands within any given product line. While related, these separate items often require different strategies. Although Kellogg's is basically in the breakfast foods business, this company has a very deep product line. Within that grouping, Kellogg's positions Rice Krispies as a fun-to-eat cereal aimed mainly at children, whereas Just Right is marketed as a tasty, nutritious cereal enjoyed by adults. The marketing mix for one product is quite different than that for another.

Bausch & Lomb pioneered the development of sunglasses over fifty years ago, and its Ray-Ban brand remains a top seller today. This initial step in the eye-care field led to the highly successful marketing of soft contact lenses during the 1970s. To accommodate this field, B&L also developed a complete line of chemicals and solutions for the care and maintenance of contact lenses. After the acquisition of the plaque fighting electric toothbrush Interplak, the

---

[6]Elaine Underwood, "Sheer shape," *BRANDWEEK*, June 13, 1994, pp. 1 and 6; Elaine Underwood, "Easy Sprit kicks off shoes for a go at support hosiery," *BRANDWEEK*, January 3, 1994, p. 12; Betsy Spethmann, "Snack Time? Give me my cereal bowl," *BRANDWEEK*, May 3, 1993, pp. 24–26.

company began to embark on an extensive marketing program to develop oral-care products. B&L's latest entry is Clear Choice mouthwash. Although Bausch & Lomb's eye-care line is deep, it carries only a few items in the dental hygiene side of its business.[7]

ow Are New Products Developed?

New product development is taken very seriously by most marketing oriented companies. Large businesses may have entire departments charged with the single responsibility of creating original goods or services. Smaller firms might have to rely on the joint efforts of several individuals. Sometimes the entrepreneur is the one who creates the products that larger businesses copy.

ACQUISITION

An easy way to establish a new line or introduce new products is through **acquisition.** Corporate buyouts and mergers are part of the saga of the American business community. For example, Colgate-Palmolive Company was a noted bystander while Procter & Gamble was expanding its product mix by buying up smaller firms. Recently, Colgate purchased The Mennen Company, expanding its mix to include toiletries for men. Nestlé, the international conglomerate from Switzerland, has purchased such well-known companies as Carnation and Hill's Bros., the coffee house. The company plans to double its sales by the year 2000 mostly through acquisition.[8]

Buyouts and mergers are especially evident in global marketing. Despite some of the grousing about Japanese imports, many of the new electronic gizmos from that country were made with American expertise and assistance. Matsushita makes the REAL video game player, but a small San Mateo, California company, 3 DO Company, designed it. In the same arena, giant Nintendo credits much of its success to Silicon Graphics Incorporated, and the joint venture between Sharp Electronics and Apple Computer helped to get electronic notepads off the ground.[9]

Not all expansion of the product mix is caused by acquisition. Most major consumer and business goods marketers increase the number of goods they offer by creating new ones. This process is not a coin toss or a hit-or-miss proposition. New products come about through a regular process of development.

---

[7]Seema Nayyar, "In your face," *BRANDWEEK,* December 12, 1992, pp. 24–31.

[8]Cara Appelbaum, "Nestlé to double in size by the year 2000," *Adweek's Marketing Week,* March 30, 1992, p. 5; Seema Nayyar, "Colgate buys its way back into the game," *Adweek's Marketing Week,* February 17, 1992, p. 4.

[9]Neil Gross and Kathy Rebello, "A tsunami or gizmos," *Business Week,* September 27, 1993, pp. 56–57.

NEW PRODUCT DEVELOPMENT PROCESS

New product development process—the evolution of a product from idea creation to commercialization.

The **new product development process** is a common procedure used by many marketers for expansion. Although it may vary slightly from firm to firm, the system generally proceeds from the spark of an idea through a series of steps that ultimately brings products to the customer. Successful product evolution requires each of these specific stages.

Idea Creation

The first step in the development of original products is the **creation of an idea.** The dreams for new products may come from a variety of sources. Research and development departments within the marketing firm may generate original concepts. The sales force and the marketing department are other good avenues for creativity. Customer needs and complaints relayed by salespeople may lead to the development of either product revisions or new items. Observations of competitive moves and input from outside marketing agencies spark creative thinking.

Marketing intermediaries may serve as sources for new product ideas. Since these firms usually handle more than one product line from different suppliers, wholesalers and retailers are in a good position to know what goods are demanded and why. Feedback from intermediaries often results in new product development. Such was the case with the PowerShot stapler from Black & Decker. Although the firm originally introduced a "kickback" free model in the 1980s, according to retailers a flimsy appearance limited sales. The redesigned product is now matching the industry leader in sales.[10]

---

[10]Joseph Weber, "Industrial strength—and looks like it," *Business Week,* June 6, 1994, p. 82.

Global Marketing: When in Rome...

It is not easy to market abroad. Too often companies are content to merely send their successful domestic brands into overseas arenas assuming that if it "...works in Peoria, it'll make it anywhere!" Just as foreign tastes are different, products and brands should adapt to their surroundings. Probably no single multinational company recognizes this fact better than does Nestlé, the world's largest branded food company.

This giant Swiss based marketer has created this position predominately by emphasizing local brands. By acquiring companies around the globe at a staggering rate over the past decade, Nestlé has been able to maintain the flavor of the country in which it operates. Although the firm has over 8,000 different brands, less than 10 percent are registered in any one nation. This strategy is especially true in the developing world, where Nestlé will alter a product to the tastes of the local consumers, then slap on a brand name that is meaningful only within that market. Although this tactic dismayed some company officials in the well-known Nescafé arena, rebranding even its coffee products proved to be an outstanding success.

The shelf life for instant coffee and condensed milk are especially attractive in many third world countries. Locally produced soya milk, for example, is more stable in Asia and South America than is cow's milk. Early on, the company also realized the tremendous size of these new markets. Southeast Asia, including Thailand, Malaysia and Indonesia, has a population that exceeds all of Europe. Although the negotiations have gone on for years, the company now has a foothold in China with powdered milk and baby cereal plants. Even the company's candy bars are adapted to local tastes in this area, being manufactured from Malaysian cocoa. Competition is catching on. . .but is it soon enough?

SOURCE: Carla Rapoport, "Nestlé's brand building machine," *Fortune*, September 19, 1994, pp. 147–156.

Screening Process

The second step in the development process is **screening.** Here, marketers discuss ideas and share prototypes with others both inside and outside the company. Marketing companies undertake feasibility studies before proceeding on product development. Checking the credibility of these ideas with customers or prospects in the ultimate marketplace can give an indication of the level of demand for the good or service. This consumer input may settle the major concern of whether this new product idea meets the requirements for successful segmentation.

Screening—product ideas and/or prototype models are discussed with customers, consultants and company employees.

Many new product failures are the result of too little effort being made in exploring the obstacles within the company. New products must fit the business's philosophy as well as its production or marketing expertise. Obviously, any firm must have the necessary manufacturing capabilities. In addition, the product should be compatible with present channels of distribution and fit the image of the company. For example, the Cadillac Division of General Motors has the production capability to build almost any type of vehicle, but a snowmobile with the Cadillac name would not be consistent with the corporate image.

Determining if the new product will have any adverse effect on the company's present product mix is important. For example, does the product being developed compete with other products already being marketed by the firm? Is the new product compatible with the present product mix, or is it creating a

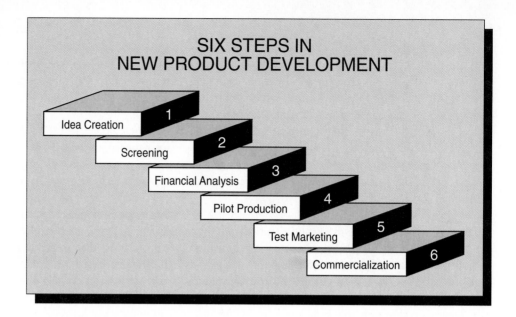

SIX STEPS IN NEW PRODUCT DEVELOPMENT

1. Idea Creation
2. Screening
3. Financial Analysis
4. Pilot Production
5. Test Marketing
6. Commercialization

new line that might not fit well with other offerings? Are distribution channels presently available?

Screening also involves a thorough study of existing and potential competition. Effort must be made to figure out how quickly a competitive firm might be able to enter the market once the new product proves successful. Hershey Company faced such questions before introducing Reese's peanut butter. As one of the world's largest candy producers, and creator of ET's favorite food, the company had to determine how a peanut butter would match its production and marketing capabilities. Facing stiff national competition from Jif, Skippy and Peter Pan, Reese's is counting on its brand familiarity to stake its claim in this new market.[11]

Financial Analysis

If the idea harmonizes with the corporate personality, the next step is a thorough financial analysis. Calculations of total market demand are made, along with revenue and cost projections. Accurate estimates of production and marketing costs need to be studied. Since few new products turn a profit in the first year, knowing projected sales and potential profit is important. If the business has to make a sizable investment in new equipment or marketing tools, the return on investment must be figured.

New product development is an expensive proposition. Many firms prefer to take a "me too" attitude. By waiting until a competitor succeeds or fails, companies may save millions in development costs. Trying to satisfy market needs can be risky. Sound financial analysis is a necessary step in the process in order to minimize the potential for loss.

---

[11] Joe Crea, "Crunchy or creamy? Think again," *The Oregonian,* March 7, 1992, p. C1; Fara Warner, "Hershey cracks the peanut butter aisle," *Adweek's Marketing Week,* January 20, 1992, p. 10.

A good example of this thorough analysis is the development of Rubbermaid's outdoor storage shed. This plastic container and housewares marketer benefited from marketing research that found consumer dissatisfaction with wood and metal sheds which rotted, rusted and deformed. Calling on its expertise in using low-cost plastics, Rubbermaid was able to produce an easily assembled, maintenance free shed for less than the competition. Although criticized for its lack of aesthetics, the product was able to fit in with the myriad of home designs. Assuring that the shed met the critical financial analysis has produced a profitable introduction.[12]

Pilot Production

If the financial picture looks promising, the business may attempt **pilot production.** In this step, a limited quantity of the product will be manufactured. Pilot production may be accomplished through an existing manufacturing unit or a brand new, small scale operation. Making finished goods at a profit is not a priority at this stage. This phase shakes down the manufacturing process and proves the practicality of making the product. Modification of design and production refinements should be worked out before introducing the unit to the entire market.

> **Pilot production**—new products are produced in sufficient quantity for test marketing.

Engineers at Cornell University offer a short cut for the pilot plant phase of the new product development process. A computer system allows marketers to create a factory simulator that can answer questions regarding new processes. This makes it possible to see in advance how modifications to a production line might affect output. Major companies such as IBM and Hughes Aircraft have funded the Cornell Simulator of Manufacturing Operations, or COSMOS for short. Several companies are now marketing simulation software packages, at prices up to $100,000, which carry out similar functions.

Test Marketing

Once a quantity of finished goods is available from the pilot plant, **test marketing** begins. The marketer sells production quantities in specific markets to determine consumer acceptance. Putting the new product into real life marketing situations is the only accurate means of gauging customer reaction. Experimenting may occur in the test marketing stage. Colors, tastes, package designs, advertising effectiveness and distribution channels will be examined closely to resolve market preferences and marketing procedures.

> **Test marketing**—production quantities are sold in specified markets to determine product acceptance.

Test marketing operates under rigid research controls. Products are not dumped into users laps with the question, "How do you like it?" Test markets are chosen because they represent the conditions that will be found in the ultimate market. Demographics in the test market should approximate those of the targeted segment. Control over the distribution and the promotion is another factor in selecting test market areas. Some locations have proven to be more informative than others.

---

[12]Zachary Schiller, "It ain't so pretty, but it works," *Business Week*, June 6, 1994, p. 83.

Test marketing is common in the personal products industry, especially in the cosmetics field. Bringing new fragrances to the market without test marketing could be quite risky. Platinum, Colgate's entry into the tooth whitener market, was test marketed in New England before nationwide introduction in 1994. Giorgio, the division of cosmetics giant Avon, used selected stores rather than geographic areas to test its scent, Wings. The campaign designed to appeal to the "woman in women" was successfully followed with a nationwide rollout in 1993.[13]

Sometimes test marketing is a hindrance to getting the jump on competition. DowBrands, Inc. the consumer arm of Dow Chemical, jumped the gun on the introduction of its Spiffits product, a line of cleanser saturated towelettes. In competition to Dow, Kimberly-Clark test marketed Once Over in Missouri. This new product development process bogged down for years, giving Dow the edge. However, Dow dumped Spiffits because the market did not prove to be big enough to be profitable.[14]

Not all new products go through the test market step. If the company has a strong indication that the product will be successful after initial screening, it may abandon this rather expensive stage in the development process. Competition may learn of a new product in the test market, giving them a jump on entering the field themselves. On the other hand, new product marketers may be able to estimate competitive reaction by what is learned during test marketing. If competition shows keen interest, the product usually has merit. Pretesting, computer modeling and overseas trials are replacing the traditional test marketing in some cases.[15]

Commercialization

Commercialization— products are made available in quantity for their intended market.

The final step in the development process is **commercialization.** Full-scale production and a complete marketing effort are undertaken once the test markets give the project a "green light." The product is now ready to be formally introduced to potential customers. It has passed the tests of each step of the development process. Initial screening, financial analysis and pilot production with test marketing have all been successfully completed. At this stage the marketer still has several options for the method to be used to place the product in front of potential buyers.

Rollout— commercialization that is gradually accomplished one region at a time.

The initial introduction may hold the clue to the product's future potential. Many companies move into this final product development stage gradually, making the product available to the selected markets on a region-by-region basis. This process is a **rollout.** PepsiCo practiced this type of commercialization with its H2Oh! sparkling waters after initial test marketing proved satisfactory. Once

[13]Pam Weisz, "Colgate sets whitener roll-out," *BRANDWEEK,* June 20, 1994, p. 8; Seema Nayyar, "Giorgio has a new fragrance for the woman in women," *BRANDWEEK,* October 19, 1992, p. 3.

[14]Terry Lefton, "DowBrands rubs out Spiffits," *Adweek's Marketing Week,* May 11, 1992, p. 4; Dan Koeppel, "Dow gives K-C the once over," *Adweek's Marketing Week,* April 17, 1989, p. 2.

[15]Christopher Power, "Will it sell in Podunk? Hard to say," *Business Week,* August 10, 1992, pp. 46–47; Associated Press release, "If it plays in Peoria, will they buy it in Boise," *Marketing News,* February 17, 1992, pp. 7 and 21.

the viability of the new product has been proven, other firms may opt to use a **blitz,** introducing the product throughout the marketing areas at the same time. Planters-Life-Savers used this commercialization tactic for GummiSavers. The decision to use the gradual or sudden method of commercialization is usually based upon cost factors. Competitive activity also plays a role in deciding how quickly to commercialize a new product.[16]

Blitz—commercialization that is accomplished within the total market area all at a given time.

The time needed to bring a new product to market will vary. From the birth of an idea to successful commercialization is not an overnight proposition for any product or company. A bulk of the decisions to abort a project come in the early exploration and screening processes, but some new ventures are dumped after they have reached full production. The competitive pressures of the nineties have proven that a quick introduction to markets is often crucial to success.

Why Do Some Products Fail?

Successful test marketing and good business planning do not always prevent failure. Over three-fourths of new products do not succeed. The reasons for product failure are many. Too often new entries are not distinctive enough from other, competing brands. Targeting the wrong market, poor timing and poor quality are other common ailments.

NOT DISTINCTIVE

Marketers have many ideas about what contributes to the success or failure of a new product. Some business people say that new items have to be as good as what is presently on the market, but priced lower. Another school of thought is that success hinges on whether the new product is better than competition but equally priced. If the product is not distinctive enough from or better than other available items, the market may reject it.

Many products introduced each year into established markets do succeed. The truly outstanding ventures offer goods that are distinctive enough to stand out from the competition. Cherry 7Up and Compaq's Deskpro 386 personal computer are examples of innovative products that have succeeded in established and crowded industries. On the other hand, Canfield's Diet Peanut Chocolate Fudge soda and the Franklin Computer did not make it in similar fields.

INEFFECTIVE TEST MARKETING

Products can fail simply because the test marketing was inconclusive. Like many manufacturers of synthetics, DuPont worked for years on the development of a substitute for leather to be used in footwear. Corfam was the apparent answer.

Distinctive product and packaging, coupled with creative advertising, helped Cherry 7Up succeed in a crowded market.

---

[16]Alison Fahey, "Perrier and Pepsi push new age drinks," *BRANDWEEK,* July 20, 1992, p. 4; Fara Warner, "A $13 million rockies crossing," *BRANDWEEK,* October 12, 1992, p. 4.

This material resisted scuffing, breathed like leather, was lightweight and practically indestructible. Furthermore, Corfam received flying colors in market tests, but that was its downfall. In practice, Corfam was found to be elastic, hence shoes made from this imitation leather had to be broken in at each wearing. Consumers rejected this feature, and the material became relegated primarily to military footwear.

For the most part, test marketing is considered essential by marketers of trade goods. Distributing products to consumers without this key step in the development process is risky. TreeSweet Products learned this fact all too well when it attempted to introduce TreeSweet Lite, a reduced calorie frozen fruit juice concentrate, without first test marketing it. The company learned the hard way that consumers are not very concerned about calories in a natural fruit drink. The product bombed, and the company fell into financial trouble.

POOR TIMING

Poor timing is often a contributing factor in product failure. Suppose test marketing occurred during times of market expansion. Acceptance could be good, for the moment. By the time full production comes on line, which may be years later, the economy takes a downturn or the market demand disappears. When the economy was booming in the late 1980s, many real estate developers were designing and planning projects. The recession of the early 1990s brought a halt to the boom and the building industry suffered.

Conditions change. What once looked like a promising market can vanish like a puff of smoke. Campbell Soups initial venture into the microwaveable meal market was far from successful. Test marketing pinned the "can't miss" label on Souper Combos, introduced in the late 1980s. Poor packaging, futile promotion and an economic downturn slowed acceptance of the soup and snack product. Competition finally killed it.[17]

COMPETITION

One of the cardinal rules of business is to never underestimate the power of competition. Doing so can result in new product failure. Sometimes entrenched businesses lower the prices of competitive lines just before the new product enters the market. Perhaps an aggressive company with a "better mousetrap" is waiting in the wings. In many ways, competition can be a major cause of product failure.

One would be hard pressed to find a more competitive U.S. market than the one for beer. The wars between major domestic brands are legendary. Yet it was into this already crowded arena that Foster's Australian Lager strode. Fueled by the popularity of the movie *Crocodile Dundee*, this imported brew hoped to carve a niche, but was quickly dispatched by the competition.[18]

---

[17]David Kiley, "Conditions that change," *Adweek's Marketing Week,* November 5, 1990, p. 25.
[18]Matthew Grimm, "Targeting a saturated market," *Adweek's Marketing Week,* November 5, 1990, p. 21.

WHY NEW PRODUCTS FAIL

1. **Poor Concept:** The product does not meet consumer needs or offer value.

2. **Insignificant Difference:** The product difference isn't significant enough from the existing products to warrant changing ("me-too").

3. **Poor Execution:** The product doesn't duplicate the original concept.

4. **Inadequate Budget:** Underestimating the budget needed to launch a new product and move it through the product life cycle.

5. **Insufficient Market Size:** The market is not large enough to produce the necessary volume for a profit.

6. **Bad Timing:** The product is introduced at the wrong time of year or in the wrong environment.

7. **Mistargeting:** The good product is designed for a group that doesn't need it.

8. **Mispositioning:** The product is designed to do one thing but positioned to appear different.

9. **Misjudging the Competition:** The company fails to read the nature of the competitive situation.

10. **Poor Estimating:** Forecast sales are overstated or costs underestimated.

11. **Market Changes:** The market environment changes between testing and launch.

12. **Wearing Blinders:** The company becomes so committed to making the product launch succeed that it overlooks the "bad news" as it progresses through the developmental steps.

SOURCE: *Business Week,* August 16, 1993, pp. 78–79.

POOR BRANDING

Poor branding can cause new products to fail even when the item itself may be useful and well planned. Because of the newness and the promotional hype, even test marketing does not always catch problem names. A men's aftershave lotion named Male Chauvinist and an instant gravy called Smooth and Easy are brands that failed. Shampoos with the monikers of Look of

Buttermilk and Touch of Yogurt did little to convince consumers that bad hair days were things of the past.[19]

Another marvelous example illustrating brand failure was Bic's venture into perfumes. The success of this company's pen and cigarette lighter lines led the firm's management to believe that the same result would be in store with scents. Bic Parfum was distributed and promoted much like pens and lighters, but consumers were not impressed. Despite a sizable marketing effort, this product line sounded too much like a Bic and not enough like a perfume.[20]

POOR QUALITY

Poor quality will spoil the market acceptance of almost any product. Too often companies do not go through sufficient product testing and pilot plant manufacturing to rid the process or the product of mistakes. Once consumers pin the poor quality label on a product, it is practically impossible to reverse the image. Certainly, the problems faced by the U.S. automobile industry during the 1980s were largely the result of poor quality. Notably, when introduced in 1987, the Cadillac Allanté was intended to compete with European imports such as BMW and Mercedes in a market that was younger and nontraditionally Cadillac. Although the car's Italian styling was attractive, it was not distinctive enough and leaky roofs, squeaks and wind noise proved to be its undoing. Cadillac took the car off the market in 1993.[21]

Inferior quality is particularly damaging to the marketing of production goods. In an industry where buyers rely upon durability and reliability, mediocrity destroys both the product and the producer. Many of the "wrinkle free" shirts that were the rage in the early 1990s proved to be less than acceptable to male consumers and an embarrassment to the marketers. Production goods appear to receive more thorough testing and longer development time than do trade goods. Most marketers in this field feel that quality assurance is more important than speed.[22]

 hat Leads To New Product Success?

Just as there are reasons why products fail, there are success factors as well. If marketing is to satisfy needs, then products should meet those needs, but customer satisfaction is not always enough to insure success. The successful introduction of new goods and services is also influenced by demographic and technological change.

[19]Christopher Power, "A Smithsonian for stinkers," *Business Week*, August 16, 1993, p. 82.

[20]Cara Appelbaum, "Overextending a brand," *Adweek's Marketing Week*, November 5, 1990, p. 21.

[21]Christopher Power, Kathleen Kerwin, Ronald Grover, Keith Alexander and Robert D. Hof, "Flops," *Business Week*, August 16, 1993, pp. 76–82.

[22]Teri Agins, "'Wrinkle free' shirts don't live up to the name," *The Wall Street Journal*, May 11, 1994, p. B1.

FITTING MARKET NEEDS

The most important factor in the success of any product is **fitting the needs of the market.** Making a product for any reason other than meeting market segment demand is foolish. Marketing graveyards are crowded with the remains of unsuccessful products that failed to fit market needs. No single factor can provide greater product success than coupling the product with market requirements.

First-aid care is certainly not a new market, especially for industry leader Johnson & Johnson. Yet even this marketing stalwart is busily creating new brands for new market segments. Realizing a need to calm the fears that kids naturally have for first-aid products, J&J introduced its No More line in 1993. No More Germies, an antibacterial liquid soap, headed the promotion, along with No More Ouchies and No More Itchies. The children's portion of the first-aid market is estimated to have an annual growth rate of about 10 percent, and Johnson & Johnson created a line to fit that segment's needs.[23]

Clever branding and packaging led to the success of the No More line of children's first aid products from Johnson & Johnson.

FAVORABLE DEMOGRAPHICS

The demographics of the United States are in a constant state of flux, a fact pointed out earlier. Marketers that keep on top of these fluctuations have a better chance for success when introducing new items. For example, women now purchase about half of the new cars sold in the United States. Automakers have learned that catering to some of the finer points creates more interest on the part of female buyers. Making hoods and trunk lids easier to lift and seats more adjustable added attractiveness for both women and men.[24]

Favorable demographics are causing marketers to take a second look at that new group of consumers, the X generation. Baby busters, as the age group of 18-to-30-year-olds are called, are typically unimpressed with advertising hype. To reach this skeptical audience, Revlon showed super model Cindy Crawford playing basketball with a racially mixed group to push its Charlie perfume to this target. Nike features a soft sell approach to Xers in ads for its sneakers. This generation also rebels against sexism in advertising, and shows a great concern for the environment. "Green marketing" appeals to this demographic segment.[25]

Rally's a fast growing, fast food chain located mostly east of the Mississippi, targets a market that McDonald's and Burger King have all but forgotten. Those people who have little time and not much cash are the prime segment for this double-drive-through operation. A Rallyburger with a 16-ounce Coke and cheese dipped fries is yours in less than a minute for around $2.00.[26]

---

[23]Seema Nayyar, "J&J teams up on Germies, Ouchies," *BRANDWEEK,* December 7, 1992, p. 2.

[24]F. Curtaindale, "Car dealers give the lady some respect," *American Demographics,* September 1992, p. 25; E. Hollreiser, "Women and cars," *Adweek's Marketing Week,* February 10, 1992, pp. 14–16; Associated Press release, "Automakers learn better roads to women's market," *Marketing News,* April 6, 1992, p. 2.

[25]Laura Zinn, Christopher Power, Dori Jones Yang, Alice Z. Cuneo, and David Ross, "Move over boomers—a portrait of Generation X," *Business Week,* December 14, 1992, pp. 74–82.

[26]Nancy J. Perry, "Hit 'em where they used to be," *Fortune,* October 19, 1992, pp. 112–113.

Like many successful marketers, PepsiCo realizes the importance of the Hispanic market. This aggressive company began importing its Miranda line of soft drinks from Mexico into California, Arizona and New Mexico in 1992. The sodas, which come in a variety of fruit flavors, have been a big hit south of the border. PepsiCo is ready to commercialize the line in other geographic areas when its initial introductions prove profitable.[27]

ADVANCED TECHNOLOGY

Many markets open today simply because the new products are so technologically advanced. Some marketing gurus continue to predict that half of the products in use ten years from now have yet to be developed. Usually, technological breakthroughs are often the result of competitive battles. On some occasions, these advancements come out of basic research.

Few markets are as competitive as the home-entertainment field. In a market long dominated by Japanese firms, Philips Consumer Electronics leads the way in interactive compact disc systems. This European giant has the task of first defining its technologically advanced products to relatively ignorant consumers. The digital video and audio systems are expected to be the state-of-the-art in entertainment for years to come.[28]

Bioremediation promises to tackle environmental problems caused by toxic wastes. Technology in this industry creates bacteria, affectionately known as "bugs," that attack such commonplace problems as sewage and industrial wastewater. The greatest hope for this technological advance is in cleaning up oil spills and hazardous chemicals such as PCBs. The future for this field appears to be unlimited.[29]

 ho Decides New Product Success Or Failure?

Unfortunately, outstanding early acceptance does not necessarily mean continued increase in sales. Hot products rarely stay hot forever. Not all ideas become new products, and not all new products are successful. The ultimate judges of any product's acceptability are its customers.

Miscalculating the rate of acceptance is a major factor in product failure. It takes time for any product to reach a volume of sales that generates enough profit. Not everyone nor every company adopts new ideas at the same rate. Over-estimating how fast the product will be accepted may lead to a shortage of funds and sizable inventories.

---

[27]Alison Fahey, "Pepsi quenches the Hispanic market," *BRANDWEEK*, July 27, 1992, p. 4.

[28]Terry Lefton, "Cutting edge CD-I beats Sony," *BRANDWEEK*, August 24, 1992, pp. 1 and 6.

[29]Reed Abelson, "Bugs clean up their act," *Forbes*, September 28, 1992, p. 144.

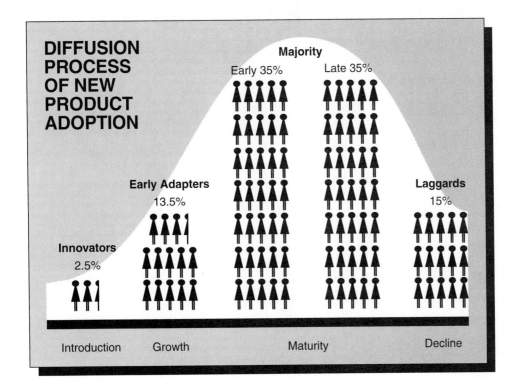

DIFFUSION PROCESS OF NEW PRODUCT ADOPTION

Majority
Early 35%   Late 35%

Early Adapters
13.5%

Laggards
15%

Innovators
2.5%

Introduction   Growth   Maturity   Decline

DIFFUSION PROCESS

Consumers and business buyers ultimately determine product success or failure. The time necessary for a new product to gain acceptance is known as the **diffusion process.** Some new products, such as Ford's Explorer and Unilever's 2000 soap bar were embraced by their markets rather quickly. Nissan's Infiniti and Irish Spring took longer.

About 15 percent of any potential market is made up of **innovators and early adopters.** These persons are the ones who crave newness and are not intimidated by skeptics. This group of young and old buyers typically has money enough to give the new product a try without too much concern over possible loss. Customers who are reluctant to grab at new items often look to these first buyers for information and guidance. In this way, innovators and early adopters are opinion leaders who usually influence other buyers.

About 70 percent of the potential buyers make up the mass market that will ultimately decide the fate of a new product. If the early buyers have a positive impact on this **buying majority,** the results may be exciting for the marketers. This majority is broken into groups of early and late adopters. Made up of moderate and conservative elements, this majority forms the backbone of any consumer group.

In any cross section of consumers, a group of **laggards** staunchly steers clear of anything that smacks of being new or different. These potential customers will be the last to try a new product, often starting to purchase just when the product is going out of style. Included with these buyers is the small

Diffusion process—
the time necessary for a new product to gain acceptance.

section of the public that will never accept new product. This sector accounts for the final 15 percent of the total market.

CONSUMER ADOPTION PROCESS

Consumer adoption process—the stages that individuals go through in deciding to buy new products.

The stages that individuals go through in deciding to buy new products is known as the **consumer adoption process.** No matter where one sits on the diffusion scale, the decision process includes the same steps. Typically, buyers become aware of new products and develop interest in them. After evaluating the need satisfying characteristics of the new item, the consumer will give it a try. At that point, the individual will either reject or accept the product.

The ability to judge new product adoption is a key to marketing success. Management that jumps into full-scale commercialization too soon may lose both potential profit and development costs. Failure to recognize a "hit" early in the game may open the door to competition or sour an eager market. Adapting the consumer adoption process to the diffusion process helps marketing managers get a handle on potential sales and profit.

How Are Products Managed?

As an integral part of the marketing mix, the product is the cornerstone on which the rest of the strategy builds. Without a product, there is no need for price, distribution or promotion. Companies work hard to create and maintain the images of their goods and services.

PRODUCTS AND ETHICS

The product is purposely listed as the beginning element of the marketing mix. Price, distribution and promotion are all important in satisfying needs, but these facets of marketing hinge upon the product. Without the proper goods and services, the rest of the marketing mix is useless. Products are sometimes causes for buyer alarm. Poor quality, planned obsolescence, lack of safety and inadequate liability protection all impact product acceptance.

PRODUCT QUALITY

Product quality relates to the ability of the good or service to carry out its intended purpose. Consumers and business buyers demand that the products they buy adhere to at least a minimum standard of quality. All purchasers recognize that the durability and reliability of products will vary according to the way they are made and their expected use. Sturdier built, more costly-to-make items are assumed by the buyer to be more durable. Regardless, any product at any level of cost or value should possess a degree of quality suitable for its intended market.

Toys and tools that fall apart and clothing that lasts for only a few washings anger consumers. Goods that arrive late or damaged are the bane of production goods buyers. Packages that misrepresent the products or that fail to protect the contents frustrate customers. Misleading warranties cause loss of both money and the use of the products.

The American automobile industry has suffered from the quality complaints of the 1970s and 1980s. Hundreds of thousands of cars were recalled for one complaint or the other. In the meantime, manufacturers from Japan and Germany were gaining large-scale consumer acceptance because of the better quality of their vehicles. Even today, as Detroit attempts to right its fallen image, the perception of American-made cars is less than perfect.

PRODUCT SAFETY

Bic, the world's largest marketer of lighters, spent years and millions developing the Child Guard.

Product safety is a problem facing many trade goods marketers. Since the Tylenol scare, several companies have come under public scrutiny because of package tampering. One positive result of this plight is the increased effort by manufacturers to develop safer packages. Tops of closures that pop up when the vacuum seal has been broken and tough plastic sealing strips around jar lids are now common. These actions by responsible marketers coupled with stiffening federal laws help eliminate tampering.

Pharmaceutical companies, working with container designers, are perfecting packages to minimize the danger of children accidentally opening them. The packaging industry is taking steps to provide greater safety, perhaps brought about largely by the Tylenol scare. The Bic Corporation, the world's largest marketer of disposable lighters, spent more than six years and $16 million developing a child-resistant model. The Child Guard version includes a plastic knob that the user must maneuver out of the way before the butane can be released and ignited. Tests showed this revision to be over 80 percent effective in keeping small children from operating the lighters.[30]

Marketing is the one arm of business that can seriously impact the types of products manufactured. As many producers are learning, this safety factor goes beyond their immediate customers. Courts have been awarding settlements in suits against firms whose faulty materials or component parts are incorporated in other items.

PRODUCT LIABILITY

Product liability laws make marketers responsible for injury or damage caused by the use of their products. Sellers must be aware of how their products are used. The paint company assumes equal responsibility with the toy maker if infants become ill from lead poisoning after chewing on painted items. Plastic manufacturers share liability with sign makers when the faces

Product liability— marketers are responsible for injury or damage caused by the use of their products.

---

[30]Terry Lefton, "Bic child-proofs its lighters," *Adweek's Marketing Week*, February 17, 1992, p. 6.

on these lighted displays fall out, injuring pedestrians. The aircraft maker has been found equally at fault with the airline in cases of fatal crashes.

The primary way to protect against product liability suits is to assure that safe products are being marketed. All aspects of that good or service must be considered in scouring product design for defects or potential danger. For example, most product liability courts consider that the package goes with the goods inside, even if supplied by an independent company. If defective aerosol cans explode in customers' hands, both the can maker and the paint manufacturer may be found at fault.

Court and jury settlements granted in injury and class-action lawsuits contribute to skyrocketing liability insurance costs. Increased rates affect the cost of doing business. For example, many individuals refuse to serve on the boards of directors of some corporations unless liability insurance is provided. Government agencies are not immune to the high cost of liability insurance. The potential for lawsuits against public bodies has raised insurance premiums to the point that many communities, counties and agencies have become self-insured.

CUSTOMER SERVICE

A major part of the marketing concept must relate to customer service. The way sellers treat buyers has a great impact upon return sales and ultimate growth. Although the concept is not new, the idea that customers need to be treated fairly and politely is receiving widespread attention lately. Marketing management must become aware that it costs more in effort and dollars to create new customers than it does to retain old ones. One study shows that decreasing the number of customers lost by only 5 percent can increase profits by over 25 percent.[31]

Customer service runs the gamut from fast, friendly response to on-time delivery to clean and well-stocked showrooms. Production goods buyers are naturally concerned with service. One manufacturer cannot afford to shut down its production lines because another did not live up to its promises. Consumers, too, are demanding better on-time performance. As competitive as today's business world has become, no marketer can afford to force customers to look elsewhere. Training and educating employees on how to provide customer-pleasing service is a major role for marketing management.

GLOBAL CONSIDERATIONS

Managing products in global markets takes on a whole new perspective. Tastes and preferences differ from culture to culture. A highly successful, easily

---

[31]Susan Greco, "Real-world customer service," *Inc.,* October 1994, pp. 36–45; Rahul Jacob, "Why some customers are more equal than others," *Fortune,* September 19, 1994, pp. 215–224.

adopted good or service in the U.S. may not even crack the surface some-where else. Designs, brands, packaging and warranties usually must be adapt-ed to the specific country into which they are being introduced. Global mar-keters quickly learn that it is better to produce to the needs of specific societies rather than try to cram American goods into markets where they are not acceptable.

The types of cake that American buyers favor are unacceptable to English tea drinkers. Nova translates into "no go" in Spanish, hardly the best name for a motor vehicle. Many Europeans prefer salad dressings in tubes, and a 70,000 mile automobile warranty in Hungary would last the lifetime of a car buyer. Marketers are wrong to assume that everyone, worldwide, shares the same tastes as Americans.

SUMMING IT UP

Products go through a life cycle. Commencing with introduction, products progress through stages of growth, maturity and, finally, decline. Marketing companies have a product mix. A product line is a single item or groups of goods that have similar characteristics or use. The width of the product mix defines the number of product lines a company owns. The quantity of indi-vidual entries in a product line describes the depth of the line.

Most marketing companies continually look for new products. The process for developing these items begins with an idea. The new product devel-opment process then proceeds through screening, financial analysis, pilot plant production, test marketing and commercialization.

Some products fail; others succeed. Failure is often attributed to ineffec-tive test marketing, poor timing, poor branding or poor quality. Success is often the result of fitting market needs, favorable demographics and advanced tech-nology. Success or failure is decided by consumers or business buyers as prod-ucts pass through the diffusion process. Product management is no easy task. Product safety and product liability are ethical concerns that managers must address.

KEY CONCEPTS AND TERMS FROM CHAPTER NINE

Blitz
Commercialization
Consumer adoption process
Depth of the product line
Diffusion process
Fad
Fashion
New product development process
Pilot production

Planned obsolescence
Product liability
Product life cycle
Product line
Product mix
Rollout
Screening
Test marketing
Width of the product mix

1. Identify the stage of the product life cycle for compact discs, designer ice creams, home permanents, monoclonal antibodies, alkaline batteries, ultra-violet filtering sunglasses.

2. Contrast the reasons why one company might limit its product mix while another chooses to expand into other fields.

3. Discuss each stage of the new product development process, citing examples where appropriate.

4. Describe the reasons that led to IBM dropping the PC Jr. after spending millions on promotion. Contrast the causes that contributed to decreased sales of the Audi 5000 versus those that led to the demise of Hot Rocks, the candy that sizzled in the mouth.

5. Identify the factors that might have hindered or helped the acceptance of under-the-counter kitchen appliances, portable computers, flea collars for pets, rabbit meat for meals.

Making Decisions 9-1: Gentlemen prefer Sara Lee.

Did you ever play a game trying to figure out which company made what products? We are continually amazed to find that a firm that we thought was in one industry shows up in another. I mean, the Chrysler Corporation making business jet aircraft? And McDonnell-Douglas peddling health insurance? Perhaps one of the most baffling of these modern conglomerates is Sara Lee . . . that well-known purveyor of hosiery!

That's right! The company whose frozen desserts share its name is the same marketer that brings us Hanes, L'eggs, DKNY and a host of other apparel items. Sara Lee jumped into the business of fashion when it acquired the Hanes Hosiery Company years ago. Few consumers realized the affiliation at the time, and corporate management has never attempted to make a serious connection between the different product lines. On its own, Hanes has grown to be the dominant firm in the women's leg coverings business, both domestically and globally. Much of the firm's spread overseas has been through acquisition, such as the purchase of Britain's Pretty Polly and France's Dim, both high-selling hosiery lines.

With its famous "Gentlemen prefer Hanes" slogan, the company's headline brand has always occupied a major position in this market. The marvelous success of the L'eggs brand moved the firm into the forefront of the hosiery field. The addition of Donna Karan's DKNY line, an upscale product selling in exclusive boutiques and department stores, Sara Lee rounded out its entry in this field. By the way, the company also markets Bali bras and lingerie and Isotoner gloves. Not bad for a corner bakery.[32]

Describe Sara Lee's product mix.

---

[32]Michael Flatow, as told to Aimee L. Stern, "Sara Lee's hosiery clings to quality," *Adweek's Marketing Week,* April 6, 1992, pp. 36–37; Editors, "Designs on Europe's knickers," *The Economist,* November 14, 1992, p. 86.

Making Decisions 9-2: Just nuke it.

No doubt about it. One of the most notable developments that has changed the way America eats is the microwave oven. Born out of the need for convenience and speed, this household staple has been the key behind the introduction of countless new products. With more women joining the workforce to provide the double incomes necessary for today's living, the radar range has become the center of kitchen activity. In answer to the cry of what's for dinner, more and more families respond "Nuke it!"

Most food marketers have joined the parade toward microwaveable products. San Francisco based Del Monte was one of them. Long known for its quality canned goods, Del Monte has entered the market for microwave foods in a big way. Like most of its competitors, this old line company has progressed into a line of shelf stable foods. These products need no refrigeration and can go straight from pantry to microwave. Del Monte has also hopped on the wellness movement train. As more and more consumers become concerned about fat content and additives, the company is developing a reputation as the upscale supplier of healthy foodstuffs.

The market for microwaveable frozen dinners is crowded. Stouffer's, Tyson, Swanson, and ConAgra are all major players. Kraft General Foods, Weight Watchers and a number of private label brands fill out the roster. Most of these marketers produce gourmet style meals as well as low fat, healthy entrees. Campbell Soup's Swanson even produced a nukable frozen dinner for kids called Fun Feast that competes with Tyson's Looney Tunes and ConAgra's Kid Cuisine lines.[33]

Identify the factors that have led to the success of microwaveable foods, while describing the consumer adoption process for these items. Analyze the problems that marketing management might face in the development of new products for this field.

Making Decisions 9-3: Hello . . . ah, er, I mean, like, HI!

The ups and downs of the automobile industry are legendary. Just when Detroit thought it was giving the American buying public what it wanted, along comes the Volkswagen Beetle. Small, economical and carrying a fun image, the little car signaled the onset of a flood of imported cars that challenged the big chrome-plated powerhouses from General Motors, Ford and Chrysler. Although it took awhile, these auto making giants got the message and began to downsize some of their lines . . . perhaps, too late.

Toyota, Nissan, Honda and Mazda quickly overtook VW, and the thrust of the imported car industry in this country shifted from Europe to Japan. Part of this move could easily be attributed to Volkswagen's ill-timed decision to dump the

---

[33]John Sinisi, "Beggar's banquet," *BRANDWEEK*, October 19, 1992, pp. 30–32; Fara Warner, "What's happening at Del Monte," *Adweek's Marketing Week*, November 16, 1991, p. 4.

Beetle, and, in so doing, destroy the image of low-cost, low-maintenance driving. As the size of cars from this German manufacturer increased, so did the prices. An edge was lost that may never be recreated. Even after the firm unveiled Concept 1, the futuristic revival of the Beetle, dealers and the industry were pessimistic that VW could survive until 1996 or 1997 when this new model is expected to hit showroom floors.

In the meantime, VW is pushing its Golf III through heavy promotion. Unfortunately, this vehicle runs head on into competition with Chrysler's highly successful Neon. Sporting safety features that include dual air bags and a price tag 25 percent less than VW's model, Neon is making its dealers smile all the way to the bank. Buoyed by the clever promotional campaign, Chrysler has a major target segment saying "Hi"

to Neon. No wonder car buyers looking for economy along with a fun image are flocking to the little car that seems to be grinning.[34]

Discuss the downfall of the Volkswagen Beetle in contrast to the rise of Chrysler's Neon in terms of failure and success factors.

---

[34]Fara Warner, "A tough road to hoe for futuristic beetle," BRANDWEEK, January 17, 1994, p. 17; David Woodruff, "Behind the friendly grin," Business Week, June 6, 1994, pp. 86–87.

10

Pricing Concepts

The Job to be Done

Determining how and where to set prices is one of the most challenging functions of marketing management. Understanding of the factors that influence buying behavior helps, but customers alone do not determine pricing policy. Chapter 10 provides the input needed to:

- define price and the ways that customers affect price,
- describe how the product and competition impact pricing policy,
- interpret the roles played by intermediaries and government in setting prices, and
- contrast the various pricing objectives of the marketing firm and their impact on the ways pricing is managed.

What Is Price?

Price means different things to different people or firms. To some, the way goods and services are priced acts to prohibit the urge to buy. Others look upon pricing as a measure of value. Marketers price their goods and services to make products attractive to potential buyers. At the same time, firms must assure that they cover their costs and produce a profit.

Competition and changing customer needs have a significant impact upon pricing policies of marketing firms. In some cases, companies are forced to reduce prices in order to maintain their present level of sales. Oshkosh B'Gosh the Wisconsin based marketer of children's clothing, faced increasing price resistance from consumers. The company embarked on a cost reduction and process overhaul program to offset the downward pressure on prices. Mercedes Benz, Philip Morris, Compaq, Burger King and Woolworth are just a few companies facing similar pressures.[1]

PERCEIVED VALUE

Sellers and buyers of goods and services place a perceived value upon the exchange of products. In terms of materials and time, sellers are giving up things

---

[1]Christopher Farrell, Zachary Schiller, Richard A. Melcher, Geoffrey Smith, Peter Burrows, and Kathleen Kerwin, "Stuck!" *Business Week,* November 15, 1993, pp. 146–155.

PRICE TERMS FOR DIFFERENT INDUSTRIES

TERM	INDUSTRY
Fare	Transportation (air fare, taxi fare, bus fare)
Fee	Law (attorney's fee), consulting, recreation (greens fees)
Tuition	Colleges and universities, private schools
Dues	Associations, clubs, organizations (monthly dues)
Charge	Utilities (telephone charge), warehousing (storage charge)
Interest	Financial institutions (price of money)
Rate	Publications (subscription rate)
Rent	Real estate
Toll	Public highways (bridge toll), ferries
Passage	Ocean transportation
Fine	Government agencies

that were costly to produce. Buyers part with money, which may be difficult to earn, as the product changes hands. Ideally, both parties reach satisfaction. This perceived value that each place upon the transaction is shown by the price of the product.

In exchange for the money spent, the buyer expects to receive utility. The benefit received depends upon the reasons for the purchase. In a matter of health or life, such as major surgery, the value of the exchange can be high for the buyer. The price of the good or service might be unimportant. Urgency, too, affects the importance of price. The person in a hurry to fly to Atlanta for a job interview may not be willing to wait for extended commitment air fare reductions. On the other hand, a trip to see Grandma might be planned well enough in advance to take advantage of special, lower air fares.

Similarly, one purchaser may not place as high a value on a particular product as will another customer. Many grocery shoppers religiously watch for specials and will shop from store to store to save the most money on their purchases. Other buyers favor a particular supermarket and will get their groceries at that outlet regardless of prices. Both customers are getting the most value as determined by their individual needs.

A MEASURE OF QUALITY

To most buyers, the price of an article is a measure of its quality. Lower prices typically mean less value. Since the amount of effort used to create the product often affects the price, customers presume that a higher priced item brings more benefit. At times values are arbitrarily raised by the buyer. For special occasions, such as anniversaries or graduations, higher priced items may be considered more meaningful. Consumers buying most specialty and many shopping goods follow this line of reasoning.

Price influences buying behavior. Marketers must control the pricing of a product to reach their basic aim of customer satisfaction. Prices of goods and services are not set arbitrarily. Many factors help marketers in deciding what buyers will be charged. Prospective customers, be they consumers or businesses, have some input, as do internal operations and competition.

The desires and needs of customers and markets are the most important items influencing price levels. A product's cost and the stage of its life cycle impact pricing policy, as does competitive action. Marketing intermediaries and government agencies can also have an impact. These factors have influence, but the marketing firm itself must resolve company objectives in setting the prices of its products.

How Do Customers Affect Price?

Customers have the greatest influence on how a firm sets its prices. The needs and wants of the marketplace are the first consideration. Marketers will not be able to sell their products at any price if there is no market demand for them. The necessity for goods and services is tempered by the status of the individual or firm. The income level of the consumer or financial situation of the business may change the degree to which products are needed or wanted. Brand loyalty or allegiance to a supplier may influence what and from whom purchases are made.

THE EFFECT OF MARKET DEMAND

Market demand—the sum of individual needs or wants for a given product.

Economists describe **market demand** as the sum of individual demand for a given product. Consumers, or business buyers, will purchase a number of goods or services out of the available choices. These choices depend upon the quantities and varieties of products that are available and the amount of money on hand at any given time. How consumers use their disposable and discretionary income to buy goods and services will vary greatly depending upon personal or social factors.

Demand for any given product may increase or decrease depending upon the value that buyers perceive that they are receiving. Poor quality will more than likely reduce the quantity desired by cumulative markets. Prices and competitive action also have an effect. Lower prices or better quality from another product will impact overall demand. Some goods and services are in greater demand than others. Consumers, on the whole, are apt to buy more hamburger than steak, more chicken than duck. Business buyers, as a rule, have greater need for computers than for stamping tools or robotic welders.

Many consumer goods were under severe price strain in the early 1990s due largely to the absence of inflationary pressure. Price wars, with marketers fighting for share of market based strictly on price, were common. From frozen

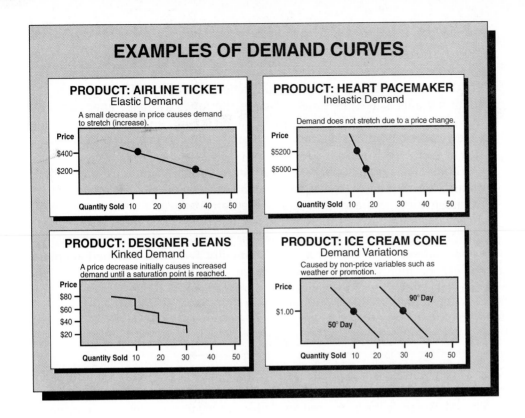

EXAMPLES OF DEMAND CURVES

PRODUCT: AIRLINE TICKET
Elastic Demand

A small decrease in price causes demand to stretch (increase).

PRODUCT: HEART PACEMAKER
Inelastic Demand

Demand does not stretch due to a price change.

PRODUCT: DESIGNER JEANS
Kinked Demand

A price decrease initially causes increased demand until a saturation point is reached.

PRODUCT: ICE CREAM CONE
Demand Variations

Caused by non-price variables such as weather or promotion.

foods to beer, major players were forced into competitive situations that were largely not anticipated. Even the high-tech field of hard-disk drives was hit with devastating price cutting. On the up side, many marketers took this opportunity to cut costs and streamline operations.[2]

Elasticity vs Inelasticity

Many consumers respond quickly to changes in price. If product sales increase rapidly with a lowering of price, market demand for that product is said to be elastic. Elasticity of demand occurs when price increases or decreases have a direct and immediate effect on the amount of goods sold. For example, a sharp drop in the price of navel oranges could trigger an increase in their consumption. In this case, the demand for oranges would be considered elastic.

Inelasticity of demand occurs when dramatic increases or decreases in price have little effect upon the number of items sold. The need or want for many goods and services is based upon more than price. The markets for textbooks or for major surgery fit this definition. A 50 percent discount in the price of biology texts would not likely cause students to flock to the bookstore or to enroll in large numbers in biology courses. Market demand for open heart surgery will not jump dramatically if physicians offered a price reduction.

---

[2]Gerry Khermouch, "Beer pressure," *BRANDWEEK*, January 10, 1994, pp. 27–32; Robert D. Hof and Peter Burrows, "Blood on the tracks," *Business Week*, July 12, 1993, p. 31; Betsy Spethmann, "Frozen in price wars, food marketers see thaw ahead," *BRANDWEEK*, June 21, 1993, p. 3.

THE EFFECT OF INCOME LEVEL/FINANCIAL STATUS

Chapter 2 explained disposable and discretionary income. The former is the amount left after taxes; the latter indicates the funds available after purchase of the necessities of life, like food, shelter and clothing. In establishing pricing policies, marketers must take into consideration the income level or financial status of their target market.

Foods, housing and clothes come with a variety of physical and associate attributes. Similarly, consumer demand for these items is influenced by how much they cost and how much they are needed. Americans have an unbelievable number of different brands and types of products to choose from. Organizations, too, have options. For manufacturers, many raw materials and component parts offer a range of quality and price. Production equipment can be highly automated or manual. Purchasers have the choice between state-of-the-art office computers or equipment that does only word processing. The buying decision often hinges upon the funds available.

THE EFFECT OF BRAND LOYALTY

Not all convenience goods are the same. These products, especially food stuffs, are often purchased with disposable income. However, individual choices are almost unlimited. To satisfy the basic need for clothes, a consumer can look to an unending array of styles, brands and quality. Organizations often have a smaller selection of products and suppliers, especially in the production goods field. Yet, even with products sold by a business to a business, the choice of product and supplier may be vast.

Strong brand loyalty often offsets elasticity of demand. Lower prices for Lucerne or Swenson's ice cream may not lure consumers who insist upon Baskin-Robbins. If Bostonian shoes offer one shopper a perfect fit, price swings in Nunn-Bush, Dexter or Kinney's may not be sufficient to overcome this brand loyalty. For these consumers, allegiance produces inelastic demand for those brands.

In business arenas, products or suppliers that provide reliable satisfaction may not lose out to a low price competitor. Production goods buyers are likely to stick with proven suppliers. Lower prices by unknown or untried vendors seldom sway savvy business buyers. With trade goods marketers, service and quality offset low prices. Loyalty to either the brand or supplier can be a major influence on pricing policy.

ow Does The Product Affect Price?

The primary way that products influence their prices is through costs. This effect includes the costs of production and marketing. Designing products to meet market demand is one thing. Establishing prices that will create healthy sales while still returning a profit is another. Positioning of the product will have a decided effect upon where the marketer sets prices. The stages of a product life cycle and the firm's product mix also impact pricing policies.

COSTS

The costs to produce and market goods and services have a direct bearing on where the firm can afford to set prices. Obviously, marketers cannot establish prices that do not bring in enough revenue to cover their expenses over a long period. No matter how great the demand for a given product, no firm wants to lose money in satisfying the market. Some costs are stable and easy to calculate. Others change for a number of reasons.

Fixed Costs

One major influence on the prices of goods or services are the costs of production. These fall into two categories, fixed and variable. **Fixed costs** do not vary with the amount of products made or sold. Production equipment, plant or buildings and many accessories are necessary for a manufacturing business to operate. Such capital purchases usually do not change as the quantities of products sold go up or down. Some expense items are also considered fixed costs. Insurance premiums, most management salaries and certain utility costs likewise do not fluctuate with increases or decreases in sales volumes.

Fixed costs—those cost items that remain the same no matter how many units are sold.

To Deere and Company, its plants and production equipment are fixed costs. For a Kmart store, rent on the building and insurance are costs that remain the same no matter how much merchandise sells. On a Delta Airline flight from Los Angeles to Atlanta, the amortized cost of the airplane and the salaries of the flight crew do not change whether there are 20 or 200 passengers. As is the case with most services, the equipment used in providing the service is a fixed cost.

Variable Costs

Variable costs are those that increase or decrease depending upon the volume of business. The ingredients used in the production of goods, such as raw materials and component parts, are variable costs. The more goods sold, the greater these expenses. Labor also fits this cost category. As sales increase, manufacturers and intermediaries often need to add personnel in order to cover demand.

Variable costs—those costs that increase or decrease with changes in the number of products sold.

To John Deere, the total cost of steel, paint, tires and transmissions will decrease if the firm builds fewer pieces of farm equipment. The total variable costs for these products depends on the number of finished goods manufactured. During special sales or before Christmas, Kmart purchases more merchandise and hires additional salespeople. With additional passengers, the weight of the Delta jet increases and so does the variable cost of fuel.

Total Costs

Total costs equal the sum of fixed and variable costs. Variable cost per unit typically decreases as production increases. In addition, fixed costs can be spread over a greater number of units. As sales volume increases, the amount of revenue used to cover fixed costs grows. While marketers are interested in all figures that affect pricing, total costs are the primary concern.

Total costs—the sum of fixed and variable costs.

The scenario of a hypothetical entrepreneur, such as a shop that decorates T-shirts, can serve as an example of the impact of costs on prices. Let's assume that this "manufacturing" concern set up shop by renting space in a shopping mall. Additional expenses include an inventory of T-shirts, silk screened designs and patterns and a stock of plastic letters and numerals. This entrepreneur would also need heat sealing equipment that presses the designs on the shirts. Our business operator then hires a person to run the equipment. For this hypothetical example, routine purchases, such as coffee, paper clips, rulers and markers, will be lumped under office supplies.

In this case, rent for the mall space and the sealing equipment would be considered fixed costs. These two expenses are needed regardless of the quantity of goods sold. Since the number of T-shirts, quantity of designs and numerals and the hours of the employee depend upon the number of goods sold, the costs for these items would be variable. The total costs would include both fixed and variable.

Marginal Revenue vs Marginal Cost

Marginal cost—the cost of producing one additional unit.
Marginal revenue—the revenue from the sale of one additional unit.

The amount that the total costs increase by producing one more unit is **marginal cost.** That figure has to be compared to the amount of increased revenue generated by the sale of one additional unit, or **marginal revenue.** The additional revenue gained by the sale of one more unit must be greater than the cost to produce it. To increase profits, the extra revenue received from the sale of one more unit must be equal to or greater than the additional cost to make it.

In the hypothetical example of the T-shirt decorator, to determine marginal cost the entrepreneur would have to total the fixed and variable costs for each piece of merchandise sold. For the sake of simplicity, suppose that the cost of materials for the average shirt is $5.00, and labor costs are $15.00 per

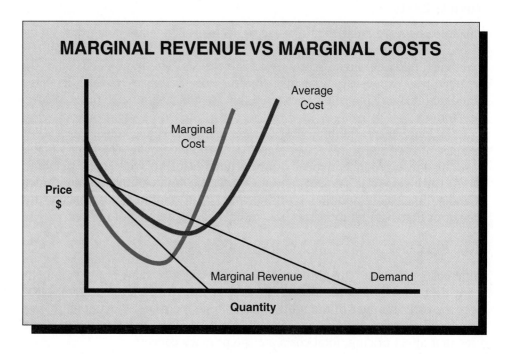

MARGINAL REVENUE VS MARGINAL COSTS

hour. Assume that our mythical shirt decorator reaches full production of ten shirts per hour, or eighty units in a typical, eight-hour day. If demand exceeds this quantity, the entrepreneur will either have to add another employee to work evenings or buy another sealing machine, or both.

When the additional demand amounts to only two shirts per hour, neither of the solutions would be wise. Sales would bring in revenue of $20.00, but the cost of materials and labor would be $5.00 each for two shirts plus $15.00 per hour for labor, or $25.00. This example does not allow for any contribution to the fixed costs of rent and equipment. In this case, marginal revenue resulting from the sale of one additional unit would not equal marginal cost of producing one additional unit.

Break-Even Analysis

Another way that costs are used in setting prices is the **break-even analysis.** Marketers need to know how many units they must sell at a given price to cover costs. To break even, that is, to show neither loss nor profit, sales revenue must cover both fixed and variable costs. Break-even analysis in service industries is often depicted showing sales dollars rather than units.[3] The formula for computing the break-even point is:

Break-even point— the number of units that need to be sold to cover both fixed and variable costs.

$$\text{Break-even Point (in units)} = \frac{\text{Fixed Costs}}{\text{Selling Price} - \text{Average Variable Costs}}$$

In the make-believe T-shirt shop, suppose the sealing equipment costs the shirtmaker $1,000, and the mall space rents for $2,000 per year. The total fixed costs equal $3,000. The selling price per shirt was $10.00, and variable costs amounted to $5.50 in material and $1.50 in labor per shirt. The break-even point equals $3,000 over $10.00 − $7.00, or 1,000 units. The owner/operator of the T-shirt store must sell 1,000 shirts to cover all costs.

Suppose the T-shirt maker finds that the retailers are buying shirts for only $8.00 each. In this case, only $1.00 would be left after subtracting variable costs from price. In this market example, 3,000 units would have to be sold to cover total costs of $3,000. The break-even point increases because there is less contribution toward covering fixed costs.

Most companies use break-even analysis in the new product development process. This study includes a **targeted return** with the fixed costs. The targeted return relates profit or return on investment. All of these items must be covered by total revenue to break even. Consequently, more units need to be sold to cover profit, or targeted return, as well as costs.

Targeted return— profit or return on investment added to fixed costs.

POSITIONING

The image of the good or service has a significant effect upon its price. Upscale or prestige items can attract higher prices. Consumers in upper end

---

[3]William R. Ransom, "Make it or break it," *Small Business Opportunities,* Fall 1993, pp. 66-82.

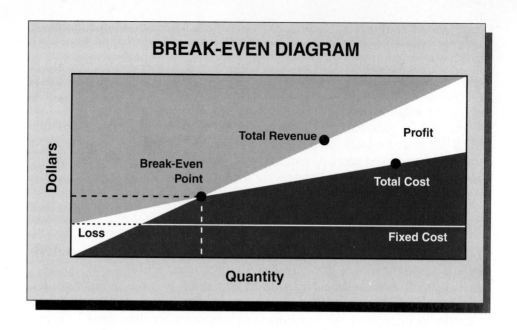

BREAK-EVEN DIAGRAM

market segments are usually willing to pay more for items that carry an aura or mystique. Marketers who position their products for upscale segments must price accordingly or risk tarnishing their image. Porsche maintains high prices because it matches the car's position. Jordache competes primarily with other upscale jeans marketers and prices to meet those competitors, not Levi or Wrangler.

Conversely, goods or services that are marketed to the masses should be priced to reflect that image. Even products that have extra perceived value might not be able to command higher prices when sold in highly competitive markets. Plainer, utilitarian goods or services fare better when priced economically. The role of positioning in pricing cannot be understated.

PRODUCT LIFE CYCLE

Many facets of goods and services affect their prices. The stages of the **product life cycle** put pressures on pricing policy. Typically, but not always, products in the introductory stage sell at a higher price than in their later phases of life. High costs of development, such as with compact disc players, cellular phones or computer software, contribute significantly to setting prices at elevated levels. Developers want to recoup some of these costs prior to the entry of competition.[4]

As competition enters the market during the growth stages, prices usually drop. To capture part of this growing market, companies introduce new products at lower price levels. Since sales quantities are increasing, production costs incurred are generally lower. Increased sales volumes by all competitors force the overall price level down.

---

[4]"Tomorrow's bulging pockets," *The Economist,* October 5, 1991.

During a product's maturity stage, marketers usually attempt to keep prices stable. Emphasis is on extending life and maintaining market share. As the product's life draws to a close, marketers can squeeze the last drop of profit by maintaining price stability. Only when the product is in the throes of death will sellers cut prices to reduce inventories.

PRODUCT MIX

The firm's **product mix** also influences price setting. Larger product mixes have a dampening effect on price changes. The price of one product within a product line is usually competitive with similar brands produced by the same company. With multiple product offerings, a company does not rely as much upon an individual unit for its profit.

To illustrate, Procter & Gamble has a significant share of the laundry detergent market. This product line is one of many for this giant consumer goods house. Therefore, differences in the pricing of Tide, Bold or Cheer do not affect total company revenue. On the other hand, the firm with only one product in a similar line could find that pricing policy dramatically impacts the bottom line.

ow Does Competition Impact Price?

The product and its cost are not the only factors influencing pricing strategies. Competition plays an important role in this process. Demand may be great and costs covered, but competitors selling at lower prices may dictate changes in strategy. There are four basic types of competitive markets; pure competition, monopoly, oligopoly and differentiated competition. Each affects pricing policy in a different manner.

PURE COMPETITION

Pure competition is a market with a large number of buyers and sellers, none of which are significant enough to affect market demand or supply. Buyers easily substitute products from one company or store for those from another supplier. A supermarket can purchase products from any number of sources at relatively the same price. At any given moment, the fruits and vegetables on the shelves of a grocery retailer may come from several different suppliers.

Entry into pure competition markets is relatively easy. Start-up costs are low and rarely does any one firm have significant technological advantages. This type of selling arena has many competitors offering similar, standardized products. Typically, in purely competitive markets, there are no price leaders. Customers generally switch back and forth between the sellers or the goods and services with the lowest prices. Generic office supplies, most agricultural products and basic raw materials are produced in these highly competitive markets.

Pure competition—a market characterized by a large number of competing firms, easy entry and standardized products.

Global Marketing: A Pocket Full of Rubles.

Not too many years ago one would be locked up and had the key thrown away for even suggesting that by 1992 the Union of Soviet Socialist Republics would be no more. Even the most vocal of Soviet bashers could not fathom that the USSR would collapse. Oh, sure . . . go through some changes, perhaps, but not cease to exist. Historians are already calling the downfall of the Soviet Union the most significant event of the second half of the century.

As the former USSR republics struggle with independence, one of the major obstacles each must face is the dive into free market economies. The freedom to set prices wherever the market will bear is difficult to cope with when one has lived so long under government control. While many citizens in the now independent countries are relishing the availability of never-before-allowed consumer goods, the ability to buy them is a problem.

In Russia, the largest of the republics, the value of the ruble is in question. Even with the opening of this nation's borders, businesses had no end of trouble

trying to tap the Russian market. PepsiCo, one of the first U.S. firms to invade the former Soviet Union, had difficulty with the currency. At least initially, the soft drink producer had to take payment in trade, swapping Pepsi for Stolichnaya vodka, which the firm resold back home. Coca-Cola has had similar experiences.

The ruble's lack of value causes delays in free trade. Today, many commodities are available on the streets of Moscow, Kiev or St. Petersburg for about what they might cost in London, Lisbon or Louisville. The one major difference is that the average Russian, Ukrainian or Georgian does not have the income to pay those prices. Once everything is sorted out for these former Soviet nations, they have the potential to collectively or independently form a mighty market.

SOURCES: Peter Galuszka and Patricia Kranz, "Welcome to the Moscow shopping mall," *Business Week*, August 19, 1991, p. 44; Richard A. Melcher, Mark Ivey, Jonathon B. Levine, David Greising and Joyce Barnathan, "For investors, 'After one step backward, it's two steps forward,'" *Business Week*, September 2, 1991, pp. 28-29; Peter Galuszka, "The ruble is dead. Long live. . . the ruble?" *Business Week*, October 14, 1991, p. 61.

MONOPOLY

Monopoly—a market characterized by a single firm that controls all activity.

A **monopoly** is simply a market that has only one supplier. Absolute monopoly is practically non-existent in America due to the anti-trust policies of the federal government. In an absolute monopoly, the lack of competition dictates that sole suppliers could peg prices wherever desired. Because of this threat to create unfair pricing, monopolies are severely restricted in their operations.

Many public utilities enjoy this status on a local basis. As a rule, there is only one electric utility, a single gas company and a lone water supplier servicing customers living in any given area. Until the breakup of AT&T, the telephone industry was in a similar position. Now, consumers and businesses have a choice of long distance telephone operators. Public utility commissions at state or local levels are available to resolve disputes and approve rates.

Another form of monopoly exists through patents. Patent protection from the federal government is limited to seventeen years, but while in force, can give the holder the ability to set price at whatever the market will bear. In other words, the patent holder will price the product at a level that will not turn off demand. Patent protection also limits competition from entering the market. When the NutraSweet division of Monsanto Chemical lost its patent on its artificial sweetener aspartame at the end of 1992, prices plummeted. Similarly, the patents held by Glaxo Holdings, Merck and Eli Lilly keep the prices on H-2 blocking ulcer drugs at a high level until the mid 1990s.[5]

OLIGOPOLY

A market dominated by a few large competitors is an **oligopoly.** Much of the industrial might of the United States operates in this type of competition. Automobiles, tires, jet aircraft, tobacco, steel and cereals are industries that show a limited number of major firms controlling most of the sales. Entry into oligopolies is limited, usually due to the high fixed costs of production or marketing. Since new firms are restricted from the competition because they cannot afford to join the game, prices are somewhat stable in these markets. Industry leaders are the ones who establish market levels for prices.

> **Oligopoly**—a market characterized by a few, large competitors, and difficult entry.

Competition within oligopolies tends to be non-price oriented. Within such a market, price wars are risky. Moves by the dominant members that cut price will usually be matched by competition. The major firms typically compete on the basis of style or brand loyalty instead of price. Procter & Gamble and Unilever experienced this price phenomenon with "ultra" detergents. Although prices were initially high, one cut led to another until all suppliers were at about the same level. Kellogg's and General Mills experienced similar results of the cereal oligopoly.[6]

DIFFERENTIATED COMPETITION

Differentiated competition, previously called monopolistic competition, is a market that has a large number of sellers offering similar, but not identical, merchandise. The larger firms are typically national in scope and have broad product mixes. The regional competitors, on the other hand, usually have a limited number of product lines that may be shallow. Jif brand peanut butter is one of

> **Differentiated competition**—a market characterized by a large number of buyers and sellers with similar products.

---

[5]Elyse Tanouye, "Price wars, patent expirations promise cheaper drugs," *The Wall Street Journal,* March 24, 1994, pp. B1 and B5; Lois Therrien, Patrick Oster, and Chuck Hawkins, "How sweet it isn't at NutraSweet," *Business Week,* December 14, 1992, p. 42.

[6]Betsy Spethmann, "Kellogg counters big G price cuts: 'Bogos' a no go June 1," *BRANDWEEK,* April 25, 1994, p. 3; Betsy Spethmann, "Ultra detergents are a hit, but makers are taking a hit," *BRANDWEEK,* December 6, 1993, pp. 30–32; Terry Lefton, "The best-laid calling plans push prices down," Superbrands supplement to *BRANDWEEK,* 1992, pp. 98–99.

TYPE OF STRUCTURE	MONOPOLY	OLIGOPOLY	DIFFERENTIATED COMPETITION	PURE COMPETITION
Number of sellers	1	Few	Many	No limit
Barriers to entry	Absolute	High	Moderate	Low
Nature of product	Few substitutes	Open	Differentiated	Homogeneous, no differences
Market share/seller	100%	High	Low	Fragmented
Influence on price	Absolute	High	Lower	Low
Examples	Electric & gas public utilities, PTTs*	Automobile, telephone companies (AT&T, MCI, Sprint)	Jeans, soft drinks, cigarettes	Commodity markets: wheat, oxide glycol

*PTTs = Postal and Telecommunications Organizations.

■　■　■　■　■

hundreds of products marketed by Procter & Gamble nationally. Adams Foods sells its competitive spread primarily in the Northwest. Anheuser-Busch, Miller Brewing, Stroh's and Coors dominate the brewing industry. Despite the presence of these industry giants, hundreds of micro-breweries are found throughout the United States.[7]

> **Product differentiation—** altering similar items slightly so that they differ yet serve the same function.

One key factor of differentiated competition is **product differentiation.** In this arena, similar items vary slightly so that they differ from one another yet serve the same general function. These differences usually include branding, but might also encompass warranties or physical characteristics. Crest, Close-Up and Aim all help to clean teeth and freshen the breath. Each, however, is different in taste, appearance and package. Consumers find a wide variety of automobiles to choose from, yet the different makes and models are distinctive to themselves.

When one firm offers a special price, others are likely to counteract with similar savings to users. The regional members of this type of competitive market tend to price their products lower. Although these smaller competitors often develop fierce followings, price can be a swaying factor.

Convenience goods marketers display most of the characteristics of differentiated competition. Grocery items, retail stores, clothing and restaurants share many similarities. In these markets, product differentiation occurs mostly by brand. Shopping goods categories may also show product differentiation. Toasters and microwave ovens bear many similarities, but different brands have distinctive characteristics. Warranties and price are often the major contrasting factors with these products.

---

[7]Gerry Khermouch, "Microbrews come of age in the ways of marketing," *BRANDWEEK,* October 18, 1993, p. 30.

How Do Intermediaries Influence Prices?

More factors than customers, cost and competition affect pricing policies. The strength and effectiveness of intermediaries influence marketers in many ways. The needs of these intermediaries often alter how manufacturers establish pricing. Trade goods marketers sell to wholesalers or retailers, but still must be concerned with the ultimate prices to consumers or buyers. If the intermediaries charge too much for the product, compared to competition, the manufacturer's sales will suffer.

More and more retail chains are developing hybrid warehouse clubs outlets. Von's has its Expo stores, and Smith's, Meijer and Lucky Stores use these types of outlets to compete pricewise with the likes of Costco/Price Club and Sam's. The buying power of these outlets also forces food marketers to cut their prices. Chances are these supermarket/warehouse club combinations will cause a continuation of the everyday low price strategies initiated by Procter & Gamble in 1993.[8]

Companies selling through intermediaries cannot govern the prices of their products at the consumer level. Laws prohibit manufacturers from controlling what a retailer may charge. Because of their inability to govern ultimate selling prices, some manufacturers channel distribution through wholly owned outlets. This strategy allows these companies to exercise a degree of control over pricing at the retail level.

MARGINS AND INCENTIVES

The **margins** required by intermediaries dictate the price of the goods to consumers. Margin is the difference between the cost of the good to the retailer and its selling price. For example, Bunn-O-Matic markets coffeemakers, a shopping good. Suppose retailers typically need a margin of $15.00 on each Pouromatic unit to cover costs and profit. If competitive brands sell for $45.00 each, Bunn must price its product to retailers at $30.00. Otherwise, this marketer will not be competitive in the consumer market.

Pricing is often used as an **incentive** to attract intermediaries. Concessions may be given or discounts offered to prod the wholesaler or retailer into promoting a particular brand. Price breaks given by manufacturers may have the effect of lowering prices to the consumer. Of course, such policies lower total revenues to the original marketing firm as well.

Margin—the difference between what a retailer pays for a good and its selling price.

What Role Does Government Play In Setting Prices?

Marketers might wish to be captains of their own destiny when setting prices. Unfortunately, outside influences affect these decisions. Government plays a

---

[8]Betsy Spethmann, "Hybrids challenge marketers on price," *BRANDWEEK,* July 5, 1993, p. 8.

Retailers have some influence over the pricing policies of manufacturers due to the profit margins that they must achieve.

significant role in pricing decisions. Whether it be through legislative action or by managing the economy, the forces of the public sector have considerable impact on pricing decisions.

MANAGEMENT OF THE ECONOMY

One way that the federal government interacts with pricing policy is through **management of the economy.** The general economy can be stimulated or stunted by government actions. Primarily through actions of the Federal Reserve Board, inflation can be controlled to a great degree. Such activities as increases in the discount rate or reserve requirements can have a dampening effect on business, which might impair a marketing program. As an additional example, taxes, levied by government, are both a major cost of doing business and a deterrent to building disposable and discretionary income.

As consumer or buyer needs for goods and services grow, more sellers enter the market, generally increasing supply and lowering prices. When available goods become too plentiful, oversupply forces price reductions. During recessions, prices on unused inventories will usually drop. These dips reflect the needs of sellers to rid themselves of excess stock and respond to lower market demand.

PRICING RESTRICTIONS

The federal government creates **pricing restrictions.** Government places conditions on policies to promote free trade so that one company does not gain unfavorable advantages over another. Federal agencies regulate prices in certain industries and serve as watchdogs on a variety of discrimination issues. Sweeping investigations of the household cleaning products industry came about as a result of alleged "deal making" between marketers and retailers.[9]

The U.S. government impacts pricing through direct pressure on consumer demand. Supply is restricted in import markets when government places quotas on the goods allowed into this country. When supply is limited, prices increase. Government also imposes import duties or tariffs on some products from overseas. These taxes increase the prices of imported items compared to domestic goods.

The federal government establishes rigid laws to keep companies from diverting from published price lists. In meeting competitive prices, firms must keep adequate, written records. Businesses may not quote special prices to individual customers if a cost savings cannot be proven. Otherwise, companies must offer similar prices on similar products sold to similar customers.

Price Fixing

Price fixing and restraint of trade are government concerns. Competitors cannot be in collusion to artificially establish the same prices. Congress passed the Sherman Act and Clayton Act to deal specifically with unfair pricing. The Federal

---

[9]Judith Springer Riddle, "Feds souring out collusive practices," *BRANDWEEK*, June 21, 1993, p. 9.

Sherman Antitrust Act (1890) Prohibits (a) "monopolies or attempts to monopolize" and (b) "contracts, combinations, or conspiracies in restraint of trade" in interstate and foreign commerce.

Federal Trade Commission Act (1914) Establishes the commission, a body of specialists with broad powers to investigate and to issue cease-and-desist orders to enforce Section 5, which declares that "unfair methods of competition in commerce are unlawful."

Clayton Act (1914) Supplements the Sherman Act by prohibiting certain specific practices (certain types of price discrimination, tying clauses and exclusive dealing, intercorporate stockholdings, and interlocking directorates) "where the effect . . . may be to substantially lessen competition or tend to create a monopoly in any line of commerce." Provides that violating corporate officials can be held individually responsible; exempts labor and agricultural organizations from its provisions.

Robinson-Patman Act (1936) Amends the Clayton Act. Adds the phrase "to injure, destroy, or prevent competition." Defines price discrimination as unlawful (subject to certain defenses) and provides the FTC with the right to establish limits on quality discounts, to forbid brokerage allowances except to independent brokers, and to prohibit promotional allowances or the furnishing of services or facilities except where made available to all "on proportionately equal terms."

Miller-Tydings Act (1937)
Amends the Sherman Act to exempt interstate fair-trade (price-fixing) agreements from antitrust prosecution. (The McGuire Act, 1952, reinstates the legality of the nonsigner clause.)

Antimerger Act (1950) Amends Section 7 of the Clayton Act by broadening the power to prevent intercorporate acquisitions where the acquisition may have a substantially adverse effect on competition.

Consumer Goods Pricing Act (1975) Prohibits the use of price maintenance agreements among manufacturers and resellers to interstate commerce.

■   ■   ■   ■   ■

Trade Commission Act and its amendments established this body as the watchdog for business activities. This federal agency is especially effective in policing pricing and advertising. Robinson-Patman was the major legislation enacted to deal specifically with restraint of trade.

To illustrate, by law Coleman must sell its outdoor and camping equipment to both Walgreen's and Wal-Mart at similar prices. Glidden must sell paint to competing retailers at the same price, but might offer a different price to mobile home manufacturers. One price fixing illustration involved steel pipe fabricators and distributors. Working in collusion, the fabricators used phony distributor prices in bidding on government contracts, splitting the differences among all parties. The FTC and the Justice Department prosecuted the offenders in this case, levying heavy fines. Sunkist was cited for working in collusion with packers to circumvent stringent government quotas that prop up citrus prices.[10]

---

[10]Amy Barrett and Laura M. Holson, "Something shady at Sunkist," *Business Week,* May 17, 1993, p. 40; E. Goldratt, "Late night discussions: Different markets, different prices," *Industry Week,* April 6, 1992, p. 58.

Deception

The FTC is particularly concerned about deceptive pricing policies. Retailers must take care when using **comparison pricing.** When comparing special sales prices to previous, standard levels, stores must assure that the original price was valid for a reasonable time. By law, retailers are not allowed to offer marked down merchandise if effort was not made to move the goods at the beginning price.

Comparison to competitor prices must be factual. It must be shown that the competition actually charged such a price. Retailers are under scrutiny regarding special offers as well. Firms offering "two-for-one" or "second-at-one-cent" sales cannot artificially inflate the original price on the first item. The Consumer Goods Pricing Act bars manufacturers from dictating prices to retailers. Many producers suggest prices, but that is the extent of their control over what a retailer charges. Manufacturers that own intermediaries must be careful not to violate the principle of this law.

Rule of Reason and Predatory Pricing

The FTC is the agency that oversees pricing within the distribution channel. This organization usually applies the **rule of reason** when hearing cases. This interpretation means that evidence of economic harm must be present for the bureau to prosecute. Suppose a retailer carrying hundreds of brands claims price discrimination from a supplier of just one of them. The FTC has ruled in such cases that the outlet has not been harmed because a bulk of the firm's income was unaffected.

Predatory pricing means a company prices its product so low that it forces competition out of business. In these cases, the FTC will usually act quickly. Dealers that threaten to withhold business unless the manufacturer makes price concessions are another target of the FTC. Manufacturers that favor wholly owned outlets to the detriment of independent distributors will also draw the wrath of this federal agency.

Rule of reason—the Federal Trade Commission bases its judgment on whether economic damage has occurred.

Predatory pricing—pricing one's product below cost to force competition out of the market.

 ## What Are The Pricing Objectives Of Marketers?

Although many outside agencies affect the pricing policies of marketers, the individual firm creates its own policies. Before determining its course of action, a marketing oriented company will take the time to outline its purposes for setting prices. Making money is not the only objective. In fact, profit may be secondary to other factors in many cases.

PROFIT

Unless firms have claimed nonprofit status, all privately owned businesses attempt to make a **profit.** Typically, the total revenues of a company minus its costs leave a positive remainder called profit. Otherwise, the firm is operating at a loss. Profit depends upon the price of the unit, the number of units sold

Retailers must be careful to avoid misleading consumers when advertising special pricing deals, such as "2 for 1."

Marketers who deal in exclusive, upscale products, such as Roll Royce, still use break-even analysis in setting prices. (Courtesy of Rolls-Royce Motor Cars Ltd.)

and the cost per unit. Obviously, a large volume of sales might offset a low selling price. Competition may force the price down to levels that leave a firm with little choice but to drastically cut costs.

Maximizing profits does not necessarily mean that firms charge the highest possible prices. When products show elastic demand, raising prices could reduce the number of units sold, decreasing total revenue. If IBM raised the price of its computers by 20 percent, business users might switch to Compaq or Macintosh. This loss of business could offset the increased revenue gained from the higher price. On the other hand, when markets display inelastic demand, an increase in prices might not impact the number of units sold. Rolls-Royce could probably raise the price of its Silver Streak by the same 20 percent and lose few sales. The break-even point for Rolls-Royce is now at 1,400 cars per year.

When demand fluctuates over time, marketers often average their profit. This method of calculating net income is particularly appropriate with seasonal products. Jantzen, the swimsuit house, may settle for lower profits during the off-season. Income will average out with high profits realized during peak periods for its predominantly summer line of clothing.

RETURN ON INVESTMENT

A good way of measuring success of pricing policies is capturing a **return on investment,** or **ROI.** This financial ratio relates profit to investment. As money is invested in a business venture, the owners expect that capital to produce income. A credible reason for setting pricing objectives is to obtain a sound return on that investment. If the business does not provide earnings on the original capital, the owners would be better off placing their moneys in bank accounts or investing in the stock market.

Some manufacturers base their pricing policy on the amount that will be earned from the amount invested. Major equipment or renovation expenses increase the amount of fixed costs that must be covered. Small firms and retailers often use return on investment as the basis for establishing pricing policies. If the business has borrowed money for its start-up costs, it wants to price its products so that its debt service is covered along with other expenses.

SHARE OF MARKET

Share of market—the percentage of the total market captured by a single product or company.

Another pricing objective of management is maintaining, increasing or reducing **share of market.** Total revenue relates to the number of units sold and their individual prices. Unfortunately, pricing to maintain share of market may be in conflict with profit maximization. Sales revenues can increase because lower prices increase the number of goods sold, but profits may dip unless corresponding decreases in costs occur. Firms with pricing objectives of maintaining share of market may lower prices to keep sales high.

The share of market that a company maintains also affects return on investment. Setting prices to maintain share of the market is common for products in the growth stage of their life cycle. Forecasting may be difficult in rapidly expanding markets. Therefore, keeping the same percentage compared with others helps to maximize profits. Many high profit products in their maturity phase are also priced using this objective, extending their total life.

Sometimes businesses wish to reduce market share. Government pressure regarding industry domination of a firm may cause management to accept a smaller share of total available sales. Other firms may have simply grown too fast to adequately service their customers. By raising prices, marketers in these positions force a lowering of demand, which in turn decreases share. Companies threatened by unwanted takeovers often use this tactic to make the business less desirable.

SURVIVAL AND MEETING COMPETITION

In bad economic times or in cases of over capacity, **survival** may dictate pricing policy. Companies with high fixed costs must generate revenues to cover this liability. Companies that cannot sell enough products at high enough prices to cover total costs may still be able to continue operating if sales revenue covers variable costs. When variable costs are not covered, the business usually shuts down. This tactic is effective for the short run only, for no business can sacrifice profits for any length of time.

Many production goods marketers set pricing policy based upon **meeting competition.** In oligopolies, the use of price reductions to gain share is quickly met by retaliation from competitors. To pursue price stability within the market, a firm may be content to set its prices at the same level as the competition. In oligopoly markets, for example, companies concentrate on non-price methods for increasing business.

One problem arises in pricing to meet competition. Pinpointing the exact source of competitive threat is difficult. Too often firms look only to immediate rivals instead of to all areas where customers can substitute products. For instance, the entertainment industry competes for the discretionary dollars of

Marketers of big-ticket items, such as construction equipment, may not be able to test market to calculate demand.

the consumer. Golf courses compete against fishing excursions, and television vies with the local pool hall. The golf course that views another country club as the only rival may be taking too shallow a view. Pricing policy needs to take into consideration all competitors, not just the obvious ones.

ow Is Pricing Managed?

The management of pricing policies is one of the most strenuous tasks facing marketers. The whims and fancies of customers are subject to constant change, which in turn dictates flexible pricing policies. This element of the marketing mix is perhaps the most vulnerable to competitive activity. Additionally, the temptation to practice unethical pricing strategy is great.

ESTIMATING DEMAND

Economics plays an important role in price setting and poses many tough problems. Estimating market demand for a single product is practically impossible. Without knowing demand, marginal revenue and cost are also difficult to compute. Sometimes test marketing will uncover high demand, but not all products can afford the luxury of test marketing. Big ticket production goods, such as construction equipment or supercomputers, are not normally test marketed. Market demand is especially difficult to predict for these types of products.

Appraising demand for new products is doubly difficult. Until the item goes through the introductory cycle and is well into the growth stage, potential market share is hard to predict. Just as sales start to grow and market estimates become feasible, competing products may appear. Sometimes, these new market entries use low prices as the ticket for gaining immediate sales.

ESTIMATING COMPETITIVE THREATS

Just as demand is difficult to predict, the actions of competitors are also beyond the marketer's control. In differentiated competition markets, lower prices may go unnoticed or ignored by competing firms. Greater demand can offset lower individual prices, but caution needs to be taken. When market demand rises, firms are inclined to increase production capacity. Then, just as maximum costs have been incurred, rivals cut their prices.

The toothpaste market offers a good example of competitive pricing. Both Colgate and Arm & Hammer were pricing their toothpaste containing baking soda at about a third higher than regular brands. Consumer demand for the extra scrubbing power of baking soda propped up these prices. When Pepsodent entered the market with a similar product at substantially lower prices, competition had no choice but to follow suit.[11]

PRICING ETHICALLY

Marketers must deal with certain **ethical** questions in setting pricing policies. It is illegal to set prices with the specific intent to drive a competitor out of business. Favoring one customer over another is another problem. In establishing strategy and policy, business people must be mindful of ethical practices. Fear of government reprisal should not be the only reason for ethical action. Many of the laws governing fair pricing are directed toward manufacturers, but wholesalers and retailers, too, must guard against discrimination in their pricing policies.

Although the same laws govern pricing by intermediaries, less attention appears to be paid to this marketing sector. Retailers, because of their numbers, are more difficult to police. The clothing store or lumberyard that advertises goods that are not in stock is less likely to be called for bait-and-switch practices than the large manufacturer. To protect themselves against claims of illegal pricing, supermarkets usually offer "rain checks" if advertised specials are out of stock.

Slotting Fees

Slotting fees (allowances)— payments made to retailers by manufacturers to obtain store shelf space.

Slotting fees, or **allowances,** are payments made by consumer goods marketers to retailers in exchange for shelf space. Whether paid for in cash or in free merchandise, such practices place a heavy burden on small competitors that may not have the financial strength to take part. Estimates are that nearly half of the

---

[11]Seema Nayyar, "Price could paste baking soda rivals," *BRANDWEEK*, November 23, 1992, p. 5.

marketing budgets for consumer goods producers go to discounts or fees. This practice also hinders the introduction of new products. With shelf space at a premium, there may not be room for such items.

Flaunting their tremendous buying power, large retailers successfully tied the hands of consumer goods houses. By forcing these marketers to pay for the privilege of using shelf space, many new products or small firms were forced out of the retail stores. While supermarket chains claim that slotting fees are a necessary evil in times of over-branding, legislatures in several states, notably California, are investigating this practice, as is the Federal Trade Commission.[12]

Transfer Fees

In today's world of megamarketers, it is not uncommon to find companies with strategic business units, or profit centers, operating as separate entities. These individual firms may have opportunities to purchase from outside sources or from other in-house divisions. Obviously, policies would dictate that in such cases the subsidiary would buy as many products as possible from within the corporation. There is nothing wrong with this philosophy. However, firms find themselves in violation of federal laws if they allow such purchases to be made at lower prices. When dealing with "sisters" within the corporate structure, a profit center must sell its goods at the same price that it offers to outside customers. The temptation exists to cut corners in dealing with in-house profit centers, but this would constitute illegal price discrimination.

Policing transfer fees is especially difficult in global marketing. Firms that own intermediaries in other countries can inflate costs so these foreign subsidiaries do not make a profit. If these puffy expenses are in reality paid by the home company, no income taxes would be accumulated in the host country. Just as was the case with in-house profit centers, pricing policies are required to be honest and reasonable.

CONTROLLING COSTS

Controlling the cost of the marketing effort, as well as production, deserves priority. Whether it is the cost of advertising or packaging or the markup taken by intermediaries, marketing is often viewed by consumers as too expensive. In reality, the functions of marketing tend to lower prices to the ultimate user by fostering competition and supplying the need for mass production. Regardless, costs should receive proper consideration by marketing managers.

Customers are upset to learn that a box of cereal or the lipstick recently purchased for dollars actually cost only pennies to manufacture. The ingredients

[12]Howard Schlossberg, "Manufacturers fighting back with alternative retail outlets," *Marketing News,* August 3, 1992, p. 9; Michael Hiestand, "Product launches are down," *Adweek's Marketing Week,* January 9, 1989, p. 4; Associated press release, "Small companies protest slotting allowances," *Marketing News,* January 16, 1989, pp. 2 and 6; Lois Therrien, "Want shelf space? Ante up," *Business Week,* August 7, 1989, pp. 60–61; Christine Donahue, "Conflict in the aisles," *Adweek's Marketing Week,* September 4, 1989, pp. 20–26; David Kiley, "California probes slotting fees," *Adweek's Marketing Week,* October 8, 1990, p. 6.

Marketing and Society: Turning the Tables on Slots!

A revolution is taking place in the aisles of America's supermarkets. Fueled by a policy change by the country's largest consumer goods marketer, Procter & Gamble, manufacturers are scrambling to win back control over trade promotions and pricing. Often, manufacturers will offer special pricing on merchandise, only to find that retailers do not pass it on to the consumer. For years companies have been wooing consumers and intermediaries alike with coupons, specials and allowances. P&G has decided enough is enough.

Supermarkets warehouse specially promoted items at low prices and sell them later at full price. Consumer goods marketers could save the expense of trade promotions, about 15 to 20 percent of the prices, by selling to discount outlets and price clubs. In addition, the inroads made by private label brands have caused more and more marketers to rethink their pricing policies. Johnson & Johnson cut 20 percent from its Immodium A-D brand of antidiarrheal in 1994 in a move to combat over-the-counter store brands. More are expected, as major consumer goods marketers battle giant retailers over lower priced private labels.

Slotting fees are another issue in this war. Major retailers, lacking in adequate shelf space, charge marketers for the privilege of displaying their goods. New products and small marketers are especially hurt by this practice. Companies making additions to their product lines either wait in line or pay dearly for shelf space. Marketers without multiple lines often cannot afford what it takes to get their goods into supermarkets or drug chains.

In 1992, Procter & Gamble initiated a policy of Everyday Low Prices, know as EDLP. By doing away with most trade promotions, P&G hopes to regain control over distribution channels and pass some savings on to consumers. Although many other marketers agree in principle with this plan, the movement to join Procter & Gamble has been slow. Retailers, having grown accustomed to the extra income from promotions and slotting fees, are reluctant to give up this major source of revenue. This battle may be fought for years to come.

SOURCES: Pam Weisz, "J&J cut may signal EDLP OTC," *BRANDWEEK*, May 2, 1994, p. 3; John Bissell, "EDLP reconsidered: What marketers are saying now," *BRANDWEEK*, June 21, 1993, p. 11; Terry Lefton, "Artzt's gamble," *Adweek's Marketing Week*, February 1, 1992, pp. 28–29; Eric Hollreiser, "Laying it out on the table," *Adweek's Marketing Week*, April 27, 1992, pp. 19–20; Seema Nayyar, "P&G answers to drug chains on pricing," *Adweek's Marketing Week*, May 4, 1992, p. 4; John Berry, "Smaller players try EDLP on request," *Adweek's Marketing Week*, April 27, 1992, p. 4.

make up a small part of the cost of breakfast goods, and the packages for many cosmetic items are often more expensive than the contents inside. However, without the promotion, distribution and protective package, cereals and lipsticks would not be available where and when buyers need them.

IN SERVICES

Pricing the service sector receives a great deal more customer input. Since consumers and businesses often have the opportunity to specify the quantity and type of service required, prices may not be standard. One beauty shop customer may prefer to shampoo at home, hence receiving a lower price than someone asking for "the works" from the stylist. The types of data requested from the marketing researcher may vary from firm to firm.

Prices for services also vary according to urgency of the need. Plumbers and electricians often charge more for weekend calls than they would during normal hours. Many accountants up their rates during the busy tax season. Although most industries formerly controlled by government bureaucracies have been deregulated, some pricing restrictions may still apply. This intervention is certainly still true with many public utilities.

IN GLOBAL MARKETS

Managing prices in global markets is particularly touchy. Unlike shipping across the border to Canada or Mexico, the time in transit can be considerable for goods sent round the world. Many things can happen to the shipment or to the economy before the goods are received. Most companies doing business overseas require letters of credit or sight drafts for payment, rather than allowing open account status.

One other factor influencing global pricing is the fluctuation of exchange rates. The value of one country's currency in relation to another changes constantly. These differences in value are affected by inflation, by supply and demand, and by government intervention. Goods shipped by boat from Seattle to Cairo may take weeks to arrive, and the exchange rate could move dramatically during that time.

SUMMING IT UP

Price is the perceived value of a good or service. It is also a measure of the quality of a product. Customers affect pricing by creating market demand. The income level and financial status of consumers and business buyers influence price levels. Brand loyalty is also an influence.

Fixed, variable and total costs of products affect their prices. Marginal revenue must be equal to or greater than marginal cost in order for a marketer to produce and sell additional items. Break-even analysis is used to determine the number of units needed to be sold to cover costs. Product life cycle and the product mix of the selling company also exert influence on pricing policy.

Competition impacts price. Pure competition affords easy entry into the market made up of many buyers and sellers. In contrast, a monopoly is a single firm acting at will in a market. Oligopoly is a market with a few, major suppliers. In differentiated competition, sellers offer many buyers a range of products that are differentiated by brand, warranty or physical characteristics. Intermediaries impact pricing through their margins and the incentives they offer. Government plays a role in price setting through management of the economy and price restrictions.

The primary pricing objective of the marketing firm is to make a profit. Other motivations include creating a return on investment, maintaining a share of market and, at times, survival. The ability to estimate demand and competition is a major concern of marketers in setting prices. Ethical pricing and the control of costs also figure prominently in management decisions.

KEY CONCEPTS AND TERMS FROM CHAPTER TEN

Break-even point	Price
Differentiated competition	Product differentiation
Fixed costs	Pure competition
Margin	Rule of reason
Marginal cost	Share of market
Marginal revenue	Slotting fees
Market demand	Targeted return
Monopoly	Total costs
Oligopoly	Variable costs
Predatory pricing	

BUILDING SKILLS

1. Explain the relationship of quality to price with higher priced goods, such as Porsche cars, prime grade beef, 18k gold jewelry, Cross pens, Noble fir Christmas trees.

2. Describe the characteristics of market demand for the following products: a United Airlines round-trip ticket to Japan, a Craftsman screwdriver, a jar of Reese's peanut butter, a carton of Diet Coke, a Ford Tempo.

3. Classify the competition for the following products: breakfast cereals, shaving cream, luggage, business aircraft, house paint.

4. Explain differences and similarities you see between the pricing policies.

5. Explain the types of government action that influence the setting of pricing policy.

6. Describe and give reasons for or against any unethical pricing practices you have seen or experienced.

Making Decisions 10-1: The Sweet Smell of Luxury.

There is, perhaps, no product sector that is subject to more ups and downs than luxury items. As the economy swings, so does the demand for upscale items. High interest rates, taxes and rising gasoline prices caused a deflation in the sale of expensive goods in the early 1980s. Then, just as the market was bouncing back, along came the Gulf War and an unexpected crash. Marketers serving this area are used to riding the roller coaster.

Many of the items sold in the upscale arena carry exotic foreign brand names, and 1994 brought renewed vigor to products such as Lalique crystal, Hermes' accessories and Christian Dior perfumes. One of the most successful marketers of luxury items is the French conglomerate LVMH. Besides the Louis Vuitton label, this large multinational also markets Moet-Hennessey champagnes and cognac and Christian Lacroix. The firm saw a jump in profits of over 30 percent in 1994.

One unique characteristic of the luxury market is its reaction to price changes. Typically, reductions create negative turns in demand for upscale products. For example, when Christofle lowered prices on its line of fine china, sales dropped over 10 percent. Comité Colbert, a French trade group handling global sales for this china maker, feels that value and quality are extremely important to buyers in this upscale market. Americans are also returning to luxury, as evidenced by a substantial increase in sales at that noted purveyor of class, Neiman-Marcus.[13]

Describe the ways that price influences the perceived value of products, especially of luxury goods.

Making Decisions 10-2: Targeting the Midscale Thigh!

The cosmetics industry often seems driven by the dreams of consumers. We do not sell [lipstick or mascara] . . . we sell hope," is a quote often attributed to Charles Revson, founder of Revlon. One would be hard pressed to discount such a statement. Scents and colorants, shampoos and conditioners, skin creams and cold creams abound, targeting both female and male audiences. Perhaps humans are searching for the fountain of youth . . . or at least for ways to "put on a happy face."

One of the startling developments in personal care products in the early 1990s was in products containing alpha hydroxy acids. Once confined to prescription acne fighting creams, these anti-agers caused quite a stir when marketed as wrinkle eliminators. When combined with aminophylline, used to treat asthma, the resulting products were touted as thigh reducers. Cellulite-plagued customers flocked to stores to snatch up this latest "miracle" of cosmetic science.

---

[13]William Echikson, "The return of luxury," *Fortune*, October 17, 1994, p. 18.

The biggest splash in this booming category was made by Dior with its Svelte Cellulite Control Complex, which was selling at about $7.00 per ounce in 1994. Most other thigh reducers, marketed by smaller firms, were in the $2.50 to $5.00 per ounce range. These inflated prices were the major reason why St. Ives took a fling at this exotic market late in 1994. Skin Zone thigh cream was introduced in a 12–ounce container that retailed for $12.99. St. Ives is counting on its well-known brand name and low price to capture some of this lucrative market.[14]

Explain the impact of competition on the pricing policy of thigh cream marketers, including other factors that might come into play.

Making Decisions 10-3: Cleaning Behind the Ears.

Soap is big business . . . $2 billion worth of big. At one time one could find few brands and, save for smell or color, little difference between them. Today, the hand soap market abounds with products that have all sorts of different characteristics. One of the latest segmentation strategies is to target the children's market with specially formulated brands, and two of the biggest players in the industry, Dial and Lever Brothers, are going head- to-head to win the 2–12 year old group. Census projections that peg over 50 million children in this range by the year 2000 make the segment very attractive.

Dial for Kids is positioned similarly to the company's flagship brand by offering antibacterial protection. In fact, the company is building on this strategy in its dish washing detergents as well. Dial for Kids comes in scents that include watermelon and bubble gum. Together with colorful packaging and clever advertising, Dial hopes to convince moms to get the kids started early with their product, in either bar or liquid pump bottles.

Lever's entry into this category is branded Baby Dove. Similar to the competition, this hand

---

[14]Pam Weisz, "Ives seeks midscale thighs," *BRANDWEEK*, September 5, 1994, p. 14.

soap is also available in either bar or liquid form. By stressing the gentle quality of its Dove brand, Lever hopes to attract parents that appreciate the softness quality that the company created for the original. Although the target market appears to be somewhat younger than Dial for Kids, Lever Brothers still expects its children's soap to be a major revenue generator.[15]

Describe the factors affecting the pricing policy of these giant hand soap marketers, the impact that wholesalers and retailers might exert on this pricing policy, and any ethical problems that these marketers might face in pricing introductory products aimed at children.

---

[15]Penny Warneford and Pam Weisz, "Dial, Lever eye baby boomlet," *BRANDWEEK*, September 19, 1994, pp. 1 and 6.

CHAPTER

11

Pricing Methods

The Job to be Done

Not all businesses sell their products for the same amount of money. Consumer goods are priced differently than those sold to businesses, and retailers use their own methods to set selling prices. In chapter 11, you will learn to:

- recognize the methods marketers use to set prices,
- define the pricing methods found in consumer goods markets,
- describe the many pricing methods retailers use,
- describe the pricing methods business goods marketers use and contrast the ways they price new products,
- understand the effect of freight costs on prices, and
- explain the factors that affect management of pricing policy.

Diablo Valley College in the San Francisco Bay area has reason to be proud of Sally Omran. Twice honoring her as "outstanding business student of the year," DVC can point to a string of achievements by this dynamic, energetic woman: sitting on the Business Advisory Board, serving as a member of the board of directors of the Contra County Ballet Foundation, organizing the first Bay Area Economic Summit, and assisting with the Kennedy King Scholarship Committee. She also managed internships with Beverages and More! and KGO-TV.

It was with KGO-TV that Sally was able to develop her bent for marketing. While working at this ABC affiliate, she produced segments for MARKETPLACE, a program with local emphasis on women in business. Her work with Beverages and More! included the development of a marketing plan for this local distributor. She designed, created and executed the media coverage for a fashion show at the Nordstrom outlet in Walnut Creek, California and handled the public relations for the Contra Costa Ballet Foundation.

Before coming to Diablo Valley College, Sally owned and operated two small businesses. One, a gourmet wine and food market located on Nob Hill in San Francisco, was featured on several occasions by noted columnist Herb Caen, writing in the *San Francisco Chronicle*. Although she achieved financial success in her business ventures, Sally felt strongly that education was the ultimate goal, and returned to college to continue her marketing studies. She handled her reentry much as she directs most of her efforts, by creating a personal marketing plan. With help from several mentors on the college staff, Sally polished her writing skills and developed her confidence. She still feels that marketing "... affects every aspect of my personal and professional life."

How Do Marketers Set Prices?

What most firms within an industry charge for similar products is pretty much the same. One supermarket may be lower priced on some items, while a competitor offers specials on others. Stores that stock jeans from Levi Strauss & Co. will usually price them at about the same general plateau. Depending upon the type of competitive market, prices on most items tend to reach a certain level. If extra value is added, such as special service or extended warranties, the selling company may be able to collect a higher amount from buyers.

MARKET LEVEL

Market level—the position of prices of similar products within a given industry.

Prices for similar products within a given industry tend to settle at a given point called the **market level.** In oligopolies, the industry leaders determine this general plane. In this type of competition, pricing policy among the few major firms is stable. In more competitive markets, amounts charged may vary from firm to firm, yet still hover in the same range. Some marketers price their products somewhat higher than the market level, while others favor going beneath the average.

Price Above or Below Market Level

Companies that **price above market level** often justify this position by giving customers something extra. Better quality or additional service are reasons why higher amounts can be charged. Firms pricing above market level strive to develop a quality image. For instance, Paper Mate, a company with a reputation for high quality, typically sells its pens slightly above the competition. Residence Inns prices its rooms higher than its competitors. By offering larger rooms and a home-like atmosphere, this subsidiary of Marriott can price above market level and still maintain a competitive posture.

On the other hand, businesses that wish to pursue high volume sales often **price below market level.** Increased revenue generated by market demand for lower prices may translate into cost savings. The additional volume tends to reduce product costs to their lowest level. Kmart and Wal-Mart built successful businesses by being low-price leaders. Employees of these mass merchandisers proudly tell customers that they will meet or beat the prices of other retailers selling nationally advertised merchandise.

In the air travel industry, price wars are common. Any lowering of the market level is commonly matched by the competition. American Airlines led the great fare wars of 1992, but the other major carriers quickly followed. Although passenger miles increased dramatically, with almost all flights running at full capacity throughout the summer months, most airline companies suffered losses. Today, Southwest Airlines is the no frills, low-price leader in this industry.[1]

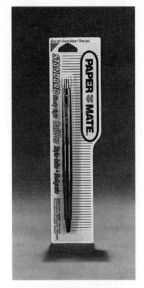

The quality of Paper Mate pens allows this division of the Gillette Company to price somewhat above the market level.

SINGLE PRICE POLICY

Following a **single price policy,** marketers offer the same price or terms of sale for a given product to all common buyers. All wholesalers, for example, no matter where they are located or what volume they purchase, would buy at the same price when manufacturers use a single price strategy. Likewise, most wholesalers sell to their retail customers at the same level. Many manufacturers favor such single price strategies because of their ease of handling, as do most retailers.

Policy decisions made by marketing firms often reflect price flexibility. The question becomes whether to offer only one price or to have a variety. In some industries, a single price policy is more efficient. Retailers with huge inventories could not afford to price each item according to individual needs or demand. In other areas, multiple prices are necessary to meet varying degrees of demand. Large ticket consumer goods, such as automobiles and furniture, are good examples.

Single price policy— the same price for a given product offered to all common buyers.

---

[1] Richard S. Teitelbaum, "Southwest Air," *Fortune,* Autumn/Winter 1993, pp. 33–34; W. Zellner, "The airline mess: Is American's Bob Crandall part of the problem—or the solution?" *Business Week,* July 6, 1992, pp. 50–55; S. Pesman, "American's new fares may clip the wings of some corporate deals," *Business Marketing,* May 1992, p. 9; Bill Saporito, "Why the price wars never end," *Fortune,* March 23, 1992, pp. 68–78.

FLEXIBLE PRICE POLICY

Flexible price policy—
different prices offered
to multiple buyers for
the same product.

A **flexible price policy** means that the seller offers different prices and terms to multiple buyers. Discounts, allowances and freight charges are part of flexible pricing policy which leaves room for negotiation. Customers can bargain with sellers that offer flexible prices. Many production goods are sold using such policies, especially where custom specifications are involved.

The seller's ultimate pricing strategy depends on the bargaining power of the markets and the policies of competition. For example, supermarkets are not likely to set up flexible pricing policies because of the cost involved and because shoppers do not demand discounts or trade-in allowances. On the other hand, the automobile and real estate industries would have difficulty surviving with a single-price policy. Car dealers, for example, usually negotiate with buyers over the amount to be paid or the offer on trade-ins. No two consumers are likely to get the same deal.

Prices in international markets also tend to be flexible, depending largely on the value of the currencies involved. What one company sells its products for in one area or country may be considerably different from what they go for in a second area. Flexible pricing is especially noticeable in trading with former members of the Soviet Union. Barter has become common in dealing with companies from Russia, the Ukraine and other Eastern European nations. PepsiCo first entered the Russian market in 1974, trading cola for vodka. Rival Coca-Cola made a similar bartering agreement, trading Coke syrup for Russian-made Lada automobiles, which the soft drink giant then sold in England.[2]

ow Are Consumer Products Priced?

Manufacturers cannot dictate prices to retailers, yet the policies of these producers ultimately affect what the consumer pays. Trade goods marketers offer incentives, discounts or rebates to retailers. As a result, these intermediaries receive lower cost merchandise. Consumers benefit from price reductions when retailers pass along their savings. Conversely, as manufacturers transfer freight charges and other associated costs to intermediaries, consumers would more than likely face price increases.

CUSTOMARY/TRADITIONAL PRICING

**Customary
(traditional) prices—**
prices for lines of
products that remain
the same over time.

Some consumer goods lines carry **customary prices,** which typically stay about the same over time. Because a product sells traditionally for a certain amount, consumers grow accustomed to paying that figure. Retailers usually do not

---

[2]Genine Babakian, "Arise, comrades, cast off your chains and go get a Coke," *BRANDWEEK*, July 20, 1992, pp. 22–24.

Candy bars and soft drinks are typical of the many products that are traditionally priced.

change customary prices. Soft drinks sell at the same level in grocery stores across the country. Coupons, discounts and specials may give one brand a short-term advantage, but traditionally, prices on these items remain constant.

Sparkling water and candy bars are traditionally priced at the consumer level. Although the cost to the retailer for imported waters may vary from maker to maker, consumers pay roughly the same for almost any brand of foreign mineral water. Evian, Calistoga and Perrier sell at the same level, as do Baby Ruth, Butterfingers, Mars and other candy bars from a variety of manufacturers, whether from the vending machine or the corner store.

PRESTIGE PRICING

Manufacturers and retailers targeting upscale markets often use **prestige pricing,** which is higher than the norm. This policy is consistent with the image of the product and the positioning strategy of the marketer. Consumers expect that Porsche automobiles will be costly. This German automobile company uses prestige pricing for its product line. What consumers pay for a Porsche is as much a part of the car's image as is its highly touted engineering. Modest decreases or increases in the price of a 944 or a Targa would not greatly affect sales.

The ice cream industry is well known for prestige pricing. The high-priced brands, such as Ben & Jerry's, Frusen Gladje and Haagen-Dazs, are taking an increasingly bigger bite out of the frozen dessert market. These premium ice creams sell for as much as four times the price of the less prestigious varieties, such as Sealtest, Carnation and Darigold. Despite the difference in cost, consumers continue to build brand loyalty. Haagen Dazs introduced its Extras line

Prestige pricing— pricing products targeted toward upscale markets.

in 1992, with flavors such as Triple Brownie Overload and Carrot Cake Passion, with suggested retail prices of up to $2.69 per pint.[3]

The real estate industry is also conscious of the prestige image. In the once hot market of Southern California, prime locations brought significantly higher prices. Many homes sell for more than similarly constructed models simply because they are in upscale neighborhoods. Once again, demand is the prime motivator for higher rates. The image of value associated with prestige areas commands more money.

Retailers such as Bullock's Wilshire, Nordstrom, Saks Fifth Avenue and Neiman-Marcus have reputations for high fashion and high quality. Merchandise from these upscale department stores typically carries prestige prices. Clothes bearing designer labels cost consumers more than over-the-counter goods. Buyers pay more for Lancome's Renergie anti-wrinkle treatment than for Procter & Gamble's Oil of Olay. One might argue about the quality of one versus the other, but it is generally the prestige image of the product or the seller that drives prices upward.

What Pricing Methods Do Retailers Use?

Retailers have special methods for setting prices. Although dictated by individual store policies and needs, some broad pricing categories are typical to these resellers of consumer goods. Competition may affect specific prices, but most retailers charge consumers based upon the cost of the merchandise, plus an amount to cover expenses and profit.

STANDARD MARKUP

Standard markup— adding a percentage to the cost of the merchandise.

Most retailers, and many wholesalers, set prices by adding a percentage to the cost of the merchandise that they purchase. This method is called **standard markup.** Stores and shops buy their goods from manufacturers at various prices from different suppliers. To cover costs and allow for profit, retailers need to add something to the cost of these items to create selling prices. Calculations of markup are explained in detail in the "Marketing in Practice" appendix at the end of this chapter. The important point is that the cost of merchandise bought by the retailer must be increased to cover expenses and profit.

For example, suppose a local store buys shoes from Dexter and Rockport. The owners of the store compute the cost of operations, including expected profit. Management then determines that a pair of shoes that cost $50 from the manufacturer should be sold for $75. The store knows that each pair of shoes purchased must be increased a corresponding amount if the venture is going to be successful. Since costs may vary, one shoe store selling Dexter or Rockport shoes may use a different markup than another that offers the same items.

---

[3]Sunita Wadekar Bhargava, "Gimme a double shake and a lard on white," *Business Week,* May 1, 1993, p. 59; Alison Sprout, "Extraa-sinful ice cream," *Fortune,* July 21, 1992, p. 115; Fara Warner, "Haagen Dazs gets behind bars," *Adweek's Marketing Week,* March 9, 1992, p. 6; J. A. Zbytniewski, "Sales snowball for frozen novelties," *Progressive Grocer,* March 1992, p. 95.

COST-PLUS PRICING

Similar to standard markup, the **cost-plus** pricing method adds a dollar figure to the cost of the merchandise. Instead of using the same percentage for the complete product line, sellers determine the exact costs of a single item, plus profit, and set prices accordingly. Cost-plus is commonly found in interior decorating and in many custom designed goods and services, such as residential construction and printing.

To arrive at an individual price per unit, sellers merely divide total costs plus profit by the number of items offered for sale. Retailers who sell a rather narrow line of merchandise may find that cost-plus is a preferred method of pricing. Computing profits on a dollar increment basis is not too difficult to compute on a limited inventory. Extensive stocks purchased from a wide variety of suppliers usually call for a percentage markup.

In spite of widespread acceptance, the use of markup and cost-plus pricing causes some problems. One difficulty facing small retailers is the inability to accurately figure costs. Overhead is especially hard to compute. For instance, what portion of executive salary or utility expenses should be charged to a specific piece of merchandise? Or, are advertising costs assigned to a single item or averaged over the entire stock? For this reason, most of consumer goods resellers simply go along with the market level of prices.

> **Cost-plus**—adding dollar figure to the cost of merchandise to cover profit.

PRICE LINING

Another popular pricing method for retailers is **price lining.** Price lining sets the same prices on different brands of similar merchandise. Costs may vary

> **Price lining**—setting the same price on similar merchandise purchased from different manufacturers.

The country's largest retailer, Wal-Mart, gains much of its success by pricing below market level.

slightly from one manufacturer to another, but using the price lining method, the retailer establishes one set of prices for the whole line of goods. For example, suppose a store purchases jeans from a variety of sources. The actual cost of each brand may vary from different suppliers, such as Levi Strauss or Wrangler, hence standard markup would create a myriad of different selling prices. Instead, the retailer establishes one line of pricing for all work jeans, another for casual pants and yet another for dressier slacks.

Many grocery supermarkets sell items within product lines, such as salad dressings and laundry detergents, at about the same level. Sporting goods stores typically sell "lines" of tennis rackets made by different companies at about the same price. Groups of merchandise, each from different manufacturers, may carry similar prices within each bracket. Most retailers use some form of price lining in tandem with standard markup.

Price lining encourages healthy competition. Many smaller retailers with limited inventory take advantage of price lining policies used by larger rivals. For example, if all brands of jeans are price lined at $24.00 by one store, the competitor who just sells Wranglers at $21.00 has a price advantage. Keep in mind that price is not the only factor in turning on consumers. Customers who do not care for this brand are not likely to buy just because they are cheaper.

UNIT PRICING

Unit pricing—a pricing method that includes the price per unit of measure, such as weight or volume.

Unit pricing is common in grocery retailing, but also finds its way into other industries. To give customers a clearer idea of the relative value of different items, prices are shown on the shelf according to the unit of measure, such as weight or volume. Instead of pricing different packages or cans individually, retailers also show the price per ounce or per pint. This policy allows shoppers to compare the value per unit among brands and package sizes.

Widely acclaimed by consumer advocates, unit pricing is used as a competitive tool leading to increased sales of store brands. These in-house or dealer labels often show a lower price per unit than manufacturer branded merchandise. Most shoppers take advantage of the posted unit prices to affect cost savings.

LOSS LEADER PRICING VS BAIT AND SWITCH PRICING

Loss leader pricing—pricing certain products at or below cost to attract buyers.

Retailers using **loss leader pricing** put certain merchandise on sale at or below cost to attract buyers. Retailers lower the price of particular goods to entice customers to come into their stores. Hopefully, while there, the customers purchase other items. Each week, supermarkets offer special prices at or below costs on selected goods. Grocers make up the loss on those items when shoppers buy other non-sale merchandise.

Automobile manufacturers use a form of loss leader pricing when they offer special packages on options such as air conditioners or automatic transmissions. By encouraging retailers to pass on the savings to the consumer, both manufacturer and dealer benefit from the increased sales of automobiles.

Retailers offering loss leader pricing must supply the goods as advertised. As a rule, if the store or shop runs out of the advertised special, substitutes or refunds will be provided. Many outlets will purposely state "supply limited" in the promotion to assure that consumers realize that this is a one-time offer. Offering "rain checks" for sold-out merchandise also enables retailers to avoid claims of bait and switch tactics.

Loss leader pricing should not be confused with **bait and switch.** With bait and switch, the retailer advertises merchandise that is not available for sale. When the consumer comes into the store or shop looking for the advertised special, the dealer attempts to switch the purchase to a more profitable item that is on hand. Bait and switch pricing practices are illegal.

Bait and switch—an illegal pricing policy offering unavailable products at low prices, then switching buyers to higher priced products.

PSYCHOLOGICAL PRICING

Many retailers use **psychological pricing** to tempt the consumer. This method sets arbitrary prices that induce sales by implying quality or savings. This practice includes prestige pricing, which was discussed previously, and **odd/even pricing.** Selling merchandise at $3.99, $39.90, or $399.00 attempts to convince consumers that these are lower prices than the next higher increment. Although buyers may mentally be aware of this scheme, most fall for this diversion.

Mass merchandisers often use this method, but price at different levels. A package of alkaline batteries sold in the supermarket at $1.99 may cost the consumer $1.82 at the discount house. In this way, the discounter avoids the onus of trying to trick the public, yet still offers a lower price. Things sold through vending machines are pegged to the nearest nickel to simplify the transaction.

The even portion of odd/even pricing refers to selling prestige items at

Psychological pricing—setting arbitrary prices that induce sales by implying quality or savings.

even prices. The mere thought of lower prices could damage the reputation of these items. Sellers of prestige goods are likely to round prices upward to the next even level. For instance, retailers of Ralph Lauren's Polo brand clothing sell shirts or ties at even dollar amounts, such as $60 or $40. Selling these prestige items at the odd prices of $59.95 or $39.95 would weaken the image that both manufacturer and retailer work hard to create.

ow Are Business Goods Priced?

Setting prices in the retail sector can be a hit-or-miss proposition. If one method does not produce results, another may be tried. Unfortunately, too much trial and error often leads to failure. The pricing policy that does not produce profitable results should be dropped immediately. Difficulty in accurately determining costs and the inability to read the competition can lead to sporadic, inconsistent policies among retailers. On the other hand, pricing by production goods marketers is usually more controlled.

BASE/LIST PRICE

Base or list price—the primary level offered by a business.

Prices for business goods are established differently than those for consumer products. As a rule, manufacturers start out with a **base** or **list price,** the primary level determined by the seller's objectives and pricing policy. Rarely does the base price stand by itself without some sort of adjustment. One way that manufacturers modify base prices is through discounts. Depending upon the costs of manufacturing and marketing, and upon competitive pricing policies, cash, quantity or trade deductions may be offered.

CASH DISCOUNT

Cash (credit) discount—a deduction based upon prompt payment.

One common adjustment in base or list prices offered to business product buyers is the **cash discount.** This discount is allowed for invoices paid within the specified terms; a reward for prompt payment. Business products are typically purchased on an open account basis, meaning that the buyer is billed for the goods at the time of shipment. Invoices specify when payment is due and if discounts are offered for quick payment.

The conditions for payment of an invoice are the **terms of sale.** The date that the total payment is due from the customer is the net invoice date. Sellers who want to improve cash flow often allow discounts for early payment. When paying prior to the discount date, buyers subtract the offered percentage. A typical method of showing a cash or credit discount on the invoice would be: "2/10, N/30." This means "a 2 percent discount may be taken if the invoice is paid within ten days, otherwise the invoice is due and payable in full in thirty days."

To avoid claims of price discrimination, sellers who offer cash discounts must treat all buyers equally. This ruling applies to risky customers as well as those who have open account status. For instance, if a customer's credit rating dictates terms of cash-on-delivery or cash-in-advance payment, this buyer would qualify for a cash discount if one is offered.

QUANTITY DISCOUNT

Many business goods sellers allow discounts based upon increased amounts purchased, or a **quantity discount.** This policy means that as the quantity of the purchase increases, the price decreases. The pricing method is commonly found in the production goods arena. Companies offering quantity discounts will usually display them on price lists broken into columns showing a range of quantities and discounts. Sometimes such price lists show percentages to be deducted. Other times the discounted prices are listed.

Quantity discount—a deduction based upon the amount purchased.

■   ■   ■   ■   ■

Sales pacer pricing: Price list showing quantity discounts

DESCRIPTION	PART NUMBER	COST PER SINGLE SIDED UNIT				SHIP WT. LBS.
		1-5	6-24	25-99	100-249	
24″ wide × 54″ high basic unit	11712454	39.08	35.95	32.82	31.26	28
packed in a UPS carton	11712454EC	38.79	35.66	32.53	30.97	28
24″ × 6″ extender panel	11712406	8.00	7.36	6.72	6.40	2.5
24″ × 12″ extender panel	11712412	10.47	9.63	8.79	8.37	5
24″ × 18″ extender panel	11712418	11.82	10.88	9.93	9.46	7
24″ × 10″ upper shelf	1171371	6.85	6.30	5.75	5.48	4
24″ × 12″ upper shelf	1171372	7.29	6.70	6.12	5.83	5
36″ width × 54″ high basic units	11713654	46.69	42.95	39.22	37.35	36
packed in a UPS carton	11713654 5BE	45.70	41.96	38.23	36.36	36
36″ × 6″ extender panel	11713606	8.38	7.71	7.04	6.70	3
36″ × 12″ extender panel	11713612	11.37	10.46	9.55	9.10	5
36″ × 18″ extender panel	11713618	13.15	12.10	11.05	10.52	8
36″ × 10″ upper shelf	1171374	8.30	7.64	6.97	6.64	5
36″ × 12″ upper shelf	1171375	8.70	8.00	7.31	6.96	7
48″ wide × 54″ high basic unit	11714854	53.03	48.78	44.51	42.42	46
packed in a UPS carton	11714854 SBE	50.89	46.64	42.40	40.28	44
48″ × 6″ extender panel	11714806	8.78	8.07	7.37	7.02	4
48″ × 12″ extender panel	11714812	11.59	10.67	9.74	9.28	7
48″ × 18″ extender panel	11714818	13.65	12.56	11.46	10.92	9
48″ × 10″ upper shelf	1171377	9.50	8.82	8.05	7.67	7
48″ × 12″ upper shelf	1171378	10.34	9.51	8.68	8.27	8

DESCRIPTION	PART NUMBER	COST PER DOUBLE SIDED UNIT				
24″ W × 54″ H × 30.75″ Deep	11752454	58.68	53.99	49.36	46.95	45
36″ W × 54″ H × 30.75″ Deep	11753654	68.73	63.23	57.73	54.98	62
48″ W × 54″ H × 30.75″ Deep	11754854	73.92	70.76	64.61	61.53	76

For woodgrain peg panels add 5.60 per square foot.
Packing: All basic units with a sign and an extender may be packed in a UPS carton. Units to be shipped with upper shelves or other accessories may require the cost of at least one additional carton in order to qualify for UPS. Please discuss custom and UPS packaging with our order desk.
Courtesy of Stor-Rite Metal Products.

■   ■   ■   ■   ■

Quantity discounts may be based upon a one-time individual purchase or may be cumulative. Companies with cumulative pricing policies will total the orders over time, and then will offer rebates or credit the account. The automotive industry bases quantity discounts on the total dealer purchases over a model year. Car dealers push end-of-the-model-year sales since each additional car sold might place the seller into the next highest discount category.

Businesses offering quantity discounts must avoid discrimination. All deductions from published price lists must be realistic. The Robinson-Patman Act, states that quantity discounts are allowed only if actual savings are realized by the manufacturer. Rohm and Haas uses a graduated price list offering lower prices as the size of orders for Plexiglas increases. This company must be able to justify those discounts, based upon cost savings from bracket to bracket. This is true of any production goods marketer.

TRADE DISCOUNT

Trade discount—a discount given to members of the trade (wholesalers or retailers).

Intermediaries often receive **trade discounts,** sometimes called functional discounts. This pricing method used by trade goods marketers provides deductions from base prices to serve as the markup for retailers or wholesalers. Companies that sell to the trade set their list prices at levels that approximate suggested retail prices. Manufacturers then offer a series of discounts to their intermediaries.

Trade discounts are usually quoted in a string or chain. A sample of trade discount pricing might read "$100, less 30, less 10." In this example, the list price is $100. Retailers buying from this manufacturer would earn a 30 percent discount, or $30. A wholesale buyer would receive an additional 10 percent, or $7. Note that the additional discount for wholesalers comes off the discounted price, not the list price. A typical less 30 less 10 discount does not add up to 40 percent, but rather is 37 percent.

PROMOTIONAL ALLOWANCES

Promotional allowance—a rebate or discount offered to intermediaries who promote products.

Trade goods marketers regularly offer allowances off their list prices to intermediaries who promote their products. Such **promotional allowances** have the effect of lowering the price to retailers carrying branded merchandise. Advertising placed by resellers generates sales for both the retailer and the original producer, hence both parties benefit.

Cooperative Advertising

The most common promotional allowance is **cooperative advertising.** When retailers promote branded products in local advertising, the manufacturer will pay a portion of that cost. Paying part of the retailer's advertising expense has the same effect as a discount. For example, if a local tire store highlights Michelin tires in its newspaper ads and radio commercials, that tire manufacturer will reimburse the retailer for a portion of the expense.

Rebates

Rebate—a price reduction offered to consumers to increase basic demand.

Sometimes, trade goods marketers offer price reductions, or **rebates,** to consumers to stimulate demand through the retailer. These concessions act as dis-

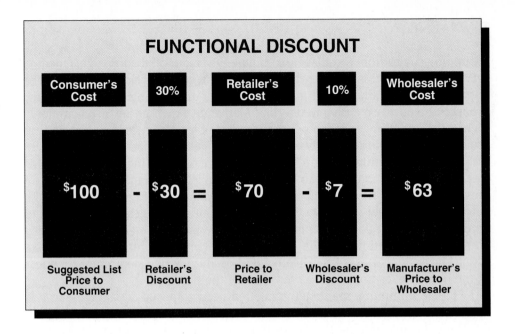

FUNCTIONAL DISCOUNT

Consumer's Cost	30%	Retailer's Cost	10%	Wholesaler's Cost
$100	- $30 =	$70	- $7 =	$63
Suggested List Price to Consumer	Retailer's Discount	Price to Retailer	Wholesaler's Discount	Manufacturer's Price to Wholesaler

counts to buyers and help manufacturers to balance production. These price reductions also provide an incentive for retailers to rid stocks of slow moving merchandise. Manufacturers of appliances and tools regularly offer rebates to consumers to increase market demand.

Push Money

As a form of promotional allowance, some companies offer cash incentives, known as **push money** or **"spiffs,"** to retail salespeople. Suppose Guess is running a special promotion on one line of its jeans. The company might offer to pay retail salespeople a small amount of cash for each pair sold. Appliance manufacturers often give spiffs to salespeople who work for their retailers. Push money acts as a bonus or commission, but is paid by the manufacturer instead of the retail outlet. Many large retailers, such as Mervyn's and J. C. Penney, take full advantage of these promotional allowances paid by the manufacturers.

Push money (spiff)— cash incentives manufacturers pay to retail salespeople.

ow Are New Products Priced?

All prices result from a combination of market demand, competition and costs. With new products, market demand may not be computable. Hopefully, costs of production were calculated during pilot plant operations, but there are a variety of charges that are nearly impossible to figure until the product is in the field. At this stage of the product life cycle, competition may not exist, or may be silently waiting until the product proves itself. Depending upon these conditions, marketers may choose to set the price high or low.

SKIMMING

Skimming—setting a high price on an introductory product to recoup development costs.

Skimming comes from the adage "skimming the cream off the top." This method sets a high price on an introductory product to recoup development costs. The hope is that the marketer will reap large returns on its initial investment. New products are often expensive to develop. Marketing expenses are also commonly high in the initial stages of a product's life. The objective of price skimming is to provide early return to cover these sometimes significant expenses.

Several conditions must be present for price skimming to succeed. This method is usually not used to enter an established competitive market. In crowded markets, new products will not command a price higher than the existing market level unless they offer significant advantages. The marketer of a new brand of dry dog food might have trouble introducing its product priced above the competition. On the other hand, a company announcing an electronic shaver that uses a laser beam could easily practice skimming. Newness of the market is as important as newness of the product.

To use skimming, manufacturers often need a special advantage that will stall the entry of competition. Patents are a good basis for such a pricing policy. The company holding this protection has, in reality, a monopoly position. Until that patent expires or competition finds a way to get around it, the holder of the grant can charge as much as buyers are willing to pay.

One of the problems with patents is that they divulge the details of the design or process to competition, which may alter the concept slightly to circumvent the patent protection. Robert Kearns is one man who has waged a battle to reform the patent process to prevent thievery. In his court case, Kearns alleged that major automobile firms copied his invention for intermittent windshield wipers. He won a sizable settlement, but the war over patent protection still rages.[4]

A highly favorable raw material position would promote a price skimming policy. If the company introducing the new product could control its ingredients, competition would be stymied. The seller could then skim enough return to cover development and promotional costs. Highly technical items are often introduced using this pricing policy.

PENETRATION

Penetration pricing—setting a low price on introductory products to gain an immediate share of the market.

Penetration is another new product pricing method. **Penetration pricing** sets low prices on introductory products to gain an immediate share of the market. This method allows the product to enter the market forcefully and capture a significant initial portion. When introducing new items into mature markets that exhibit highly elastic demand and many competitors, marketers often prefer this type of pricing. For the penetration policy to work successfully, buyers must be willing to switch brands based upon price alone. Products that have high brand loyalty are not likely to be affected by competitive penetration pricing.

---

[4]Alan L. Adler, The Associated Press, "Kearns wins wiper battle but not patent principle war," *The Oregonian*, June 12, 1992, p. G1.

Global Marketing: That's A Close Shave!

For centuries man has been struggling with that purely masculine problem regarding what to do with the hair on one's face. While beards have gone in and out of fashion, most men opt for shaving. This daily ritual, often accompanied with nicks and cuts, has proven to be the bane of most adult males. Some opt for blade razors, even the throwaway types, which are less expensive. Others choose one of the electric models, which may be a significant initial investment.

Blade users swear by the closeness of the shave that they get. Those who go electric laud the no-mess ease provided by this method. Although electric shavers have been used for decades, only recently has the market heated up. The Philips Consumer Electronics division of giant Dutch owned Philips NV, which markets under the Norelco brand in the United States, owns a major share of this business, thanks in part to its "floating head" feature. Yielding to the shape of the face, the patented lift-and-cut rotary blades have been able to convince many a blade user to switch to this more convenient shaving method.

Late entries from the makers of blade razors include flexible models that bend with the curve of the face. Not to be outdone, Braun, the German electronics giant owned by Gilette, entered the market with its Flex Control. This electric shaver has a head that pivots so that the platinum coated foil screen is always at right angles to the skin no matter what the arm position might be. Braun has four models to choose from, with suggested retail prices pegged at $70, $90, $110 and $150. These prices are somewhat higher than market leader Norelco.

SOURCE: Alison Sprout, "Pivoting shaver," Products to Watch column, *Fortune*, May 18, 1992, p. 101. (Photo courtesy of Gillette Company)

Penetration pricing appears most often when development costs are not significant. Without large capital expenditures, marketers can price their new products low enough to significantly impact buyers. Even with high development costs, Chrysler introduced its LH line in 1992 using penetration pricing. These new styles were expected to completely reposition this old line car

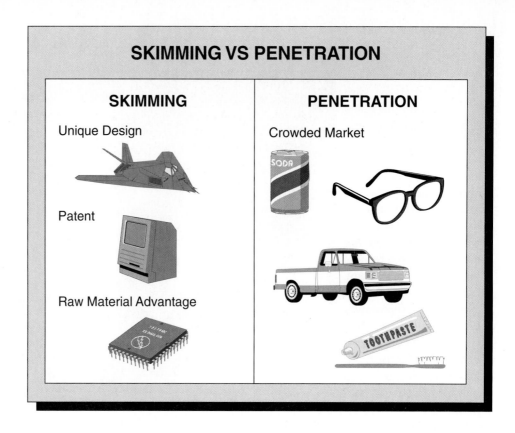

SKIMMING VS PENETRATION

SKIMMING	PENETRATION
Unique Design	Crowded Market
Patent	
Raw Material Advantage	

manufacturer as an innovative, forward thinking automobile designer. Dubbed the Intrepid, Vision and Concorde, these midsized family sedans compete head to head with the Honda Accord, Ford Taurus and Toyota Camry.[5]

Preemptive Pricing

In new markets, penetration pricing has the effect of chasing competition away. Sometimes called **preemptive pricing,** this low, new product price takes away the incentive for other companies to enter the market because of poor promise for profits. This is especially true if the marketer has uncovered a brand new field with a brand new product. Penetration pricing preempts the competition.

How Does the Cost of Freight Affect Prices?

Few products are picked up at the manufacturer's place of business. Some goods are shipped around the globe, while others travel only to the next coun-

[5]Brian S. Moskal, "Hot wheels for big wheels," *Industry Week,* October 4, 1993, pp. 24–25; Alison L. Sprout, "Products of the year," *Fortune,* December 28, 1992, pp. 64–69; David Woodruff, "Chrysler yells 'look at me' to an upscale audience," *Business Week,* May 25, 1992, p. 30; David Woodruff, "A new Eagle gets an eagle eye," *Business Week,* May 25, 1992, p. 31.

ty. Whatever the distance, there is a cost associated in moving products from seller to buyer. These freight charges become an integral part of pricing. Whether sellers recover transportation costs in their price or buyers pay them directly, the customer ultimately pays for freight.

Another major consideration for both seller and buyer is who has title to the merchandise during shipment. No matter how much care and concern freight carriers show toward their cargoes, some damage may occur in transit. Who owns the goods plays a major role in which company must file a claim. Both the cost of delivery and the ownership of the freight depend upon competition and the selling firm's policies.

FREE-ON-BOARD (FOB)

The selling term **F.O.B.** means free on board. Literally, this phrase means that the seller will place the goods on board a specified carrier. The F.O.B. position determines where ownership of the goods transfers from seller to buyer. The terms of sale will specify this significant point, which is critical in determining the party that handles any claims for freight damage.

F.O.B.—Free On Board, the point where title to the goods transfers from the seller to the buyer.

FOB SHIPPING POINT (POINT OF ORIGIN)

During the early industrialization of the United States, the sale of most business goods carried terms of **F.O.B. Shipping Point** or **Point of Origin.** This term of sale indicates that title transfers from seller to buyer when the goods are loaded on board a carrier at the seller's place of business. At this point the products become the property of the buyer. Buyers, then, are responsible for the cost of transportation and any claims that could result from damage to the merchandise.

Increase in competition brought the realization to business goods sellers that making the customer pay freight might lose sales. For example, if a buyer in St. Louis had the option of purchasing from sellers in either Boston or Chicago, the logical choice would be the latter. Chicago is closer to St. Louis and freight costs would be lower. The Boston manufacturer might not be competitive simply because of transportation charges.

F.O.B. Shipping Point (Point of Origin)— title transfers from seller to buyer when the goods are loaded on board a carrier at the seller's place.

FOB DESTINATION (DELIVERED)

Manufacturers often must absorb freight costs just to remain competitive. These sellers may adopt terms of sale stating **F.O.B. Destination,** or **Delivered,** which means that title does not transfer until the goods reach the customer's place of business. Since ownership of the merchandise remains with the seller, that company is responsible for processing damage claims, and will typically pick up the transportation costs as well.

When shipping merchandise over long distances, the chances for goods being damaged are significant. Making long distance claims against the freight

F.O.B. Destination (Delivered)—title transfers from seller to buyer when goods arrive at the buyer's place.

carrier can be a nuisance and a problem. When customers receive damaged merchandise that has been shipped F.O.B. delivered, buyers' only choices are to refuse to accept the shipment. At this point, the seller still owns the goods. Negotiations with the carrier can be difficult, and sometimes the shipment must be returned to the point of origin for inspection.

FOB SHIPPING POINT, FREIGHT ALLOWED

F.O.B. Shipping Point, Freight Allowed (Absorbed)-title transfers from seller to buyer when goods leave the seller's place, but seller pays transportation costs.

Many business goods shippers use terms of sale that read **F.O.B. Shipping Point, Freight Allowed.** This policy means that title transfers to the buyer when the goods leave the seller's place, but the seller pays transportation costs. This procedure simplifies problems regarding damage claims and allows the seller to remain competitive with rivals located closer to the customer. Sometimes called "freight absorbed," this is the preferred method of handling freight charges when the distance between the parties is great or the merchandise is fragile and/or expensive.

Using "FOB Shipping Point, Freight Allowed," the buyer holds title and is the party who files claims for freight damage. If the shipment arrives damaged, the buyer deals directly with the carrier for settlement. The selling firm remains price competitive with other firms because the transportation costs are absorbed. Using this method, since buyers own the products during shipment, they usually select or specify the freight carrier.

REGIONAL (ZONE) PRICING

Regional (zone) pricing—selling terms with different prices depending upon the distance of buyers from the shipping point.

To reduce the effect of freight charges, many sellers use **regional** or **zone pricing.** This policy establishes different prices depending upon the distance of buyers from the shipping point, usually in concentric circles. Sellers charge all customers located within a given zone the same price for delivered merchan-

COMPARISON OF FOB SYSTEMS

Type Of System	Who Has Title	Who Pays Freight
FOB Shipping Point	Buyer	Buyer
FOB Shipping Point, Freight Allowed	Buyer	Seller
FOB Delivered	Seller	Seller

dise. Many freight forwarders use zone pricing, including the U.S. Post Office and United Parcel Service. Many catalog sellers commonly use regional pricing.

hat Affects the Management of Pricing Policy?

Many marketing executives feel that pricing is the most important element of the marketing mix. Revenue and profit depend upon selling prices. If too high, fewer products will be sold. While low prices may generate greater demand and sales, total income may not be sufficient to cover costs. All facets of the operations come into play in determining price.

PRODUCT QUALITY

Price and **product quality** are inseparable. Sellers indicate the value of their products when setting prices. Buyers perceive the quality of the product based upon that price. Consumers are likely to assume that higher priced articles provide greater satisfaction. These presumed values are not limitless.

Price is the avenue that sellers use to express their belief in the value of the product. To maintain credibility with the buyer, perceived value must equal actual value. Underpricing a quality product is as harmful to its image as overpricing an inferior one. Cross pens and Patek Philippe watches rarely go on sale. To offer these goods at bargain prices would tarnish the perception of quality adopted by consumers.

The garment industry provides an interesting illustration of this quality versus price issue. Many of the world's top designers offer lower priced lines of merchandise carrying their signatures. Based primarily on reduced costs of fabrics and buttons, plus economies of scale in production, these less expensive lines are distributed through a wider range of ready-to-wear.

For example, Donna Karan, one of America's top designers, sells both her high end goods and the DKNY line through her New York showroom to fashion boutiques and upscale retailers. Garments from the exclusive Donna Karan Collection are handled by most image conscious retailers, such as Saks, Bloomingdales and Neiman-Marcus. The DKNY line of clothing and jeans is produced in quantity, is relatively less expensive and, while carried by these same upscale department stores, can also be found at Macy's and Harrod's.[6]

DISTRIBUTION

Distribution is a major factor in formulating pricing policy. Trade goods marketers must be constantly aware of the profit needs of its wholesale and retail customers. Establishing prices that provide a satisfactory return to the marketing company are of little good if intermediaries cannot resell them profitably.

---

[6] Susan Caminiti, "The pretty payoff in cheap chic," *Fortune*, February 24, 1992, pp. 71–73.

DONNAKARAN
NEW YORK

Products priced too high to members of the distribution channel may cause intermediaries to earn lower profits or become noncompetitive. Very low pricing to intermediaries will increase demand, but lower product quality image. One of the major sources of conflict among the members of the distribution channel is pricing. Unhappy wholesalers or retailers typically will not promote as heavily for products with lower quality images.

Customer Service

Price affects **customer service.** Higher priced items usually command more attention by sellers. Lower priced goods and services do not generate the income necessary to support major customer service. Individual attention requires trained and capable personnel. This can amount to a significant expense to the marketer and intermediary alike. Retailers simply cannot afford to give an extremely high degree of service without a corresponding level of revenue.

The retail industry clearly demonstrates this principle. Stores and shops offering higher priced merchandise, such as Jerry Magnin's and Geary's of Beverly Hills, provide customer services that include such perks as valet parking, free alterations and complimentary champagne. The May Company and G. K. Gill's are largely self-service and offer few amenities. The profit margins earned by most retail outlets enable or prohibit the providing of fringe benefits for customers.

PROMOTION

Promotion, too, has an effect upon pricing. Consumer goods often require substantial promotion. Price is the marketing mix factor that produces the income necessary to support heavy promotional programs. Promotion is expensive and needs a price structure that will support these costly programs.

Many marketers ignore flashy advertising and aggressive selling. By strictly emphasizing price, some manufacturers can move merchandise profitably in markets dominated by large consumer product houses. This principle is especially true in differentiated competition. Store or distributor brands of butter, such as Safeway's Lucerne or TV brand distributed by Fleming Companies are priced considerably lower than Land O' Lakes or Darigold. Inexpensive fragrances, such as Georgy Girl from Deborah International Beauty or Turmoil from Parfums de Coeur, easily compete with major perfumes. These similar scents carry lower prices than Avon's Giorgio and Dior's Poison.[7]

---

[7]Pat Sloan and Kate Fitzgerald, "Coty targets scent invaders," *Advertising Age,* May 4, 1992, p. 4.

Marketing and Society: Hold the Phone!

The federal government protects the general public and businesses from price discrimination. Many laws are on the books which deal with such things as tying contracts, collusion and price fixing. The Justice Department also takes a dim view of predatory pricing. With all of the bureaus and agencies watching over a business's shoulder, it would appear difficult if not impossible to be unfair in setting pricing policies.

When the Feds decided to break up the near monopoly that giant AT&T held in the telephone business, a host of competitors jumped into this huge market. Most of the pretenders to the throne are long gone, leaving MCI and Sprint as the two major rivals for Ma Bell. Although AT&T holds the lion's share of this lucrative communications industry, these two smaller firms are formidable opponents. The battle has taken place largely on television. In this medium, the competitors joust, each seeming to refute each other's claims regarding price savings and special offers. One sometimes wonders how much these promotional costs impact monthly charges.

Some consumers and businesses question the judgment of the government action to create more competition in the telephone business. The claims are that service has deteriorated and prices have not gone down. The promotional battles between the "big three" have left many dazed. On the other hand, competitive markets typically bring lower, more realistic pricing. No matter whose claims one believes, there can be little doubt that long distance telephoning is a price competitive market.

SOURCE: Terry Lefton, "The man from Mars' game plan for Sprint," *Adweek's Marketing Week*, May 25, 1992, p. 12; B. G. Yovovich, "Marketing after the break-up: AT&T, Baby Bells, and rivals in a free-for-all," *Business Marketing*, November 1991, pp. 12–14. (Art courtesy MCI Communications Corporation)

ETHICS

Marketers are in the business of seeking profit while striving for customer satisfaction. Company profits derive from income from the sale of goods and services. If priced too low, profits sag, investors scream, businesses fail. When prices are higher than those of competitors, lower sales result, which impacts the bottom line. In pursuit of profit, management walks a tightrope.

In tough economic times, many organizations and business people are apt to take short cuts in pursuit of hard-to-come-by profits. Management too often looks the other way. In one case, wholesalers and retailers filed a class action suit alleging price fixing against the three largest marketers of instant baby formula. Although the firms denied any wrong doing, Abbott Laboratories, Mead Johnson and American Home Products settled out of court in the summer of 1992.[8]

---

[8]Carolyn Skorneck, "Infant-formula makers accused of bid rigging," *The Oregonian*, June 12, 1992, p. G1; Bob Lewis, The Associated Press, "Mead Johnson & Co. offers settlement," *The Oregonian*, July 3, 1992, p. C12.

The publicity received by shady practices appears to be awakening many American businesses. Both large and small firms are taking more interest in ethical behavior. Citicorp uses a game to teach ethical behavior, while General Electric uses a computer program. Texas Instruments employees run a "Dear Abby" type of mailbag to answer questions on ethics. Hewlett-Packard runs seminars covering everything from gratuities to pricing to conflicts of interest.[9]

Marketers offering trade discounts use caution to avoid discrimination. Members of the distribution channel on the same level must receive fair and equal treatment. All retailers receive the same discount, and all wholesalers must be treated in a similar manner. Special care must be taken by manufacturers to avoid giving extra discounts to retailers owned by the company. The federal government views any pricing policy that gives unfair advantage to any one customer as discriminatory.

SUMMING IT UP

Typically, prices for goods and services fall into a general area known as the market level. Although most firms would sell at this plane, some may price above market level and others below. Some firms follow a single price policy where all buyers pay the same price for the same amount of the same merchandise. Items such as automobiles and real estate are more often priced using a flexible policy with the buyer being able to negotiate with the seller.

Many consumer goods marketers set prices traditionally, where all items are in the same general level. Prestige pricing is used by marketers of upscale goods and services. Marketers of some production goods and many consumer services use negotiated prices.

The primary pricing method for retailers is standard markup, where the store or shop adds a percentage to the cost of its merchandise. Cost-plus is a variation of standard markup, usually in a dollar amount. Price lining involves pricing similar goods from different suppliers at the same level. Unit pricing, used mostly in the grocery industry, displays prices by unit of measure for easy comparison. Some retailers price several items at or below cost to attract buyers for other goods, or loss leader pricing. Bait and switch is an illegal method that advertises nonexistent items. Psychological pricing includes prestige pricing and odd/even prices.

Business goods are usually pegged at a base or list price, from which discounts may be offered. A cash discount offers buyers a percentage off the net invoice amount for prompt payment. Quantity discounts are awarded for increased order sizes. Trade discounts go to wholesalers and retailers when trade goods marketers set list prices at suggested retail levels. Some firms also give promotional allowances, such as cooperative advertising, spiffs and rebates, which have the effect of discounts.

New products are either priced by skimming (a high price) or penetration (a low price). Freight is a factor in pricing because of its impact on costs. The FOB point is where title transfers from seller to buyer. Freight terms may be FOB Point of Origin, FOB Destination or Freight Allowed. Some companies use

---

[9]Kenneth Labich, "The new crisis in business ethics," *Fortune*, April 20, 1992, pp. 167–176.

a regional or zone pricing method, with different prices based upon the distance from the shipping point.

Product quality has a decided impact upon price. Trade goods marketers must be aware of intermediary needs as well as those of consumers. Customer service has an effect upon cost and customer perception. Promotion and positioning affect the way the product is priced. In managing prices, marketers must avoid discrimination.

KEY CONCEPTS AND TERMS FROM CHAPTER ELEVEN:

Bait and switch
Base or list price
Cash (credit) discount
Cost-plus
Customary (traditional) prices
Flexible price policy
F.O.B.
F.O.B. Delivered (Destination)
F.O.B. Shipping Point, Freight Allowed (Absorbed)
F.O.B. Shipping Point (Point of Origin)
Loss leader pricing
Market level

Penetration pricing
Prestige pricing
Price lining
Promotional allowance
Psychological (odd/even) pricing
Push money (spiff)
Quantity discount
Rebate
Regional (zone) pricing
Single price policy
Skimming
Standard markup
Trade discount
Unit pricing

BUILDING SKILLS

1. Describe the pricing method that would be best for marketing table linens, cosmetics, pickup trucks, peppermint candy, decorated T-shirts.

2. Contrast the retail pricing methods used by golf course pro shops, dry cleaners, women's shoe store, auto parts store, used car lot.

3. Explain the kinds of discounts that manufacturers would likely give in pricing engines for lawn mowers, snowmobiles and jet skis, fasteners for the aerospace industry, office furniture, packaged noodles and pasta.

4. Suppose a wholesaler places an order with a manufacturer under terms of sale of "F.O.B. shipping point, freight allowed." A whole-

saler buyer asks the seller to drop ship the order to its retail customer. Which company has title to the merchandise during shipment: the manufacturer, the wholesaler or the retailer? Which one picks up the cost of freight?

5. Contrast the pricing methods that the following organizations might use based upon the company image desired: Wal-Mart, Kinney shoes, Neiman-Marcus.

6. Contrast the pricing methods most likely to be used while introducing a new line of sports shoes, laser printers, microwave ovens, skis, cancer drugs.

Making Decisions 11-1: A Winning Smile.

The dollar sales figures for some categories of consumer goods are often mind boggling. For instance, it is difficult for one to imagine that almost $450 million worth of toothbrushes are purchased in the United States annually. That sort of volume would be enough to attract any marketer, and some rather big names play in that arena.

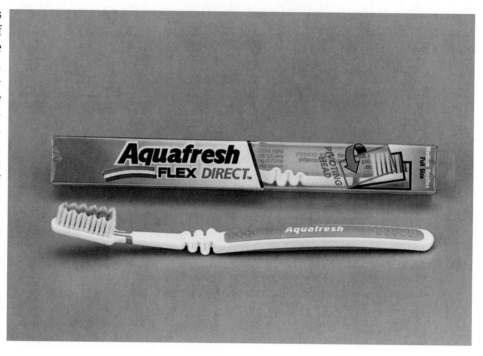

Not surprisingly, the oral care market is rather high tech. Although it does not buzz with the whir of computers, many everyday products in this field are rather scientific, and new designs win over new customers. SmithKline introduced its Aquafresh Flex Direct toothbrush in 1994 as a breakthrough in dental hygiene. The flexible neck and pivoting head of this product make it unique, and SmithKline ads claim that the design allows it to reach places that competitors cannot.

The Flex Direct is just one example of the continual upgrading of this product category. Premium items carrying higher price tags have become more popular since Chesebrough-Ponds came out with its Mentadent toothpaste. Generally, firms in the oral care field are finding that aging baby boomers are willing to pay extra for healthy mouths. Building on that philosophy, Oral-B created Ultra Floss, made with special fibers that stretch thin to fit between the teeth and then return to the original width to scrub away plaque. Oral-B expects this premium line to capture a significant part of the over $100 million floss market.[10]

Identify the type of introductory pricing SmithKline used for Flex Direct and the product features and/or market conditions that would have influenced this pricing policy. Explain the different types of discounts you would expect a firm such as Oral-B to offer to wholesaler customers.

---

[10] Pam Weisz, "SmithKline, Oral-B up ante in oral care," *BRANDWEEK*, September 26, 1994, p. 3.

Making Decisions 11-2: The Moving Finger Writes, and Having Writ. . . .

Few would argue the fact that computers have changed the lives of almost everyone. In one way or another, each of us is touched daily by these electronic marvels. From the time pieces we wear on our wrists to the ignition of the cars we drive, computers play a major role in the ways we work and play. The checkout stands at the stores where we shop are automated. The car wash works electronically, as do the elevators we ride in and the coffeemaker and toaster that prepare our breakfast.

Electronic machines and gadgets are especially important to business. Computers handle everything from production processes to printing checks. Telephones are programmable and voice mail collects messages when no one is there to answer. The facsimile machine, better known as FAX, has staked a major claim on the business community. The world's second largest computer marketer has taken a major bite out of this electronic transmission system. Say hello to Apple's entry into consumer electronics, the Newton.

This book-size device is a pen-based computer. It has no keyboard, but is programmed to recognize handwriting. Much of the liquid crystal display and miniaturized hardware is made for Apple by Sharp Electronics Corporation in Japan. As state-of-the-art as it might be, the sophisticated software is what really sets the Newton apart. This electronic notebook even produces a sound of rippling pages when the user thumbs through the address book. Up against some seasoned competition in Casio's Boss line of electronic organizers and Hewlett-Packard's palm top PC, Apple must price its product to compete yet produce a good return on its significant investment.[11]

Discuss the different pricing options for new products and the conditions affecting each.

Making Decisions 11-3: En garde!

To the warriors of old, the strength of their sword blades was truly a matter of life and death. Although some movie swashbucklers might throw away the broken stub and win the battle with a shovel or a curtain rod, real sword fighters were in deep trouble if their weapon shattered. Europeans learned during the Crusades that swords forged from Damascus steel were stronger than any other. Unfortunately, the secret of that process was lost through the ages.

In the early 1970s, Oleg Sherby, a Stanford University professor, developed "superplastic" steel that shows many of the same characteristics that ancient sword fighters attributed to Damascus. Both have a high carbon content and a similar molecular structure. These properties create a steel that is stronger and harder, yet is easier to form than most other types. As great as the prospects were for this product, two decades passed without it reaching the market. Apparently the problems producing

---

[11]Bradley Johnson, "Chastened Newton turns 1 with hopes intact," *Advertising Age,* August 1, 1994, p. 4; Kathy Rebello, "Apple's Newton: The start of something big?" *Business Week,* May 25, 1992, p. 122.

superplastic steel in bulk are about to be solved.

This remarkable metal's resistance to corrosion and heat make it a natural for applications such as engines. Compared to conventional steel that cracks when stretched more than 50 percent, superplastic steel can be pulled up to 11 times its original length. The material's moldability allows it to be easily molded into parts such as gears and sprockets. Although initially expected to carry an expensive price tag, superplastic steel is expected to dramatically lower the processing costs of forging or casting in the long run.[12]

Assume you were the marketing manager of a firm introducing superplastic steel into the market, describe how you would set your prices, including the production goods pricing options that are available to you.

---

[12]Alison L. Sprout, "Back to the future with flexible steel," *Fortune*, May 16, 1994, p. 71.

Marketing in Practice: Accounting for Marketing Decisions

What Does Accounting Have To Do With Marketing?

Marketing does not perform in a vacuum. All facets of any commercial venture interact with each other to form the complete business entity. Survival of the whole depends upon the good health and well being of each part. Marketing is a dynamic, creative aspect of both domestic and international trade, but accounting functions provide management with information regarding how the business is progressing toward its goals.

Accounting and accountants are often considered the watchdogs of business activity. The task of measuring and controlling the activities of a firm lies with the financial arm. The statements and books of record that controllers create and analyze contain a wealth of valuable information that is needed to manage the marketing group. Students and executives alike would be wise to become knowledgeable about the relationships that exist between these two seemingly incomparable sectors of business.

A key function of marketing managers is planning. During that process, marketers establish goals and objectives. Whether long range or short, attainment of these missions is crucial to the success of the marketing effort and the business. The information that relates to these accomplishments, or their lack, can be found in the statements of financial position of the company.

The income statement, sometimes called the profit-and-loss statement, provides a picture of the business activities over time. This financial document is required for tax purposes only at the end of the calendar or fiscal year, but most marketing oriented firms demand this information semi-annually or even quarterly. The end of the year is often too late. Problems need to be solved as they arise, and the need to know the income position is imperative to these decisions.

To grasp the true importance of the income statement, that document needs to be examined in detail. Although some of the entries may seem insignificant and purely financial, many parts of this report are pertinent. As a guide to understanding what information marketer's need to garner from an income statement, here is a hypothetical example:

Out-of-Shape Sporting Goods Company
Income Statement
for the year ending December 31, 19X1

Revenue:			
Sales			$350,000
Less: Sales returns/allowances		6,000	
Sales discount		9,000	
Net sales			$335,000
Cost of goods sold:			
Beginning inventory		$ 45,000	
Purchases	$145,000		
Add: Freight in	25,000		
	170,000		
Less: Returns/allowances	$4,500		
Purchase discounts	5,800	10,300	
Net purchases		159,700	
Goods available for sale		204,700	
Less: Ending inventory		47,200	
Cost of goods sold			157,500
Gross profit			$177,500
Operating expenses:			
Selling expenses			
Salaries expense		25,400	
Commissions expense		12,400	
Advertising expense		10,425	
Supplies expense		9,925	
Automotive expense		5,850	
Payroll tax expense		3,500	
Total Selling Expense		67,500	
General and administrative expenses:			
Salaries expense		20,000	
Supplies expense		4,150	
Utilities expense		7,600	
Rent expense		12,800	
Taxes expense		2,950	
Payroll taxes expense		7,700	
Telephone expense		5,300	
Freight-out expense		3,400	
Depreciation expense		11,100	
Total G&A		75,000	
Total operating expense			142,500
Net profit			$ 35,000

ow Do Marketers Use Income Statements?

Several key areas of the income statement are of particular importance to marketers. To begin with, all marketing people need to know the volume of **Sales,** for this is the figure that shows how well the program is operating. To avoid being mislead, readers of the income statement should be sure to subtract **Returns, Allowances, and Discounts** from that figure to arrive at **Net sales.**

The amounts subtracted from total revenue are revealing because they are an indication of product quality and pricing policies.

In calculating **Cost of goods sold, Freight-in** becomes important in determining the effectiveness of the firm's buying. If the marketing group can help the purchasing department in locating cost saving suppliers, pricing may be dramatically affected. **Purchase returns, allowances, and discounts** provide valuable information for setting prices.

This income statement example provides some additional, helpful cost information, which is important in setting prices. The headings **Selling expenses** and **General and administrative expenses** contain data that are necessary in establishing pricing structures. In addition, comparing selling expenses to the amount of sales generated give the marketing manager clues regarding the efficiency of the field sales force. The **advertising expense** figure can be used as a comparison with industry averages and against benefits received.

As useful as this information is to marketing management, additional benefit is available by using the figures from the income statement to generate some key ratios. For instance, **Turnover rate,** or the number of times per year that stock is sold and replaced, is especially vital to retailers. These figures allow a comparison that shows whether sales performance is at, above or below averages found in any specific industry. In addition, turnover rate can be used to pinpoint members of a product line that are not performing well.

Turnover rate is calculated as follows:

$$\text{Turnover rate} = \frac{\text{Cost of goods sold}}{\text{Average inventory}} = \frac{\text{COG}}{\dfrac{(\text{beginning} + \text{ending inventory})}{2}}$$

For our mythical company, Out-of-Shape Sporting Goods, the turnover rate would be:

$$\frac{\$157,500}{\$\ 92,200} \text{ or } 1.71$$

This figure by itself may be meaningless, but, when used to compare with similar firms in the same line of business, turnover rate becomes an important management tool. Computing this ratio for separate products within the mix provides even greater assistance for marketers.

Another helpful piece of information that can be derived from the income statement is **Profit margin.** Sometimes referred to as **Return on sales,** this ratio provides a comparison between net income and total sales. As a formula, Profit margin is written like this:

$$\frac{\text{Net income}}{\text{Net sales}}$$

For Out-of-Shape Sporting Goods, the figures would be:

$$\frac{\$35,000}{\$335,000} \text{ or } 10.44\%$$

For a retail business, this profit margin should look favorable to management. The owners would certainly do better investing in this firm than they would by putting their capital in the bank. To make the figures more meaningful, the ratio should be used to compare this firm with similar ventures. While 10.44 percent looks good, if competitors are earning a greater return than this company may not be doing as well as it should.

The income statement can offer a variety of other comparisons. For instance, any of the categories can be compared to net sales. The **Sales efficiency ratio** weighs gross sales against net sales. By equating cost of goods sold to net sales, the firm develops the **Cost of goods sold ratio.** The same comparison can be made with the heading of selling and operating expenses. By dividing net sales by either of these expense areas, the firm gains a relative judgment regarding the effectiveness of its operations. Both **Selling expenses ratio** and **Operating expense ratio** are indicators of the efficiency of the operation.

Although the income statement is of great assistance in helping marketers determine costs and prices, retailers, in particular, must compute their selling prices without this information. To calculate these figures, knowledge of standard markup and markdown is necessary.

 ## How Is Standard Markup/Markdown Calculated?

Mathematical calculations are used in the pricing of products. In particular, retailers have need to compute the prices at which to sell their goods based upon the costs of the items and the expenses of the operation. Most resellers of consumer products use **standard markup** in determining prices. The retailer must add dollars or cents to the cost of the goods it buys in order to cover their expenses and to allow for a profit.

Standard markup is usually calculated by using a percentage. Predetermining this figure often with the help of industry associations or government agencies, allows retailers to apply one formula in computing its ultimate prices. These prices can be figured either as percentage of the selling price or of the merchandise cost. Standard markup formulas are written as follows:

$$\text{Markup percentage (at cost)} = \frac{\text{Selling price} - \text{merchandise cost}}{\text{Merchandise cost}}$$

or

$$\text{Markup percentage (on selling price)} = \frac{\text{Selling price} - \text{merchandise cost}}{\text{Selling price}}$$

Putting these standard markup formulas to test, suppose that an item costs a retailer $15 and that store sells the good for $22.50. The markup on cost would be:

$$\frac{\$22.50 - \$15.00}{\$15.00} = 50\%$$

On the other hand, markup on selling price is:

$$\frac{\$22.50 - \$15.00}{\$22.50} = 33\%$$

Retailers can use these same figures to calculate the amount to be used to markdown goods, such as for sales or clearance events. Usually, the selling store will want to cover more than just the cost of its merchandise when trying to clear out slow movers. After all, some expenses have incurred while the goods were in inventory, and these amounts should be added on the original price to determine a new cost base. If the retailer determines that $2.50 additional needs to be added to the original cost, the new base would be $17.50. If the store is willing to sell the merchandise at this figure, the mark down percentage, to be used for advertising purposes, would be:

$$\text{Markdown percentage} = \frac{\text{Original selling price} - \text{new selling price}}{\text{New selling price}}$$

$$\text{Markdown percentage} = \frac{\$22.50 - \$17.50}{\$17.50} = 28\%$$

The retailer can then advertise that this merchandise is on sale for 28 percent off and still cover costs plus some previous accrued expenses.

12

Distribution Systems

■　　■　　■　　　■　　　■　　　■　　　■　　　■　　　■　　　■　　■　　■　　■

The Job to be Done

Products, priced reasonably, provide customer satisfaction if they can be purchased when they are needed and at convenient locations. Providing time and place utility is the role of distribution. This chapter provides the answers to:

- explain the functions of distribution and describe the different channels of distribution,
- explain the factors of the product, the market and the firm that affect the size and shape of channels,
- contrast the depth and width of the distribution system based upon the product life cycle, the product and the marketer,
- recognize the methods of inventory control for trade goods and production goods,
- describe the characteristics of the modes of transportation, freight carriers and storage facilities, and
- understand and analyze the problems facing the management of channels of distribution.

James Jennings

When thinking of the field of distribution, it is easy to get trapped into considering only marketing intermediaries, such as wholesalers or retailers. Although many opportunities are available with these channel members, the whole world of physical distribution also holds great promise. Freight carriers, storage facilities and major shippers all have need for marketing-oriented employees. Wholesale and retail operations also require warehousing personnel who understand the importance of customer service and on-time delivery.

After receiving his associate degree from Essex County College, James Jennings went on to the New Jersey Institute of Technology, receiving his bachelors degree in Industrial Management and masters degree in Marketing. His first work experience in the distribution field was with People Express Airlines, where he was trained as a customer service representative. He moved on to become Intermodal Coordinator for P&O Container, where his primary responsibility was the routing of ocean freight containers around the world. Most recently, James accepted a position with Costco Northamerica Inc. as Assistant National Intermodal Manager. In this position he oversees the inland cargo container operations for this international steamship company.

Throughout his career in distribution systems, James has maintained his business as a part-time marketing consultant. Much of this work has been with the Duralens Corporation, a contact lens manufacturer. In this capacity he designed and managed marketing research projects and headed the company's promotional efforts. Although he credits many of his marketing courses for leading the way to his career choice, James also applauds Delta Epsilon Chi, the college division of Distributive Education Clubs of America. The hands-on activities in which he participated through DEC helped build his confidence and hone skills. Feeling strongly the importance of "giving a little back," James remains active with this organization, serving as advisor and judge in the New Jersey area.

What Are The Functions Of Distribution?

The quality of a product means little if it cannot be obtained. Features and benefits can only bring satisfaction when consumers or businesses can buy and have use of the good or service. Distribution is the element of the marketing mix that solves the where and when needs of customers. The physical transport and storage of goods and the availability of services are important to both the customer and the marketer.

REDUCE TRANSACTIONS

One key function of intermediaries is to **reduce the number of transactions** between the manufacturer and the ultimate user. In doing so, the channel member makes it easier for sellers to move their products, while simplifying the task of buying. The sheer numbers of retailers could overwhelm many manufacturers. By buying in large quantities, wholesalers make it easier and more economical for goods to move to the ultimate user.

By distributing their products through wholesalers and retailers, firms such as Kraft General Foods, Coca-Cola, Kodak and Procter & Gamble have fewer customers to service. Without intermediaries, mass merchandised goods would bog down en route to consumers, who would not be able to find necessary items to produce satisfaction.

BREAK BULK

Another function of intermediaries is **breaking bulk.** Wholesalers buy merchandise in large lots and resell in smaller quantities. These resellers buy Post cereals from Kraft General Foods by the truckload and break the order down into case lots for sale to retailers. These stores and shops continue breaking bulk by offering individual units to consumers. This process makes it easier for each member of the channel to make purchases.

Breaking bulk— intermediaries buy in large quantities and resell in smaller lots.

Breaking bulk benefits all members of the distribution system, as well as the ultimate consumer. Producers reduce their costs by being able to ship in large quantities. The retailers are able to buy in smaller quantities from wholesalers than would be possible from manufacturers. These resellers tie up less of their capital in inventory, purchasing only the amounts needed, when required.

PROVIDE AN ASSORTMENT

Intermediaries also **provide an assortment** of goods. Not all consumers want the same items, hence retailers purchase just what is required by the publics they serve. Wholesalers carry a tremendous assortment of merchandise. Because of the size of these stocks, retailer customers can pick and choose the items needed by their customers.

Wholesalers must anticipate retailer needs. By purchasing an assortment of products from a variety of manufacturers, these resellers actually transmit

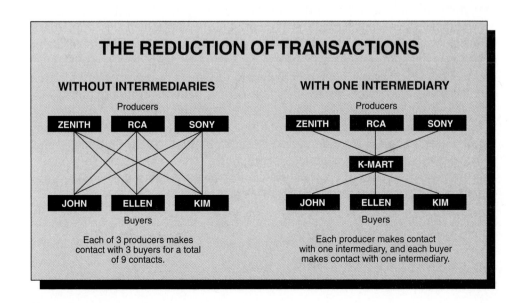

THE REDUCTION OF TRANSACTIONS

WITHOUT INTERMEDIARIES

Producers

| ZENITH | RCA | SONY |

| JOHN | ELLEN | KIM |

Buyers

Each of 3 producers makes contact with 3 buyers for a total of 9 contacts.

WITH ONE INTERMEDIARY

Producers

| ZENITH | RCA | SONY |

K-MART

| JOHN | ELLEN | KIM |

Buyers

Each producer makes contact with one intermediary, and each buyer makes contact with one intermediary.

the needs of the ultimate consumer, relayed through the retailers they serve, back to the manufacturers. The grocery store in Dallas may require a decidedly different mix of products than a Houston supermarket, and the wholesaler supplying these retailers carries an assortment of goods to satisfy both.

STORAGE AND TRANSPORTATION

One activity conducted by intermediaries that benefits manufacturers is product **storage.** By providing the physical area where quantities of goods are inventoried, wholesalers remove a burden from manufacturers. Product storage also benefits retailers. Without facilities close to the customers needing the goods, time and place utility may be lost. The drug store, auto parts house or health foods retailer cannot survive with empty shelves.

Firms exporting goods to the United States are especially keen on developing storage through wholesalers. These firms often have no distribution centers stateside for new product lines. For example, when Toshiba introduced electronic ballasts and halogen lamps in 1992, the Japanese company actively recruited American lighting wholesalers. The Lamps and Components division of Toshiba America needed U.S. firms that could provide the storage capacity needed for this merchandise.[1]

Intermediaries often provide **transportation.** Many wholesalers run their own fleet of trucks to assure on-time arrival of goods to their retail customers. Since these resellers act as the primary source of merchandise for the retail industry, the ability to service these customers with fast, efficient delivery is important. When the retailer is out of goods to sell, no one benefits. Consumer, retailer, wholesaler and manufacturer all suffer.

PROMOTION

Intermediaries are active in **promotional activities.** Manufacturers may spend vast sums on advertising or mass audience media, but wholesalers and retailers often use sales staffs as their promotional tool. Wholesale salespeople pass on product availability information to retail customers. Since these resellers often carry huge lines of merchandise, sales staffs are often overwhelmed. One innovative manufacturer, Schrader Bellows, produces training videos to educate its wholesaler's sales forces on the uses and benefits of its products.[2]

Marketing intermediaries provide the key promotional link between the manufacturer and the consumer. Promotional campaigns and materials from the manufacturer pass through the wholesale and retail chain. Producers send point-of-purchase displays and sale merchandise to the wholesaler for storage and ultimate distribution. The sales staff for these resellers then redistribute the promotional materials to their retailer customers.

---

[1]Editors, "Toshiba seeks lighting houses," *Industrial Distribution,* At Press Time column, April 1992, p. 7.

[2]Editors, "Schrader Bellows promotes videos," *Industrial Distribution,"* At Press Time column, February 1992, p. 7.

Retailers are major advertisers. Manufacturers' promotional messages create desire and stimulate demand, but retailers must provide consumers with the information about where products can be found. While wholesalers spend little effort on mass media promotion, retailers advertise extensively in their selling areas. These intermediaries complete the promotional cycles begun by manufacturers.

MARKETING RESEARCH AND SPECIAL SERVICES

Intermediaries conduct valuable **marketing research,** although it is often informal. Many times consumers will relate specific needs or trends to retailers, who in turn pass the word up through the pipeline through their suppliers. Indirectly, the orders wholesalers place weave a pattern that gives the producer information about what is hot and what is not. By supplying feedback to the manufacturer, resellers furnish data that affects design or alters product development.

As members of the distribution channel, intermediaries must carry out any number of tasks to satisfy the ultimate needs of consumers. Value added service has become an important competitive tool for wholesalers and retailers. More and more intermediaries realize the value of assisting their customers in reaching decisions. Some provide training, both in sales and management. Many help in designing store layout and security. Others have adopted policies that offer financial record keeping.

Super Valu has set up its own electronic marketing department to assist its clients with Electronic Data Interchange (EDI). Common Brothers, an upstate New York drug wholesaler, assigns every customer an employee "buddy." These members of the firm's management team are equipped with pagers and portable computers and are on call 24 hours a day to handle problems. Sysco, the giant

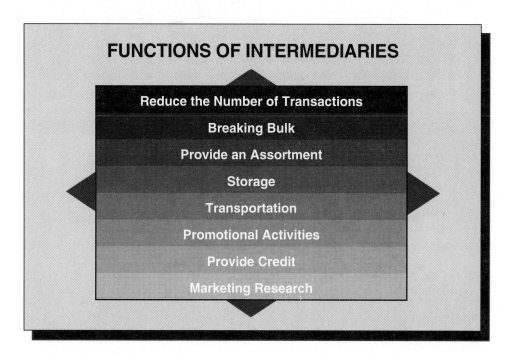

FUNCTIONS OF INTERMEDIARIES

Reduce the Number of Transactions

Breaking Bulk

Provide an Assortment

Storage

Transportation

Promotional Activities

Provide Credit

Marketing Research

food service wholesaler, helps its restaurant clients design their kitchens and lay out their menus.[3]

One company that understands the role played by intermediaries in supplying time utility is 800-FLOWERS. This entrepreneurial firm specializes in gifts for the last-minute shopper. Using the Inventory Express program offered by United Parcel Service, the firm stashes boxes of candy and fresh flowers in Louisville. 800-FLOWERS then transmits its orders directly to UPS for immediate shipment from this central distribution point.[4]

What Are Channels Of Distribution?

Consumer and business satisfaction is often dependent upon efficient performance of marketing intermediaries. These members of the distribution system provide the channels through which goods and services flow through en route from seller to buyer. Channels of distribution differ from product to product.

800-FLOWERS is a marvelous example of how marketing intermediaries provide time utility. (Courtesy of McCann Erickson)

---

[3]Iris Rosendahl, "Drug wholesaler always on call for its customers," *Drug Topics,* January 21, 1991, p. 73; Editors, "Help from wholesalers," *Progressive Grocer,* January 1991, p. 52.
[4]Editors, "Everybody knows his number," *RoundUPS,* Spring 1992, p. 5.

CHANNELS DEFINED

Channels of distribution are the firms and individuals forming a pathway to move products from manufacturers to ultimate users. Some producers deliver directly to the party who will be putting the product to use. Colgate-Palmolive buys peppermint oil for its toothpaste directly from the distiller. The corner bakery produces and sells its wares to the consumer without going through other firms. Most consumer goods, however, proceed through channels with help from marketing intermediaries.

Channel of distribution—the firms and individuals forming a pathway to move products from manufacturer to ultimate users.

TRADE GOODS CHANNELS

Most of the merchandise that the general public purchases travels through trade goods channels. Manufacturers sell trade goods to marketing intermediaries. These firms purchase goods for resale to other companies or to consumers. The tremendous number of brands and package sizes in this arena dictate the need for wholesalers and retailers. There are a number of different pipelines for channeling these items to the final buyer.

Direct

The simplest system used to service individuals is from the **manufacturer to the consumer.** Not many trade goods travel this short channel. Roadside stands sell produce directly from the farmer to consumers. Some small independent retailers make and market their own goods. Bakeries, cabinet makers and dressmakers are examples of companies that manufacture and sell direct. Except in this direct channel from manufacturer to consumer, **only the retailer sells to the consumer.**

Using Retailers

A more frequently used channel of distribution for trade goods is from **manufacturer to retailer to consumer.** In this channel, stores and shops become the selling intermediary. These retailers have the responsibility for supplying many of the utility factors that provide ultimate satisfaction. A poor selling outlet can spoil the good image developed by the manufacturer through product design and promotion.

The apparel industry is one of the most notable group of sellers to use channels directing the flow from manufacturer to retailer to consumer. Many clothing suppliers have salespeople who call on department stores and other larger retailers. Others use the services of independent selling agencies. Firms in the automobile industry also sell directly to retail establishments, as do computer, furniture and some major appliance manufacturers.

Using Wholesalers and Retailers

From **manufacturer to wholesaler to retailer to consumer** is the most common channel trade goods marketers choose. Wholesale firms buy and stock

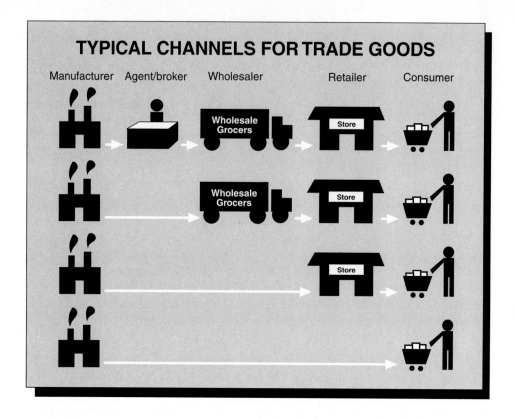

TYPICAL CHANNELS FOR TRADE GOODS

Manufacturer   Agent/broker   Wholesaler   Retailer   Consumer

merchandise in substantial quantities, which they in turn resell to retailers and manufacturers within their competitive sphere. Most grocery products stocked by supermarkets travel through wholesalers. These resellers also supply much of the inventory found in drug and hardware stores.

Changes in existing markets or the development of new ones may create nontraditional channels. To illustrate, Campbell Soup Company distributes its products through grocery wholesalers. When marketing research uncovered an outstanding, untapped market for Chunky brand soups among college students, Campbell had to rethink its traditional methods of distribution. The firm chose college bookstores as the key intermediaries to reach this market. Other firms marketing in this arena use free samples and sponsorship of extracurricular activities to tap this lucrative market.[5]

Using Agents/Brokers

Agents and brokers are special types of intermediaries who typically carry out only the selling function of marketing. Some consumer goods and services are channeled from **manufacturer through agent or broker to wholesaler or retailer to consumer.** Agent/brokers sometimes sell manufacturers products to

---

[5]Editors, Marketing Solutions Column, "Campbell's campus caper targets fast-food generation," *Adweek's Marketing Week,* January 9, 1989, pp. 58–61; Eben Shapiro, "New marketing specialists tap collegiate consumers," *The New York Times,"* February 27, 1992.

wholesalers and on other occasions deal directly with the retailer. Smaller firms producing specialty items often use these selling intermediaries.

Agent/brokers are also common in the consumer service sector. These selling intermediaries typically handle stocks, bonds, insurance and real estate. Most travel arrangements are made through agent/brokers, and a number of nonprofit organizations use the services of independent agencies. To illustrate, United Way serves as the intermediary, collecting and dispersing donations for many independent causes.

PRODUCTION GOODS CHANNELS

Production goods channels vary slightly from their consumer goods counterparts. In most cases, these pipelines are shorter than those used to move products to the ultimate consumer. Consumers are not involved in the purchase of productions goods. The organizations that buy these items often need technical help or require custom specifications. Intermediaries may not have this type of expertise.

Direct

Most raw materials, component parts and production equipment travel directly from **manufacturer to user,** as business product purchasers are called. It is a common practice for industrial producers to employ their own salespeople who deal person-to-person with purchasers from other businesses. Firms such as Weyerhaeuser, Burlington Mills and Intel use these in-house personnel to call on other product manufacturers. Production goods marketers also sell directly to intermediaries, government and institution buyers. Georgia Pacific, Merck and American Hospital Supply employ salespeople who receive orders from both wholesalers and medical facilities.

Using Agent/Brokers

Another method production goods sellers frequently choose is from **manufacturer through agent/broker to user.** Many firms choose independent professionals to carry out the selling function instead of hiring their own staff. Although these intermediaries do not purchase the merchandise, they facilitate the transfer of title from seller to buyer. B. F Goodrich uses manufacturers representatives for several of its divisions, as do DuPont, Jefferson Electric and Owens-Illinois.

Using Wholesalers

A less common channel for the distribution of production goods is from **manufacturer to wholesaler to user.** Marketers of operating supplies and small, inexpensive parts often use this type of channel. These wholesalers sell to other manufacturers and wholesalers. Since these firms do not handle trade goods, they do not resell to retail outlets. Wholesalers handling production goods are usually called industrial distributors. Items handled by these resellers include janitorial supplies, lubricants, electric motors, safety gear, nuts and

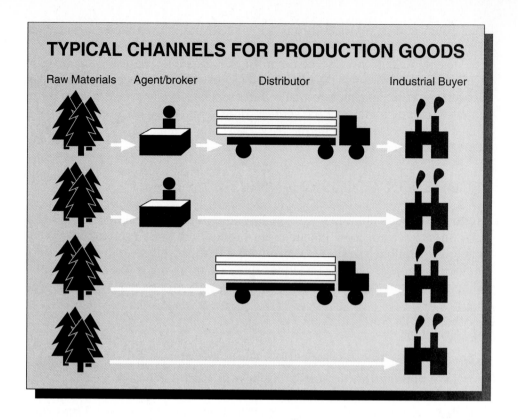

TYPICAL CHANNELS FOR PRODUCTION GOODS

Raw Materials Agent/broker Distributor Industrial Buyer

bolts, abrasives and electrical supplies. Larger, more expensive merchandise usually moves directly from seller to buyer.

SERVICES CHANNELS

While it is difficult to think of services in terms of distribution channels, time and place utility is still needed to assure satisfaction. Although not physical, the benefit supplied by these products must be transferred from the provider to the customer. Sometimes the seller of the service performs work for the buyer, and on other occasions, as in the case with equipment based services, customers may use the facilities owned by another. Perhaps now one can envision services flowing, in a way, from the service provider to the service receiver.

Direct

The primary distribution channel for services is direct from supplier to user. Because of the personal nature of many people-based services, whether professional or semi-skilled, benefit and satisfaction is gained directly from the source of the service. The massage therapist assists the patient in gaining full use of body parts following surgery without going through intermediaries. Similarly, services provided by bookkeepers and trash collectors do not reach businesses and consumers after first being handled by wholesalers or retailers.

In the case of equipment based services, the customer typically receives the use of the facilities without help from intermediaries. People use playgrounds and parks, watch movies and attend concerts, go through the car wash or get a haircut in direct contact with the person or firm creating the service. Although payment may be made using credit cards, another type of service, there are usually no dealers or distributors involved in the transactions.

Using Agents

Some consumer services are distributed from provider to customer with the help of agents. One of the best examples is the use of travel consultants for those taking a trip or booking an airline flight. Just as in the case with goods, these marketing intermediaries are independent businesses that help bring buyer and seller together for a fee or commission. Other consumer service agents would include insurance brokers, ticket sellers and real estate rental agencies.

Travel agents and insurance brokers work in both the consumer and the business service markets. There are some firms, however, that only supply to other firms. Advertising, for example, is typically placed in the media by a business with the help of an agency. The actual service is the air time or print space provided by the television station or magazine. The advertising agency facilitates these services for its business clients. Other agents operating in this arena would include public relations companies and property management firms.

hat Affects The Size And Shape Of Channels?

Distribution channels vary in size and shape. The number and types of intermediaries used differs from company to company. Depending upon factors that include tradition, the product, markets and the producer, the channel for one type of good can be very different from that for another. Even within the same category of goods, one may find variations simply because of differences in philosophy among the different marketers.

TRADITION

Typically, manufacturers form their distribution channels. Often these systems evolve from **traditional** ways of doing business. Historically, the saw mill sells lumber through brokers to distributors to lumberyards. A new manufacturer entering this industry would probably use similar channels. Clothing, for example, typically moves from the garment maker directly to retailers, often with the help of agent/brokers. A new firm in this field would probably not look for an apparel wholesaler, even if one were available.

The increasing dominance of mass merchandisers has had a tremendous impact on the breakup of traditional distribution channels. Manufacturers that normally sell their products through wholesalers often must abandon customary channels when faced with the buying power of large retail chains. Suppose Kmart, for example, refuses to buy cameras, toasters or sneakers

Global Marketing: Keep on Pedaling.

Distribution in overseas markets can be a real headache. Many countries have established networks of wholesalers, distributors, dealers, jobbers and retailers that are difficult to circumvent. Often the rule seems to be "do business our way, or do not do business." Japan's distribution system has proven to be especially difficult for many manufacturers. One company that successfully markets in that country after solving its maze of intermediary channels is Cannondale, the bicycle manufacturer from Georgetown, Connecticut.

Thanks in part to the tremendous popularity of the mountain bike, U.S. production of two wheelers has soared in the past few years. In the meantime, exports of Japanese-made bikes have gone in the opposite direction. Initially, Cannondale used Mitsubishi as its sales agent in Japan. When this gigantic firm insisted that Cannondale add another level of distribution through wholesalers, the U.S. firm took a different route.

Avoiding the high costs and bureaucratic maze of Tokyo, Cannondale set up a distribution center in the Osaka area. Using a team of Japanese-speaking American professional bikers, the U.S. company makes calls directly on dealers. This move brings the company closer to the consumer, providing a wealth of marketing research data regarding preferred colors and designs for its products. Although its bikes cost an average of $400 more than competitive Japanese models, Cannondale sales quadrupled since its first year in this Asian country.

SOURCE: Andrew Tanzer, " 'Just get out and sell'," *Forbes,* September 28, 1992, pp. 68–72. (Photo opposite courtesy of Cannondale)

through traditional pipelines. The manufacturers of these goods would either have to sell direct or risk losing the business.

PRODUCT CHARACTERISTICS

The number of intermediaries within a channel depends upon more than tradition. **Product characteristics** influence the size of the channel and the types of channel members selected. The nature of some products requires certain types of special handling. For others, an entirely different set of needs might dictate channel size or shape. Although product characteristics come into play, the individual firm must choose the avenues that best suit its strategies.

Perishability

Products with greater **perishability** use shorter channels. Fresh produce and many baked goods are delivered directly from producer to retailer. Foods for eating establishments sometimes bypass intermediaries, being delivered directly to the restaurant or hotel. Bread and rolls found in supermarkets usually arrive fresh from the bakery, unless made in-house.

Easily damaged products also travel shorter channels. Fragile or delicate goods are safer if handled fewer times. Production goods or accessories with limited shelf life, such as certain chemicals, plastics and agricultural products, have short channels of distribution. Items that might be easily damaged, such as hospital equipment or electronic parts, hold up better when handled less.

Perishable goods, such as bread from Oroweat Bakeries, typically travel through short, direct channels.

Size

Physical size dictates the number of intermediaries that can handle the product. Larger products are more costly to move from place to place. Therefore, machinery and equipment manufacturers use shorter or regional distribution channels. Farm implement marketers avoid the use of wholesalers, preferring to deal directly with retail equipment outlets. Massey-Ferguson and Kubota would not benefit by selling their tractors to wholesalers instead of directly to farm equipment outlets.

Automobiles are shipped from the manufacturer by train, cargo ship and truck. Additional channel members, such as wholesalers, would create unnecessary loading and unloading at each stop. Besides, automobile dealers usually have sufficient storage space and capital to deal directly with the car manufacturer or importer. Machine tools, stamping dies, injection molding machines and steam turbines are too large to be shipped and reshipped through many intermediaries.

Value

Product **value** is another consideration in setting up distribution systems. Channels are usually shorter when the value of the merchandise is greater. Lengthy channels have the potential for loss through damage or theft. Inexpensive items travel through widespread distribution systems. Ballpoint pens, chewing gum, film and most convenience goods pass through at least one wholesaler before reaching the retailers shelves.

Specialty goods and many shopping goods generally move directly from maker to retail seller. Crystal and jewelry, car tires and refrigerators bypass wholesalers. Channels for high value trade goods often include agent/brokers to facilitate the sale. Within the production goods category, lower priced operating supplies and accessories sell through distributors, while bigger ticket items move directly from the manufacturer to the user.

Complexity

Product **complexity** is another factor that determines length of channel. Some items may require complicated installation or service that is beyond the capabilities of intermediaries. In those cases, manufacturers may choose to sell direct or through agent/brokers. Supercomputers and commercial aircraft are examples. Standard products may pass through several hands in the channel, but customized units usually travel direct to the ultimate user. Businesses with strong, well-established distribution systems often refuse to accept orders for custom-made goods. Those which do deal in such items usually use direct channels.

MARKET CHARACTERISTICS

Market characteristics contribute to the shape and size of distribution channels. As we have seen, trade goods typically travel through longer channels than do production goods. With the exception of some commodity type items, raw materials, component parts and production equipment reach the end user after a very short trip, often directly from the manufacturer. Industrial distributors carry operating supplies, such as lubricants and janitorial cleaners, and office supply houses provide the copier paper and paper clips needed by business entities.

Order Size

The **size of the order** has a bearing on the size of the channel. Consumers purchase in relatively small quantities. Therefore, channel members that can break bulk are required to meet the needs of these buyers. Storage of these items benefits both the marketer and the consumer. By providing wide assortments of merchandise, retailers allow a broad field of choice to the individual buyer.

Production goods buyers use greater quantities of goods. Channels for large orders can be quite short. Shipping in large quantities benefits both seller and buyer. Generally, distribution systems provide greater efficiency when goods pass through fewer hands. To manufacturers, fewer intermediaries means less damage to the goods, less lost merchandise, less miscommunication and less confusion.

PRODUCER CHARACTERISTICS

Producer characteristics influence channel shape or size. Large, multi-product line, trade goods marketers are capable of carrying out most marketing functions themselves. These firms look to intermediaries to provide assistance primarily in the areas of storage and transportation. Marketers such as Borden, Whirlpool and Stanley Tools need little marketing assistance.

Marketers with smaller staffs or fewer product lines may seek out intermediaries for both distribution and marketing assistance. Members of the distribution channel may be used to supplement those areas not covered by the product manufacturer. For example, because of the expense of operating a full-time sales staff, the small manufacturer may require the use of agents. In another case, the marketer may lack funds for promotion, and retailers provide an additional service when they advertise items available in their stores.

Size of the Product Mix

Marketers with a **broad product mix** have the opportunity to minimize selling costs because their sales forces offer numerous items to many customers. Such firms usually sell directly to wholesalers or retailers. These intermediaries have the capability of stocking large quantities of goods, and the manufacturer can count on its entire mix receiving attention. Granted, these resellers usually stock a variety of goods from many manufacturers, but individual firms still benefit from mass coverage.

Firms with limited product lines may need the services of agent/brokers to receive the desired coverage. For such companies, contracting with an additional intermediary offsets the lack of a large sales force. Smaller marketers with few products may also select specialty intermediaries. Their limited lines may receive more attention than if distributed through large channels.

Financial Strength

Financial strength can dictate channel size. The functions carried out in distribution channels are costly. Firms having sufficient funds often want to control as many activities as possible. By governing the complete distribution process,

Procter & Gamble has an extremely wide product mix, including everything from potato chips to paper towels, distributed through long channels.

they can assure that their products reach the ultimate customer in the manner that the marketer desires. Large, multiple line, trade goods marketers carry an aura of strength and power that leads to greater channel control.

Companies of lesser financial strength may have to farm out some of the marketing activities to channel members. Intermediaries may then assume control of the channel from these small manufacturers. Such marketers usually experience trouble in getting a reasonable share of display space or dealer promotion. Once again, these companies often turn to specialty wholesalers to help in securing the greatest impact on their markets.

How Deep Or Wide Should The Distribution System Be?

The size and shape of a distribution system for trade goods marketers can be measured by its depth or its width. The depth of the channel refers to the amount of different levels of intermediaries found between the manufacturer and the ultimate consumer. The width of the channel relates to the number of retailers handling the products. For some marketers, the channel is deep and wide. Others may wade in shallower and narrower waters.

INTENSIVE DISTRIBUTION

The number of channel members a marketer uses depends largely on the market demand for its products. Chewing gum, deodorant and camera film are needed by large, diverse markets. Most convenience goods receive **intensive distribution,** using many intermediaries. Wrigley's, Gillette and Kodak want their products handled by as many retailers as possible, including vending machines.

At times, intensive distribution is not possible. In the grocery industry, shelf space is at a premium. Large and small convenience goods marketers are in a constant wrestling match with supermarket managers to secure display areas for their wares. While fighting the battle of slotting fees, the firms with less clout and shallower lines may not receive as much distribution.

Intensive distribution—using as many intermediaries as possible.

SELECTIVE DISTRIBUTION

Producers of shopping goods often prefer a **selective distribution** system. This method limits the number of intermediaries geographically, by size or by number. Restricting the number of retailers carrying their lines allows these marketers to concentrate on those establishments that will maintain the desired image or provide greater service to the ultimate customer. Jordache sells its jeans through select department stores, avoiding the negative image that might be raised using mass merchandisers. With the exception of sparsely populated, rural areas, auto manufacturers limit the number of dealers carrying any one line.

Selective distribution is common with specialty goods. Firms that market upscale items often restrict coverage to those retailers who fit the image of the

Selective distribution—limiting the number of intermediaries geographically, by size or by numbers.

product itself. At the other end of the scale, low priced utility items may also travel through a limited number of outlets for the identical reason. Matching the image of the store with the product is part of positioning. Rolex distributes its watches through fine jewelry stores, not Wal-Mart.

EXCLUSIVE DISTRIBUTION

Exclusive distribution—rigidly limiting the number of intermediaries.

As the name implies, **exclusive distribution** rigidly limits the number of intermediaries. Gasoline refiners establish regions in which their wholesalers work, and agricultural chemical marketers allot exclusive territories to distributors. Some specialty goods sell through exclusive channels, especially imported items. Louis Vuitton luggage is sold mainly through company owned outlets, and Kaiser Porcelain is distributed exclusively by Ebeling & Reuss.

Once again, the selection of this type of distribution is based mainly upon demand. High demand for a trade good usually requires wider coverage. More people buy breath mints than sterling silver flatware. In cases where fewer people have need for the item, marketers can pick and choose the retailers more carefully. New product marketers may initially opt for more restrictive systems, then widen the channel as demand grows.

ow Do Marketers Control Inventories?

Inventory control is the responsibility of all members of the distribution channel. Trade goods houses require good communication between suppliers and intermediaries. Stockouts hurt everyone. Consumers rarely wait for retailers to order additional merchandise from wholesalers or manufacturers. Production goods firms need raw materials, component parts, production equipment and other manufacturing requirements to avoid shut downs and delayed shipments.

IN TRADE GOODS CHANNELS

For intermediaries in trade goods channels, efficient management of stocks of merchandise is crucial for success. Wholesalers and retailers must continually be aware of what is on hand and how long it takes to receive new goods. In the sometimes fickle retailing arena, a store or shop that does not have the right product on hand may lose the sale, and, too often, the customer. To keep shelves and racks full, intermediaries often call on the speed and accuracy of computerized systems.

Electronic data interchange (EDI)—on-line computer ordering system connected with electronic inventory gathering devices.

Electronic Data Interchange

Computers allow for increased logistical efficiency. **Electronic data interchange (EDI)** uses on-line computer ordering procedures coupled with electronic wands. These tools collect inventory information according to bar codes. The use of Universal Product Codes, UPCs, on packages and shipping cartons greatly simplifies inventory data collection. Not only does EDI reduce the time lag in placing orders, it provides intermediaries with up-to-the-minute data regarding fast and slow moving items.[6]

Storage facilities and warehousing are necessary to maintain the stocks of merchandise needed to service markets. When the consumer runs out of flour, the grocery store, not Pillsbury, satisfies time and place utility. If the supermarket runs low on this staple, it contacts the wholesaler, who in turn buys from the mill. Each of these channel players must work as part of a team to bring the ultimate service to the consumer.

Customer Service

The main objective of inventory control is to provide **customer service.** The distribution system is the key to getting the right product to the right person at the right time. Making sure that buyers return is a major concern of all marketers, but providing customer service can be difficult. There are no manuals that spell out appropriate procedures. One customer's demands may be unlike any other.

Whether using automated order systems or relying on personal contact, an important task for all channel members is servicing the ultimate consumer. The primary goal of distribution is to keep merchandise where it is needed, when it is required. Intermediaries have the job of maintaining the proper levels of inventory. Having too little on hand produces customer dissatisfaction. Having too much in stock hurts efficiency and profits.

IN PRODUCTION GOODS CHANNELS

Time is often the enemy of production goods marketers. Incoming goods needed for production and outgoing finished goods desired by customers must be managed efficiently and accurately. Producers strive to establish ordering practices that promise to provide enough materials, equipment and supplies.

America's leading motorcycle manufacturer, Harley Davidson, is a strong proponent of just-in-time inventory control.

[6]J. A. Tompkins, "Quick response: Slow but inevitable," *Industry Week,* September 9, 1994, p. ADCM8; Myron Magnet, "Who's winning the information revolution," *Fortune,* November 30, 1992, pp. 110–113; F. Gebhart, "McKesson opens up EDI system to its customers," *Drug Topics,* January 20, 1992, p. 68; W. Gruber, "Are you ready for the 21st century?" *Industrial Distribution,* February 1992, p. 35; J. Pellet, "Partnership: A fundamental," *Discount Merchandiser,* November 1991, pp. 18–19.

Reliability includes the need to ship and receive the right parts while meeting time constraints. Shipments that arrive on time are worthless if they do not contain the right products.

A final objective of any distribution operation is efficient delivery while minimizing **costs.** Many factors make up the total cost of an inventory system. The cost of the merchandise can be calculated readily. How one measures the cost of losing an order or a customer is more difficult. Managing these factors is the key to proper inventory control.

Just-In-Time

Just-in-time—stocks of parts and materials are delivered at the precise moment needed.

Just-in-time is an expansion of the philosophy created by Toyota called Kanban. This inventory control system assures that the right products arrive at the point of production just as they are needed. It is an entire process of scheduling, manufacturing and controlling stocks of parts and materials. JIT is more than an inventory control system; it is a problem solving technique. Just-in-time is proving to be successful in this country and around the world.

As production efficiency increases, manufacturers find that they rely upon fewer suppliers. Xerox, a proponent of just-in-time, has eliminated 4,700 companies from its vendor list. Harley-Davidson cut the number of its sources by more than 50 percent. Apple Computer and Caterpillar Tractor penalize suppliers who do not deliver on time. These companies consider early arrival almost as devastating as tardiness.[7]

Who Carries The Freight In Distribution Systems?

Those individuals and firms that transport goods are, to a great degree, responsible for channel success. Manufacturers may produce and contract to ship their goods to meet order requirements, but if the truck or train is late delivering, the customer blames the shipper not the transportation company. When carriers do not perform, wholesalers and retailers are without goods to sell. No just-in-time system can work if the critical timing of product delivery is not met.

MODES OF TRANSPORTATION

Mode of transportation—the method used to move the goods from seller to buyer.

The **modes of transportation** provide the methods for moving goods from seller to buyer. Without these efficient systems, neither trade goods nor production goods channels can function successfully. These transportation methods provide the customer service, timing and reliability necessary for the operation of any channel. In comparing these means of transporting freight, marketers typically evaluate each by flexibility, cost, speed, types of goods carried and reliability.

---

[7]Lewis J. Perelman, "Kanban to kanbrain," *Forbes,* June 6, 1994, p. 84; Howard Gleckman, Zachary Schiller and James B. Treece, "A tonic for the business cycle," *Business Week,* April 4, 1994, p. 57; Editors, "Manufacturing management: I want it now," *The Economist,* June 13, 1992, p. 78; S. McDaniel, "The effect of JIT on distributors," *Industrial Marketing Management,* May 1992, pp. 145–149.

Truck

Many shippers favor motor carriers, or **trucks,** over other modes of transportation due primarily to flexibility. Trucks deliver to more destinations than any other freight method. Shipping by truck is not the least expensive way to transport goods. One major cause for the high costs of trucking is **deadheading.** Motor carriers that haul freight to one destination often return empty to the original shipping point. The empty return run is known as deadheading.

Trucking typically hauls finished goods, leaving most of the bulky, raw material transportation to other modes. Motor carriers are diversified and have the capability of handling a wide variety of products. Trucks are one of the more reliable methods of shipping freight, in terms of both on-time performance and lack of damage to the goods.

Much of the transcontinental shipping is **intermodal,** or involves more than one mode of transportation. The most noted system is "piggyback," or putting truck trailers on trains. Piggyback results in lower costs on long hauls through less fuel consumption and fewer driver hours. Other forms of intermodal transportation are trucks on ships, or "fishyback," and trainships which combine rail and water.

Intermodal—more than one mode of transportation used for shipment.

Train

Trains, or rail transportation, have long been noted as the mainstay of the American freight system. About one-third of all intercity freight, that which moves between metropolitan areas, is hauled by rail. This percentage has been steadily declining, primarily because of the lack of flexibility using this mode. Many smaller, rural markets are not serviced by rail. Hauling freight by train is

Doublestacking makes intermodel containerization economically feasible for both domestic and global shipments. (Courtesy of Burlington Northern Railroad)

low cost. Second only to water, rails offer economical transportation, but loading and unloading is expensive.

A major disadvantage of shipping by rails is the lack of speed. If goods are needed to meet tight schedules, trains are not the first choice. Although trains can haul many types of freight, rail shipment generally carries large, bulkier goods. Specially designed railcars can accommodate many bulk cargoes, such as grain, lumber, plastic resins, scrap iron, coal and wood chips. Trains are not particularly reliable. Freight inside railroad cars often suffers damage. Rail carriers use many modern types of dunnage, such as foam or air bags, to secure freight within the railcar, but damage still occurs.

Water Transportation

Water transportation includes ocean going ships and barges that travel inland waterways. Hauling over water is not very flexible, meaning that freight cannot be shipped to many or various customers. Cost is the one area where ships and barges shine. Although increased gas and oil prices have impacted water shippers, the use of containers lowers the cost of loading and unloading. Containerization reduces the damage caused by handling and improves security by lowering pilferage.

Water shipping is slow. Depending upon the destination and the carrier selected it can take months to move cargo port to port. Usually water transports haul large, bulky items, such as grain and fruit from the rich Eastern Oregon and Washington agricultural areas that float down the Columbia River, later to be transshipped worldwide. Coal barges travel the Mississippi and Ohio rivers fueling the industrial might of the Midwest. Iron ore travels in special cargo vessels across the Great Lakes to reach the steel mills in Gary, Indiana. Low reliability is also a disadvantage of this mode. Although containerization significantly reduces damage to cargo, some still occurs.

Air Freight

The fastest growing mode of transportation is **air freight.** Air carriers, such as United Air Freight, UPS and FedEx, fly cargo all over the world. Since many areas do not have facilities to handle large planes, air freight is not known for its flexibility. The biggest negative regarding air freight is cost. Although automated terminals help reduce expenses, the growth of this mode is somewhat restricted because of high operating costs. A contributing factor to the growth of the air freight industry is speed. The benefit of fast delivery from shipping by air becomes available to more shippers as the size of aircraft increases to accommodate larger shipments.

Air freight has limited capability. Although today's larger planes allow for the shipment of full trucks and other large items, air freight is not noted as a bulk cargo carrier. High value, low cubic measure items are the best bet for air freight. The reliability of air freight is excellent. In part because of the special care given to the handling of more valuable cargo, less damage occurs with air freight than with most other methods of shipment. Weather affects air carriers less than it does their overland competitors, so on-time delivery is common.

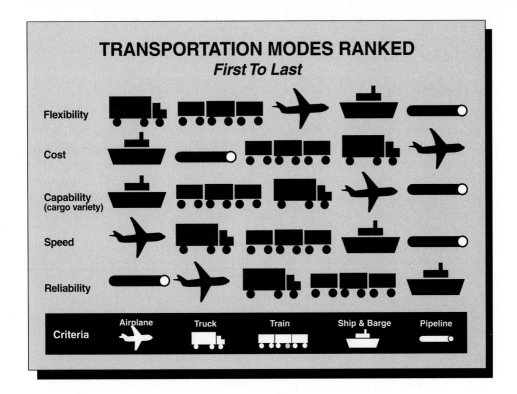

TRANSPORTATION MODES RANKED
First To Last

Pipeline

Pipelines are major transporters. Although they are not heard and are rarely seen, pipelines quietly go through the process of shipping liquids and gases across the country. Although not very flexible, the over 200,000 miles of pipelines that crisscross the continent carry their cargo to every major city. Freight shipment by pipeline is rather inexpensive, despite the high initial cost of the pipes. Since liquids flow through these pipelines at only three to four miles per hour, the actual time to pump might be lengthy. However, since the product flows as soon as the valve is opened at the receiving end, delivery seems instant.

Pipelines ship only liquid or gaseous cargo, and the petrochemical industry is the largest user of this mode. Pipelines excel in reliability. Cargo shipped by this mode suffers almost no damage in shipment, and the weather conditions have little or no effect on speed or quality. When the receiver turns on the "spigot," the goods are on hand. This mode of transportation is the most effective and efficient means for moving bulk petroleum cargoes.

How Are Freight Carriers Categorized?

Individual freight carriers use different modes of transportation. Some restrict themselves to single modes, while others operate using a wide variety of transportation methods. Burlington Northern plies the skies as well as rails, and

Southern Pacific uses both train and truck. Some carriers haul freight for only one company. Others provide service to a variety of shippers. Many use published rates, while a few work under contracts with shippers.

PRIVATE CARRIER

Private carrier—a shipper owned freight hauler.

Many companies that ship large, continuous quantities of freight own their transportation systems. Shipper owned freight haulers are called **private carriers.** These freight carriers transport the owner's merchandise on company operated or leased vehicles, usually using company employees. Typically, these firms are found in trade goods channels hauling finished goods to intermediaries. Marketers such as Frito-Lay, Nabisco and McDonald's operate their own fleets of vehicles as private carriers.

Some of these types of freight carriers look to pick up cargoes from other shippers on the voyage home to avoid deadheading costs. By charging others for return haul freight, private carriers reduce overhead. Manufacturers, such as Pozzi Window Company, pick up raw materials, component parts or operating supplies from vendors when returning from a cross-country delivery of wood windows and doors.

COMMON CARRIER

Common carrier—a freight hauler that carries cargo for any shipper under published tariffs.

A **common carrier** is a freight hauler that carries cargo for any shipper under published tariffs, or price lists. These carriers accept freight for delivery according to their established routes and schedules. Some common carriers operate within limited geographical areas, while others haul freight nationwide. Common carriers are the most widely used type of freight hauler.

Common carriers operate within every mode of transportation. System 99, Burlington Northern Railroad, Matson Line, Emery Air Freight and Tenneco are all common carriers. Although now deregulated, freight haulers still face rigid controls. In this industry, prices, routes, schedules and cargoes are watched closely by the Interstate Commerce Commission to assure no restraint of trade occurs.

CONTRACT CARRIER

Contract carrier—a freight hauler that contracts exclusively with one shipper.

As the name implies, **contract carriers** haul for shippers under contract terms. Although regulated to a degree, contract carriers have much more freedom than common carriers. Some of these transporters operate under contract in only one direction. This allows the carrier to pick up additional work on the backhaul. Contract carriers are common in the oil and chemical industries.

Gypsy—a contract carrier that hauls freight on return trips at less than normal rates.

Many contract carriers operating out of California haul produce to the Midwest. These freight companies often return with equipment or pallets of boxed goods destined for the West Coast. Such contract carriers are often called **gypsies.** Shippers love the low rates these haulers offer, but often

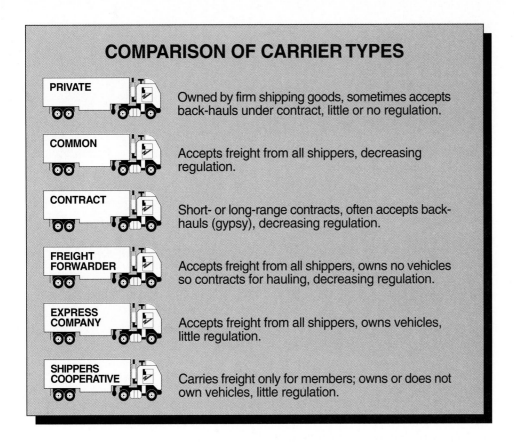

COMPARISON OF CARRIER TYPES

PRIVATE — Owned by firm shipping goods, sometimes accepts back-hauls under contract, little or no regulation.

COMMON — Accepts freight from all shippers, decreasing regulation.

CONTRACT — Short- or long-range contracts, often accepts back-hauls (gypsy), decreasing regulation.

FREIGHT FORWARDER — Accepts freight from all shippers, owns no vehicles so contracts for hauling, decreasing regulation.

EXPRESS COMPANY — Accepts freight from all shippers, owns vehicles, little regulation.

SHIPPERS COOPERATIVE — Carries freight only for members; owns or does not own vehicles, little regulation.

suffer because of the lack of scheduled departures. Gypsy carriers are not noted for reliability.

FREIGHT FORWARDERS AND EXPRESS COMPANIES

Freight forwarders are carriers that do not own their own equipment. These transshippers collect small shipments from a variety of customers and then transport the amassed cargo by common or contract carrier. Operating from large metropolitan areas, these transportation companies send freight to many different destinations on any given day. The speed of departure from the shipping point depends upon the amount of freight accumulated.

Express companies, such as United Parcel Service and FedEx, collect small shipments from a variety of sources, just as do freight forwarders. The difference between these carriers being that express companies own their vehicles. These companies operate fleets of aircraft, trucks and vans and often guarantee overnight delivery.

UPS, for example, can affect a variety of services by ground and by air including next day and same day delivery. Parcels picked up by truck during the day travel by air to distribution centers where workers sort packages and

Freight forwarder—a freight carrier that does not own its own equipment.

Express company—a freight hauler that collects small quantities and ships them using its own vehicles.

One of the world's leading express carriers, the UPS trucks and planes are easy to spot. (Courtesy of United Parcel Service)

documents throughout the night. Planes leave these areas early in the morning, transporting goods around the country, where ultimate delivery is made by truck. Express companies are more in demand due to the greater emphasis on the timing of deliveries to firms using JIT.[8]

Who Provides Merchandise Storage?

While some trade goods marketers maintain physical inventories at their manufacturing locations, many rely upon intermediaries to carry out this function. Wholesalers and retailers typically maintain stocks of goods needed to fill customer orders. Yet to insure customer service, large consumer goods houses often establish warehousing facilities in key locations across the country.

DISTRIBUTION CENTERS

Distribution center—a regional storage facility owned by the producer or intermediary.

Producers and large intermediaries that do not have the necessary space or who wish to provide faster service to customers often use regional storage facilities called **distribution centers.** Locating storage capacity in large market

---

[8]Adam Bryant, "The newest name in the overnite delivery business," *New York Times,* June 24, 1994, p. D6, Danna K. Henderson, "FedEx updates tracking system," *Air Transport World,* March 1993, p. 48; Tom Eisenhart, "On target delivery: Federal Express scores big with Via FedEx," *Business Marketing,* April 1992, p. 52; Seth Lubove, "Vindicated," *Forbes,* December 9, 1991, pp. 198–202.

areas, allows manufacturers to provide substantial finished goods inventories close to the ultimate user. Large retailers with broad geographic coverage may ship to individual stores from their own distribution centers. Lucky Stores, the California grocery chain, and Wal-Mart maintain regional distribution centers.

Often freight costs can be minimized by shipping in large quantities to distribution centers, from which small shipments move directly to company outlets. By automating the storage and retrieval process, shipping errors are becoming less of a crisis. With bar codes placed on cartons and packing crates, warehouses use laser devices to determine exact contents of the package. Computer controlled robots then travel the aisles selecting merchandise for shipment or restocking the shelves with fresh goods.

PUBLIC WAREHOUSES

Shippers also rent space from **public warehouses.** These independently owned facilities are available for general use by any business. Manufacturers using this type of warehouse benefit from lower storage costs. Public warehouses are particularly advantageous to smaller firms that cannot afford to carry large stocks of finished goods.

Public warehouse—a storage facility that accepts freight from any shipper.

Companies entering new geographic markets often minimize costs by using public storage. The high, fixed costs associated with private warehousing can be postponed until the market grows to the point where a distribution center is needed. Sometimes the quantity of goods shipped to a region does not warrant investing in a company owned facility. On the negative side, these facilities offer limited access due to their hours of operation and can increase product damage or theft.

ow Are Channels Of Distribution Managed?

In most cases, the individuals and firms operating within distribution systems are independent from the seller or buyer. Although some agents may work under an exclusive agreement for one or the other, many intermediaries, freight carriers and storage facilities are available for a variety of marketers. Because of this unique relationship between manufacturers and channel members, a variety of concerns and problems must be addressed. Good working relationships between all parties in the distribution system does much to help deliver the when and where satisfaction needed by customers.

ETHICS

The ethical concerns about **exclusive distributorships** relate to restraint of trade. Manufacturers are leery about assigning restrictive territories that may eliminate or hamper fair competition. Exclusive geographical territories awarded to wholesalers or retailers might be held by the courts to be restraint of trade.

The depth and width of distribution systems often breeds more than legal problems. Intensive distribution can create scenes where larger intermediaries demand more attention or lower prices than less powerful resellers. Selective distribution can leave territories uncovered. Exclusive distribution may limit entry of capable dealers. Whichever system the marketer selects, channel conflict can arise.

CHANNEL CONFLICT

Conflict between producer and intermediaries is common. One partner in the distribution system often feels that another is not carrying its load. Sometimes the clash is between the manufacturer and its wholesaler or retailer customers. On other occasions, the friction is among the intermediaries. Managing the entire distribution system to assure customer satisfaction while minimizing conflict is a major management task.

Manufacturers look to wholesalers to provide adequate market coverage. This is especially true when it comes to following up on leads generated by the producer. When introducing new products, many manufacturers select the best performers among their wholesale accounts. Manufacturers should be mindful of the needs of their wholesalers, including incentives to increase the net income of these channel members. Quantity discounts and special allowances have a direct effect on improving profit margins, along with joint sales calls and cooperative advertising.[9]

A classic conflict situation arises when manufacturers bypass wholesalers to sell directly to a retailer or industrial user. Strife may also arise between channel members operating on the same level. Retailer pitted against retailer often creates an atmosphere ripe for discrimination. Territorial battles may cause manufacturers to make decisions that cannot please any involved parties. Channel conflict is the major rationale for the formation of integrated distribution systems.

INTEGRATED DISTRIBUTION SYSTEMS

Integrated distribution system—an internally managed channel where the producer assumes direct control.

An **integrated distribution system** is one where the producer assumes complete control. In these distribution channels, sometimes known as vertical marketing systems, the manufacturer owns or manages the intermediaries that handle its merchandise, primarily retailers. By exercising management over these resellers, the system leader assures that the needs of the marketplace are met. At the same time, the manufacturer guarantees that its products receive the utmost in promotion and display at the retail outlet.

Manufacturers must maintain control over their products at the retail level. If independent stores and shops cannot guarantee that the consumer will

---

[9]Elizabeth J. Wilson and Arch G. Woodside, "Marketing new products with distributors," *Industrial Marketing Management*, February 1992, pp. 15–21; Allan J. McGrath and Kenneth G. Hardy, "Manufacturer services for distributors," *Industrial Marketing Management*, May 1992, pp. 119–124.

The independent tire dealer is a fixture in consumer markets. Found in almost every city and town, these retailers stock and service a wide range of rubber for cars and trucks. Some of these stores are members of chain operations. Others are completely independent from manufacturer as well as from a national or regional organization. Still other tire retailers are franchise operations.

There was a time when most of the major American tire companies welcomed franchisees. B. F. Goodrich, General Tire, and U.S. Rubber (now Uniroyal) reached consumers through licensed independent stores. The cause of the demise of franchised distribution in the tire industry can be laid on foreign competition. When independent merchants were blocked from buying tires made in the United States, manufacturers from Europe, Japan and Korea quickly filled the void. In today's market, Goodyear Tire and Rubber is one of the few firms that still sells through franchised stores, and that may not be for long.

In 1992, Goodyear inked a contract to sell its tires through Sears. This opened a tremendous opportunity for both firms, but caused no end of concern to Goodyear's franchisees. The pinch was felt especially hard in smaller communities, where these licensed retailers had a difficult time competing with a major chain such as Sears. Many of these franchisees are threatening to either dump Goodyear completely or take on additional lines from overseas.

SOURCE: Zachary Schiller, "Goodyear is gunning its marketing engine," *Business Week,* March 16, 1992, p. 42.

be adequately serviced, the producer may choose to establish its own retail outlets. Birkenstock owns or franchises shoe stores, as does Florsheim. Men's clothing manufacturer Hartmarx operates the Kuppenheimer chain of clothiers. Standard Oil of California sells through company owned Standard stations as well as through Chevron dealers. If a consumer wants to buy Sinclair paint, she or he must go to a Sinclair paint store.

Some manufacturers have set up their own wholesale operations to better control the flow of their products. Appliance manufacturer Whirlpool created its in-house subsidiary, Quality Express, for this purpose. By dedicating its trucks, space and personnel to wholesaling, this firm services its total market from eight locations. Delivery of Whirlpool, KitchenAid, Estate and Roper appliances occurs within 24 hours to over 90 percent of the company's retailer customers. By taking these distributor functions in-house, Whirlpool reduces the amount of capital tied up in inventory by retailers.[10]

---

[10]Editors, "Whirlpool's Quality Express a JIT distribution system for retailers," *Appliance Manufacturer,* February 1992, p. 6.

OF SERVICES

The distribution of services is usually direct from the provider to the customer. Gardeners and auto mechanics do not work through wholesalers. The advertising agency and management consultant deal directly with their clients. In some occasions, brokers act as intermediaries, especially with consumer services. Travel agents and real estate brokers are good examples.

The expansion of the distribution of services usually requires adding additional facilities or personnel. An accounting office can only handle so much work. As the load increases, computerization becomes increasingly important. At some point, added bookkeepers or tax experts may be the only answer. Some service providers increase their hours of operation to handle larger numbers of customers. Some banks are even open on Saturdays.

IN GLOBAL MARKETS

The major distribution concern for global marketers is managing within the often cumbersome framework of existing channels. This is especially true in Pacific Rim countries, particularly Japan, where multiple levels of intermediaries are common. Instead of selling through wholesalers to retailers as may be the case in the U.S., a trade goods exporter may face four or five different distributors in the typical Japanese channel. Many firms, when faced with these challenges, resort to direct marketing.

The sometimes poor infrastructure found in many foreign countries adds to the distribution burden. Inadequate roads and railways often translate into sizable delays in reaching markets. The lack of sufficient or refrigerated storage facilities also creates problems for multinationals. Businesses from advanced industrialized nations typically export more services, including the engineering and development of infrastructure, due to the problems of physical distribution.

SUMMING IT UP

Distribution systems are the pipelines through which products flow. Marketing intermediaries provide the functions of limiting the number of transactions, breaking bulk, sorting and assorting, storage and transportation, promotion, marketing research and special services. Trade goods are channeled from the manufacturer through wholesalers, sometimes agents or brokers, and retailers to the ultimate destination, the consumer. Production goods channels are usually direct from manufacturers to user, sometimes with the help of agents. Some operating supplies are channeled through industrial distributors.

The size and shape of the channel is determined by product, market and producer characteristics. Larger, more valuable, perishable or complex goods travel shorter channels. Market size and order size have impact. The manufacturer's product mix and financial strength is influential. The extent of the distribution system can be intensive, selective or exclusive. In trade goods channels, electronic data interchange is a common method of inventory control. Just-in-time is prevalent in production goods arenas.

The modes of transportation include highway, rail, water, air and pipeline. Trucks offer the most flexible service, reaching the most locations. Trains are less expensive than trucks, but are limited where they can travel and are less reliable. Water transportation is the least expensive, but is slow and does not offer as much cargo protection. Air freight is the speediest mode of transportation, but is the most expensive. Pipelines are the most reliable in on-time performance and lack of damage, but are limited to liquid or gas cargoes.

Private freight carriers are owned by the shipper. Common carriers collect freight from multiple shippers under published rates and schedules. Some shippers contract with independent firms for their freight needs. Freight forwarders do not own their own vehicles, but collect small shipments that they then send by common or contract carriers. Express companies specialize in quick delivery of small parcels.

Storage of trade goods is often handled by distribution centers owned by manufacturers or retailers. Some firms use public warehouses. Management of distribution systems evolves around fair and equitable treatment for all channel members. Channel conflict and competition are additional concerns.

KEY CONCEPTS AND TERMS FROM CHAPTER TWELVE

Break bulk
Channel of distribution
Common carrier
Contract carrier
Distribution
Distribution center
Electronic data interchange
Exclusive distribution
Express company
Freight forwarder

Gypsy
Integrated distribution system
Intensive distribution
Intermodal
Just-in-time
Mode of transportation
Private carrier
Public warehouse
Selective distribution

BUILDING SKILLS

1. Describe the functions of intermediaries handling tomato ketchup, automobiles, woodworking tools, stationery and writing implements, designer jeans.

2. Contrast the distribution channels for Esprit apparel, Tom's peanuts and snacks, Rockport footwear, Sharp copying machines, Timex watches.

3. Explain how a JIT system works and the types of businesses that would benefit from just-in-time.

4. Identify the modes of transportation that might work best for shipping wheat and corn from Iowa to an export center for shipment to the Mideast, transporting silicon chips from San Jose to Boston, sending 400 cases of Wheaties from General Mills in Minneapolis to a distribution center in Atlanta.

5. Discuss transportation systems, commenting on the differences between the types of carriers.

6. Contrast the warehousing systems that might be best for a peanut butter producer located in Spokane, Washington, expanding to cover Texas and Oklahoma, General Motors introducing a new pickup truck, Coca-Cola opening up markets in Russia.

7. Discuss channel conflict and its impact on integrated distribution systems.

Making Decisions 12-1: Takin' a Coke break.

The coffee break is a tradition of American industry. Many firms spell out the rules and times for these rest periods in hiring policies and union contracts. Other companies follow more liberal procedures allowing workers to take time away from their stations whenever necessary. The methods used may differ, but the intent is the same. A break in the work schedule benefits both the worker and the business.

Although rest periods have long been called coffee breaks, a variety of other drinks and snacks are part of "the break." Many office areas and employee lounges are equipped with microwave ovens. The marvelous aromas of popcorn or baked sweet rolls wafting out of these regions draw other employees to take a break. Some forward thinking firms equip these areas with vending machines that dispense a variety of "nukable" merchandise.

To take advantage of this American business custom, the Coca-Cola Company introduced a countertop, soft drink dispenser. The Breakmate machine, sold or leased through Coca-Cola bottlers, fits comfortably in small areas where larger cola dispensers would be out of place. Offices with twenty to fifty employees and small retail operations are the primary targets for this equipment. So far, Coca-Cola has distributed over 50,000 Breakmates, and the outlook for greater numbers looks good.[11]

Describe the distribution channel selected by Coca-Cola and the factors that have affected the shape and size of this system.

Making Decisions 12-2: Beep, Beep!

Much of the industrial growth of America can be traced to the development of sophisticated transportation systems. The spread of commerce across this vast continent would have been a nearly impossible task without trains and trucks. Initially, the "iron horse" opened up the west, but as rail systems grew so did the need for local delivery by highway. Soon the flexibility offered in shipping by truck was realized by manufacturers and intermediaries everywhere. The ultimate in cooperation between these modes of transportation is the development of intermodal "piggyback" systems. Today, much of the freight hauled by trains travels in the bellies of trucks riding the rails.

The influence of trucks on the growing economy was felt most in 1980, when the deregulation of the industry led to growth by smaller firms. Prior to this time, the federal government controlled and doled out the operating rights between major cities; major carriers received most of the grants. When government decided to get out of the trucking industry, the door was opened for smaller, more efficient and lower cost shippers. Werner Enterprises was one of those companies that blossomed.

This contract carrier, operating out of Omaha, Nebraska, has grown to a fleet of over 3,000 trucks, and twice that number of trailers.

---

[11]John R. Emshwiller, Michael J. McCarthy, "Coke's soda fountain for offices fizzles, dashing high hopes," *The Wall Street Journal*, June 14, 1993, p. A1; "Fountain business opens up in offices," *Beverage World*, February 1991, p. 48; David Kiley, "Coke's Breakmate machine finds wide acceptance," *Adweek's Marketing Week*," September 25, 1989, pp. 38–39.

The company hauls for retailers such as Sears and Target, as well as for trade goods marketers like Kellogg and Frito-Lay. Expansion into temperature-controlled rigs has opened up even more opportunity.

Advanced equipment and new technologies have increased the versatility of the trucking industry. Computerization of tracking systems and sophisticated loading operations help truckers adapt to the just-in-time philosophy required of modern transportation systems. All Werner trucks are

(Courtesy Werner Enterprises)

equipped with portable computers connected to headquarters via satellite. In addition, a change in marketing attitude is leading toward more cooperation with other modes, notably rail, to increase proficiency and performance. Stressing the need to provide customer service, trucks are expanding their image as the most flexible member of the transportation industry.[12]

Describe the various modes of transportation evaluated, including the industries or products that benefit the most from each.

aking Decisions 12-3: Reebok on the run.

Few manufacturers would claim that their distribution systems are flawless. Making sure that their products reach consumers in the best manner has long been the goal of marketing managers. While many trade goods houses have excellent, time proven channels, it does not mean that all members of the system are equally cooperative. Conflict is common in these pipelines.

Sometimes the channel members are at fault for not giving proper service to the makers' brands. On other occasions it may be the manufacturer who drops the ball. Whatever the cause, when channel conflict appears, no one benefits.

The sneaker game is especially competitive. Nike and Reebok are the stars, and the battle is fierce. One area that Nike has dominated is sales

[12]John Labate, "Werner Enterprises," Companies to Watch section of *Fortune*, November 29, 1993, p. 105.

to local schools. In late 1991, management at Reebok decided to go after this market in a big way. Number 2 in sales, Reebok created a team-sales department that began making direct calls on athletic departments at high schools and colleges. This strategy generated increased sales for Reebok in this market, but alienated a number of the company's retailers.

Some Reebok outlets actively sought out this lucrative, volume business. When Reebok began taking orders direct, it cut these stores out of the market. The manufacturer countered with the argument that many of its outlets were pushing shoes from arch rival Nike rather than Reeboks. When the channel conflict flared up, Reebok managers quickly developed the Team Sports Network, which included cross-referenced local retailers, tying them into an 800 number system. Hopefully, such cooperative efforts will soothe the touchy situation.[13]

Discuss how channel conflict arises and how it can be minimized.

---

[13]Debra Aho and Jeff Jensen, "Reebok gravitates to cyberspace," *Advertising Age,* June 13, 1994, p. 24; Matthew Grimm, "Reebok's direct sales spark retail revolt," *Adweek's Marketing Week,* December 2, 1991, p. 7.

Figure #11—ad reprint—Dysan

Dysan uses clever advertising to promote the value of its products. (Courtesy of Dysan International)

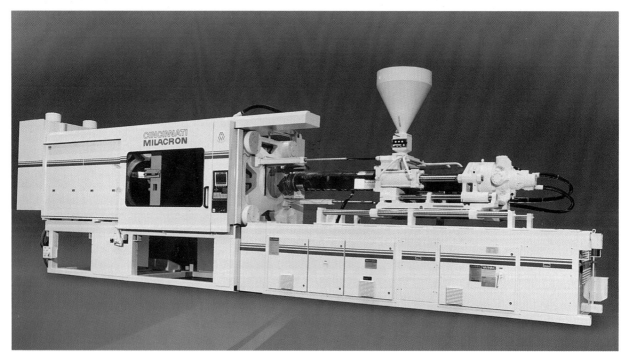

F igure #13—ad reprint—Milacron machinery
Heavy, bulky production equipment, such as this injection molding machine from Cincinnati Milacron,
demands short channels of distribution (Courtesy of Cincinnati Milacron)

You don't have to dress up to strip anymore.

Now there's a paint and varnish remover that doesn't require protective clothing: new Safest Stripper™ Paint and Varnish remover from 3M. It's easy. It's effective. And, because it contains no methylene chloride, it has no unpleasant odors, no harmful fumes and it won't harm wood or skin. Just apply a thick coat and let

©1989 3M

it set to fully soften the old finish. It won't lose its effectiveness, even after sitting all night. So you can complete the entire project at once. It's part of the wood refinishing system from 3M. With a fresh new approach to virtually every refinishing problem, the

system is available at finer stores everywhere. For the dealer nearest you, call us toll free at 1-800-548-6527 or in Canada 1-800-263-2856. Because when it comes to refinishing, 3M has you covered.

3M

Figure #14–ad reprint–3M

With a widely diversified product mix, 3M advertises using a variety of media and messages (Courtesy of 3M)

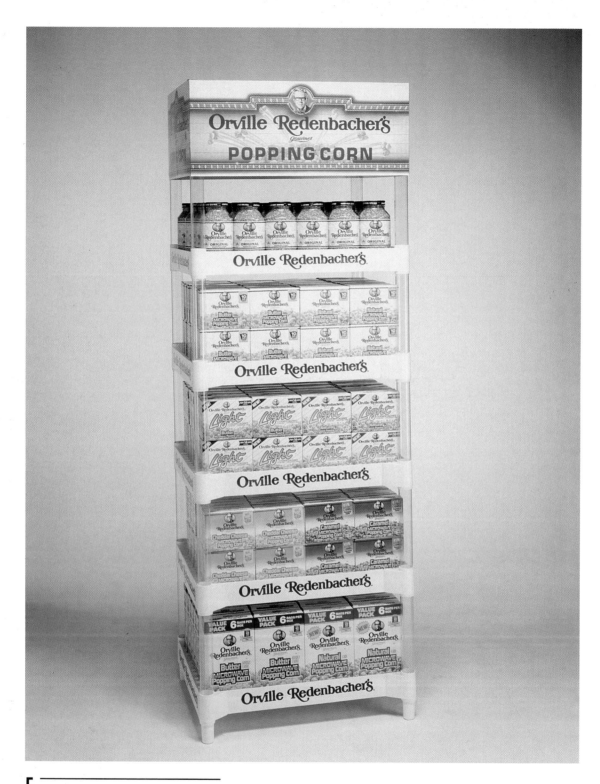

Figure #15—photo—Reddenbacher display

The Orville Reddenbacher division of Hunt-Wesson expands its distribution by placing these attractive point-of-purchase displays in video rental stores. (Courtesy of Hunt-Wesson Inc.)

13
Wholesaling

∎　∎　∎　∎　∎　∎　∎　∎　∎　∎　∎　∎　∎

The Job to be Done

Trade goods make a few stopovers en route to consumers. Most of these products go through wholesalers, businesses that buy and resell products to other businesses. Chapter 13 explores the roles played by these intermediaries, enabling the student to:

- describe wholesaling and the functions of wholesalers,
- contrast the benefits and the problems in using wholesalers,
- categorize wholesalers by type, function and industries served, and
- recognize and analyze the factors influencing the management of wholesaling.

Mike Arlint

Wholesalers form an integral part of the distribution system for many trade goods marketers. These intermediaries provide much more than just the storage of goods. Serving as an extension of the manufacturing company, these intermediaries form a link between the producer and the consumer. Buying, sorting, stocking and transporting goods through retailers, these distributors must keep in touch with the pulse of the market. Wholesaler salespeople form the connection that keeps the entire channel of distribution humming.

Glacier Wholesalers Inc., operating out of Kallispell, Montana, is typical of the many firms in the distribution system. Locally owned, the firm has been in operation for over fifty years. Although the mainstay of the business has been the distribution of candy and tobacco products to local retailers, the firm also handles meat and produce to the restaurant trade. Glacier has doubled its capacity in recent years, adding lines of paper goods which it sells to hotels and food purveyors. Servicing customers within a 100-mile radius, this wholesaler relies upon its salespeople to not only handle its retailers but to bring back information regarding market conditions. Mike Arlint is just such an employee.

Mike is a product of the Trend Colleges system, a professional business school chain that operates in the Northwest. Besides the usual coursework, including an emphasis on marketing, he credits a strong attendance policy and strict dress code with preparing him for the world of business. The role-playing exercises that Trend emphasized in sales classes helped prepare him for the rigors of professional selling. Although Mike is on the road a lot in the Big Sky country that he calls home, his duties include overseeing customer service and new account development for the entire company. Mike Arlint epitomizes the entrepreneurial spirit and dedication that make wholesaling such an important part of the American business scene.

What Is Wholesaler?

The federal government classifies all sales that are not made directly to the consumer as wholesale transactions. This description would obviously take in all business goods. However, most of this market involves the sale of products by manufacturers to other producers. To clarify the position and functions of these intermediaries, this text considers wholesaling as the reselling of trade goods to retailers and supplies to industrial users.

One reason why many people have difficulty understanding wholesaling is that most of us never come into contact with this type of business. Consumers make their purchases from retailers. Many assume that stores and markets receive their merchandise directly from the manufacturer. On the contrary, most consumer goods pass through wholesalers en route to the retail establishment.

WHOLESALER DEFINED

Wholesaler—
marketing intermediary that resells goods to other businesses.

Wholesalers are marketing intermediaries that resell the products that they purchase to other businesses, primarily to retailers. Although some resellers advertise "wholesale to the public," wholesale businesses do not sell to consumers.

As members of the distribution system, these firms perform many of the functions necessary to satisfy retail customers. Without these intermediaries, the shelves of grocery, hardware and drug stores would be practically empty.

Manufacturers sell in large quantities to wholesalers, who in turn sell smaller lots to retailers or other businesses. While fewer in numbers than outlets selling to consumers, these resellers form a substantial part of the distribution system. It is sometimes suggested by an uneducated public that wholesaling does little more than contribute cost to goods without adding benefits. On the contrary, if these businesses did not carry out specific tasks, these functions would have to be borne by another firm within the distribution system.

The wholesale trade forms the closest link to the manufacturer. Therefore, prices paid for goods are lower on the wholesale level than they are in retail. Since consumer goods may pass through several resellers, the wholesale industry is greater than its retail counterpart.

hat Benefits Do Wholesalers Provide?

For those who understand distribution systems, the value of wholesalers cannot be questioned. The margin of profit in the wholesale industry is very low, yet these resellers are invaluable channel members. These firms furnish benefits to the manufacturer, to other members of the distribution system and ultimately, to the consumer. Wholesalers provide freedom of choice, cost savings, financial assistance and special services to all parties within the channel.

CHOICE

One of the major benefits of a free market society is the **freedom of choice.** Consumers are royalty when it comes to dictating what goods and services are needed. If consumers neither need nor want any given product, manufacturers will not produce it. It is the distribution systems that provide the vehicles for maintaining consumer sovereignty. Wholesalers are an important part of that system.

For example, the number of outlets where the consumer can purchase Pepsi Cola or Wrigley's spearmint gum are staggering. Servicing of these millions of retail firms would be an impossible task for either PepsiCo or Wrigley. By selling to a limited number of wholesalers, manufacturers of these consumer goods make their distribution systems manageable. Without these intermediaries, producers might have difficulty realizing wide distribution of their products.

In trade goods channels, retailers benefit from having one source for a wide variety of goods. Wholesalers buy many more items than soft drinks or chewing gum. The number and variety of goods offered by these resellers benefits retailers by providing the assortment of merchandise that consumers demand. Without wholesalers, consumer selection could suffer.

Global Marketing: Has China Gone Green?

American agriculture is unquestionably the most fruitful in the world, with levels of technology and productivity not found elsewhere on the globe. It is a point of frustration for many famers that the crops they raise in abundance are often stymied from going to other economies worldwide. Too often the blockage seems to stem from the resistance to imported goods by other countries. China is no exception.

As the worlds most populous country, China holds much promise as a market for many goods. Still largely an agrarian economy, the "Giant Dragon" is lurching toward acceptance of many free market tenets. Much of the agriculture in this huge territory is still quite primitive. In many provinces, tilling the land is still done using animals for power. Irrigation, when pre-

sent, often consists of crude, gravity feed devices long ago abandoned in America.

Yet, with a seemingly large potential for importing farm products from the United States, China still blocks such trade activity. For example, although a small portion of American wheat contains a fungus, Beijing uses this excuse to limit the tonnage allowed to cross its borders. No, China has not suddenly "gone green," but rather is simply trying to protect its own agricultural community from outside, more efficient competition. Producer cooperatives in this country face the constant battle of trying to get around provincial Chinese regulations.

SOURCE: Douglas Harbrecht and Joyce Barnathan, "And you thought Japan's trade hurdles were high," *Business Week*, December 12, 1994, p. 57.

COST SAVINGS

The use of wholesalers can produce a **cost savings.** For instance, the manufacturer's selling costs are lower when using wholesalers. Fewer customer contacts mean fewer dollars spent. Retailers also benefit from the reduced number of transactions. To illustrate, instead of making thousands of telephone calls or internet messages to fill its shelves, a typical supermarket deals with only one or two wholesalers. The time savings by using these intermediaries reduces personnel requirements and frees management for customer related tasks.

Additionally, transportation costs go down. Shipping in larger quantities results in lower freight rates. By using wholesalers, manufacturers ship in bulk, knowing that these intermediaries will break the shipment into smaller, more manageable units. Offering a wide and deep assortment of merchandise from a variety of manufacturers, wholesalers fill large and diverse orders to many retailers. To better affect delivery, many of these resellers run their own vehicles.

Storage costs go down when using a multiple member distribution system. Retailers do not have to carry as much inventory if the wholesaler has a backup stock readily available. Retail establishments occupy more expensive floor space than do wholesalers, hence a reduction in the room needed to store

Wholesaler services

FOR MANUFACTURER	FOR RETAILER
Reduction of storage space at producer's place by warehousing finished goods	Additional storage capacity as a readily available backup for retailer's inventory
Purchase of finished goods as produced providing immediate income and ready cash-flow	Providing wide assortment of merchandise from a variety of manufacturers creating less paperwork for retailer and allowing greater choice for ultimate consumer
Increasing the selling activity for the manufacturer, thereby lowering selling costs and improving efficiency	Supplying a variety of value-added services for retailers, including store layout/design, automated ordering and improved product
Reduce both credit problems and risk by eliminating need for manufacturer to deal with small, credit-risk retailers	Enhancing retailer buying power supplying credit and financial assistance to small, credit-risk retailers

■ ■ ■ ■ ■

goods can mean sizable savings to these firms. Wholesale firms, on the other hand, usually locate in lower cost industrial areas, where larger space is not as expensive. This reduction in overall costs often means lower prices to the ultimate consumer.

FINANCIAL ASSISTANCE

All three of the major members of distribution systems benefit from the financial assistance wholesalers offer. Manufacturers have to carry fewer accounts, which translates into less headaches and lower costs. Since wholesalers and retailers share a kindred relationship within the system, credit between them is usually handled more easily. Manufacturers might be hesitant to grant open account status to small retailers, but wholesalers may bend a little to help these firms.

New markets for the merchandise stocked by wholesalers grow through the credit function. As these retailers are able to gain financial assistance from their suppliers, they in turn are in a better position to pass similar arrangements on to their customers. Without the credit assistance from wholesalers, many small retail shops and stores might not be able to offer consumer credit.

SPECIAL SERVICES

As members of the distribution channel, wholesalers must carry out any number of tasks to satisfy the ultimate needs of consumers. Retailers are typically called upon, when necessary, to add value to the product to please the consumer. It may be rare that wholesalers would provide extras that actually reach the ultimate buyer, but these firms can deliver services to their customers. Value added service has become an important competitive tool for wholesalers in any field.

More and more wholesalers realize the value of assisting their retailer customers. Some provide training, both in sales and management. Many help in designing store layout and security. Others have adopted policies that offer financial record keeping.

Marketing functions can be carried out by the manufacturer or by other channel members. No matter who does the work, the work must be done. If the producer cannot or will not supply the needed activities, the intermediaries must, or the product will simply die. Wholesalers are an important part of the entire marketing picture. These resellers provide benefit to the producer, retailer and consumer.

How are Wholesalers Categorized?

Wholesalers come in many shapes and sizes. Those firms common to one industry may be considered out of date in others. Since there is such a variety of wholesale functions and industries which are served, placing these resellers in little niches is a bit difficult. Fortunately, these intermediaries can be separated according to their basic functions. Some of these resellers carry out most of the intermediary operations; others provide only a few services. Most wholesalers work entirely within a given industry, but there are those that serve across product lines.

MERCHANT WHOLESALERS

Merchant wholesaler— intermediary that takes title to the merchandise.

Merchant wholesalers take title to the merchandise that they handle. There resellers account for over 75 percent of the sales of the entire wholesaling industry. Merchant wholesalers have a variety of names, such as distributor and jobber, and carry an unbelievable assortment of goods. They supply groceries, cosmetics, tools and a host of other consumer goods to supermarkets, drug stores and hardware outlets. These three industries account for a significant portion of the sales of non-automotive consumer products in the United States.

Although fewer in number, wholesale operators also deal in production goods. Called industrial distributors, these firms typically handle production and operating supplies. A typical plastics distributor, for example, will carry acrylic sheet, nylon and teflon rod, acetate and vinyl film, fiberglass and polyester resin, molded parts and a raft of other industrial polymers for any and all types of businesses.

Full Function vs Limited Function

Full function merchant wholesaler— carries out all of the intermediary functions.

These resellers are additionally classified by the number of intermediary functions that they perform. **Full function** merchant wholesalers buy and sell, sort and assort, store and arrange for transportation, offer credit, promote and break bulk. This category of wholesaler satisfies the needs of both marketer and retailer by economically providing the services necessary to channel products into the hands of consumers.

McKesson Drug Company, for example, is a full function merchant wholesaler working in the pharmaceutical industry. This firm supplies drug stores with a majority of the products needed to satisfy consumers. This full-service reseller supplies a wide assortment of prescription drugs, over-the-counter medicines, sundries and notions to its retailer customers. United Grocers and Fleming, full function merchant wholesalers in the grocery business, provide a similar service to supermarkets.

Although full function resellers are plentiful, many do not offer all these services. The **limited function** merchant wholesaler, as the name implies, omits several of the standard reseller activities. Some do not provide storage, and others eliminate offering credit to their retailer customers. Any reseller that does not provide the full range of functions is a limited function merchant wholesaler. These resellers can be found in any trade goods channel.

Limited function wholesaler—a merchant wholesaler carrying out a limited number of intermediary activities.

For example, in the restaurant supply industry, Sysco and Continental Food Services provide eateries with a full range of services. These wholesalers carry a wide assortment of merchandise, which they store, break into smaller quantities and deliver to customers, offering credit and marketing assistance as well. These same restaurants purchase much of their fresh produce from local vendors that are usually paid at the time of delivery. Other food brokers serving this industry often carry limited supplies of goods, preferring to have manufacturers drop ship to the ultimate customer.

General Line vs Specialty

Full function merchant wholesalers are usually classified as either generalists or specialists. A **general line** merchant wholesaler carries a variety of merchandise for a specific industry. Retailers within that field could purchase most of their needs from such a generalist. These firms are common in the grocery, hardware and pharmaceutical businesses. For example, General line grocery wholesalers carry most of what the average supermarket needs, including produce and dairy products.

General line wholesaler—serves a specific industry with a broad and deep line of merchandise.

General line wholesalers may provide either full or limited service. These giant resale organizations offer a full array of functions to their retailer customers. Fleming and United Grocers are general line wholesalers serving large supermarket chains and small, independent grocers. McLane provides similar services to the convenience market arena. In the pharmaceutical field, McKesson plays a similar role. Since more than one wholesaler is usually available to major buyers, competition is keen.

A **specialty line** distributor serves a specific industry with a limited line of merchandise. Specialty distributors supply certain key areas of grocery goods, such as frozen foods, seafood or gourmet items. These types of firms would provide drug outlets with soft goods, paper items and fishing tackle found in those retailers. In the hardware trade, general merchandise firms handle most of the goods needed by the multi-product building products or home improvement center. A specialty line house might carry only power tools from Skil.

Specialty line wholesaler—a merchant wholesaler serving a specific industry with a limited line of merchandise.

For nearly four decades, Carpenter high temperature alloys have quietly been doing their jobs.

We haven't earned the confidence of jet engine manufacturers by shouting about our high temperature alloys. Instead, for almost 40 years, we've produced alloys that have consistently met precise specifications and successfully done their jobs in high temperature environments.

Our alloys have demonstrated their ability to meet user specifications for mechanical properties and strength levels at elevated temperatures. Users have also confirmed benefits including easier fabrication and greater productivity. The strong performances of Carpenter high temperature alloys can be attributed to the modern, statistically controlled processes by which they are made. For example, our premium melting techniques, singly or in combination, produce alloys with consistently reliable structural integrity. Then, our rotary forge press, state-of-the-art rolling mill, bar finishing facilities

and immersion ultrasonic testing equipment are put to work . . . allowing us to make sure our alloys meet your critical specifications, lot to lot, order after order.

We back up these superior manufacturing capabilities with the support of metallurgists and other specialists who can help you meet material challenges and make the best use of your high temperature alloys.

When your operations demand high temperature grades with a proven track record, look to Carpenter. Your nearby service center is a mere phone call away.

CARPENTER TECHNOLOGY

CARPENTER STEEL DIVISION • READING, PA 19612

CARTECH®

High Temperature Alloys Ad # 1-89/90

Carpenter uses trade journal advertising to generate leads for its wholesaler customers. (Courtesy Carpenter Technology Corporation)

Manufacturers of major product lines often use specialty line wholesalers. These marketers believe that large, multi-line intermediaries might not provide the aggressive promotion that their products need. Smaller, specialty wholesalers are usually the answer. In addition, these resale outlets handle product lines that are a nuisance or bother to larger firms. Gourmet foods provide a substantial profit margin for supermarkets, but the small volume in these areas make it unattractive for giant, general merchandise wholesalers. A specialty line house would be more than happy with lower volume but substantial profit.

Rack jobbers fill retailer shelves, usually in non-food areas like magazines, with consignment merchandise.

Rack Jobber

The **rack jobber** is an unusual full function merchant wholesaler. Similar to general merchandise and specialty line resellers, rack jobbers take title to the merchandise and perform most of the intermediary functions. In addition, these firms stock their retailer customers' shelves with consignment merchandise. Besides carrying out inventory functions, rack jobbers often waive payment until after the retailer's fixtures have been refilled.

For example, these merchant wholesalers handle many of the nonfood items found in supermarkets and grocery stores. Rack jobbers handling magazines, toys, hardware or clothing fill the allotted spaces in supermarkets or drug emporiums every week or two. After counting the missing goods during the process of restocking the shelves, these wholesalers present an invoice to the store for the items that moved during the past period.

Rack jobber—a merchant wholesaler that stocks retailers' shelves with consignment goods.

Drop Shipper

Drop shippers are limited function merchant wholesalers. These firms purchase goods directly from the manufacturer, but do not take possession of them. Instead, the merchandise is shipped directly to the wholesaler's customers. Since drop shippers do not carry out the standard intermediary function of storage, they qualify as limited function merchant wholesalers.

When a drop shipper places an order with a manufacturer, the goods are billed to the wholesaler, but possession is never taken. Instead, the products travel straight to a retailer or other customer designated by the buyer. Drop shippers usually deal in bulky, difficult to handle goods, such as grains, lumber and heavy equipment.

Drop shipper—a merchant wholesaler that does not take possession of goods shipped directly to its customers.

Truck Jobber

Truck jobber—a merchant wholesaler that sells produce from its vehicles to grocery retailers on a cash basis.

Truck jobbers work in the grocery business. This type of distributor does not store the merchandise and often will not grant credit. These retailers qualify as typical limited function merchant wholesalers. As their name implies, truck jobbers usually use their own vehicles to pick up and deliver the merchandise. This type of wholesaler can also be found, in limited numbers, distributing tobacco, candy and dairy products to a variety of industries.

The fruits and vegetables general merchandise wholesalers sell are usually collected at a distribution center and held in refrigerated areas until reshipped to the retailer. Truck jobbers gather produce from local farmers and deliver directly to the grocery store or supermarket. The produce these wholesalers carry is fresher and of higher quality. Truck jobbers are usually paid in cash at time of delivery.

Producers Cooperative

Producer cooperative—a limited function merchant wholesaler, owned by its suppliers, that collects and resells farm products.

Producer cooperatives are another form of wholesaler common to the food industry. These firms are limited functions wholesalers, owned by their suppliers, that collect and resell farm products to the grocery processing industry. Coops vary in the number of tasks carried out, ranging from complete, full function organizations to one that only store the goods. Typically, growers create these intermediaries so that they can have a united voice in the marketing of their farm products.

Many cooperatives are publicly owned organizations that sell and promote private label goods nationally. Some of the better known names among producer cooperatives include Sunkist, Welches, Ocean Spray and Land O'Lakes. These wholesalers add the service of branding to their operations. By marketing agricultural products under a single brand name and symbol, the producer cooperative gains status and position that would be nearly impossible for individual growers.[1]

Cash-and-Carry Wholesalers

Cash and carry—a limited function merchant wholesaler that does not offer credit or delivery.

Cash-and-carry wholesalers are limited function merchant resellers that usually do not offer credit or delivery service. These intermediaries were prominent during the depression years of the 1930s, but have dwindled since. Today, cash-and-carry wholesalers typically service small grocery outlets and restaurants. They carry rather limited lines of merchandise and do very little promotion.

The quantity of merchandise these intermediaries carry is usually low. In addition, these resale houses often feature a few select products that may be closeouts or over orders from manufacturers. Restaurants often create their menus based upon what particular food or beverages a cash-and-carry wholesaler features on a given day. Restaurateurs who utilize these intermediaries often will not put together a bill of fare without assurance that the ingredients are available.

---

[1]Steve Dwyer, "Farm co-ops raising stakes at retail level," *National Petroleum News*, July 1993, p. 16; Corie Brown, Mary Pitzer, and Teresa Carson, "Why farm co-ops need extra seed money," *Business Week*, March 21, 1988, p. 96.

Wholesaler types and the functions performed

TYPE	FUNCTIONS
General merchandise	Break bulk, sort and assort, storage, transportation*, promotion, credit, marketing research
Specialty line	Break bulk, sort and assort, storage, transportation*, promotion, credit, marketing research
Rack jobber	Break bulk, sort and assort, storage, transportation, promotion, credit, marketing research, restock**
Drop shipper	Break bulk, sort and assort, promotion, credit
Producer cooperative	Sort, storage, promotion, credit, marketing research
Truck jobber	Break bulk, sort and assort, storage, transportation
Cash-and-carry	Break bulk, sort and assort, storage, transportation* promotion
Mail order	Break bulk, sort and assort, storage, promotion

*not all firms in all cases

**fill shelves for retail customers

Note: The promotion activity of wholesalers is primarily a selling function, including telemarketing.

■ ■ ■ ■ ■

Mail-Order House/Desk Jobber

An additional type of limited function merchant wholesaler is a **mail-order house.** These firms should not be confused with retail establishments. Mail-order wholesalers, sometimes called **desk jobbers,** promote through catalogs. Like cash-and-carry firms, these wholesalers are few in numbers. They process orders received from their retail customers by phone, computer or mail. Typically, these companies carry a rather narrow and shallow inventory of merchandise.

Mail-order house—a limited function merchant wholesaler, often called desk jobber, that promotes through catalogs.

These firms fill requirements from stock, and ship by common carrier or express company. Desk jobbers are most common in the jewelry, cosmetics, sporting goods and automotive parts markets. Along with retailers, government agencies are major customers for mail-order wholesalers.

AGENTS AND BROKERS

Agents and brokers serve as a sales liaison between seller and buyer in many distribution channels. Unlike merchant wholesalers, these intermediaries do not take title to the merchandise, performing limited functions in their roles. As a rule, they do not break bulk, transport merchandise or offer credit. Agents and brokers are primarily salespeople. Although they can work for the buyer, these intermediaries usually represent the seller. Agents and brokers are compensated, as a rule, using straight commission.

Agents and brokers—marketing intermediaries serving as sales liaison between seller and buyer.

Many manufacturers who use representatives find that agents or brokers are more economical than salaried sales staffs. Since these intermediaries do not receive commissions until after the sale has been made, principals using agents incur no up-front selling costs. In addition, representatives cover their own expenses, including insurance policies, health benefits and retirement plans.

Besides being more economical, agent brokers add an air of professionalism to selling programs. Experts with years of experience in their fields staff these independent organizations. By concentrating on single industries, agents and brokers build closer relationships with customers. Company salespeople often carry multiple lines and frequently transfer from territory to territory.

As a rule, agents are considered to have long lasting relationships with the companies or individuals with whom they do business. These intermediaries typically work under a long term contract arrangement. A broker's job is usually of shorter term, often a one-time transaction. Although brokers have a contractual relationship with those who they represent, the duration is usually not as long.

Manufacturers' Representatives

**Manufacturers'
representative**—an
agent that sells for
several manufacturers,
or principals.

Agents and brokers are known by many names, including selling agents, commission merchants and merchandise brokers. Although the functions of these types of intermediaries vary slightly, they are correctly labeled **manufacturers' representatives** or **agents.** These intermediaries personally sell the merchandise made by the principals whom they represent. Principal is the name given to the manufacturing companies. Manufacturers' representatives commonly operate in production goods industries. For example, Owens Corning Fiberglass acts as the principal contracting with manufacturers' representatives who sell that firm's line of glass fibers and cloth.

Depending on the industry, a manufacturers' representative may carry a single line, representing just one company, or may have several principals. Most commonly, the agent, or agency, handles six to eight product lines from different producers or principals. Some of these agencies are individuals, while others are multi-person corporations.

Many producers'
cooperatives market
their own private label
brands.

Manufacturers' representatives typically have a long term, contractual relationship with principals. Selling agents sometimes earn a retainer or some form of salary, but usually manufacturers' representatives receive a commission on the products that they sell. Depending upon the industry, commissions can range from 1 to 15 percent.

Although there are exceptions, manufacturers' representatives typically do not carry competing lines. Most of the principals represented by agents manufacture complimentary products. A manufacturers' representative in the packaging industry, for example, might handle several different material and machinery lines that do not compete for the same business. In calling upon potential customers, the representative can offer solutions to a variety of problems because of the different items carried.

Food Brokers

Food brokers are manufacturers' representatives unique to the grocery industry. These representatives typically carry merchandise lines from several manufacturers. Similar to other agents, these companies do not store or deliver merchandise. Most brokers carry sampling stock. This small quantity of goods provides test quantities and sometimes helps customers in emergency situations.

Consumer Services Brokers

Real estate and **stock brokers** are agents commonly found in consumer services industries. Because these sellers are more familiar to the average person, their functions are easy to understand. These intermediaries carry out exactly the same tasks as manufacturers' representatives handling production goods. Their limited activities consist primarily of selling.

Consumer services brokers usually work on a sale-by-sale basis. After the property or stock is sold, the relationship between agent and principal ceases. This is contrary to the role of manufacturers' representatives who often enjoy a long-term contractual relationship with their principals. Agents working for buyers are more common in real estate than in other industries.

Auction Houses

Another type of broker deserving mention is the **auction house.** This type of intermediary sells both consumer and business goods. Tobacco, livestock, used cars and works of art typically sell through auction houses. Like other brokers, these firms provide sales assistance and do not take title to the merchandise. Auction houses conduct sales either at their own places of business, the seller's location or in public areas.

Branch Office and Sales Office

Many manufacturers conduct business through branch or selling offices. These locations act similarly to agents, but are not independently owned and operated. Manufacturer's branch offices are typically warehouse facilities that operate in much the same manner as wholesalers. These extensions of the producer stock merchandise and ship against orders received. As a rule, branch offices carry out selling and administrative functions as well.

Sales offices are merely outposts owned and managed by the manufacturer that house a selling staff. These outlets are extensions of the sales department of the manufacturer. An Alcoa office in Rochester, the General Dynamics group in Houston and the sales staff of Duracell in Southern California are units of the parent corporation. Although often mistakenly called intermediaries, branch offices are truly extensions of the selling and marketing arm of the manufacturer, not an agent or broker.

Marts

In some industries, notably home furnishings, accessories, jewelry and garments, agents often work out of a central location called a **mart.** A mart is a location, not an intermediary. Manufacturers and representatives alike share floor space in these large buildings, normally located in major metropolitan areas. Retailers and other business clients travel to these locations and visit the many outlets that are available.

By locating in marts, selling agencies attract buyers who can view the merchandise in a showroom setting and visit more than one supplier. Retailers in certain fields find the use of marts to be a convenient way to do their "shopping." Marts also sell to professional specialists, such as interior designers, and are not generally open to the public.

What Influences the Management of Wholesaling?

As is the case in the management of any facet of marketing, there are no set rules covering the governing of wholesalers. Some manufacturers lose sight of

Duracell operates regional sales branches throughout the country.

the fact that these resellers are independent businesses. A heavy handed, autocratic style usually does not sit well with any type of intermediary. Although they should not necessarily be pampered, wholesalers should be treated with the same respect and consideration that would be paid to any customer.

TRENDS IN WHOLESALING

The world of wholesaling has gone through major changes in the past decade and faces even more upheaval. Once dominated by small, "mom and pop" warehouses, this area of distribution now features large, marketing oriented aggressive organizations. Weak or unimaginative resellers have been acquired or have merged with bigger, well-managed intermediaries. Once the doormats of the channel, wholesalers are taking their places as vital, sometimes controlling, members of their systems.

Once somewhat ignored by regulatory agencies, wholesalers are now being carefully watched by the Federal Trade Commission. To assure fair trade, the FTC keeps a wary eye on mergers and acquisitions. As more intermediaries join forces in quest of greater power and control, a greater potential for restraint looms. To combat the increased might of giant wholesale firms, manufacturers often develop their own, integrated channels.[2]

In times of recession, wholesalers suffer along with other resellers. When consumer purchasing is down, retail sales decline, causing a resultant drop in business for wholesalers. Distributors grow in strength as they learn to make their organizations more efficient. For example, early in the 1990s, Merisel International Incorporated, a wholesale house handling personal computers, inked a deal with Compaq. This agreement strengthened the wholesaler's position in its market. Ace Hardware Corporation and W. W. Grainger Incorporated, two well-known names in industrial distribution, fared well in tough times by increasing efficiency and expanding product lines.[3]

VALUE-ADDED SERVICE AND DEALER BRANDS

At one time, the primary function of wholesalers was storage. Firms in this field were content to warehouse goods for manufacturers and contributed little else in the way of intermediary activity. The selling effort to retailer consisted of phone calls to ask if anything was needed. Since retailers were limited in the number of product sources that were available, wholesalers became a complacent lot.

As the wholesaling market heated up, retailers found more than one firm handling the goods they needed to fill their shelves. The sting of competition woke up this sleepy market. Well-managed wholesalers realized that their companies had to offer more to both their suppliers and their customers. Looking for ways to beat rivals, the wise intermediaries began to offer extras to satisfy manufacturers and retailers.

---

[2]J. Uhlenberg, "Who needs distributors?" *Industrial Distribution*, November, 15, 1991, p. 25.
[3]Joseph Weber, "It's like somebody shot the postman," *Business Week*, January 13, 1992, p. 82.

The computerized order handling and billing system at C&S Wholesalers provides management with up-to-date information while servicing customers.

The concept of value-added services, old hat in the retailing arena, blossomed among wholesalers. These resellers began to provide more service to both supplier and customer. Computerized systems offering current and complete marketing research information to producers are now common. Both McKesson and Bergen Brunswig, the country's two largest drug wholesalers, provide in-store design and merchandising assistance to their accounts. C&S Wholesale, Incorporated, a grocery reseller working the Northeast, provides custom billing systems that give retailers more flexibility in dealing directly with manufacturers. This computerized system provides forecasting models and management reports to C&S's customers and suppliers.[4]

Many wholesalers joined the value added bandwagon, only to find profits dwindling. In offering additional services, some firms neglected to determine costs and failed to charge for them. Many of these options are expensive. In tight times, no firm can afford to ignore the added cost for value-added service. At the same time, companies most be mindful of competition. Charging for services when rivals do not can force customers to look elsewhere. A software package for value-added services is available.[5]

Another trend in wholesaling is the increased offering of dealer brands. To the dismay of some manufacturers, over 30 percent of these intermediaries stock their own branded merchandise. Since profit on house brands is higher than other merchandise, wholesalers are inclined to push these goods over other items. The use of dealer brands is bound to increase through the nineties, and manufacturers are making an effort to combat this trend.

[4]Kenneth Harris Jr., "Wholesale change is now, so wholesalers must change," *BRANDWEEK*, March 7, 1994, p. 14.

[5]Steve Zurrier, "Do you charge for Value Added?" *Industrial Distribution,* May 1992, pp. 30–32.

MANUFACTURER NEEDS

As in any business venture, there are pluses and minuses involved with the use of wholesalers. In the same fashion, some of these resellers do a better job than others. Depending upon the industries served and the intermediaries that are available, producers have the option on which wholesaler to use or not. Those who opt not to distribute through wholesalers find other ways to handle the functions often carried out by these resellers.

Many trade goods marketers realize the need for wholesalers. The rise of aggressive, customer oriented resellers is just what many producers have been looking for. On the other hand, manufacturers worry about the possible loss of control. As wholesalers become bigger and more powerful, they tend to exert more pressure to conduct business in a way that benefits them the most.

Manufacturers still look to wholesalers for storage and transportation of goods. Without this step, many trade goods marketers would be unable to function properly in supplying goods to the ultimate consumer. Producers also expect these intermediaries to provide adequate market coverage. Wholesalers need to show that they have the sales force and in-house staff necessary to cover the selected area.

Wholesalers provide help for the manufacturers whose products they sell and for their customers. Although these intermediaries are an integral part of many trade goods channels, there are some disadvantages in using them. Many producers feel more comfortable providing the services directly. Others rely more on their retailer channel members.

Many grocery wholesalers carry their own private label brands, such as United Grocers' line of Western Family products.

Loss of Control

The more members within the distribution chain, the more cumbersome inventory control becomes. The ultimate in control occurs when the producer sells directly to the consumer or user. Feedback on product and pricing is immediate. It would be a real advantage to greet the customer face-to-face and learn firsthand whether your products are satisfying or not. Few trade goods are sold through such a short channel.

The addition of intermediaries to the distribution system makes life easier for the manufacturer. However, this ease of operation often results in the loss of control. Trade goods producers have a more difficult time keeping attuned to the needs of the ultimate buyer when the distribution system becomes large and unwieldy. Without feedback from consumers, the risk of dissatisfaction grows. By selling directly to retailers, manufacturers have a closer link to the market.

Since intermediaries carry a variety of products from many manufacturers, the producer loses promotional control. Wholesalers or retailers may give time and emphasis to competing brands. Because of this lack of control, manufacturers may find their products bogged down in the system and not reaching the consumer when needed. Expensive promotional campaigns are fruitless when intermediaries fail to perform.

Competition

Competition from intermediaries is a major concern for manufacturers. Many wholesalers and some retailers carry their own brands of private label merchandise. Since the profit may be greater on these items, intermediaries often promote in-house over the other products that they carry. Competition from within the distribution system creates conflict.

Competition from other manufacturers dramatically affects channel make-up. Producers who use wholesalers may be in a noncompetitive situation when a rival chooses to bypass the wholesaler and sell direct. For example, if Procter & Gamble decided to sell its products directly to retailers, competitors who use channels that include wholesalers could be at a disadvantage. The added cost tacked on by these intermediaries might increase prices to the final customer, the consumer. By eliminating one intermediary, the retail prices on Procter & Gamble products might be less than those of its rivals.

Although many manufacturers in the food industry have abandoned these intermediaries, often over conflict with private label brands, wholesaling accounts for over 55 percent of the sales in this arena. The subject of control is touchy between the manufacturer and intermediary, yet wholesalers are expected to remain a dominant player in this field. While resellers need to be more aware of the needs of consumer goods suppliers, manufacturers also need to place greater emphasis on dealing with this important link with the retail trade.[6]

---

[6]Bill Wyman, "Marketers shouldn't give up on wholesalers just yet," *BRANDWEEK*, July 5, 1993, p. 13.

New Product Support

When introducing new products, manufacturers look to wholesale members of the channel for support. Producers typically select the best performers for these initial offerings. However, these firms need customer service and dealer education packages to succeed. Good communication is needed from both parties for the new items to move into the growth stage of the product life cycle. The objective of the manufacturer should be to move from selective to intensive distribution as soon as feasible.[7]

With competing firms available in many regions and industries, these resellers should provide service to the firms whose goods they handle. Producers prefer to deal with wholesalers that have good inventory control systems and that provide quick and accurate delivery. The computerization of distribution systems requires well-managed, trained and competent staffs at all levels.

WHOLESALER NEEDS

Although the term "middleman" is archaic, wholesalers are indeed in the center of the distribution channel. These firms must be continually aware of the needs of their manufacturer suppliers. At the other end of the pipeline, retailers also have specific requirements. These customers exert pressure on wholesalers to provide more than just goods.

Customer service oriented wholesalers, such as PepsiCo bottlers, provide more than just storage facilities.

[7]Elizabeth J. Wilson and Arch G. Woodside, "Marketing new products with distributors," *Industrial Marketing Management,* February 1992, pp. 15–21.

[8]Allan J. McGrath and Kenneth G. Hardy, "Manufacturer services for distributors," *Industrial Marketing Management,* May 1992, pp. 119–124.

Intermediaries are motivated by profit. Retailers look to their wholesalers for the goods that will produce a healthy bottom line. The wrong assortment of merchandise can be detrimental to all channel partners. The critical element in this relationship between buyer and seller is the supply of products. Stockouts create real problems for retailers. On time and accurate delivery, too, are vital.

Manufacturers must keep the needs of their wholesalers in mind when offering services. Providing "extras" without thought as to their benefit simply increases costs and lowers trust. Producers should look for incentives to increase the net income of its channel members. Quantity discounts and special allowances have a direct effect on improving margins. Other manufacturer efforts that lower wholesaler expenses or increase merchandise turns include joint sales calls, spiffs and cooperative advertising.[8]

Wholesalers must carry the assortment necessary to meet the needs of the many customers in the areas they serve. Brands, styles, shapes and prices may vary greatly between the stores and shops covered. Inventory control is crucial to success. Retailers often prefer to limit the number of suppliers with which they do business. Once these alliances are formed, they remain rather permanent. Retailers also look to their wholesaler suppliers for reasonable credit terms. At the crucial times of special sales or seasonal demands, retailers must feel confident that their wholesalers support them and their efforts.

ETHICS

Manufacturers have the basic desire to control the destiny of their products. They can accomplish this by establishing smooth running, efficient channels of distribution. Trade goods marketers can also manage the flow of their finished goods to the consumer by owning the intermediaries. Many manufacturers have purchased either the wholesaler or retailer sectors of the distribution system. Such practices are legal, so long as these in-house resellers do not receive merchandise or prices that are not available to independent intermediaries.

Wholesalers, too, are integrating with retailers. SuperValu, one of the largest wholesalers in the country, owns several retail operations, including Twin Valu and Cub. This firm must exercise unusual caution in dealing with all of its customers to assure that its own retail outlets do not receive preferential prices or treatment. Wholesalers that own retailers must be especially careful to avoid direct competition by establishing one of its own stores in areas serviced by other customers.

TECHNOLOGICAL CHANGE

One of the most significant steps made by wholesalers involves electronic data interchange. This inventory control and ordering system speeds the processing and delivery of most merchandise from most distributors. With more and more supermarket and drug chains opening their own distribution centers, prompt service becomes increasingly important for wholesalers. America's

Marketing and Society: Some Kind of Pipeline!

No segment of the business world is without sin. Money has a tendency to corrupt, and the business of business is to make money. On a large part, business people are law abiding and honest. As in any profession, a few bad actors are inclined to spoil the overall image of any marketing area. The metal pipe industry seemed to collect quite a few rotten eggs over the past twenty years. Most of these bad actors ended up in a trade association known as the Pipe Fabrication Institute.

This now defunct organization was actually the clearinghouse for one of the biggest price-fixing conspiracies in the history of American business. The members of PFI were wholesalers and fabricators of metal pipe. Steel mills, which were never implicated in the scam, sold their pipe products through industrial distributors, who in turn supplied the fabricator. Pipe customers, notably power companies, refineries, and chemical plants, purchased special orders from the fabricators on a cost-plus basis. The wholesalers, partly through their association in PFI, acted in collusion to artificially inflate the cost to the fabricators, splitting the differences with their customers.

This long-lasting con game began to unravel when the Washington Public Power Supply System got into trouble in the mid 1980s. WPPSS sold millions of dollars worth of bonds to finance nuclear power plants. Massive price overruns and lengthy delays eventually led to the demise of Washington's largest utility. Subsequent investigations began to turn up the nationwide collusion among pipe wholesalers and fabricators. Years will pass before all of the civil and criminal actions are settled.

SOURCE: William P. Barrett, "Bent Pipe," *Forbes*, March 30, 1992, p. 83.

largest food wholesaler, Fleming Companies in Oklahoma City, connects its retailers with its EDI system for fast, accurate order response. McKesson, the country's leading drug distributor, provides standard software for its retailer and hospital clients.[9]

Electronic data interchange is commonplace in wholesaling. Producers use these computer-controlled inventory management systems to keep wholesaler stocks at the most efficient level. Bearing Incorporated connects its over 3,000 industrial distributor customers on line. Many wholesalers couple EDI with completely automated retrieval systems. Using robotics, manufacturers and wholesalers can fill orders and load pallets without people. Although the initial investment may be high, overall cost reductions occur through higher output with less labor expense.[10]

SUMMING IT UP

Wholesalers are marketing intermediaries that resell goods to other businesses, either retailers, producers or organizations. Wholesalers provide benefit to manufacturers and to retailer customers. These firms increase the available merchandise choice to buyers. They also produce a cost savings within the distribution system and supply financial assistance to the channel.

Merchant wholesalers take title to and possession of the merchandise. Full function merchant wholesalers include general line and specialty line firms. Rack jobbers provide the additional service of stocking the retailer customer's shelves. Drop shippers, truck jobbers, producers cooperatives, cash-and-carry wholesalers and mail-order houses are limited function intermediaries. Agents and brokers are intermediaries that do not take title to the merchandise. These individuals and firms carry out selling functions for their principals. Manufacturers' representatives, food brokers, consumer services brokers and auction houses are typical agents and brokers.

The management of the wholesaling function is influenced by trends in wholesaling. More and more of these firms are adding value and service to the products they carry. Manufacturers and wholesalers have sometimes divergent needs that managers must address. Ethical considerations, as always, impact decisions regarding distribution channel members. To the manufacturer, wholesaling often means a loss of control. Competition and conflict within the channel are additional problems producers face.

---

[9]Steve Weinstein, "The best buy and sell," *Progressive Grocer,* August 1994, pp. 40–42; Anthony Baldo, "Food fight: Why supermarket chains are making life difficult for wholesalers such as Fleming Cos.," *Financial World,* January 8, 1991, pp. 40–41; Fred Gebhart, "Foremost-McKesson opens up EDI system to its customers," *Drug Topics,* January 20, 1992, p. 68.

[10]Philip Van Ness, "BI sets EDI goal for 1993," At Press Time column, *Industrial Distribution,* January 15, 1992, p. 7; Editors, "Automating at the point of shipment," *Distribution,* January 92, p. 64.

KEY CONCEPTS AND TERMS FROM CHAPTER THIRTEEN

Agents and brokers
Break bulk
Cash-and-carry
Channel captain
Drop shipper
Full function wholesaler
General merchandise wholesaler
Limited function wholesaler
Mail-order house

Manufacturers' representative
Merchant wholesaler
Producers cooperative
Rack jobber
Specialty line wholesaler
Truck jobber
Wholesaler
Wholesaling

BUILDING SKILLS

1. Contrast the advantages and disadvantages of using wholesalers.

2. Describe the functions wholesalers perform that benefit manufacturers, retailers and consumers.

3. Categorize the different types of wholesalers, explaining why these intermediaries operate in the different manners.

4. Compare the types of wholesalers that typically distribute specialty ice creams, snack foods in drugstores, snow tires and chains, magazines, hand tools.

5. Contrast the reasons for using agents or brokers in handling metal castings sold to the aerospace industry, the sale of a home or business, the purchase of bulk cotton, stocks and bonds.

6. Explore some of the problems confronting the management of wholesalers.

Making Decisions 13-1: Food Fight!

The distribution of food to restaurants, fast food outlets, hospitals and other institutions is big business. This $80-billion-dollar-a-year market is dominated by small, local operators, yet a number of major companies are fighting for greater shares. With this kind of market potential, there are no holds barred in the fight for servicing food outlets.

With Americans now spending about 35 cents out of every food dollar outside of the supermarket, the prospects for growth in this industry are excellent. Food distributors calling on restaurants and institutions carry everything from soup to nuts to aprons. Because the person eating out may be a little more fussy than the grocery shopper, firms such as Sysco are conscious of quality.

Sysco is America's largest wholesaler of food and other items to restaurants, hospitals and prisons. The company has experienced remarkable growth in recent years, primarily at the expense of the small operators. Sysco's purchase of several midwestern distributors selling largely in the fast food field promoted the rapid growth of this aggressive marketing intermediary.

With giant, fast food franchise accounts at stake, Sysco is in a battle that now involves prices. Although food purveyors in this industry have typically competed based upon quality and service, customers who are franchise operations may be able to win some price concessions by pitting one distributor against the other. These food wholesalers could then put the squeeze on their suppliers and processors for lower prices.[11]

Describe benefits provided by food distributors to restaurant and institutional food markets.

Making Decisions 13-2: Through Rose-Colored Glasses.

Not all distribution channels run smoothly. To the contrary, most suffer through a few hitches and glitches while delivering goods and services down the pipeline. International channels are often the most difficult to manage. Many countries have laws that restrict the introduction of foreign made goods. Others have extensive channels that are difficult to penetrate. Even doing business in the United States is not an easy task for all. Just ask Luxoticca Group SpA of Italy.

The world's largest maker of eyeglass frames has faced some difficult distribution problems throughout the world, including the United States. Producing well-known and pricey designer brands, such as Byblos, Giorgio Armani and Yves St. Laurent, Luxoticca carves a sizable notch out of the middle to upper-end market for frames. Over the past five years, this Italian company reduced its costs dramatically, making it one of the more profitable firms in the industry.

---

[11]Martin Kahn, "Corporate America's most powerful people: John Woodhouse," *Forbes,* May 27, 1991, p. 230; Suzanne Loeffelholz, "Voracious appetite," *Financial World,* April 18, 1989, pp. 72–73.

Unfortunately, the firm learned that its wholesalers were not passing these savings on to retail optical shops. Consumers ended up paying top dollar. Management at Luxoticca began buying up its distributors around the world, delivering directly to its retail customers. To better service its 28,000 U.S. customers, the company has taken over the wholesale functions. Luxoticca equips the small eyeglass marts with computer software that allows these retail clients to check stocks and place orders from the firm's distribution centers for overnight delivery.[12]

(Courtesy Luxoticca)

Analyze and discuss the methods Luxoticca used to overcome channel conflict.

Making Decisions 13-3: SuperValu is Super!

Just walking through a major grocery wholesale operation can be mind boggling. The sheer size of the storage facilities for these intermediaries staggers the imagination. Although there are some 300 of these distributors in the United States, only a handful are giant-sized. One of the largest is SuperValu, whose sales from its wholesale operation alone will exceed $9 billion by 1995. Among its peers, SuperValu is also noted for its charitable work, notably in helping young people and the unfortunate finish their education.

SuperValu grew in the eighties through the acquisition of several retail chains. This aggressive firm owns Cub Foods, Twin Valu and Bigg's, all in the megaretailing class. SuperValu also purchased Food Giant, an Atlanta-based supermarket chain that was one of the wholesaler's largest customers. The company recently divested itself from ShopKo, a mass merchandiser. However, the firm still derives over 80 percent of its income from its wholesale operations.

---

[12]Bill Saporito, "Cutting out the middleman," *Fortune,* April 6, 1992, p. 96.

Management at SuperValu still looks on its major role as servicing its 3,000 plus grocery store customers. Most of these clients are independent or small chain operations, and SuperValu prides itself on helping these retailers compete against the huge supermarket conglomerates. The company has among the highest profit margins in its industry, thanks to an efficient, cost monitoring management. SuperValu works closely with its retailer customers, assisting them in store design, promotion and electronic data interchange.[13]

Describe SuperValu's operations and analyze the potential for conflict between SuperValu and its customers.

---

[13]"Super Valu + Wetterau," *Progressive Grocer,* July 1992, p. 7; Anthony Baldo, "Best-practice companies: Super Valu Stores," *Financial World,* September 17, 1991, pp. 43–44; Steve Weinstein, "Accent on education," *Progressive Grocer,* December 1990, pp. 27–28.

14

Retailing

■ ■ ■ ■ ■ ■ ■ ■ ■ ■ ■ ■

The Job to be Done

Retailing is the final phase in trade goods distribution. The shops and stores that resell to consumers provide time, place and possession utility. Chapter 14 discusses the role and types of retailers, providing the information that will enable you to:

- distinguish retailers from other members of the distribution system and understand their relationship with other marketing functions,
- identify the specific types of retail establishments by service offered, ownership and merchandise assortment, including nonstore retailers,
- understand the characteristics of different retail locations including central business districts and planned shopping centers, and
- recognize the factors affecting management of retailing operations and be able to discuss the impact of ethics and technological advances on this sector of distribution.

Marketers at Work

Lourdes Lozano

Lourdes Lozano had to struggle to make her dreams come true. After migrating to San Francisco from her birthplace in Mexico, she yearned to enter the glamourous world of fashion. Overcoming her father's objections, she enrolled in the Fashion Institute of Design and Merchandising in Los Angeles. Earning her Associate of Arts degree, she fulfilled her dream by entering the garment industry.

After spending five years learning the ropes in retail selling, Lourdes quickly climbed the ladder from the wholesale side of the business. As Western Sales Manager for the Weekend Exercise Company, she gained a reputation for outstanding promotion and customer service savvy. She was hired away to become Vice President, Sales for LCA Intimates in 1992. Her marketing skills were largely responsible for the tremendous success of two new lines launched under her guidance. Under her management, LCA sales increased by 50% over three years.

Lourdes has always smoldered with an entrepreneurial spirit, and finally reached her ultimate goal, a business of her own. As co-owner of 9TZ (pronounced "nineties,") she relaunched a line of men's and women's contemporary casual sportswear in 1995. The clothing is casual, yet nice, at moderate price points. The firm expects to add a children's line at a later date.

Although Lourdes recognizes the importance of her education, she admits that her success is due largely to her drive. While there is no substitute for knowledge and experience, the will to work hard and smart is the key to making it in today's highly competitive market. With desire, any goal can be reached. Lourdes Lozano certainly has attained hers.

What Is Retailing?

Consumers would be in a sorry state were it not for retailers. Almost everything that the general public needs it buys from these intermediaries. The drug store, coffee shop, supermarket, hardware seller, automobile dealer and appliance emporium are retailers. Often called the final step in the distribution process, these resellers are the backbone of the American economy. In times of recession, the first indicator of recovery is increased sales in the retail sector.

RETAILER DEFINED

Retailer—marketing intermediary that sells goods and services to consumers.

Retailers are businesses that sell merchandise or services directly to consumers. These organizations and people carry out almost all of the standard intermediary functions. Most retail businesses occupy stores, but consumers may also purchase from nonstore sources. Although many people do not understand the role of wholesalers nor see their value, few would dispute the need for retailers. Shopping, as we know it, would be impossible without stores and markets. The services they offer to the buying public are necessary and endless.

Retailing is big business. In the United States, more than two million retail stores ring up sales of over $1.25 trillion per year. As might be expected, the major metropolitan areas account for the greatest portion of both the

RANK	BRAND NAME(S)	COMPANY	1993 SALES $ BILLIONS
1	Wal-Mart	Wal-Mart Stores	67.3
2	Kmart	Kmart	34.1
3	Sears	Sears Roebuck	26.3
4	Kroger	Kroger Co.	22.3
5	Mervyn's, Target, Dayton	Dayton-Hudson	19.2
6	J.C. Penney	J.C. Penney	18.2
7	Jewel, Lucky Stores, Sav-on	American Stores	18.7
8	Safeway	KKR	15.2
9	Lord & Taylor, Payless	May Dept. Stores	11.5
10	Albertsons	Albertsons	11.2
11	Winn-Dixie	Winn-Dixie Stores	10.8
12	Marshall's, Thom McAn	Melville	10.4
13	A&P	Tengelmann (Ger.)	10.3
14	Foot Locker, Woolworth	Woolworth Co.	9.6
15	Home Depot	Home Depot Inc.	9.2
16	Walgreen	Walgreen Co.	8.2
17	Toys " Я " Us, Kids " Я " Us	Toys " " Us	7.9
18	Price*	Price Co.	7.6
19	Food Lion	Food Lion	7.6
20	Costco*	Costco	7.5

*merged in 1994

SOURCE: National Retail Federation, as presented in *SUPERBRANDS*, October 17, 1994, p. 122.

■　　■　　■　　■　　■

number of retail establishments and the volume of sales. Retail volume has always been a bellwether watched by economists to read the state of business activity. This means that sales by retailers is an indication of the strength or weakness of the general economy. As consumer spending increases, other sectors follow.

Individual entrepreneurs often flock to the retail field. Entry into this industry may be easy and relatively inexpensive, especially in the service sector. On the other hand, beginning a store or shop that requires large inventories of goods or highly experienced personnel complicates the startup. Making a success of a retail venture is much more difficult than many entrepreneurial types reckon with. Although some retailers succeed and become financially independent, many small store owners struggle or fail. Retailers account for the majority of small business failures.

ow Are Retailers Classified?

Retailers differ according to the service provided, the products carried and their form of ownership. Some firms offer little in the way of personal assistance.

Others cater to their customers lavishly. Product lines can be general in nature or highly specialized. Some of the most familiar names in the retailing arena are part of giant corporations or conglomerates, yet most retailers are independently owned.

BY SERVICE PROVIDED

The trend toward convenience shopping in the last two decades brought about an increased emphasis on self-service. Many stores that once offered a full line of customer amenities have opted to let consumers choose and select on their own. Labor cost savings are a major contributor to this movement. If the goods are not expensive and are widely available, it just makes good sense to let the buyer shop without the added pressure of salespeople.

Self-Service

The range of customer convenience provided by retailers varies from completely **self-service** to 100 percent full service. In the clothing business, stores such as Mervyn's, May Department Stores Co. and Miller's Outpost are almost totally self-service. Although some help is available, customers at these establishments usually select items and take them to centralized cashiers, similar to those in supermarkets.

Self-service retailers are evident in every type of market. Certainly, the grocery industry typifies this do-it-yourself operation. Perhaps the supermarket started the concept of shopping without help. Merchandisers, such as Kmart, Sears and Wal-Mart have expanded this shopping scheme to include a whole new group of products. Newer retail ventures, such as membership stores, built upon this help-yourself method of shopping. Most consumers buy most of their necessities from self-service retailers.

Full-Service

At the other end of the scale from help-yourself stores are a smaller group of retailers that prosper by providing complete customer service. Often found more at high-end or upscale stores, full-service retailers thrive on pampering the consumer. The boutiques on Rodeo Drive in Beverly Hills and smaller shops on New York's Fifth Avenue provide everything from free champagne to valet service to pet sitting.

One need not shop at an upscale boutique to receive complete service. Many department stores employ professional salespeople who provide a full range of customer services. Even lower end appliance outlets give consumers a variety of extras that could not be found in self-service emporiums. Some gas stations even offer to check your oil or clean your windshield. Any retail operation that helps in the selection of merchandise or volunteers to add some value can be considered a full-service retailer. Shoe stores are another example of full-service retailers. Customers at some discount outlets select their own shoes, but usually fitting at shoe boutiques is done individually by satisfaction oriented salespeople.

Global Marketing: The world's greatest department store.

"Retailing should be exciting, like theater," expounds Mohamed Al Fayed, the owner of Harrods, London's quintessential department store. Unlike most of its rivals, this grand dame of retailers is noted for its showmanship. From the grandeur of its building to its unique products to the live music and art objects found in its halls, Harrods is indeed an unusual retail store. This grandiose emporium attracted Al Fayed, who gained his wealth through oil and shipping, and in 1985, along with relatives, added Harrods to his other European purchase, the Ritz hotel in Paris.

Although he had little experience in retailing, Al Fayed knew where to go for help. The former CEO of Neiman-Marcus, Stanley Marcus, was hired as a consultant, and he brought with him a business philosophy of putting customer interests ahead of profits. The eleven million people who visit Harrods annually are notoriously poor shoppers, and as a consequence the store's financial performance is not the greatest. Still, sales have been rising steadily, and the owners are content to bask in the glory of the Harrods mystique. Al Fayed's theory of retailing is summed up simply when he says, ". . . what they do in America is just sell merchandise. Bloomingdale's is like a supermarket."

Not only does the store carry an assortment of rare merchandise, but the retailer is noted for its customer service. Although it is only half the size of Marshall Field's Chicago location, Harrods employs over 800 more people. No matter what the season, one can always find an abundance of salespeople willing to help with the slightest of details. Suppliers often find that it costs more to do business with Harrods, but usually agree that it is well worthwhile to be display in what is regarded worldwide as the most prestigious address in retailing.

SOURCE: Kevin Helliker, "Harrods: Grandeur comes at a grand cost," *The Wall Street Journal*, December 1, 1993, p. B1.

BY OWNERSHIP

The retail industry is made up of a tremendous number of different types of businesses. Most of these outlets are local in nature, serving a limited geographical market. Some retailers are part of gigantic nationwide chains, while others are independently owned and operated. Success in retailing is not limited to either type of ownership.

Chain Store Operations

Much of America's retail business is owned by giant corporations, consisting mostly of chain operations. Mass merchandisers such as Wal-Mart, Kmart and J.C. Penney, enjoy the advantage of buying merchandise in large quantities at the best prices possible. Specialty stores, like Kinney's Shoes, Waldenbooks, The Gap and other organizations with multiple outlets similarly dictate volume purchases, often meaning lower prices.

With the almost unlimited choices available to consumers, many chain operations have had to rethink their strategies. The recession of the early 1990s brought a number of well-known retail names to the brink of financial disaster. Department stores, for example, are learning to follow the lead of firms such as Neiman-Marcus, Sak's and Sears, by placing a premium on customer service. With their frequent shopper programs labeled Incircle, Saks First, and Sears Best Customer, these retailers have reinvented the meaning of customer service.[1]

Some of the changes in this industry were the result of changes in the customer. Fewer individuals can afford the luxury of casual shopping. Today's consumer demands quality merchandise at reasonable prices from service-minded retailers. Whether self-service or highly personal, to succeed today retailers must embody the very essence of the marketing concept.

Many of today's major retailers, such as Target, are chain operations.

[1]*Colloquy,* Vol. 4, Issue 3, 1994; Laura Zinn, Christopher Power, Julia Flynnsiler, Gail DeGeorge, and Wendy Zellner, "Retailing: Who will survive?" *Business Week,* November 11. 1990, pp. 134–144.

Independent Ownership

Despite large chain competition, small, entrepreneurial firms can still find room to prosper in retailing. Independent stores and shops often pool their buying power to create economies of scale. By combining orders from several businesses, a group of retailers may command competitive pricing on their merchandise buys that are comparable to larger purchasers.

Many independently owned stores and shops are quite profitable. Carrying product lines that are in demand often sets these entrepreneurs apart. By offering services that chain operations cannot afford, many small retailers attract customers that do not care to shop in the bigger, less personal marts. The corner grocery store may stock certain brands or cash checks without a big to-do, both of which are important services to many buyers. The dry cleaner that remembers customer names and preferences may be of more interest to a consumer than the chain operation that merely sells for less.[2]

Franchising

Franchising is a system of ownership that grants the rights to use a company's name or products to an independent, retail owner/operator. This popular contractual agreement links the **franchisor,** or rights granting company, with the **franchisee,** or the individual or firm running the retail establishment. Franchisors supply managerial and fiscal training and support in return for fees and royalties. The reputation and expertise of the franchisor benefits the franchisee by creating instant recognition and sales.

Franchising—granting the rights to use a company's name or products to an independent owner/operator.

By using the franchise system, manufacturers gain tighter control over their distribution system, but the franchisees still maintain an aura of independence. Franchisors set rigid quality standards for the contracted outlets. The franchise agreement limits competitive pressure because the retailer has little or no choice over the products it wishes to sell. Chevron dealers cannot sell Texaco or Mobil gasoline. Coast to Coast Hardware Stores carry a variety of nationally advertised merchandise and some private label items, but the franchisor still approves the lines carried by individual franchisees.

Several major consumer goods marketers have entered the franchise arena by licensing independent retail operations. PepsiCo purchased Taco Bell and Pizza Hut years ago. These fast food franchisers naturally sell a sizable amount of Pepsi soft drinks in the course of a year. The Oscar Mayer division of Kraft General Foods began its Hot Dog Construction Company outlets in malls; as roll out continues, it is expected that these fast feeders will go franchise. ConAgra, Sara Lee and Heinz are also experimenting with carts and kiosks in malls.[3]

---

[2]Mike McDermott, "The revenge of the little guy," *Adweek's Marketing Week,*" September 17, 1990, pp. 21–27.
[3]Betsy Spethmann, "Frankcise," *BRANDWEEK,* May 16, 1994, pp. 1 and 8.

BY TYPE OF OPERATION

Retail operations come in all sizes and types. Some are self-serve, others offer the utmost in assistance. Many operate under a corporate or conglomerate umbrella, others are "mom and pop" outlets. Retailers occupy gigantic complexes filled with all sorts and kinds of assorted merchandise, or are housed in tiny, one room slots in a mall or downtown area. Separating these intermediaries by their types of operation helps to clarify how they provide service and satisfaction.

Department Stores

The original general store provided the base for much of today's retailing strategy. Frontier people needed a variety of goods that were available from one establishment. **Department stores,** the off-spring of these general stores, carry a broad and deep assortment of merchandise separated into specific sections, or departments. Each area employs merchandise buyers trained to handle particular lines.

Unlike its predecessor, the department store rarely sells grocery items or farming needs, although many do offer gourmet food sections and nurseries. Department stores offer credit to customers and often provide delivery services. Some of these retailers supply a myriad of other services, from cooking classes to jewelry design. Many of the departments in these stores, such as photography studios, restaurants, or travel bureaus, lease to independent owners. In exchange for a rental fee, these firms operate the department as if it were a separate business entity.

Department store—a large retailer offering a broad and deep assortment of merchandise separated into specific sections.

Department stores, such as Emporium, offer a broad and deep line of diversified merchandise.

Sweden's largest department store, Nordiska Kompaniet, or NK, expands this basic concept dramatically. Facing increasing rental costs in the locations of its three stores and five fashion units, this innovative retailer leases out almost all of its departments. This network of entrepreneurs includes fashion names such as Gant, Ralph Lauren's Polo line, and Levi Strauss. Each department, while run as an independent business, still carries the NK logo, and the retailer also maintains a degree of managerial control over its tenants.[4]

Customer Service

Customer service within department stores ranges from self-serve to high quality assistance. Some of these retailers, such as The Broadway, Emporium and May Company, are basically serve-yourself operations. Neiman-Marcus, Garfinckle's and Nordstrom, on the other hand, offer complete sales assistance. The amount of service depends upon the specific department. Expensive clothing areas and cosmetics groups usually provide more help. Most sundries, some accessories, and linens tend to be self-serve.

Most major department store chains take pride in offering a variety of goods and customer services. These retailers do not attempt to compete based upon price, but rather offer more in the way of personal attention and convenience. Department stores typically carry shopping and specialty goods, and augment their product lines with services such as free alterations, bridal registries, and charge accounts. Nordstrom recently inked a joint venture to serve Starbucks coffee in its in-store cafes, adding exposure to both firms.[5]

Trends In Department Stores

In the past decade or two, department store sales may have suffered. These retailers are traditionally located downtown in major metropolitan areas. Fewer suburban shoppers are driving to the inner city. Furthermore, the increase in specialty stores and discount houses has taken big bites out of department store revenues. Unfortunately, many of these retailers are saddled with tremendous real estate investments in the city cores that drain profits.

Most department store chains are embarking on programs to counteract this downward sales trend. Much of the pressure on these retailers eases through the success of branches located in suburban malls. These planned shopping centers feature specialty stores of all types that attract more consumers. Department store outposts located in malls are usually quite successful.

In addition to locating in suburban malls, many department store chains are going through complete face-lifts. To combat the competition from specialty stores, owners are trying to inject excitement and innovation into the humdrum

[4]Mary Krienke, "Sweden's NK: Nordiska Kompaniet takes bold new step," *Stores*, May 1992, pp. 26–32.

[5]Joan Oleck, "The tap won't cut it at Starbucks," *Restaurant Business*, January 1, 1994, p. 32; John Sinisi, "Starbucks, Nordstrom Au Lait-up," *BRANDWEEK*, September 28, 1992, p. 7; Editors, "Saks embraces best customers," *Colloquy*, vol. 3, issue 2, pp. 1, 4, and 5.

department store image of the past. Some chains eliminate departments such as major appliances to cut space in some branches. Displays need to be updated more frequently, and the salespeople require training to develop a more upbeat attitude. Cost reductions and better customer service help overcome price competition from discounters and specialty stores.[6]

Some independent department stores exist, but giant holding companies own most of these large retailers. Because of the troubled times endured by department stores, many of these chains acquire other retail outlets to survive. Major holding companies own several department store groups, operating supermarkets, specialty stores, and other retailers.

Mass Merchandisers

Mass merchandiser— retailer offering a broad but shallow assortment of merchandise, projecting a lower priced image.

Mass merchandisers, while related to department stores, carry a broad but shallower assortment of merchandise. These firms sell based upon lower prices and project a lower quality image. Before the 1980s, both Sears and J.C. Penney were considered mass merchandisers. Now that these giant retailers have adopted quality images, the category into which they fall is blurry, following more of the department store image. Penney's began to sponsor young, local talent with the hope that as their careers blossom, so will the store's image.[7]

Mass merchandisers carry name brand goods and operate almost entirely as self-service retailers. Although floor help is available in a pinch, customers usually fend for themselves. Cashiers, located near the exits, serve to check out and bag the customer's selections, but are not usually expected to give personal service. Most mass merchandisers are chain operations with large stores. These retail operations grew rapidly during the 1960s and 1970s. Today, the spread is slowing somewhat, and many companies are working to upgrade present locations instead of adding new ones.

Although Sears slipped a notch a few years ago, this granddaddy of mass merchandisers appears to be headed back toward solid ground. Some industry experts claim that the recent drop in sales was due largely to the merchandising concept Sears initiated in the late 1980s. By stocking more nationally branded merchandise and selling at everyday low prices, the chain dramatically changed its image. In addition, nationwide publicity on the "customer bilking" charges at some Sears auto centers had a definite impact on sales.[8]

Discounters

Discounter—mass merchandiser offering low prices across their entire line of merchandise.

One of the credos of mass merchandisers is lower prices for less service. Some of these retailers go one step further, promoting themselves as discounters, offering to "meet or beat" the prices of any other store or shop. **Discounters** are mass merchandisers that offer lower prices across their entire line of merchandise. Wal-Mart, Kmart, Bi-Mart and Target are examples of these types of retailers.

---

[6]Francesca Turchiano, "Death of department stores: Inevitable or avoidable?" *BRANDWEEK,* September 6, 1993, p. 14.

[7]Elaine Underwood, "Penney ties to regional talent," *BRANDWEEK,* August 1, 1994, p. 5.

[8]Susan Chandler, "Sears' turnaround is for real—for now," *Business Week,* August 15, 1994, pp. 102–103; Gilbert Fuchsberg, "Sears reinstates sales incentives in some centers," *The Wall Street Journal,* March 7, 1994, pp. B1 and B6.

Like other mass merchandisers, discounters carry a broad but somewhat shallow assortment of merchandise. Most have separate automotive and garden departments, and a number also include restaurants. By putting a lower markup on their merchandise, discounters cater to consumers who are willing to sacrifice service for low prices. The world's largest retailer, Wal-Mart, which classifies itself as a discounter, continues to show rapid expansion and growth. The company that was founded in the folksy image by Arkansan Sam Walton, is now bigger than Kmart and Sears combined and almost as large as the entire department store industry. Discounters typically locate in shopping centers and malls, although they are sometimes found in freestanding locations.[9]

Superstores

Another discount operation appearing on the retail scene is an outlet labeled a superstore. Usually owned by major chains, these shopping marts feature a broad mix of merchandise in a concentrated area. For example, Pet Care, PETsMART and Petstuff are superstores that cater strictly to pet owners. Averaging about 10,000 square feet in size, these retailers feature everyday low pricing, convenience and amenities appealing to dog and cat fanciers. Superstores also are common in the office supply and electronics arenas.[10]

Hypermarkets

Yet another recent development in consumer shopping is the **hypermarket.** Containing as much as 330,000 square feet, these huge one-stop shopping sites are true megaretailers. Services located within these complexes may include barber shops, computer stores, auto repair facilities and banks. Besides groceries, hypermarkets sell building materials, major appliances, garden supplies, toys, clothing and hardware. The Fred Meyer chain, located in the Pacific Northwest, is one of the fastest growing and most successful of these retailers.[11]

Hypermarket— multi-section mass merchandiser carrying a wide variety of dissimilar merchandise in very large facilities.

In spite of some consumer discomfort, these gigantic resellers are here to stay. With stores that can turn the tills at a rate of greater than $1.5 million per week, there is no shortage of companies joining the parade. Carrefour USA, offshoot of the original megamarketing chain from France, has opened a 330,000 square foot store in Philadelphia, and has another blockbuster scheduled for Texas. Bigg's, a midwest retailing giant and one of the first to open a big-big store in the United States, is expanding its chain of Hyper-Bigg's.[12]

Even Wal-Mart is into hypermarkets in a big way with its supercenters. For this "king of the mass merchandisers," megaretailing has not been a bed of roses. After opening four megastores, Wal-Mart is downsizing its future developments. Although it does not call itself a hypermarket, Leedmark has all

[9]Bill Saporito, "And the winner is still. . . Wal-Mart," *Fortune,* May 2, 1994, pp. 62–70.

[10]Tim Triplett, "Superstores tap into bond between owners and pets," *Marketing News,* April 25, 1994, pp. 1–2.

[11]Heikki Rinne, Bill Swinyard, "Discounters: a competitive study," *Stores,* December 1992, pp. 54–57; Robert L. Hill, "In with the New," *Oregon Business,* June 1987, pp. 21–26.

[12]"Wal-Mart to open supercenter stores at accelerated pace," *The Wall Street Journal,* September 15, 1994, p. B6; Kevin Kelly and Amy Dunkin, "Wal-Mart gets lost in the vegetable aisle," *Business Week,* May 28, 1990, p. 48.

Hypermarkets, such as Fred Meyer, are giant retailers that carry a huge selection of merchandise, offering "one stop shopping." (Courtesy of Fred Meyer Corporation)

the characteristics of a megaretailer. This over 300,000 square foot emporium features such customer comforts as CNN television viewing in checkout lines and computerized store directories.[13]

Like other mass merchandisers, hypermarkets are largely self-service, having as many as sixty checkout counters or cashiers. Like department stores, many of the individual sections in hypermarkets, such as the photography or the optometry areas, may be leased to outside, independent owners. These retailers usually locate near major commercial areas, often standing alone.

Off-Price Stores

Off-price store— retailer that sells distressed merchandise at greatly reduced prices.

Off-price stores are smaller retailers, usually stocked with distressed merchandise, selling at greatly reduced prices. Stocks found at these outlets are often irregulars or seconds. Goods might also consist of excess purchases from other retailers, or manufacturers overruns. Off-price retailers carry everything from low price goods to designer labels, although, in the latter case, the labels are often removed.

These retailers usually specialize in specific lines of merchandise instead of carrying a broad range of goods. Dallas-based Tuesday Morning for example, carries quality women's fashions at very low prices. This retailer buys overruns and seasonal items directly from manufacturers or from fashion boutiques and

---

[13]"Discounters borrow supermarket tactics," *Chain Store Age Executive,* December 1991, pp. 24B–25B; Faye Brookman, "Can hybrid make hypermarket concept work in the U.S.?" *Drug Topics,* September 9, 1991, p. 68; Marianne Wilson, "Leedmark: A hypermarket by any other name," *Chain Store Age Executive,* August 1991, pp. 28–31.

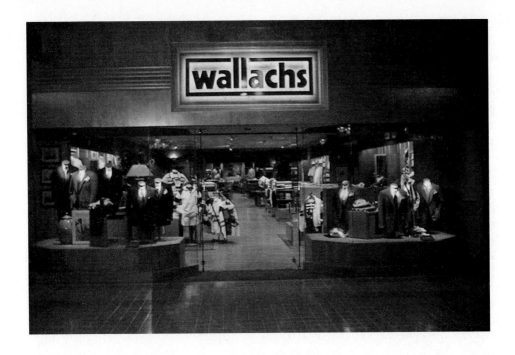

Many of America's retailers, such as Wallach's, fall into the specialty store category. (Courtesy of Hartmarx)

sells them out of dingy basements in strip malls. Buyers who know their merchandise can find great bargains at off-price stores, but inventories vary. Items available one week may not be the next.[14]

Many off-price outlets locate in shopping centers that cater to this category of retailer. Loehmann's, as an example, developed a series of small malls all over the country. Ross Clothes For Less stores, on the other hand, are typically found in residential shopping centers. Some mass merchandiser holding companies own off-price operations. Two of the fastest growing of these chains, Marshall's and T. J. Maxx, are owned respectively by Melville and by Zayre.

Specialty Stores

Specialty stores are retailers that offer narrow but deep assortments of merchandise. Clothing and shoe stores, bath boutiques and ice cream parlors, sporting goods outlets and pet stores are typical of wide variety of specialty stores. Unlike their larger competitors, these retail establishments carry limited quantities of merchandise from relatively few manufacturers.

Specialty stores range from primarily self-service to providing very strong sales assistance. Specialty clothing retailers, prominent in malls and shopping centers, offer shoppers racks of self-service merchandise. Casual Corner, Kaufman's and Foxmoor thrive on low overhead operations where sales help is at a minimum. Self-service ice cream parlors, on the other hand, would be neither practical nor sanitary. Food service retailers naturally offer more individual attention, with the possible exception of salad bars.

Specialty store— retailer offering narrow but deep assortments of merchandise.

---

[14]Kevin Helliker, "Discount chains are squeezed by competition," *The Wall Street Journal,* April 13, 1994, pp. B1 and B12.

The Gap is typical of a specialty store chain that has succeeded very well. This retailer owns Banana Republic, babyGap and GapKids. The company specializes in classic, well-made clothing at reasonable prices. Once noted for carrying nationally advertised lines such as Levi Strauss, the inventory in these specialty stores now carries mostly Gap labels. This megaretailer chain surpassed Liz Claiborne to become the second ranked U.S. clothes brand behind Levi. Newer openings of Gap stores are heading toward central business districts rather than malls.[15]

Some very successful specialty store chains limit their product lines to a very narrow base. By handling only toys, Toys `R´ Us carved a niche that most multi-line operations envy. Similarly, Radio Shack, Ikea and Sportmart concentrate their efforts on consumer electronics, home furnishings and sports or outdoor equipment respectively. Although limited in width of mix, these specialty stores are anything but small. Barnes & Noble, the book retailer that features espresso bars and classical music, typically has 15,000 square feet under one roof in its freestanding superstores.[16]

Supermarkets

Supermarket— grocery retailer carrying a broad and deep assortment of mostly food items.

A typical **supermarket** offers a broad and deep assortment of mostly food items. An average store produces upwards of $5.5 million in annual sales. These grocery retailers are primarily self-service and offer little in the way of consumer amenities, other than carryout assistance. A few scattered supermarkets accept credit cards, but generally these stores are cash-and-carry retailers. There is a growing trend with these giant grocery sellers to increase space to accommodate delicatessens, frozen yogurt stands and even full-service, sit-down restaurants.[17]

About 90 percent of all operating supermarkets use computer controlled cashier centers with laser scanners. In addition, most modern facilities have computers for management's use. Order handling, payroll and work schedules are electronically controlled in these efficient grocery centers. One of the latest experiments, imported from Europe, is a self-service scanning system. Using a hand-held wand, shoppers scan the bar codes on products and place the selected items in carts lined with plastic totes, which eliminate bagging. Once the scanners are returned, a receipt is printed and the shopper proceeds to a cashier. Krogers is also looking at such an automated system.[18]

Andersen Consulting offers Smart Store 2000 Act II as a training ground for grocery industry marketers. This experimental station offers opportunities from store layout to the latest in technology to Andersen clients. This

---

[15]Susan Caminiti, "How the Gap keeps ahead of the pack," *Fortune*, February 12, 1990, pp. 129–131; Russell Mitchell, "The Gap," *Business Week*, March 9, 1992, pp. 58–64.

[16]Sunita Wadekar Bhargava, "Espresso, sandwiches and a sea of books," *Business Week*, July 26, 1993, p. 81; Carrie Goerne, "Now book browsers can munch brownies as they shop for Browning," *Marketing News*, July 6, 1992, pp. 1 and 9.

[17]Eleena de Lisser, "Catering to cooking-phobic customers, supermarkets stress carryout, add cafes," *The Wall Street Journal*, April 5, 1993, pp. B1 and B3.

[18]Tim Triplett, "Scanning wand makes checkout lines disappear," *Marketing News*, July 4, 1994, pp. 6 and 11.

RETAILING MIX

Store Type	Product Line Width	Product Line Depth	Pricing	Customer Service	Product Quality	Store Image
Department Store	Wide	Deep	Medium	Medium/High	Medium	Medium
Discount Store	Wide	Shallow	Low	Low	Low/Medium	Low
Specialty Store	Narrow	Deep	Medium/High	Medium/High	High	High
Off-price Store	Moderately Wide	Deep	Low	Low	Medium/High	Low
Hypermarket	Wide	Deep	Low	Low	Low/Medium	Low/Medium
Supermarket	Wide	Deep	Medium	Low	Medium/High	Low
Convenience Store	Narrow	Shallow	High	Low	Medium	Low
Warehouse Store	Very Wide	Moderately Deep	Low	Low	Low/High	Low

interactive system includes a state-of-the-art kitchen allowing supermarket and grocery managers to learn about shopping in the future. The increased use of electronic technology, both in the home and in the store, is expected to have a significant influence over how the supermarket of the future is designed and controlled.[19]

High Volume, Low Profit

Low profit margins in this industry force supermarkets to rely on volume sales to produce net income. To increase profits, supermarkets look to nontraditional services and products. Nonfood items are good sources for additional income, accounting for over 20 percent of the sales of an average supermarket, and that percentage continues to increase. In search of profits, grocery retailers add items such as health and beauty aids, small appliances, auto accessories, linens, toys, clothing and a variety of other nonedibles.

Supermarkets are fast approaching what the general store was years ago. A Richmond, Virginia, supermarket chain, Ukrop's, attracts customers with personal service and product selection. Byerly's, a Minneapolis retailer, offers the epitome of an upscale grocery store for yuppies, complete with carpeting, restaurants and a jewelry counter. The Byerly's name now adorns a variety of

[19]Tim Triplett, "Smart store challenges executives to change," *Marketing News,* July 4, 1994, pp. 6 and 11; Howard Schlossberg, "Tomorrow's retailing technologies on display today at Smart Store," *Marketing News,* January 20, 1992, p. 2.

frozen dinners and soups that are available from grocery retailers in over half of the United States.[20]

In 1992, a war began between supermarket chain store operations, which account for about 75 percent of all grocery sales, and major trade goods marketers. Traditionally, manufacturers offered special sales and promotions to these retailers with the idea that any savings would be passed on to the consumer. Flaunting their tremendous buying power, many of these retailers took advantage of the discounts, but pocketed the differences. Led by Procter & Gamble, several packaged goods houses have done away with these incentives. This battle for power in the grocery market is likely to last. Wal-Mart even went so far as to ask some suppliers to provide a "business planning" packet.[21]

Warehouse Clubs

Warehouse club— retailer requiring membership fees that offers a broad but shallow assortment of merchandise.

Similar in concept to mass merchandisers, **warehouse clubs** offer a broad but shallow assortment of merchandise to members only. Often called **wholesale clubs,** these retailers offer their goods on a self-service basis in austere surroundings. Warehouse clubs typically locate in industrial tracts and carry brand name merchandise often purchased from manufacturers' excess inventory. Although several competitive brands appear in some store sections, individual areas may stock only a few items that are overruns or factory seconds. The growth of this industry has been staggering, but overcrowding has hurt profits.[22]

Because of their purchasing patterns, warehouse stores suffer stockouts more often than other retailers. For example, if Whirlpool offers a carload of washers or dryers at reduced prices to a given store, when that stock sells out it cannot be replaced with similar goods. Warehouse clubs charge membership fees. Costco/Price Club, out of Kirkland, Washington; Pace Membership Warehouse, headquartered in Aurora, Colorado; The Wholesale Club in Indianapolis; and DECE Warehouse Club in Minneapolis are examples of these retail outlets. Even Vons, the Southern California supermarket chain, has entered the field with its Expo stores.[23]

[20]Elaine Underwood, "The changing supermarket," *Adweek's Marketing Week,* April 29, 1991, pp. 28–29.

[21]Zachary Schiller, "Not everyone loves a supermarket special," *Business Week,* February 17, 1992, pp. 64–68; Michael McCarthy, "P&G takes back the supermarket," *Adweek's Marketing Week,* April 13, 1992, pp. 4–5; Howard Schlossberg, "Grocers seek peace treaty in war with manufacturers," *Marketing News,* June 8, 1992, pp. 16–17.

[22]Gerry Khermouch, "Sizing up profits," *BRANDWEEK,* May 3, 1993, p. 32; Wendy Zellner, "Warehouse clubs butt heads—and reach for the ice pack," *Business Week,* April 19, 1993, p. 30.

[23]Betsy Spethmann, "Vons opens hybrid megamarket," *BRANDWEEK,* June 28, 1993, p. 4; James M. Degen, "Warehouse clubs move from revolution to evolution," *Marketing News,* August 3, 1992, p. 8; Andrew Kopfer, "The final word in no-frills shopping," *Fortune,* March 13, 1989, p. 30.

PETsMART typifies the new breed of superstore specializing in deep, but narrow, product lines.

Convenience Stores

Convenience stores are another type of retailer that primarily handles fast food items. The outlets are small, averaging about 3,000 square feet of floor space, and carry a limited inventory of products. Selling at higher-than-average prices, these retailers offer few services. By locating in neighborhood areas and offering extended hours, convenience stores fill a consumer need not available through other sources.

The Southland Corporation, recently purchased by Japanese interests, operates over 7,000 7-Eleven stores worldwide and is the largest convenience store owner. Beer, soft drinks, cigarettes, fast food, candy bars and dairy products produce a significant portion of sales for this firm. Other major chains include Circle K, Stop-N-Go, and am/pm Mini Marts, the latter owned by gasoline giant Arco. A major portion of the sales of convenience stores includes gasoline, when and where available.

Convenience store— small retailer, usually franchised, carrying fast food, grocery and sundry items.

CONSUMER SERVICES PROVIDERS

A large percentage of both the discretionary and disposable income of consumers goes toward the purchase of services. These specialty retailers deserve special mention. Beyond rent or mortgage payments, the greatest portion of these expenditures appears to be in repairs. Automobiles, appliances, computers and electronics gadgets do not last forever. As consumers continue to purchase more "toys," more specialists will be in demand to fix them.

Financial Institutions

Banks, savings and loans, credit unions and insurance firms make up a significant part of the service industry. These organizations provide consumers and business clients with everything from money storage to investments to credit.

Most people transact their business through banks. A checking account is the way of life for most Americans. Financial institutions also offer a safe haven for funds, whether in demand or time accounts.

In recent times, these firms expanded the types and amount of services they provide. The public looks to banks, savings and loans associations and credit unions for loans to buy houses, cars and appliances. In many cases, these institutions offer investment opportunities through IRA accounts or certificates of deposit. Some can now sell stocks and bonds as well.

Food Service Purveyors

One of the largest and fastest growing fields of this sector is food service. Restaurants, coffee shops, fast food outlets and bistros take a major portion of the consumer dollar. Whether serving a meal for four at a fancy dinner house or providing a bag full of hamburgers and fries, foods services are a prominent sector of retailing. A few of these specialty retailers, such as cafeterias, offer self-service, but most food purveyors service customers through employee contact.

Many food service retailers are chain operations. This is especially true of the fast food industry. Taco Bell, Domino's Pizza, Orange Julius and Coco's are all part of multi-outlet operations. Most of these chains sell through company owned stores as well as franchises. McDonald's, Burger King and Wendy's exploded over the past two decades to become multi-billion dollar operations. Some full-service restaurants are also large corporate entities, but most of these food suppliers are independently owned.

■ ■ ■ ■ ■

Retail real estate

RANK	RETAILER	NUMBER OF U.S. OUTLETS
1	McDonald's	9,100
2	Subway	7,990*
3	Pizza Hut	7,489
4	Radio Shack	6,600
5	Burger King	6,124
6	7-Eleven	5,600**
7	Blockbuster	2,381
8	Kmart	2,324
9	Wal-Mart	2,020
10	J.C. Penney	1,266
11	Sears***	799
12	Home Depot	273

*U.S. and U.S. possessions
**U.S. and Canada
***Department stores only
SOURCE: *BRANDWEEK*, March 21, 1994, p. 24.

■ ■ ■ ■ ■

What Are Nonstore Retailers?

Although an overwhelming portion of retail sales channel through stores and shops, consumers can still satisfy their needs through several other types of retailers. Many shoppers purchase goods and services in the comfort of their homes or from dispensing machines. The advent of cable television and home computers has increased the use of nonstore retailers.

DIRECT MARKETING

Direct marketing allows consumers to purchase products in the comfort of their homes without going through a store or shop. The firms in this industry are for the most part retail operations, although some manufacturers also use this method of selling. This form of retailing is one of the fastest growing segments of marketing. Customers may respond to promotions received through the mail, by television or over the telephone. Direct response advertising provides prospective buyers with the means to respond. The media used include direct mail, television and electronic communications.

Mail-Order Houses

The fastest growing segment of nonstore retailing is through **mail-order houses.** Originally the domain of major retailers such as Sears and Montgomery Ward, mail-order retailing has become widespread with thousands of companies involved. Although most mail-order houses deal in clothing, almost any type of consumer product can be purchased through these retailers, including computers. Two of the fastest growing direct marketing firms of early 1990s, Gateway 2000 Inc. and Dell Computer Corporation, sell PCs by mail order.[24]

Some of the best-known mail-order houses are Land's End, L. L. Bean and Spiegel which offer clothing. Williams-Sonoma handles kitchen equipment and supplies, while Breck's offers an array of flower producing bulbs. REI features outdoor clothing and equipment, and The Rose sells an eclectic assortment of gifts and apparel. One of the most successful mail-order ventures, Lillian Vernon, carries a bit of everything.

Having gained a reputation and a consumer following, many mail-order retailers are now opening stores. Talbot's and Banana Republic are two firms that are expanding their selling base by establishing their presence in malls. These moves increase their customer potential. Many of the shoppers at the mall stores are not presently on the mailing lists these firms use. Clerks promote the buy-by-mail feature of these retailers to people who visit the store.

Typically, the quality of merchandise offered through mail-order houses is good, and prices are normally competitive for similar products. Catalogs are complete, and telemarketing representatives are trained to be knowledgeable

---

[24]Kyle Pope, "Once very hot, mail-order PCs are cooling off," *The Wall Street Journal,* December 1, 1993, p. B1.

Mail order houses are a form of non-store retailers that are booming due to the explosion in direct marketing.

and helpful. Product selection may be skimpy, and the inability to see or try on the merchandise turns off some shoppers. Much of this negativism is overcome by the quality of the goods and by the liberal return policies offered by mail-order firms.

Video Marketing and Teleshopping

Video marketing— using cable television as the medium to generate direct sales.

Video marketing is increasing as the use of cable television expands. This nonstore retailing outlet allows for the products to be viewed on television along with buying information. Customers order by phone or mail according to the instructions given on the television screen. Although selection is sometimes limited, competition is nonexistent and prices are generally low. Once considered a toy for middle-aged women, video marketing generally appeals to a young, well-educated and affluent audience that includes men.[25]

Electronic shopping— service carried by phone or cable lines to home television screens.

Video marketing is the forerunner of **electronic shopping,** which many predict will be the consumer buying wave of the future. The Videotex system travels over phone or cable lines direct to the consumer's television screen. By selecting the appropriate menus, the consumer can choose merchandise, charge the purchase by credit card, and give shipping instructions without leaving the confines of the easy chair. Video marketing requires only a TV set

[25]Laura Zinn, Gail DeGeorge, Rochelle Shoretz, Dori Jones Yang and Stephanie Anderson Forest, "Retail will never be the same," *Business Week,* July 26, 1993, pp. 54–60.

and a telephone. The next step in electronic retailing, interactive shopping, requires a computer terminal as well.

Capitalizing on carnival atmospheres similar to those on game shows, these shop-at-home viewings are hooking many viewers. Offering everything from power tools and furniture to Italian porcelain and clocks, shopping networks buy in bulk from liquidation and closeout sales. Usually requiring viewers to call in while the product is on the screen creates an air of urgency that is exciting and catching. Tele-retailers are expanding their operations to include more upscale merchandise and direct ordering without having the television set tuned in. Although skeptics feel that the craze will not last, cable networks are jumping on this bandwagon by the droves. Cable television networks, such as QVC and Home Shopping Network (HSN) have become billion dollar businesses.[26]

IN-PERSON, AT-HOME SELLING

Other at-home retailing involves personal contact made by salespeople. This nonstore form of retailing has made great headway in recent years. Professional approaches have been traded for much of the slick-talking, hard-selling techniques of the past. At-home sellers contact clients in advance for appointments, and the actual sales presentations are rarely pushy.

Much of the success of door-to-door retailing is attributable to the quality of the salespeople. Companies using this nonstore method put the selling staffs through quality training programs. Commissions are high for these salespeople, and the quality of the merchandise is usually above average. Cosmetics, health care products, household items and jewelry marketed by companies such as Avon, Shaklee, Mary Kay, Stanley, Jafra and Sarah Coventry distribute their wares through door-to-door retail operations.

Party plans are another form of at-home retailing. The use of the party plan for presenting products originated with Tupperware. A salesperson presents the merchandise at a neighborhood gathering in someone's home, using a promise of free gifts for the host, depending upon the volume of sales generated. The host invites potential customers, who are usually more inclined to purchase through a friend instead of a stranger.

VENDING MACHINES

Another type of nonstore retailer is the **vending machine.** Standing alone or in groups, these retail operations dispense all types of merchandise in exchange for the quarters, dimes and nickels consumers press into the slots. Vending machine operations continue to grow as consumers demand more convenience. Many office lunchroom or break facilities contain banks of these

---

[26]Elaine Underwood, "QVC, HSN explore next level of branded tele-retailing," *BRANDWEEK*, October 17, 1994, p. 9; Patrick M. Reilly, "TV shopping hooks high-toned viewers," *The Wall Street Journal*, November 16, 1993, pp. B1 and B10; Howard Schlossberg, "Picture still looks bright for TV shopping networks," *Marketing News*, October 23, 1989, p. 8.

mechanical devices that dispense everything from microwaveable foods to espresso.

Vending machines are especially popular for filling emergency or after-hours needs. The traveler who forgot to pack toothpaste and the hungry student cramming for an exam are typical customers. Many industry lunchrooms service the workforce with a variety of foods and beverages dispensed from machines. Kodak is now selling disposable cameras as well as film through these "silent retailers." In Europe, one can find vending machines that peddle Levi's 501 jeans.[27]

Where Do Retailers Locate?

Retailers locate their businesses in convenient areas. Establishments that are hidden or difficult to find are often the first to fail. Several options are usually available for retail site selection. Downtown and shopping centers compete for rental space, offering different advantages.

Location is an important aspect of retail strategy. More retail businesses have difficulty because of poor location than for any other factor, with the exception of poor management. Selecting the proper place to put the business is a critical decision for retailers. Without satisfactory locations, the most needed products or best promotion may not bring success.

Retailers flock together. Rarely does a retail establishment locate by itself, with the possible exception of hospitality and entertainment businesses. The two most popular congregating points for retailers are the central business district, otherwise known as downtown, and the planned shopping center.

CENTRAL BUSINESS DISTRICT

Central business district (CBD)—the commercial center of a metropolitan area, often called "downtown."

The **central business district,** or CBD, became the commercial center of any size town or city because of its closeness to population. Usually, these areas are on main thoroughfares, accessible by mass transportation. Department stores established themselves in these core areas, soon to be followed by specialty stores looking for the leftover shoppers from the larger retailers.

When people migrated away from downtown locations into the suburbs, CBDs began to deteriorate. High property values in downtown areas led to high taxes, causing a financial drain on inner-city locations. These factors and others caused the decline of many major metropolitan central business districts.

Most metropolitan areas have a downtown revitalization program. Fanned by government money and creative plans such as tax increment financing, these refurbishing projects have breathed new life into many blighted areas. Many urban renewal projects are attracting retailers to the core area for the same reasons that they left decades ago: reasonable rents and plenty of cus-

---

[27]Betsy Spethmann, "Kodak vending focus sharpens," *BRANDWEEK,* August 30, 1993, p. 3.

When refurbishing its downtown area, the city of Eugene, Oregon blocked off streets to create a "city center mall."

tomers. Taking advantage of the numbers of workers in downtown areas, stores with "star" status such as Toys ' Я ' Us, Kmart, Target and Filene's Basement are coming to central business districts in droves.[28]

PLANNED SHOPPING CENTERS

More and more retailers locate in **planned shopping centers.** These commercial areas usually develop in suburbs away from the central business district. The average shopper prefers these retail locations that offer consumers a collection of shops and stores with easy parking and public transportation. Because of the purposely planned mix of stores within the mall, shoppers discover "one-stop shopping." The atmosphere and attractiveness of modern malls also serve as an entertainment bonus to consumers. Retailers want to be "where the action is," which often means locating in the planned shopping center.

Any location decision has its disadvantages. Retailers selecting planned shopping centers must prepare their operations to pay higher rents. In addition to paying more per square foot, retailers lose a good deal of independence when signing a lease in a mall. Shopping center management dictates the hours of operation, instead of store owners. Malls can impose restrictions on the merchandise individual stores carry, and expect retailers to take part in all planned promotions. Because of such policies, the entrepreneurial drive may be lost when retailers move into a planned shopping center.

Planned shopping center—a collection of retail outlets clustered to provide convenient shopping.

[28]Gregory A. Patterson, "All decked out, stores head downtown," *The Wall Street Journal*, February 15, 1994, pp. B1 and B7.

Neighborhood Center

As cities grow and population spreads from the central business district, neighborhood shopping areas sprout. These **neighborhood centers,** occupied mostly by specialty stores, typically evolve at major street intersections. The term "strip center" arose because the stores and shops are often physically placed in a row. Rental rates are typically lower in neighborhood centers than they are in central business districts. Therefore, these locations afford an excellent opportunity for new retail businesses to take root. This group of retailers provides shoppers with many necessities, such as groceries, baked goods, dry cleaning services and banks.

Community Shopping Center

Community shopping centers emerged with the spread of urbanization. Larger than the neighborhood strip, these planned centers may sprawl over an area the size of several city blocks. Usually located in suburban communities, community centers are typically located on major thoroughfares, taking advantage of public transportation.

Community shopping centers herald the appearance of a retailer unique to the planned development, the **anchor tenant.** Located at the ends or corners of the shopping areas, anchors command the dominant position among the tenants. Anchor tenants usually receive preferred lease arrangements from the center owners. These major stores in community shopping centers are usually supermarkets and drug store chains.

Regional Mall

The largest of planned shopping centers is the **regional mall.** These arenas can occupy as much as fifty acres and have over a million square feet of floor space leased to hundreds of retailers. Parking is ample, and public transportation is usually available. Branches of major department stores typically anchor regional malls. Several anchor tenants may be wooed by the developers of these giant planned shopping centers. Similar to community centers, the major tenants in regional malls receive preferential treatment and rental rates.

Regional malls have blossomed into entertainment centers and shopping meccas. Many newer versions come complete with theaters and restaurants. Atlanta's Omni Center, the Clackamas Town Center near Portland, Oregon, and the Peninsula Center in Southern California, include ice skating rinks. Strolling musicians, child care centers and art shows are all part of the effort to attract more shoppers. The Annapolis Mall opened a lot of eyes with innovative features such as family rest rooms.[29]

Lately, malls have become overbuilt. Some market areas have several shopping centers without the population and buying power to support them. Ready capital for the development of these trading areas has led to their abun-

---

[29]Editors, "Amenities set the pace at Annapolis Mall," *Chain Store Age Executive,* May 1992, p. 86.

Outlet malls, featuring manufacturer's discount stores, have become popular planned shopping centers.

dance, but enough appears to be enough. Competition between malls is common, as managers of these planned centers fight for consumer dollars. Retailers are subsidizing the costs of renovating malls in some areas. The Limited leads the way in upgrading these planned shopping centers. Outdoor sights in refurbished downtown areas appear to be a more profitable venture for retail developers.[30]

Outlet Mall

A relative newcomer to the mix of planned shopping centers is the **outlet mall,** a collection of discount or off-price stores. Many of these planned centers cropping up around the country are developed by the same firms. As a rule, these centers do not have anchor tenants. Many of the stores located in outlet malls are owned by manufacturers and are used to funnel overrun or irregular goods out of the typical retail channels. Some of the names commonly associated with outlet malls include London Fog, Mikasa, Van Heusen and Bali.

A recent trend in outlet malls finds some going upscale. Accent lighting and snazzy displays are transforming the "bare-bones" image into one of glitz and high fashion. Some of these centers now sport sidewalk cafes serving croissants and espresso. Along with the upgraded image comes upraised prices, turning off many consumers. Some manufacturers are shipping first-rate

Outlet mall—collection of discount or off-price stores located in the same center.

---

[30]Cara Appelbaum, "The Limited gives America's malls a new lease," *Adweek's Marketing Week,* March 23, 1992, p. 4; Michael J. McDermott, "Too many malls are chasing a shrinking supply of shoppers," *Adweek's Marketing Week,* February 5, 1990, pp. 2 and 3.

goods directly to company-owned outlet stores, creating their own integrated distribution system. In this scenario, outlet malls risk losing their low-priced image.[31]

What Affects the Management of Retailing?

In this age of powerful retailers, marketing management often has its hands full in trying to maintain control. It is easy for large, dominant chains to assume the role of channel captain, dictating policy to both manufacturers and wholesalers. Distribution systems with many intermediaries are more prone to develop conflict.

ETHICS

Just as with wholesale members of the channel, marketers must assure that retailers handling their products are treated equally. Special care should be taken when a manufacturer sells to both independent and company-owned outlets. Pricing and promotional assistance must be equal among competitors. Allowing one retail customer an advantage over another is illegal as well as unethical.

Retailers, too, must be careful not to discriminate. Although in most areas these resellers maintain the right to refuse service to anyone, the courts have held that such practices may be subject to prosecution. The owners or managers need to have good reasons for rejecting a prospective buyer. Making a case against a store or shop may be more difficult because of the regional nature of many retailers and the nature of the refusal to serve. Consumers often keep the pressure on wayward outlets through peer group pressure and local publicity.

Resellers also owe a degree of loyalty to the manufacturers whose goods they carry. One company's items may have distinct advantages over another's, and stores and shops are certainly free to voice opinions about their merchandise. However, inaccurate or biased product bashing increases channel conflict. A lack of loyalty on the part of the retailer often leads to consumer distrust of both producer and reseller.

Smart retail managers stock product lines that meet the needs of their target markets. Many large, chain operations in the clothing field receive complaints regarding their merchandise, where selection in larger sizes is often limited. Stores in major metropolitan areas are sometimes criticized for ignoring the black community. Kmart and J.C. Penney are two retailers that have made a real effort to stock merchandise that appeals to the African-American segment.[32]

---

[31]Christina Duff, "Brighter lights, fewer bargains: Outlets go upscale," *The Wall Street Journal,* April 11, 1994, p. B1.

[32]Carry Goerne, "Retailers boost efforts to target African-American consumers," *Marketing News,* June 22, 1992, p. 2.

Marketing and Society: Green = Gold!

In today's era of heightened awareness regarding the environment, it is not too surprising to see more and more companies involved with "green marketing." Manufacturers that offer safer, cleaner products abound. As the international consumer increasingly focuses attention on products that are safe to use and safe for the environment, businesses turn their efforts toward meeting that demand.

Although the manufacturing sector may lead the way in this movement, retailing is not far behind. Many stores and shops that have offered healthy alternatives in food and other staples are finding a growing number of products to appeal to their target segment. Paper goods made from recycled products are in particular demand. Cosmetics and cleaners that are nontoxic and biodegradable also receive considerable attention from earth conscious consumers.

Eco-retailers with names such as Ecology Box, Whole Earth Products and Ozone Brothers are cropping up all over the country. Shower curtains, paint, light bulbs and linens are among the over 1,000 items that these stores stock. Natural foods stores, which blossomed during the 1980s, have enjoyed good success, as more consumers look toward organic produce and additive free groceries. Many of these emporiums, such as Devore's, have expanded their merchandise base to include wines

SOURCE: Laurie Freeman, "Eco-retailers turn green into gold," *Stores,* October 1991, pp. 50–51.

Like manufacturers, some retailers are joining the movement toward green marketing. Although health or natural food stores have long been a part of the American scene, more emporiums are in operation that carry a wide range of environmentally sound products than ever before. Consumer advocacy groups are calling upon the retail community to join manufacturers in the effort to recycle and conserve.

TECHNOLOGY ADVANCES

Retailers and manufacturers alike are caught up in the wave for more advanced inventory and order handling systems. Electronic data interchange is common among this reselling sector. Many manufacturers find that the lack of computerized logistics hinders expansion. Retailers are becoming selective, opting to carry merchandise lines that are the easiest to use. Two shoe producers, Brown and Stride Rite, supply their resale customers with complete setups.[33]

Upscale cosmetics is one segment of the industry that in the past rejected bar codes and laser readers as being ugly. With new package designs, Estee Lauder, a leading high-end makeup house, lifted the veil that allows for the use of EDI. This use of advanced technology greatly increases the efficiency of retail operations. Estee Lauder joins other cosmetics marketers in speeding up delivery cycles to lower the stock requirements of its customers.[34]

Many of the power relationships between supplier and buyer are breaking down due to the massive computer and communication networks. Manufacturers may now have the opportunity to link directly with consumers to bypass intermediaries entirely. Instant access through information technology has had impact on the auto glass replacement and repair industry, where insurance companies now put owners in direct contact with networked local providers. Travel agents are concerned that similar services will be available from airlines and resorts in the near future, negating the need for intermediaries.[35]

Since consumer goods appeal to different markets, it is not surprising to find a tremendous variety in types of stores and management problems. Although thought of as being uniquely American, retailing is international in scope and growing rapidly in third world countries. This exciting facet of marketing is truly "where the action is."

SUMMING IT UP

Retailers purchase their merchandise from manufacturers or wholesalers and sell to consumers. Typically, these intermediaries are classified by the service provided, by ownership and by type of operation. Retailers are either self-service or full-service. These intermediaries may be part of large

---

[33]William McKee, "A customer service remedy," *Distribution*, June 1994, pp. 38–40; "Sears takes direct approach: EDI speeds furniture from warehouse to home," *Chain Store Age Executive*, March 1994, p. 68; Tony Seideman, "Getting started with EDI," *Distribution*, February 1994, p. 38; Gary Robins, "EDI: Small independents stay in step," *Stores*, March 1992, pp. 38–40; Bill Stack, "Small firms can reap benefits with electronic data interchange," *Marketing News*, April 1, 1991, p. 14.

[34]Bruce Fox, "EDI lifts sales of cosmetics," *Chain Store Age Executive*, March 1992, pp. 34–35.

[35]Zachary Schiller and Wendy Zellner, "Making the middleman an endangered species," *Business Week*, June 6, 1994, pp. 114–115.

chain organizations or independently owned. A number of retailers are franchised operations.

Department stores carry a wide and deep assortment of merchandise. These operations are large in size and provide a variety of customer services. Mass merchandisers carry a wide range of products, but offer a rather shallow selection in each line. Many of these organizations are discounters. Hypermarkets are really mass merchandisers with the addition of grocery lines. These huge complexes carry a broad line of goods and services, but depth is a weak point. Specialty stores carry a narrow assortment of merchandise, but with deep lines.

The grocery business is dominated by supermarkets. These resellers operate on large volume but low margin. Off-price stores are smaller types of retailers that typically carry distressed merchandise. Like hypermarkets, warehouse clubs have prospered in the past decade. These members-only outlets carry a wide assortment of merchandise, but somewhat shallow lines.

Some special consumer service providers include financial institutions and food purveyors. Retailing also includes a number of nonstore members. Direct marketing, or selling without a store, has fostered mail-order houses, video marketing and electronic shopping. In-home salespeople and vending machines round out the list of nonstore retailers.

Retailers locate either in downtown central business districts or in planned shopping centers. Neighborhood centers are common in residential areas. Community shopping centers are most often found in suburbia, and introduce the anchor, or major tenant. Regional malls are giant complexes anchored by department stores and mass merchandisers. Outlet malls are planned shopping centers occupied by off-price retailers.

Ethics is a consideration in managing marketing operations in any field. Technological advances have greatly enhanced the efficiency of retail operations but have also created the need for increased control.

KEY CONCEPTS AND TERMS FROM CHAPTER FOURTEEN

Anchor
Central business district (CBD)
Community shopping center
Convenience store
Department store
Discounter
Electronic shopping
Franchising
Full service retailer
Hypermarket
Integrated distribution systems
Mail-Order House

Mass merchandiser
Neighborhood (strip) center
Off-price store
Outlet mall
Planned shopping center
Retailer
Supermarket
Regional mall
Specialty store
Video marketing
Warehouse club

BUILDING SKILLS

1. Describe the benefits retailers provide to manufacturers and consumers.

2. What types of consumer goods would one find in self- versus full-service outlets? Why?

3. What factors might have led to the mergers and acquisitions of retailers? What advantages or disadvantages do chain operations offer to manufacturers?

4. Describe the differences between department stores, mass merchandisers, hypermarkets and warehouse stores.

5. What environmental factors have caused the increase in the number and types of nonstore retailers?

6. What societal changes have fostered the increase in planned shopping centers? What advantages do these areas offer? Describe the differences between a neighborhood (strip) center, a community shopping center and a regional mall.

7. How has information technology influenced retailing?

Making Decisions 14-1: A Computer For M'Lady?

Most computer retailers offer a rather stark, businesslike atmosphere. One would be hard pressed to call the decor or ambiance feminine. Perhaps this is so because the computer has its roots in the office, in a world still too often dominated by males. Maybe there is a lingering of that chauvinistic attitude that electronics are "too complicated" for women. Whatever the reasoning, Tandy Corporation is making a step in the right direction.

The parent company of Radio Shack feels that many computer-electronics stores are hardware dominated, presenting a heavy, macho image that may turn off female buyers. Another division of Tandy, The Edge in Electronics, positions itself to better capture this market segment. These retail outlets present almost a boutiquelike atmosphere. Curved glass cases and marble tile, coupled with personalized service, give these computer emporiums an upscale, yet soft appearance.

Tandy management undertook a major effort to avoid cannibalizing Radio Shack. The product mix at The Edge in Electronics definitely tends toward the upper end. Brand names such as JVC, Sharp, Panasonic and Memorex are not as a rule found in the lower end stores. The product mix at The Edge also tends to be more personal and portable. High-tech telephones, calculators and entertainment devices are big items for The Edge.[36]

Based upon service provided, ownership and merchandise mix, describe The Edge in Electronics and the marketing functions this firm carries out.

Making Decisions 14-2: Join the Club.

Trade goods marketers walk a tightrope in servicing intermediaries. Manufacturers must be constantly alert to avoid discrimination. Special care is necessary when the producer owns members of the distribution channel, whether those are wholesale or retail outlets. While fair pricing policies is the foremost concern, packaging and special offers can also be cited as restraints of trade. The water has become a bit more muddied with the advent of wholesale clubs.

Although these resellers are actually retailers, in many ways they operate as if they were wholesalers. These warehouse stores offer a small variety of goods at very low prices. They are likely to run contrary to most of the strategies used by retailers. These membership outlets do not try to offer as many "facings" as possible, nor are they likely to carry more than a few major brands. These super stores also like to get special packaging on the goods that they resell. By wrapping several units into one big pack or offering giant-sized containers of mayo or relish, these megastores can provide a service that other retailers only dream about.

---

[36]Nancy Cohen, "The Edge aims high," *Stores,* June 1991, pp. 58–59; Dawn Smith, "Tandy seeks a feminine edge," *Adweek's Marketing Week,* November 12, 1990, p. 42.

The hooker is, how does a trade goods marketer treat these resellers? Are they wholesalers, as they would like to have their suppliers believe, or are they really just glorified discounters? Can a manufacturer offer these outlets special pricing or packaging without discriminating against other wholesale or retail buyers? As firms such as Costco/Price Club, B. J.'s Wholesale Club and Sam's continue to spread, manufacturers will be forced to face ethical dilemmas head on.[37]

Contrast the differences between wholesalers and retailers, including suggestions for solving the ethical problems in selling through these outlets.

Making Decisions 14-3: You Ain't Seen Nothin' Yet!

America's largest center opened in 1992 in Bloomington, Minnesota. Mall of America boasts over 400 stores, fourteen movie houses, seven restaurants, and almost five million square feet of shopping. Many analysts question whether such a giant will survive. This huge complex was developed by Triple Five Corporation, the same company that created the world-famous West Edmonton Mall in Canada. The latter shopping center has been especially successful catering to vacationers.

The recession of the early nineties and troubled times with two of the major tenants slowed the development: Bloomingdale's, of Federated Department Stores, which emerged from court protection before the mall opened, and a Macy's store, belonging to R. H. Macy & Co., which entered Chapter 11 protection later. These two anchors join Nordstrom and Sears in holding down the corners in the Mall of America.

---

[37]Dori Jones Yang, "Bargains by the forklift," *Business Week,* July 15, 1991, p. 152; Fara Warner, "Campbell, Kellogg 'bulk' their brands for wholesale clubs," *Adweek's Marketing Week,* April 29, 1991, p. 26.

Triple Five, citing statistics showing 4.8 million people living within a 150-mile radius, hope to prove the analysts wrong by making this giant a success. An additional five times that many potential shoppers reside within a day's drive. The developers are counting on that short distance to bring consumers from Kansas City, Chicago and Winnipeg in Manitoba province to shop and have fun. No questions about it, Mall of America will have something for everybody, if everybody only comes.[38]

Describe the different types of planned shopping centers and the sorts of anchor tenants each would have. Discuss the advantages and disadvantages of planned shopping centers versus central business districts.

---

[38]David Greising and William Symonds, "Guys and malls: The Simon's crapshoot," *Business Week,* August 17, 1992, pp. 52–53; Laura Baenen, "Mega-mall opens doors to shoppers, the curious," *The Oregonian,* August 12, 1992, p. C5; Donald Woutat, "Nation's newest destination resort: The Mall of America," *Los Angeles Times/Bend Bulletin,* August 2, 1992, p. C1; Associated Press, "Nation's largest mall seeks big niche," *Marketing News,* April 27, 1992, p. 2; Jimmy Golen, "Mall of America to be nations's largest," *The Oregonian,* March 29, 1992, p. R13.

15

Promotion Concepts

The Job to be Done

What good is a product if no one knows about it? How can wholesalers and retailers provide time and place utility without customers? The entire marketing mix depends upon promotion to spread the word about goods and services. This chapter provides you with the tools to:

- comprehend the role of promotion in marketing and the communications process used by promoters,

- identify the elements in the promotional mix and grasp the effect of the product, its image, the product life cycle, price, distribution and market conditions on these elements, and

- describe the methods of budgeting for promotion and understand the problems and solutions in managing promotional campaigns.

Marketers at Work

Sherri Haibeck

Many students are attracted to advertising because it is one of the more glamorous aspects of marketing. Advertisers and advertising agencies are always looking for talented writers and artists, and many students opt for this creative end of the business. Others seem more interested in the business end of the business, helping clients to get the most bang for their buck. Sherri Haibeck chose this latter route after gaining her diploma in marketing from British Columbia Institute of Technology. She still credits the number of oral presentations required by the BCIT faculty in helping her to succeed in the world of marketing.

Upon graduation, Sherri went to work for McKim Advertising, which was later purchased by BBDO. Her early positions provided real learning experience, allowing her the opportunity to examine every aspect of the advertising industry. Western Canada's largest agency, Palmer, Jarvis Advertising, lured her away to become Director of Media Services for this firm. Climbing the ladder, she ultimately became a member of the management team. She then was able to focus the efforts of the entire organization on satisfying client and consumer needs. Sherri recently served as President of ABCOM, the Association of Broadcast Communicators.

After doing an outstanding job for Palmer, Jarvis, this energetic young woman was hired away by Moffatt Communications, the parent company for Vancouver radio stations CKLG/CFOX. As Regional Sales Manager, Sherri is now on the other end of the business, selling her firm's media outlets to advertising agencies and advertisers in her area. She is now working every bit as hard promoting radio as she did boosting the agency. As an added measure of her success, the British Columbia Institute of Technology has hired her as an adjunct instructor in its continuing education program. Sherri has also co-authored the textbook *Introduction to Media,* used in courses throughout Western Canada.

What Is The Role Of Promotion?

Promotion—marketing communication that informs, reminds or persuades.

Promotion is marketing communication, or, more specifically, promotion that informs, reminds or persuades. This final element of the marketing mix informs consumers or users about product characteristics or availability. Promotion serves as a reminder for products that exhibit a strong brand loyalty following. Marketers attempt to persuade prospects to their goods and services by describing the features that benefit customers. Promotion can be directed toward a broad based, large group of potential customers or can be concentrated on an individual.

TO INFORM

At times, merely **informing** prospects that certain goods and services are available is enough. People who have already defined their needs often know what product or products will bring satisfaction. Additional information about product uses or ingredients might serve to better inform an audience. The more detail that potential buyers have about a good or service, the greater the chances that they will buy it. Most individuals, and especially businesses, do not purchase blindly.

Television commercials describe the safety features of the car. A couple picks up the local newspaper to see what is playing at the movie theaters. Voters study pamphlets describing the issues and candidates before entering the booth. Promotion also informs markets and buyers of product attributes, in particular the advantages of one product over another. Competition touts the attributes of its goods or services to overcome entrenched buying habits for other brands. In this way, promotion fosters competition.

TO REMIND

Consumers are constantly being **reminded** of brand names. A typical marketing strategy calls for the isolation of market segments and modification of the marketing mix aimed at satisfying that target. Development of brand loyalty among buyers in the selected market is a key task. Promotion is also used to remind customers where to make their purchases.

Marketers commonly develop an image for their products that is in character with the target audience. Once that image is set, marketing oriented companies continue to remind the market of product attributes. The reminding objective of promotion helps to keep buyers from changing their minds or experimenting with competitive brands. The protection of brand loyalty and the strengthening of product position are major functions of promotion.

TO PERSUADE

Promotion tries to **persuade** the buying public to purchase one product or another. Consumers and business buyers are often reluctant to change brands or suppliers. Marketing communication may be needed to convince these customers to continue their present habits or to persuade them to make a switch. Promotion may be the only way to persuade prospects to make the switch.

■ ■ ■ ■ ■

Promotion functions

TYPE OF PROMOTION	FUNCTION
Television commercial for Lever 2000	Persuade
Point-of-purchase display for Lever 2000	Remind
Billboard for political candidate	Persuade
Direct-mail piece for political candidate	Inform
Newspaper ad for appliance dealer	Persuade
Salesperson working at appliance dealer	Inform/persuade
Magazine ad for computer	Persuade
Magazine article about computer	Inform
Public service announcement for United Way	Inform/persuade
Direct-mail piece for United Way	Remind/inform/persuade
News coverage of airline disaster	Inform
Advertising, publicity from airline	Inform/persuade

■ ■ ■ ■ ■

Many of today's markets have reached or neared saturation. In these areas, product awareness may not be enough to establish a satisfactory share of the market. Recalling the brand name will not suffice. The audience for promotional efforts must respond by buying. Since brand loyalties can be deep rooted, assertive persuasion is necessary, which is perhaps the most crucial role of promotion.

hat Is The Communication Process?

To transmit a message there must be someone who sends and someone who receives. Promotion begins when the sender puts together a promotional message in a way that will attract the attention of the receiver, or potential customer. The transmitted message may travel through mass media or individual communication. A television commercial for Carnival cruise lines, an eye-catching point-of-purchase display for Trifari jewelry or the discussion with a salesperson at Computerland are all examples of promotion.

Whichever methods of transmission are used, communication stops if the message is not received. If a TV viewer leaves the room during a commercial, the sender's advertising goes unheeded. Shoppers who do not notice the merchandising display never receive its promotional impact. When the browser leaves the store as the salesperson approaches, communication does not take place.

SENDER ENCODES/TRANSMITS MESSAGE

As in any form of communication, the **sender** transmits the message using a form of code. By **encoding** the transmission in words and pictures, the promoter desires to move beyond the attention stage to create interest or desire. A problem promoters face occurs in this critical stage of moving the receiver from an awareness state to a position of developing a preference. If the desired communication stops, negative reaction may result. The salesperson may "turn off" a prospect if the encoded message is garbled or the delivery is too pushy.

The promotional message must be encoded to appeal to the groups targeted by the marketer. To the prospective Mercedes owner, a message stressing available colors will likely have little appeal. Performance and prestige are the attributes that interest luxury car buyers. Sunkist does not inform consumers about the cost of its produce, but about the superior taste and consistent quality of its products.

RECEIVER DECODES/INTERPRETS MESSAGE

After an audience receives the message, it must be decoded. As important as it is for the marketer to put the proper information into the message, it is equally necessary that what is said be understandable. Marketers often prepare different versions of commercials and ads for the same product to reach a greater audience. One consumer may be interested in Jell-O gelatin dessert because of its taste. Another may be turned on by its fun image and a third may appreciate the fact that it is a non-cholesterol treat. To insure proper decoding of the message, the marketing communication must address all of these concerns.

One of the biggest obstacles that marketers must overcome is noise in the transmission channel. Interference, in the form of clutter or other activity, disrupts the flow of information. The driver's need to focus on the road during bad weather diffuses the effect of the billboard. Conversation during television commercials or too many ads on one page of the newspaper constitutes noise or interference.

RECEIVER SENDS FEEDBACK TO SENDER

After the message is received and decoded, feedback returns to the sender. If the response to marketing communication is a purchase that satisfies, the promotion was successful. On the other hand, with mass communication in particular, it is difficult to assess the results of the promotional effort. Some receivers may purchase Michelin tires because the television commercial was convincing, but others may buy on the recommendation of a friend. The question of how many potential buyers opted for the purchase based upon the advertising is unknown.

In personal selling, feedback is direct. The professional salesperson is continually probing to identify the needs of the prospect. The process of sending messages and receiving feedback is standard among salespeople.

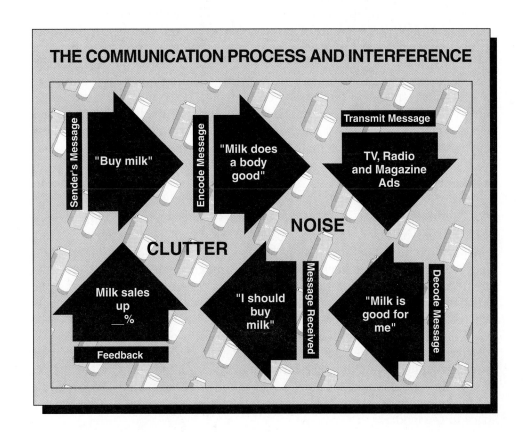

THE COMMUNICATION PROCESS AND INTERFERENCE

Sender's Message — "Buy milk"

Encode Message — "Milk does a body good"

Transmit Message — TV, Radio and Magazine Ads

NOISE

CLUTTER

Decode Message — "Milk is good for me"

Message Received — "I should buy milk"

Feedback — Milk sales up ___%

Sellers learn about the needs of the customer and whether or not satisfaction is possible through this communication. The feedback received from the prospect gives the sender the information necessary for further encoding of the message.

What Is The Promotional Mix?

Promotional mix— the elements of advertising, publicity, sales promotion and personal selling.

Marketers have a variety of tools available to promote products, known as the **promotional mix.** The promotional mix includes advertising, publicity, sales promotion and personal selling. The art of employing these tools effectively, economically and entertainingly often spells the success of the marketing program. Mass communication includes advertising, publicity and sales promotion. Selling is a more personal and individual form of marketing communications.

ADVERTISING

Advertising— impersonal marketing communication directed toward a mass audience, carried by the media and paid for by an identifiable sponsor.

Advertising is the most visible of the promotional tools. This impersonal form of promotion is directed toward a mass audience. Advertising is paid for by an identifiable sponsor, who controls the content of the message and how it is transmitted. The channels used to communicate the advertised message are known as the **media.** Broadcast media include radio and television, while newspapers, magazines and direct-mail compose the print media. Outdoor billboards and signs and placards on transit vehicles form the final member of the team. Advertising is purchased time or space on any of these six media.

Some advertising experts argue that the media should be expanded to include commercial messages placed anywhere. Those promotional blurbs on park benches, in movie theaters or on shopping bags certainly have value. Rented videos often contain promotional bits, and the Goodyear blimp flashes all sorts of hype as it floats through the nighttime sky. In the near future these supplementary vehicles may be included as regular media members.

PUBLICITY

Publicity— free informative marketing communication, usually carried by the media.

Differing from advertising, **publicity** does not include a sponsor who purchases media time or space. Sometimes called "free advertising," publicity is more difficult to control than advertising. For example, the company putting out a press release regarding a new product breakthrough receives no guarantee that the media will use that information. Because of time or space limitations, the radio station or newspaper may have to edit the copy. In addition, the media may editorialize or not report the message favorably.

Publicity promotes either the organization or its products. News releases, press conferences or general news disseminated about the company and its image are public relations efforts. These forms of promotion may benefit the firm as the general public becomes better informed. Information about product advancements or breakthroughs is also publicity if it is not purchased time or space in the media.

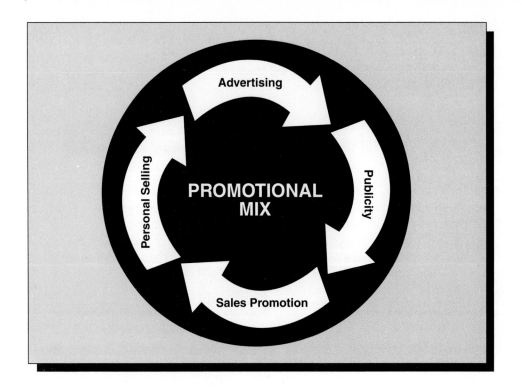

SALES PROMOTION

The purpose of **sales promotion** is to stimulate customer action. As with publicity, these short-term incentives are not purchased media space or time. Sales
promotion encompass a variety of means to promote products and stimulate
buying. Some examples include coupons, free samples, contests, point-of-purchase displays, trade shows and sponsorship of sporting events.

    Sales promotion benefits the corporate image or promotes the sale of
products. Consumers may not run to the store for cans of STP motor treatment
just because a race car pictured on TV sported a decal. However, the image of
this product coupled with racing cars does have promotional value. Kemper
Insurance does not notice a huge increase in activity immediately following the
company sponsored golf tournament, but this promotion does help the company image. Although the results are difficult to measure, these types of sales
promotion are important to marketers and to the goods and services they sell.

Sales promotion—
short-term incentives
to purchase, such as
coupons, contests or
trade shows.

PERSONAL SELLING

Selling is the only element of promotion that is personal. By not playing to the
masses, personal selling involves more direct feedback than the other forms of
marketing communications. If the salesperson does not state the case clearly, or
if a phone call distracts the prospect, communication stops. In mass promotion,
the message is lost when breaks occur. In personal selling, the exchange can
continue after an interruption. Buyers and sellers may restate questions or
points until the understanding is complete.

Personal selling—
persuasive or informa-
tive interpersonal mar-
keting communication.

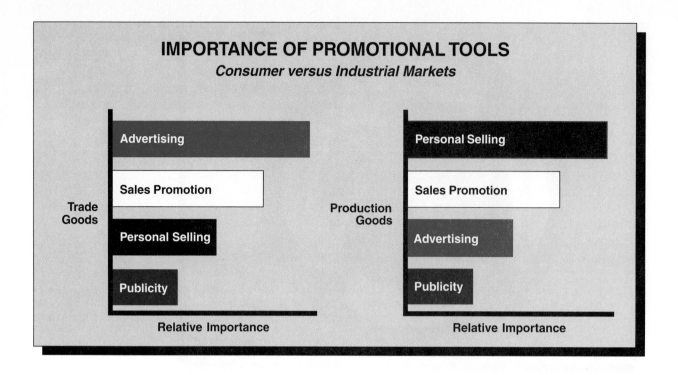

IMPORTANCE OF PROMOTIONAL TOOLS
Consumer versus Industrial Markets

Although personal selling is an effective marketing communications tool, it is also costly. Marketing firms pay salaries and commissions, fringe benefits and insurance as part of their selling costs. Marketers of trade goods could hardly be expected to hire salespeople to convince individuals or households to buy goods or services. On the other hand, because the customers are fewer and the order size larger, production goods marketers make good advantage of the effectiveness of personal selling.

What Factors Affect The Use Of The Promotional Mix?

Marketers blend the use of the elements of promotion together to create the best results. Depending upon several factors, the mix varies, with more of one or another promotional tool used in given situations. Since any form of promotion is costly, wise marketers determine what mix is necessary before investing heavily in marketing communications. Establishing objectives and priorities is important for the success of any campaign.

PRODUCTS

Products influence promotion. The characteristics of the product, its image and the stage of product life cycle all impact marketing communications. To one buyer, a personal computer is used for keeping the household records; for someone else, it takes the place of a typewriter. Still others think of computers as entertaining toys for adults and children. Each target segment creates the need for different types and styles of promotion.

Trade Goods

Product type influences the promotion mix. Marketing communications will vary depending upon whether the product is sold to consumers or to business buyers. **Trade goods** promoters rely heavily on advertising because these items are bought by mass audiences. Marketers for Best Foods mayonnaise, Head and Shoulders shampoo, Sure deodorant, Chevy Lumina and Residence Inns advertise using a variety of media.

Manufacturers of trade goods, for whom branding is important, use both advertising and sales promotion extensively. Media presentations and a host of other activities are designed to persuade and remind consumer audiences. Since trade goods are distributed through intermediaries, marketers use contests and premiums to promote products to wholesalers or retailers. Merchandise awards and vacation trips are examples of incentives that manufacturers use to fire up their intermediaries.

Consumer products distributed through self-service retailers do not need personal selling. Details on how Nabisco puts the holes in Lifesavers is not a significant selling point that needs to be explained to the grocery shopper. Personal assistance is necessary for some consumer items, especially shopping or specialty goods. Many drug stores and most department stores have consultants available for help in the cosmetic sections. Computer retailers must offer aid to sometimes squeamish customers to overcome fear or uncertainty.

Production Goods

Marketers of **production goods** typically rely on personal selling as the prime method of promotion. This type of promotion works well because of the limited number of customers in concentrated locations common in these markets. The need for close interpersonal relationships between buyer and seller also dictates the use of personal selling.

Production goods marketers may use some advertising to soften the market for personal selling efforts that follow. The salesperson's visit is more meaningful if the prospect is aware of the company and its products beforehand. Production goods advertising also generates leads for the selling force. For sales promotion, manufacturers of raw materials and production apparatus rely more on incentive programs for the field sales force.

Image

Product **image** influences the promotional mix. Prestige items rarely use coupons or point-of-purchase displays. Cadillac does not promote by sponsoring ski races, but Chevrolet does. Cross Pens relies upon distinctive advertising to promote its products. Paper Mate uses coupons, contests and a variety of sales promotion items.

The image of the media selected for advertising campaigns must match the position of the product. One would not expect to find commercials for

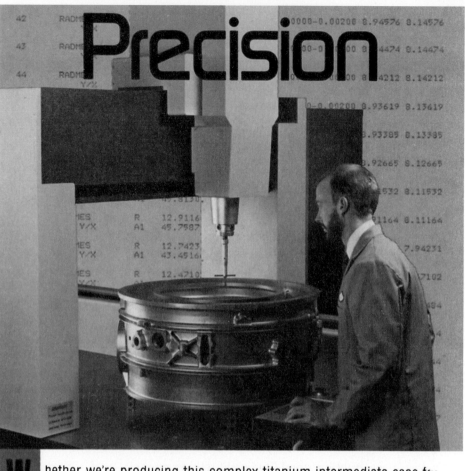

Precision

W hether we're producing this complex titanium intermediate case for an RB199 engine—or a 60-inch casting with a wall thickness of .060 inches—accuracy is everything.

Precision. It's in our name—and in every product we manufacture.

For more information, contact Tom Allen at 44-0625-827042, Telex: 44-0625-827844,

or write:
Tom Allen
P.O. Box 56
Macclesfield
Cheshire SK10 4XG
England.

Precision Castparts Corp.

Personal selling is an important promotional activity for marketers of produciton goods, such as Precision Castparts. (Courtesy of Precision Castparts Corp.)

Hartmann luggage on the soap opera "All My Children." Advertisements for Liz Claiborne women's wear would be inappropriate in *Penthouse*. The premiere marketer of automobile hoses and belts, Gates Rubber Company, would receive little value from advertising placed in *Reader's Digest*. The media selected and the message transmitted must be consistent with the image of the product.

Product Life Cycle

The promotional mix varies with the stage of the **product life cycle.** Because products are unknown in the introductory stage, mass communication is the obvious choice. Advertising tends to be somewhat general during this initial phase. The "new age" drinks category of flavored sparkling waters grew sharply during the early 1990s due largely to combined promotional efforts of companies such as Perrier Group of America and PepsiCo. Promotion for these new products included point-of-purchase displays and radio ads.[1]

During the growth stage of a product, advertising becomes more specific as the product gains its own identity. The entry of competition in this phase creates the need to differentiate between brands. Bausch & Lomb, noted for eye care products, moved into the oral hygiene arena when it purchased Interplak, the electric toothbrush with rotating brushes. Once into the dental products business, B&L increased its presence with a patented mouthwash, Clear Choice. As its mint-flavored alcohol-free mouthwash began to grow, the company's advertising stressed the differences between its product and the competition. Product comparisons are common in this stage of the PLC.[2]

As products enter their maturity stage, profits peak and competition intensifies. Early in a product's "adulthood," promotional efforts abound. The purpose of advertising and sales promotion is to retain brand loyalty by using constant reminders. A number of mature brands dominate the automobile market. Although model changes are common, there is often little to differentiate one make from another. In tightly competitive markets where mature brands abound, the use of heavy, hard-hitting promotion often makes the difference in share of market.[3]

Advertising tapers off as products begin to enter the declining stage. As the product nears the end of its useful life, many marketers cease advertising entirely, counting on lingering sales promotions to keep the good or service alive. Publicity efforts are aimed at providing a "hall-of-fame" image. Marketers direct promotional efforts toward allowing the product to die respectfully. Companies also strive to assure that the death of a product does not affect the overall corporate image.

PRICE

The **price** of a good or service has a bearing upon the promotional mix. Many lower priced items receive heavy sales promotion activity to supplement advertising. Marketers of products carrying higher prices seldom use contests, coupons and sampling, and often employ more personal selling efforts. As an example, Toyota and Ford use a variety of sales promotions, including contests, giveaways and sponsorship of racing events. Mercedes Benz and Lincoln rely upon more sophisticated advertising and personal selling by their retailers.

---

[1]Alison Fahey, "Perrier and Pepsi push new age drinks," *BRANDWEEK*, July 20, 1992, p. 4.
[2]Seema Nayyar, "Bausch & Lomb mouthwash: $13M," *BRANDWEEK*, September 14, 1992, pp. 1 and 6.
[3]Fara Warner, "Toyota puts $40M into momentum," *BRANDWEEK*, September 7, 1992, pp. 1 and 6.

■ ■ ■ ■ ■

Promotion functions within product life cycle

STAGE OF PLC	PROMOTIONAL OBJECTIVES	PROMOTIONAL ACTIVITY
Introductory	Develop product awareness	Advertising, publicity
	Stimulate product testing	Advertising, sales promotion
	Engage initial distribution	Advertising, personal selling
Growth	Create product differentiation	Advertising
	Expand distribution	Advertising, personal selling
	Develop brand loyalty	Advertising, sales promotion
Maturity	Maintain brand loyalty	Sales promotion
	Maintain distribution system	Personal selling, sales promotion
	Create new markets	Advertising, sales promotion
Declining	Create respectable death	Publicity, advertising
	Maintain company image	Publicity

■ ■ ■ ■ ■

Price and position go hand in hand. The perceived quality of a product usually affects the selection of media as well as the message portrayed. Big ticket items can afford and often require more personal selling. On the other hand, marketers cannot afford to have salespeople spending precious and expensive time promoting lower priced goods or services. Advertising and sales promotion are more effective on less costly items.

DISTRIBUTION

Distribution may influence the size and shape of the promotional mix. For instance, intensely distributed products need heavy promotional emphasis to move the goods through the channels. By creating ultimate buyer demand, promotional efforts clear the storage spaces of intermediaries. Marketers that rely heavily on wholesalers and retailers may need additional promotional effort to help build ultimate demand.

MARKET CHARACTERISTICS

Characteristics of the **market** affect promotion. The tremendous numbers of consumers dictate a mass communication policy for goods aimed at this market. Production goods buyers, on the other hand, are smaller in number and more concentrated geographically. When markets converge in one area, personal selling is the most effective promotional tool. The cost of making individual sales calls may be prohibitive if buyers are widespread.

Another aspect of market conditions that affects promotion is competition. Market share often depends upon presenting an image. Matching the promotion efforts of competitors becomes important in an oligopoly, where vying for business is not price oriented. The major producers of No Nonsense and L'eggs pantyhose, for example, promote the features and benefits of their products and strive to create brand loyalty.

Dominated by General Mills, Kraft General Foods' Post brand and Kellogg, the dry cereal market thrives on promotion. Both advertising and sales

Global Marketing: Nothing But Lip Service!

To the lay person, the global arena appears to be reserved for the "big boys." Certainly the company names that are bantered about read like a Who's Who of international business. In the cosmetics industry alone the lineup is full of giants. Unilever, the Anglo-Dutch megamarketer is heavy into world trade with its Arden and Ann Klein divisions. L'Oreal is another major name player, and many of the Procter & Gamble lines are poised for even bigger efforts overseas.

Hardly seems to be the right place for a New York based lipstick manufacturer names Creative Cosmetics, but this runt among Goliaths controls about 20 percent of the lipstick market in Japan. This is the firm that staggered the fashion industry when it introduced is multihued line of Moodmatcher lipsticks. These are the lip colorings that appear green, silver, yellow or even black while in the tube. Once applied to warm skin, however, the wild colors turn into natural looking shades of red and pink, depending upon the body chemistry of the wearer.

After an exhausting round of testing, Creative Cosmetics was able to gain approval for its products from the Japanese Ministry of Health. Asian buyers also imposed strict quality control standards on the American company, which ended up being a boon to domestic business as well. Once its products were approved, this exporter carried out an extensive, ongoing promotional campaign to assure the success of the Moodmatcher brand. Advertising related directly to Japanese culture, while building on the appeal of Western products and ways of life.

SOURCE: Cyndee Miller, "U.S. firm gives lip (coloring) service to Japan," *Marketing News*, March 16, 1992, p. 6; Seema Nayyar, "Unilever makes power move on Arden," *Adweek's Marketing Week*, June 22, 1992, p. 10. (Photo courtesy of Wilson Marketing Enterprises, Inc.)

promotion are prominent promotional tools. Major brands are heavily advertised on television and in magazines, and coupons and point-of-purchase displays create additional incentives. In oligopolies, where price is typically not used as a competitive weapon, promotion may be the answer to product differentiation.[4]

---

[4]John Sinisi, "Bursting with health," *Superbrands,* 1992, pp. 80–87.

MARKETER CHARACTERISTICS

With many firms historical positions determine present planning. If the marketer can afford a major personal selling effort, advertising and sales promotion may not be as necessary. As a rule, this form of production is more effective than mass communication.

The size of the firm's product mix affects the extent of its marketing communications efforts. As the width of the mix increases, more advertising effort is necessary. The multiple product lines from Procter & Gamble illustrate product mixes that receive maximum promotional effort. With a family brand policy, many products may be boosted by the efforts in promotion of just one item within the line. Television commercials for Tide, for example, benefit all of the individual brands of laundry detergent marketed by Procter & Gamble.[5]

ow Do Marketers Budget For Promotion?

No accurate mathematical model to compute the perfect budget for marketing communications exists. Obviously, marketers will spend money on promotion if it produces results. Not all advertising or sales promotion is profitable. Successful promoters view the cost of these efforts as an investment rather than an expense. Promotional budgeters use four methods to estimate costs: percentage of sales, competitive equality, return on investment, and objective and task.

Percentage of sales— budgeting for promotion based upon a percentage of previous or forecasted sales volume.

PERCENTAGE OF SALES

One common method of budgeting for promotion is **percentage of sales.** This fixed percentage can be based upon the revenues generated in a previous

· · · · ·

Factors affecting use of promotional mix

FACTORS	PROMOTIONAL MIX USAGE
Trade products	Heavy advertising and sales promotion
Production products	Greater use of personal selling and publicity
Company image	Upscale products use fewer sales promotions
Technical products	Personal selling required; advertising very detailed
Product life cycle	Sales promotion heavy in introductory and maturity stage; advertising dominates growth stage
Price	Sales promotion heavy with low priced items; advertising and personal selling dominate "big ticket" items
Distribution	All forms of promotion heavy in widely distributed products
Marketing company	Smaller firms rely on personal selling and some forms of trade promotion; larger firms use all types of promotions

· · · · ·

[5]Alison Fahey, "Ads up $12-18M: Seeks new media," BRANDWEEK, July 20, 1992, pp. 1 and 6; "Nabisco rolls out twelve new products," BRANDWEEK, July 13, 1992, pp. 1 and 6.

period or computed on forecasted sales. Although used by many businesses, notably the automobile industry, this form of budgeting is not considered to be the most effective by advertising experts.

Percentage of sales budgeting seems to suggest that sales cause promotion instead of the other way around. During times of declining sales, promotion may be the exact tool needed to reverse the downward trend. The percentage of sales budgeting method would reduce spending at a time when marketing efforts should increase.

COMPETITIVE EQUALITY

Another method of budgeting relates to **competition.** Budgeting based upon competition is common in oligopolies where the actions of the leader are closely monitored by the other members. Marketers construct a correlation between what the competition is spending for a similar volume of sales and apply the same formula to their own budget. For example, if Company A has 25 percent of the market and spends $5 million per year on promotion, Company B with 20 percent of the market would budget $4 million.

Just because one company spends a certain amount on promotion does not mean that a similar expenditure by a competitor will produce like results. What works for one firm or one product may not succeed for another. Additionally, the possibility exists that the competitor may be astutely hiding some of its marketing communications dollars in other categories. This action throws off rivals who are copying promotional budgets.

Competitive equality— budgeting for promotion based upon being equal to the competition.

RETURN ON INVESTMENT

Some firms base promotional budgeting on **return on investment.** Using this budgeting method, the marketer earmarks dollars that will maintain or increase the present share of market. Suppose Hunt-Wesson spends a specific amount of money to maintain a 40 percent share of the ketchup market. By considering that expenditure as an investment, the company can judge the return in profit against the original budget.

In operation, this type of allocation is almost impossible to compute. Expenditures based on producing a return are long range in nature, but spending on marketing communications is immediate. Also, return on investment is tied to sales revenue, which does not increase solely through promotion. For example, how much should Hunt-Wesson spend to increase its share of market by 5 percent or 15 percent?

Return on investment—budgeting for promotion based upon a desired return on investment.

OBJECTIVE AND TASK

The favored system for budgeting system is **objective and task.** This method places emphasis on programs needed to reach specific goals. By defining the objectives and then targeting the promotional tasks necessary for success, the marketer takes control of the entire program. Some products and programs may require different amounts of marketing communication effort, and by treating each item separately, budgeting becomes more meaningful. Kraft General Foods

Objective/task— budgeting for promotion based upon determining the objectives desired and the tasks necessary to reach those goals.

may not need to spend as much on promotion for mayonnaise as it doles out to push Cheez Whiz. General Motors will budget more to promote new models, such as its Saturn, than for models that are moving slowly or are less profitable.

The objective/task method is the preferred way of budgeting for promotion. Still, small, nonmarketing oriented firms may have a difficult time in implementing this procedure. Many factors affect how sales respond to advertising and sales promotion. Marketers must establish the objectives of the promotional campaign before addressing specifics relating to advertising, publicity, sales promotion or personal selling.

ow is Promotion Managed?

Marketing oriented businesses want to receive the most benefit from the dollars they spend on promotion. Since many factors affect this choice, the promotional mix varies from firm to firm and from product to product. Marketers must define the desired objectives from the use of marketing communications. Using the budget as a guide, the promotional mix can then be modified to create the best chance for success in reaching those goals.

PRODUCTION GOODS AND SERVICES

For **production goods** marketers, distribution channels are typically short. Personal selling works well in this setting because products do not travel through several hands, and the buyers are generally knowledgeable. In addition, the interpersonal relationships and complexity of the products found in this arena dictate the need for this type of promotion. Although the other elements of the promotional mix are used, selling remains dominant.

Production goods are often highly technical. Reaching audiences for these products cannot be done through consumer oriented media. Most business buyers subscribe to media that relate to their specific field or interest. Timken does not use television to advertise its bearings, and it would be ridiculous for Caterpillar, the heavy equipment manufacturer, to promote over radio or in newspapers. Similar to most production goods sellers, these firms reach their prospects through advertising in business magazines and through salespeople.

Similarly, the providers of business services tend to select nonconsumer media. Consultants, advertising agencies and engineering firms advertise using magazines that are going to best reach their target audience. Some business service firms select specific television programs where statistics show a high percentage of viewing by managerial types, such as the evening news. Generally, such firms avoid the typical consumer media.

TRADE GOODS

With **trade goods,** the ultimate user is not usually the customer. Although women are the ultimate consumers of Giorgio's new Wings scent, the company's

Trade journals, the favorite media for production goods marketers, cover every subject imaginable.

original buyers are wholesalers and retailers. This cosmetics house, now a division of Avon, uses television and magazines to promote Wings to consumers, while relying upon personal selling and trade journals to reach intermediaries. Consumer goods manufacturers have to promote to both the final user and the intermediate buyer.[6]

Trade goods use longer channels of distribution, and promotional efforts must include intermediaries. Marketing communications in these arenas can either push the product through the channel or pull it. By promoting to the intermediary, the manufacturer fills the distribution system, which in turn must act to rid itself of the merchandise. On the other hand, promotion aimed at the consumer creates the demand which then entices wholesalers and retailers to stock the products.

PUSH STRATEGY

The **push** strategy aims promotion toward wholesalers and retailers. Push strategies involve advertising, publicity, sales promotion and personal selling. Advertisements in specific magazines tend to make intermediaries aware of the

Push strategy—directs promotional efforts toward marketing intermediaries.

[6]Editors, "Giorgio answers its critics with new fragrance," *BRANDWEEK.* February 22, 1993, p. 26; Seema Nayyar, "Giorgio has a new fragrance for the woman in women," *BRANDWEEK,* October 20, 1992, p. 3.

goods, and articles in these same journals create interest in the company as well as its products. Contests and premiums aimed at wholesalers and retailers have the effect of loading the shelves with the manufacturer's merchandise, which must be turned. All these efforts assist the sales staff that calls on these intermediaries.

Suppose Spalding, the sporting goods manufacturer, offers a vacation for two to Hawaii for the retailer with the greatest one month increase in sales. This special promotion has the effect of encouraging intermediaries to push more merchandise. Manufacturer and retailer both benefit from increased sales.

In-store promotion is another sales promotion method gaining in favor. Promotional messages on aisle signs, shopping carts, and at the checkout stands are common. One of the leading firms in the in-store promotional fields is ActMedia. This innovative company markets instant coupon machines and live sampling to supermarkets and drugstores. More recently, ActMedia has developed POP Radio which pipes FM-style music, plus commercial messages, through some 15,000 stores nationally. These types of promotion may be a cost to the retailer, but in turn generate sales.[7]

PULL STRATEGY

Pull strategy—directs promotional effort toward the ultimate user or consumer.

Pull strategies create market demand. By encouraging the ultimate buyer or consumer, products will be pulled through the distribution system. As consumers demand goods and services, the marketing system provides them. The key promotional tool used in the pull strategy is advertising, reaching audiences in widespread locations. Properly used, advertising is accurate in targeting both segmented markets and undifferentiated ones.

Sales promotion used in pull strategies aims at consumers instead of intermediaries. Contests, samples and coupons help boost demand. Sponsorship of sporting events produces publicity coverage through newspaper, magazine, radio and television. The constant reminder of brands reinforces the loyalty that pulls products through the distribution system.

The "Heinz has your number" promotion targeted consumers who matched the last four digits of their phone number with the last numbers on the UPC bar code on twelve Heinz products. This pull type promotion livened the market for ketchup, pickles and tartar sauce. Inflatable Image Industries markets replicas of containers in the form of cold air balloons placed in parking lots. These attracters are sold to promoters such as Kraft General Foods and PepsiCo.[8]

Marketers of production goods and services have also discovered the benefits of pull strategies. Advertising and sales promotion aimed at the ultimate user become tools in selling to other manufacturers. Briggs & Stratton conducted a heavy promotional campaign aimed at the buyers of garden equipment. By promoting to consumers, this manufacturer of gas engines created demand for its customers' products, such as lawn mowers and mulchers. This demand created increased orders for Briggs & Stratton engines.

---

[7]Chuck Stogel, "Quest for the captive audience," *Superbrands,* 1992, pp. 106–107.
[8]Editors, "So much cold air," *Adweek's Marketing Week,* February 3, 1992, p. 20.

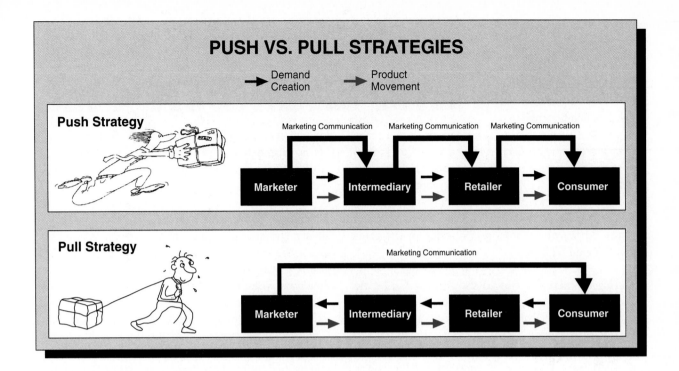

PUSH VS. PULL STRATEGIES

Demand Creation   Product Movement

Push Strategy

Marketing Communication   Marketing Communication   Marketing Communication

Marketer → Intermediary → Retailer → Consumer

Pull Strategy

Marketing Communication

Marketer ← Intermediary ← Retailer ← Consumer

COMBINATION STRATEGY

Most major, trade product marketers use a **combination** of push and pull promotional strategies. By developing promotional plans that benefit the reseller and attract the consumer, marketers gain the best of two worlds. These marketers use a pull strategy to create consumer demand while offering push incentives to their intermediary customers. Determining the objectives of promotion in advance allows marketers to use the available tools efficiently.

The combination of pull and push is clearly seen in the building supply industry. Manufacturers of windows and doors, such as Andersen and Pella, for example, employ salespeople to call on architects and builders for specifications. These producers also direct advertising at the ultimate consumer to stimulate demand. Contests, point-of-purchase displays and trade shows promote to lumberyards and home improvement centers.

ETHICS

Promotion is an area of marketing that receives heavy public complaint. Deceptive or distasteful advertising is of major concern. Continual upgrading of media presentation will help in overcoming the stigma that many attach to advertising. On the other hand, many ads are artistically and sensitively produced, and others offer refreshing entertainment.

Green Marketing

Making environmental claims about products or their packages is still a wise marketing decision. Naturally, these assertions must be accurate. Many

Marketing and Society: Way to Go Liz!

Starting a new business or product line is an exciting, but difficult, challenge. New ventures that fail exceed those that make it by a great margin. Such evidence would be reason enough for most to expect little when Liz Claiborne Inc. entered the highly competitive women's fashion arena over a decade ago. This upstart company, led by its designer-founder, quickly climbed the charts and shattered growth records. In 1992, sales for the company topped $2 billion.

During its meteoric rise to the top, Liz Claiborne Inc. grew from its signature sportswear line into a variety of other fashion areas. Lizwear and Lizsport brands were joined by the upscale Dana Buchman line. Three moderate brands—Russ, Crazy Horse and Villager—also proved successful. Accessories and fragrances joined the product mix, along with shoes and jewelry. The opening of free-standing boutiques has long been awaited, and the Elisabeth Stores, carrying large-size women's apparel, added to the firm's retail ventures. The latest Liz Claiborne Inc. move is into home furnishings, with the line of Liz at Home bed, bath and related products. The company also opened a midtown Manhattan store in 1995.

Liz Claiborne Inc. is well aware of its social responsibility. The charitable arm of the company, The Liz Claiborne Foundation, supports a variety of programs in the arts, education and human services. Employee volunteerism is strongly encouraged. In addition, the company established a domestic violence awareness program called Women's Work. Liz Claiborne Inc. dramatically demonstrates that marketing and social responsibility do mix, while maintaining its dominant position in the women's fashion industry.

SOURCE: Elaine Underwood, "Can Liz still work?" *BRANDWEEK*, December 5, 1994, pp. 27–31.

consumers have been turned off by statements that were either not true or were meaningless. The Federal Trade Commission and the National Advertising Division of the Council of Better Business Bureaus are cracking down on the use of broad, generalized statements such as "environmentally safe" or "biodegradable."[9]

For some marketers, ethical green marketing has paid off both in sales and in helping society. Most soft drinks, for example, bear labels saying "Please Recycle." Cartons for Sunshine Biscuits and Arm & Hammer Fabric Softener state that they are made from recycled paper. Lever Bros. not only claims that it uses recycled plastics, but encourages consumers to recycle its containers through a message on its packages. Although the ground swell of green marketing has ebbed somewhat, those marketers that swear by accuracy and honesty continue to reap additional sales.[10]

---

[9]Allan Glass, "Does a green message still belong on your package," *BRANDWEEK*, October 13, 1992, pp. 26–28.

[10]Adam Snyder, "The color of money," *Superbrands*, 1992, pp. 30–32.

Puffery

Legislation requiring "truth in advertising" has helped to resolve the accuracy issues of commercials and ads. In their promotional efforts, marketers must present their products' attributes accurately. General Foods cannot advertise that Betty Crocker cake mixes will cure acne, and Jordache cannot claim that wearing its blue jeans will make the consumer look like Brooke Shields.

Puffery, on the other hand, is common in advertising. This term describes the sometimes meaningless statements made about products that are considered harmless. Kraft General Foods can state that Betty Crocker makes great tasting cakes and Jordache can allow that the comfort and fit of its clothing is superb. Converse can even claim a "77% better energy return than Nike air" without actually defining energy return. Budweiser's claim as "The king of beers" and the allegation that Pepsi is the favorite of ". . . the younger generation" are also puffery.

Perhaps because they are so used to puffery, a number of major consumer goods houses have been caught stretching the truth in their promotions. The Kellogg Company came under fire for branding one of its cereals Heartwise. Under pressure from government agencies, the Battle Creek, Michigan, company changed the name of this high-fiber breakfast food to Fiberwise. Similarly, Procter & Gamble changed the label on its Citrus Hill Fresh Choice orange juice because it was not fresh. The FTC ordered Sandoz Nutrition Corp., of Minneapolis, to stop unsubstantiated claims about its liquid diet product and forced First Brands Corporation of Danbury, Connecticut, to remove misleading environmental labels from Glad trash bags.[11]

The Food and Drug Administration also scrutinizes advertising claims. General Mills used the words "reduce cholesterol" sixteen times on each package of its Benefit cereal, including a statement regarding lowering the chances for a coronary incident. Pfizer's Plax is advertised as reducing plaque and tartar, decreasing the potential for contacting gingivitis. The FDA usually disallows such claims unless substantiated. Mayonnaise marketers are in a tizzy because this government agency has ruled against the use of the words "light" or "cholesterol free" on labels for mayo. This action resulted from initial industry standards, approved by the FDA, which spelled out the ingredients for true mayonnaise.[12]

The federal government also polices comparative advertising. Revisions to the Lanham Act, effective late in 1989, strengthened the legal position of those products and firms that are named in competitor's promotion. Prior to passage of the Trademark Revision Act of 1988, an advertiser could only be sued for making false claims about its own products. With the new law, civil action may

Puffery—blustery and pompous statements about products that, while not being deceptive, are somewhat meaningless.

---

[11]Helen Kahn, Jim Henry, "Volvo agrees to $150,000 penalty for monster truck ads," *Automotive News,* August 26, 1991, p. 33; Fara Warner, "What happened to the truth?" *Adweek's Marketing Week,* October 28, 1991, pp. 4 and 5.

[12]Dan Koeppel, "After five years, the FDA decides 'light' mayo is not what it seems," *Adweek's Marketing Week,* October 15, 1990, p. 6; Dan Koeppel, "Will the FDA swallow big G's Benefit," *Adweek's Marketing Week,* April 17, 1989, p. 2; Editors, "Hey, whatever happened to 'tooth' in marketing," *Adweek's Marketing Week,* January 9, 1989, pp. 26–30.

be taken against a promoter for any misrepresentation. Selective survey results are especially vulnerable.[13]

Delicate Subjects

How to handle sensitive subjects has always been a problem for promoters. As audiences become more receptive to the mention of body functions and activities, advertisers for feminine hygiene products, laxatives and hemorrhoid preparations became a little bolder. Most of these promotional efforts are tastefully done. Others are not. Sending free samples of maxi-pads to a blind mailing that included male as well as female students was senseless and thoughtless.

Although today's society is more open minded about subjects previously considered too personal to discuss publicly, there is a limit to what audiences will tolerate. A good example is the debate over condom advertising. The AIDS epidemic has certainly created more interest in these products, but many are not ready to accept television commercials just yet. As a general rule, if advertising is created tastefully and sensibly, audiences are more willing to be receptive.

Pressure Selling

High pressure personal selling, while on the decline, still persists in many industries. Rude presentations by hucksters create bad images for both the product and the company. The increase in the number of professional, problem-solving salespeople will go a long way toward eliminating pushy or intimidating individuals in the selling field. Unfortunately, there are no government or industry regulations that restrict distasteful selling habits, although dishonest or misleading presentation are cause for legal action.

In most cases, marketing oriented companies prefer to correct their mistakes before they become public knowledge. When the Parker Brothers Toy Company learned that the deaths of two children were attributed to parts off its Riviton toy, the company immediately withdrew the product from the market. Procter & Gamble removed its Rely brand tampon from stores the moment it learned of the problem of toxic shock syndrome suffered by women using the product. If businesses do not react in the same responsible manner shown by these two companies, buyers and consumer groups usually will turn to the government for protection or relief.

PROMOTIONAL CLUTTER

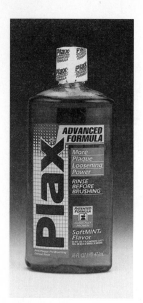

When Pfizer advertises that its Plax reduces tartar and plaque, the marketer must be able to back up those claims.

Promotional clutter— the overwhelming quantity of advertising.

The unending onslaught of advertising, called **promotional clutter,** is a constant target for criticism. Excess advertising on commercial television networks has prompted many viewers to turn to cable TV or public television. Radio ads interrupt the music and news programming. Over half of the average newspa-

---

[13]Leah Rickard, "New ammo for comparative ads," *Advertising Age,* February 14, 1994, p. 26; Cyndee Miller, "Demonstrating your point," *Marketing News,* September 27, 1993, p. 2; Dan Koeppel, "Bashing brand X will no longer be as easy as ABC," *Adweek's Marketing Week,* June 12, 1989, p. 17.

per is devoted to advertising, and there are about five thousand magazines in print in this country alone. Citizen complaints have led to a reduction in the number of billboards found alongside the country's highways.

Although the amount of advertising can be annoying, these commercial messages pay for the programs we watch and the articles we read. The travel tips, gardening advice and recipes found in *Sunset* magazine are made possible through advertising dollars. Those firms who use the pages of this popular journal to promote their products and places to visit contribute much more to the costs of printing and distributing the magazine than do subscription rates. The evening news, "60 Minutes" and sitcoms such as "Home Improvement" are possible because of advertising.

AIDA

Communication clutter adds to promotion's task of persuading potential buyers. To deliver the message regarding the benefits or attributes of a product, marketers must first penetrate the communication maze. If this breakthrough does not happen, markets and customers remain unaware of necessary goods and services. Promoters follow the acronym **AIDA** in combating clutter.

Aida—acronym for Attention, Interest, Desire and Action.

Grab Attention

The first step in any promotional program is to attract the **attention** of the audience. With so much promotional activity, trying to get an audience to focus on one subject is an accomplishment, but advertisers have an extensive arsenal of attention getters for breaking through the communication chaos.

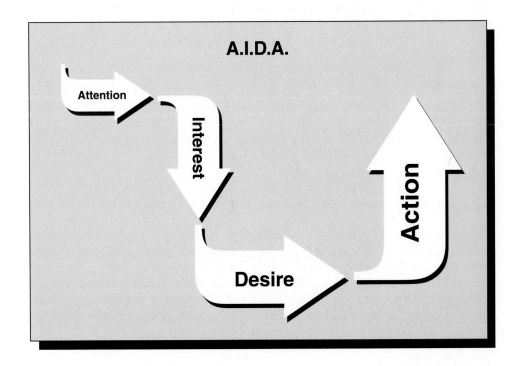

A.I.D.A.

Attention
Interest
Desire
Action

Among these techniques for attracting the prospect's attention are appealing personalities, pictures, colors and headlines. Coupons and contests are great for pulling customers into the retailer's store or shop. Banners and displays help to grab buyers as they stroll the aisles. Considerate and informing assistance from a salesperson gains the attention of the prospective buyer.

Create Interest and Build Desire

After getting the audience's attention, marketing communication must increase **interest** or build **desire.** Persuasion to develop preferences for products builds brand loyalty. If people become interested in a particular good or service, they will likely buy it. That interest helps turn product features into customer benefits. Interest and desire peak when the promotional effort points out specific product attributes that will satisfy individual needs.

Interest and desire may be generated by the copy of an advertisement or by the explanation received from a salesperson. Sometimes trying a sample is what develops the appeal and whets the appetite. Advertising for Nuprin states that the product effectively combats headache pain. The salesperson at the stereo store explains the features of the Sony compact disc player. The next door neighbor claims that his Weber grill is the best he has ever owned. Each of these forms of communication helps in building interest and desire.

IN GLOBAL MARKETS

Certainly, cultural differences create an interesting challenge to firms in global markets. The meaning of words or phrases used to describe a product to an American audience may sound ridiculous or lewd when heard by people from other cultures. Even brand names take on new meanings when translated. Some television commercials seen in Europe would be X-rated in the U.S., yet much of our advertising would be considered too risqué by many Asian or Arabic cultures.

Additionally, many markets overseas are not blessed or burdened with the number of media outlets that are found here. In the countries of Eastern Europe, much of the television capability is still government owned, which restricts the availability of commercial time. Newspapers and magazines are not found in most societies in the diversity and quantity to which Americans are accustomed. In many poorer nations, the often maligned outdoor billboard is the primary advertising medium.

Produce Action

The ultimate goal of marketers is to sell the merchandise or service that produces satisfaction. To reach this end, promotion must produce **action.** Purchasers prefer the feeling of buying instead of being sold. Promotion attempts to convince prospects that satisfaction will result from the purchase. Television commercials for Nuprin pointedly ask viewers to buy the product. The salesperson at the Builders Emporium or rebate offers from the manufacturer exhort customers to purchase the Weber barbecue.

SUMMING IT UP

The role of promotion is to inform, remind or persuade customers and markets about products and their features or benefits. In the communication process, promoters send a coded message to the audience. The receivers must then decode the communication and return feedback to the original sender. The input returned from this marketing communication process often is in the form of product sales.

The promotional mix includes advertising, publicity, sales promotion and personal selling. Advertising is impersonal communication directed toward mass audiences. This form of promotion is paid for by an identifiable audience and carried by the media. Publicity is often carried by the media, but is not purchased time or space, hence is more difficult to control. Sales promotion includes all of those nonmedia events that provide incentives for customers to buy. This category includes coupons, contests and trade shows. Personal selling is the only form of promotion that is direct communication between individuals. While it is most effective, selling costs are high.

The promotional mix for trade goods differs from that for production goods. Trade goods marketers use both advertising and sales promotion. Production goods marketers favor personal selling. The image and positioning of the product affects the selection of promotional methods. Upscale, sophisticated products call for less sales promotion and a greater amount of personal selling. In the introductory stage of the product life cycle, advertising, sales promotion and publicity are used to awaken mass audiences. All forms of promotion are hefty in mature phases of product life, and dwindle rapidly as the product goes into decline.

Large channels of distribution, such as those found in many trade goods arenas, call for intense advertising and sales promotion. The shorter channels used in production goods markets are a natural for personal selling. Similarly, the characteristics of the market and the marketers influence the amount and types of promotion used. Widespread, highly competitive markets call for mass communications. Large product mixes within financially strong businesses will receive greater promotion.

Percentage of sales is a common way of budgeting for promotion. Competitive parity and return on investment are also popular. The most effective budgeting method is objective and task, where the marketer matches what needs to be done with the means of accomplishing those goals. Management of promotion is dictated by the types of products and markets involved. Push strategies target intermediaries, building desire for product at the wholesaler and retailer level. Promotion aimed at building ultimate consumer or buyer demand is a pull strategy. Trade goods marketers typically use a combination of both.

Ethics in marketing is a major concern. Puffery, the pompous bluster of advertising, may be distasteful, but it is not illegal. Deception, on the other hand, is actively policed by the Federal Trade Commission. The promotion of delicate subjects poses sensitive issues. Promoters have the task of breaking through the clutter that abounds in the world of marketing communication. Marketers first attempt to grab the attention of an audience. The next task is to build interest and desire, culminating in product sales.

KEY CONCEPTS AND TERMS FROM CHAPTER FIFTEEN

AIDA
Advertising
Available funds
Competitive equality
Marketing communication, promotion
Objective/task
Percentage of sales
Personal selling

Promotional clutter
Promotional mix
Publicity
Puffery
Pull strategy
Push strategy
Return on investment
Sales promotion

BUILDING SKILLS

1. Explain the purposes of the following forms of promotion: a television commercial for FedEx, the Southland Corporation involvement with the Muscular Dystrophy Association, a coupon in the Sunday newspaper for Ragu spaghetti sauce.

2. Define the differences in the communication process for the various elements of the promotional mix.

3. Analyze the types of promotion which would be the best choice for the following products: gourmet frozen dinners, the Dallas Cowboys, lubricating oils for industrial machinery, fiction best-sellers, aluminum ingots.

4. Explain how the factors of the product or market would influence a promotional campaign for Holiday Inns, the introduction of the Chrysler LH model automobiles, a rate decrease by Sprint long distance telephone service.

5. Describe each method of budgeting for promotion and explain why objective and task is preferred.

6. Discuss the differences between "push" and "pull" strategies, pointing out specific cases where a combination occurs.

7. Discuss the ethical concerns in the management of promotion.

Making Decisions 15-1: Still Going.

Perhaps it's the unbelievable amount of it. Maybe consumers just get tired of all the hype and fuss. Sick, silly or stupid commercials certainly are not a help. Whatever the reasons, many people grow weary of the same old stuff on television. Does the American public need any more females portrayed as bimbos cavorting in beer commercials? Are two scoops of raisins really going to make us stop what we are doing and grab a bowl of cereal? Where has all the fun in advertising gone?

And as for that silly rabbit beating the drum. . . . Wait a minute. Now you're talking. The seemingly ever-present character representing Energizer batteries is approaching cult symbol status. Not only is this fuzzy pink fur ball with the dark glasses traipsing across the television screen, but toys and gifts have been created around the bunny. This funny bunny has become

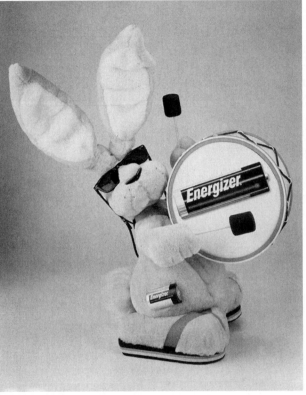

one of the top vote getters among memorable advertising characters.

For a long time, using humor in commercials was considered taboo. Many of the leaders in the industry felt that, while humor might make an audience remember the commercial, it would not get them to buy the product. Today, humor has become a mainstay of television advertising. The "Where's the beef?" ads for Wendy's, Nike's efforts featuring Bo Jackson and the clever commercials for Alaska Airlines are classic examples of the return of humor in advertising. It appears that most viewers prefer these comic interludes to the typical fare served up on the tube.[14]

Describe how humorous advertising satisfies the functions and objectives of promotion.

[14]Susan Bady, "How to use a little humor to get a lot of sales," *Professional Builder*, March 1994, p. 24; Edmund O. Lawler, "Campaigns all use humor," *Business Marketing*, January 1994, p. 20; Craig Bloom, "Madison Avenue, where humor can get some respect," *The Wall Street Journal*, August 19, 1990.

Making Decisions 15-2: The Pen Is Mightier . . . .

Lately, upscale appears to be the "order of the day" for marketing. Consumer are bombarded with so called "premium" products. From cars to cat box filler, frozen dinners to shampoos, or circular saws to television sets, products of better-than-average quality appear in almost every conceivable category. Premium products also carry premium prices. Few industries escape the introduction of products that target a more affluent clientele, wooing them with images of exceptional durability and quality served in an aura of exclusiveness.

The writing implement field is no different. The return of "wet" ink pens has been in progress for a while, but now many of these old timers are coming in premium grades. The Paper Mate Division of Gillette introduced its version of the "yuppie" pen in the late l980s. Manufactured in France, this fine writing implement features an 18k gold nib and a body that receives a seven step lacquer coating that must be applied in a clean-room setting. The fifty separate inspections guarantee the customer the ultimate in pens.

Gillette uses a three-pronged promotional campaign for this pen. Media presentations in upscale magazines such as *Vogue* and *Gentlemen's Quarterly* lead the effort. An educational program directed at retailers describes the sophisticated manufacturing techniques used to make the pens. Store personnel and shopkeepers are then in a position to pass along this interesting and persuasive information to prospective buyers. In addition, attractive point-of-purchase displays are used to lure the consumer.[15]

Describe the elements of the promotional mix Gillette uses, including the types of strategy ("push" or "pull") that each element uses, and the factors of product and market that impact those choices.

Making Decisions 15-3: Take It Off!

The promotion of some products is, well . . . just sexier than that for others. The advertising for its jeans gained some notoriety for Jordache during the early nineties. Male and female models wearing little if anything more than a pair of Jordache jeans seemed somewhat risqué even by today's standards. And who can forget the classic ads for Calvin Klein's Obsession cologne. The totally nude models in those print offerings were the brunt of much criticism.

Perhaps no modern promoter has been more daring than Quintessence Incorporated, the Chicago-based marketer for Jovan Musk. The steamy television commercials heated up the tube. Although most of the sensuous shots were flashed in quick review, it did not take a rocket scientist to get the point.

[15]William H. Miller, "Gillette's secret to sharpness," *Industry Week*, January 3, 1994, pp. 24–26; Laura Bird, "Marketers sell pen as a signature of style," *The Wall Street Journal*, November 9, 1993, p. B1; Diane Schneidman, "Gillette plans three-prong U.S. marketing blitz for upscale pens," *Marketing News*, April 11, 1988, p. 30.

Although the obvious sexual implications received much comment and criticism, the networks ran them with apparent abandon. Not so with the thirty-second spots created for Jovan's twentieth anniversary sale.

These cute but spicy commercials began with a portrayal of a stuffy looking and sounding character intended to be a network censor. The action flashes back and forth between a man and woman playfully taking off their clothes much to the concern of the censor. The punch line was "Hey, it's our sale. We'll take off as much as we want." The three major networks refused to run the ad until it was cut and changed. So much for journalistic freedom.[16]

Describe the ways that management can reduce or eliminate consumer and industry complaints about promotion.

---

[16]Cyndee Miller, "No sex, please; we're censors," *Marketing News,* March 16, 1992, pp. 1 and 7; Seema Nayyar, "For Jovan, ad bans are all in a day's work," *Adweek's Marketing Week,* March 9, 1992, p. 7.

16

Advertising, Publicity and Sales Promotion

■　　■　　■　　■　　■　　■　　■　　■　　■　　■　　■　　■

The Job to be Done

Products can be promoted in many ways. A television commercial or radio spot is advertising. Articles about products and companies that appear in magazines and newspapers are publicity. Coupons, contests and point-of-purchase displays are among the many incentives to buy that are called sales promotion. Chapter 16 provides students the information needed to:

- describe the various types of advertising and show how each pertains to marketing situations,

- identify the advertising media and analyze how the advantages and disadvantages of each relate to specific types of products or marketers,

- compare the functions of advertising agencies and explain how advertising is evaluated,

- explain the role of public relations in marketing and the function of publicity within that role, and

- recognize the types of and uses for sales promotion along with the factors affecting the management of this promotional tool.

459

How Is Advertising Classified?

Advertising is a relatively inexpensive way to communicate marketing messages to mass audiences. The intent may be to inform about product benefits, or simply to remind listeners or readers about goods or services to maintain brand loyalty. Most advertising is intended to persuade people that a particular good or service is the best buy or offers the most benefit. Advertising is typically classified as being either product or institutional, as consumer or business.

PRODUCT ADVERTISING

Product advertising— media messages that promote goods or services.

Most advertising promotes products. **Product advertising** creates or develops a desire for consumers or businesses to buy goods or services, either now or at some future time. The intention of the magazine ad for Reebok sneakers and the television commercial for Delta Airlines is to produce sales for those advertisers. By describing the attributes of their products, advertisers bank that consumers will choose the good or service being promoted.

To guarantee future and present sales, product advertising attempts to establish or maintain brand loyalty. This promotional effort should correspond with the positioning strategy that the marketer develops. Allegiance for a specific good or service is difficult to break, so advertisers continually remind customers of brand

RANK				TOTAL U.S. AD SPENDING		
1993	1992	COMPANY	HEADQUARTERS	1993	1992	% CHG
1	1	Procter & Gamble Co.	Cincinnati	$2,397.5	$2,164.3	10.8
2	2	Philip Morris Cos.	New York	1,844.3	1,977.5	−6.7
3	3	General Motors Corp.	Detroit	1,539.2	1,345.2	14.4
4	4	Sears, Roebuck & Co.	Chicago	1,310.7	1,166.3	12.4
5	5	Pepsi Co	Purchase, N.Y.	1,038.9	929.6	11.8
6	6	Ford Motor Co.	Dearborn, Mich.	958.3	794.8	20.6
7	18	AT&T Co.	New York	812.1	623.7	30.2
8	10	Nestle SA	Vevey, Switzerland	793.7	731.1	8.6
9	11	Johnson & Johnson	New Brunswick, N.J.	762.5	717.4	6.3
10	7	Chrysler Corp.	Highland Park, Mich.	761.6	756.3	0.7
11	8	Warner-Lambert Co.	Morris Plains, N.J.	751.0	751.0	−0.0
12	12	Unilever NV	London/Rotterdam	738.2	690.4	6.9
13	9	McDonald's Corp.	Oak Brook, Ill.	736.6	743.6	−0.9
14	16	Time Warner	New York	695.1	637.9	9.0
15	14	Toyota Motor Corp.	Toyota City, Japan	690.4	648.9	6.4
16	21	Walt Disney Co.	Burbank, Calif.	675.7	553.0	22.2
17	15	Grand Metropolitan	London	652.9	646.3	1.0
18	17	Kellogg Co.	Battle Creek, Mich.	627.1	630.3	−0.5
19	13	Eastman Kodak Co.	Rochester, N.Y.	624.7	686.0	−8.9
20	25	Sony Corp.	Tokyo	589.0	517.0	13.9

SOURCE: *Advertising Age,* September, 1994.

■   ■   ■   ■   ■

names. Frequent advertising of these product identifiers strengthens brand position in the mind of the consumer or business buyer.

Comparative Advertising

Some consumer product advertising is **comparative.** By comparing their goods or services with competition, some marketers feel that they can convince consumers to switch their brand loyalty. Although many consumers find these promotional "wars" distasteful, marketers use this type of promotion to accurately point out the differences between competitive products. Comparative advertising is prevalent during the growth stage of the product life cycle.

Comparative advertising is usually not practiced by marketers whose brands or companies are considered industry leaders. These firms would prefer not to mention the competition at all. Other marketers use this type of advertising to defend their market or product positions. Whether appreciated or not, comparative advertising is part of the promotional scene.

Comparative advertising—product advertising that compares competing brands.

Cooperative Advertising

Cooperative advertising is product advertising placed by retailers that is at least partially paid for by the manufacturer. This type of promotion provides incentives for intermediaries to promote manufacturers' products. Marketers that offer such programs agree to cooperate in the advertising effort with the

Cooperative advertising—product advertising placed by retailers that is partially paid for by the manufacturer.

retailers or wholesalers that carry and resell their merchandise. By paying for a portion of the media work done by retailers, marketers help these intermediaries promote products to consumers. Cooperative advertising arrangements usually pay as much as 50 percent of the actual media costs.

Co-op advertising benefits both the producer and retailer by generating additional sales for both. Retailers culminate sales with consumers, and by helping these resellers promote their merchandise, manufacturers maintain some degree of control in reaching the ultimate buyer. Retailers, on the other hand, receive an extra boost to their promotional efforts. The total advertising budgets expand by the moneys available from manufacturers. Cooperative advertising from trade goods marketers is typically directed toward newspapers. Production goods marketers cooperate through training sessions, join sales calls and a variety of other innovative means.[1]

BUSINESS ADVERTISING

Business product advertising—product advertising directed toward buyers of business goods and services.

Business product advertising is directed toward buyers of business goods and services. Audiences for business product advertising include industry, the trade, buyers of professional services and the agricultural community. Industrial advertising is for production goods and services. Advertising to the trade is directed toward marketing intermediaries. The medical, legal and financial professions place a minimum amount of advertising with media, primarily in directories. Farm advertising is directed toward the agricultural community.

Industrial Advertising

Industrial advertising targets the buyers and specifiers of production goods. This type of business product advertising appears in magazines especially designed to appeal to these individuals. Business-to-business advertisers also use direct mail to reach their audiences. Promotional messages using these media usually go into great detail about the goods or services being presented.

One of the primary functions of industrial advertising is to make prospects aware of product attributes and availability in advance of a personal call by a salesperson. Softening the market with business product advertising makes the job of the sales force easier. Prospects who learn of the product first through advertising are often more receptive to salespeople. Potential customers may learn so much about a company's products through advertising that they are presold toward making the purchase.

Marketing companies frequently reprint their advertising to be passed out to the sales force as customer handouts. Since the ads that appear in business publications are usually more detailed and technical than consumer product promotions, such reprints are often very informative. In addition, handouts given to prospects serve as reminders about companies and their products.

---

[1]Julie S. Newhall, "The care and feeding of a cash cow," *Sales & Marketing Management*, May 1992, pp. 40–47.

Owens-Corning Fiberglas tones its message to intermediaries to reflect the value derived from handling their merchandise. (Courtesy of Owens-Corning Fiberglas)

Trade Advertising

Trade advertising is business product advertising directed toward marketing intermediaries. If wholesalers or retailers are the buyers of the products, this type of media promotion describes how the manufacturer's merchandise will benefit resellers. Since profit motivates most intermediaries, trade advertising shows wholesalers and retailers the income advantages of handling a particular line of goods.

Some trade advertising is for other items used in these types of businesses. Shelving, racks and display fixtures are important to wholesale and retail buyers. Information regarding material handling equipment, computers and even janitorial supplies are regularly advertised to members of the trade. Any media presentation that is used to inform or persuade intermediaries to buy merchandise or supplies is classified as trade advertising.

Trade advertising— business product advertising directed toward marketing intermediaries.

Professional Advertising

Professional advertising is placed by professionals, such as doctors, dentists, attorneys and accountants. Advertising in the medical and law communities is somewhat new, and many professionals in these fields still find such commercialism degrading. Some professional organizations, such as the American Medical Association and the American Bar Association have strict policies regarding what type of advertising is or is not allowed.

Despite this tendency to avoid promotion, physicians and lawyers face increased competition, which creates greater need to contact prospects and clients. Tastefully produced advertisements are one way of informing the public of special expertise. Some attorneys regularly use newspaper and local television to inform audiences of their services. Accountants use a variety of business oriented media to attract potential clients.

Professional advertising—business advertising placed by professionals such as doctors, attorneys and accountants.

Nonbusiness advertisers have similar objectives. Although products are not involved, agencies and organizations try to attract contributors or participants through advertising. United Way advertises on professional football telecasts, and the American Heart Association places ads in magazines and newspapers. These promotional efforts show the publics of nonprofit organizations how and where their contributions are put to use.

Farm Advertising

Farm advertising— business advertising directed toward the agricultural community.

Another type of business advertising targets the agricultural community. Manufacturers of products used in agriculture promote through **farm advertising.** Direct mail and outdoor are two of the favored media for this type of promotion, but newspaper and magazines segmenting this business community are available. Farmers are both the target of and users of advertising. Many individuals and companies advertise their agricultural products to producer cooperatives and other marketing agents through these media.

INSTITUTIONAL ADVERTISING

Institutional advertising— business advertising promoting the company rather than its products.

Not all business advertising relates directly to products. **Institutional advertising** promotes the company rather than its products. Although this form of promotion may ultimately provide increased sales or customer interest, the primary purpose is not to sell goods or services. Business and nonprofit entities use this form of media promotion. Often called nonbusiness or corporate advertising, this type of promotion is used to enhance company or product image.

Positioning the marketer is as important as positioning the products of the marketer. In the eyes of buyers the company and its products are inseparable, and the image of one can have either a beneficial or detrimental effect on the other. Institutional advertising also attracts investors or personnel. At times this type of promotion simply informs a general public about activities of interest within the firm.

Build Product or Company Image

Public relations relies heavily on institutional advertising. Coupled with standard publicity practices, this type of promotion benefits the image of marketers and their products. The promotional efforts targeting image or positioning should not be taken lightly. As much care should be given to image building promotion as is spent on product development.[2]

For instance, Monsanto regularly spends advertising money telling the general public how valuable chemicals are in our daily lives. Such promotion benefits the entire industry, not just Monsanto. This marketing communication accomplishes more than just public awareness of the marketer. Stock brokerage Drexel Burnham Lanham will likely carry a negative image for years due to its junk bond scams. Advertising is one tool this securities trader is using to try to overcome that poor reputation.

---

[2]Bob Lamons, "If you don't care about your company image, who will," *Marketing News*, June 8, 1992, p. 13.

Global Marketing: The Body Beautiful.

Anita Roddick is not what you might call your ordinary, run-of-the-mill entrepreneur. Oh sure, like all entrepreneurs, she created a business out of an idea. Some kind of business! The Body Shop, which Roddick founded in 1976 in Brighton, England, now has 1,000 stores in some forty–five countries around the world. All of this based upon a shrewd combination of manufacturing and selling natural ingredient products mixed with a healthy dose of social activism.

From the beginning, Roddick has not wavered from her philosophy toward environmental protection. All of The Body Shop's products are biodegradable, and the company refuses to test its cosmetics on animals. However, the company goes much farther than simply being attuned to "green" marketing. In each of her company owned and franchise operations, Roddick displays literature and posters regarding ozone depletion, Romanian orphans and other humanitarian issues and causes.

The latest promotional move by The Body Shop is the creation of an exclusive group that shares Roddick's desire to make this world a better place. The Body Shop Club solicits members to join in a variety of conservationist causes for a nominal $25 annual fee. Besides receiving the latest information about company products, T-shirts and campaign buttons, members get quarterly issues of a newsletter that updates causes and issues The Body Shop supports. The company, in return, uses the club to gain valuable demographic and personal information, while maintaining continuing contact with its customers.

SOURCE: Editors, "The Body Shop Club: Frequency marketing for politically correct cosmetics," *Colloquy*, Vol. 3, Issue 1, pp. 8–9.

Attract Investors or Personnel

One of the purposes of institutional advertising is to **attract investors.** By promoting the company in a good light, this promotional effort makes the firm appear appealing to the financial community. Brokers often take out ads in *The Wall Street Journal, Business Week* and *Fortune* informing readers about stock offerings and bond issues. This form of marketing communication spreads the word to an audience that is keen on investing.

In addition, businesses use institutional advertising to **attract personnel.** This does not include classified ads placed to fill vacant positions, but rather display ads or commercials describing firms in terms of the atmosphere and opportunity available to prospective employees. Dow Chemical runs a series of advertisements in *Time* magazine and commercials on national television each spring with the intention of luring graduating college students to work for that firm.

Advocate a Position

Institutional advertising is used by businesses wishing to take a stand on an issue. **Advocating a position** is a prime use of these media presentations. Firms use advertising to assure that inaccurate reporting does not change their image. For example, media personnel often edit publicity that they receive in the form of a press release or interview. Such editing may destroy the original intent of the promotion. On the other hand, institutional advertising reads exactly as the company desires.

Although the use of institutional advertising does not promote products directly, advertisers obviously hope to gain some promotional value. Mobil Oil advertises

Is it time to teach an old law new tricks?

Just because a law is old doesn't mean it's necessarily good or bad. But when over the years an industry changes dramatically, it seems reasonable that the laws governing it should also change. For example, America's financial services are governed by a law enacted before computer technology, globalized capital markets, and a wide variety of instruments became part of our financial system.

That law, the Glass-Steagall Act, was passed in the crisis atmosphere of the Great Depression in response to stock market abuses. This 54-year-old law keeps commercial banks from breaking into the Wall Street cartel that dominates stock and bond underwriting and has created a division of services that's outdated and harmful.

By creating a monopoly on certain lines of corporate business, Glass-Steagall has kept the cost of raising capital artificially high. And, ironically, it has prevented U.S. commercial banks from conducting business at home they can successfully pursue overseas—underwriting bonds in London but not in New York, for instance.

Chemical Bank supports appropriate regulation. But we believe that regulations must be removed if they perpetuate unfair competition, hinder our domestic banking system, or raise prices for our corporate clients. If we fail to repeal these archaic regulations, we'll continue to use yesterday's laws to govern today's markets. And that seems to us like the tail wagging the dog.

CHEMICAL BANK
The bottom line is excellence.

Member FDIC
© 1991 Chemical Bank

Many marketers use institutional advertising to promote their corporate image. (Courtesy of Chemical Bank)

in *Time* and *The Wall Street Journal* advocating positions regarding the press and the federal government. The only reference to the oil company is the credit at the bottom of the page. Mobil suspects that people who agree with their position or who appreciate their straightforward presentation will buy Mobil products.

Distribute Information

Another specialized use of business advertising is to **inform** customers and channel members of changes. Confusion often prevails when companies purchase other firms. Through advertising, marketers are able to pass along the word regarding the change in ownership and how it might affect business. When RJR merged with Nabisco, the new company placed ads in business magazines announcing future plans. KKR used the same tactic when it subsequently bought RJR Nabisco.

Name changes are other events that receive advertising attention. For example, Navistar advertised heavily to promote its new name for an old company, International Harvester. Companies use advertising to pass on facts and information to have the control over promotion that publicity often lacks. By purchasing media time or space, the marketer assures that its message will be aired or printed.

What Are The Advertising Media?

Advertising media are the channels that carry promotional messages from marketer to the targeted audience. Television, radio, newspaper, magazine, direct mail and outdoor are the typical promotional vehicles for both product and institutional advertising. The use of media is what distinguishes advertising from other forms of marketing communications. To qualify as advertising, promotional messages must be purchased time or space in these media.

Advertising media—
the channels that carry promotional messages from marketer to audiences.

Each of these channels has different characteristics and capabilities and offer distinct advantages for different marketers. Cosmetics houses, such as Estée Lauder, Calvin Klein and Clinique, choose magazines. Soft drink and beer houses, such as Coca-Cola, PepsiCo, Coors and Stroh's concentrate on television. Stores and shops typically find newspaper and radio the most advantageous. Automobile manufacturers use a combination of all of the media.

Many other advertising vehicles, or **supplementary media,** are options for marketers. These include yellow page and industrial directories, flyers and internal business publications, such as house organs or annual reports. Many promoters are developing these in-house magazines to reach selective audiences. These slick and expensive publications are used by many major marketers, such as bootmaker Timberland, telephone giant MCI and Federal Express.[3]

---

[3]Ripley Hotch, "Refined desktop publishing," *Nations Business,* August 1994, p. 50; Lura K. Romei, "Desktop publishing: Image is everything," *Managing Office Technology,* January 1994, pp. 8–9; Joshua Levine, "Self-made press lords," *Forbes,* December 9, 1991, pp. 302–304; Kate Bertrand, "Volcanic activity," *Business Marketing,* April 1992, pp. 22–24.

EVALUATION CRITERIA

Reach—the number of people who can be contacted by a given medium.

Lead time—the time in advance of the actual printing or airing that the order must be placed.

To compare their advantages and drawbacks, evaluators use certain criteria to compare each of the media. For instance, **reach** is the coverage of broadcast media or circulation of print media. Reach means the total number of people who can be contacted by use of that medium. **Cost** is computed using "cost per thousand" people contacted, or CPM. Each member of the media has a different cost/benefit ratio.

Lead time refers to the time in advance of the printing or airing that the order must be placed. Lead time varies greatly between media members. Less flexibility occurs as the lead time increases, making message changes more difficult. **Durability** relates to how long the impression continues to attract attention. The length of time that a given advertisement or commercial is in front of the audience increases its impact and retention.

The **artistic quality** offered by a medium may be the difference between gaining or losing the attention of the reader or viewer. Those media that are better at capturing the attention of the audiences usually provide the advertiser with greater potential. Another criteria is the ability of the media to reach a **segmented audience.** Since so many products target specific groups of people or firms, the media selected must penetrate the clutter and deliver those potential buyers.

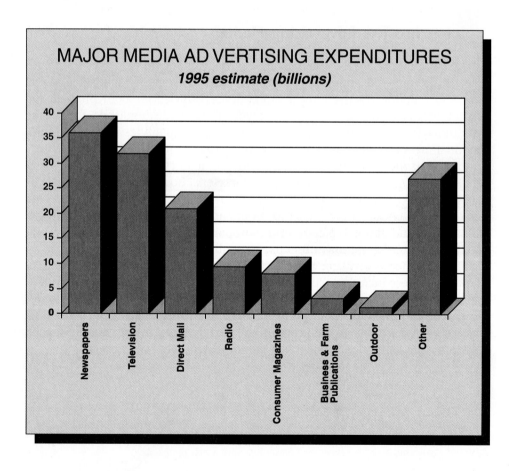

TELEVISION

Television, the newest of the six media, is noted for its reach. About 99 percent of U.S. households own at least one TV set, and many have more than one. Television is the favorite of manufacturers who distribute consumer products nationwide and is the only medium on which products can be demonstrated. Advertisers likely favor television because of the vast numbers of people that can be reached through this vehicle.

Television advertising is generally expensive. Other than commercials aired over small, independent stations, the total cost of advertising on television is high. Considering the excellent reach of this medium, cost per thousand can be reasonable for major network presentations. Cable television has made sizable gains in terms of viewers changing from the major networks.

Television may face a challenge from another communications veteran, the telephone company. "Baby bells," regional successors born out of the breakup of AT&T, since switching to glass fibers, would be a natural medium for programming such as home shopping and movies. Cable TV firms are lobbying hard against this move.[4]

Lead time for placing ads on national networks can be two to three weeks. In addition, production for shooting the commercials can be lengthy. Television spots are fleeting, and this lack of durability is a drawback to both broadcast media. The artistic quality of the medium is outstanding, being the only vehicle to impact both video and audio senses. Because of the variety of programs available on television, minimally segmented audiences can be reached, but television is not noted for its ability to grasp a specific target market.

Production Details

Since television impacts both video and audio senses, dramatic attention grabbers are not as necessary as they might be with other media. Shots of moving automobiles, celebrities, or computer generated artwork is often enough to capture the concentration of television viewers. Musical presentations, problem/solution formats and comedy are typical methods used to gain attention. The advertising agency for Nestle's Tasters Choice instant coffee created a continuing romantic interlude to gain a lasting memory.

Television commercial producers start their artistic layout with a device called a **storyboard.** A storyboard is a series of pictures and dialogue put on paper to simulate the television screen. This presentation allows the advertiser to get an idea of how a facsimile of the finished product will appear before spending large sums on video production. The entire commercial can be shown in bits and pieces prior to production by using storyboards.

Television commercials follow several forms. By showing a slice-of-life, the ad places the product in a typical setting. Procter & Gamble uses these

Storyboard—a device used in creating TV commercials using sketch forms to depict the scenes.

---

[4]Gail Edmondson and Patrick Oster, "Waltz of the media giants," *Business Week,* September 12, 1994, pp. 52–53; Gary Samuels, "Partner or die," *Forbes,* September 12, 1994, p. 128; George Gilder, "Cable's secret weapon," *Forbes,* April 13, 1992, pp. 80–84.

types of presentations to promote the benefits of all-temperature Cheer laundry detergent. Narrative commercials tell a story and may be humorous. The ads for Keebler cookies and crackers gain audience attention through the clever use of animation while using the narrative approach.

One somewhat recent approach to television advertising is the infomercial. These usually half-hour long, dedicated programs gain new impetus during election years. The success of this type of advertising has attracted a raft of mainstream advertisers, including GM Saturn, Sears, Apple Computer, McDonalds, Pepsi and Eastman Kodak. Although initially panned by some media and agency executives, infomercials appear to be growing in popularity.[5]

RADIO

Radio is often a support vehicle, being paired with other advertising media in a promotional campaign. Retailers use radio along with newspaper advertising to reinforce the message of special offerings or sales. Although its reach is not as great as television, the vast number of sets in operation give radio good coverage. Radio is a low-cost medium, which gives radio an advantage over more expensive outlets. Short lead time, usually within seventy-two hours, is another advantage for radio. As with television, durability is a weak point. Listeners are inclined to "tune out" when the radio commercial is aired, hence catchy, well-written copy is needed to keep the ear of the listener.

Because radio appeals only to the sense of hearing, commercials must work hard to capture attention of the audience within the first few seconds of a spot. Developing memorable ads for this medium is one of the more difficult jobs in advertising. A commercial with a recognizable tune or voice grabs the attention faster than the words spoken by a local announcer. The variety of programming available from stations allows radio to reach different audiences. Ads on stations featuring country and western tunes may differ from those featuring classical music. Despite these programming policies, radio is not noted for its segmenting ability.

Production Details

Radio copywriters realize that they have a scant three seconds to grab the ear of the listener. Humor is one of the tools radio copywriters use, as is music, particularly memorable jingles. The creative people hope that the listener will keep humming or whistling that tune heard over the air as a constant reminder of the product. Using the same audio track found in television commercials helps to reinforce the message that the listener hears. This technique of radio advertising supports the attractive television commercials, while the TV presentation builds interest in the radio message.

---

[5]Tim Triplett, "Big names crown the infomercial airwaves," *Marketing News,*" March 28, 1994, pp. 1 and 2; Rinler Buck, "Infomercials: History repeats itself," *BRANDWEEK,* July 19, 1993, p. 11; Howard Schlossberg, "Infomercial industry enjoys growth; still faces some hurdles," *Marketing News,* August 3, 1992, p. 13.

Many creative copywriters refer to radio commercials as the "theater of the mind." Using words, these ad people paint a mental picture of the scenario so that listeners can actually imagine what is happening. The Stiller and Meara commercials for Blue Nun wine and United Van Lines caught listeners' attention because of the distinctive voices of the characters and the humor of the scenario. Listeners could conjure up their own vivid, mental pictures of the scenes these two characters verbally painted.

NEWSPAPER

Newspapers attract many advertising dollars even though reach is rather poor. This medium features local news items, which creates interest among people living within the circulation area. The cost of newspaper advertising is one of its best features. No other media can boast a lower rate in reaching an audience. Copy can be inserted easily in newspapers within three days of press time. This short lead time, along with low cost and local news, make this medium the darling of retailers.

The durability of newspaper is better than that of the broadcast media. Advertisements still attract buyers days after the copy is printed. If the edition survives without being used to start the fire in the fireplace or line the bird cage, chances are the advertisement will be seen again and again. However, a major disadvantage of newspaper advertising is its lack of artistic quality. With its black on white format, newspaper ads do not attract attention as easily as other media, and color ads are more expensive. With an average of over 50 percent of

Our holiday
tag sale will
knock your
stockings off!

25-50% OFF our already
low Rack prices.

Grab the nearest one-horse open sleigh. Hitch a ride with a reindeer. Any way you can, dash into the Nordstrom Rack and save a bundle on selected apparel for the whole family. You'll also find great deals on ornaments, accessories, terrific gift items—there's something for everyone! Hurry for best selection. All markdowns will be taken at the register.

NORDSTROM
RACK

Due to the local nature of the content, low cost and short lead time, newspapers are the favored media of the retail industry.

each newspaper dedicated to advertising, an individual ad often becomes lost in a sea of ink. Different sections within the paper may appeal to specific people, but newspapers are not noted for reaching segmented audiences.

Production Details

Newspaper advertisers use headlines and photos as the attention getters. Although there are many types and styles of headlines, the key to this portion of the ad is to grab the audience. Further, if the headline can lead the reader into the rest of the copy, it has done its job. Many retailers use photographs of the merchandise to attract the newspaper reader's interest.

One method of gaining reader attention is through separate advertising sections. Also known as **free standing inserts,** or **FSI,** these separate publications are usually printed by outside sources and carried by the newspaper for a fee. This method of advertising devotes an entire piece to the merchandise offered by one store or shopping center. Colorful tabloids or inserts, often printed on slick paper, are more eye-catching than black-and-white ads that may become lost in a sea of editorial copy.

Many trade goods marketers consider free standing inserts an integral part of their promotional mix. Once considered archaic and on the verge of extinction, FSIs, are showing a steady and consistent growth pattern. One reason for revival is the ability to tailor the coupons or materials in these inserts to fit the demographics of specific regions. Cities, for example, can be broken into sections with different free standing inserts delivered to each. Marketers can experiment with product and pricing strategies that fit the specific needs of these segments.[6]

Free standing insert (FSI)—separate advertising publication inserted in newspapers.

MAGAZINE

The reach of **magazines** is somewhat limited. Advertisers would have to use many different publications to impact a significant number of people. Such extensive coverage may not be practical. One area where magazines shine is in reaching segmented audiences. With publications available for almost every type of vocation and avocation, the medium's ability to impact a targeted market is excellent, making its high cost more acceptable.

To increase their segmenting capability, magazines are often printed with different issues for specific geographic areas. Reader's of *Time* in New York find different ads than audiences in Houston or Seattle. Magazine publishers also tailor articles or editorial content to appeal to widespread markets. Early in 1990, subscribers to *Sports Illustrated* found an advertisement for Isuzu with their own name printed on the insert card. Issues of *Sunset* also had personal messages to subscribers.[7]

---

[6]Frank LaRonca, "The FSI: Thinking about the marketing 'No brainer,'" *BRANDWEEK*, July 4, 1994, p. 13; Fara Warner, "Hold the comics, sports, and give me that FSI," *BRANDWEEK*, March 21, 1994, pp. 40–42.

[7]Heidi Schultz, "City and regionals: Building strength," *Folio: the Magazine for Magazine Management*, August 1992, pp. 57–59; David Jacobson, "Magazines increasingly become customized," *The Sunday Oregonian*, January 7, 1990, p. D4.

■ ■ ■ ■ ■
The top twenty magazines in paid circulation

RANK	MAGAZINE	1993 CIRCULATION	AD REVENUES ($ MILLIONS)
1	Modern Maturity	22,398,630	52.2
2	Reader's Digest	16,261,968	131.3
3	TV Guide	14,122,915	322.2
4	National Geographic	9,390,787	46.8
5	Better Homes & Gardens	7,600,960	188.7
6	Good Housekeeping	5,162,597	206.9
7	Ladies' Home Journal	5,153,565	127.8
8	Family Circle	5,114,030	163.2
9	Woman's Day	4,858,625	146.3
10	McCall's	4,605,441	102.5
11	Time	4,103,772	344.2
12	People Weekly	3,446,569	367.4
13	Playboy	3,402,617	46.0
14	Sports Illustrated	3,356,729	302.0
15	Redbook	3,345,451	94.5
16	Prevention	3,220,763	NA
17	Newsweek	3,156,192	260.7
18	Cosmopolitan	2,627,491	140.8
19	Southern Living	2,368,678	87.7
20	Glamour	2,304,769	102.0

SOURCE: *Competitive Media Reporting,* as seen in *BRANDWEEK,* February 18, 1994, p. MQ23.

■ ■ ■ ■ ■

Another major advantage of magazine advertising is outstanding durability. Promotional messages in this medium go on selling for months and even years, as evidenced by the older issues found in the offices of doctors and dentists. "Pass-along readership," meaning copies are read by more than one buyer, is another plus. Magazine advertising can be artistic, which helps counteract its high initial cost. The use of photographs and full-color printing enhances the ability to attract attention. Lead time can be as much as two to three months, meaning that advertising must be planned well in advance.

Business Magazines, or Trade Journals

Business magazines are called **trade journals.** Trade journals come with a variety of titles and make up roughly 75 percent of published magazines. Some of these publications are broad in coverage, having content that is pertinent to business men and women in any industry. *Business Week, Sales & Marketing Management, Industry Week* and *Purchasing* are good examples of such **horizontal trade journals.**

Vertical trade journals are magazines with content that relates to a specific field or type of industry. *Apparel* and *Women's Wear Daily* target the fashion industry. *Bakery, Progressive Grocer* and *Prepared Foods* are vertical trade journals for food purveyors. *Iron Age* relates to the metals industry, whereas

Horizontal trade journal—business magazine with content of interest to a variety of businesses.
Vertical trade journal—business magazine with content of interest to a select industry.

Chemical Week and *Chemical Engineering News* are of interest to workers in any phase of the chemical industry. Readers appreciate the articles, which are considered publicity, and the advertising for products pertinent to that field.

Production Details

Advertisers use many methods to snare the attention of magazine readers. Headlines can be much splashier than those produced on newsprint. Illustrations and photographs are particularly effective, especially with the added appeal of color. The outstanding printing available with magazines give this medium an edge over newspapers in attracting their audience. Unique to magazines, "scratch and sniff" is a method of impregnating the ink used in printing the ad so that it gives off a scent when rubbed.

To escape from the clutter often found in magazine advertising, some art directors effectively use mini-spreads. Placing two thirds of the ad on one page and the remaining one third of the facing page creates the illusion of a two page presentation at a considerable saving. A mix of black and white with color achieves additional cost reductions. Advertising using this medium can be versatile along with being attractive and eye-catching.

DIRECT MAIL

Another media member designed to reach highly segmented audiences is **direct mail.** The medium is a favorite of business-to-business advertisers because it can target a select audience. Mail lists can be rented, bought or accumulated for almost any market segment. Significant reach is possible with this medium, but cost is high. With the increase in third-class postage rates, many bulk mailers are using their own delivery systems. Inserts in newspapers are one inexpensive yet effective way of delivering direct mail.[8]

For interesting, well-produced direct mailings, lead time is quite long. As with any printed medium, attractive artwork and full-color production is not created overnight. Durability is rather good for direct mail. If it survives the initial reaction to trash it, the material may stay active days or even weeks and months. This is especially true with merchandise catalogs, which often have extended life. Direct-mail houses such as Spiegel and Banana Republic are doing very well. Cataloger Lands' End mixed prosaic copy from award-winning playwright David Mamet along with ads for chinos in order to extend interest, hence durability.[9]

Production Details

Users of direct mail advertising must gain the receiver's attention before unveiling the message. If the addressee does not open the envelope, the contents are

---

[8]"The consumer perspective," *Direct Marketing,* May 1994, pp. 21–22; Terry Lefton, "Cadillacs. Scotch. Pizza. Chips. It's in the mail," *BRANDWEEK,* July 13, 1992, pp. 16–22; Frances Seghers, "Will junk mailers make their own rounds?" *Business Week,"* March 21, 1988, pp. 53–54.

[9]Cyndee Miller, "Lands' End goes literary as it touts chinos," *Marketing News,* April 11, 1994, p. 7; Cyndee Miller, "Catalogues alive, thriving," *Marketing News,* February 28, 1994, pp. 1 and 6.

lost, and on the average only 2 percent of direct-mail recipients respond. Creative advertisers use a variety of special effects, such as printing teasing messages on the outside, to prompt the receiver to look inside. *The Wall Street Journal* promoted subscriptions in a direct mail campaign that featured cartoons on the outside of the envelope using the addressee's name. Computer-assisted printing allows the sender to personalize either the envelope or the message inside.

The words "Urgent" and "Confidential" are often seen on mass mailers to lure the addressee into opening the envelope. Hand-written envelopes, instead of address labels, create the illusion that the mailer does not contain a promotional piece. Recipients are more likely to open an envelope addressed to them personally. Once opened, like any other media the direct-mail piece must lead the audience through the copy to complete the message.

OUTDOOR

Outdoor advertising includes highway billboards, messages on and in transit vehicles, and even bus stops and train stations. Reach is amazingly good using outdoor, because of the many motorists and travelers who come into contact with this medium. This is especially true with billboards, where the message can be rotated within a given market area. The advent of "Superflex," a flexible, vinyl-coated fabric, gives outdoor advertisers greater flexibility to move a message from billboard to billboard without destroying it.

The expense of renting billboard space is nominal, but production costs can be high. Production time to prepare a printed message for posters or a

Direct mail can reach highly segmented audiences and is often used by business-to-business advertisers.

painted bulletin is relatively short, but many communities have moratoriums on the placement of additional billboards. Since customers often wait in line to rent available space, lead time can be lengthy.

Durability is a drawback with outdoor advertising. Although the physical structure may be up for a long time, the advertiser has but an instant to present the message. Since time available to capture attention and leave an impression on the motorist is brief, outdoor advertising must be short and to the point. A unique application of outdoor advertising involves putting messages on the sides of long haul trailers. Using contract carriers, whose vehicles as a rule are not decorated, advertisers carry their messages around the country.[10]

Production Details

Outdoor advertisers gain attention through pictorials and spectaculars. The message copy must be short with this medium, usually fewer than eight words, and the headline or pictorial often says it all. For traffic safety reasons, flashing lights and moving parts are not allowed in many urban areas. In the countryside, however, outdoor advertising has a freer rein. The Coppertone ads showing the dog tugging at the youngster's bathing suit is a memorable example of eye-catching billboards.

The outdoor advertising industry has had a tough go of it in the past few decades. Most areas have imposed moratoriums on the spread of billboards, and some recent Congressional effort wanted to ban outdoor completely. Advertisers must settle for those locations that are in place, and demand for space is great in most locales. Industry leader Gannett Outdoor Group created a series of artistic billboards to show the general public that this medium can be very creative.[11]

■ ■ ■ ■ ■

Media comparison

MEDIUM	REACH	COST	LEAD TIME	DURABILITY	ARTISTIC	SEGMENTING
Television	Excellent	High	Long	Poor	Excellent	Moderate
Radio	Very good	Low	Short	Poor	Poor	Moderate
Newspaper	Fair	Low	Short	Fair	Poor	Moderate
Magazine	Fair	High	Very long	Excellent	Excellent	Excellent
Direct mail	Fair	High	Moderate	Good	Good	Excellent
Outdoor	Good	Low	Moderate	Poor	Fair	Poor

■ ■ ■ ■ ■

---

[10]K. Riddell, "Truck ads drive home benefits of rolling billboards," *Marketing,* February 17, 1992, p. 17; Editors, "Study confirms effectiveness of mobile advertising displays," *Marketing News,* February 29, 1988, p. 26.

[11]Kevin Goldman, "Billboards gain respect as spending rises," *The Wall Street Journal,* June 27, 1994, p. B8; Ricardo A. Davis, "Competition ignites outdoor spending," *Advertising Age,* April 11, 1994, p. 32; Cyndee Miller, "Outdoor advertising weathers repeated attempts to kill it," *Marketing News,* March 16, 1992, pp. 1 and 9; Richard R. Szathmary, "The great (and not so great) outdoors," *Sales & Marketing Management,* March 1992, p. 81.

hat Are Advertising Agencies?

An **advertising agency** is an independent organization that conducts promotional activities for its clients. Some marketing oriented companies may have advertising experts on their staff. Others hire agencies. Typically, the expertise available through outside professionals is worth the expense, but cost is rarely a concern. Expenses using agencies are on a par with those generated by company advertising departments.

Many advertisers treat agencies as though they were partners, and this close relationship benefits both parties. Personnel at these firms, especially account executives, often operate as if they were directly on the payroll of their clients. Advertising agencies plan the entire promotional campaign, create messages and place ads or commercials with the appropriate media.

Advertising agency— independent company that conducts promotional activities for clients.

FULL-SERVICE AGENCY

The **full-service agency** is a company that conducts all of the promotional functions required by its clients. Staffed with creative people and media buyers, this type of agency can take control of the entire promotional effort. Many carry out marketing research functions, especially with regard to new product branding or packaging decisions. Additionally, full-service firms typically handle public relations campaigns or efforts for their clients.

Full-service agency— advertising agency that carries out all advertising functions.

With the marvelous communications networks available in the business arena, effective agencies often take root in smaller towns and cities. Although New York City is still the mecca for this industry, professionally recognized agencies locate in areas around the country. For example, Wieden & Kennedy, the Portland, Oregon, agency, has won national acclaim for its creative work on the Nike and Microsoft accounts.[12]

Marketing campaigns include product design and packaging, which are tied to promotional efforts. Therefore, full-service agencies prefer to make early input with the marketing program during product design. By contributing to packaging and branding decisions, advertising people can direct the promotional program from its infancy. In this regard, marketing research often becomes an additional task for advertising agencies.

MEDIA BUYING SERVICE

A **media buying service,** as the name implies, is an advertising agency that does nothing but direct the purchase of media time or space. With thousands of potential choices available to the marketer, proper media selection for the message is a prerequisite to success. The greatest ad or most interesting commercial is of little benefit if it does not reach the right audience.

Media buying service—advertising agency that only directs the purchase of media time or space.

[12]Jim Barnett, "Portland firm maps campaign for Microsoft," *The Oregonian*, November 11, 1994, pp. E1 and E6; C. Taylor, "Risk takers: Widen & Kennedy, *Adweek's* agency of the year," *Adweek's Marketing Week*, March 23, 1992, pp. 26–27.

The staff of a media buying service concentrates on the placement part of the advertising business. Their knowledge of markets and promotional channels can be invaluable to advertisers. Media selection is not just a choice between television or newspaper. Picking out the specific television stations or choosing the most appropriate dailies that will give the best coverage for the dollar is a demanding task.

BOUTIQUE AGENCY

Boutique—advertising agency that works only on the creative aspects of promotion.

Another type of advertising agency works only on the creative aspects of promotion. **Boutique** agencies write the copy, produce the artwork and lay out the complete advertisement or commercial. These firms do not handle placement of the materials with the media. Staffed with writers and artists, these organizations are particularly helpful to the smaller marketer.

Many advertisers have local or regional markets with limited media potential. Les Schwab distributes tires only in the Northwest, and Goldwater's has department stores mainly in Arizona. For these marketers, perhaps the primary task involves the creation of the advertising, rather than media selection. Boutique agencies provide a needed service for such companies that need first-rate copy and artwork, but for whom media selection is uncomplicated.

MEDIA COMMISSIONS

Media commissions— payments made to advertising agencies by media members, usually at a rate of 15 percent.

Advertising agencies receive compensation in a number of ways. Most of the revenues for these independent operators comes in the form of payments from media members, or **media commissions.** When an agency places advertising with a magazine or television station for its clients, the broadcaster or publisher pay commissions for that service. Media commissions normally run 15 percent.

For example, on a $100,000 television campaign for Scope mouthwash, the network or participating stations would bill Procter & Gamble for the full amount of the advertising. When the advertiser pays the media member, the media member remits 15 percent of the total billing as a commission to the advertising agency making the placement. Many broadcast stations, newspapers, magazines and outdoor advertising firms pay commissions to agencies from distant cities with whom they have had no personal contact.

OTHER COMPENSATION

Some advertising agencies work with clients on a **retainer.** This method of compensation means that the advertiser pays the agency a flat fee to develop the necessary materials and campaigns. This retainer may be on top of or in lieu of commissions. Agencies that are heavily involved with product development and marketing research prefer this compensation method. Similar to the retainer, many agencies charge their clients **fees,** usually based on an hourly rate. The creation of the advertising message can take varying amounts of time and may not be relative to the amount of media commissions. In these cases, fees are a better means of covering the out-of-pocket costs of the agency.

World's top advertising organizations

RANK 1993	RANK 1992	ADVERTISING ORGANIZATION, HEADQUARTERS	U.S.-BASED AGENCY BRANDS INCLUDED	WORLDWIDE GROSS INCOME 1993	1992	% CHG
1	1	**WPP Group,** London	**Ogilvy & Mather Worldwide:** Cole & Weber; Ogilvy & Mather Direct; A. Elcoff & Co.; Morton Goldberg Associates; **J. Walter Thompson Co.:** Brouillard Communications; J. Walter Thompson Direct; Deltakos; Thompson Recruitment; **other U.S. units:** Einson Freeman; Ferguson Communications Group; Mendoza, Dillon & Asociados	$2,633.6	2,592.6	1.6
2	2	**Interpublic Group of Cos.,** New York	**Lintas Worldwide:** Dailey and Associates; Fahlgren; Del Rivero Messianu Lintas; Long, Haymes & Carr; Lintas Marketing Communications; **Lowe Group:** Lowe & Partners/SMS; Lowe Direct; LCF&L; The Martin Agency; Stenrich Group; **McCann-Erickson Worldwide:** McCann Direct; McCann Healthcare; McCann Universal Group	2,078.5	2,054.5	1.2
3	3	**Omnicom Group,** New York	**BBDO Worldwide:** Baxter, Gurian & Mazzel; Frank J. Corbett Inc.; Doremus & Co.; Harrison, Star, Weiner & Beitler; Lavey/Wolff/Swift; **DDB Needham Worldwide:**Bernard Hodes Group; Kallir, Phillips, Ross; Puskar Gibbons Chapin; **other units:** TBWA Advertising; Alcone Sims O'Brien; Altschiller Reitzfeld; Goodby, Berlin & Silverstein; Merkley Newman Harty; Ralnoldi Kerzner Radcliffe; Rapp Collins Worldwide	1,876.0	1,820.5	3.1
4	5	**Dentsu Inc.,** Tokyo	Dentsu Corp. of America	1,403.2	1,387.6	1.1
5	4	**Saatchi & Saatchi Co.,** London/New York	**Saatchi & Saatchi Advertising;** Saatchi & Saatchi/CMS; Saatchi & Saatchi Direct; Team One; Conill Advertising; Cliff Freeman & Partners; Klemtner Advertising; Rumrill-Hoyt; **Backer Spielvogel Bates Worldwide:** BSB/Dryden & Petisi; AC&R Advertising; Kobs & Draft; **CME KHBB**	1,355.1	1,397.4	–3.0
6	6	**Young & Rubicam,** New York	Young & Rubicam; Chapman Direct; CMF&Z; Muldoon Agency; Sive/Young & Rubicam; Sudler & Hennessey; Wunderman Cato Johnson Worldwide	1,008.9	1,058.7	–4.7
7	7	**Euro RSCG Worldwide,** Neuilly, France	Robert A. Becker Inc.; Cohn & Wells; Hadley Group; Lally, McFarland & Pantello; Messner Vetere Berger McNamee Schmetterer; Stranger & Associates; Tatham Euro RSCG	864.8	932.1	–7.2
8	8	**Grey Advertising,** New York	Grey Advertising; Beaumont Bennett Group; Font & Vaamonde; Grey Direct Marketing Group; Gross Townsend Frank Hoffman	765.7	728.1	5.2
9	12	**Hakuhodo Inc.,** Tokyo	Hakuhodo Advertising America	667.8	608.7	9.7
10	9	**Foote, Cone & Belding Communications,** Chicago	Foote, Cone & Belding Communications; FCB Direct; Borders, Perrin & Norrander; IMPACT; Vicom/FCB; Wahlstom & Co.	633.7	661.5	–4.2
11	10	**Leo Burnett Co.,** Chicago	Leo Burnett Co.	622.4	643.8	–3.3
12	11	**Publicis Communication/ Publicis-FCB,** Paris	Publicis/Bloom	572.0	623.0	–8.2
13	13	**D'Arcy Masius Benton & Bowles,** New York	D'Arcy Maslus Benton & Bowles; Clarion Marketing & Communications; Medicus Intercon International	553.6	558.4	–0.9
14	14	**BDDP Group,** Boulogne, France	McCracken Brooks Communications; Wells Rich Greene BDDP	278.8	293.0	–4.8
15	15	**Bozell Worldwide,** New York	Bozell Worldwide; Poppe Tyson: Temerlin McClain	269.9	247.3	9.1
16	16	**Tokyu Agency,** Tokyo	NA	181.8	185.6	–2.0
17	17	**Daiko Advertising,** Osaka, Japan	NA	181.5	175.9	3.2
18	18	**Asatsu Inc.,** Tokyo	Asatsu America	171.3	165.9	3.3
19	20	**Ketchum Communications,** Pittsburgh	Ketchum Advertising; Botto, Roessner, Horne & Messinger; DiFranza Williamson	140.4	132.8	5.7
20	19	**Dai-Ichi Kikaku,** Tokyo	Kresser/Craig DIK	135.3	151.4	–10.7

Advertising agencies may purchase materials from outside sources for their clients. When this occurs, the firm will often **mark up** these items as a means of compensation. Suppose an advertiser has the agency develop a series of printed outdoor posters or new company letterhead. The price of these materials from the graphics house will be marked up by the agency as compensation for its efforts. Agencies and their clients work closely together.

ow Is Advertising Evaluated?

Whether the advertising message is created by the marketing company or an independent agency, the effectiveness of the promotion is hard to assess. Higher sales may be the most accurate indicator, but not always. Increases in sales can be the result of competitive failure, product improvement or the consequence of a successful advertising campaign. For example, General Mills introduced new versions of Cheerios and Wheaties in 1994, bolstered by extensive advertising and sales promotion. Consumer acceptance of these "new" products was everything the company had hoped for, but was it the promotion or the new taste and texture? To evaluate how much of the increase in sales was the result of the advertising campaign would be practically impossible.

Advertising is evaluated by both the public and the advertising industry. Sometimes the media presentations that win the plaudits and awards of colleagues are also the favorites of consumers; sometimes the reverse is true. In either case, the ads and commercials may be great but the products don't sell. All facets of the promotional effort work together to create desire and demand, and one clever, well-accepted commercial usually does not do it on its own. Still, smart marketers use a variety of methods to test the effectiveness of their advertising.[13]

PRE-TEST VS POST-TEST

The first step in evaluating advertising often occurs before the campaign begins. Almost all successful advertising ventures proceed through some sort of **pre-test.** Pre-testing is often part of the marketing research or test marketing phases of product development. In the pre-test of a commercial or advertisement, potential product users are shown several versions. Focus groups are a favorite tool for this evaluation. The participants are tested and quizzed regarding their attitudes toward and the appeal of the creative work.

Most **post-testing** involves recall of the advertisement, along with brand recognition questioning. Random samples of the audience are asked if they recall seeing a certain ad or commercial. Other surveys ask audiences if they recognize the brands advertised. If the image of a product in the consumer's mind has changed after an advertising campaign, it can be assumed that the commercial message has done its job.

---

[13]Laura Bird, "Loved the ad. May (or may not) buy the product," *The Wall Street Journal,* April 7, 1994, pp. B1 and B7.

Balloons, such as this one from Planters, are a good example of sales promotion efforts. (Courtesy of Planters LifeSavers Company)

Several private firms or agencies evaluate advertising. Arbitron and A. C. Nielson poll television viewing audiences and establish ratings for individual shows and stations. These ratings and share of audience figures provide the basis from which broadcasters develop advertising rates. Cost of newspaper and magazine ads are based upon circulation, and outdoor advertisers pay more for locations that have heavier traffic counts.

What Is Public Relations?

Public relations— promoting the image of the business or organization to its publics.

Public relations, or **PR,** is used to promote the image of the business or organization to its various publics. These groups include customers, industry, employees, stockholders and the local business community. The relationship that a business has with the publics it serves may ultimately affect the sale of its products. Public relations can include philanthropic activities or participation in worthwhile causes, but publicity and advertising are the tools used to promote such activities.

Public relations involves the organization's image with several groups. Customers are important, and firms must respect their customers to find success. Employees and labor unions are another public. Companies cannot mistreat workers without running the risk of creating negative images. Stockholders, many of whom may also be customers, must be appeased. The local business community where the company operates is very much a part of the public relations effort, as are competitors and industry associations.

Businesses often seek outside assistance in positioning the firm. Public relations experts, whether working directly for the company or for independent agencies, protect and maintain a positive corporate image. Good PR is especially needed in times of trouble, such as when the cyanide scare stopped sales of Tylenol. However, public relations should not be a one-time promotion that arises only because of disaster. Continuous effort to build favorable positions in the eyes of the public helps businesses fare better when bad times come.

Excellent knowledge of and relationship with the media are assets for public relations practitioners. The markets covered by the media, their deadlines and required publicity formats must be known. Poorly executed publicity that arrives past the deadline has a negative effect on the print or broadcast members whom public relations efforts intend to impress.

How Is Publicity Used In Promotion?

The primary promotional tool used by public relations experts is **publicity.** Similar to advertising, publicity uses the media. Advertisers purchase media time or space, so what is said, how it is said and who says it are all controlled by the company paying the bill. Since the media do not charge for publicity, companies using this promotional tool have no control over content or comment once placed with the media. Public relations plays a key role in any promotional campaign, and positive publicity creates a good company image.

Trade shows offer small companies with limited budgets an excellent opportunity to compete side by side with larger competitors.

Publicity advises the public about such things as awards won by company employees or the donation of a plot of land for a community playground. These types of corporate contributions build good public relations. Announcing them is publicity. This promotional tool is also used to announce breakthroughs in new product design or reductions in prices. Articles appearing in trade journals about performance or design help promote product acceptance. Information about changes in marketing plans or strategies help marketers stay ahead of competition.

NEWS RELEASES

Some of the most effective tools used in publicity are **news releases,** which are articles about the company, its products, or its employees. These written commentaries are directed to the appropriate media for insertion as news items. The lack of control when using publicity occurs after the media has received the release. Newspapers, magazines, televisions and radio broadcasters can either choose to use the material or not. In addition, media members may edit the copy, which can undo what the promoters had in mind.

News release—article describing company events or products sent to the media.

News releases typically follow a journalistic style and should be in the proper form to be accepted in whole or in part by news media. Unlike advertising copy, news releases should not hype the product or the company, but instead should report the facts. Media members who feel that the publicity only promotes products are likely to refuse to use the materials. On the other hand, newsworthy reports of product or company developments are likely to be considered.

PRESS CONFERENCES AND PUBLIC FORUMS

Press conferences are difficult to control. When publicists call a group of media together for an announcement, the news given out must be significant or the gathering will be unsuccessful. A standard rule of publicity states that if

Press conference—meeting held by company spokesperson(s) to make an announcement to the media.

the information can be adequately covered in a news release, do not hold a press conference. News of major product breakthroughs, mergers or purchases, changes in management or rebuttals of bad publicity might be suitable reasons for holding press conferences.

Occasionally company officials will be called to appear at **public forums.** Giving speeches to trade associations or attending conferences are all part of the process of publicity. When asked, management should be prepared to handle these assignments so that the company receives the most benefit. Speakers who are unprepared or inept do little to further the corporate image.

Advertising and publicity are valuable members of the promotional mix, but these tools do not operate alone. Campaigns typically try to involve all of the possible tools that are appropriate. Trade and production goods marketers use a large group of effective devices called sales promotion.

How Is Sales Promotion Used?

Sales promotion consists of those other tools of mass communications that do not fall into the categories of advertising or publicity. Marketers pay for these promotional devices, but they do not, as a rule, appear in the media. Usually coupled very closely with advertising, these extrapromotional efforts often overcome the lack of durability found in media advertising. This element of the promotional mix includes many of the incentives used to keep the product or company names before buyers.

POINT-OF-PURCHASE DISPLAYS

Point-of-purchase display—product merchandiser or rack placed in retail stores.

Point-of-purchase displays, or **P-O-Ps,** are a type of sales promotion. Offered by the product manufacturer, either free of charge or at nominal cost, these merchandisers encourage resellers to stock the product. By providing a point-of-purchase package, manufacturers give intermediaries an incentive. The marketer's objective is to fill the distribution channel and encourage intermediaries to push the merchandise. For example, Schlage Lock Company offers retailers a merchandising display while a competitor does not. The hardware or building supply store may prefer Schlage because the P-O-P will create more sales, producing greater profit.

Many trade goods marketers feel that their products have a better chance of selling if they are displayed on custom merchandising displays rather than on store fixture shelves. Offering a special collection of goods along with a display rack, the manufacturer is assured that its products stand out from the competition. Retailers benefit from lower prices or a free display. Procter & Gamble increased the use of P-O-Ps for Revlon's Almay brand cosmetics while lowering advertising expenditures. Isotoner, a division of Sara Lee, provides its retailers with elaborate displays during the holiday crunch.[14]

---

[14]Cara Appelbaum, "P&G cuts back on ads, but forges ahead with its beauty blitz," *Adweek's Marketing Week,* March 4, 1991, p. 5; Howard Riell, "Isotoner has to stretch its tactics to exploit brief selling season," *Adweek's Marketing Week,* April 1, 1991, p. 12.

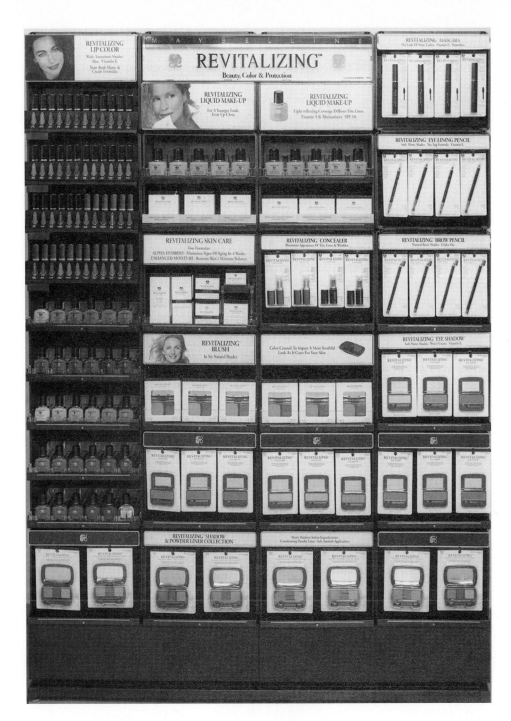

Point-of-purchase displays, such as this one created for Maybelline by Advertising Display Company, Inc., are an effective sales promotion tool. (Courtesy of Advertising Display Company, Inc.)

INCENTIVES

Sales promotion provides **incentives** either to buy or sell. When targeted towards the end user, sales promotion becomes an inducement for consumers to purchase. Such incentives include coupons, contests and premiums. Although much has been said and written about the demise of coupons, this sales promotion item seems to be gaining in popularity. Although some firms, notably General Mills and H. J. Heinz, have cut these incentives altogether, Kraft General Foods and Borden have tested in-store electronic coupon kiosks. Denver based In-Store Media Systems has experimented with a swapping that allows shoppers to exchange unwanted coupons for instant rebates.[15]

Premiums have come a long way since two boxtops were good for a secret code ring. Today, expensive, quality merchandise may be purchased as premiums coupled with many consumer products. Although it may be advertised on television or in magazines, the premium itself is a form of sales promotion. Many consumer goods marketers include premium offers in monthly billings to charge customers. Oil companies are notorious for using this method to present premiums.

Incentives to sell sometimes target the sales force and intermediaries. Many production goods sellers establish quotas and reward salespeople who reach their goals with merchandise premiums. Trade goods marketers also motivate their customers, wholesalers and retailers with special offers. Used as a tool to promote specific merchandise, rewards of a Caribbean cruise or a Tahitian vacation can motivate sellers and resellers to move merchandise more aggressively.

Sampling is another form of incentive used in sales promotion. Trade goods marketers often distribute free samples of new or revised products to consumers by mail or through newspaper delivery. In-store sampling is popular on weekends when families often collect what amounts to a free lunch by strolling the aromatic aisles of supermarkets and warehouse clubs. This type of incentive is especially useful for local or regional marketers who may not have extensive advertising or sales promotion budgets.[16]

PRODUCT BROCHURES

Another form of sales promotion business goods and services producers use is the product brochure. To soften the market by making buyers aware of products before the salesperson calls, firms send printed or electronic brochures to prospects beforehand. Printed literature explaining product benefits sometimes goes unread, so some companies create videocassettes to tell the same story. These mailings are usually in response to inquiries received from advertising in trade journals.

Desktop publishing has made it economical for even small businesses to produce quality promotional literature. Laser printers coupled with computers create sales letters, brochures, catalogs, newsletters and other printed pieces in superb quality. Some firms have in-house desktop publishing capability, while others farm it out to companies specializing in this activity. Either way,

---

[15]Tim Triplett, "Report of couponing's death has been greatly exaggerated," *Marketing News,* October 14, 1994, pp. 1 and 2; Tim Triplett, "Cereal makers await reaction to General Mills' coupon decision," *Marketing News,* May 9, 1994, pp. 1 and 2; Karen Benezra, "Heinz cut coupons, trade $," *BRANDWEEK,* March 21, 1994, p. 5; Betsy Spethmann, "Marketers test coupon swaps," *BRANDWEEK,* January 3, 1994, p. 4; Betsy Spethmann, "KGF, Borden test new coupon kiosks," *BRANDWEEK,* October 4, 1993, pp. 1 and 6.

[16]Gabriella Stern, "With sampling, there is too a free lunch," *The Wall Street Journal,* March 11, 1994, pp. B1 and B3.

the quick response and relative low cost of this printing method has become a popular sales promotion tool.[17]

Another technological development in this area of sales promotion is the video brochure. Electronic presentations add an aura of professionalism to products and companies. Video brochures are especially helpful in assisting salespeople handling highly technical or complex products. Tektronix, a marketer of fiber optics testing equipment, uses this sales promotion tool to soften the market and train customers after the sale.[18]

TRADE SHOWS

Trade shows and **exhibitions** are prime sales promotion tools. Although great for smaller companies, almost all marketers participate in the trade shows conducted for their industries. Representation at trade fairs can consist of a standard 10' x 10' booth with a few chairs and some handout literature. Other marketers use elaborate spectaculars covering thousands of square feet, using robots, professional models or actors. Difficult to describe in all of their splendor, some of these theatrical trade show presentations cost hundreds of thousands of dollars. The Exhibit Registry, an innovative Southern California company, buys up used displays and rents or resells them to noncompetitive users.[19]

Trade shows are a favorite promotional tool used for wooing intermediaries. When these conclaves convene at major convention centers throughout the country, the meetings usually include seminars and speakers along with the customary booths where exhibitors show their wares. Most business product industries have conventions or exhibitions that pertain to their field. Hardware, housewares, candy, packaging, dairy products, restaurant fixtures, lumber equipment, paint and decorating and hundreds of other industries conduct trade shows.

What Affects The Management Of Sales Promotion?

Because of the unusual nature of sales promotion, the efforts are sometimes overdone. In trying to create the action to buy, marketers may be inclined to overwork and overhype the use of these specialty items. The media besiege the consumer with continuous promotional messages, and at every turn there

---

[17]Sue Kapp, "Farming it out," *Business Marketing,* April 1992, pp. 34–36; Len Strazewski, "Desktop publishing: Powerful marketing communications aid," *Marketing News,* November 7, 1988, pp. 2 and 29; 22.

[18]George Griffin, "Going beyond the newsletter," *Graphic Arts Monthly,* January 1994, pp. 78–80; Lynn Wallford, "Desktop publishing capabilities grow while prices shrink," *The Office,* April 1993, p. 30; Bristol Voss, "Video revelations and revues," *Sales & Marketing Management,* April 1992, pp. 64–78.

[19]Stefane d'Avad, "Making the old 'new' once again," *Business Marketing,* April 1992, p. T4.

appears to be still more in the way of gimmicks and turn-ons to persuade the buyer. The amount of money spent on sales promotion in the United States is almost equal to what is doled out for advertising . . . about $150 billion per year.

TRADE VS PRODUCTION GOODS

Typically, trade goods receive more sales promotion effort than production goods. The nature of the market and size of the purchase make consumers more susceptible to incentives and premiums. A coupon worth fifty cents off on a box of Cheerios or a contest awarding a picnic table to buyers of Kingsford charcoal make a considerable impact on purchase decisions. Similar promotions offered to buyers of industrial robots or carloads of polyester resin just do not make sense.

There are some sales promotion tools that do attract business buyers. Trade shows, conventions and sales meetings are important sales promotion tools in both trade goods and production goods arenas. Many of these activities are coupled with training sessions, which benefit both manufacturer and intermediary. Typically, production goods firms hold annual sales meeting for the field staff. These meetings are often held at vacation resorts where business is mixed with recreational activities. Marketers in this field also reward their salespeople with trips and merchandise for outstanding effort.

PROMOTIONAL STRATEGY

The types of sales promotion selected for any promotional campaign depend upon the basic strategies of the marketer. Branding, segmentation and especially positioning influence the presentation of the product. Coupons, contests and free samples may work well with convenience goods, but might not be as effective with higher priced merchandise. Upscale products, or those with more sophisticated images, might find their position tarnished if coupled with mass merchandising gimmicks.

Promotion today has become a multi-media, multi-tool challenge impacting all marketers. Using a single element of the promotional mix rarely gets the job done. Savvy marketers combine and blend all of the tools available to them to gain the best from their available budgets. Product positioning and company personality will dictate what type of promotion will be used, but each must interact and agree with the other. Advertising and sales promotion smooth the way for the salesforce, which in turn supplies customer feedback to assist other promotional efforts.[20]

---

[20]Bill Burke, "Position, personality, not price, should frame consumer messages," *BRANDWEEK*, September 19, 1994, p. 20; Cyndee Miller, "A little pizzazz in the ad punches up the pitch," *Marketing News*, April 25, 1994, pp. 6 and 11.

ETHICS

Sales promotion may be the kicker that turns a want into a purchase. Sometimes those purchases may not be truly necessary. Most of us would find the promotion for a Mounds candy bar or a McDonald's Big Mac tempting, even though we might not need those additional calories. On the other hand, assuming that adult buyers are capable of making sensible decisions, sales promotion cannot force consumers to buy anything.

Because of the relative low cost of production of many sales promotion tools, these incentives often provide an opportunity for fraud. Coupons, for example, are especially easy to counterfeit. Bogus coupon printing and redeeming operations are uncovered by the Federal Trade Commission regularly. It is tempting for companies offering contests to be less than fair in awarding prizes. Favoring certain customers in sales promotion is just as much an illegal restraint of trade as is unfair pricing.

SUMMING IT UP

Product advertising promotes goods and services. Comparative advertising contrasts the characteristics of competitive brands. Trade goods marketers that offer to pay a portion of their retailer customer's promotion are providing cooperative advertising. Business product advertising is broken down into industrial, trade, professional or agricultural categories. Institutional advertising is used to promote the company or product image rather than sell products. Additional functions of institutional advertising are to attract investors or personnel, advocate a position, or distribute information.

The advertising media consist of television and radio, newspaper and magazine, direct mail and outdoor. Television has tremendous reach and is favored by national consumer goods marketers. Radio is low cost and has a short lead time, making it an attractive medium for retailers. Newspapers are also favored by retailers due to cost and the local nature of news coverage. Magazines offer outstanding segmenting ability, coupled with durability. Horizontal and vertical trade journals are business magazines. Direct mail is the favorite medium of business goods marketers, and, like magazines, can reach highly segmented audiences. Outdoor advertising, while not commanding a high percentage of advertising expenditures, is still viewed as an effective medium.

Each of the media handle creativity differently. Television production begins with a storyboard which describes the sequence of video and audio that make up the commercial. Getting audience attention through radio is difficult. Many radio copywriters practice the art of creating a theater of the mind to help audiences "see" the commercials. Newspaper advertising is mostly black and white, a difficult creative hurdle. Free Standing Inserts are a way of lending colorful, higher quality printing, especially for regional or national stores or products.

The color and printing quality of magazine advertising lend an aura of pizzazz to advertising. New techniques, such as scratch and sniff, allow this

Marketing and Society: Getting clipped.

The American consumer has much to complain about. Products that fall apart or that are not safe head the list. Prices that have no basis other than "what the seller can get" are another major protest. Certainly deceptive or tasteless advertising registers high on the scale of promotional goofs. With all these major areas of concern, it would be very easy to overlook the measly coupon. Afterall, how could such an inane thing as a little piece of paper clipped from a magazine, newspaper or free standing insert be unethical?

Well, it is not the coupon itself that is unethical, but rather the people or firms redeeming the coupon. As it happens, coupon fraud is no penny ante matter. Estimates range up to $800 million per year that are paid out to retailers or consumers who do not earn them. Procter & Gamble, General Mills, Nestle, Kraft General Foods, RJR Nabisco and the like redeem hundreds of millions in coupons annually. As in any other business venture, it didn't take too long for con artists to seize an opportunity. Some coupon fraud occurs when crooks set up dummy store fronts. These operators buy ducats from such unsuspecting organizations as charity groups or women's club raising money for worthy causes. Other examples of illegal activity include counterfeiting of coupons or proofs of purchase. Some manufacturers such as Gillette are shortening the redemption cycle to thwart fraud, while others are using sophisticated scanning devices or inks that change under photocopier lights.

Coupons are also providing a tremendous amount of data to marketers and retailers. Although only slightly more than 2 percent of the coupons issued are redeemed each year, they have become useful as marketing research tools. Nabisco, for example, tracks both consumer preferences and retailer stocking policies. In this age of electronic fantasia, there is one firm, Acu-Trac, that provides a black box that will disgorge coupons on request from the television watcher.

SOURCE: Betsy Spethmann, "Coupons shed low-tech image," BRANDWEEK, October 24, 1994, p. 30; Christopher Power, "Coupon scams are clipping companies," Business Week, 6/15/92, pp. 110–111.

medium to expand its sensual appeal. The object of direct mail creators is to get the recipient to open the piece. Much of the creative activity evolves around this goal. Billboards are limited in the number of words of copy that can be used to attract passing motorists.

Full service advertising agencies handle all facets of promotion for their clients. Media buying services are concerned strictly with the placement of advertising with the media. Agencies that tackle only the creative function are called boutiques. Advertising agencies earn most of their income through media commissions, usually at 15 percent. Retailers, fees and markups are additional forms of compensation for agencies.

Public relations promotes the company rather than its products to many different publics. Publicity, in the form of news releases, press conferences and public forums, is the primary tool of public relations. Sales promotion includes all of those other promotional items that help trigger the actual purchase. Point-of-purchase displays, coupons, contests and banners help attract consumers to one brand over another. Trade shows, conventions, and product brochures are some of the tools used by business goods marketers. Strategies and ethics impact the management of sales promotion.

KEY CONCEPTS AND TERMS FROM CHAPTER SIXTEEN:

Advertising agency
Boutique
Business product advertising
Cooperative advertising
Farm advertising
Full-service agency
Horizontal trade journal
Institutional advertising
Lead time
Media buying service
Media commissions

News release
Point-of-purchase display (P-O-P)
Press conference
Product advertising
Professional advertising
Public relations
Reach
Storyboard
Trade advertising
Vertical trade journal

BUILDING SKILLS

1. Contrast the objectives of product advertising with those of institutional advertising.

2. Describe which media would work best for advertising golf shoes, designer ice cream, sunglasses, disk brake pads, laser printers.

3. Describe the different types of advertising agencies.

4. Explain the tasks public relations addresses, and how publicity affects the effort.

5. Identify the types of sales promotion that would be appropriate for cold remedies, a classical music concert, wall decorations, frozen orange juice, steam irons.

aking Decisions 16-1: Think again.

The camera focuses in on the bronzed figure, and immediately the viewer recognizes it as Rodin's *The Thinker*. In the background, birds chirp and a bell tolls. As the lens slowly makes its way around the seated, crouched over figure, the narrator begins. "If you think you have only two choices for business computer systems . . ." Just at that moment the statue moves to put its chin in the other hand, and the voice over completes the message with, ". . . think again."

Hewlett-Packard Co.'s award-winning television commercial marked a return to television for the company after a five-year absence. What is more, this type of campaign was unusual for business-to-business advertisers. Generally, one does not think of the television medium as being the best choice for such a narrowly targeted audience. The firm's advertising agency, Saatchi & Saatchi Pacific/San Francisco wanted to reach the business decision maker using the mass medium and key trade journals.

H-P's advertising agency selected some key programs to increase the potential of these commercials. Using cable TV, the spots were broadcast during golf, professional basketball, tennis and the America's Cup yacht races. The advertisement received further coverage airing over CNN, CNBC and on American Airlines' video magazine. The campaign also included print ads running in *The Wall Street Journal*, *Time*, *Computerworld*, *Fortune* and *Sports Illustrated*.[21]

Describe this type of advertising H-P used, comparing with the other types, giving examples to support your descriptions. Describe the types of activities carried out by the different types of advertising agencies.

aking Decisions 16-2: One tough mother.

Gertrude "Gert" Boyle is the chair of the board of Columbia Sportswear, a leading marketer of skiing, outdoor and casual clothing. She has a reputation for being a tough, perfection seeking executive, and her looks back up that image. "Mother Boyle," as she is affectionately known by employees and customers, has built Columbia into one of the most respected firms in its field. The company is noted for high quality, fair pricing and excellent customer service.

In the late 1980s, as a newcomer to a crowded field, Columbia searched for new ways to promote their company. Although possessing a rather modest promotional budget, the marketing staff wanted to make the most of their advertising. After trying a variety of themes and strategies, the promotional team, together with its advertising agency, hit upon the idea of using "Mother Boyle" as the company spokesperson. Building on the image of a tough female executive that would not be satisfied with anything less than top quality, the ads appearing in magazines and trade journals were a smashing success.

As Columbia grew rapidly, so did its product line. Wanting to tackle the lucrative jeans market, the product design team created a comfortable, attractive pair of pants. Capitalizing on the amazing success of its advertising campaign, the company added the finishing touch by labeling them "Tough Mothers." Just like the ads featuring Mother Boyle, the jeans were an instant success,

---

[21]Kevin Goldman, "Nike, H-P gamble on new sales pitches," *The Wall Street Journal*, April 8, 1994, p. A5; Kate Bertrand, "H-P returns to television with a bang," *Business Marketing*, July 1992, pp. 30–34.

which prompted the firm to expand its promotional efforts to include television. Although a hit in the United States, the campaign had to be adapted in many overseas markets, principally South America, where a strong woman image might be a little less acceptable.[22]

Describe the advantages and disadvantages of the different advertising media, citing examples of products that have used each successfully.

Making Decisions 16-3: It's a dog's life.

Pet foods mean big business. Once dominated by names such as Carnation and Ralston-Purina, the market turned inside out during the 1980s as lean and mean animal product houses entered the field. Iam's and Hills led the wellness movement for dogs and cats. Other smallish companies joined the parade, producing a wide variety of new and nutritious products. Even distribution systems for pet foods changed, with both the veterinarians and feed stores joining the channels.

Enter Famous Fido's Specialty Foods, a Chicago marketer of healthy doggie treats. Branded with clever names like Petzels, Doggie Donuts, Beagle Bagels and Terrier Twists, these snack foods for pooches are every bit as healthy as they are tasty. Unlike some of the doggie treats that dogged the market in the past, these snacks contain neither sugar or salt. Made from ingredients such as wheat flour, honey, oatmeal and garlic, the gourmet items are not manufactured from meat by-products, which the company owners claim are a health concern.

---

[22]Editors, "Getting the message," *The Oregonian,* July 14, 1994, pp. B1 and B6.

Generally, the animal medical profession agrees that these vegetable-based treats are good for their animal users. Packaged four to a plastic bag and priced at four for a dollar, they are distributed through pet stores. If the pet is traveling to Chicago, it can stop by Famous Fido's Doggie Deli for a complete three-course meal, but, of course, reservations are required.[23]

Plan a promotional campaign for Famous Fido's line of Doggie treats, using as many elements of the promotional mix as are appropriate.

---

[23]Alison Sprout, "Doggie delicacies," *Fortune*, July 27, 1992, p. 107.

17

Personal Selling and Sales Management

The Job to be Done

Selling is often called the final step in the marketing process. Some marketers feel that this form of personal promotion is really the beginning. Chapter 17 looks at the role of personal selling, and gives students the answers to:

- explain personal selling and its role in marketing,
- describe the various types of salespeople, the industries in which they work and the functions they perform,
- define the selling process and the role of telemarketing within that process, and
- explain the function of sales management.

Cheri Mason Naudin

rofessional selling is not for everyone. To achieve any degree of success, one has to have a genuine care for and interest in others, but being a "people person" is usually not enough. Salespeople need to be self-starters and achievers. Long hours and constant pressure often take a toll on those who need constant direction and want to work a regular nine-to-five day. Similarly, sales management requires a special type of person. Although some field representatives rise through the ranks to leadership positions, many filling these seats are from other disciplines.

Sales managers must control the activities of the sales force for maximum company benefit. This process starts with hiring the right people. Since not everyone has what it takes to produce in this arena, initial selection is the key to establishing an efficient and workable team. Training recruits in territory control and time management is necessary for anyone in sales management. Above all, sales managers need to motivate. Often this posi-

tion is described as being a combination of mother hen, scout leader and fiscal wizard. Cheri Mason Naudin fits that description to a tee.

Cheri is Manager, Inside Sales for Air Touch Cellular, a group with an annual budget in excess of $10 million. She rides herd over some eighty telemarketers who produce sales of between 3,000 and 11,000 cellular units per month. Prior to accepting her present position, she spent almost five years in the business-to-business cellular division as Direct Sales Manager. Cheri captured the Sales Manager of the Year awards for her company in both 1992 and 1994. She became interested in this lucrative business through marketing and selling courses at Rancho Santiago College, and is presently pursuing a Bachelors degree through the University of Phoenix. Cheri fills up her "spare"

What Is Personal Selling?

Personal selling fits the description of marketing communications to a tee. In fact, selling is the only form of promotion that is personal, direct and flexible. It is personal because it occurs between individuals. Because of the direct relationship between prospect and seller, the opportunity exists for an exchange of feelings and information that is not available with other forms of promotion. Personal selling is not prerecorded, allowing the seller flexibility to handle immediate feedback and to change the presentation to adapt to the needs of the audience. Selling is dynamic.

Many people call selling the final step in the marketing process. After the rest of the marketing mix performs satisfactorily, selling brings products together with those who need them. This definition does not mean that marketing stops once a product is sold. A constant flow of information from customers must be maintained to assure that product design and distribution systems continue to satisfy. Personal selling provides the ongoing information input that nourishes the marketing program.

Some marketers view selling as the first step in the marketing program. All of the pre-testing in the world does not take the place of a satisfied customer. Without the sale, production ceases, pipelines are not filled and accounts are not paid. **Nothing happens in business until something is sold.**

Profile in quality #14: Driveability.

The sophisticated engineering of today's Ford Motor Company cars and trucks is truly remarkable. For instance, today's Mercury Cougar XR7 and Ford Thunderbird Super Coupe have a speed sensitive electronic rack and pinion steering system that provides optimum driving control. Their new adjustable suspension system monitors driving conditions, automatically making adjustments to optimize ride and handling. And both cars are equipped with four-wheel disc anti-lock brakes. If your goal is to build the highest quality cars and trucks in the world—you don't do it any other way.

Ford, Mercury, Lincoln, Ford Trucks. Our goal is to build the highest quality cars and trucks in the world.

Buckle up—together we can save lives.

FORD MOTOR COMPANY

F igure #16—ad reprint—Ford
The Ford Motor Company has gained a lot of mileage with its "Quality Is Job 1" motto. (Courtesy of Ford Motor Company.)

De secretaresse die beslist een Ricoh copier wilde.

Ricoh heeft in Nederland misschien nog niet de allergrootste naam als het om kopieerapparatuur gaat. Maar in bedrijven en kantoren oogst Ricoh steeds meer waardering. Horen mensen die voor Ricoh kozen, steeds weer dat ene, alleszeggende woord 'bedankt'.

Een bedankje van de directeur voor 't verhogen van de efficiency. Een bedankje van de financieel manager voor het verlagen van de servicekosten. En een heel bijzonder bedankje van alle collega's voor duidelijke, perfecte kopieën. Dankbetuigingen die voortvloeien uit de simpele bedrijfsfilosofie van Ricoh: je verplaatsen in de positie van een ander. In die van de directeur. De financieel manager. De inkoper. En, natuurlijk, de gebruiker. Een filosofie die leidt tot arbeidsbesparende technologie, deskundige service en strenge kwaliteitseisen.

Ricoh. De naam die voor duizenden gebruikers synoniem is geworden met 't begrip 'betrouwbaar'. Al in meer dan 130 landen. Met als hoogtepunt de marktleiderspositie in de copier-markt van Japan. Het land waar, zoals u weet, ze wel verstand hebben van efficiënt zaken doen.

OFFICIËLE SPONSOR
RUGNUMMERS
TOUR DE FRANCE

TECHNOLOGY WITH A HUMAN TOUCH

RICOH

Ricoh Europe B.V., Postbus 114, 1180 AC Amstelveen, Fax 472006, Telex 11384, Tel. 020-5474111/G.K.N., Postbus 868, 3800 AW Amersfoort, Fax 033-12710, Tel. 033-635694/Kentie B.V., El. Rooseveltlaan 110-112, 1183 CL Amstelveen, Fax 020-472884, Tel. 020-470106/Kentie B.V., Binckhorstlaan 151, 2516 BA Den Haag, Fax 070-474491, Telex 32745, Tel. 070-859504.

Figure #17—ad reprint—Ricoh
European advertising such as this ad for Ricoh business machines, often portrays a different culture than found in U.S. media. (Courtesy of Ricoh)

Congratulations.

You've made it.

WHAT'CHA GONNA DO?

Buy more clothes?

A new car?

More gym shoes?

WHAT'CHA GONNA DO?

Remember the neighborhood?

The teacher who wouldn't let you quit?

The coach who was on 24 hour call?

WHAT'CHA GONNA DO?

Donate sports equipment?

Picket a crack house?

Replace an old hoop at the park?

WHAT'CHA GONNA DO?

Feed the hungry?

Help a kid study for the SAT?

Coach Boys & Girls Club games?

WHAT'CHA GONNA DO?

Just Do It.

Figures #18 and 19—ad reprint—Nike

Advertisements for Nike often promote more than just the firm's products, as evidence by these messages encouraging multicultural harmony. (Courtesy of nike and Muse Cordero Chen, Inc.)

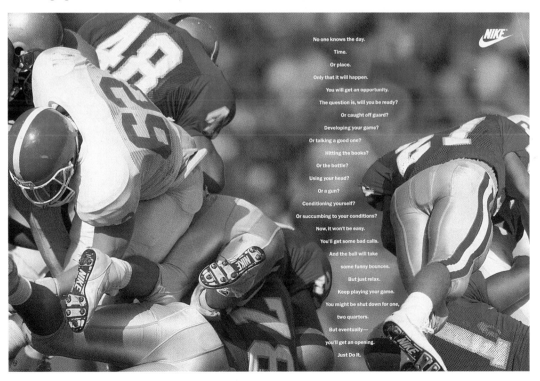

No one knows the day.

Time.

Or place.

Only that it will happen.

You will get an opportunity.

The question is, will you be ready?

Or caught off guard?

Developing your game?

Or talking a good one?

Hitting the books?

Or the bottle?

Using your head?

Or a gun?

Conditioning yourself?

Or succumbing to your conditions?

Now, it won't be easy.

You'll get some bad calls.

And the ball will take some funny bounces.

But just relax.

Keep playing your game.

You might be shut down for one, two quarters.

But eventually— you'll get an opening.

Just Do It.

Figure #20—ad reprint—California Dept. of Health Services
Nonprofit organizations use advertising to effectively promote their causes as evidenced by this clever and powerful ad used by the California Department of Health Services in its anti-smoking campaign. (Courtesy of California Department of Health Services)

THE SALE

Many products would not reach the consumer or business buyer without passing through an intermediary. With trade goods, the wholesaler or retailer actually completes the sale. A **sale** is simply a business transaction where the ownership or use of products transfers from seller to buyer. With the sale of physical goods, the product becomes the property of the buyer. In the sale of services, title does not change hands. Instead, the buyer gains the use of or is treated to the activity offered.

> **Sale**—a business transaction where ownership or use of a product transfers from seller to buyer.

This transaction that completes the exchange process occurs when a need or perceived need is satisfied. Sellers supply buyers with products and receive something of value in return. With business goods, transactions occur between companies, but individuals are usually involved either as direct participants or as facilitators.

SALESPERSON

A **salesperson** serves as the liaison between buyer and seller, facilitating the sale. Whether in the direct employ of the seller or acting as an independent agent, salespeople arrange for the transfer of the good or service. Professionals selling for Omark, a manufacturer of saw chains, call on manufacturers such as Homelite, McCulloch and Husqvarna. Sales representatives from Squibb contact the doctors and hospitals promoting medicines. Consultants working in the better dress salon at Saks persuade customers to buy the latest in fashions. These individuals operate as professional salespeople.

> **Salesperson**—one who serves as liaison between seller and buyer, facilitating the sale.

The salesperson helps both parties to the transaction. By bringing benefit to the buyer in the form of satisfaction, the salesperson works on behalf of the person or firm that is purchasing. On the other hand, the selling organization also receives benefit. Salespeople act as agents for the seller and have a fiduciary responsibility to the firm paying for their services. This means that while bringing satisfaction to customers, salespeople must remain loyal to and follow the policies of the seller.

Owens Illinois, the firm making plastic bottles for shampoo and detergent marketers, employs salespeople to promote its business. Precision Castparts, a metal die casting company, producing pedestals for picnic umbrellas or housings for transformers, depends upon personal selling to get the message to its

■　　■　　■　　■　　■
Top sales forces

COMPANY	PRODUCT	1993 SALES	STAFF	AVG. TIME WITH FIRM
Northwestern Mutual Life	Insurance	$5.9 billion	7,100	12.3 years
Moore Medical Corporation	Pharmaceuticals	$275 million	20	5.2 years
Val-Pak Direct	Coupon ads	$110 million	1,300	n.a.
Eastman Chemical Company	Chemicals	$4 billion	500	16 years
PruCare of Austin	Health care	$31 million	14	n.a.

■　　■　　■　　■　　■

potential markets. The sales staff at Dow Chemical calls directly on manufacturers to help them reduce dangerous 1,1,1-Trichloroethane emissions. These salespeople carry out important promotional functions.[1]

How Are Salespeople Classified?

Although previously classified as **order getters** and **order takers,** these descriptions do not do justice to the selling job. Titles that more accurately describe the functions of salespeople are **active** and **passive.** Some professional sellers take a "hands-on" approach to solving customer problems and satisfying needs. Others who work in the field of sales may do much to help the selling effort but not actually become involved with searching for and satisfying needs.

In today's market, the selling company often receives the buyer's purchase order by mail or telephone. In this case, an active salesperson may satisfy the needs of the customer through personal contact yet not physically receive the order. Order getter does not fit the job that such sellers perform. Passive sellers carry out many tasks in helping the sales effort other than just take orders. Classifying these sales assisters as just order takers ignores the many other facets of personal selling.

ACTIVE

Active salesperson— creative professional seller who actively seeks out needs, offering specific solutions.

An **active salesperson** takes a dominant role in the purchase decision process. This type of seller delves into the buyer's need to offer solutions that satisfy those requirements. The active salesperson strives to complete the transaction, but does not always get the order. In the process of satisfying needs, this seller may actually refer the prospect to another source of supply. Salespeople employed by production goods marketers are usually of the active type.

Creative salespeople go by many names, including but not limited to consultative, needs oriented or client related. Whatever the description, the active salesperson commands a reputation for professionalism in business-to-business markets. In these arenas, where close relationships and trustworthy performance are crucial to buyers, salespeople play a vital role and are highly regarded.

Customer Oriented

The creative salesperson is **customer oriented.** Many of these active sellers prefer to be called needs finders rather than problem solvers. By truly caring about the prospect's needs, customer oriented salespeople may occasionally not culminate the sale. As members of the business-to-business selling team, these professionals provide the ultimate link between seller and buyer.

---

[1]Editors, "Eaton's no-holds-barred approach wins Sawyer Award," *Business Marketing,* January 1992, pp. 26–29.

■ ■ ■ ■ ■
Active and passive sales people by job

JOB	SALESPERSON TYPE
Automobile salesperson	Active
Life insurance salesperson	Active
Department store clerk	Active/passive*
Pharmaceutical representative	Passive
Customer service agent	Passive
Travel agent	Active/passive*
Stock broker	Active/passive*
Specialty wholesaler salesperson	Passive
Dry cleaners counter person	Passive
Lumber broker	Active
Chemical company sales representative	Active
Route driver	Active/passive*
Manufacturers' representative	Active

*May be either, depending upon the company

■ ■ ■ ■ ■

Not all salespeople have the answers to all customer problems, and it is sometimes necessary to refer the client elsewhere for solution. When searching for customer needs, the salesperson may realize that another product from another company is the better solution. In this case, the professional may make a referral instead of pushing his or her own merchandise. The creative salesperson has met a need, yet has not personally completed the transaction. Customers often remember the salespeople who helped them solve a problem, even those who recommend a competitor.

Nonmanipulative

Creative sales people are **nonmanipulative.** These promoters refrain from using canned presentations and are not pushy. The customer oriented seller probes to resolve the true needs of the prospect and then uses her or his company's products to create a satisfactory solution. If the active salesperson does not have the solution for satisfying the specific needs of a prospect, referral to another qualified source is a standard procedure.

The most highly regarded and often most successful salespeople are ethical and considerate individuals. Consultative sellers strive to give their undivided attention to prospects and customers. These salespeople assure that every aspect of the good or service is understood and its use fully explained. Since buyers gain confidence in products when they trust the salesperson, these professionals often sell themselves first, then promote the product.

PASSIVE

Passive salespeople handle the transfer of merchandise or use of services, but do not take a major role in finding solutions to customer needs. These members

Passive salesperson— salesperson who does not actively participate in finding solutions to customer needs.

of the selling team take payment, package the merchandise or take orders from catalogs. Many sales personnel working for self-service retailers and general line wholesalers fit this description. The salesclerk at Kmart and the vendor from Central Janitorial Supply are typically passive sellers.

The retail clerk who collects the money from the customer and places the self-serve merchandise in a bag is typical of the passive salesperson. Such employees carry out necessary functions with many retailers, such as The Broadway, Wal-Mart and Kroger. Creative selling is not appropriate with these self-service outlets. For convenience goods, selecting one's own merchandise is an efficient and economical method of shopping.

Sales performance receives little emphasis in stores handling low- and medium-priced merchandise. On the other hand, exclusive boutiques and upscale department stores such as Bullock's Wilshire, I. Magnin and Saks Fifth Avenue provide considerable personal selling assistance. This satisfaction of customer needs is critical in the consumer exchange process.

It is difficult for stores or shops to provide customer satisfaction when retail salespeople are poorly trained. Many retail stores would fare better if more time were spent educating their staffs in the art of needs oriented selling. Too often satisfaction goes wanting simply because the retailer has not tried to determine the need of the customer.

Sales Assister

Some salespeople facilitate the exchange, but do not directly participate in the decision process. Among passive salespeople, **sales assister** is a prominent classification and accurately describes many retail employees. This person helps the actual sales transaction to occur, but, as a rule, does not creatively satisfy needs. Sales assisters are regularly called **order takers,** and are often found working for predominantly self-service type retailers. These types of salespeople are seldom called upon for creative assistance.

Other passive sellers act as support staff. Although these people do not aid the actual transaction, their help in developing interpersonal relationships between buyer and seller is often the clue to making the sale. Members of the support staff have the responsibility of assuring that the selling company's products and policies are presented in a complimentary light to the buyer. This team effort enhances the active salesperson's success.

Technical Specialists

Technical specialist—
a member of the sales support staff who assists customers after the sale is made.

Technical specialists, typically found in production goods marketers, receive specific training to help customers use the product effectively and efficiently. Usually, these passive sellers carry out their duties after the sale is made. By adapting the product to the specific needs of the customer, these experts are a key link in assuring ultimate satisfaction. Technical specialists are particularly useful in today's high-tech arenas.

Many companies that produce highly technical products, such as Sandvik, Honeywell, and Rohm and Haas, employ these specialists to act as troubleshooters. Creative salespeople working for high-technology companies may have engineering backgrounds, but may not be as highly trained in other pertinent areas.

Global Marketing: I love Japan!

Although Japan has become a dominant force in world trade, many U.S. companies avoid doing business in this fascinating country. The language barrier certainly contributes to this hesitancy. Cultural differences, too, scare off many firms. Yet while many shun this major market, the need for increased exports to Japan grows greater daily. American electronics marketers are especially averse to trying to crack a market where Japanese firms have international renown.

One company that is successful selling in Japan is Conner Peripherals Incorporated, a Silicon Valley manufacturer of computer disk drives. According to industry analysts, Conner sells about three-fourths of all of the 2.5-inch disk drives for Japan's laptop and notebook computers. Most surprisingly, Toshiba, the Japanese multinational that manufactures both computers and disk drives, chose Conner over its own in-house division.

Conner contributes its company philosophy of "Sell, design, build" to its success in this market. Using a sales organization based in Japan, the firm prides itself on close customer relations. The staff, composed mostly of Japanese nationals, includes service technicians and quality assurance reps to assist the selling effort. In addition, Conner advertises in Japanese trade journals and participates in exhibits and conferences.

SOURCE: Kate Bertrand, "Conner's Japanese success drive," *Business Marketing,* December 1991, pp. 18–20. (Photo Courtesy of Conner Peripherals)

Once the sale is made, it is the job of the technical specialist to help the customer get the best use out of the products purchased.

Missionaries

Another support member of the sales force is the **missionary,** a seller used to gain product specifications. These individuals work to develop basic demand with specifiers, those people or firms who decide what goods or services others will use. Often called detail people, missionaries call on clients, primarily

Missionary—a passive salesperson used to gain product specifications.

in the medical or construction fields, who do not actually purchase the products offered. Although their selling task can be aggressive and customer oriented, these salespeople are most often listed in the passive group.

Drug salespeople from Pfizer call on doctors to convince them to prescribe their company's medicines. The actual customer is the pharmacist who stocks the medicines, but without the doctor's prescription, consumers cannot buy. Building products manufacturers, such as Texlite or U.S. Gypsum, use missionaries to call on architects and engineers. These detail persons sell prospects on specifying their firm's products in construction jobs that are in the design stage.

Where Are Professional Sellers Employed?

Placing sales representatives from whole industries or types of business into one category or another is difficult. For example, the route driver for one Pepsi Cola distributor may be creative, while a person in a similar position with a different company acts as just an order taker, or a passive type of salesperson. Generally, certain industries or particular types of goods or services require professional selling.

Both active and passive salespeople appear in a variety of different types of industries and businesses. Creative sellers are commonly, but not exclusively, found in production goods markets. In business-to-business selling, the close working relationships needed between buyer and seller call for needs oriented selling. Many of these marketers employ creative sellers for direct contact with prospects and customers and passive salespeople for other roles. Technical service representatives and detail salespeople are also commonly found in these markets.

PRODUCTION GOODS MARKETS

Perhaps the marketing arena that has the largest concentration of creative salespeople is the production goods field. Selling products from one manufacturer to another usually requires the special, creative talents of active sellers. Probing for needs and concern for satisfaction are trademarks of these consultative agents. Prospects and buyers of production goods need this type of assistance. Salespeople working for Ashland Chemical, Hewlett-Packard, Allen-Bradley, Owens-Corning and Uniroyal have the aptitude and training to be active, creative sellers.

Some grocery manufacturers maintain separate sales forces to handle the actual buyer, general line wholesalers or supermarkets. The individuals calling on these resellers are needs searching, customer oriented sellers. This group strives to discover and satisfy the requirements of the actual purchaser, the intermediary, while other members of the sales support staff take care of the in-store work. Some marketers of grocery items combine these selling duties by employing a single representative to do both jobs.

WHOLESALERS

Generally, wholesalers employ passive, order taking types of salespeople. These intermediaries carry an enormous line of products. The sales force usually has little choice but to see what the customer is lacking and fill out an order form, a passive role. Sales representatives employed by these resellers may not have the opportunity to be very creative. The main task for a typical wholesale representative is to take orders.

Without representation wholesale distributors would be lost. Although their jobs may be passive, wholesaler salespeople still perform very necessary functions. This group often provides the only form of promotion that the wholesaler may use. The classification of passive salesperson does not mean to imply that these employees are unnecessary. On the contrary, active and passive sellers are equally important in carrying out any marketer's goals.

The Business Imaging Systems division of Eastman Kodak Co. uses a multi-tiered selling organization. Besides direct sales representative, the firm has a system of broker/distributors and components marketers. The key to the success of this program is the integration of responsibilities and assistance. Each member of the organization receives credit and/or compensation for sales within the assigned areas. Kodak successfully minimizes channel conflict with this partially integrated system.[2]

CONSUMER SERVICES

Consumer services markets also rely heavily upon personal selling. Real estate, insurance and securities brokers feature active salespeople. The intangible nature of services make these products more difficult to understand. Therefore, salespeople who can probe for needs and solve problems are in greater demand for selling consumer services than consumer goods. Some of these sales professionals are independent agents; others work as company representatives.

In each of these fields, the need to probe for customer needs is mandatory. Creative real estate sellers ask questions and listen carefully to responses to learn of the client's requirements. Insurance agents must be aware of the purposes behind the purchase of risk protection. In the securities industry, salespeople determine if prospects are looking for income or for speculation in their investments.

DIRECT-TO-CONSUMER MARKETING

Direct-to-consumer marketers also employ client oriented salespeople. Even though Avon is experimenting with in-store distribution, most of the sales revenue for this cosmetics giant derives from the consultants who see customers in their homes. Shaklee, Mary Kay and Electrolux are other companies employing in-home sales representatives. Such direct-to-consumer salespeople are truly creative types.

---

[2]Thomas E. Ferguson, "Customers' diverse needs require diverse channels," *Business Marketing*, March 1992, pp. 64–66.

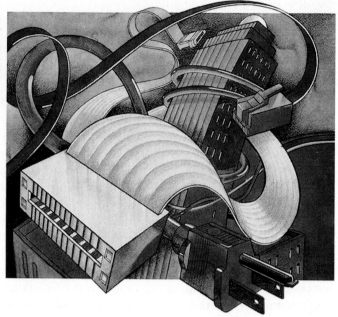

UNTANGLING YOUR ENERGY MANAGEMENT PROBLEMS BEFORE THEY TIE UP YOUR FACILITY.

When you hear complaints about comfort, see your utility bills go up, or your building's equipment go down, you know you have an energy management problem.

If your facility is more than 10 years old, you may have less obvious problems. Aging equipment, outmoded technology and changing building usage may be the culprits.

Johnson Controls brings over 100 years of experience in recognizing and solving these money-wasting problems. We're sensitive to the unique energy management requirements of your facility, whether it's a hospital, retail store, warehouse, school, or office building of any size.

We can design and implement solutions that provide greater cost-effectiveness with no compromise in occupant comfort. And you'll take comfort in the prompt payback of your investment and our flexible financing packages.

Don't wait for an energy management crisis before you call Johnson Controls. Call now at 1-800-972-8040 and avoid one. In Wisconsin, call 1-800-472-6533. Or write, Johnson Controls, Systems and Service Division, C19, Milwaukee, WI 53201-0423.

Johnson Controls Facility Management System forecasts cooling requirements based on predicted weather conditions for the next day to optimize the totally electric HVAC system at The Crescent, in Dallas.

© 1990 Johnson Controls, Inc.
JC9063C

JOHNSON CONTROLS
Exceeding Your Expectations!

Like many business goods marketers, Johnson Controls uses advertising to develop leads for its salesforce. (Courtesy of Johnson Controls Inc.)

Categorizing salespeople is not simple, as generalizations often backfire. Although much of the retail field employs passive sellers, many intermediaries recognize the need for creative salespeople. Wholesalers may find that customers have needs beyond just ordering merchandise. These firms recognize the need to be more consultative in their selling effort. Many marketing oriented companies in those industries that typically use passive salespeople are changing their promotion efforts to become more creative.

How Do Salespeople Allocate Time?

Just as it is difficult to place salespeople into predetermined niches, it is equally challenging to describe how sellers operate. What might be true regarding the types of activity for one person or one company might be dramatically different for others. It is reasonably safe to say that business-to-business salespeople have some regular duties that take up a portion of their work days.

The role of the professional salesperson has changed dramatically over the past few decades. The days of the prepared presentation and hard sell tactics are gone. The creative salesperson works toward determining the needs of potential customers and finding the means to bring satisfaction. This new breed of seller is often called facilitator instead of peddler.

PERSONAL CONTACT

A day in the life of a salesperson is not entirely spent in the company of customers. Professionals spend only about one-third of their time in **personal contact** with customers and prospects, and the amount of face-to-face interaction has been steadily declining. Although direct contact is down, primarily due to increased travel costs, salespeople must still maintain the relationships that are so important to business goods transactions.

To counteract less personal contact, the average salesperson spends more and more time on the telephone. Triggered by the dramatic increases in fuel costs during the 1970s, phone calls allow for continued personal contact yet are less costly. Once used mostly to arrange appointments, the telephone is important for carrying out a variety of selling tasks.

PAPERWORK

Processing **paperwork** often requires 20 percent or more of a salesperson's time, but this drain is also diminishing. Laptop computers and other types of electronic office equipment drastically reduce the hours that business goods salespeople spend on reports and office work. Many professional sellers carry laptops with them and take the opportunity while traveling or waiting to complete paperwork drudgery.

Technological improvements in equipment have simplified report filing and correspondence. Many salespeople use battery operated recorders while traveling or during waiting periods. Portable FAX machines, connected with computers, are popular. Using these selling aids, professional salespeople find that less time spent on paperwork means more time for productive face-to-face contact.

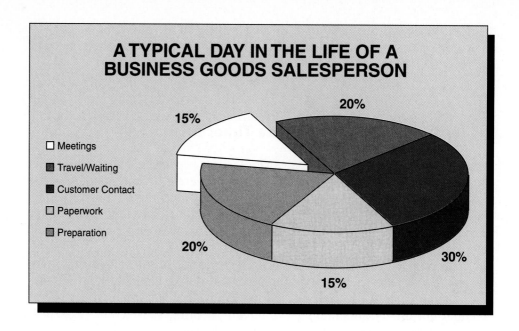

A TYPICAL DAY IN THE LIFE OF A BUSINESS GOODS SALESPERSON

- □ Meetings
- ▨ Travel/Waiting
- ■ Customer Contact
- □ Paperwork
- ▨ Preparation

15% 20% 30% 15% 20%

TRAVEL

A significant portion of the business-to-business salesperson's day is spent on **travel.** These journeys may be around the city or around the country, but some is usually necessary. Since most salespeople visit customers at their places of business, traveling can use up valuable time. Whether riding a taxicab in New York City or flying a private plane to cover New Mexico, time spent on the road is subtracted from what is available to meet directly with customers and prospects.

Travel dramatically impacts the costs associated with selling. Many firms are taking some substantial steps to reduce the expensive use of automobile and airplane. Using other forms of communication can be a significant help to sales minded companies and individuals. Telephone, FAX machines and Internet will gain added application as more marketers equip the sales forces of the future.

WAITING

Companies often establish specific hours when purchasers can meet with vendors. When large numbers of representatives call on the same prospect, some **waiting** is inevitable. Many times the salesperson waits even when appointments have been made. Routine business can be conducted over the telephone, reducing the need for traveling and waiting. Yet, as necessary as the telephone has become to the salesperson, nothing can replace the need to establish good working relationships through personal calls.

To gain the efficiency and productivity demanded of the position, professional salespeople must be accurate planners. Each customer or prospect visit must be organized for optimum results, but the selling process itself involves more than just talking with potential buyers.

What Is The Selling Process?

Professional salespeople carry out a variety of activities in the process of satisfying customer needs. No matter which industry or field the seller is working, the fundamentals of conducting sales are similar. The active salesperson follows a routine that varies little from market to market. The **selling process** is broken into three distinct areas; preparation, presentation, and post-sale activities.

Selling process—preparation, presentation and post-sale activities.

PREPARATION

Preparation for selling includes prospecting for potential customers and laying the groundwork for successful interaction in the presentation stage. All successful sellers pride themselves on product knowledge. This information is not learned in a day. Salespeople should also thoroughly understand the companies they represent, the industries they operate within, and the markets they service. To a true professional salesperson, preparation is not something to be taken lightly.[3]

Time is important to both the salesperson and the marketing firm. Proper budgeting and management of the hours available for presentation with prospects and customers are the marks of a professional. In addition to time assigned for visitations, a certain portion of the salesperson's week must be set aside for developing potential customers. While this function is important, time cannot be wasted when it comes to looking for new clients.

Prospecting

Prospecting means searching for new customers, but this is not the simple act of deciding where to call next. This process involves learning of interested parties and determining if they are potential buyers. The prospecting process begins with leads, found either by the seller or the marketing company. Prospecting does not stop with the receipt of a lead.

Prospecting—searching for new, potential customers.

A **lead** is a company or an individual having an interest in the salesperson's product, and can be generated from several sources. Advertising provides many sales leads. Companies that respond to trade journal ads have shown an interest in the product. Leads also evolve from satisfied customers and from researching through publications or directories. In business-to-business, salespeople may receive leads from each of these sources.

Lead—potential customer that has shown interest.

The lead itself is not sufficient reason for a salesperson to spend precious time making a personal visit. Just because companies or individuals show interest does not mean they are in a position to purchase. Before the seller hits the streets and interacts with an interested party, needs should be verified. A lead that has demonstrated need is a **prospect.** The telephone is an excellent tool for determining potential needs.

Prospect—lead that has demonstrated need.

---

[3]John P. Kirwan, Jr., "The precision selling payoff," *Sales & Marketing Management,* January 1992, pp. 58–61.

Our glasses are designed to bring out the best in a beverage. "Excelsior," our prize-winning stemware series, is a good example.

Nature has ingeniously created the shapes and colors of flowers to appeal to the taste of "guests" needed to preserve the species.

© Schott Corporation

With a diversified line that includes trade goods and operating supplies, Schott uses its advertising to appeal to a variety of business buyers. (Courtesy of Schott America)

happen by chance.

Qualifying

Qualified prospect— prospect that has the ability and authority to purchase.

Prospects must be **qualified.** This process includes checking on the ability of the potential customer to pay its bills. Companies who have poor payment records or insufficient financial strength are not good prospects for salespeople. A firm's credit department or outside resources such as Dun & Bradstreet are often useful in uncovering a prospect's ability to pay. Once this financial data is known, qualifying takes another step.

The next step in the qualifying process is determining the proper person to see. Professionals can save valuable time by calling only on the key people involved with the buying decision. Pinpointing who these decision makers are in advance is part of the prospecting process. Nothing is more frustrating to a salesperson than calling on a likely prospect but not being able to determine who makes the buying determination. Although most firms have purchasing departments or people, the one whose decision counts may work in engineering or manufacturing.

Cold call—an unannounced visit on a lead.

A salesperson's unannounced visit on a lead is known as a **cold call.** Conducting cold calls is a poor use of a professional seller's time. Visiting a lead for the purpose of determining need or ability to pay is counterproductive. Since cost effective selling dictates that salespeople spend their time interacting with prospects and customers, cold calls are not efficient.[4]

Gaining Knowledge

Another aspect of preparation involves laying the groundwork for the sales call on qualified prospects or customers. Salespeople must be knowledgeable. Knowing the policies and procedures of the selling company is the first step in preparing to make sales calls. A complete understanding of the prospect's business is also important.

Interaction with potential customers will be more beneficial to both parties if the salesperson is well prepared. Sellers need to recognize the business problems and needs of prospects. The preparation process includes gaining knowledge of the products the prospect handles and the markets where the prospect sells the products.

Salespeople need complete knowledge of the industries of both buyer and seller. Prospects and customers need solutions to their problems. Awareness of market conditions, including competition, helps the professional find alternatives and solutions to problems or needs. Well-prepared salespeople are in the best position to offer the proper answers.

PRESENTATION

Presentation—probing for needs, handling objections and closing.

The second step in the process of selling is **presentation.** This phase includes all of the activities and functions carried out during face-to-face or telephone

---

[4]Jack Green, "Training your TSRs—essential to telemarketing success," *Telemarketing,* August 1992, pp. 16–17; Martin Everett, "Talk it up," *Sales & Marketing Management,* October 1993, pp. 128–131; K. Baker, "Ten sales techniques for telemarketing success,"*Telemarketing,* July 1992, pp. 18–20; Richard L. Bencin, "How to start a business-to-business telemarketing program," *Marketing News,* March 16, 1987, p. 8.

contact with prospects and customers. Professional salespeople rarely use "canned" presentations. Since the process of selling involves the discovery of prospect needs and presenting a satisfactory solution, preplanned or canned sales pitches miss the objective.

Probing

Since selling involves the satisfaction of needs, the first step in the presentation process is **probing.** Full determination of the nature of needs is necessary before the selling process can continue. The lay person might feel that problems can be uncovered merely by asking questions, but in reality, salespeople must be detectives. Not all of the clues are evident. Probing is usually a continual process that takes place over several sales calls.

Probing—asking open-ended questions to discover needs or problems.

Handling Objections

Presentation includes **handling objections.** Prospects may raise questions or place demands that salespeople must overcome to proceed toward the goal of satisfaction. Not all problems have solutions that can be controlled by salespeople. The seller's product may not be the best one for the job, or the prospect may not be in a position to take full advantage of the attributes of the good or service offered.

The process of handling objections and countering with suggestions is a necessary part of determining true needs of the prospect. Many buyers do not voice their real requirements. By probing and discussing the objections and obstacles placed in the path, the professional can discover what is needed and offer satisfying solutions.

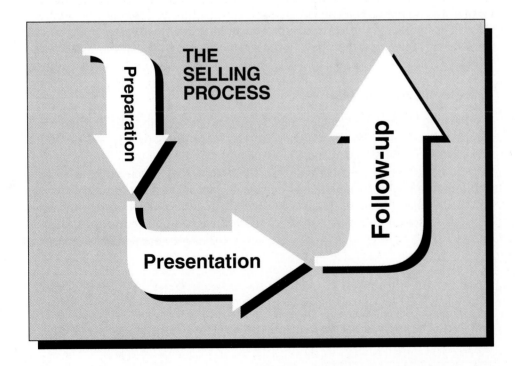

THE SELLING PROCESS

Preparation

Presentation

Follow-up

Closing

Closing, or **receiving an order,** is the final step in the presentation process. Although some prospects need to be pushed into placing the actual order, most professional salespeople obtain purchase orders by making sure that the prospect's needs have been satisfied. Leading prospects to buy instead of selling to them helps assure satisfaction.

Many "techniques" have been proposed for closing the sale. The safest bet is for the salesperson to correctly perform everything that leads up to getting the order. If the presentation process has been properly concluded, the prospect will make the decision to buy if the products proposed satisfy needs. Customer's do not continue to look to sellers who cannot satisfy those needs.[5]

POST-SALE ACTIVITIES

Many questions prospects and customers raise cannot be answered on the spot. Special requests or price demands may be different from stated company policy. The salesperson may have to resubmit information or gain approvals from the selling company. During these negotiations, it is important for the professional to properly represent the selling company. Promoting the capabilities of the company offering the product is as important as selling the product itself.

The final step in the selling process relates to **post-sale activities.** Once a prospect becomes a customer, the work has just begun. Giving an order does not create satisfaction with the buyer. Receiving the merchandise or service that solves problems is what satisfies. Professional salespeople must assure that the purchased products deliver on time, arrive as ordered and function as they have been represented to do.

Many inexperienced sellers are content to receive orders. Proper training emphasizes that the goal of any salesperson should be long-term customers instead of immediate orders. Once prospects turn into customers, professional salespeople really earn their pay. In the competitive arenas of today's business-to-business markets, rivals can easily turn a customer into a former customer.

Reinforce Buyer's Decision

The development of the satisfied, repeat customer is a major part of the reward for the seller. Some buyers, whether they are consumers or businesses, might suffer from cognitive dissonance. Professional salespeople try to put their customers' concerns to rest by assuring them that their decision was sound. **Reinforcement** of the customer's decision to buy is part of the followup portion of the selling process. A customer who is uncertain whether the purchase decision was a good one is less likely to be pleased upon receipt of the good or service.

---

[5]Tom Searcy, "The best techniques for closing the sale," *Telemarketing,* October 1993, pp. 82–83; J. Falvey, "For the best close, keep an open mind," *Sales & Marketing Management,* April 1990, p. 10; Mack Hanan, "Let the customer close for you," *Sales & Marketing Management,* August 1986, pp. 68–70.

Customers feel more secure assuming that they have made a purchase rather than they have been sold. Although the events leading up to the close may have supported that feeling, consultative sellers make sure that their buyers are really "sold" on the product and the supplier. Professional salespeople continue to reassure the customer even after the product is received. Such support tends to reduce the occurrence of cognitive dissonance.

A professional approach is necessary to please business-to-business buyers. Because time is limited for both buyer and seller, salespeople who come to the point quickly and do not waste time are appreciated by purchasing managers and product buyers. Knowledge, appropriate dress, good listening habits and the ability to reassure the buyer after the order has been placed are qualities that business goods buyers appreciate.

Order Tracing

The product itself is a necessary element in producing satisfaction, but there are many other factors that must be considered. Delivery of the product where and when needed is paramount, especially if the buyer is using the just-in-time process. The professional salesperson must coordinate with the selling company to make certain that the right goods ship at the right time. **Order tracing** is a necessary task that salespeople carry out to assure proper delivery.

What Is The Role of Telemarketing?

Telemarketing is the use of the telephone for prospecting or to make sales presentations. With the constant increase in selling expenses, the use of telephones

Telemarketing—using the telephone for prospecting or sales presentations.

Selling is the one form of promotion that is personal.

has become mandatory for selling efficiency and productivity. If information can be gathered or transmitted through the wires instead of over the road, more time will be available for interaction with the client.

Although consumers may have a negative reaction to telemarketing, this selling tool is embraced in business-to-business markets. New laws have clamped down heavily on the fraudulent use of the telephone to solicit business, giving states and citizens expanded authority to sue in federal courts. As a rule, telemarketing in business arenas has not needed policing. On the contrary, both production and trade goods marketers use this cost savings method of marketing communications to good advantage.[6]

PROSPECTING

Telemarketing is most helpful for **prospecting.** The high cost of putting a salesperson on the road is reason enough for the groundwork to be handled through telemarketing. A well-trained person can often qualify leads easily over the telephone. Determining the level of need and ability to purchase in advance of the salesperson's visit saves time and money.

The information gathered by experienced callers can give the seller needed information for the presentation. Many a market can be softened through the use of telemarketing. Experienced telephone callers can lead a prospect through many of the intermediate steps of the selling process. For example, sample orders may be placed and receipt verified before the salesperson makes the first visit.

MAKING PRESENTATIONS

The preparation step in the selling process is not the only beneficiary of telemarketing. Today's marketers conduct **complete presentations** over the phone. Because buyers are also busy, many prefer to deal by telemarketing instead of in face-to-face interviews. Purchasing people can pick up a phone and receive needed information on the spot. Capable inside salespeople who answer questions and give technical advice over the telephone are a boon to any marketing program. The ability to measure and control the selling effort becomes a major advantage, as telemarketers can gain immediate feedback and waste little time.

Video brochures have greatly enhanced the effectiveness of telemarketing presentations. Following up the telephone call with a direct mail campaign helped companies such as Soloflex, the Oregon exercise equipment marketer. For Hagerty Marine Insurance, of Traverse City, Michigan, a video brochure became the centerpiece. A direct mail campaign first targeted a market offering the free tape. Telemarketers then followed up the responses to create a tremendous response.[7]

---

[6]"FTC says National Art ran scheme to sell posters via telephone," *The Wall Street Journal*, April 12, 1994, p. A5.

[7]Richard L Bencin, "Telefocus: Telemarketing gets synergized," *Sales & Marketing Management*, February 1992, pp. 49–53.

TELEMARKETING APPLICATIONS
Advantages & Disadvantages

APPLICATIONS

- Taking customer orders
- Inbound telemarketing
- Reactivating customers who haven't bought recently
- Contacting marginal accounts
- Providing service
- Maintaining goodwill
- Handling customer complaints
- Answering customer inquiries
- Prospecting
- Setting sales appointments
- Notifying customers about special deals
- Outbound telemarketing
- Informing customers about new products and services

ADVANTAGES

- Yields higher profits
- Low cost
- Convenient
- Flexible
- Saves time
- Can reach almost anyone

DISADVANTAGES

- Easier for prospect to say "no"
- Persuasive messages must be brief
- Lacks multisense (sight, touch, smell) appeal
- Can't observe demographic information (age, race, sex)
- Cost of telephone calls

MARKETING RESEARCH

Telemarketing is a natural method for collecting **marketing research** information. Well-trained telephone people can obtain data regarding products and markets from busy buyers more easily than the salesperson. Buyers are usually more inclined to give a few minutes of phone time to a qualified telemarketer than a longer period needed to talk to a visiting salesperson.

Telemarketing is not the only answer for management. Although proving to be a less costly method of operation, it is by no means a cure-all. This selling tool receives some criticism, especially in the consumer sector, but several states have action through "asterisk" bills that allow consumers who do not want calls to have their directory listing starred. Other legislation involving telemarketing regards how the use of these sellers should be taxed and whether automatic transmitting devices should be allowed.[8]

What Is Sales Management?

While many professional salespeople work independently, management of the sales staff is a major responsibility. A major part of the efficiency of any sales staff directly relates to sales management. Usually, the people selected for this task come from the ranks of the salesforce, but some companies find that management personnel from other disciplines are a wiser choice to lead the selling staff. Besides, leaving good sellers in the field where they excel is often more desirable than replacing them with new, untried rookies.

SALES MANAGERS

No matter what field of expertise she or he might bring to the job, the key to the success of a sales manager is the word manager. Managing the field sales force is not that much different than running any other business operation. The functions of planning, staffing, leading and measuring describe the sales manager's job. The one difference might be that the selling staff is typically a bit more independent than many other groups within a business.

For sales management, planning includes the staffing requirements needed in the future and keeping the present organization efficient and motivated. Although by nature salespeople respond to incentives and other compensation, other factors come into play. Controlling costs and working cooperatively with other sectors of the marketing team are important considerations for sales managers.

STAFF EVALUATION AND ORGANIZATION

Along with quotas and compensations, sales management is responsible for development of a system for **evaluation.** The methods used are as important to morale as the compensation paid. Sellers with large geographical areas to cover might need extra incentives based on factors other than sales. New accounts might need special treatment, or the promotion of a particular line of merchandise may require a different commission schedule.

---

[8]D. Lipman, "Congress hastens enactment of telemarketing legislation," *Telemarketing*, April 1992, pp. 12–15; Editors, "FCC hangs up on autodialers and faxes," *Direct Marketing*, January 1992, p. 7.

Salespeople and territories must be **organized.** Sales managers must spend valuable time establishing geographical or customer areas and setting quotas. Management must assure that all potential areas of business receive coverage. On the other hand, territories that are so large and sparsely populated often hamper motivation. A representative who must spend excess time traveling finds it difficult to reach quotas or earn incentives.

RECRUITING AND HIRING

Sales management is responsible for **recruiting** and **hiring** the sales staff. Finding good salespeople takes more than putting an ad in the paper and signing up those who respond. With the emphasis placed upon consultative or client oriented selling, specific abilities and aptitudes are necessary for a person to succeed as a professional seller. Recruiting and hiring these special people require management input regarding employment criteria.

Marketing oriented firms take considerable time in the hiring process. Companies must assure that the applicants can hold up under the rigors associated with personal selling. Placing an emphasis on nurturing and caring traits produces salespeople who probe deeper for needs, and who truly want to produce solutions. Salespeople today need to be level headed, self-confident and thoughtful to gain the most for their firms from the interpersonal relationships found in business.

TRAINING

Sales management is responsible for **training.** Proper preparation of the sales staff is mandatory for the success of the selling program. Initial training acquaints sellers with company policies, procedures and products. Other instruction with new sales trainees deals with people awareness and techniques in verbal and nonverbal communication. The emphasis on these people skills helps in the entire selling process.

Training does not stop with the sales beginners. Increased emphasis on retraining and refresher courses for experienced members of the sales staff has created new challenges for sales managers. Older, more knowledgeable professionals may not be as willing to learn new techniques as young tyros. The methods of presenting new ideas to these veterans are often different. For maximum efficiency of the entire selling team, sales management must continually strive to improve the knowledge and skills of each member.[9]

---

[9]Melissa Campanella, "Sales training: Can managers coach?" *Sales & Marketing Management,* July 1994, pp. 58–64; Earl D. Honeycutt, John B. Ford, and John F. Tanner, Jr., "Who trains salespeople?" *Industrial Marketing Management,* February 1994, pp. 65–70; Dennis Fox, "The fear factor: Why traditional sales training doesn't always work," *Sales & Marketing Management,* February 1992, pp. 60–64; Robert G. Head, "Systemizing salesperson selection," *Sales & Marketing Management,* February 1992, pp. 65–68; Gerald A. Bricker, "Performance agreements: The key to increasing motivation," *Sales & Marketing Management,* February 1992, pp. 69–70.

IF IT PROTECTS AGAINST BOTH BURNS AND CUTS, KEVLAR® HAD A HAND IN IT.

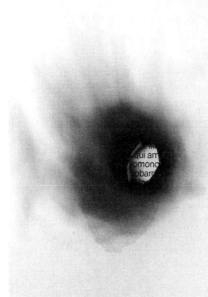

And it fits Mazda's safety needs like a glove.

Mazda was after a single safety standard with the best possible protection. Yet each production area in its Flat Rock plant posed a different worker hazard: sharp edges, moving parts, high temperatures. The right safety glove had to protect against all this, while providing excellent dexterity, comfort and durability.

Gloves of Du Pont KEVLAR® aramid were the choice. It's the only glove that provides both burn and cut protection. This protection is unsurpassed by any other synthetic fiber glove or traditional materials like leather.

And KEVLAR gives you extraordinary strength; it's five times as strong as steel on an equal weight basis.

Dual protection from a single source. Gloves of KEVLAR.

UNCOMMON PROBLEMS.
UNCOMMON SOLUTIONS.
KEVLAR FROM DU PONT.

DU PONT
REG. U.S. PAT. & TM. OFF.

Send for free information. Write to: Gloves of KEVLAR, Room H-13664-1 P.O. Box 80029, Wilmington, DE 19880-0029. Or call 1-800-4-KEVLAR.

Name
Title
Company
Address
Phone
City, State, ZIP
Principal Products

Complex technical products, such as DuPont's Kevlar, require highly trained sales staffs. (Courtesy of DuPont)

COMPENSATION

Sales personnel are typically among a firm's highest paid employees, often receiving greater compensation than groups in comparable positions. Salespeople receive compensation in a variety of ways. Some firms reward the sales staff with high salaries, while others offer incentive plans. The type of industry and the type of selling necessary dictate the method of pay. Products and markets that require creative selling usually offer some sort of incentive to salespeople in the field.

One of the prime responsibilities of sales management is to develop a fair and equitable compensation plan. Financial incentives motivate salespeople, but how bonuses or commissions are earned and by whom can create problems among the members of the team. If these rewards are based strictly upon sales increases, the promotion of new products or more profitable lines might be downplayed or avoided entirely. Management must assure that incentives are set up so that no portion of the product line suffers.

Since the entire product line must prosper, including new or slower moving items, compensation plans should reward performance and contribute to company progress and profits. Often the system pays extra incentives for creating markets for new products or slower moving items. Also, money is not the only motivator used in compensation plans. Points earned toward trips and prizes are an additional way to assure that slow moving items are given proper attention.

Straight Salary vs Straight Commission

Compensation plans vary. As a rule, few business-to-business marketers reimburse salespeople using the **straight salary** method. Although once popular in some production goods markets, straight salary does not give the seller immediate reward for increased accounts or orders. Most professional, active salespeople do not favor the straight salary method. This compensation type is more common among passive sellers.

Straight commission is the standard method for paying manufacturers' representatives. Salespeople in the direct employ of a marketer may have difficulty adapting to a straight commission form of remuneration. Since time is needed to develop territories and build accounts, salespeople using this incentive plan would be without income if this were the only form of compensation. For this reason, company employed salespeople are generally paid a base salary plus incentives. Agents and brokers, on the other hand, have other lines in established arenas, hence this straight commission is common for them.

Combination Incentive Plans

Among the forms of compensation that include an incentive on top of base, **salary plus bonus** is a favorite. In this plan, the salesperson receives an incentive at stipulated times of the year, usually tied to a targeted quota. Once reaching that milestone, the seller becomes eligible for this extra sum. Another favored incentive method is **salary plus commission.** While similar to the bonus program, this compensation method rewards success more quickly. Instead of waiting until quarter or year end, the salesperson receives commissions along with salary.

Many firms put an upper limit, or cap, on the incentives. This means that when using a bonus or commission plan, the salesperson will only be able to earn a stipulated amount over the base salary. To many professionals in the sales field, such a limitation is counterproductive. If salespeople are motivated by financial reward, putting a cap on the amount of incentive pay would dictate a limit on the amount of sales effort.

The entire subject of salesperson compensation is cloudy. No single line of reasoning prevails in the setting of incentives. Management is torn between desire for maximum performance and the need to minimize costs. Merchandise awards are one method of reducing incentive expense.[10]

Salesperson compensation is only one part of the high cost of selling. Putting salespeople on the road is also a costly proposition. A small portion of the typical day in the life of a seller is spent interacting with prospects or customers. Efficiency and time management are needed to hold costs down. Most management estimates show the average cost for a business goods salesperson to call on one account is over $250.00. Many sales managers would claim that this figure is too low.[11]

MANAGING SELLING COSTS

Selling costs include several factors, including a portion of administrative **overhead.** Office personnel support the efforts of the sales staff and contribute to its success. Determining this expense in offices where workers share duties with other departments can be difficult. Some **advertising** expense may also be charged to the cost of making sales calls. Since the primary purpose of business-to-business promotion is to soften the market and generate leads, the cost of selling must bear some of this expense.

The cost of making a sales call includes the direct cost of the salesperson. **Salary** and **incentive** moneys contribute to the $250 figure, but **entertainment** and **travel** must be included. Management uses these costs, plus a percentage for miscellaneous items, in computing the cost-per-sales-call figure. This number has been rising steadily for the past two decades. As the price of making a personal sales call increases, continued use of the telephone makes more sense. By decreasing driving expenses and time, the overall efficiency of the sales staff increases.[12]

Selling costs vary from industry to industry and from area to area. In dense, metropolitan areas such as Manhattan or San Francisco, the number of sales calls made in a day might be significantly higher than calls made in less compact cities or in rural areas. Even in Southern California, a seller can easily drive 50,000 miles in one year just calling on customers and prospects in that territory.

---

[10]Editors, "Incentives—making the right moves," *Sales & Marketing Management,* September 1991, Special Advertising Section.

[11]As reported on p. 5 of the September 12, 1988 *Marketing News,* the Laboratory of Advertising Research, a division of McGraw-Hill Research has pegged the average cost of sales call at $251.63.

[12]Editors, "Hey! Where's my Survey of selling costs," *Sales & Marketing Management,* March 1991, pp. 42–45.

TIME MANAGEMENT

One of the best attributes that a salesperson can possess is a good sense of **time management.** Because of the high cost of selling and the small amount of time available to deal directly with prospects and customers, the salesperson who is a good organizer is an asset to the selling firm. Squeezing out extra time for face-to-face interaction increases the chances for successful selling.

Salespeople who schedule one visit in one part of town and the next call miles in the opposite direction are not efficient. Although too little attention is paid to constructive time management, a little training can often produce spectacular results. Once sellers learn how efficiency can impact the number of opportunities to make calls, most become good territory managers. For sales managers, the task of teaching good time management to the sales force is a most important duty.

MOTIVATION

Managers must be **motivators.** Selling is not always an easy job, and many salespeople are easily discouraged. Monetary rewards alone are seldom enough to motivate most people. Teaching professional sellers to overcome the disappointment of losing a sale or failure to communicate with the prospect is a difficult job. Burnout is common among salespeople, especially in business goods industries. While most sellers are more than adequately paid, the constant pressure to succeed and personal concern for approval take their toll.

A common complaint that salespeople voice about management is the failure of these leaders to give recognition. Knowing that they are performing their job well is important to the sales force. Sometimes financially, but more often emotionally, sales management often fails to give credit when and where

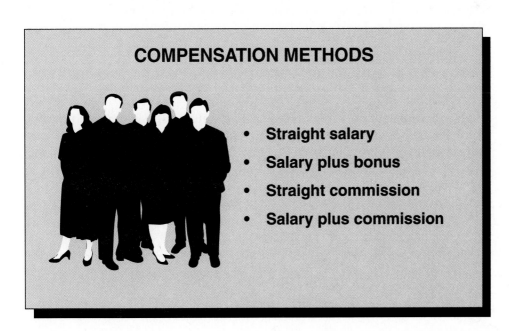

COMPENSATION METHODS

- **Straight salary**
- **Salary plus bonus**
- **Straight commission**
- **Salary plus commission**

it is due. Too often, management is quick to criticize and slow to praise. Salespeople, like all employees, appreciate receiving feedback on their performance. The nature of sales work calls for continual reinforcement by supervisors to maintain morale.[13]

Another registered complaint from salespeople is the unwillingness of managers to let the individual correct his or her own mistakes. Most sellers realize the mistake when it occurs and are in a better position to rectify the error than anyone else. Salespeople appreciate management that respects the professionalism and abilities of the sales staff.

ETHICS

In no other area of marketing is ethical behavior more important and more evident. Professional selling is personal, one-on-one communication. Salespeople who abuse the interpersonal relationships demanded of their field hurt the firms that they represent and often destroy their own careers. Unethical sellers cannot be tolerated in any industry, and are usually quickly removed.

Privileged Information

In the preparation phase of the selling process, the salesperson strives to learn about the company represented, the market and the industry. A strong bank of knowledge about all aspects of these areas helps the salesperson toward success. Information about company projects or finances may be delicate. Although the sales staff must know many factors about the firm, that does not mean that such data is pertinent to others outside the company.

In the very nature of this work, a professional salesperson discovers many things about prospects and customers. Much of the information gained in the process of trying to solve problems and service needs may be confidential. Professional sellers remain conscious of the sensitivity of the knowledge they possess or acquire. Leaking production or process information to competitors could be disastrous for the salesperson and selling company. Such privileged information is considered to be private property.

Pressure Selling

High pressure selling, while on the decline, still persists with some people in some industries. Rude presentations by hucksters create bad images for both the product and the company. The increase in the number of professional, problem-solving salespeople goes a long way toward eliminating pushy or intimidating individuals in the selling field. In spite of the drift toward professionalism in the field of sales, the lure of the rewards for successful selling still draws some bad characters.

Talking prospects into buying products that they neither need nor can afford are hopefully a technique of the past. IBM salespeople used to call such

---

[13]Edwin E. Bobrow, "Reps and recognition: Understanding what motivates," *Sales & Marketing Management,* September 1991, pp. 82–86.

pressure selling "pushing metal," and the Xerox team titled the same practice "slamming metal." Although when it comes time to meet quotas many professionals still resort to a little arm wrestling, sales management today stresses partnering with buyers and total quality teamwork. Even the automobile business, noted for pushy tactics, is turning toward the "Saturn" way of making sales.[14]

Unfortunately, no government or industry regulations are available to restrict distasteful selling habits. Although dishonest or misleading presentations may be cause for legal action, the obnoxious seller only gains a bad reputation. On the other hand, most industries possess an informal network that quickly passes the word about such individuals. Professionalism is respected and encouraged in business-to-business selling arenas.

Relationship Selling

Professional selling usually involves the development of interpersonal relationships between seller and buyer. As a rule, business-to-business marketers are especially aware of the importance of maintaining close working ties with customers. Many firms are facing complete realignment of sales forces to streamline their operations and free up staff to handle larger product lines to fewer accounts. Such reorganization helps sellers develop more personal contact with customers and prospects.

Asea Brown Boveri, a Swiss-based industrial equipment marketer, found that its salespeople overloaded with prospects for narrow product lines. ABB sales staff often passed each other in customer lobbies without knowing one another. The company's retraining program equipped each seller with knowledge of the full product line to be carried to a trimmed down customer list. Hyatt Hotels did a similar reorganization with remarkable success. Trade goods houses, such as Kraft General Foods and Lipton-Lawry's, also adopt relationship selling to allow the sales force to get closer to the supermarket's operation.[15]

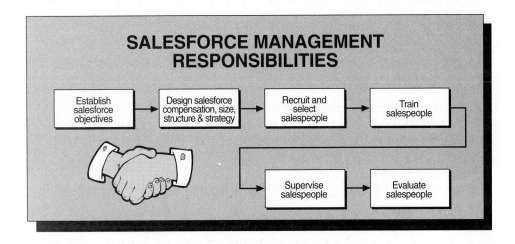

---

[14]Jaclyn Fierman, "The death and rebirth of the salesman," *Fortune,* July 25, 1994, pp. 80–91.

[15]Christopher Power, Lisa Driscoll, and Earl Bohn, "Smart Selling," *Business Week,* August 3, 1992, pp. 46–48; Patricia Sellers," How to remake your sales force," *Fortune,* May 4, 1992, pp. 98–103.

Team Selling

Many firms in the business-to-business field have adopted a team approach to selling. Realizing that products alone cannot satisfy the needs of prospects, groups from different disciplines may have the expertise to solve multiple needs or problems better than a single, well-trained salesperson. Additionally, by including people from other areas within the company, such as production or finance, sales managers help make the entire company more marketing oriented.

Xerox is one company that has been especially successful in team selling. When handling major accounts, such as AT&T, this marketer may have upwards of two hundred people assigned to one squad. Ranging from top executives to service personnel and located in over sixty districts in the United States, this selling group assures that its customer receives daily contact. By including all levels of management on its teams, Xerox also makes sure that those at the top understand and realize the importance of those on the firing line.[16]

NEW TECHNOLOGY

Technological developments occur so rapidly in today's marketing arenas that many salespeople have trouble keeping up. Changes in products, competitive offerings and different ways to conduct the business of selling can leave the sales force floundering and confused. Developments in hardware and software appear almost daily. For many representatives, change, and especially technological change, is frightening. Laptop and notebook computers may save time and money for the company and for the salesperson, but first these new items must be accepted. The job of convincing the sales force lies with the managers.[17]

Selling and sales management also have found the computer to be a useful tool. Useful for data collection, spreadsheet and wordprocessing, the computer helps sales operations gain efficiency. Coupling the computer with an order system and a trained telemarketer holds very real promise in many fields employing passive salespeople. Computer assisted telemarketing reduces the number of calls made by outside salespeople and decreases selling costs. This combination is a natural for wholesalers.

Not all technological developments seem logical to the salesforce. For instance, professionals have heard the advice for ages that the telephone should not be used if a personal call is possible. Today, telemarketing is often preferred for many selling situations. As personal selling progresses toward the twenty-first century, changes in technology will greatly impact the ways professional salespeople operate. Regardless of the requirement to adapt to new procedures and equipment, marketers will continue to call upon the services ⁓⁓sional sellers. After all, **nothing happens until something is sold.**

, "Team selling works," *Personal Selling Power,* September 1994, pp. 52–58.
ɪn, "On the cutting edge," *Sales & Marketing Management,* June 1994, pp.
Goldenberg, "Automation: Pointers on process," *Sales & Marketing Management,*
, pp. 71–73; Steve Silva, "Are your sales systems focused on your customers?"
ɪketing Management,* January 1992, special advertising section from Digital
Corporation.

SELLING AND SALES MANAGEMENT

Marketing and Society: Say please!

Few would argue that the days of the wisecracking, backslapping, huckster are gone. Today's salespeople are largely professionals who enjoy the freedom and financial rewards found in the field of selling. In most business-to-business arenas, one finds sales forces who are articulate, well trained and customer oriented. The industrial salesperson of the 1990s exudes the essence of professionalism.

The world's largest manufacturer of commercial aircraft, Boeing Co. of Seattle, naturally employs just such professionals. When thinking of "big ticket" items, one could hardly find a larger or more expensive product than a Boeing 747. To sell such airplanes, the salesforce had to develop close ties with the airline customers it served. The importance of personal relationships were obvious. Recently, this marketer retrained its selling staff in the art of good manners.

Failure to return telephone calls promptly was a major complaint from customers. Other subjects covered in the retraining sessions included too

(Photo courtesy of Boeing Co.)

much informality, bad mouthing competitors and inattention to codes of conduct in different countries. Sales management also was aware of reports that some salespeople were ignoring smaller clients in favor of the "biggies" when at air fairs and trade shows. Boeing determined that relationship selling demanded good etiquette.

SOURCE: Kate Bertrand, "Boeing reps schooled in the art of the 'mannered sell,'" *Business Marketing*, May 1992, pp. 48.

SUMMING IT UP

Personal selling is a major factor in the promotion of some consumer and most business goods. A sale is the transaction where ownership or use of products passes from seller to buyer. Salespeople facilitate this transaction. Salespeople are classified as either active or passive. Active, or customer oriented, sellers are nonmanipulative and needs oriented. Passive salespeople include sales assisters, technical specialists and missionaries.

Professional salespeople are most commonly found in production goods markets. Wholesaling and consumer services also provide areas where personal selling is a common method of promotion. A day in the life of a typical professional salesperson involves personal contact with customers and prospects, as well as paperwork, travel and waiting.

The selling process includes preparation, presentation and post-sale activities. Prospecting, qualifying and gaining knowledge are all parts of the preparation stage. The presentation portion of the selling process includes probing for needs, handling objections and closing the sale. During post-sale followup, salespeople reinforce the customer's decision to buy and trace the order to assure customer satisfaction. Telemarketing plays an increasing roll in prospecting, presentation and the gathering of marketing research data.

The management of salespeople includes establishment of compensation methods and managing selling costs. Sales managers are also active in evaluating the sales staff, recruiting and hiring, training and motivating selling personnel. The responsibilities of sales management includes teaching ethical behavior, especially in the areas of handling privileged information, controlling high-pressure tactics and tempering interpersonal relations.

KEY CONCEPTS AND TERMS
FROM CHAPTER SEVENTEEN

Active salesperson	Prospect
Closing	Prospecting
Cold call	Qualified prospect
Lead	Salesperson
Missionary	Selling process
Passive salesperson	Technical specialist
Post-sale followup	Telemarketing
Presentation	The sale
Probing	

BUILDING SKILLS

1. Explain why salespeople are required for promoting the sale of a commercial office building, an inquiry from a wholesaler wishing to handle a manufacturer's line of auto parts, a request from a hospital to bid on carpeting for resident physicians' offices.

2. Describe the type of salesperson that would likely be employed by Cincinnati Milacron, Kraft General Foods, Wal-Mart, Wausau Insurance Company, Barnes & Noble bookstores.

3. Identify any industries or types of products where salespeople still use canned pitches or presentations.

4. Describe the types of markets or products that would be appropriate for telemarketing.

5. Explain the compensation method you would select for paying salespeople handling new cars, construction equipment, designer apparel, office supplies, textbooks.

6. Categorize the typical tasks of a sales manager, explaining how you would go about motivating a salesforce. Explain how you would address your representatives regarding ethics.

Making Decisions 17-1: In all the right places.

Most of today's marketing oriented companies realize the need for a well-trained, customer oriented, professional sales staff. Whether operating in trade goods channels or production arenas, the bottom line is getting the orders. One would be hard pressed to find a selling organization that is not schooled in the basics of customer satisfaction. Yet, there is always the lingering decisions regarding in-house sellers or manufacturers' representatives.

Size alone does not dictate whether the selling team should be company folk or outsiders. Economics has a great deal to do with the decision. Bigger firms, with the funds available to hire, train and finance large staffs, often opt for the proprietary group. Smaller organizations often decide to place their lot with independent professionals. In selecting agents, some marketers are lost.

Manufacturers' representatives are often the creme-de-la-creme of professional sellers. These individuals or organizations are capable, knowledgeable and competent salespeople. In looking for the right combination between manufacturer and selling staff, companies should first check with their customers and prospects. Salespeople who impress the firms they are targeting ought to be hired. Although the commissions may appear high, the marketer should remember that with independent sales staffs, there are no costs until something is sold.[18]

Contrast and give examples of the different types of salespeople, including the types of industries in which they operate and the types of functions they perform.

Making Decisions 17-2: Ring, Ring!

The telephone is not a new gadget for the business world. Almost from the moment that Mr. Bell first created this sometimes nerve-racking device, the world of commerce embraced the opportunities telecommunications provided. It would be difficult to fathom what might happen to the world of business were the telephone not available. In the field of personal selling, the phone has taken on new importance and new dimensions.

One of the most frustrating tasks for salespeople is qualifying prospects. When a company's advertising efforts successfully produce leads, the field salesforce is often left on its own to develop those inquiries into customers. With the high cost of individual sales calls, the field staff finds it frustrating to run into dead ends when those leads prove to be futile. Executone Information Systems Incorporated discovered a way to make its sales force more productive.

Executone, a marketer of telephone systems, turned to the very product that it sells. Employing capable telemarketers, the company found that it could pre-sell prospects at the same time that it was qualifying leads. Arming its sales representatives with

---

[18]Susan Greco, "Looking for reps in all the right places," *Inc.*, July 1992, p. 117.

the names of the decision makers and a clear definition of customer needs, Executone increased productivity and success. The closing records of the sales staff indicate that the telemarketing ploy is working.[19]

Describe the functions of and advantages in using telemarketing.

M aking Decisions 17-3:
If a real live human answers. . . .

Without question, the most effective form of marketing communications is personal selling. A major problem confronting marketing oriented companies is how to continue this effective means of promotion in the face of constantly increasing costs. No one argues that the personal touch adds a great deal to the sale of any product, but face-to-face selling is expensive. Increases in the cost of energy and the high remuneration commanded by good salespeople have led many companies to question whether they can continue to put capable people in the field.

The advent of the computer greatly influences the careers of salespeople. Instant information is a boon to any peddler. Salesforces throughout the world are becoming equipped with all sorts of electronic gadgetry. Although the training of salespeople has new significance with this electronic explosion, few would argue against its effectiveness.

Picture, if you can, the salesperson of the future. Armed with a miniature computer, the intrepid sales rep makes a call on a tough prospect. As each objection is fielded, the salesperson consults with the computer and receives up-to-the-minute suggestions on restructuring the presenta-

(Courtesy of Apple Computer Inc.)

tion. "Intelligence agents" imbedded in laptop PCs would be capable of offering such advice to salespeople as they are actually making their calls. Who knows that selling robots are not just around the corner?[20]

Discuss how technology might influence personal selling today and tomorrow.

---

[19]Martin Everett, "Instead of fishing for leads, Executone navigates," *Sales & Marketing Management*, October 1991, pp. 86–88.

[20]Thayer C. Taylor, "A glimpse into the future of information technology," *Sales & Marketing Management*, April 1992, p. 61.

18

Global Marketing

*T*he Job to be Done

Global marketing creates a feeling of foreign intrigue. Exotic languages and customs add to the mystery of dealing overseas. Foreign commerce today is an integral part of our lives. Although examples of global marketing have appeared throughout this textbook, this chapter examines the subject in detail, asking the student to:

- contrast the differences between the world's societies,
- understand why companies trade overseas and explain how global marketing is conducted,
- describe the impact of environmental changes on global marketing, and
- pinpoint where U.S. firms market around the world, and define the problems in managing global marketing.

Marketers at Work

Eric Ericksen

Eric Ericksen is a doer. He never rests on his laurels and is constantly striving toward newer and bigger successes. While at Spokane Community College, he picked up not one but four Associate of Applied Science degrees. To support his education, Eric worked the graveyard shift at Albertson's supermarkets. Upon graduation, he entered the workforce in the employ of a food broker in the Spokane area. His one regret was missing his graduation ceremonies at SC. He was continuing the real business education at work, on the road selling S&W coffee in western Montana.

Eric reentered the educational arena to pick up his BA from Eastern Washington University, where he received the Direct Marketing Institute award for developing a catalog for outdoor/camping gear. After graduation he hired on as a salesperson with Ryder Transportation Resources, where he quickly showed his talent by winning "Rookie of the Year." Never content with the status quo, Eric is now enrolled at Whitworth College working toward a masters degree in International Manage-

ment. He hopes to become fluent in Russian, German and Chinese as well.

While at Whitworth, Eric has participated in an overseas internship and has become involved with a special project to further his education: creating his own outsourcing for a line of camping gear that he has designed. The sewing patterns for the sleeping bags, backpacks and tents are created in Spokane, then contacts are made through U.S. embassies overseas to get quotes on manufacturing the items. The gear will then be dropshipped to wholesalers and brokers around the globe. Additional promotion opportunities are being explored using general purpose catalogs and the Internet. With an eye to the future, Eric plans to pursue a PhD to position himself as a global marketing consultant, ultimately to return to the community college market as an instructor.

How Do The World's Societies Differ?

The economies of most nations differ significantly from ours. Although Americans have a high standard of living, other countries, such as Sweden, Japan and Germany, also enjoy economic prosperity. Some countries produce in abundance while others do not create enough to provide for their own needs. Industrialized countries manufacture and export goods to those nations that do not have production capability. Countries lacking industrial resources or manufacturing capacity offer lower standards of living for their inhabitants.[1]

Advanced industrialized economies— countries with a high standard of living, industrial base and modern economy.

ADVANCED INDUSTRIALIZED ECONOMIES

Using Gross Domestic Product as a measuring stick, the nations of the world classified according to standard of living. **Advance industrialized economies,**

---

[1]Aaron Bernstein, "The good life isn't only in America," *Business Week,* November 2, 1992, p. 34.

also known as **AIE**s, have a reasonable standard of living, strong industrial bases and modern economies. Most of the inhabitants of these societies have sufficient income to maintain a moderate lifestyle. Many societies from Europe, North and South America and the Pacific Rim fall into the category of advanced industrialized economies.

AIEs provide a bulk of the world's manufacturing power. From television sets to cars, tractors to buses, these countries produce most of the physical goods people and businesses consume. Some of these goods are exported for use by other societies, and others are consumed at home. Regardless of where the ultimate customer resides, the industrial output of these societies fuel the standards of living around the globe.

NEWLY INDUSTRIALIZED ECONOMIES

Newly industrialized economies, or **NIE**s, are those countries that have made recent gains in standard of living by increasing their industrial base. Many of these societies were considered lesser developed countries just a few decades ago. Although these nations may not as yet have reached a standard of living or per capita income associated with advanced industrialized economies, they are approaching that status.

Newly industrialized economies—countries with growing industrial bases and increasing standards of living.

Most newly industrialized economies are strengthening their investment bases and beginning to actively participate in global marketing. As trade increases, so does employment, followed by per capita income and standard of living. This new business activity fuels more private capital, which in turn spreads the industrial base. The Pacific Rim includes many of these NIEs. Certainly Korea, Taiwan, Hong Kong, Indonesia and Singapore fit this definition.

As the industrial might of Asian countries increases so does their wealth. A decided swing in the world's power base from North America and Europe to the Pacific Rim has occurred over the past few decades. One Singapore banker which will only handle accounts of more than $1 million lists over eight thousand clients from Asian countries. The growth of the affluent class in Southeast Asia is mind-boggling, and their consumption patterns are equally astounding.[2]

LESSER DEVELOPED COUNTRIES

Lesser developed countries are those that have a low standard of living and no modern economy. These societies are struggling to achieve better conditions for their populations. The majority of people from these third world nations have lower levels of income and do not enjoy the wide variety of goods and services that are available in industrialized countries. Kenya, Jamaica, Sri Lanka, Afghanistan and Surinam can aptly be labeled lesser developed countries.

Lesser developed countries—any country with a low standard of living and no modern economy.

The emerging world of developing economies is struggling toward improving living standards, often resulting from capitalizing on raw material

---

[2]William Glasgall, Pete Engardio, and Joyce Barnathan, "Asia's wealth," *Business Week,* November 29, 1993, pp. 100–111.

The growth of the Pacific Rim area has opened new markets for U.S. firms such as Bank of America.

positions. Finding sources of these building blocks of industrial development can provide a poor society with the opportunity for growth. Bauxite deposits in Jamaica and forests in Surinam illustrate this point. Not too long ago, Arab sheikdoms of the Middle East were underdeveloped economies. Today, some of these principalities are among the wealthiest in the world, thanks to an unbelievable source of raw material . . . oil.

FREE MARKET ECONOMIES

Free market economy—country where trade is determined by consumer demand.

Most countries with high levels of income and living standards are **free market economies.** In free market economies, the consumer dictates what is to be made and in what quantities. Business ventures in these societies produce those goods and services that the public demands. Consumer sovereignty governs the markets in these economic entities. The United States, Japan, Canada, the countries of the European Community, Brazil and many other Western nations operate free market economies.

Since in free market economies the consumer decides what products are to be marketed, government's role is to act as a referee. Buoyed by consumer demand, free market economies move toward increased benefit for the publics they serve. When businesses act contrary to the will of the public, product failures occur and, if the misadventure is illegal, government will intervene. When business acts to benefit the consumer, little regulation or interference is necessary.

Trade between free market countries most often occurs from company to company. Toyota, Carling and Unilever do not sell their products to the U.S. government. Instead, these marketing firms distribute goods directly to businesses located in this country. Owens-Illinois has a plant in Panama that makes glass bottles. This firm sells its output to Central American companies, not to the nations of Costa Rica or El Salvador.

The world's largest industrial corporations

RANK 1993			SALES $ MILLIONS	PROFITS $ MILLIONS	EMPLOYEES
1	General Motors	U.S.	133,621.9	2,465.8	710,800
2	Ford Motor	U.S.	108,521.0	2,529.0	322,200
3	Exxon	U.S.	97,825.0	5,280.0	91,000
4	Royal Dutch/Shell Group	Brit./Neth.	95,134.4	4,505.2	117,000
5	Toyota Motor	Japan	85,283.2	1,473.9	109,279
6	Hitachi	Japan	68,581.8	605.0	330,637
7	Intl. Business Machines	U.S.	62,716.0	(8,101.0)	267,196
8	Matsushita Electric Industrial	Japan	61,384.5	227.0	254,059
9	General Electric	U.S.	60,823.0	4,315.0	222,000
10	Daimler-Benz	Germany	59,102.0	364.0	366,736
11	Mobil	U.S.	56,576.0	2,084.0	61,900
12	Nissan Motor	Japan	53,759.8	(805.5)	143,310
13	British Petroleum	Britain	52,485.4	923.6	72,600
14	Samsung	South Korea	51,345.2	519.7	191,303
15	Philip Morris	U.S.	50,621.0	3,091.0	173,000
16	IRI	Italy	50,488.1	N.A.	366,471
17	Siemens	Germany	50,381.3	1,112.6	391,000
18	Volkswagen	Germany	46,311.9	(1,232.4)	251,643
19	Chrysler	U.S.	43,600.0	(2,551.0)	128,000
20	Toshiba	Japan	42,917.2	112.5	175,000

SOURCE: *Fortune*, July 25, 1994, p. 143.

CONTROLLED MARKETS

Consumers in **controlled markets** purchase only those goods and services that the government dictates will be available. In these countries, market demand is dormant. Business in nations such as Russia, China and much of Eastern Europe have traditionally operated economies that feature central planning. In these economies, the government determines what is to be manufactured and offered to the people. Because of this control, international business with these nations often involves contracts with the state or government.

Controlled market— country where government manages all economic activity.

Trade between countries or between companies within different countries is a vital part of the economy of most nations. Advanced and newly industrialized economies alike engage in global trade. A company within one country producing products more economically or of better quality than those from a firm in another country will more than likely experience a demand for those goods overseas. This is the essence of global marketing.

GLOBAL MARKETING

Trade between business firms results from the same supply and demand forces that manage an internal free market economy. The United States, for example, produces agricultural products more efficiently than many other nations. These goods form a major portion of the exports from this country. In turn, more labor intensive goods, such as clothing or small machines, can be produced less expensively in developing countries. American businesses import these goods when there is an economic advantage.

Global marketing involves transactions between domestic organizations and businesses abroad. In some cases, the marketing effort between firms in other nations is similar to that conducted domestically. For the most part, dealing with foreign companies or in different countries creates a variety of new and interesting ventures. Marketers undertake these challenges for a number of reasons.

Why Do Companies Trade Overseas?

Global marketing is an important aspect of doing business for any sized company. Large or small, firms today realize that foreign markets offer a major market potential. Similarly, foreign manufacturers look to U.S. intermediaries to move their products through distribution channels. It just makes good sense to market globally.

MAXIMIZE PROFITS

The primary reason that companies participate in global marketing efforts is to **maximize profit.** Overseas markets often create new demand for products, which in turn, expands profit. When domestic markets become saturated, global opportunities often pick up the slack. Many foreign markets are freer from competition than those at home. Therefore, companies with stagnant business stateside often look overseas for expansion.

A good example of this practice is the American meat industry. With domestic markets stagnant, or in some cases dropping, beef producers expanded into European, Asian and South American markets. ConAgra, the world's largest meat processor, leads the way in export. Although many barriers to trade still exist, especially in Japan and Korea, meat exporters are thriving. While shipments of beef overseas is bursting, the agri-business still is learning to modify production to please a variety of tastes.[3]

SMOOTH OUT SEASONAL TRENDS

Seasonal trends in a company's business provide another good reason for investigating overseas markets. If demand for a firm's output varies at different times of the year, global selling in the off-season makes sense. When sales slip during slow seasons, economies of scale can suffer. Because of the lower efficiency often found with decreased production, firms marketing seasonal products suffer additional dips in profits. In this case, global marketing evens out production.

---

[3]"World beef trade—at a glance," *Food Review,* January/June 1992, p. 18; Dale McDonald, "The export jungle," *Beef Today,* March 1992, pp. 32–37; Steve McGill, "Beef producers eye the Japanese market," *The Furrow,* March 1992, pp. 7–8; Steve Kay, "Globe-trotters," *Beef Today,* February 1992, pp. 37–38.

Ski manufacturers look for markets in South America and New Zealand during the summer months. Jantzen and other swimming suit manufacturers sell to south-of-the-equator countries during the off-season months to even out the cyclical nature of their business. Sporting goods companies can smooth out the peaks and valleys of their production by selling golf clubs in winter and racket ball gear in summer to markets in the southern hemisphere.

REDUCE COSTS

Global marketing provides the possibility for **cost reduction.** When domestic markets are at capacity, entering foreign trade may increase production and lower costs. For example, suppose a company operates two shifts per day, five days per week, to manufacture a product. If it were more economical to run a third shift or operate for seven days, the firm could reduce costs on its entire production. Seeking additional business in the global market could be the answer.

While many companies begin their global marketing ventures by selling products overseas, production in other countries may result from the successful lowering of costs in domestic production. Goodyear Tire & Rubber has had outstanding success with its high-performance tires in the domestic market. Now, with foreign auto makers such as Porsche and Ferrari demanding the Eagle VR Gatorback, Goodyear makes the tire in Europe.

RECIPROCITY

Reciprocity is just as much a factor in global marketing as it is in domestic business. Perhaps an overseas source of raw materials can use the finished goods that are produced from that stock. Importing raw wool to be made into

■　■　■　■　■

Reasons for conducting global marketing

REASON	EXAMPLES
Profit maximization	Saturated domestic market (toothpaste, shaving cream), new market opportunity (McDonald's in Russia, Coke in China, Campbell's in Japan)
Seasonal variations	Different climates between Northern and Southern Hemispheres (ski equipment to New Zealand and Argentina, Wilson golf clubs and tennis balls in Australia, Fieldcrest cottons in India, Zaire and Saudi Arabia)
Reduced costs	Economies of scale and increased work week (Harley-Davidson in Europe, Black & Decker in Mexico, Owens-Illinois in Malaysia)
Reciprocity	Giving business back to companies who shared in development (made in America Hondas to Japan, Cincinnati Milacron machine tool technology to Taiwan)
Extend product life	Create new markets for mature products (Unilever's Lux in Japan, Caterpillar earthmovers in Brazil)

■　■　■　■　■

fabric which would in turn be exported for garment production would be an example. Similarly, a manufacturer might need to export to protect its source of supply, even selling at a breakeven point, if necessary, to meet competition.

Reciprocity may also result from transactions with domestic customers. Major stateside buyers may put pressure on marketers to offer products to foreign subsidiaries or other international friends. Loctite found that when its adhesives were specified at Nissan and Honda, those companies began to purchase for their U.S. assembly plants in addition to those in Japan.[4]

EXTEND PRODUCT LIFE

Overseas business can **extend product life.** Although domestic markets may view a particular product as obsolete, foreign buyers could find that same item quite advanced. While Unilever's Lux is on the edge of the declining stage in this country, Nippon Lever built the same product into the number two selling handsoap in Japan. Promotion in Japan for Lux parallels the original campaigns of the 1950s in the United States by using movie stars in advertising.

In a reverse scenario, Cadillac will begin selling the Omega from its German Opel subsidiary in 1996. This General Motors division hopes to strengthen the position in designing global cars. Although entirely manufactured by Opel, the automobile will be marketed under the Cadillac name, through Cadillac dealers. The firm hopes that the European design and features will liven up a somewhat sluggish luxury car market.[5]

How Is Global Marketing Conducted?

Just as the reasons for doing business overseas vary from company to company, so do the methods of global marketing. The procedures chosen for trading in foreign countries depend upon the product, company philosophy, opportunity and government intervention. Many firms start their global marketing ventures using one method, only to switch to a different form as business develops.

EXPORT/IMPORT

Export/import—the direct sale of products to a company in another country.

The simplest and most common way to conduct business globally is through the **export** or **import** of products. Either of these trade functions can be conducted directly with foreign buyers. With small firms, export and import activities often travel through intermediaries. Wholesale brokers who deal exclusively in global marketing offer assistance to companies that are not well versed in buying or selling abroad. Export/import brokers and wholesalers are acquainted with the problems in dealing overseas and are readily available to provide expertise.

[4]T. Smart, "Why ignore 95% of the world's market," *Business Week,* October 23, 1992, p. 64.
[5]Audrey Choi, "Turning an Opel into a Cadillac: GM goes global," *The Wall Street Journal,* March 11, 1994, pp. B1 and B2.

Top U.S. industrial exporters

COMPANY	PRODUCTS	1993 SALES (millions)
1. General Motors	Motor vehicles and parts	14,913
2. Boeing	Commercial aircraft	14,616
3. Ford Motor	Motor vehicles and parts	9,483
4. General Electric	Jet engines, turbines, locomotives	8,498
5. Chrysler	Motor vehicles and parts	8,397
6. IBM	Computers and related equipment	7,297
7. Motorola	Communications equipment	4,990
8. Hewlett-Packard	Measurement equipment	4,738
9. Philip Morris	Tobacco, beer, foods	4,105
10. Caterpillar	Heavy machinery	3,743
11. United Technologies	Jet engines, helicopters	3,503
12. E.I. duPont de Nemours	Specialty chemicals	3,500
13. Intel	Microcomputer components	3,406
14. McDonnell Douglas	Aerospace products	3,405
15. Archer Daniels Midland	Protein meals, vegetable oils	2,900
16. Eastman Kodak	Imaging and health products	2,242
17. Raytheon	Electronic systems	2,063
18. Compaq Computer	Computers and related equipment	1,922
19. Digital Equipment	Computers and related equipment	1,800
20. Lockheed	Aerospace products	1,743

SOURCE: *Fortune,* August 22, 1994, p. 132.

Global marketing is not limited to the mighty. Presentables-Cinzia Inc., a small California marketer of giftware, could not find suitable U.S. manufacturers willing to handle the small, startup quantities that the company needed. PCI found that Taiwanese firms were more than capable of meeting this company's needs. Now, with sales over $10 million, Presentables could meet the domestic order requirements, but chooses to stay with their trusted overseas suppliers.

LICENSING

Another method of conducting global marketing is by **licensing.** Instead of exporting products made from a manufacturing process, the domestic company sells the rights to an overseas company and collects fees and royalties for its use. This method of trade is particularly helpful for companies that do not have the capacity to produce for export.

Licensing does not have to involve manufacturing. Contracts can be arranged with selling agents or intermediaries to handle a firm's business in a specific area. Instead of proceeding through export/import brokers, the seller sets up the foreign based operative under a contractual arrangement for the exclusive sale of its products. Some U.S. firms also perform global marketing through management contracts, considered a form of licensing.

Franchising

Franchise agreements are a type of licensing. As in domestic operations, the franchisor establishes foreign companies or individuals to operate under the corporate name. McDonald's, Wendy's and Burger King have franchisees all over the world. These types of businesses feature a relatively low capital outlay, compared with starting a firm from scratch. The tremendous consumer acceptance of the franchisers' names make this type of licensing agreement very popular.

JOINT VENTURE

A **joint venture** with a foreign company provides another method of conducting global marketing. Just like domestic operations, overseas joint venture agreements involve two or more parties who establish an entirely new entity. This company then divides its profits among the owners according to the pre-arranged percentage. The Coca-Cola Company has a joint venture with the city of Moscow. This operation is very Western in nature, marketing Coke and Fanta for rubles. Although both Coca-Cola and PepsiCo have been doing business in Russia for a long time, this is the first joint venture by either soft drink company directly with a government entity.[6]

Toyota and General Motors have a joint venture agreement called New United Motor Manufacturing Incorporated. NUMMI builds the Nova automobile and Toyota pickup in California. Each company shares in the profits of the joint venture partnership. One of the better partnerships in foreign trade exists between Ford and Mazda. The Japanese firm provides much of the engineering and technical know-how that goes into the Taurus, Probe and F series pickups sold by Ford. In addition, Mazda engineered the highly successful Explorer, and Ford assembles the Navajo for Mazda.[7]

Joint ventures may be the only way of doing business when countries have specific laws restricting foreign ownership. As with domestic joint ventures, some of these partnerships result from financial reasons. Joint venturing also can be used to overcome negative images. The new company formed by the joint venture may have a better chance of succeeding because its products are perceived by customers as being domestic.

DIRECT INVESTMENT

Global marketers also conduct business through **direct investment.** By setting up manufacturing or marketing facilities in other nations, multinational com-

---

[6]W. Konrad, "Cola wars: All noisy on the Eastern front," *Business Week,* January, 27, 1992, pp. 94–95; W. Konrad and I. Reichlin, "The real thing is thundering eastward," *Business Week,* April 13, 1992, pp. 96–97.

[7]Karen Lowry Miller and James B. Treece, "The partners," *Business Week,* February 10, 1992, pp. 102–107.

Methods of conducting global marketing

METHOD	ADVANTAGES	DISADVANTAGES
Export/import	Least amount of capital expenditure, speed of entry, understanding customs and language handled by experts in field	Potential government intervention at receiving end, special versions of product may be needed
Licensing	No direct involvement in management, expert assistance available	Less potential income, cross-culture conflict, government red tape
Joint venture	Circumvent government restrictions, increase management talent	Contracting may prove difficult, different ethics may pose problems
Direct investment	Maximize profit, create base for further overseas development, largest potential for recognition	Unstable government, greatest demand for understanding of customs and languages

panies reap the benefit. Most American soft drink manufacturers have bottling plants in foreign countries, and many major breweries have established operations overseas. Colgate-Palmolive has been especially successful with a manufacturing facility in Poland.[8]

Shell Oil, a Dutch firm, and Nestlé, based in Switzerland, are examples of European companies that have well-established business in this country. English brewer Bass PLC owns Holiday Inns. British Airways bought 20 percent of USAir in 1993, and KLM owns a portion of Northwest Airlines. Even the Pillsbury doughboy talks with a slightly British accent, courtesy of parent company Grand Metropolitan PLC. The banking industry often resembles a global melting pot, as financial institutes representing dozens of countries can be found in any major U.S. city.[9]

Political unrest in some foreign countries may cause global marketers to steer clear of direct investment. The possibility of losing facilities during government upheaval is real, and in some nations, periods of unrest seem ongoing. American interests can be confiscated or nationalized in these hot spots, causing tremendous losses. In Cuba, for instance, American sugar plantations and production facilities were seized when the Castro regime came into power. Despite these problems, investing in overseas facilities may be the most profitable way to conduct global marketing.

---

[8]Gail E. Shares, "Colgate-Palmolive is cleaning up in Poland," *Business Week,* March 15, 1993, pp. 54–56.

[9]Dan Blake, "British companies increasingly find expansion attractive in United States," Associated Press release, *The Oregonian,* June 13, 1993, p. K1.

How Do Environmental Changes Impact Global Marketing?

Global marketers face the same environmental factors that impact domestic producers. No matter what method of conducting foreign trade is chosen, changes in economic, cultural, political, technological and competitive factors impact the ways firms do business overseas. Swings in these areas can be much more dramatic then those found at home. Savvy global players strive to keep on top of environmental changes to assure against what could be catastrophic failure.

ECONOMIC

The **economic** environment worldwide is a concern for global marketers. Traders must be well versed with the economic conditions in other countries and with the internal financial facilities that are available. If the nation is in a recession, the global trader may have trouble finalizing its transactions. The ability to buy or sell without concern over matters of banking and currency exchange greatly assist the global marketer.

The country's economic climate can be either a hindrance or a help to global marketing. The U.S. economy typically acts as a bellwether for economic activity around the world. When things stateside slipped in the early nineties, the impact was felt in countries everywhere. Although business in America rebounded dramatically in the past few years, the world economy dragged a bit during this period. By early 1994, however, most industrialized nations were experiencing solid growth, which translated into an export boom for American firms.[10]

CULTURAL

Ethnocentrism—the belief that all cultures are affected by the same stimuli as your own.

The **culture** of a country has a significant impact on global marketing. Many U.S. businesses assume that people in the rest of the world behave in the same manner as Americans. This belief that all societies are affected by the same stimuli as your own is called **ethnocentrism.** This global marketing philosophy is fatal to the development of business overseas. Cultures vary greatly, and the possibility of offending potential buyers is high. No firm should embark upon a multinational policy without thoroughly studying the culture of the countries where it intends to do business.

Language differences can be troublesome even among English-speaking countries. In translating words and brand names to other languages, care must be taken to be sure that the terms mean the same in other countries. Brand names take on new meaning when translated. Many are humorous, others are suggestive, some outright lewd. Since packaging and instructions must be printed in a variety of languages and dialects, marketers often go through an

---

[10]Rob Norton, "Strategies for the new export boom," *Fortune,* August 22, 1994, pp. 124–130.

entirely different branding process to satisfy multiple markets. For example, the literal Chinese translation for Coca-Cola is "bite the wax tadpole," hardly an appetizing name for a soft drink.

Color takes on different meanings in different societies. The color of a package might be acceptable in one country and unacceptable in another. The importance of color in a country or culture must be part of the consideration when designing packaging for products for export. **Customs** of other cultures affect product acceptance. Certain meat products are often taboo, such as beef in India or pork in Arab nations. The status of women, too, varies from country to country. Only recently have females begun to show up in the ranks of managers in Japan. In fact, during the recession of the early 1990s, women were laid off in far greater numbers than men. This and other discriminatory practices has led to a tremendous increase in the number of Japanese business startups owned by women.

POLITICAL/LEGAL

The **political/legal environment** can present obstacles to global marketing. Although trade generally occurs between companies rather than countries, the policies and laws of nations have a definite bearing on the business climate. Most developed countries impose trade restrictions on certain imports. The major reason for barriers to trade is for the protection of local industry. Government action sometimes provides a haven to new business ventures. By protecting infant industries, the country assures growth without competition. Japan protects its electronics industries by limiting imports or establishing tariffs. The United States has similar barriers on firms that export fabrics and clothing from Asia to this country.

Trade Quotas

By setting **trade quotas,** or a limitation on the quantity of imports, a country gives its own businesses a chance to grow and prosper. Other companies in different societies might be able to produce better products at lower prices, but by allowing free import of those goods, the local businesses could suffer. To protect its own industries, some countries limit the number of acceptable imports.

Japan and the United States established trade quotas on imported autos in 1980. This five-year agreement limited the number of cars shipped into this country. During this period, the American auto industry returned to the practice of building bigger, flashier models. In 1985, the pact was not renewed, and Detroit found that the buying public preferred the size and quality of Japanese cars. Today, one would be hard pressed to find a single automobile, either Japanese or American, that is 100 percent "made in America." To bolster its image among American buyers, ads for the Toyota Camry tout that the car is mostly made in the United States, but competitors are quick to challenge this statement.[11]

One does not have to be a huge industrial company to be a multinational, as illustrated by Original Mink, which sells its lubricative products worldwide. (Courtesy of Original Mink Oil, Inc.)

Trade quota—a barrier to trade that sets a limitation on the quantity of imports.

[11]James B. Treece, "Toyota's Camry: Made in the USA—sort of," *Business Week*, November 22, 1993, p. 6.

Tariffs and Embargoes

Tariff—a barrier to trade that places a duty or tax on imports.

The most common method of limiting the impact of imports is the imposition of a **tariff.** By charging import duties, or taxes, a country makes the imported goods more expensive. For instance, if the United States imposes a duty on imported goods such as clothing, consumer prices of these imports would rise. This artificial increase makes domestically produced articles more competitive.

Sometimes tariffs are used in retaliation for actions by other countries. By paying farmers who grow soybeans, France made prices on U.S. exports of this commodity noncompetitive. When negotiations between the governments failed, the United States proposed stiff tariffs on imported French wines and cheese. This move, naturally, brought instant retaliation by France.[12]

Embargo—government restriction on entry of foreign goods.

In time of severe stress between nations, embargoes may occur. An **embargo** is a government restriction on the entry of a foreign good. Although seldom used, this policy has come into play when political relations between countries deteriorate. This ultimate in trade barriers may be against all goods from a particular country, or may selectively target only certain items. For example, for years the United States has had an embargo against the importation of Cuban cigars.

Laws and Domestic Policies

Governments sometimes take overt actions over and above imposing trade restrictions. The creation of **laws** or **regulations** to protect certain industries or businesses is common practice in both developed and undeveloped countries. Japan, for example, often uses product specifications or inspection criteria to limit strategic imports. Rather than using tariffs or quotas, the country drowns companies bringing in goods in a sea of red tape. For example, Petrofsky's International, an exporter of frozen bagel dough, had difficulty getting through Japanese food inspectors because the product contained "active bacteria," which was actually yeast.[13]

Domestic policies may impact trade with foreign countries. Commonly, policies established by government are the result of opposition from constituents. For example, countries throughout the world have reacted to South Africa's system of apartheid. Citizens of nations in all parts of the globe reacted to that country's prosegregation government. Politicians came under pressure from disapproving voters and acted to impose trade sanctions against South Africa.[14]

TECHNOLOGY

In any society, the degree of **technological** expertise offered by other countries can be a source of irritation and confusion. Too often businesses from technologically advanced nations attempt to force the "modern" philosophy on peoples

---

[12]Paul Magnusson, Bill Javetski, and Patrick Oster, "Is Washington giving up on GATT?" *Business Week*, November 9, 1992, p. 42.

[13]"Strategies for the new export boom," Rob Norton.

[14]Cyndee Miller, "S. Africa market opens up," *Marketing News*, April 27, 1992, pp. 1 and 2.

unable to comprehend them. In addition, the different means of measurement and styles of design can be troublesome for global marketers. Most of the world uses the metric system, and many U.S. importers fail to comprehend the problems in dealing with different systems. Knowing the technological status of the targeted society is necessary to conduct global marketing.

As an illustration, Becton-Dickinson, the large U.S. medical instruments house, standardized its complete line of syringes to be competitive overseas. The Boeing Corporation found that runways in underdeveloped nations were generally short and soft. Technological changes to the undercarriage on its 737 aircraft made them more acceptable to foreign airline companies serving lesser developed countries. Bike manufacturer Cannondale found that its technologically advanced mountain bike was widely accepted in Japan and Europe. These multinational firms adapted their products to satisfy foreign markets.[15]

COMPETITION

Competition around the world behaves differently from country to country. Business in some societies is much more ruthless than what many U.S. companies face at home. While it is not suggested that global marketers conduct themselves in the same manner, awareness of the difference can at least lead to understanding of the problem. Learning these competitive ropes could be essential for survival in a joint venture arrangement.

The customs of conducting business in foreign countries can have a startling effect on American multinationals. In many cultures, it is common when conducting business to offer payment to high officials within the trading company or within government. While a standard operation in other societies, this

■ ■ ■ ■ ■

Effects of environmental changes on global marketing

CHANGE	EFFECTS
Economic	Different business cycles, confusing financial institutions, less available information
Demographic	Ranges of age groups may differ, fewer women in work force, less migration within economy, lower standards of living and wealth
Cultural	Different languages concern branding, colors impact buyer acceptance, customs affect product use and packaging
Political/legal	Import restrictions, confusing laws, political strife, lack of stability, currency exchange rates
Technological	Different measuring and calculating systems, aversion to modernization, illiteracy
Competitive	Different morals create unusual competitive climate, strong support for domestic producers, graft

■ ■ ■ ■ ■

[15]Ron Stodghill II, "Joe Montgomery's wild ride," *Business Week,* April 19, 1993, pp. 50–52.

action amounts to bribery in the eyes of Americans. Although U.S. companies are prohibited from such activities, many societies look upon these payments as little more than gratuities. Understanding the differences in competitive posturing can save face and fortune.[16]

Policing such illegal activity is one of the major problems facing the global marketplace. The U.S. Department of Justice tries to monitor U.S. companies that step out of bounds, but has little clout in international law circles. A non-profit group called Transparency International, founded by former World Bank officials, tries to stem bribery by using some persuasive "arm twisting." Hopefully, governments and businesses will realize the destructiveness of such shady practices.[17]

Where Do U.S. Firms Conduct Global Marketing?

The American market is facing increased competition from imported goods. As imports increase, manufacturers in the United States will have to look to foreign markets for the sale of their products. The increase in imported industrial goods causes a corresponding decrease in many American industries. Many U.S. firms locate new plants overseas in the hope of cutting labor costs and becoming more competitive in global markets. Typically, products cost less to make in developing economies.

Outsourcing— producing parts overseas for domestic assembly.

The importing and exporting of products also includes services. American Express buys low cost software from Bombay, India. **Outsourcing,** the production of low-cost component parts overseas for assembly in this country, is a growing practice. The U.S. auto industry is heavily into this practice of global marketing. Mexico is fast becoming known as "Detroit South," as GM, Ford and Chrysler establish plants in our southern neighbor. The Ford facility at Hermosillo, which was designed by Mazda engineers, is touted as being the state-of-the-art automobile manufacturing facility in the world.[18]

ASIA

Japan is the United States' second largest trading partner. A majority of the consumer electronics, or "yuppie toys," enjoyed by U.S. buyers originated in Japan. This Asian country has become a dominant player in global economics. As the value of the yen changes in relation to other world currencies, notably the dollar, franc and mark, people in countries all over the world feel the

[16]Catherine Yang and William Spindle, "Commerce cops," *Business Week,* December 13, 1993, pp. 69–70; Karen Pennar, Peter Galuszka, David Lindorff, and Raphael Jesurum, "The destructive costs of greasing palms," *Business Week,* December 6, 1993, pp. 133–138.

[17]Karen Pennar, "A new globo-cop for crooks in high places," *Business Week,* December 6, 1993, p. 136.

[18]Stephen Baker, David Woodruff, and Elizabeth Weiner, "Detroit South," *Business Week,* March 16, 1992, pp. 98–103.

impact. As the exchange rate dropped to one hundred yen for one dollar in 1993, the price of imported goods from Japan rose markedly. Production goods marketers using a variety of Japanese items from lenses to robots found their costs increasing dramatically.[19]

Korea, Taiwan, Singapore and Hong Kong, often referred to as the **"little dragons,"** were the fastest growing Asian economies of the 1980s. Typically noted for the export of cheap merchandise, companies from these countries captured major portions of world markets as product quality improved. Taiwan is now the world's largest producer of vinyl plastics and is entering the semiconductor field, two areas of highly sophisticated production. Malaysia and Indonesia strive to join Singapore to form a triangle of global power in Southeast Asia.[20]

The largest market in the world is beginning to slowly open its doors to global marketers. **China,** with nearly one-third of the world's population, is becoming active in foreign trade. Many experts feel that the impact of Chinese-made goods on world markets will be much greater than the export boom experienced by Japan in the past decade or two. Many prospective marketers have found that the masses are still too poor to buy many Western goods, yet firms such as Gillette, Motorola and Coca-Cola are making major investments on the mainland. The potential of trade with the People's Republic of China is vast, but so are the problems.[21]

Bidding to become a member of the "little dragons," is the Chinese coastal province **Guangdong.** Shortly after the Tiananmen Square tragedy in 1989, Shunde county officials in this area increased production of a major industry, refrigerators, in defiance of Beijing. To everyone's surprise, the central government of China soundly endorsed this aggressive plan. Today, industrial growth in Guangdong averages over 20 percent annually. As China continues to awake from its slumber, more of this type of development is expected.[22]

EUROPE

In the **European Community,** formerly known as the **Common Market,** member countries formed an unusually cohesive front to gain competitive parity or advantages with the United States and Russia. Business among members and between nonmembers enhances this alliance. Typically, such trading blocs emerge when countries feel that they have a common purpose. Although alliances for trade have existed for centuries, there is a new emergence of economies and groups with common goals.

"Little dragons"—the smaller Asian countries, including South Korea, Taiwan, Singapore and Hong Kong.

European Community (Common Market)— Belgium, Denmark, France, Greece, Ireland, Italy, Luxembourg, Netherlands, Portugal, Spain, United Kingdom and Germany.

---

[19]Valerie Reitman, "Global money trends rattle shop windows in heartland America," *The Wall Street Journal,* November 26, 1993, pp. A1 and A5.

[20]Louis Kraar, "Asia's hot new growth triangle," *Fortune,* October 5, 1992, pp. 136–142; Editors, "Ito-Yokado roles a 7-Eleven," *Chain Store Age Executive,* January 1992, p. 6.

[21]Jennifer Reese, "A boom year for China," *Fortune,* June 28, 1993, p. 11; Brenton Schlender, "China really is on the move," *Fortune,* October 5, 1992, pp. 114–122; Louis Kraar, "A new China without borders," *Fortune,* October 5, 1992, pp. 124–128.

[22]Pete Engardio and Lynne Curry, "The fifth tiger is on China's Coast," *Business Week,* April 6, 1992, pp. 42–43.

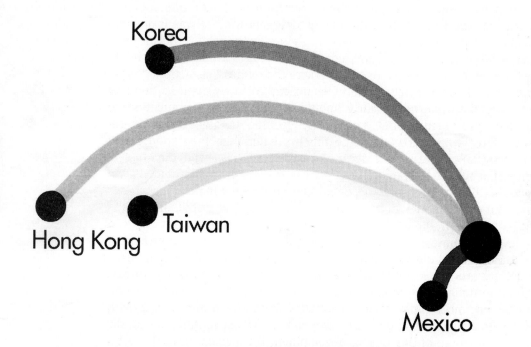

WHY GO ANY FURTHER WHEN MEXICO OFFERS SOME OF THE WORLD'S LOWEST PRODUCTION COSTS?

Why indeed?

Mexico is much nearer to your markets and your headquarters.

But being nearby wouldn't go very far if it weren't for another advantage: Mexico's labor costs are among the lowest in the world.

Which is why hundreds of U.S. and worldwide firms have set up assembly plants, called maquiladoras, in Mexico.

Add to the advantages of a low-cost labor force close by, our country's very favorable tariff policy, our well-developed infrastructure and the superior skills of our work force and you have the

solution to your production cost problems.

Banca Serfin can help you arrive at that solution.

We're one of Mexico's most innovative banks. The oldest, too. So our dedicated Maquiladora Department has years of experience to share.

Banca Serfin offers comprehensive financial services. Experts to help you select sites, services and personnel, as well as access to superior legal and customs guidance.

So talk with Banca Serfin and explore Mexico's Maquiladora program.

After all, if you can find some of the world's lowest production costs close by, why look anywhere else?

BANCA SERFIN
Helping you make it in Mexico.

Mexico City	New York	Tokyo	London	Toronto	Los Angeles	Nassau
Justo Fernández del Valle	Jaime de la Torre	Jose Landa	Marcos Mendoza	Gaston Alegre	Alejandro Garcia	Jaime de la Torre
(526) 512-1413	(212) 635-2300	(813) 273-5911	(441) 408-2151	(416) 360-8900	(213) 624-6610	(212) 635-2300

Many foreign banks, such as Banca Serfin from Mexico, advertise their services in U.S. media. (Courtesy of Banca Serfin and AF-GL Inc.)

The Pan-European unification of 1992 opened new doors for this market. Common currencies and product specifications simplify business dealings across the Atlantic. On the other hand, one of the central issues in the new European Community is the promotion of trade among its members to the exclusion of others, notably American firms. Prior to EC 1992, U.S. multinationals scrambled to invest while the opportunity still existed. Meanwhile, nationalism among these countries slowed progress toward unification. A united Germany has a stronger role in Europe, and will likely continue this dominant position.[23]

Retailing has led much of the recent development in Western Europe, often changing the face of society on the way. Many countries of the EC have either laws or long-standing customs of being closed over weekends. The invasion of megaretailers from the United States and England have changed some of these customs, as consumers have become accustomed to the American tradition known as "shop till you drop." Because Belgium has no ban on Sunday shopping, shoppers from both France and Germany flooded stores there until legislatures modified their stance.[24]

The explosive events in Eastern Europe also fan hope for global marketers. The former communist bloc countries offer hundreds of millions of customers clamoring for Western goods and lifestyles. Economic revolutions in Poland, Czechoslovakia, Bulgaria, Hungary and Romania thrust these countries headlong into the world marketplace. Although bitter ethnic clashes among the Balkan countries threatened many of these economies, the opportunity for growth remains strong.

Much work needs to be done in Eastern Europe for those countries to become active participants in global marketing. Most of these nations lack the infrastructure for conducting overseas operations. Currencies often have no value in world markets, and distribution systems can be nonexistent. Still, freeing Eastern Europe holds a promising future for global marketers everywhere. Colgate-Palmolive is especially active marketing in Poland.[25]

One of the shining lights of Eastern European recovery is Hungary. Exhibiting the same strong individualistic character that it has for centuries, this once member of the Warsaw Pact of Soviet domination is embracing a free market makeover with as much gusto as it can manage. Much of the foreign

---

[23]John Templeman, Gail E. Shares, Stewart Toy, and William Glasgall, "Germany takes charge," *Business Week,* February 17, 1992, pp. 50–58; John Rossant, Richard Melcher, and Stewart Toy, "Is Europe's express train to unity slowing down?" *Business Week,* February 3, 1992, p. 46; Richard Melcher, Patrick Oster, and Stewart Toy, "Europe, too, is edgy about imports—from America," *Business Week,* January 27, 1992, pp. 48–49; Shawn Tully, "Europe 1992: More unity than you think," *Fortune,* August 24, 1992, pp. 135–142.

[24]Paula Dwyer, Karen Lowry Miller, Stewart Toy, and Patrick Oster, "Shop till you drop hits Europe," *Business Week,* November 29, 1993, pp. 58–59.

[25]Gail E. Schares, "Colgate-Palmolive is really cleaning up in Poland," *Business Week,* March 15, 1993, pp. 54–56; Richard A. Melcher, Jonathon B. Levine, and Patrick Oster, "The best-laid plans of multinationals. . .," *Business Week,* October 7, 1992, pp. 37–38; Stewart Toy, John Templeman, Richard A. Melcher, John Rossant, and Stanley Reed, "Europe's shakeout," *Business Week,* October 14, 1992, pp. 44–51; Carla Rapoport, "Europe looks ahead to hard choices," *Fortune,* December 14, 1992, pp. 144–149.

CLASS ATTRACTS CLASS

American truck marketer Peterbilt has found a sizable market for its big rigs in global markets. (Courtesy of Peterbilt)

investment in Hungary is going toward improving environmental conditions. Privatization of industry and financial institutions have increased productivity and freed up private capital. Hungary is one of the brightest lights in this newly created market arena. [26]

---

[26]Special advertising section, *Fortune*, October 18, 1993.

RUSSIA AND THE FORMER SOVIET UNION

The breakup of the Soviet Union brought about dramatic economic change. Russia, and the other newly formed republics, look forward to trade with companies in the United States and other Western nations as a means of bolstering their poor standards of living. The vast petroleum reserves in these areas may be the bargaining chips for gaining the products and productivity so badly needed by the people. Freeing up the private ownership of property will also speed the growth of this area. The addition of this "capitalistic" motivator will likely cause an increase in productivity in Russia, something long lacking in its economy. [27]

One of the biggest obstacles for businesses dealing in Russia is the low value of its currency, the ruble. Until the ruble is accepted as a medium of exchange, most of the trade with this country remains through barter. As the pain and chaos of the political action smoothes, Russia, Ukraine and the other independent countries will begin to share more in global marketing.

American firms are investing heavily on the planned recovery of this region. The newness of dealing with free markets in Russia and the other republics creates a whole new research dilemma. Profiles of the Russian consumer have never before been available. Marketers are finding that this new arena is nearly as diversified as markets in the rest of the world. Not only has McDonald's found Moscow, but that quintessential American firm Ben & Jerry's is serving up ice cream in Petrozavodsk in northern Russia.[28]

LATIN AMERICA

American companies are looking to our southern neighbor, **Mexico,** as more than just a source of low-cost labor. Increased per capita income is beginning to provide a marketplace for U.S.-made goods as well. Manufacturing facilities have sprung up along the border from Tijuana to Matamoros, producing everything from waterbeds to refrigerators. The Mexican worker can maintain an improving standard of living on wages that American labor could or would not accept. There is pent up demand for goods from the United States.[29]

The North American Free Trade Agreement, or NAFTA, was signed by the United States, Mexico and Canada in 1993. This far-ranging pact will eventually eliminate all tariffs between those countries. While generally conceded to be of benefit to workers in each economy, American exports have blossomed through exports. Some Mexican manufacturers, especially those that are outmoded and inefficient, are facing stiff competition from modern U.S. factories.

---

[27]Adi Ignatius, "New shade of red," *The Wall Street Journal,* January 27, 1994, pp. A1 and A10.

[28]Stephen Seplow, "Russians get a big scoop of Americana," *San Jose Mercury News,* April 16, 1993, p. 21a; Betsy Spethmann, "Raking in the rubles with scratch-and-win," *BRANDWEEK,* March 1, 1993; Rose Brady, Deborrah Stead, and Igor Reichlin, "After Yeltsin's strong medicine, a few twitches of life," *Business Week,* March 2, 1992, pp. 50–51.

[29]Stephen Baker, "Free trade isn't painless," *Business Week,* August 31, 1992, pp. 38–39; Luane Hellmann Hill, "Selling south of the border," *Oregon Business,* February 1992, pp. 12–15.

Small retailers are also struggling, as lower priced imports from north of the border cut into their customer base.[30]

Change is occurring throughout Latin America. Governments are stabilizing and prosperity is creeping in. Led by the four nation bloc known as Mercosur, the entire area clamors for goods and services, largely from the United States. The countries of Brazil, Argentine, Uruguay and Paraguay dominate the economy of South America. Together they form one of the fastest growing trade groups in the world. Once favoring protectionist policies, Latin America now opens its doors for investors from around the globe. Ford, Eastman Kodak and Monsanto, to name a few, formed joint ventures with Mercosur firms.[31]

CANADA

Canada remains this country's largest trading partner. Trade agreements with the neighbor to the north have greatly increased both exports and imports. Since NAFTA, American investments in Canada have increased dramatically, and goods flowing south are growing as well. Canada's Northern Telcom, for example, receives 50 percent of its revenues from the United States. Even with NAFTA, some Canadians feel resentful and uneasy about the United States.

American products are commonplace on Canadian store shelves, yet some of them are a bit different than what we see stateside. For instance, PepsiCo markets a sugar free Pepsi Max throughout Europe, where diet drinks notoriously receive a cold reception. In Canada, Pepsi Max is a mid-calorie soft drink that may end up on supermarket shelves in the States. Many U.S. firms use this neighbor to the north as a testing ground for new products.[32]

One of the most successful firms in Canada is also making strong waves south of the border. Loblaw International Merchants, the distributor of President's Choice products, supplies dozens of chains and thousands of stores in the United States. As one of the largest private label marketers in the world, Loblaw continues to expand into American markets and is setting its sights on Asia and Europe as well.[33]

---

[30]Geri Smith, "Free trade isn't coming cheap," *Business Week*, December 6, 1993, pp. 58–59.

[31]"NAFTA is not alone," *The Economist*, June 18, 1994, pp. 47–48; Santiago Perez del Castillo, "Mercosur: History and aims," *International Labor Review*, 1993, pp. 639–653; Bill Hinchberger, "Mercosur on the march," *Institutional Investor*, March 1993, pp. 107–108; Stephen Baker, Geri Smith, Kevin Kelly, and Elizabeth Weiner, "Making a yanqui boodle south of the border," *Business Week*, February 10, 1992, pp. 40–41; Editors, "Latin America cheers up," *The Economist*, April 18, 1992, pp. 11–12; Geri Smith and John Pearson, "The new world's newest trade bloc," *Business Week*, May 4, 1992, pp. 50–51.

[32]Karen Benezra, "Double entendre: The life and the life of Pepsi Max," *BRANDWEEK*, April 18, 1994, p. 40.

[33]Betsy Spethmann, "Dave Nichol: Marketer of the year," *BRANDWEEK*, November 8, 1993, pp. 46–47.

One of the largest private brand marketers in the world, Loblaw International Merchants, sells its products under the President's Choice label.

How Is Global Marketing Managed?

American firms have several problems in dealing with customers in global markets. Products may not be universally acceptable in all countries. Similarly, pricing methods and buying practices vary greatly among different economies. In many areas of the world, distribution systems are inadequate, at best. American promotion tactics may be obnoxious to some people, a turnoff to others. Managing global marketing is truly a challenge.

PRODUCT

Products offered to domestic markets may not be acceptable overseas. Many firms have learned the hard way that consumers from other societies do not always have the same needs or tastes as American buyers. Manufacturers have sometimes found that either modifications or completely new products are necessary to capture the international market. For example, Germans buy salad dressings packaged in tubes, and attempts to market bottled salad dressings have not been successful. The cakes preferred by the English at tea time are heavy and solid. American cake mixes produce a moist, crumbly cake that Britishers have trouble picking up with their fingers while sipping their brew.

Sometimes products vary because of the availability of raw materials in other countries. McDonald's has over 2,000 outlets outside the United States, but faces difficulty maintaining the same type of operation in other countries.

The hamburger chain prides itself on its French fries made from Idaho Russet Burbank potatoes. Since these large spuds are not grown in many countries, and the local varieties make poor fries, McDonald's now raises its own potatoes in over twenty countries.

Branding is especially difficult overseas because typically American verbiage may have different interpretations in other languages. Firms often must create an entirely separate name for the same product. Colgate-Palmolive is one company that benefited from extensive marketing research when introducing its antibacterial, plaque fighting toothpaste, Total. This marketer designed a formulation, image and package that would translate across national boundaries. Total now sells in almost one hundred countries worldwide.[34]

PRICE

Pricing is a problem when dealing in other countries, as foreign exchange rates affect both sales and receipts. One challenge that faces marketers in this area is to remain competitive while still covering the added costs of exporting. Packing and shipping cost more for overseas delivery. Tariffs imposed by the receiving country are costs that impact the ultimate price to the foreign consumer.

Dumping—selling goods for a lower price in export markets than in domestic arenas.

When an exporter sells goods to a foreign market at a price lower than that charged domestically, it is called **dumping.** The exporter may claim that extra business results in economies of scale to reduce costs, but domestic competition usually cries foul. By dumping products on a foreign market, the exporter can gain or retain an unfair competitive advantage. Many countries, including the United States, have laws against dumping. Such government legislation is easy to circumvent and difficult to police. Many U.S. firms simply import parts, or have their products assembled in a third country, to avoid dumping charges.[35]

DISTRIBUTION

Distribution is critical when trading globally. Successful multinationals realize that differences exist and modify their efforts accordingly. In Japan, some products may travel through as many as five intermediaries before they reach the consumer. Procter & Gamble met with difficulty breaking through Japan's tight distribution channels. When the U.S. megamarketer introduced new Ultra Pampers disposable diapers, it bypassed secondary and tertiary wholesalers by offering incentives to the primary intermediaries.[36]

In selling to companies in lesser developed countries, the international marketer may find inadequate or nonexistent distribution channels. In many

[34]Pam Weisz, "Border crossings: Brands unify image to counter cult of culture," *BRANDWEEK,* October 24, 1994, pp. 24–28; Jon Berry, "How big is your umbrella? Maybe not so big after all," *BRANDWEEK,* December 6, 1993, p. 22–23.

[35]Janet Novack, "It's like a big balloon," *Forbes,* July 20, 1992, p. 48.

[36]Karen Lowry Miller, "Psst! Wanna buy into Japan Inc.?" *Business Week,* March 30, 1992, pp. 41–42.

Many countries of the world do not have the sophisticated distribution systems taken for granted by American businesses.

emerging nations, consumers do not have adequate cold storage facilities. Lack of refrigeration in some lesser developed countries dictates the use of smaller packages to minimize spoilage. Family sized packs of chicken or fish would not go over well in Trinidad or Sri Lanka. Poor roads or lack of rail service also affect the size and shape of the distribution systems.

PROMOTION

Global marketers must adapt their **promotion** to fit the tastes of new audiences. Many foreign consumers would be offended by the typical American television commercial. For example, the appearance of women in advertising would be totally unacceptable in Arab countries. The framework for promotion may also be different overseas. Many foreign countries do not have commercial radio stations. Others have several newspapers, but few magazines. Many cultures find personal selling offensive. Developing nations frequently lack television coverage, while outdoor advertising is prominent.

Positioning

Positioning is as important in global marketing as it is in dealing with domestic markets. Products sold in foreign markets develop images in the minds of buyers just as they do when sold in the United States. Products thrown into an overseas market with little regard for how these goods and services are perceived by the new buyers rarely succeed. Knowing the market and the factors affecting foreign buying behavior, successful multinationals position their products to suit those cultures.

One company that has done well in positioning to Japanese standards is Nippon Lever. For example, this Dutch firm's Timotei shampoo is the best-selling hair care product in Japan. Nippon Lever recognized that Japanese women shampoo their hair as often as six times weekly and are heavy users of conditioners and hair cleaning products. Timotei is positioned as a mild shampoo using natural herbs. This subsidiary of Unilever promotes the ingredients of Timotei as wild European grasses instead of Japanese herbs to lend an aura of the unusual to this product.

ETHICS

Since the ethical codes of different societies vary greatly, dealing with overseas customers or suppliers can pose problems. Many firms find it easy to stray from their established methods of doing business, to "cheat just a bit." Levels of sophistication in many countries, especially developing nations, creates opportunities to take advantage of less savvy business people. On the other hand, many foreign contacts find American dealers naive and soft.

Many U.S. firms take advantage of lower wage rates to have their products manufactured, at least partially, overseas. In setting up production facilities in other countries, an American multinational would have little difficulty exploiting ignorant and uninformed employees. Levi Strauss is one company that has shown concern for personnel abuses. With more than 50 percent of its jeans and shirts being made overseas, this San Francisco clothing giant imposes strict guidelines over the manufacture of its products. The company will not allow below scale wages, child labor or excessive working hours.[37]

Ethical considerations are not limited to only U.S. multinationals. Of major concern to the global economy is the increase of counterfeit products in worldwide markets. At one time brand piracy was primarily limited to consumer goods such as designer jeans and upscale watches. Now software imitating Microsoft's Windows and Excel pour out of China to markets in Latin America and Asia. Recordings and books are other intellectual property being counterfeited in China.[38]

Despite the many obstacles facing global marketing, overseas trade is an increasingly important facet of business operations. The trend is definitely toward increased commerce with companies in other societies. Even small firms find that very lucrative ventures are available in foreign markets. Advanced communications systems and ever expanding technology place the world economy at the fingertips of business people everywhere.

SUMMING IT UP

The world's societies differ in many ways. Developed nations are those with high standards of living and sophisticated production capability. Those coun-

---

[37]Brian Dumaine, "Exporting jobs and ethics," *Fortune,* October 5, 1992, p. 10.
[38]Amy Borrus, Pete Engardio, and Richard Brandt, "Will China scuttle its pirates?" *Business Week,* August 15, 1994, pp. 40–41.

Marketing and Society: Is it a Conspiracy?

There is little question that American businesses and business people are into global marketing in a big way. As a society, our involvement with products and companies from foreign lands will go nowhere but up. Certainly the American consumer is not going to stop buying foreign-made goods so long as the quality and prices remain attractive. The only way to achieve some sort of balance between imports and exports is to ship more goods and services overseas.

Business in the United States is relatively free from government intervention; other societies cannot boast the same. Many of the rules and laws under which commerce operates in America are not the same overseas. Interlocking directorates, where members from different companies serve on each other's boards of directors, are outlawed in the United States. When it comes to overseas operations, however, things are different. This interconnection between the boards of directors exists with sixteen of the world's top twenty-five multinationals.

A surprisingly large number of multinationals are connected in more ways than just buyer and seller. Using the joint venture mechanism, many of the largest businesses in the world are tied together. Fiat, the Italian conglomerate, is in partnership with Ford, General Electric, Motorola, Nissan and formerly with the government of Libya, to name just a few. DuPont and Merck work together in overseas operations, as do DuPont and AT&T. Nestlé and General Mills have an alliance that minimizes competition from Kellogg. A construction project in the Far East was jointly financed by Citicorp and Mitsubishi Bank.

The concentration of wealth and power in the hands of a few giant multinationals is alarming. The temptation to use those advantages to restrain trade or manipulate prices is great. All global partners and governments must continue efforts to promote fair and ethical relationships among all global marketers.

SOURCE: Janet Lowe, *The Secret Empire*, (Homewood, IL: Business One Irwin, 1992).

---

tries that are still struggling to improve their lot are known as emerging nations. In free market economies, consumers determine what will or will not be marketed, whereas government decides the product mix in controlled markets.

Global marketing is conducted between businesses in different countries. Multinational companies trade overseas for profit. Other reasons for global marketing include smoothing out seasonal fluctuations, cost reduction, reciprocity and expanded markets extending product life. Global marketing is conducted by export/import, through licensing, joint venture and by direct investment, the riskiest method.

Global marketing is affected by the same changes in environment that impact domestic operations. Economic fluctuations are even greater in foreign countries than in the United States. Many cultural obstacles impact global marketing, including language and customs barriers. The political climate in many foreign countries is unstable. Many governments impose trade barriers, such as quotas and tariffs. Exchange rate fluctuations and domestic policies influence trade abroad. Technology and competition play roles. In many foreign societies, standards for ethical business behavior are quite different from ours.

U.S. multinationals conduct business in many arenas. Asia, including Japan, the "little dragons," and China, offer unique opportunities and problems. Europe, with the consolidation of 1992, is trading more as a block in the future. Russia and the former Eastern bloc of nations are still trying to cope with newfound free market economies. Latin America and Canada, while closer to home, still offer challenges.

Products, including packaging, must be designed with foreign tastes in mind. Pricing can be a problem, especially with fluctuating foreign exchange rates and dumping. In many countries, multitiered distribution channels are difficult to penetrate. In others, the lack of infrastructure makes physical distribution tricky. Global promotion does not follow the same rules as those found domestically, and the media are less developed in many cases. Positioning is just as important overseas as it is in the United States. Good marketing ethics, while different in many societies, are as important in global market as in the United States.

KEY CONCEPTS AND TERMS FROM CHAPTER EIGHTEEN

Advanced industrialized economies
Controlled market
Dumping
Embargo
Ethnocentrism
European Community (Common Market)
Export/import

Free market economy
Global marketing
"Little dragons"
Newly industrialized economies
Outsourcing
Tariff
Trade quota

BUILDING SKILLS

1. Contrast the global marketing differences between advanced industrialized nations and lesser developed countries.

2. Explain the reasons for global marketing for companies from the following industries: major appliances, California wine, petroleum products, swimsuits, vitamins.

3. Discuss the pros and cons of exporting, licensing, joint venture activities and direct overseas manufacturing.

4. Compare the effect of economic, cultural or political/legal environ-

mental changes on global marketing for supercomputers, automobile seat belts, candy bars, lingerie, coffee makers.

5. Discuss how the marketing mix elements of product, price, distribution and promotion might be different for successful overseas marketing.

6. Describe the markets that American businesses will be dealing with in the future, including the factors that might adversely affect global marketing.

Making Decisions 18-1: An Apple a Day.

Whether speaking domestically or internationally, computers are a very competitive market. Although IBM got an initial jump in the global market, Apple is coming on strong. This is especially true in Japan, the most rapid consumer electronics market anywhere. Apple, the Cupertino, California, based company surpassed IBM in this market in 1992, to join the top five in sales. The other members on this lofty perch are all Japanese companies.

(Courtesy of Apple Computer Inc.)

Apple does well in this Asian arena because of smart marketing. The company continually courts the intermediaries that will succeed in slugging it through Japan's complicated, and often frustrating, distribution channels. Brother Industries, Mitsubishi, Sharp and Minolta, all major suppliers to the country's businesses, handle the Macintosh. The company also supplies its unique software systems to a variety of joint venture partners, including Sony and Sharp.

Savvy management at Apple built a solid reputation in this often ticklish society through a series of shrewd promotional moves. The marketer sponsored the Tokyo performance of Janet Jackson. This popular star was a smashing success, and each patron at her concerts received a lap full of literature from Apple. The company sponsors a stop on the Japanese Ladies Professional Golf Association tour, with T-shirts, mugs and other specialty items bearing the Apple logo on sale everywhere.[39]

Describe the reasons Apple had for expanding its global marketing efforts, noting any special problems that hamper doing business in Japan.

Making Decisions 18-2: Turn Out the Lights.

Global marketing affects almost every facet of the U.S. economy. Politicians are quick to point out that manufacturing overseas takes jobs away from Americans. What is sometimes lost in this discussion is the creation of jobs because of international activity. The imbalance of trade is narrowing, and, in some areas of the globe, notably Europe, this country is presently running a surplus. When trade in services, such as movies, insurance and software, is included in the statistics, the effect is negligible.

[39]Niel Gross and Kathy Rebello, "Apple? Japan can't say no," *Business Week,* June 29, 1992, pp. 32-33.

One example of increased domestic production due to expanded overseas operations is the Emerson Electric Company of St. Louis, Missouri. This marketer of electric motors, pressure measuring equipment and other production goods began its global marketing operations by building overseas manufacturing facilities. Today, because of the firm's presence in foreign markets, international sales from its U.S. facilities are growing geometrically. Emerson's domestic workforce has more than doubled in the last decade.

Changes in international trade figures do not occur overnight. As disastrous as the difference between imports and exports was in 1970, today's figures are marching in the right direction. A couple of pluses are worth examining. Low-cost imported goods squeezed profit margins in the United States. This forced companies to streamline, and American business today is the most productive in the world. Secondly, as people in the emerging countries earned more by exporting their goods to this country, they put themselves in the position to afford to buy our exports. "Made in America" is more in demand today worldwide than ever before.[40]

Detail the methods of global trade that Emerson selected and describe the environmental factors that affect global marketing for a production goods house.

Making Decisions 18-3: A Thorough Cleaning!

Most U.S. marketers are sophisticated enough to realize that they must develop a complete profile of their market before rushing out to sell products. Without knowing what potential customers need and how they buy, any marketing effort is facing a tough, uphill climb. When American businesses travel abroad to sell their wares, the same information may be more difficult to amass. Not all societies act the way that ours does, nor do people around the globe have similar needs.

Conventional wisdom would assume that the many different cultures that form the European Community would provide a mixed bag of needs and wants. One might accurately predict that developing a profile of the typical Euro-shopper would be difficult at best. Yet large appliance manufacturer Whirlpool is bucking the tide. Recognized as a leader in marketing research in Europe, Whirlpool has successfully built a market based upon a standard product.

The industry generally conceded that model designs, brands and distribution systems would need to be individualized for each country serviced. Top loading washers are preferred in France, and front loaders in Germany. The British typically buy their large appliances at giant superstores, while Italians prefer to deal with small, independent retailers. Whirlpool decided that these differences could be overcome by good marketing. This U.S. multinational determined that Europeans would trade off their preferences if they were given products with superior performance, environmental economy and reliable quality. Using this philosophy, Whirlpool is cleaning up.[41]

Contrast the factors of the marketing mix in global marketing with doing business domestically.

---

[40]Howard Banks, "The world's most competitive economy," *Forbes,* March 30, 1992, pp. 84–88.

[41]William Echikson, "Inventing Eurocleaning," *Fortune,* Autumn/Winter 1993, pp. 30–31.

/9

The Future of Marketing and Social Responsibility

The Job to be Done

Marketing and marketers face an exciting future. New technology promises a wealth of possibilities, yet some people fear or distrust marketing. Marketers must recognize problem areas, and propose remedies that are acceptable. Chapter 19 gives you what you need to:

- understand and explain the events and trends affecting the future of marketing,

- describe society's concerns about marketing and how marketers are responding, and

- define responsible marketing and the rewards for social responsibility.

Marketers at Work

Brenda Daly

At one time it looked as though math would be Brenda Daly's Achilles heel. Her business and computer courses were a snap, but algebra kept rearing its ugly head. Squeaking by with little room to spare, Brenda conquered the Xs and Ys and received her Associate of Applied Science degree from Central Oregon Community College. Although she majored in information systems, her experience in Delta Epsilon Chi tweaked her interest in marketing.

Her career path first led south to the Santa Cruz, California area, where she was originally hired as a data entry clerk by the Visitors' Bureau. Brenda's marketing acumen began to show, and she was snatched up by the Cathedral Hill Hotel in San Francisco to work in sales. Soon another lodging organization recognized her capabilities, and she was recruited by Shilo Inns to be its Regional Sales Manager. In this position, she was in charge of booking conventions and other events for this fast-growing chain of hotels and resorts.

The lure of her native Oregon with its beautiful mountains and clear streams, brought Brenda back home, where she began her own business, Central Oregon Group Sales. This organization is responsible for booking tours to some of the region's many attractions. The numerous golf courses, museums and recreation facilities in the area soon began to see dramatic increases in tourist numbers due, at least in part, to her efforts.

One of the attractions that she fell in love with is the Crooked River Dinner Train, which she serves as Marketing Director, on top of running her own business. This dining experience wends its way through spectacular countryside and, thanks to Brenda's creativity, offers a variety of exciting and colorful distractions such as a mock train holdup, mystery theater and strolling troubadours and magicians. In the summers, after a scrumptious Champagne Brunch, the train makes a stop at an authentic cattle ranch, where riders take part in a Western hoedown, followed by an early evening barbecue. Recalling her roots, Brenda also provides marketing expertise to Kaneeta Resort, owned by the Confederated Tribes of Warm Springs.

What Events and Trends Will Affect the Future of Marketing?

No one with a crystal ball could accurately predict the future of marketing, yet some trends are clear. A number of changes have already occurred that will have further impact, and additional developments will continue to influence marketers and their decisions. The decades ahead will be challenging as well as rewarding.

CONTINUED DEINDUSTRIALIZATION

Deindustrialization—the reduction in the number of firms and people involved in manufacturing goods.

Since 1952, the **deindustrialization** of our economy has reduced the number of people in our society working to make tangible products. More people are employed in creating and providing services than in the production and marketing of goods. The loss of production jobs will continue due to outsourcing. While manufacturers look for lower cost labor in overseas pools, the rise in the standards of living worldwide in turn increases the demand for products made in the United States.

Some of America's fast growing small businesses

COMPANY (LOCATION)	TYPE OF BUSINESS
Object Design (Burlington, MA)	Database software
CardMember Publishing (Stamford, CT)	Services to credit card holders
Rasna (San Jose, CA)	Software for mechanical engineers
Furst Group (Shamong, NJ)	Long-distance telephone services
MicroVoice Applications (Minneapolis, MN)	Voice responsive software
Access America Telemanagement (Chesterfield, MO)	Telecommunications systems
Travelpro Luggage (Deerfield Beach, FL)	Manufacturer/distributor luggage
Tivoli Systems (Austin, TX)	Systems management
Duracom Computer Systems (Irving, TX)	Computer/computer peripherals distributor
PC & More (Freemont, CA)	Computer/computer peripherals distributor
Midcom Communications (Seattle, WA)	Resells long distance telephone services
Vektron International (Grand Prairie, TX)	Computer/computer peripherals distributor
United Vision Group (Ossining, NY)	Consumer goods manufacturer/importer
Quik-Pak (Lafayette, IN)	Shipping, freight forwarding services
Oasis Imaging Products (Hudson, NH)	Remanufacturing laser printer cartridges
Payroll Transfers (Tampa, FL)	Temporary employment services
America II Electronics (St. Petersburg, FL)	Wholesale integrated circuits and semiconductors
Diamond Multimedia Systems (Sunnyvale, CA)	Designs/manufactures computer boards
Spectrum Astro (Gilbert, AZ)	Satellites for space stations
Washing Systems (Cincinnati, OH)	Industrial laundry products

SOURCE: Editors, *Inc. 500,* 1994, p. 117.

■ ■ ■ ■ ■

Although the actual number of goods manufactured in this country may be declining, the U.S. production sector remains among the most creative in the world. Our industrial community is in the midst of a renovation phase. Old products and processes are being replaced with creative goods and automated, highly efficient ways of getting things done. The "Fortune 500" list of America's largest companies shows an increasing number of smaller, more innovative young firms joining the ranks.

THE INFORMATION AGE

The computer led us into the **information age,** where more people work in the transmission of ideas than in the manufacturing of goods. Today, the automated office is common, robots control production processes and the electronic home is fast approaching. Computers control automobile engines and manage the car's interior environment. Our wrists carry microprocessors in watches, and the appliances that make our toast and morning coffee are controlled electronically.

Information age—the present era where more people are employed in information processing.

Artificial Intelligence

Artificial intelligence, or **AI,** where computers think, learn and invent seems awesome, but neural-net systems are starting to show promise of doing just that. These developments attempt to duplicate on silicon chips the way the human

Artificial intelligence—computers that behave and react in a manner similar to the human brain.

brain handles information. Early success has led to the development of the first products using a limited form of AI. Neural networks and genetic algorithms from Norad Incorporated are producing sophisticated corporate bond trading systems. Apple Computer's Newton is another example of this growing technology.[1]

Automation and information processing open new frontiers for marketing. Many of the products that consumers and users will be enjoying by the year 2000 have yet to be created, let alone marketed. The use of computers to control production processes will continue to expand. While automation may initially create concern in the workforce, the retraining and educating of the labor force will create new opportunities for people in the field of marketing. In addition, the service sector is expanding to include the repair and maintenance of these new products.

High-Tech Developments

The creation of new products from automated production lines could increase the need for storage and transportation facilities. Old distribution systems will be revamped or new ones created to handle a new generation of goods. The facsimile machine, or FAX, has made communication more efficient. These data transmission tools are now found in planes, trains and automobiles. High-definition television, or HDTV, is creating heavy global competition. The firms who are "first out of the blocks" with this consumer development are reaping large rewards.[2]

Shopping malls, libraries and even automobile showrooms display one of the most dramatic developments of the information age. Electronic kiosks placed in well-traveled public areas offer a wide range of data and services. Touch-screen monitors on these computers beckon the passerby to get job information, order meals, receive directions or order birth certificates. Some experiments with electronic kiosks by the state of California promise to reduce workloads and lower costs.[3]

THE GLOBAL ECONOMY

Global economy— emphasis on world-wide markets rather than limiting efforts to domestic operations.

In addition to these technological advances, there is an increased emphasis on a **global economy.** In this arena, marketing oriented firms concentrate their efforts worldwide rather than solely on domestic areas. U.S. consumers buy more imported goods, and American business exports more expertise. This country's engineering and technology remain important exportable commodities.

---

[1]Catherine Arnst and Amy Cortese, "PDA: Premature death announcement," *Business Week,* September 19, 1994, pp. 88–89; Evan I. Schwartz and James B. Treece, "Smart programs go to work," *Business Week,* March 2, 1992, pp. 96–105; Kate Bertrand, "Apple joins the battle of the notebooks," *Business Marketing,* December 1991, p. 12.

[2]Mark Lewyn, Lois Therrien, and Peter Coy, "Sweating out the HDTV contest," *Business Week,* February 22, 1993, pp. 92–94; Jon Pepper, "Office machines: More for less," *Nation's Business,* February 1992, pp. 44–47; L. G. Coleman, "Report: It's a wild fax future for marketers," *Marketing News,* October 28, 1991, p. 5.

[3]Evan I. Schwartz, Paul M. Eng, S. Lynne Walker, and Alice Cuneo, "The kiosks are coming, the kiosks are coming," *Business Week,* June 22, 1992, p. 122.

Electronic kiosks are appearing in shopping centers and malls everywhere.

More and more companies are talking about the benefits of globalization, but to compete in global markets, American business had to change its ways. Costs had to come down, while efficiency increased, making productivity the catchword of the manufacturing community. Markets around the world require products in different forms than those found in domestic arenas. To satisfactorily feed these needs, mass production has given way to customized production in many cases.

THE QUALITY MOVEMENT

The globalization of business produced many unexpected results. For one, U.S. manufacturers are now more aware of the demand for quality. Finding that their goods were unacceptable by many foreign standards, American industry worked hard to change an image that had been decades in growing. Japanese investments in America brought with it that society's penchant for quality. Together these factors led to jumps in productivity and efficiency in U.S. businesses. Perhaps nowhere is this movement to quality more evident than in the American auto industry. Copying the Japanese bent toward superior relations with suppliers, Detroit is cutting costs while increasing the quality of its product.[4]

The new found emphasis on quality also impacts domestic markets. Better made, more attractive and longer lasting products are in as much demand locally as they are overseas. Better quality in American goods led to a shift in demand away from many imported items. Although the consumer goods markets will continue to see increases in imported items, U.S. goods are regaining customer favor.

Total Quality Management (TQM)

Total quality management (TQM)— a philosophy that empowers employees to increase productivity while preserving customer satisfaction.

Total quality management is labeled as the "buzzword" of the 1990s. The **TQM** concept is a philosophy first promoted by consultant W. Edwards Deming. After being somewhat rebuffed in the United States, Deming introduced this new concept in Japan to overcome the cheap image accompanying products from that country at the close of World War II. The philosophy is simple: the production of goods and services should be customer driven. Under TQM, management pushes all facets of the company to strive for customer satisfaction. In this way, total quality management is similar to the marketing concept.

Taking this concept one step further involves rewarding employees who really create customer satisfaction. One company that puts total quality management to good use is Hewlett-Packard. This computer firm created an employee compensation plan based upon TQM. Salespeople are not only rewarded by making sales quotas, but also receive incentives based upon customer satisfaction. Total quality management is not a new concept, rather it is just a new way of putting old ideas into an understandable, acceptable, controllable format.[5]

Although some management gurus now minimize the worth of TQM, it appears that the quality aspect of doing business has taken root. Total quality management has given way in some instances to "reengineering" or "continuous process improvement," which deal with the same theory: customers are attracted by quality of both product and service. It is rare that a marketer which has adopted the principles of TQM will revert to old processes or outmoded procedures.[6]

---

[4]David Greising, "Quality," *Business Week,* August 8, 1994, pp. 54–59; Alex Taylor II, "The auto industry meets the new economy," *Fortune,* September 5, 1994, pp. 52–60; Laurie Petersen, "A patriotic pitch that few can buy," *Adweek's Marketing Week,* February 2, 1992, p. 9.

[5]Kerry Rottenberger and Richard Kern, "The upside-down Deming principle," *Sales & Marketing Management,* June 1992, pp. 39–44.

[6]Rahul Jacob, "TQM: More than a dying fad," *Fortune,* October 18, 1993, pp. 66–72; Cyndee Miller, "TQM out; 'continuous process improvement' in," *Marketing News,* May 9, 1994, pp. 5 and 20.

One of the keys to success of TQM is the acceptance of employees as being part of the "customers" who need to be satisfied. For example, Chaparral Steel, a somewhat small manufacturer of I-beams and reinforcing bars for building construction, treats its employees as adults. Managers at Chaparral do not adhere to the typical "coat and tie" apparel common in business. Even more important, executives give workers a full rein on making production decisions. The employees are rewarded with higher than average industry salaries plus a share of the profits.[7]

While many large organizations struggle with total quality management, small businesses have been quicker to adopt the concept. Since TQM requires the total, top-down commitment by management, the hierarchy typical with larger firms usually translates to longer adoption times. One of the keys to TQM is the empowerment of employees to make on-the-spot decisions regarding what is good for the customer while benefiting the company. Alphatronix is one smaller firm that has happily relinquished the responsibility to all members of the team. Like many manufacturers, this high-tech company, located in the Research Triangle Park, North Carolina, couples TQM with just-in-time to produce ultimate efficiency.[8]

THE HUMAN FACTOR

Amidst the rush toward a high-tech society, tempered by global developments and new management concepts, marketers cannot lose sight of the human element. The Japanese economy is often referred to as "high tech, high touch." This means that much of the sophisticated development in that country goes toward improving quality of life on a nonmaterial level. As a greater portion of our daily living falls under the control of electronic marvels, people may cry out for greater emphasis on the personal touch.

To have a minimum family existence, many American families face the need for two incomes. This necessity to produce income creates additional burden on personal requirements, such as child care and recreational needs. Businesses are accepting this challenge, and in-company and independent child care facilities are appearing. Paternal as well as maternal leave is recognized by many industries and firms, as is the need for increased assistance for both new and single parents. These human relations features create a variety of marketing opportunities.

Health and Wellness

Health care is a major problem in our society. Estimates are that health care costs will account for 20 percent of the average American's budget by the year

---

[7]Brian Dumaine, "Unleash workers and cut costs," *Fortune,* May 18, 1992, p. 88.

[8]Michael Barrier, "Small firms put quality first," *Nation's Business,* May 1992, pp. 22–32; Michael Barrier, "Spreading the word: Quality," *Nation's Business,* August 1992, p. 56; Editors, "Total quality by satellite," *Nation's Business,* March 1992, p. 49; Rose Knotis, "Rambo doesn't work here anymore," *Business Horizons,* January-February 1992, pp. 44–46.

One word tells the whole story.

And what a story it is.

Beginning with our supply. The largest year-round supply of fresh, quality citrus in all of North America.

Add to that an organization whose reputation for integrity and trust is unequaled in the citrus business.

And a trademark which means a guarantee of quality because fruit with Sunkist written on the outside means quality on the inside.

Sunkist. It's a story of excellence. Quality. And high standards. A story with many great chapters yet to be written.

You have our word on it.®

Sunkist, Sunkist, and "You have our word on it" are registered trademarks of Sunkist Growers, Inc. © 1990 Sunkist Growers, Inc.

The name Sunkist on the outside signifies the quality on the inside. (Courtesy of Sunkist Growers Inc.)

2000. Medical advances are praised by most, yet these steps forward are not without costs, social as well as financial. The need to tackle the rising price tag on medical care is a challenge for business, not just government. Many companies already accept this opportunity by creating innovative plans for meeting increasing obligations. The future holds as much in the way of promise as it does in the way of problems.[9]

---

[9]Albert G. Holzinger, "Building the American future," *Nation's Business,* March 1992, pp. 18–26.

Society can expect new products for physical fitness and health care. In addition to exercise equipment, programs designed to enhance fitness while relieving stress will grow. Wilderness training programs, such as those initiated by Outward Bound, provide techniques for eliminating stress and building teamwork awareness. General Electric has a similar in-house training program for managers.

People are developing healthy habits, including the foods they eat. Cereal marketers are producing more whole grain and fiber rich products for a growing, health-conscious market. A greater number of fruit bars without sugar are appearing in the frozen dessert sections. Magazines and cookbooks featuring lighter, fat free eating are selling well, and gourmet stores specializing in healthful foods are popping up across the continent. Meatless recipes appear regularly in *Bon Appetit, Gourmet* and *Cooks,* and vegetarian restaurants are common.

One firm has been very successful by concentrating on egg substitutes and meat alternatives. Worthington Foods Inc., a pioneer in health foods, started selling its soybean-based meat alternatives to religious groups over fifty years ago. The company now distributes its Morningstar line through supermarkets, but faces a battle with the major food marketers trying to find shelf space.[10]

In addition to changing the way we eat, we are changing the way we spend our free time. As manufacturing diminishes in importance and as technology expands, fewer people will produce more products. The number of hours that people spend at work will diminish, creating additional leisure time and recreational activities. Demand for both the space and the equipment needed for the enjoyment of this added time will increase.

Developments in Education

As our economy expands into new areas, including health care, wellness and leisure time, trained marketers will be needed. Hospitals and medical clinics embrace a more marketing oriented operation as competition among service providers grows. In a field where few practitioners have much in the way of a business background, a void of marketing people exists. As an example, a noted doctor in the Northwest pioneered and perfected treatment for endometriosis, and then sent an assistant through a college marketing program to learn how to promote this breakthrough.

Success stories in the wellness arena abound. Equipment manufacturers, such as Nautilus and Nordic Trak, blossomed as exercise became an important part of most people's lives. Programs in wellness and leisure studies are cropping up at universities nationwide. Businesses, realizing the importance of healthy employees, include exercise and fitness as part of their human resources agenda. Marketing positions in companies involved with recreation and health service are becoming plentiful.

---

[10]Richard Phalon, "Thin in the wrong places," *Forbes,* June 8, 1992, pp. 62–66.

Marketing and Society: Taking It Off!

There is probably no group of people in the world more obsessed with getting thin than Americans. Of course, there is probably no group that should be more concerned. A major direction of the wellness movement focuses on weight loss, as added emphasis is placed on no-fat or low-fat diets. Eating well has become an important part of living well. Dieting is no longer just a cosmetic treatment.

Capitalizing on the increased awareness of good health and fitness, weight reduction devices and diet centers sprouted like weeds. Some of the more intense programs include counseling, exercise and special foods sold exclusively by those organizations. One of the simpler methods for getting off those extra pounds is to select a can of flavored powder or frozen dinner off the supermarket shelf. Advertising for these quick fix types of products are under scrutiny by the FTC to assure that no exaggerated claims are being made.

Therein comes the rub. Most of the special diets offered by companies such as Nutri/System Incorporated and Jenny Craig Incorporated are quite expensive. The recession that led off the 1990s made it difficult for some would-be skinny minnies and Jack Sprats to maintain the programs. The federal government entered the fray to question the results of some treatments. The Federal Trade Commission, for instance, required advertising for weight loss programs to show representative samples of their clients, not just the stars. In addition, the FTC is conducting ongoing investigations of the entire diet product industry.

SOURCES: Larry Armstrong and Maria Mallory, "The diet business starts sweating," *Business Week*, June 22, 1992, pp. 32–33; Cyndee Miller, "Anti-diet forces, health report assail weight-loss programs," *Marketing News*, May 25, 1991, pp. 1 and 14.

Emphasis on Environmental Solutions

The protection of our environment is a major issue for everyone. No society and no economy can escape this responsibility. As the realization of potential damage to our ecosystems emerge, individuals and governments join in the search for solutions. While not everyone agrees with either the causes or the solutions, assuring environmental safety creates needs in many marketing areas. Sometimes the solutions are neither easy nor pleasant. For example, the 1990 Clean Air Act forces major bread bakers to eliminate the emission of ethanol which is a natural result of the baking process. Gone, too, will be the marvelous aroma enjoyed by many.[11]

Businesses are more aware than ever of the need to clean up the processes and the products that threaten air and water pollution. While addressing the issues of environmental protection, many firms realize gains in efficiency and lower costs. For example, Carrier Corporation in spending $500,000 to eliminate toxic lubricants found an annual saving in production costs in excess of $1.2 million. By eliminating an ozone depleting chemical from its printed circuit board manufacturing process, AT&T cut $3 million per year in expenses.[12]

Another company that has accepted its environmental responsibility is Marcal Paper Mills, a small New Jersey paper towel and bathroom tissue marketer. Scooping industry giants Kimberly-Clark and Procter & Gamble, Marcal heeded the plea from local post office officials regarding the disposal of undeliverable, third class mail. Overcoming the hurdle of the windows and gummed labels found on much of this mail, the company developed methods to recycle these paper goods.[13]

No area of the globe is in greater need for cleanup than Eastern Europe. Under the restrictive regimes of the past, these countries paid little heed to the damage being done to the atmosphere and to water supplies. Industrial production by smoke-belching, coal-burning factories sooted the skies. Rivers and streams were used for little more than sewers. Much work is to be done as these economies emerge into free markets, and control over the environment in Eastern Europe will tax the abilities of businesses and marketers worldwide. Proactive thinking by individuals and companies is needed to solve the challenges of cleaning up our environments and protecting against future damage.

RELATIONSHIP MARKETING

Some experts say that the impersonalness of the high-tech movement creates the need for more individual contact. Others claim that mass marketing and mass advertising has lost its momentum and appeal. Whatever the reasons, relationship marketing has arrived. By increasing direct contact with customers, firms establish bonds akin to that achieved with personal selling. In the attempt to communicate more on a one-to-one basis with their customers, marketers search for ways to promote directly.

[11]Charles McCoy, "Businesses are battling environmentalism with its own laws," *The Wall Street Journal,* April 28, 1994, pp. A1–A6; Bridget O'Brien, "An illegal pleasure: The smell in the bread being baked," *The Wall Street Journal,* April 13, 1994, p. A1.

[12]William K. Reilly, "Environment Inc.," *Business Horizons,* March-April 1992, pp. 9 Winsemius and Ulrich Guntram, "Responding to the environmental challenge," *Business Horizons,* March-April 1992, pp. 12–20.

[13]Terry Lefton, "A thrifty green brand called Marcal," *Adweek's Marketing Week,* 1992, p. 6.

Marcal, a paper products marketer in New Jersey, recycles undeliverable third class mail for use in its products.

Emphasis is switching from customer acquisition to customer retention. Once again, the computer proves to be the instrument of change. The ease of building and maintaining data bases simplifies the use of relationship marketing. Kimberly Clark, the giant disposable diaper manufacturer, sends letters to expectant mothers regarding the care and feeding of infants. After the child is born, coded coupons for the firm's Huggies brand trace the effectiveness of the contacts from the database. This is a good example of relationship marketing.[14]

Relationship marketing also relates to communicating with customers after the sale. Production goods marketers rely on such post-sale attention as a matter of course. Keeping the same types of communication lines open in consumer goods markets was difficult before the advent of computers, laser readers and toll-free telephone numbers. Today, most major trade goods marketers depend on customer information files.[15]

Customer service is a natural result of relationship marketing. Retailers and business goods marketers alike realize that happy customers become return buyers. Businesses can no longer survive by smugly hiding behind policies that do not provide service as well as products. Marketers are learning that products alone do not produce satisfaction. Buyers who are treated fairly and happily want to return.[16]

[14]Jonathan R. Copulsky and Michael J. Wolf, "Relationship marketing: Positioning for the future," *Journal of Business Strategy,* July/August 1990, pp. 16–20.

[15]Terry G. Vavra, *After-marketing* (Homewood, IL: Business One Irwin, 1992).

[16]Barry Farber and Joyce Wycoff, "Customer service: Evolution and revolution," *Sales & Marketing Management,* May 1991, pp. 44–48.

COLLABORATIVE MARKETING

In this age of super-competition, one might have trouble visualizing two or more rival companies working cooperatively on a project. Not so in today's markets where joint ventures are common. General Motors and Toyota got together years ago to form NUMMI for the manufacture of Novas. In the auto industry, Ford and Mazda have a smooth running relationship, and Nike and Coke collaborate on a variety of sports related promotions. The agreement between computer giants IBM and Apple is another example of collaborative marketing.

Many of today's collaborative efforts find competitors sharing their prowess for increased marketability. Movie studio Pathé Entertainment joined with Bantam Books to promote the movie based upon John LeCarré's book, *The Russia House*. Kmart and Little Caesar's Pizza joined forces to set up fast-food operations in stores. One of Canada's largest brewers, Labatts, brews up Budweiser under a licensing agreement from Anheuser-Busch. In a move that benefits society as well as bottom lines, Toys 'Я' Us picks up the tab for playrooms in hospitals for pediatric patients when the medical facility buys the playthings from the donor.[17]

DIRECT MARKETING

Another growth area in marketing is selling to consumers without the use of stores, or **direct marketing.** The development of fiber optics and digital transmission has been instrumental in the tremendous increase in this shopping medium. Video shopping is already offering 24–hour shows, and a union of television and computer has made an electronic catalog viable. The breakup of AT&T marked a starting point in the direct marketing revolution because it opened the door for electronic competition.

Direct marketing— marketing to the ultimate consumer or user without the use of stores.

Direct marketing allows consumers to purchase products in the comfort of their homes. This form of retailing is one of the fastest growing segments of marketing. Customers may respond to promotions received through the mail, by television, or over the telephone. Many direct marketers also run retail operations through stores and outlets. Talbot's, Eddie Bauer and Banana Republic are major catalog retailers that also have stores in malls.

A company that can deal directly with the ultimate consumer often feels as though it has a closer touch on the pulse of the market. Marketing research can be simplified and enhanced by gathering and recording the information built into the selling medium. Demographic data can be collected at the time of sale, instead of hoping that a card might be returned after the consumer receives the product.

Direct marketing also offers the consumer some benefits. Many discount operations are switching to this method for shoppers. Dial-A-Mattress sells top-of-the-line beds for considerably less than the average department or furniture store, and this retailer also delivers. Many of these types of appliance

---

[17]Matthew Grimm, "Dream Team II?" *BRANDWEEK*, February 15, 1993, pp. 1 and 6; Allan J. Magrath, "Collaborative marketing comes of age—again," *Sales & Marketing Management*, September 1991, pp. 60–64.

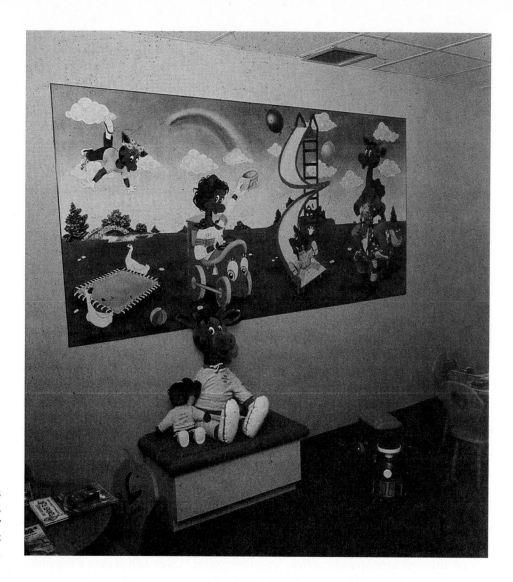

Toys 'Я' Us, the world's largest toy retailer, sponsors hospital play rooms for pediatric patients.

and decorating outlets have a Spartan appearance and may offer little sales assistance, but for bargain hunters, the price is right.[18]

The financial-services industry, once thought of by many as stuffy as their banking cousins, uses direct response advertising with great success. Respondents clip coupons from print ads or telephone 800 numbers to receive information and place orders. Most brokerage houses now require extensive telemarketing training for their salespeople. These services are used to educate and inform potential investors, rather than to just drum up business with hot tips.[19]

[18]Patricia Sellers, "A 1990s consumer goes shopping," *Fortune,* July 29, 1991, p. 122.
[19]Judy Abel, "For the love of money," *Adweek's Marketing Week,* April 27, 1992, pp. 26–27.

How Do Marketers Prepare for the Future?

Trends are not overnight events. Many marketers caution about jumping on bandwagons prematurely, but on the other hand, firms that miss opportunities rarely get second chances. The planning model previously described is a good guide toward preparing for the future. There is no substitute for knowing your strengths and weaknesses when planning marketing growth.[20]

Opportunities for using marketing know-how continue to grow. As dynamic changes impact society, the need for some goods and services will increase, while the requirements for others will decline. Success in the marketplace of tomorrow requires a major planning effort. The marketers of the future will have to be flexible, creative and responsive.

ETHICAL CONSIDERATIONS

Savvy marketers will take advantage of the many opportunities heading their way in the twenty-first century. Technological advances make it easier for firms to know their markets and track company performance. These same electronic marvels can be used to the detriment of society and individuals. Protection of privacy will be a major issue as marketing moves toward and into the next era, and consumers, businesses and organizations struggle to combat unethical behavior.

The right to privacy extends beyond consumer markets to the workplace. Just as computer data bases have helped marketers get a better handle on their customers, these same means can be used to provide information about employees to overzealous managers. At one time, the Ford Motor Company sent social workers to employees' homes to determine their fitness for bonuses. Although those days are gone, employers do retain the rights to make background checks and conduct drug testing. Many of the issues relating to privacy rights have yet to be settled by the courts.[21]

Companies that violate the trust of buyers will lose customers. The change in attitude toward increased customer service and relationship selling applies to firms of any size. The small retailer must remain as conscious of customer relations as the giant corporation. The public is slowly, but ever so surely, refusing to let marketers get away with shoddy products, poor service, or deceptive advertising.

SOCIAL RESPONSIBILITY

More and more marketers follow the "Ben & Jerry's" formula. These two self-pronounced "hippies" created the ultimate in company philosophy. Simply

---

[20]Eric Miller, "What if they announced a trend and nobody came," *Sales & Marketing Management,* December 1991, pp. 112–113.

[21]Lee Smith, "What the boss knows about you," *Fortune,* August 9, 1993, pp. 88–93; K. Labrich, "The new crisis in business ethics," *Fortune,* April 20, 1992, pp. 167–176; F. K. Sonnenberg and B. Goldberg, "Business ethics: An oxymoron," *Industry Week,* April 6, 1992, pp. 53–54.

stated, Ben & Jerry's Homemade, Incorporated serves the community and makes a profit selling ice cream. In its mission statements, the company states it will make and distribute only the finest quality, all-natural product. It will also strive to improve the quality of life of society, creating financial rewards for its employees.[22]

Other marketers continue to become more socially conscious. Dayton Hudson, corporate owner of Target and Mervyn's, sponsors a "Child Care Aware" campaign. The firm donated startup costs of $2.8 million to provide information for parents and prospective parents regarding child care facilities. The effort helps to raise the quality of child care in America.[23]

hat Are Society's Concerns About Marketing?

While striving to satisfy needs, marketers sometimes go overboard. Through product development or excessive promotion, marketing may lead people to desire too much. The tendency to create the need to buy things becomes especially annoying when a significant portion of society struggles to buy the basics and cannot afford more attractive products. Although products can and do enhance people's lives, they do little to improve the nonmaterial needs of a society.

MATERIALISM

In an economy with a high standard of living, the marketing system supplies the goods and services that the population enjoys. However, the same system can affect demand, hence promoting materialism. One of the primary characteristics of a free market society is the tremendous range and diversity of goods and services available to consumers and businesses. With the creation of such high demand for these products, production may increase to the point of over supply.

Marketers counter the charges of materialism by arguing that the consumer is the final judge. If buyers do not need or want the products, goods and services will not be bought. By hitting the producers where it hurts most, in the pocketbook, the buying public has the ultimate control over the number, as well as the types, of products offered for sale. Advocates of a lesser marketing effort argue that the system is too powerful to be controlled by the actions of buyers. Too many products and too much hype confuse consumers.

---

[22]"The iceman goeth," *The Economist,* June 18, 1994, p. 70; Suein L. Hwang, "While many competitors see sales melt, Ben & Jerry's scoops out solid growth," *The Wall Street Journal,* May 25, 1993, p. B1; Jennifer J. Laabs, "Ben & Jerry's caring capitalism," *Personnel Journal,* November 1992, pp. 50–57; Ben & Jerry's 1991 Annual Report.

[23]Gordon Oliver, "Child-care campaign kicks off in Portland," *The Oregonian,* July 14, 1992, p. B3.

Global Marketing: Made in Japan.

Japan does not have a corner on the market for new products. All of the major industrial nations produce their share of innovative and creative designers. The United States is renown as a leader in industrial engineering. The French have a reputation in the garment industry, and many interesting furniture creations come from Scandinavia. Germans are known for their engineering prowess, and a racier image follows Italian designers.

In the past few decades, Japanese industry developed an aura in electronics. Television, VCR, computer peripherals and camcorders are just a few products that people associate with Japan. Cameras, CD players, stereo equipment, and telephones also come to mind. And, of course, there is the automobile. Japanese carmakers have probably done more

to advance the art of this industry than any other group. Daihatsu, for example, is experimenting with a recyclable aluminum frame.

The Japanese economy was the first to adopt robotics for manufacturing. One Japanese firm, Tomy, markets a robot toy, complete with a radio controlled system that enables it to walk and nod to commands. Toshiba created a robotic hand that is so close to the real thing that it can write. Japanese designers also create some very functional, yet beautiful, products such as glassware and china. Pentax markets flexible, twistable eyeglass frames made from nickel-titanium.

SOURCE: *Business Tokyo*, April and May 1992, pp. 10–14.

POWER

Marketing can lead to the creation of **power,** becoming an awesome force in fashioning opinions. The most visible source of strength can be found in the clout created from advertising dollars. When major, consumer products marketers spend billions with television, radio, magazine and newspaper, critics argue that editorial content of those media is influenced. When a woman wearing no makeup was featured on the cover of a popular womens' publication, many cosmetics advertisers canceled their ads. Market dollars do exert some influence over editorial content.

As marketing contributes to the growth and recognition of business interests, government officials are pressured by lobbyists to argue the cases for these wealthy contributors. On the other hand, despite pressure by business interests in the heavy industry centers, Congress voted for stringent air quality controls. Although lawmakers do not always move rapidly when confronted with powerful business interests, citizens groups have proven to be an important counterforce to bring about change.

MARKETING TO CHILDREN

Marketing to **children** is big business. The spending power of children is awesome, and almost all of the typical child's income is discretionary. Although having complete control over the moneys they spend, most children are unable to differentiate between desire and need. Marketing aimed at influencing children often contributes to stress in parent/child relationships.

Some companies target schools as a place to begin developing brand loyalty, and are often accused of being exploitative. Posters and photos adorn classroom walls, all with the prominent logo of the supplying firm. Some questionable marketers supply study guides or educational materials that are blatantly commercial. Other products offer kids coupons on its packaging that can be traded for computer equipment. Such aggressive marketing to children can create strong public backlash.[24]

One company that couples good marketing and children is Sylvania. This light bulb marketer launched a major program urging Americans to turn off television and turn on a lamp to read a book. Although the promotion aimed at adults, the buyers of light bulbs, children were the recipients of its benefits. Sylvania coupled the advertising campaign with a number of other promotional schemes that generated funds for books for school systems and libraries.[25]

Overuse of Television

An average child watches twenty-eight hours of television per week, and approximately 15 to 20 percent of the material viewed is advertising. Research shows

Parker Brothers leads the parade in marketing safe, entertaining toys and games for children of all ages. (Courtesy of Parker Brothers)

[24]Alice Z. Cuneo, "Not in my house, parent exclaims," *Advertising Age,* February 14, 1994, p. S12; James U. McNeal, "Kids: The new big spenders," *The Oregonian,* November 27, 1992, pp. C1 and 6; Laurie Petersen, "Risky business: Marketers make a beeline for the nation's schools," *Adweek's Marketing Week,* May 14, 1990, pp. 18–22; Christine Donahue, "A limit on children's advertising," *Adweek's Marketing Week,* July 17, 1989, p. 2.

[25]Laurie Petersen, "Sylvania's pitch to keep the reading lamp lit," *Adweek's Marketing Week,"* February 10, 1992, p. 9.

that young viewers are especially affected by commercials and that small children want almost everything they see promoted on the tube. In addition, a 1993 survey by EDK Forecast found that a majority of parents will buy once their kids start clamoring. Children may also be influenced by "adult" ads. Commercials for patented medicines can leave the impression on young minds that a pill can make the difference between suffering and feeling good.[26]

Tobacco and Alcohol Promotion

Many groups place wine cooler and beer advertising in the same distasteful category as marketing directed toward children. Some feel that alcohol purveyors are improperly influencing young adults. Although the industry adopted a voluntary policy to use no models under the age of twenty-five in commercials, some beverage marketers obviously skirt that credo. Molson Ice from Miller Brewing came under fire in 1994 for clearly showing its alcohol content, a violation of federal law. Because of this abuse and consumer concern, federal and state governments are looking at limiting or eliminating all ads for alcoholic beverages.[27]

Tobacco marketers are increasingly under fire. Although smoking continues to show a decline, a concerned public sees an apparent effort to lure the younger audience. Joe Camel, the symbol for Camel cigarettes, is a topic for debate because of the brand recognition it creates in children. Tobacco symbols and logos on T-shirts and other apparel is under fire. The increased use of snuff, or smokeless tobacco, worries health minded publics.[28]

To Whom Are Marketers Responsible?

There was a day when marketers needed only to report to their management or to stockholders. If the good or service produced satisfaction among buyers and profit to the company, marketers must be doing their jobs well. Such is not the case today. As the most visible of business activities, marketing carries the burden of being responsible to many publics. Still, the most viable and demanding of these groups are customers.

---

[26]Cyndee Miller, "Parents tend to buy what their children see on TV," *Marketing News,* January 31, 1994, p. 2; Laura Bird, "Gatorade for kids," *Adweek's Marketing Week,* July 15, 1991, pp. 4 and 5; Jon Berry, "Did marketers overhype the kids' market," *Adweek's Marketing Week,* December 12, 1990, pp. 18 and 19.

[27]Eben Shapiro, "Molson Ice ads raise hackles of regulators," *The Wall Street Journal,* February 25, 1994, pp. B1 and B6; R. E. Bunzel, "Industry faces ongoing beer ad threat," *Broadcasting,* December 2, 1991, p. 44.

[28]Kevin Goldman, "A stable of females has joined Joe Camel in controversial cigarette ad campaign," *The Wall Street Journal,* February 18, 1994, pp. B1 and B8; Fara Warner, "Novello throws down the gauntlet," *Adweek's Marketing Week,* March 16, 1992, pp. 4–5.

TO CUSTOMERS

Customers are of prime importance, but are not the only responsibility faced by marketing companies and people. In being accountable to the buyers of their goods and services, marketers have an obligation to present the marketing mix in a fair and ethical manner. Customers need to be satisfied, not duped.

The goal of customer satisfaction is reachable in different ways. Marketers within the same industry may use a variety of tactics to reach this end. Whatever the industry in which the marketer operates, the mission of satisfying customers does not justify the use of any available means. Customer satisfaction cannot be used as an excuse for unfair competition or misleading promotion.

Society has established systems of checks and balances, and when a business venture oversteps the bounds of proper ethics, consumers and users will react. Adverse public opinion can result in a negative image for the marketer, which in turn leads to loss of business. Penalties assessed by government for unethical behavior can be even more severe.

TO THE BUSINESS COMMUNITY

Another public that marketing serves is the **business community.** This responsibility includes the obligation to treat competitors fairly. No one argues against healthy rivalry which benefits consumer and business buyer alike. The competition that aims to destroy or undermine other businesses or products is predatory. Marketers that practice predatory pricing policies or inaccurate promotion can expect a reaction from the competition. These actions may be taken by the companies involved in the disagreement or instigated by government agencies.

Responsibility to other businesses requires more than practicing fairness with competitors. Each business entity is a member of its community. Stores and shops are part of the retail family and are citizens of the business district or planned shopping center where they are located. Marketers have an obligation that results from being citizens of these sub-societies, which include loyalty to the industry groups within which the firm operates. Dining establishments belong to restaurant associations, bankers are members of financial communities and manufacturers are responsible to industry trade groups. Firms that are part of such organizations are encouraged to conduct their business in a manner that does not tarnish the industry.

Unethical business practices are especially hard to police overseas. Many of the laws and mores of foreign countries differ from those found in the United States. Of special interest to the American drug industry is patent protection. For decades many global markets have not prosecuted local businesses for drug rip-off. Recent strong support from the federal government has won some battles against patent pirates overseas.[29]

---

[29]John Pearson, Geri Smith, Joseph Weber, and Mark Maremont, "The patent pirates are finally walking the plank," *Business Week,* February 17, 1992, pp. 125–127.

THE ADVERTISING PRINCIPLES
OF AMERICAN BUSINESS*

TRUTH

Advertising shall tell the truth, and shall reveal significant facts, the omission of which would mislead the public.

SUBSTANTIATION

Advertising claims shall be substantiated by evidence in possession of the advertiser and advertising agency, prior to making such claims.

COMPARISONS

Advertising shall refrain from making false, misleading, or unsubstantiated statements of claims about a competitor or his products or services.

BAIT ADVERTISING

Advertising shall not offer products or services for sale unless such offer constitutes a bona fide effort to sell the advertised products or services and is not a device to switch consumers to other goods or services, usually higher priced.

GUARANTEES AND WARRANTIES

Advertising of guarantees and warranties shall be explicit, with sufficient information to apprise consumers of their principal terms and limitations or, when space or time restrictions preclude such disclosures, the advertisement should clearly reveal where the full text of the guarantee or warranty can be examined before purchase.

PRICE CLAIMS

Advertising shall avoid price claims which are false or misleading, or savings claims which do not offer provable savings.

TESTIMONIALS

Advertising containing testimonials shall be limited to those of competent witnesses who are reflecting a real and honest opinion or experience.

TASTE AND DECENCY

Advertising shall be free of statements, illustrations or implications which are offensive to good taste or public decency.

* Adopted by the American Advertising Federation Board of Directors, March 2, 1984, San Antonio, Texas.

TO SOCIETY

Marketers have a responsibility to **society** as a whole. Our world, our country and our cultures depend upon ethical and competent behavior by business. Besides providing for an improved standard of living through satisfaction of needs, marketers must take a part in the preservation of the quality of life of its society by helping to protect its environments.

No society has succeeded in abolishing unethical behavior. The fact that some members have misbehaved is not grounds for mass punishment. Business suffers from the actions of dishonest members. The insider trading scams of the 1980s have left a bad taste with many. The companies for whom these con artists were employed have suffered through embarrassment and loss of customers. Although many of those involved in shady dealings have served time in prison, few have paid the total amount of the assessed fines.

The banking industry was rocked by scandal in the early 1990s. Bank and savings and loan failures ran considerably higher than normal, causing bailouts by the federal government using taxpayers' money. The banking crisis touched the political arena, involving a number of ranking senators and other government officials. All of these failings of businesses and business people affect public opinion.

What is Responsible Marketing?

Marketing has both critics and supporters. Criticism of marketing practices can strengthen the industry. Public assessment provides the impetus to management to correct or modify the marketing mix and business operations. Without such continuous evaluation, marketing might not have progressed as far as it has, yet there is always room for improvement.

Responsible marketing—providing products to satisfy customer needs while benefiting society.

Marketers have the opportunity to assume a major role in educating the business community in the area of **social responsibility.** Making a profit is no longer enough. Goods and services must be presented to needy markets in a manner that benefits a full range of society and future generations, not just those who buy and sell. The repercussions of any marketing move need to be analyzed before the products reach the markets, not after.

Many socially responsible firms believe that marketing is the most visible part of their businesses. With this visibility comes responsibility. When all the world can observe their actions, wise marketers strive to assure that they receive applause, not brickbats. Marketing wields the power to bring about change and innovation, and has the responsibility to do so.

WITH PRODUCTS

The product is often a cause for complaint. Toys that fall apart and clothing that lasts only a few washings anger consumers. The lack of service availability for the repair of damaged or inoperative products is another concern. Buyers rightfully expect the things they purchase to be safe, durable and useful. Packages that misrepresent the products or that fail to protect the contents frustrate buyers.

Planned obsolescence—products that have limited life, forcing customers to buy replacements.

Planned Obsolescence

An additional complaint about automobiles and other products is what buyers call **planned obsolescence.** This phrase means that marketers sell products that are

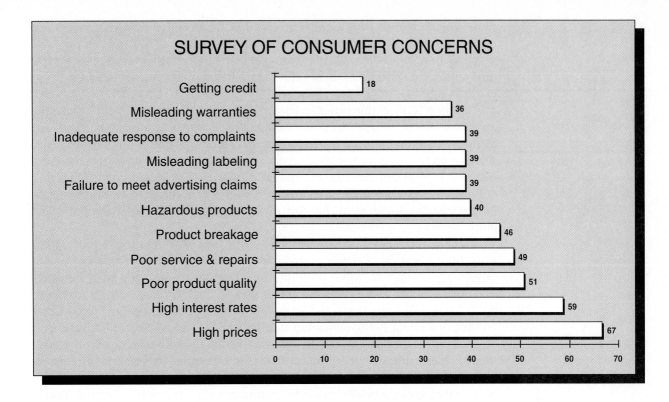

SURVEY OF CONSUMER CONCERNS

Concern	Value
Getting credit	18
Misleading warranties	36
Inadequate response to complaints	39
Misleading labeling	39
Failure to meet advertising claims	39
Hazardous products	40
Product breakage	46
Poor service & repairs	49
Poor product quality	51
High interest rates	59
High prices	67

known to have limited life, forcing buyers to purchase replacements. Consumers become irate when the transmission fails or the brakes go out just after the warranty expires. These same customers often fail to recall the years of good service provided by many products. Cars are not the only recipients of consumer ire. Toasters, washing machines, table saws, television sets and computers from a variety of different manufacturers have been targets of buyer hostility.

On the other hand, many consumer goods have records of excellent quality and service. Lexus and Mercedes continue to rank high among auto buyers for their overall quality and resale value. Among major appliances, Maytag is renown for its durability, and many retailers, large and small, are noted for good customer service and generous warranty policies.

Product safety is a matter of concern for marketers. Since the Tylenol scare, several companies have come under public scrutiny. A positive result of package tampering is that manufacturers have increased efforts to develop safe packages. Tops of closures that pop up when the vacuum seal has been broken and tough plastic sealing strips around jar lids are becoming common. These actions by responsible marketers coupled with stiffening federal laws can help eliminate tampering.

WITH PROMOTION

Many legislators clamor for health warnings on all advertising for alcoholic beverages. Additional flak is being fired at brewers by consumers incensed over the use of scantily clad females to promote their products. Sexual harassment charges filed against Stroh's for that company's commercials featuring the Swedish Bikini Team led to further outcry about the "bimboism" used by beer marketers. The major player in this market, Anheuser-Busch, announced in 1992 that it would eliminate exploitation of women in its advertising.[30]

At one time, women in advertising were rarely portrayed without wearing an apron. Today, females in promotional efforts appear as attorneys, pilots and business executives. Blacks, Hispanics, Asians and other ethnic groups, once missing from advertising's portrayals of consumers, now take their rightful places on television screens and magazine pages. The stereotyping of men in commercials is also under attack. Men's Rights Incorporated vigorously campaigns against advertising that portrays men as "jerks," citing the television work for Kellogg's Nutri-Grain cereals as an example.[31]

Many advertising people still follow the "sex sells" motto. Without question, pretty bodies of either gender are attention grabbers. Some of today's advertisers attempt to add a bit of humor to sexual scenes. The Sansabelt television commercials built around the slogan "what women look for in men's pants" received both raves and pans. Former pro-football center Randy Cross complained about being unknown in a Miller Light ad, but when he bent over to pick up a dropped purse he was immediately recognized by a woman patron. Men's Rights Incorporated made no comment on either of these presentations.

Social responsibility is gaining ground among advertisers. General Motors spends advertising dollars promoting the use of seat belts in automobiles. Several brewers, including Coors, promote the responsible use of alcoholic beverages. Texize and Maxell have joined Project Kids-Care in spreading the word among children and parents on avoiding drug abuse. Ralston Purina sponsors the Pets for People program, especially targeted toward the elderly. Georgia-Pacific offers premiums of stuffed animals representing endangered species on its packages of MD bathroom tissue, donating the proceeds to The World Wildlife Fund.

What Are the Rewards for Social Responsibility?

Historically, marketing has fueled our standard of living. Today, marketers are learning that protection and promotion of the quality of life as an integral part of our standard of living have become major objectives. This goal enhances the aim of customer satisfaction. By producing safe products while protecting the environment, business people assure that their markets will not diminish. These are the tasks of socially responsible marketers.

[30]Matthew Grimm, "Bud, Coors mull 'media' strategy to blunt critics," *Adweek's Marketing Week,* November 11, 1991, p. 5.

[31]Mary Jung, "Watchdog group lashes out at ads that demean men," *Marketing News,* March 27, 1989, pp. 2 and 21.

Brewing beer has been a

topic of conversation around my family's

house since I can remember.

SO BELIEVE ME,

I know you might think about

drinking before you're 21.

But do us

AND **YOURSELF** A

favor, *please don't.*

We'll wait for your business.

Pete Coors, Coors Brewing Company

For more information on Coors Alcohol Programs
and Policies, call **1-800-328-6785.**

© 1994 Coors Brewing Company, Golden Colorado 80401

Many marketing orient-
ed companies spend
advertising dollars to
promote socially
responsible causes,
such as this timely
example from Coors.

PUBLIC OPINION

Negative **public opinion** is disastrous for marketers. An easy way to reverse
this powerful force is to practice social responsibility. The creation of beneficial, safe and durable products, and the practice of protecting the environment will do much to satisfy a demanding buying public. With so many

Public opinion—
either positive or
negative reaction of
the public at large to
business operations.

goods and services from which to choose, the power of the consumer cannot be denied.

In free market economies, consumer sovereignty is a powerful energy when unleashed against irresponsible marketers. Not only can public opinion affect specific products, it can be used as a deterrent for irresponsible marketing. Led by consumer organizations, many buyers boycott products marketed by companies that have acted irresponsibly. Pressure from competitors and industry associations is often brought to bear on poor performers because one unsafe toy hurts the entire industry, not just the manufacturer of the defective product.

ECONOMIC FREEDOM

Economic freedom— business operations that are generally unconstrained by government action.

The **economic freedom,** with businesses enjoying freedom from government intervention, may be at stake. Socially responsible marketing behavior could be the major factor in saving business as we know it. The cooperative effort among manufacturers, marketers, consumers and regulatory agencies is needed to preserve the environment and culture desired by society. To gain these benefits, social responsibility has become an integral part of any marketing program.

Perhaps it is time to restate the marketing concept, bringing it in line with today's politically correct thinking. Those businesses that channel all of their efforts towards the satisfaction of customer needs *in a socially responsible manner* are endowed with the marketing concept.

SUMMING IT UP

The continued deindustrialization of the American economy will exert influence on marketing. The information age provides new opportunities in artificial intelligence, and additional high-tech developments will produce change in the ways that business conducts business. The impact of the global economy will grow as greater opportunities in foreign business appear at home and abroad.

The quality movement has arrived. Total quality management places the emphasis on empowering employees to provide customer service. Added emphasis on health and wellness brings increased potential for marketing, as does environmental concern. Relationship marketing, collaborative marketing and direct marketing provide new thinking as to the way marketing operates within businesses and in the economy.

In preparing for these future developments, marketers must heed ethical restrictions and develop social responsibility. Concerns about materialism and the abuse of power must be addressed. Marketing to children, especially in the areas of overuse of television presents an increasing concern to parents. Tobacco and alcohol promotion will change. Marketers are being pressured to be responsible to customers, the business community and society. Responsible marketing addresses the issues of product and promotion while seeking the rewards of positive public opinion and economic success freedom.

KEY CONCEPTS AND TERMS FROM CHAPTER NINETEEN

Deindustrialization
Direct marketing
Economic freedom
Global economy

Information age
Public opinion
Responsible marketing
Total quality management

BUILDING SKILLS

1. Discuss the effects of deindustrialization, the information age, global economy, and health and wellness on the future of marketing.

2. Define and contrast relationship, collaborative and direct marketing.

3. Describe some specific products that have been unsatisfactory, pointing out the methods used to purge them from the market.

4. Give some examples of advertising that is "unfit for human consumption," including the specific reasons for this criticism. In contrast, cite some examples of artistic, moving or entertaining ads, explaining the basis for your praise.

5. Describe the ways that government can best interact with business in promoting responsible marketing.

6. Discuss some businesses that have behaved in a marketing sense that shows social responsibility.

Making Decisions 19-1: I've got your number.

There was a time when we could all be relatively assured that a person could lead a private life if desired. Granted, social security numbers could give government agencies a certain amount of information about an individual, but that was somewhat limited. Certainly no one suspected that companies could gain access to personal information such as birthdays, buying preferences or lifestyle. NOT! The magic of the computer has spawned database marketing, and today's marketers know a lot about a lot of people.

Database marketing, as it is called, simply means using the information collected and stored by a variety of businesses to direct personal promotional effort toward individuals. The storage capabilities of these systems is staggering, and this ability to collect and retrieve data quickly and accurately allows marketers to pinpoint target markets at will. Rather than use the shotgun approach that advertising generally provides, the promoter of today can direct messages to specific individuals. Subscribe to a magazine and do not be surprised to find an ad for Toyota or Kraft General Foods using your name.

Much of the increase in database information comes from credit cards. When applying for plastic money, individual applicants must provide rather detailed information. Notice how many marketers now promote their own Visa or MasterCard cards. The GM or the BP Oil credit card gives these companies access to that information. Use that bit of plastic to verify a check while buying groceries, for example, and suddenly the products you buy become database fodder available to anyone who has the key. Similarly, send in a warranty, enter a contest or join a consumer group and your life unfolds in a computer memory system.[32]

Comment on the ways that technology influences marketing today and the ethical consequences to those using such technology.

Making Decisions 19-2: Pursuing the Cure.

Medical science never stops researching for wonder drugs, nor should it. There was a time when most of the exploratory effort was found in universities and hospitals. Today, the lure of profit transfers those activities to private industry. Biotech is big business and is growing rapidly. Companies involved with basic research used to number in the dozens. Now such firms are cropping up everywhere. Armed with large staffs or fistfuls of chemists and doctors, these pioneering businesses seek the answers to humankind's diseases and problems.

Bristol-Myers Squibb is a giant in this industry. The firm is one of the leaders in seeking to synthesize taxol, the cancer fighting element found in the bark of yew trees. Ironically, the source of this promising drug lies in the spotted owl habitat of the Pacific Northwest. The federal government faces

---

[32]Jonathon Berry, John Verity, Kathleen Kerwin, and Gail DeGeorge, "Database marketing," *Business Week*, September 5, 1994, pp. 56–62.

the dilemma of appeasing the environmentalists by protecting the old growth forests or allowing harvest of this species. It takes three mature yew trees to produce enough taxol for a single treatment, making its costs prohibitive. If scientists can create a synthetic equivalent, thousands of lives may be saved.

Cancer is not the only plight that medical research tackles. Diseases affecting the brain, notably Alzheimer's and Parkinson's are also major targets. Regeneron Pharmaceuticals Incorporated is one of a small group of research firms focusing on the brain. This firm is a leader in the development of ciliary neurotrophic factors, CNTF, for treatment of Lou Gehrig's disease. Regeneron expects to have similar drugs to treat Alzheimer's and Parkinson's victims by the mid–1990s.[33]

Equate the marketing mix to firms conducting basic medical research.

Making Decisions 19-3: Demons Begone!

Bugs are everywhere. Getting rid of them safely is a universal problem. Many of the insecticides produced in the fifties and sixties have proven to be unsafe for humans. DDT contamination still exists throughout the world, even though that chemical killer is no longer in use. The insecticide industry has made great strides in developing safer products, yet these chemicals are still tricky to handle and difficult to control.

This was the problem facing ICI Americas Incorporated manufacturers of Demon brand roach insecticide. The product, a very fine powder, is mixed with water by extermination contractors. A dispenser had to be created that would keep the product and the final solution off the hands of the workers and surrounding area. ICI Americas selected the industrial design team headed by Peter Bressler. The final product won a gold in the 1992 Industrial Design Excellence Awards (IDEA).

Since the dispenser was given away with jugs of the insecticide, it had to be inexpensive. Working closely with their client, BresslerGroup designed a stopper-like apparatus that fits the top of the insecticide container. Tipping the jug over, the exterminator twists the dispenser filling it with the precise amount of roach-killer. The dispenser is then placed over the water container, and another twist drops the powder into the liquid. No mess, no fuss, no danger. The dispenser is designed to visually communicate its operations, so that no complicated directions are necessary. What's more, the whole thing is recyclable.[34]

Comment on how the concepts of relationship marketing, collaborative marketing, the wellness movement and social responsibility relate to the Demon Dispenser.

---

[33]Gene Bylinsky, "The race for a rare cancer drug," *Fortune,* July 13, 1992, pp. 100–102; Fleur Templeton, "Regeneron has research on the brain," *Business Week,* July 27, 1992, pp. 78–79.

[34]Bruce Nussbaum, "Flub-proof bug control," *Business Week,* June 8, 1992, pp. 58–59.

Marketing in Practice: Careers and Entrepreneurship in Marketing

What is Needed for a Career in Marketing?

The field of marketing offers a wide variety of occupations. These positions are especially geared for the knowledge, talents and training that marketing people possess or acquire. As in any career position, good communication skills are necessary for success in finding the right employment opportunity and for advancing within a given company or field.

In the marketing arena, people skills are especially important. The ability to work with others and deal with the problems of customers or suppliers is necessary in carrying out the day-to-day tasks of a marketing job. Whether working in sales for a production goods marketer, as a continuity director for a member of the media or in the traffic department of a wholesaler, people in marketing are typically "people people."

While the skills and knowledge gained at college are important in finding a position and performing well on the job, most careers in marketing are specialized. Degrees in this field are not mandatory. Many firms are looking more closely at liberal arts majors, preferring people with a broad, unconcentrated education. In either case, specific training will be provided on the job. One gains specific job-oriented knowledge more through experience than through education.

What Types of Marketing Jobs Are Available?

Although the job titles and descriptions will vary from industry to industry and firm to firm, there are some general categories of positions that are somewhat similar. The list of opportunities presented in the next section does not attempt to be exhaustive or exclusive. Under the broad subjects of product, price, distribution and promotion, the list provides general job description. As they relate to the marketing mix categories, specific industries and business areas are also suggested.

Many of the positions are managerial, and most new employees will not start at such an elevated level. Depending upon the size of the firm, many openings for assistant managers or management trainees may exist. The general duties will be similar in each case, with the degree of authority and responsibility being the major distinction between grades.

IN THE PRODUCT FIELD

Product management—often called brand managers, people qualifying for this position usually have considerable company and product knowledge. Although not always necessary, a bachelor's degree is commonly required, and some larger firms prefer an MBA. These people typically manage the complete marketing mix for the individual product assignment. Management trainees and assistants often work on branding, warranty policy, or product enhancement. Specific jobs may also be available in production areas that relate to product design or development.

Packaging specialist—This position may be highly technical in nature. With major consumer product manufacturing firms, packaging experts are likely to be designers as well as marketers. People in these positions must be well acquainted with legal restrictions regarding the use of materials and disposability. Not all packaging jobs require design or engineering skill. Many product management trainees start out in the packaging area, working in areas such as test marketing or sampling programs.

Market researcher—People in this field usually have at least a bachelors degree, but there are a number of rewarding opportunities open to "people people" as survey conductors. Whether working for independent agencies or as part of a marketing department, interviewers are in demand. Research analysts, those people who examine and evaluate data, usually have advanced degrees. Much of the report writing and data presentation may be performed by individuals without specific educational background.

Purchasing—Some of the more rewarding jobs in marketing are on the buying end instead of selling. Knowledge of marketing is a tremendous assistance to this position. Jobs in purchasing are open in the organizational goods arena and with intermediaries. Some experience in sales serves as an excellent background for purchasing, but no specific educational requirements may be necessary. Excellent pay and advancement opportunities are available through purchasing, especially in retail buying. Consumer goods merchandisers, especially in the garment industry, are in demand. Buyers usually spend a training period in sales before joining the buying ranks, but this step will depend upon individual firms.

Service sector—This area offers an excellent opportunity for marketers, especially in nonbusiness or nonprofit organizations. Professional offices, government agencies and hospitals are all becoming more marketing oriented, as are attorneys, health centers and clinics, and local and federal government agencies. The tourist industry deserves special note. Hotels, resorts, restaurants and parks all require the type of talent usually associated with marketers. Tourism is becoming a major factor in economic development throughout the United States, and marketing positions are plentiful. Even government agencies, such as the Forest Service and National Parks Service are employing marketers.

IN THE AREA OF PRICE

Credit manager—Most employees filling this position would typically have backgrounds in finance. Accountants and financial managers are typically hired in credit positions, and, as a rule, people in these positions report to the Chief Financial Officer. In smaller firms, a person with a marketing background and an aptitude for numbers could lend a lot to this job. Employees with good people skills are often placed in credit departments as customer service representatives. These workers gain credit information from prospects, handle complaints and special requests from customers, and follow up on delinquent accounts.

Pricing specialist—Someone who truly understands economics has an unusual opportunity available in this position. Many large corporations hire "number crunchers" to help compute demand and price accordingly. Typically, a bachelors degree is necessary for this work. "Mystery shoppers" are often hired in the retail fields. These employees call on competitive stores to purchase products and/or note prices. Such positions inside the marketing operation serve as a continual check on service rendered by the retailer's selling staff.

IN DISTRIBUTION

Traffic manager—With large firms, these positions normally require bachelors degrees. Some management personnel rise up through the ranks, and experience is often as important as education. Typically, positions in traffic will include control of both incoming and outgoing freight. Many transportation companies and freight carriers hire people to call upon the traffic managers at shippers. These missionary sellers gain specifications from traffic departments for the use of a specific carrier or company.

Inventory control manager—Although inventory control managers are usually assigned to the production department, marketing background and aptitude would be helpful in this position. Typically, people working in inventory control forecast demand for on-hand inventories and process requisitions for replacements. In the age of just-in-time, this position receives more emphasis. Inventory control personnel work closely with marketing, sales and traffic departments as well as with production.

Warehouser—Assistant traffic management jobs often include starting in the warehouse. These positions are usually stepping stones toward higher positions, but are still rewarding. Scheduling shipments and receipt of cargo are extremely important parts of the marketing scheme. Warehouse management positions are also widespread in marketing intermediaries. Wholesalers and retailers both need accurate and efficient control of inventories. While automation has helped in reducing waste in and mishandling of orders, people must manage the systems.

Wholesale management—A variety of job opportunities exist in wholesaling. Management positions tend to relate to inventory control, sales, purchasing, and traffic. Depending upon the size of the firm, positions may be available for trainees or assistants in any of these areas. Good rapport with suppliers, customers, transportation carriers and local government agencies often dictates a need for marketing talent.

Retail management—The retail industry has a substantial need for management personnel. Many beginning retailers start out "on the floor" and leave the firm before the opportunity for advancement arrives. For those who stick it out there is an outstanding opportunity for financial and individual growth. As mentioned above, buyers are especially in demand in retail fields. Retailers in pharmaceuticals, hardware, automobiles, sporting goods and especially in the garment industry need good buying expertise. Many salespeople in the retail arena progress into buying positions with their firms or competitors.

IN THE PROMOTION FIELD

Sales—Most marketing managers begin in sales. Whether selling for a production goods marketer or merchandising for a trade goods house, boundless opportunities are available for salespeople. Selling is a rewarding marketing career, both in the way of advancement and from a compensation standpoint. A real problem solving and people pleasing attitude is a plus in sales positions.

Production goods marketers are a major job source. The typical salesperson for such companies goes through a training program, which may include inside selling, before being assigned to a sales territory. Advancement is often rapid and management opportunities are great. **Trade goods marketers** employ both active and passive sellers. Creative type salespeople are hired to service wholesaler and retailer accounts. Sales assisters, or merchandisers, typically call upon retailers to set up displays and arrange stock. Some firms use their salesforce to carry out both jobs.

The retail field can be especially lucrative for salespeople. Individuals who work on a commission basis for firms selling consumer services or large ticket consumer goods can make a fine living. While the hours are often long and the job trying, for those with the temperament and talent for selling, the rewards are great. Missionary sales positions are available in the pharmaceutical and building products industries. These salespeople call upon doctors and architects/engineers to gain specifications for their products. Often the positions lead to more active selling roles or management seats.

Customer service—Many career salespeople begin in customer service. Order handling and processing is a key area in this field. Telemarketing has moved the customer service specialist into the forefront of marketing effort.

Advertising—Typical positions in advertising range from account executive to copywriter to artist to media analyst. Many jobs require artistic or journalistic acumen, but some positions are open to people who are simply interested in promotion and who are people orientated. Employment is available in marketing departments of companies as well as with advertising agencies. Positions in advertising agencies can range from being strictly creative to people oriented. Any advertising venture needs copywriters and artists. Salespeople and account executives are also needed.

Media salespeople are in constant demand. The increasing numbers of radio and television stations and the host of publications require salespeople to survive. The opportunities for financial reward in this field are excellent. The advertising media also use traffic and continuity people, and any job in this arena can lead into management positions. Media buying experts work specifically on the placement end of advertising and can be employed by agencies or advertisers.

Sales promotion specialist—Although often linked with advertising, sales promotion can be a separate career field. Whether working for a consumer goods marketer or an advertising agency, sales promotion specialists work with design and in implementation. Artistic talent is not always needed for these positions. A strong marketing sense and an understanding of the client's products and distribution channels are helpful.

Journalism—Somewhat of a kissing cousin to marketing, journalism leads the way to many opportunities within the field of promotion. Ranging from speechwriters for politicians to public relations careers, people who can write, and who are marketing oriented, are in great demand. These positions can be with marketing firms or with advertising and public relations agencies.

ENTREPRENEURSHIP

Another avenue open to marketers is their own business venture. Not all marketing oriented people go to work for others. Many students, especially the nontraditional or older than average types, seem drawn toward going into business for themselves. While the hours are long and the risk is great, the rewards for entrepreneurs are great.

An entrepreneur is a person who turns an idea into a business venture. Innovative men and women abound in the United States. Each year over 600,000 Americans start their own businesses. Few succeed. Entrepreneurial ventures fail for many reasons. Lack of marketing planning is a major one. Whether introducing a new product or service or embarking on a new retail venture, marketing expertise can make a difference between success and failure.

Entrepreneurs are not limited to one industry or field. They abound wherever opportunity exists. The continuing rise in the service sector has spawned considerable entrepreneurial effort. As new products evolve in this and other technological areas, the need for service will continue. While marketing expertise is needed in all business ventures, the success of entrepreneurs is often directly attributable to their prowess in managing the product, its price, distribution systems and promotion.

The ability to establish plans and satisfy customer needs can be learned. The important first step is to assign proper significance to the **role of marketing.** The ability to attract loans or venture capital often depends upon having a good marketing program. Managerial skills are also important for entrepreneurs. These skills are necessary to run the marketing portion of the business and supervise personnel. Knowledge of marketing and its importance to the business plan is imperative to small business management.

Opening up a store or manufacturing facility may bring a sense of pride, but there is little point to being in business for oneself if no profit occurs. Understanding the need to satisfy is an important step on the road toward profitable operation. If the entrepreneurial venture involves a new product, little can be accomplished without a marketing plan. Entrepreneurs need to know where they are going, and the **marketing plan** is an effective device for showing the way. A marketing plan should be put together before investing money in the business effort. Attention must be paid to each element, and the plan must be committed to writing.

A **feasibility study** should be made prior to embarking on any entrepreneurial venture. SWOT analysis is just as important to small planners as it is for large firms. Determining the market dimensions and competitive threats in advance will help assure success. Whether checking the market needs for products or the potential success for a new store or shop, general information regarding the marketing area needs to be gathered. This step is also helpful in determining location for the venture, which is paramount in the retail trade.

Positioning is not a fancy concept reserved for major corporations. Every retail store has its image, and the way that a business positions itself in the minds of the customers may be the clue to success. In positioning, avoiding a "me too" image is important, no matter what the business venture. Entrepreneurs often owe their success to "going against the grain," or doing something different from the rest of the crowd. If the product is not significantly different or better than others on the market or if the store is similar to others in the area, it has little chance of success.

Timing is especially important to the implementation of the marketing plan. When the action is taken is often as important as what action is taken. All products or stores are vulnerable to competition. Sooner or later others will follow the path that the entrepreneur has forged. Being ready for the "new kids on the block" is better than being surprised. When products will be ready for sale and shipment and how that timetable will affect cash flow are important requirements for the entrepreneur. Promotion should not be undertaken until there is something to sell.

Many community colleges and universities provide service and consulting specifically for small businesses. **Small Business Development Centers** are staffed by professionals and assisted by capable volunteers ready to help put the entrepreneur on the road to profitability. Funded by both federal and state governments, SBDCs provide educational programs and consulting services for the benefit of small businesses. These training centers are chartered to provide assistance to existing firms and to new ventures. Another source of assistance is the Small Business Administration. Located in most metropolitan areas, this federal organization has information available to any business operation. From statistics about markets to financial goals for most types of business, the SBA can be a real partner.

How Does One Get a Job in Marketing?

The process for hiring in the marketing field is similar to that for other business positions. Typically, prospects make application, submit a résumé, and, hopefully, sit for interviews. When looking for work, there is no substitute for determination. Those who sit back and wait for an opportunity to happen normally miss the boat. While each position and each company will vary, there are some general rules for looking for employment that are good to follow. Preparation often means the difference between success and failure. Here are a few tips which might make the job search a little easier:

1. Know your desires and capabilities—The time to decide the type of field or position that might interest you is in advance of the interview. Check out the industry and the company before submitting an application. The research done in advance will also help later should an interview be granted. Preparing a personal inventory will assist in filling out applications and drawing up résumés.

2. Make résumés specific—Each job is different and the résumé should reflect this fact by being directed toward a specific position with a specific company. Mass produced résumés are often too general to be helpful when applying for a particular position. This tool should be specific, concise and attractive. Résumés get interviews. Interviews get jobs.

3. Be prepared—The job interview is a time for the applicant to learn about the company, as well as vice versa. Proper preparation allows the interviewee to ask intelligent and thoughtful questions, instead of merely being an answering machine. Homework done on the job and the company make the application sound and look more desirable.

SUMMING IT UP

Career opportunities in the marketing field have never been more plentiful. As our society becomes increasingly gripped by the marketing age and more businesses embrace the marketing concept, people with this background and interests become a valuable asset to any firm. Marketers are the backbone of any business or nonprofit organization.

Jobs in marketing are available in all industries and businesses. Work in product areas and pricing are just two of the opportunities. Distribution channels offer many employment slots. The promotion fields often provide the greatest number of openings for fledgling marketers, especially in the area of personal selling. As for specific industries, tourism and other service orientations are targeted for rapid expansion. Marketing opportunities abound everywhere, even in government agencies and professional services. Giving marketing its proper attention can be an important part of the success of any business and can bring gratification from the efforts of that business adventurer, the entrepreneur.

Appendix A

■ ■ ■ ■ ■ ■ ■ ■ ■ ■ ■ ■ ■ ■

Starship Takes a Nosedive!

The general aviation, or business aircraft, market has suffered much lately. From a peak in 1977, when almost 18,000 units were sold, sales fell to less than 1,000 in 1993—a loss of almost 95 percent of the market over a decade and a half. Most all of the major producers of these small airplanes—Cessna, Piper, Beech, Mooney—either suffered huge losses or went out of business. In 1989 Beech Aircraft, a division of Raytheon, made a bold move, and Starship was born.

From the outset, it was clear that this was more than a standard general aviation product. Researchers and engineers at Beech completely changed the design of business aircraft. To begin with, Starship is an all-composite airplane, made with plastics and carbon fibers. These space-age materials are three times stronger than aluminum, yet are lighter by almost twenty percent. The turbo-prop engines are mounted in the rear, almost eliminating noise.

The flight deck has so much space that it seems like a commercial airliner. The aerodynamics are outstanding, and initial test models handled like a dream. Pilots loved the airplane . . . but pilots don't buy, companies do! Still, most first-time buyers raved about the plane's comfort and stability. To say that the cabin is luxurious is like saying that Sophia Loren and Mel Gibson are fairly attractive people.

In spite of its striking good looks and many innovative features, Starship never really got off the ground. Beech sold less than half of the initial production run. Even an attractive leasing program brought few results. Many of these futuristic flyers are now gathering dust parked in hangars around the country. In the summer of 1994, Beech halted production. Although company officials still claim that the bird may be manufactured again, some day, no plans are in the offing for this most innovative of general aviation aircraft.

If the plane is that good, why is it a flop? To begin with, Beech ran afoul of government bureaucracy. Not having seen a plane of this nature before, FAA inspectors demanded changes, including the addition of metal support frames rather than the composite materials used throughout. Airplanes like Starship with wings in both the front and back cannot stall, yet the FAA required Beech to include heavy, costly anti-stall devices. These moves increased the weight of the plane, which in turn required larger engines, which in turn required more fuel, which in turn meant still more weight.

At that point, the FAA placed Starship in the commuter aircraft category, which meant that two pilots were required rather than one. With the additional weight and added costs, the price of the plane rose faster than its climbing speed. Soon the selling price rivaled that of jets, but with propeller driven performance. The company's initial plans to offer the market a state-of-the-art, high performance, moderately priced plane vanished. The plane took six years finally to get into production, and many original prospects canceled orders. Beech dealers, too, were disgruntled as the company tried to force policies on the distribution system that forced incomes and motivation down. In the fall of 1994, Raytheon announced the merger of its two aircraft units, Beech Aircraft Corporation and Raytheon Corporate Jets, into one entity, the Raytheon Aircraft Company.

Describe the environmental changes that both brought about the design of this innovative airplane and caused its demise. Analyze any changes in the marketing strategy that might have prevented the downfall of Starship.

etting the Big Picture!

Much to the delight of couch potatoes everywhere, television programs have increased tremendously in both quantity and quality over the last few decades. Pioneers in commercial broadcasting probably had no idea that the big box with the small black and white screen would become such an important part of American culture. Much of the rapid growth of television as an entertainment medium can be attributed to hardware innovations. Color, wide screens, improved clarity and satellite systems have vastly increased the number of viewing options and the quality of the presentations. Technological advances in the telecommunications industry, notably fiber optics, also contributed to this growth.

One of the latest moves in broadcast television is Direct Satellite Service, or DSS. Created by RCA, a division of French-owned Thompson Consumer Electronics, this innovation became operative late in 1994. Once one million units are sold, Sony will also be licensed to manufacture dish systems. With the ability to beam over 150 channels into a subscriber's home, this system promises to change the way that many view television. Featuring a satellite dish not much bigger than a large pizza, coupled with a receiver the size of a standard VCR, DSS produces uncanny video and audio reception. Clarity of picture and CD-quality sound have turned on early adopters. A clear, unobstructed path to the south is necessary to pick up the signals.

Although these systems are not inexpensive, many compare with standard cable. With initial installation included, subscribers must cough up close to $1,000. In addition, there is a standard monthly charge for programming. So far two firms, USSB and DirectTV, offer delivery of Digital Satellite Service. The former offers MTV, Comedy Central, HBO, Nickelodeon, Cinemax and Showtime, while DirectTV concentrates on sports, news and pay-per-view movies. The cost for viewers begins at under $8 a month, but, as with cable, most subscribers opt for more expensive packages. While DSS delivers a wide range of sporting events and entertainment programs, FCC regulations do not permit transmission of network or local broadcasting.

Initially, cable providers scoffed at this new development. Competitors also point out that foul weather can foul up reception from these 18-inch dishes. The inability of RCA to produce the units quickly and in quantity slowed the adoption process, feeding ammunition to competitors. Improved cable systems, such as Primestar, have been used to offset the initial clamor for DSS units. Most big cable operators, notably Time Warner, are increasing their capacity and working on quality. The competitive battle really boils down to one of price versus quality. For those consumers who relish the clarity of picture and superb sound reproduction offered by DSS, the high cost may be no barrier. Those who would rather play golf or tennis than watch all of the NFL football games would probably not buy the unit anyway.

Analyze and discuss the factors of consumer buying behavior that would influence the purchase of a DSS system. Describe the features of a marketing plan that might be used by a cable TV company in offsetting this competitive threat.

Snow's Up!

For any surfing enthusiast, riding the waves has produced a unique vocabulary. Who can forget the popular Hang Ten logo, referring to the placement of one's toes on a surfboard, appearing on sportswear through the 1960s and 70s? *Shredding* is another term with which most Generation X Southern Californians are quite familiar. Today, more shredders hang out on the ski slopes than at the beach, as snowboarding has become the "in" sport among young people. Although an increasing number of those who are older are strapping on these elongated skateboards without wheels, the typical snowboarder remains a male between the ages of 16 and 25, usually clad in a "grunge" outfit.

Snowboarding got its start during the 1980s, with manufacturers such as Burton leading the way. However, the big burst in the sport came early in the next decade when single-skiing literally exploded. Much of the impetus comes from non-skiers, especially from city kids who have mastered the techniques of skateboarding. Although the medium is different, many of the moves and the coordination required are similar. Skiing and skateboarding are not without their physical risks: Snowboarders are subject to injury, especially of the wrists.

Those experienced skiers who take up snowboarding typically opt for stiffer, alpine boards, that are best for making the carved turns that are common to the double ski sport. Younger buyers prefer the more flexible models that are perfect for stunt boarding. Either way, prices for a typical snowboard range from $300 to $700. Although some teenagers still wear high-topped sneakers as part of the Generation X uniform on the slopes, a pair of proper boots will jack up the cost of getting into the action by several hundred dollars.

Because of the rapid rise in popularity of this sport, mountains have become increasingly crowded with snowboarders. Much to the dismay of avid skiers, the sight of youngsters swooping and dipping down the slopes has become commonplace. The increase in snowboarding activity has caused a dilemma for many winter recreation spots. Since most shredders do not come from the skiing venue, they may not have learned proper etiquette on the slopes. In addition, few take lessons where they might learn good manners relating to the use of the mountain.

This lack of etiquette, coupled with the general distrust between adult populations and Xers, is creating a standoff. Equipment marketers which use questionable branding or promotion make the situation worse. Names such as Aggression and Boneless seem to cry out for reckless behavior, and ads that feature bikini-clad females tend to turn on young shredders while turning off the older population. Some in the industry, including Transworld Snowboarding magazine, feel that preaching safety and protocol would fall on the sometimes deaf ears of teenagers.

Ski resorts face a true dilemma. With almost a million and a half avid participants, snowboarding accounts for close to fifteen percent of the traffic on the slopes. Since few of these activists are former skiers, this number represents a true growth in overall sales. Some resorts segregate shredders from skiers, while others have banned snowboarding completely. In a brave move, Big Air Green Valley dedicated its slopes entirely to snowboarders. Most ski areas are trying to accommodate both shushers and shredders, perhaps realizing that as more skiers realize that snowboarding is easier on the knees they are likely to be converts.

Analyze the factors affecting the pricing of both snowboarding equipment and skiing areas. Sketch a marketing plan for a line of clothing for shredders.

Putting the Pedal to the Metal!

The aerodynamic design is sleek and contemporary, leaving a sense of speed even when it is standing still. The power plant brims with high-tech know-how, including fuel injection and computerized ignition. Inside, one senses the roominess and comfort, maximized by the air conditioning and state-of-the-art stereo system. The dashboard looks like the control panel of a jet airliner, and the safety features are truly mind boggling. Is it a late model car? A powerboat? How about a truck! A semi, baby! The business end of an eighteen wheeler. The tractor part of a tractor-trailer rig.

Today's big rigs are a far cry from the lumbering, ugly, cramped trucks of a few decades ago. One cannot help but be awed at the modern look, feel and performance of Class 8 vehicles. Even the noise levels for which these behemoths are known have been greatly reduced. The firm that has jumped to the head of the class in this industry is Freightliner, headquartered in Portland, Oregon. Much of this company's success can be attributed to the streamlined design of its products, which many ascribe to parent Daimler Benz. Access to that German firm's engineers and wind tunnels is credited for the superior aerodynamics of Freightliner rigs.

The market for heavy trucks grew dramatically in the early 1990s. Industry analysts expect 1995 to be the peak year for this trend. Many shipping companies found themselves with outdated and worn-out rigs at the end of the last decade, and the new designs of these highway haulers promised better fuel mileage and lower maintenance. The availability of better, more efficient trucks juxtaposed with the aging of fleets caused shippers to place orders for Class 8 trucks in increasing quantities. Industry experts also credit the increased use of just-in-time inventory control systems with the expanded demand for the more flexible transportation provided by highway carriers. All of the major truck suppliers reported sold out capacity for 1995–96.

The highway brutes, weighing up to 33,000 pounds, are not inexpensive. Big rigs can cost as much as $65,000 with options, forcing some freight carriers to overhaul present equipment rather than buy new. Even medium-duty trucks, an area dominated by Ford, General Motors and Navistar, carry price tags from $25,000–40,000. While Freightliner is eyeing this market for future growth, it may be tougher to crack than the Class 8 field. Then again, parent Daimler Benz has a great deal of experience worldwide in this smaller truck arena.

Freightliner leads the industry in sales, capturing about 25 percent of the market. Paccar, the Bellevue, Washington marketer of Kenworth and Peterbilt trucks, is a close second. Navistar, out of Chicago, is hanging tough in third place. Together these three firms account for over two-thirds of the heavy truck market. One major reason for Freightliner's rapid rise to the number one spot is its dominance in international markets. Due largely to the experience of Daimler Benz in global arenas, the company now sells in more than twenty countries around the world.

Analyze and describe the factors contributing to the growth of the heavy truck market. Outline a marketing plan that would carry Freightliner into the 21st century.

The Right Stuff!

The American business community, perhaps like none other in the world, appears to be under constant pressure to toe the line. Few societies embrace the ethical and responsible roles of businesses and business people as does ours. Despite the many laws and regulations that the U.S. has adopted governing price discrimination, product safety, environmental concerns and consumerism, the general public still casts a wary eye on the world of commerce. Certainly, scandals such as those that rocked the investments arena in the late 1980s do not allay the concerns of the citizenry. Even putting those shady inside traders behind bars did little to improve the reputation of business.

Unquestionably, business does have its share of "bad apples." One would be hard pressed to look at any field without finding some who were less than perfect. The medical and legal occupations have their share of less desirable or incapable members, and even the religious sector cannot hide the charlatans who have brought dishonor to the profession. Because of its more exposed position in the limelight, business often receives unjust criticism. Exemplary companies and executives are numerous, and none typify the concept of social responsibility better than Levi Strauss & Co. and its CEO Robert D. Haas.

As the great-great-grandnephew of company founder Levi Strauss, Haas believes that companies are ethical entities. His philosophy is that any business ought to leave the world a little bit better off, even as it strives to maximize profits. This aspiration not only embraces environmental concerns and corporate ethics, but includes striving for workforce diversity, open communications and empowerment. Although some calloused management gurus might scoff at such outspoken social responsibility, doing the right thing for the right reasons has certainly not harmed Levi Strauss & Co. The world's largest clothing manufacturer posts record profits on sales of over $6 billion annually.

Levi Strauss & Co. is certainly not alone in its efforts to conduct business in a socially responsible manner. Other companies include MCI, Xerox and Johnson & Johnson, which promote diversity by hiring and advancing employees regardless of age, gender or ethnic background. Similarly, Microsoft, FedEx and Nike are major firms noted for empowering employees at all levels. Yet despite this definite trend of the 1990s toward greater social responsibility by the global business community, Levi Strauss & Co. stands out among the crowd.

Levi posts its "Aspiration Statement," printed on paper made from recycled blue denim, on walls and pillars throughout its facilities. This company-wide distribution of top management's corporate philosophy does not necessarily translate into a warm and fuzzy climate that ignores normal business goals. For example, human resource policies that call for peer evaluation, along with appraisal by supervisors, are often stringent. Workers find that fellow workers are often more critical, especially in the areas of "aspirational" behavior, than might be the bosses.

Concerns for societal needs and protection are not merely limited to the office and production facilities occupied by Levi Strauss & Co. The company was a leader, for example, in pulling out of China in protest over human rights violations. Levi Strauss also boasts a tough policy regarding subcontractors overseas. Such firms must practice the same level of employee safety and fair practices as do Levi's own plants. Additionally, the company will not cotton with suppliers who pay less than a fair wage rate. Other of the firm's projects range from paying tuition for young female workers in Bangladesh to providing health benefits for partners of gay employees.

Create a marketing plan for a fictional company that includes social responsibility.

SOURCES: Russell Mitchel and Michael Oneal, "Managing by values," Business Week, August 1, 1994, pp. 46–52; G. Pascal Zachary, "Levi tries to make sure contract plants in Asia treat workers well," The Wall Street Journal, July 28, 1994, p. A1.

Index